MACHINE LEARNING

McGraw-Hill Series in Computer Science

Senior Consulting Editor

C.L. Liu, University of Illinois at Urbana-Champaign

Consulting Editor

Allen B. Tucker, Bowdoin College

Fundamentals of Computing and Programing
Computer Organization and Architecture
Computers in Society/Ethics
Systems and Languages
Theoretical Foundations
Software Engineering and Database
Artificial Intelligence
Networks, Parallel and Distributed Computing
Graphics and Visualization
The MIT Electrical and Computer Science Series

Artificial Intelligence

Bowen: *Prolog and Expert Systems Programming*
Fu: *Neural Networks in Computer Intelligence*
***Horn:** *Robot Vision*
Jain, Kasturi, and Schunck: *Machine Vision*
Levine: *Vision in Man and Machine*
Mitchell: *Machine Learning*
Rich and Knight: *Artificial Intelligence*
Schalkoff: *Artificial Neural Networks*

*Co-published by the MIT Press and The McGraw-Hill Companies, Inc.

For Meghan, Shannon, and Joan

CONTENTS

PREFACE

The field of machine learning is concerned with the question of how to construct computer programs that automatically improve with experience. In recent years many successful machine learning applications have been developed, ranging from data-mining programs that learn to detect fraudulent credit card transactions, to information-filtering systems that learn users' reading preferences, to autonomous vehicles that learn to drive on public highways. At the same time, there have been important advances in the theory and algorithms that form the foundations of this field.

The goal of this textbook is to present the key algorithms and theory that form the core of machine learning. Machine learning draws on concepts and results from many fields, including statistics, artificial intelligence, philosophy, information theory, biology, cognitive science, computational complexity, and control theory. My belief is that the best way to learn about machine learning is to view it from all of these perspectives and to understand the problem settings, algorithms, and assumptions that underlie each. In the past, this has been difficult due to the absence of a broad-based single source introduction to the field. The primary goal of this book is to provide such an introduction.

Because of the interdisciplinary nature of the material, this book makes few assumptions about the background of the reader. Instead, it introduces basic concepts from statistics, artificial intelligence, information theory, and other disciplines as the need arises, focusing on just those concepts most relevant to machine learning. The book is intended for both undergraduate and graduate students in fields such as computer science, engineering, statistics, and the social sciences, and as a reference for software professionals and practitioners. Two principles that guided the writing of the book were that it should be accessible to undergraduate students and that it should contain the material I would want my own Ph.D. students to learn before beginning their doctoral research in machine learning.

A third principle that guided the writing of this book was that it should present a balance of theory and practice. Machine learning theory attempts to answer questions such as "How does learning performance vary with the number of training examples presented?" and "Which learning algorithms are most appropriate for various types of learning tasks?" This book includes discussions of these and other theoretical issues, drawing on theoretical constructs from statistics, computational complexity, and Bayesian analysis. The practice of machine learning is covered by presenting the major algorithms in the field, along with illustrative traces of their operation. Online data sets and implementations of several algorithms are available via the World Wide Web at http://www.cs.cmu.edu/~tom/mlbook.html. These include neural network code and data for face recognition, decision tree learning code and data for financial loan analysis, and Bayes classifier code and data for analyzing text documents. I am grateful to a number of colleagues who have helped to create these online resources, including Jason Rennie, Paul Hsiung, Jeff Shufelt, Matt Glickman, Scott Davies, Joseph O'Sullivan, Ken Lang, Andrew McCallum, and Thorsten Joachims.

ACKNOWLEDGMENTS

In writing this book, I have been fortunate to be assisted by technical experts in many of the subdisciplines that make up the field of machine learning. This book could not have been written without their help. I am deeply indebted to the following scientists who took the time to review chapter drafts and, in many cases, to tutor me and help organize chapters in their individual areas of expertise.

Avrim Blum, Jaime Carbonell, William Cohen, Greg Cooper, Mark Craven, Ken DeJong, Jerry DeJong, Tom Dietterich, Susan Epstein, Oren Etzioni, Scott Fahlman, Stephanie Forrest, David Haussler, Haym Hirsh, Rob Holte, Leslie Pack Kaelbling, Dennis Kibler, Moshe Koppel, John Koza, Miroslav Kubat, John Lafferty, Ramon Lopez de Mantaras, Sridhar Mahadevan, Stan Matwin, Andrew McCallum, Raymond Mooney, Andrew Moore, Katharina Morik, Steve Muggleton, Michael Pazzani, David Poole, Armand Prieditis, Jim Reggia, Stuart Russell, Lorenza Saitta, Claude Sammut, Jeff Schneider, Jude Shavlik, Devika Subramanian, Michael Swain, Gheorgh Tecuci, Sebastian Thrun, Peter Turney, Paul Utgoff, Manuela Veloso, Alex Waibel, Stefan Wrobel, and Yiming Yang.

I am also grateful to the many instructors and students at various universities who have field tested various drafts of this book and who have contributed their suggestions. Although there is no space to thank the hundreds of students, instructors, and others who tested earlier drafts of this book, I would like to thank the following for particularly helpful comments and discussions:

Shumeet Baluja, Andrew Banas, Andy Barto, Jim Blackson, Justin Boyan, Rich Caruana, Philip Chan, Jonathan Cheyer, Lonnie Chrisman, Dayne Freitag, Geoff Gordon, Warren Greiff, Alexander Harm, Tom Ioerger, Thorsten

Joachim, Atsushi Kawamura, Martina Klose, Sven Koenig, Jay Modi, Andrew Ng, Joseph O'Sullivan, Patrawadee Prasangsit, Doina Precup, Bob Price, Choon Quek, Sean Slattery, Belinda Thom, Astro Teller, Will Tracz

I would like to thank Joan Mitchell for creating the index for the book. I also would like to thank Jean Harpley for help in editing many of the figures. Jane Loftus from ETP Harrison improved the presentation significantly through her copyediting of the manuscript and generally helped usher the manuscript through the intricacies of final production. Eric Munson, my editor at McGraw Hill, provided encouragement and expertise in all phases of this project.

As always, the greatest debt one owes is to one's colleagues, friends, and family. In my case, this debt is especially large. I can hardly imagine a more intellectually stimulating environment and supportive set of friends than those I have at Carnegie Mellon. Among the many here who helped, I would especially like to thank Sebastian Thrun, who throughout this project was a constant source of encouragement, technical expertise, and support of all kinds. My parents, as always, encouraged and asked "Is it done yet?" at just the right times. Finally, I must thank my family: Meghan, Shannon, and Joan. They are responsible for this book in more ways than even they know. This book is dedicated to them.

Tom M. Mitchell

CHAPTER 1

INTRODUCTION

Ever since computers were invented, we have wondered whether they might be made to learn. If we could understand how to program them to learn—to improve automatically with experience—the impact would be dramatic. Imagine computers learning from medical records which treatments are most effective for new diseases, houses learning from experience to optimize energy costs based on the particular usage patterns of their occupants, or personal software assistants learning the evolving interests of their users in order to highlight especially relevant stories from the online morning newspaper. A successful understanding of how to make computers learn would open up many new uses of computers and new levels of competence and customization. And a detailed understanding of information-processing algorithms for machine learning might lead to a better understanding of human learning abilities (and disabilities) as well.

We do not yet know how to make computers learn nearly as well as people learn. However, algorithms have been invented that are effective for certain types of learning tasks, and a theoretical understanding of learning is beginning to emerge. Many practical computer programs have been developed to exhibit useful types of learning, and significant commercial applications have begun to appear. For problems such as speech recognition, algorithms based on machine learning outperform all other approaches that have been attempted to date. In the field known as data mining, machine learning algorithms are being used routinely to discover valuable knowledge from large commercial databases containing equipment maintenance records, loan applications, financial transactions, medical records, and the like. As our understanding of computers continues to mature, it seems inevitable that machine learning will play an increasingly central role in computer science and computer technology.

A few specific achievements provide a glimpse of the state of the art: programs have been developed that successfully learn to recognize spoken words (Waibel 1989; Lee 1989), predict recovery rates of pneumonia patients (Cooper et al. 1997), detect fraudulent use of credit cards, drive autonomous vehicles on public highways (Pomerleau 1989), and play games such as backgammon at levels approaching the performance of human world champions (Tesauro 1992, 1995). Theoretical results have been developed that characterize the fundamental relationship among the number of training examples observed, the number of hypotheses under consideration, and the expected error in learned hypotheses. We are beginning to obtain initial models of human and animal learning and to understand their relationship to learning algorithms developed for computers (e.g., Laird et al. 1986; Anderson 1991; Qin et al. 1992; Chi and Bassock 1989; Ahn and Brewer 1993). In applications, algorithms, theory, and studies of biological systems, the rate of progress has increased significantly over the past decade. Several recent applications of machine learning are summarized in Table 1.1. Langley and Simon (1995) and Rumelhart et al. (1994) survey additional applications of machine learning.

This book presents the field of machine learning, describing a variety of learning paradigms, algorithms, theoretical results, and applications. Machine learning is inherently a multidisciplinary field. It draws on results from artificial intelligence, probability and statistics, computational complexity theory, control theory, information theory, philosophy, psychology, neurobiology, and other fields. Table 1.2 summarizes key ideas from each of these fields that impact the field of machine learning. While the material in this book is based on results from many diverse fields, the reader need not be an expert in any of them. Key ideas are presented from these fields using a nonspecialist's vocabulary, with unfamiliar terms and concepts introduced as the need arises.

1.1 WELL-POSED LEARNING PROBLEMS

Let us begin our study of machine learning by considering a few learning tasks. For the purposes of this book we will define learning broadly, to include any computer program that improves its performance at some task through experience. Put more precisely,

> ***Definition***: A computer program is said to **learn** from experience E with respect to some class of tasks T and performance measure P, if its performance at tasks in T, as measured by P, improves with experience E.

For example, a computer program that learns to play checkers might improve its performance *as measured by its ability to win* at the class of tasks involving *playing checkers games*, through experience *obtained by playing games against itself*. In general, to have a well-defined learning problem, we must identity these

- Learning to recognize spoken words.

  All of the most successful speech recognition systems employ machine learning in some form. For example, the SPHINX system (e.g., Lee 1989) learns speaker-specific strategies for recognizing the primitive sounds (phonemes) and words from the observed speech signal. Neural network learning methods (e.g., Waibel et al. 1989) and methods for learning hidden Markov models (e.g., Lee 1989) are effective for automatically customizing to individual speakers, vocabularies, microphone characteristics, background noise, etc. Similar techniques have potential applications in many signal-interpretation problems.
- Learning to drive an autonomous vehicle.

  Machine learning methods have been used to train computer-controlled vehicles to steer correctly when driving on a variety of road types. For example, the ALVINN system (Pomerleau 1989) has used its learned strategies to drive unassisted at 70 miles per hour for 90 miles on public highways among other cars. Similar techniques have possible applications in many sensor-based control problems.
- Learning to classify new astronomical structures.

  Machine learning methods have been applied to a variety of large databases to learn general regularities implicit in the data. For example, decision tree learning algorithms have been used by NASA to learn how to classify celestial objects from the second Palomar Observatory Sky Survey (Fayyad et al. 1995). This system is now used to automatically classify all objects in the Sky Survey, which consists of three terrabytes of image data.
- Learning to play world-class backgammon.

  The most successful computer programs for playing games such as backgammon are based on machine learning algorithms. For example, the world's top computer program for backgammon, TD-GAMMON (Tesauro 1992, 1995), learned its strategy by playing over one million practice games against itself. It now plays at a level competitive with the human world champion. Similar techniques have applications in many practical problems where very large search spaces must be examined efficiently.

TABLE 1.1
Some successful applications of machine learning.

three features: the class of tasks, the measure of performance to be improved, and the source of experience.

A checkers learning problem:

- Task T: playing checkers
- Performance measure P: percent of games won against opponents
- Training experience E: playing practice games against itself

We can specify many learning problems in this fashion, such as learning to recognize handwritten words, or learning to drive a robotic automobile autonomously.

A handwriting recognition learning problem:

- Task T: recognizing and classifying handwritten words within images
- Performance measure P: percent of words correctly classified

- Artificial intelligence

  Learning symbolic representations of concepts. Machine learning as a search problem. Learning as an approach to improving problem solving. Using prior knowledge together with training data to guide learning.
- Bayesian methods

  Bayes' theorem as the basis for calculating probabilities of hypotheses. The naive Bayes classifier. Algorithms for estimating values of unobserved variables.
- Computational complexity theory

  Theoretical bounds on the inherent complexity of different learning tasks, measured in terms of the computational effort, number of training examples, number of mistakes, etc. required in order to learn.
- Control theory

  Procedures that learn to control processes in order to optimize predefined objectives and that learn to predict the next state of the process they are controlling.
- Information theory

  Measures of entropy and information content. Minimum description length approaches to learning. Optimal codes and their relationship to optimal training sequences for encoding a hypothesis.
- Philosophy

  Occam's razor, suggesting that the simplest hypothesis is the best. Analysis of the justification for generalizing beyond observed data.
- Psychology and neurobiology

  The power law of practice, which states that over a very broad range of learning problems, people's response time improves with practice according to a power law. Neurobiological studies motivating artificial neural network models of learning.
- Statistics

  Characterization of errors (e.g., bias and variance) that occur when estimating the accuracy of a hypothesis based on a limited sample of data. Confidence intervals, statistical tests.

TABLE 1.2
Some disciplines and examples of their influence on machine learning.

- Training experience E: a database of handwritten words with given classifications

A robot driving learning problem:

- Task T: driving on public four-lane highways using vision sensors
- Performance measure P: average distance traveled before an error (as judged by human overseer)
- Training experience E: a sequence of images and steering commands recorded while observing a human driver

Our definition of learning is broad enough to include most tasks that we would conventionally call "learning" tasks, as we use the word in everyday language. It is also broad enough to encompass computer programs that improve from experience in quite straightforward ways. For example, a database system that allows users to update data entries would fit our definition of a learning system: it improves its performance at answering database queries, based on the experience gained from database updates. Rather than worry about whether this type of activity falls under the usual informal conversational meaning of the word "learning," we will simply adopt our technical definition of the class of programs that improve through experience. Within this class we will find many types of problems that require more or less sophisticated solutions. Our concern here is not to analyze the meaning of the English word "learning" as it is used in everyday language. Instead, our goal is to define precisely a class of problems that encompasses interesting forms of learning, to explore algorithms that solve such problems, and to understand the fundamental structure of learning problems and processes.

1.2 DESIGNING A LEARNING SYSTEM

In order to illustrate some of the basic design issues and approaches to machine learning, let us consider designing a program to learn to play checkers, with the goal of entering it in the world checkers tournament. We adopt the obvious performance measure: the percent of games it wins in this world tournament.

1.2.1 Choosing the Training Experience

The first design choice we face is to choose the type of training experience from which our system will learn. The type of training experience available can have a significant impact on success or failure of the learner. One key attribute is whether the training experience provides direct or indirect feedback regarding the choices made by the performance system. For example, in learning to play checkers, the system might learn from *direct* training examples consisting of individual checkers board states and the correct move for each. Alternatively, it might have available only *indirect* information consisting of the move sequences and final outcomes of various games played. In this later case, information about the correctness of specific moves early in the game must be inferred indirectly from the fact that the game was eventually won or lost. Here the learner faces an additional problem of *credit assignment*, or determining the degree to which each move in the sequence deserves credit or blame for the final outcome. Credit assignment can be a particularly difficult problem because the game can be lost even when early moves are optimal, if these are followed later by poor moves. Hence, learning from direct training feedback is typically easier than learning from indirect feedback.

A second important attribute of the training experience is the degree to which the learner controls the sequence of training examples. For example, the learner might rely on the teacher to select informative board states and to provide the correct move for each. Alternatively, the learner might itself propose board states that it finds particularly confusing and ask the teacher for the correct move. Or the learner may have complete control over both the board states and (indirect) training classifications, as it does when it learns by playing against itself with no teacher present. Notice in this last case the learner may choose between experimenting with novel board states that it has not yet considered, or honing its skill by playing minor variations of lines of play it currently finds most promising. Subsequent chapters consider a number of settings for learning, including settings in which training experience is provided by a random process outside the learner's control, settings in which the learner may pose various types of queries to an expert teacher, and settings in which the learner collects training examples by autonomously exploring its environment.

A third important attribute of the training experience is how well it represents the distribution of examples over which the final system performance P must be measured. In general, learning is most reliable when the training examples follow a distribution similar to that of future test examples. In our checkers learning scenario, the performance metric P is the percent of games the system wins in the world tournament. If its training experience E consists only of games played against itself, there is an obvious danger that this training experience might not be fully representative of the distribution of situations over which it will later be tested. For example, the learner might never encounter certain crucial board states that are very likely to be played by the human checkers champion. In practice, it is often necessary to learn from a distribution of examples that is somewhat different from those on which the final system will be evaluated (e.g., the world checkers champion might not be interested in teaching the program!). Such situations are problematic because mastery of one distribution of examples will not necessary lead to strong performance over some other distribution. We shall see that most current theory of machine learning rests on the crucial assumption that the distribution of training examples is identical to the distribution of test examples. Despite our need to make this assumption in order to obtain theoretical results, it is important to keep in mind that this assumption must often be violated in practice.

To proceed with our design, let us decide that our system will train by playing games against itself. This has the advantage that no external trainer need be present, and it therefore allows the system to generate as much training data as time permits. We now have a fully-specified learning task.

A checkers learning problem:

- Task T: playing checkers
- Performance measure P: percent of games won in the world tournament
- Training experience E: games played against itself

In order to complete the design of the learning system, we must now choose

1. the exact type of knowledge to be learned
2. a representation for this target knowledge
3. a learning mechanism

1.2.2 Choosing the Target Function

The next design choice is to determine exactly what type of knowledge will be learned and how this will be used by the performance program. Let us begin with a checkers-playing program that can generate the *legal* moves from any board state. The program needs only to learn how to choose the *best* move from among these legal moves. This learning task is representative of a large class of tasks for which the legal moves that define some large search space are known a priori, but for which the best search strategy is not known. Many optimization problems fall into this class, such as the problems of scheduling and controlling manufacturing processes where the available manufacturing steps are well understood, but the best strategy for sequencing them is not.

Given this setting where we must learn to choose among the legal moves, the most obvious choice for the type of information to be learned is a program, or function, that chooses the best move for any given board state. Let us call this function *ChooseMove* and use the notation $ChooseMove : B \rightarrow M$ to indicate that this function accepts as input any board from the set of legal board states B and produces as output some move from the set of legal moves M. Throughout our discussion of machine learning we will find it useful to reduce the problem of improving performance P at task T to the problem of learning some particular *target function* such as *ChooseMove*. The choice of the target function will therefore be a key design choice.

Although *ChooseMove* is an obvious choice for the target function in our example, this function will turn out to be very difficult to learn given the kind of indirect training experience available to our system. An alternative target function—and one that will turn out to be easier to learn in this setting—is an evaluation function that assigns a numerical score to any given board state. Let us call this target function V and again use the notation $V : B \rightarrow \Re$ to denote that V maps any legal board state from the set B to some real value (we use $\Re$ to denote the set of real numbers). We intend for this target function V to assign higher scores to better board states. If the system can successfully learn such a target function V, then it can easily use it to select the best move from any current board position. This can be accomplished by generating the successor board state produced by every legal move, then using V to choose the best successor state and therefore the best legal move.

What exactly should be the value of the target function V for any given board state? Of course any evaluation function that assigns higher scores to better board states will do. Nevertheless, we will find it useful to define one particular target function V among the many that produce optimal play. As we shall see, this will make it easier to design a training algorithm. Let us therefore define the target value $V(b)$ for an arbitrary board state b in B, as follows:

1. if b is a final board state that is won, then $V(b) = 100$
2. if b is a final board state that is lost, then $V(b) = -100$
3. if b is a final board state that is drawn, then $V(b) = 0$

4. if b is a not a final state in the game, then $V(b) = V(b')$, where b' is the best final board state that can be achieved starting from b and playing optimally until the end of the game (assuming the opponent plays optimally, as well).

While this recursive definition specifies a value of $V(b)$ for every board state b, this definition is not usable by our checkers player because it is not efficiently computable. Except for the trivial cases (cases 1–3) in which the game has already ended, determining the value of $V(b)$ for a particular board state requires (case 4) searching ahead for the optimal line of play, all the way to the end of the game! Because this definition is not efficiently computable by our checkers playing program, we say that it is a *nonoperational* definition. The goal of learning in this case is to discover an *operational* description of V; that is, a description that can be used by the checkers-playing program to evaluate states and select moves within realistic time bounds.

Thus, we have reduced the learning task in this case to the problem of discovering an *operational description of the ideal target function V*. It may be very difficult in general to learn such an operational form of V perfectly. In fact, we often expect learning algorithms to acquire only some *approximation* to the target function, and for this reason the process of learning the target function is often called *function approximation*. In the current discussion we will use the symbol $\hat{V}$ to refer to the function that is actually learned by our program, to distinguish it from the ideal target function V.

1.2.3 Choosing a Representation for the Target Function

Now that we have specified the ideal target function V, we must choose a representation that the learning program will use to describe the function $\hat{V}$ that it will learn. As with earlier design choices, we again have many options. We could, for example, allow the program to represent $\hat{V}$ using a large table with a distinct entry specifying the value for each distinct board state. Or we could allow it to represent $\hat{V}$ using a collection of rules that match against features of the board state, or a quadratic polynomial function of predefined board features, or an artificial neural network. In general, this choice of representation involves a crucial tradeoff. On one hand, we wish to pick a very expressive representation to allow representing as close an approximation as possible to the ideal target function V. On the other hand, the more expressive the representation, the more training data the program will require in order to choose among the alternative hypotheses it can represent. To keep the discussion brief, let us choose a simple representation: for any given board state, the function $\hat{V}$ will be calculated as a linear combination of the following board features:

- x_1: the number of black pieces on the board
- x_2: the number of red pieces on the board
- x_3: the number of black kings on the board
- x_4: the number of red kings on the board

- x_5: the number of black pieces threatened by red (i.e., which can be captured on red's next turn)
- x_6: the number of red pieces threatened by black

Thus, our learning program will represent $\hat{V}(b)$ as a linear function of the form

$$\hat{V}(b) = w_0 + w_1x_1 + w_2x_2 + w_3x_3 + w_4x_4 + w_5x_5 + w_6x_6$$

where w_0 through w_6 are numerical coefficients, or weights, to be chosen by the learning algorithm. Learned values for the weights w_1 through w_6 will determine the relative importance of the various board features in determining the value of the board, whereas the weight w_0 will provide an additive constant to the board value.

To summarize our design choices thus far, we have elaborated the original formulation of the learning problem by choosing a type of training experience, a target function to be learned, and a representation for this target function. Our elaborated learning task is now

Partial design of a checkers learning program:

- Task T: playing checkers
- Performance measure P: percent of games won in the world tournament
- Training experience E: games played against itself
- *Target function:* $V\text{:}Board \rightarrow \Re$
- *Target function representation*

$$\hat{V}(b) = w_0 + w_1x_1 + w_2x_2 + w_3x_3 + w_4x_4 + w_5x_5 + w_6x_6$$

The first three items above correspond to the specification of the learning task, whereas the final two items constitute design choices for the implementation of the learning program. Notice the net effect of this set of design choices is to reduce the problem of learning a checkers strategy to the problem of learning values for the coefficients w_0 through w_6 in the target function representation.

1.2.4 Choosing a Function Approximation Algorithm

In order to learn the target function $\hat{V}$ we require a set of training examples, each describing a specific board state b and the training value $V_{train}(b)$ for b. In other words, each training example is an ordered pair of the form $\langle b, V_{train}(b)\rangle$. For instance, the following training example describes a board state b in which black has won the game (note $x_2 = 0$ indicates that red has no remaining pieces) and for which the target function value $V_{train}(b)$ is therefore $+100$.

$$\langle\langle x_1 = 3, x_2 = 0, x_3 = 1, x_4 = 0, x_5 = 0, x_6 = 0\rangle, +100\rangle$$

Below we describe a procedure that first derives such training examples from the indirect training experience available to the learner, then adjusts the weights w_i to best fit these training examples.

1.2.4.1 ESTIMATING TRAINING VALUES

Recall that according to our formulation of the learning problem, the only training information available to our learner is whether the game was eventually won or lost. On the other hand, we require training examples that assign specific scores to specific board states. While it is easy to assign a value to board states that correspond to the end of the game, it is less obvious how to assign training values to the more numerous *intermediate* board states that occur before the game's end. Of course the fact that the game was eventually won or lost does not necessarily indicate that *every* board state along the game path was necessarily good or bad. For example, even if the program looses the game, it may still be the case that board states occurring early in the game should be rated very highly and that the cause of the loss was a subsequent poor move.

Despite the ambiguity inherent in estimating training values for intermediate board states, one simple approach has been found to be surprisingly successful. This approach is to assign the training value of $V_{train}(b)$ for any intermediate board state b to be $\hat{V}(Successor(b))$, where $\hat{V}$ is the learner's current approximation to V and where $Successor(b)$ denotes the next board state following b for which it is again the program's turn to move (i.e., the board state following the program's move and the opponent's response). This rule for estimating training values can be summarized as

Rule for estimating training values.

$$V_{train}(b) \leftarrow \hat{V}(Successor(b)) \tag{1.1}$$

While it may seem strange to use the current version of $\hat{V}$ to estimate training values that will be used to refine this very same function, notice that we are using estimates of the value of the $Successor(b)$ to estimate the value of board state b. Intuitively, we can see this will make sense if $\hat{V}$ tends to be more accurate for board states closer to game's end. In fact, under certain conditions (discussed in Chapter 13) the approach of iteratively estimating training values based on estimates of successor state values can be proven to converge toward perfect estimates of V_{train}.

1.2.4.2 ADJUSTING THE WEIGHTS

All that remains is to specify the learning algorithm for choosing the weights w_i to best fit the set of training examples $\{\langle b, V_{train}(b)\rangle\}$. As a first step we must define what we mean by the *best fit* to the training data. One common approach is to define the best hypothesis, or set of weights, as that which minimizes the squared error E between the training values and the values predicted by the hypothesis $\hat{V}$.

$$E \equiv \sum_{\langle b, V_{train}(b)\rangle \in \text{ training examples}} (V_{train}(b) - \hat{V}(b))^2$$

Thus, we seek the weights, or equivalently the $\hat{V}$, that minimize E for the observed training examples. Chapter 6 discusses settings in which minimizing the sum of squared errors is equivalent to finding the most probable hypothesis given the observed training data.

Several algorithms are known for finding weights of a linear function that minimize E defined in this way. In our case, we require an algorithm that will incrementally refine the weights as new training examples become available and that will be robust to errors in these estimated training values. One such algorithm is called the least mean squares, or LMS training rule. For each observed training example it adjusts the weights a small amount in the direction that reduces the error on this training example. As discussed in Chapter 4, this algorithm can be viewed as performing a stochastic gradient-descent search through the space of possible hypotheses (weight values) to minimize the squared error E. The LMS algorithm is defined as follows:

LMS weight update rule.

For each training example $\langle b, V_{train}(b)\rangle$

- Use the current weights to calculate $\hat{V}(b)$
- For each weight w_i, update it as

$$w_i \leftarrow w_i + \eta\ (V_{train}(b) - \hat{V}(b))\ x_i$$

Here η is a small constant (e.g., 0.1) that moderates the size of the weight update. To get an intuitive understanding for why this weight update rule works, notice that when the error $(V_{train}(b) - \hat{V}(b))$ is zero, no weights are changed. When $(V_{train}(b) - \hat{V}(b))$ is positive (i.e., when $\hat{V}(b)$ is too low), then each weight is increased in proportion to the value of its corresponding feature. This will raise the value of $\hat{V}(b)$, reducing the error. Notice that if the value of some feature x_i is zero, then its weight is not altered regardless of the error, so that the only weights updated are those whose features actually occur on the training example board. Surprisingly, in certain settings this simple weight-tuning method can be proven to converge to the least squared error approximation to the V_{train} values (as discussed in Chapter 4).

1.2.5 The Final Design

The final design of our checkers learning system can be naturally described by four distinct program modules that represent the central components in many learning systems. These four modules, summarized in Figure 1.1, are as follows:

- The **Performance System** is the module that must solve the given performance task, in this case playing checkers, by using the learned target function(s). It takes an instance of a new problem (new game) as input and produces a trace of its solution (game history) as output. In our case, the

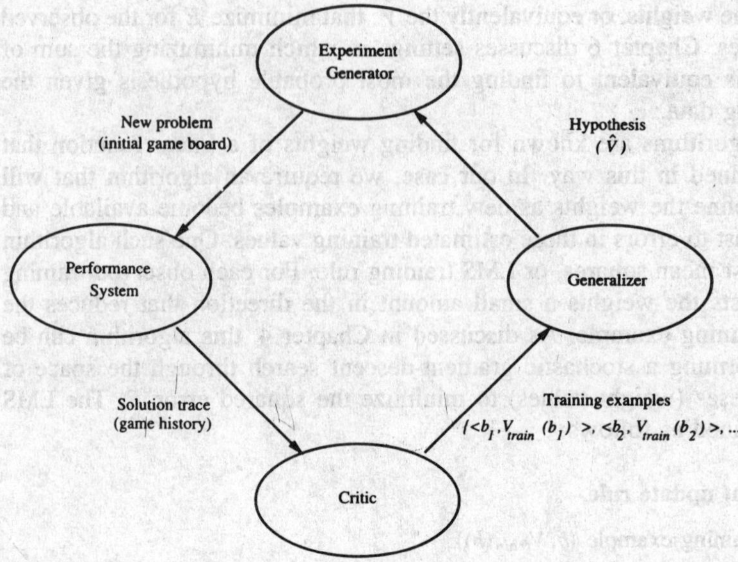

FIGURE 1.1
Final design of the checkers learning program.

strategy used by the Performance System to select its next move at each step is determined by the learned $\hat{V}$ evaluation function. Therefore, we expect its performance to improve as this evaluation function becomes increasingly accurate.

- The **Critic** takes as input the history or trace of the game and produces as output a set of training examples of the target function. As shown in the diagram, each training example in this case corresponds to some game state in the trace, along with an estimate V_{train} of the target function value for this example. In our example, the Critic corresponds to the training rule given by Equation (1.1).
- The **Generalizer** takes as input the training examples and produces an output hypothesis that is its estimate of the target function. It generalizes from the specific training examples, hypothesizing a general function that covers these examples and other cases beyond the training examples. In our example, the Generalizer corresponds to the LMS algorithm, and the output hypothesis is the function $\hat{V}$ described by the learned weights $w_0, \ldots, w_6$.
- The **Experiment Generator** takes as input the current hypothesis (currently learned function) and outputs a new problem (i.e., initial board state) for the Performance System to explore. Its role is to pick new practice problems that will maximize the learning rate of the overall system. In our example, the Experiment Generator follows a very simple strategy: It always proposes the same initial game board to begin a new game. More sophisticated strategies

could involve creating board positions designed to explore particular regions of the state space.

Together, the design choices we made for our checkers program produce specific instantiations for the performance system, critic, generalizer, and experiment generator. Many machine learning systems can be usefully characterized in terms of these four generic modules.

The sequence of design choices made for the checkers program is summarized in Figure 1.2. These design choices have constrained the learning task in a number of ways. We have restricted the type of knowledge that can be acquired to a single linear evaluation function. Furthermore, we have constrained this evaluation function to depend on only the six specific board features provided. If the true target function V can indeed be represented by a linear combination of these

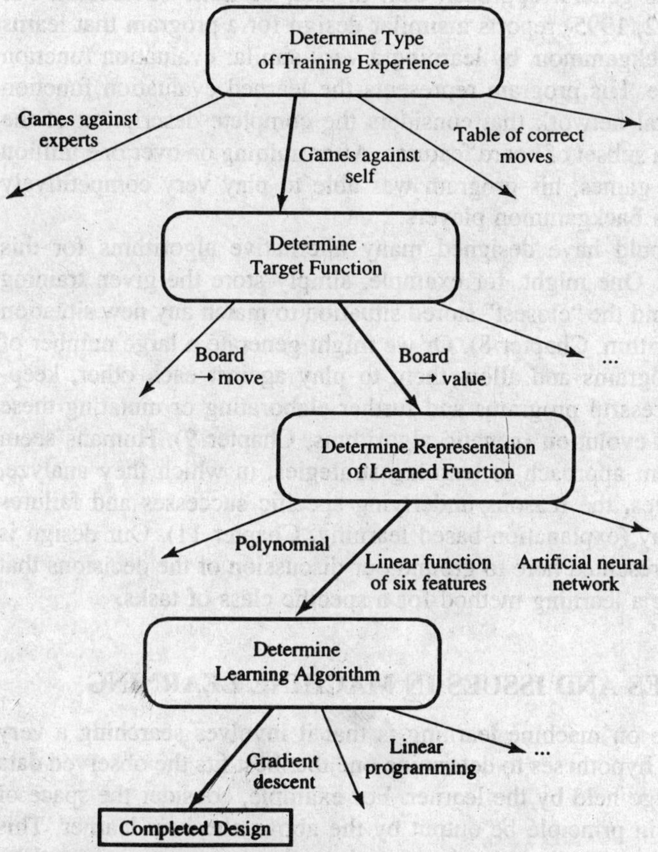

FIGURE 1.2
Summary of choices in designing the checkers learning program.

particular features, then our program has a good chance to learn it. If not, then the best we can hope for is that it will learn a good approximation, since a program can certainly never learn anything that it cannot at least represent.

Let us suppose that a good approximation to the true V function can, in fact, be represented in this form. The question then arises as to whether this learning technique is guaranteed to find one. Chapter 13 provides a theoretical analysis showing that under rather restrictive assumptions, variations on this approach do indeed converge to the desired evaluation function for certain types of search problems. Fortunately, practical experience indicates that this approach to learning evaluation functions is often successful, even outside the range of situations for which such guarantees can be proven.

Would the program we have designed be able to learn well enough to beat the human checkers world champion? Probably not. In part, this is because the linear function representation for $\hat{V}$ is too simple a representation to capture well the nuances of the game. However, given a more sophisticated representation for the target function, this general approach can, in fact, be quite successful. For example, Tesauro (1992, 1995) reports a similar design for a program that learns to play the game of backgammon, by learning a very similar evaluation function over states of the game. His program represents the learned evaluation function using an artificial neural network that considers the complete description of the board state rather than a subset of board features. After training on over one million self-generated training games, his program was able to play very competitively with top-ranked human backgammon players.

Of course we could have designed many alternative algorithms for this checkers learning task. One might, for example, simply store the given training examples, then try to find the "closest" stored situation to match any new situation (nearest neighbor algorithm, Chapter 8). Or we might generate a large number of candidate checkers programs and allow them to play against each other, keeping only the most successful programs and further elaborating or mutating these in a kind of simulated evolution (genetic algorithms, Chapter 9). Humans seem to follow yet a different approach to learning strategies, in which they analyze, or explain to themselves, the reasons underlying specific successes and failures encountered during play (explanation-based learning, Chapter 11). Our design is simply one of many, presented here to ground our discussion of the decisions that must go into designing a learning method for a specific class of tasks.

1.3 PERSPECTIVES AND ISSUES IN MACHINE LEARNING

One useful perspective on machine learning is that it involves searching a very large space of possible hypotheses to determine one that best fits the observed data and any prior knowledge held by the learner. For example, consider the space of hypotheses that could in principle be output by the above checkers learner. This hypothesis space consists of all evaluation functions that can be represented by some choice of values for the weights w_0 through w_6. The learner's task is thus to search through this vast space to locate the hypothesis that is most consistent with the available training examples. The LMS algorithm for fitting weights achieves this goal by iteratively tuning the weights, adding a correction to each weight each time the hypothesized evaluation function predicts a value that differs from the training value. This algorithm works well when the hypothesis representation considered by the learner defines a continuously parameterized space of potential hypotheses.

Many of the chapters in this book present algorithms that search a hypothesis space defined by some underlying representation (e.g., linear functions, logical descriptions, decision trees, artificial neural networks). These different hypothesis representations are appropriate for learning different kinds of target functions. For each of these hypothesis representations, the corresponding learning algorithm takes advantage of a different underlying structure to organize the search through the hypothesis space.

Throughout this book we will return to this perspective of learning as a search problem in order to characterize learning methods by their search strategies and by the underlying structure of the search spaces they explore. We will also find this viewpoint useful in formally analyzing the relationship between the size of the hypothesis space to be searched, the number of training examples available, and the confidence we can have that a hypothesis consistent with the training data will correctly generalize to unseen examples.

1.3.1 Issues in Machine Learning

Our checkers example raises a number of generic questions about machine learning. The field of machine learning, and much of this book, is concerned with answering questions such as the following:

- What algorithms exist for learning general target functions from specific training examples? In what settings will particular algorithms converge to the desired function, given sufficient training data? Which algorithms perform best for which types of problems and representations?
- How much training data is sufficient? What general bounds can be found to relate the confidence in learned hypotheses to the amount of training experience and the character of the learner's hypothesis space?
- When and how can prior knowledge held by the learner guide the process of generalizing from examples? Can prior knowledge be helpful even when it is only approximately correct?
- What is the best strategy for choosing a useful next training experience, and how does the choice of this strategy alter the complexity of the learning problem?
- What is the best way to reduce the learning task to one or more function approximation problems? Put another way, what specific functions should the system attempt to learn? Can this process itself be automated?
- How can the learner automatically alter its representation to improve its ability to represent and learn the target function?

1.4 HOW TO READ THIS BOOK

This book contains an introduction to the primary algorithms and approaches to machine learning, theoretical results on the feasibility of various learning tasks and the capabilities of specific algorithms, and examples of practical applications of machine learning to real-world problems. Where possible, the chapters have been written to be readable in any sequence. However, some interdependence is unavoidable. If this is being used as a class text, I recommend first covering Chapter 1 and Chapter 2. Following these two chapters, the remaining chapters can be read in nearly any sequence. A one-semester course in machine learning might cover the first seven chapters, followed by whichever additional chapters are of greatest interest to the class. Below is a brief survey of the chapters.

- Chapter 2 covers concept learning based on symbolic or logical representations. It also discusses the general-to-specific ordering over hypotheses, and the need for inductive bias in learning.
- Chapter 3 covers decision tree learning and the problem of overfitting the training data. It also examines Occam's razor—a principle recommending the shortest hypothesis among those consistent with the data.
- Chapter 4 covers learning of artificial neural networks, especially the well-studied BACKPROPAGATION algorithm, and the general approach of gradient descent. This includes a detailed example of neural network learning for face recognition, including data and algorithms available over the World Wide Web.
- Chapter 5 presents basic concepts from statistics and estimation theory, focusing on evaluating the accuracy of hypotheses using limited samples of data. This includes the calculation of confidence intervals for estimating hypothesis accuracy and methods for comparing the accuracy of learning methods.
- Chapter 6 covers the Bayesian perspective on machine learning, including both the use of Bayesian analysis to characterize non-Bayesian learning algorithms and specific Bayesian algorithms that explicitly manipulate probabilities. This includes a detailed example applying a naive Bayes classifier to the task of classifying text documents, including data and software available over the World Wide Web.
- Chapter 7 covers computational learning theory, including the Probably Approximately Correct (PAC) learning model and the Mistake-Bound learning model. This includes a discussion of the WEIGHTED MAJORITY algorithm for combining multiple learning methods.
- Chapter 8 describes instance-based learning methods, including nearest neighbor learning, locally weighted regression, and case-based reasoning.
- Chapter 9 discusses learning algorithms modeled after biological evolution, including genetic algorithms and genetic programming.

- Chapter 10 covers algorithms for learning sets of rules, including Inductive Logic Programming approaches to learning first-order Horn clauses.
- Chapter 11 covers explanation-based learning, a learning method that uses prior knowledge to explain observed training examples, then generalizes based on these explanations.
- Chapter 12 discusses approaches to combining approximate prior knowledge with available training data in order to improve the accuracy of learned hypotheses. Both symbolic and neural network algorithms are considered.
- Chapter 13 discusses reinforcement learning—an approach to control learning that accommodates indirect or delayed feedback as training information. The checkers learning algorithm described earlier in Chapter 1 is a simple example of reinforcement learning.

The end of each chapter contains a summary of the main concepts covered, suggestions for further reading, and exercises. Additional updates to chapters, as well as data sets and implementations of algorithms, are available on the World Wide Web at http://www.cs.cmu.edu/~tom/mlbook.html.

1.5 SUMMARY AND FURTHER READING

Machine learning addresses the question of how to build computer programs that improve their performance at some task through experience. Major points of this chapter include:

- Machine learning algorithms have proven to be of great practical value in a variety of application domains. They are especially useful in (a) data mining problems where large databases may contain valuable implicit regularities that can be discovered automatically (e.g., to analyze outcomes of medical treatments from patient databases or to learn general rules for credit worthiness from financial databases); (b) poorly understood domains where humans might not have the knowledge needed to develop effective algorithms (e.g., human face recognition from images); and (c) domains where the program must dynamically adapt to changing conditions (e.g., controlling manufacturing processes under changing supply stocks or adapting to the changing reading interests of individuals).
- Machine learning draws on ideas from a diverse set of disciplines, including artificial intelligence, probability and statistics, computational complexity, information theory, psychology and neurobiology, control theory, and philosophy.
- A well-defined learning problem requires a well-specified task, performance metric, and source of training experience.
- Designing a machine learning approach involves a number of design choices, including choosing the type of training experience, the target function to be learned, a representation for this target function, and an algorithm for learning the target function from training examples.

- Learning involves search: searching through a space of possible hypotheses to find the hypothesis that best fits the available training examples and other prior constraints or knowledge. Much of this book is organized around different learning methods that search different hypothesis spaces (e.g., spaces containing numerical functions, neural networks, decision trees, symbolic rules) and around theoretical results that characterize conditions under which these search methods converge toward an optimal hypothesis.

There are a number of good sources for reading about the latest research results in machine learning. Relevant journals include *Machine Learning*, *Neural Computation*, *Neural Networks*, *Journal of the American Statistical Association*, and the *IEEE Transactions on Pattern Analysis and Machine Intelligence*. There are also numerous annual conferences that cover different aspects of machine learning, including the International Conference on Machine Learning, Neural Information Processing Systems, Conference on Computational Learning Theory, International Conference on Genetic Algorithms, International Conference on Knowledge Discovery and Data Mining, European Conference on Machine Learning, and others.

EXERCISES

1.1. Give three computer applications for which machine learning approaches seem appropriate and three for which they seem inappropriate. Pick applications that are not already mentioned in this chapter, and include a one-sentence justification for each.

1.2. Pick some learning task not mentioned in this chapter. Describe it informally in a paragraph in English. Now describe it by stating as precisely as possible the task, performance measure, and training experience. Finally, propose a target function to be learned and a target representation. Discuss the main tradeoffs you considered in formulating this learning task.

1.3. Prove that the LMS weight update rule described in this chapter performs a gradient descent to minimize the squared error. In particular, define the squared error E as in the text. Now calculate the derivative of E with respect to the weight w_i, assuming that $\hat{V}(b)$ is a linear function as defined in the text. Gradient descent is achieved by updating each weight in proportion to $-\frac{\partial E}{\partial w_i}$. Therefore, you must show that the LMS training rule alters weights in this proportion for each training example it encounters.

1.4. Consider alternative strategies for the Experiment Generator module of Figure 1.2. In particular, consider strategies in which the Experiment Generator suggests new board positions by

- Generating random legal board positions
- Generating a position by picking a board state from the previous game, then applying one of the moves that was not executed
- A strategy of your own design

Discuss tradeoffs among these strategies. Which do you feel would work best if the number of training examples was held constant, given the performance measure of winning the most games at the world championships?

1.5. Implement an algorithm similar to that discussed for the checkers problem, but use the simpler game of tic-tac-toe. Represent the learned function $\hat{V}$ as a linear combination of board features of your choice. To train your program, play it repeatedly against a second copy of the program that uses a fixed evaluation function you create by hand. Plot the percent of games won by your system, versus the number of training games played.

REFERENCES

Ahn, W., & Brewer, W. F. (1993). Psychological studies of explanation-based learning. In G. DeJong (Ed.), *Investigating explanation-based learning*. Boston: Kluwer Academic Publishers.

Anderson, J. R. (1991). The place of cognitive architecture in rational analysis. In K. VanLehn (Ed.), *Architectures for intelligence* (pp. 1–24). Hillsdale, NJ: Erlbaum.

Chi, M. T. H., & Bassock, M. (1989). Learning from examples via self-explanations. In L. Resnick (Ed.), *Knowing, learning, and instruction: Essays in honor of Robert Glaser*. Hillsdale, NJ: L. Erlbaum Associates.

Cooper, G., et al. (1997). An evaluation of machine-learning methods for predicting pneumonia mortality. *Artificial Intelligence in Medicine*, (to appear).

Fayyad, U. M., Uthurusamy, R. (Eds.) (1995). *Proceedings of the First International Conference on Knowledge Discovery and Data Mining*. Menlo Park, CA: AAAI Press.

Fayyad, U. M., Smyth, P., Weir, N., Djorgovski, S. (1995). Automated analysis and exploration of image databases: Results, progress, and challenges. *Journal of Intelligent Information Systems*, 4, 1–19.

Laird, J., Rosenbloom, P., & Newell, A. (1986). SOAR: The anatomy of a general learning mechanism. *Machine Learning*, 1(1), 11–46.

Langley, P., & Simon, H. (1995). Applications of machine learning and rule induction. *Communications of the ACM*, 38(11), 55–64.

Lee, K. (1989). *Automatic speech recognition: The development of the Sphinx system*. Boston: Kluwer Academic Publishers.

Pomerleau, D. A. (1989). *ALVINN: An autonomous land vehicle in a neural network*. (Technical Report CMU-CS-89-107). Pittsburgh, PA: Carnegie Mellon University.

Qin, Y., Mitchell, T., & Simon, H. (1992). Using EBG to simulate human learning from examples and learning by doing. *Proceedings of the Florida AI Research Symposium* (pp. 235–239).

Rudnicky, A. I., Hauptmann, A. G., & Lee, K. -F. (1994). Survey of current speech technology in artificial intelligence. *Communications of the ACM*, 37(3), 52–57.

Rumelhart, D., Widrow, B., & Lehr, M. (1994). The basic ideas in neural networks. *Communications of the ACM*, 37(3), 87–92.

Tesauro, G. (1992). Practical issues in temporal difference learning. *Machine Learning*, 8, 257.

Tesauro, G. (1995). Temporal difference learning and TD-gammon. *Communications of the ACM*, 38(3), 58–68.

Waibel, A., Hanazawa, T., Hinton, G., Shikano, K., & Lang, K. (1989). Phoneme recognition using time-delay neural networks. *IEEE Transactions on Acoustics, Speech and Signal Processing*, 37(3), 328–339.

CHAPTER 2

CONCEPT LEARNING AND THE GENERAL-TO-SPECIFIC ORDERING

The problem of inducing general functions from specific training examples is central to learning. This chapter considers concept learning: acquiring the definition of a general category given a sample of positive and negative training examples of the category. Concept learning can be formulated as a problem of searching through a predefined space of potential hypotheses for the hypothesis that best fits the training examples. In many cases this search can be efficiently organized by taking advantage of a naturally occurring structure over the hypothesis space—a general-to-specific ordering of hypotheses. This chapter presents several learning algorithms and considers situations under which they converge to the correct hypothesis. We also examine the nature of inductive learning and the justification by which any program may successfully generalize beyond the observed training data.

2.1 INTRODUCTION

Much of learning involves acquiring general concepts from specific training examples. People, for example, continually learn general concepts or categories such as "bird," "car," "situations in which I should study more in order to pass the exam," etc. Each such concept can be viewed as describing some subset of objects or events defined over a larger set (e.g., the subset of animals that constitute birds). Alternatively, each concept can be thought of as a boolean-valued function defined over this larger set (e.g., a function defined over all animals, whose value is true for birds and false for other animals).

In this chapter we consider the problem of automatically inferring the general definition of some concept, given examples labeled as members or nonmembers of the concept. This task is commonly referred to as *concept learning*, or approximating a boolean-valued function from examples.

Concept learning. Inferring a boolean-valued function from training examples of its input and output.

2.2 A CONCEPT LEARNING TASK

To ground our discussion of concept learning, consider the example task of learning the target concept "days on which my friend Aldo enjoys his favorite water sport." Table 2.1 describes a set of example days, each represented by a set of *attributes*. The attribute *EnjoySport* indicates whether or not Aldo enjoys his favorite water sport on this day. The task is to learn to predict the value of *EnjoySport* for an arbitrary day, based on the values of its other attributes.

What hypothesis representation shall we provide to the learner in this case? Let us begin by considering a simple representation in which each hypothesis consists of a conjunction of constraints on the instance attributes. In particular, let each hypothesis be a vector of six constraints, specifying the values of the six attributes *Sky, AirTemp, Humidity, Wind, Water,* and *Forecast*. For each attribute, the hypothesis will either

- indicate by a "?" that any value is acceptable for this attribute,
- specify a single required value (e.g., *Warm*) for the attribute, or
- indicate by a "Ø" that no value is acceptable.

If some instance x satisfies all the constraints of hypothesis h, then h classifies x as a positive example ($h(x) = 1$). To illustrate, the hypothesis that Aldo enjoys his favorite sport only on cold days with high humidity (independent of the values of the other attributes) is represented by the expression

$$\langle ?, Cold, High, ?, ?, ? \rangle$$

Example	*Sky*	*AirTemp*	*Humidity*	*Wind*	*Water*	*Forecast*	*EnjoySport*
1	Sunny	Warm	Normal	Strong	Warm	Same	Yes
2	Sunny	Warm	High	Strong	Warm	Same	Yes
3	Rainy	Cold	High	Strong	Warm	Change	No
4	Sunny	Warm	High	Strong	Cool	Change	Yes

TABLE 2.1
Positive and negative training examples for the target concept *EnjoySport*.

The most general hypothesis—that every day is a positive example—is represented by

$$\langle ?, ?, ?, ?, ?, ? \rangle$$

and the most specific possible hypothesis—that *no* day is a positive example—is represented by

$$\langle \emptyset, \emptyset, \emptyset, \emptyset, \emptyset, \emptyset \rangle$$

To summarize, the *EnjoySport* concept learning task requires learning the set of days for which $EnjoySport = yes$, describing this set by a conjunction of constraints over the instance attributes. In general, any concept learning task can be described by the set of instances over which the target function is defined, the target function, the set of candidate hypotheses considered by the learner, and the set of available training examples. The definition of the *EnjoySport* concept learning task in this general form is given in Table 2.2.

2.2.1 Notation

Throughout this book, we employ the following terminology when discussing concept learning problems. The set of items over which the concept is defined is called the set of *instances*, which we denote by X. In the current example, X is the set of all possible days, each represented by the attributes *Sky*, *AirTemp*, *Humidity*, *Wind*, *Water*, and *Forecast*. The concept or function to be learned is called the *target concept*, which we denote by c. In general, c can be any boolean-valued function defined over the instances X; that is, $c : X \rightarrow \{0, 1\}$. In the current example, the target concept corresponds to the value of the attribute *EnjoySport* (i.e., $c(x) = 1$ if $EnjoySport = Yes$, and $c(x) = 0$ if $EnjoySport = No$).

- **Given:**
  - Instances X: Possible days, each described by the attributes
    - *Sky* (with possible values *Sunny*, *Cloudy*, and *Rainy*),
    - *AirTemp* (with values *Warm* and *Cold*),
    - *Humidity* (with values *Normal* and *High*),
    - *Wind* (with values *Strong* and *Weak*),
    - *Water* (with values *Warm* and *Cool*), and
    - *Forecast* (with values *Same* and *Change*).
  - Hypotheses H: Each hypothesis is described by a conjunction of constraints on the attributes *Sky*, *AirTemp*, *Humidity*, *Wind*, *Water*, and *Forecast*. The constraints may be "?" (any value is acceptable), "Ø" (no value is acceptable), or a specific value.
  - Target concept c: $EnjoySport : X \rightarrow \{0, 1\}$
  - Training examples D: Positive and negative examples of the target function (see Table 2.1).
- **Determine:**
  - A hypothesis h in H such that $h(x) = c(x)$ for all x in X.

TABLE 2.2
The *EnjoySport* concept learning task.

When learning the target concept, the learner is presented a set of *training examples*, each consisting of an instance x from X, along with its target concept value $c(x)$ (e.g., the training examples in Table 2.1). Instances for which $c(x) = 1$ are called *positive examples*, or members of the target concept. Instances for which $c(x) = 0$ are called *negative examples*, or nonmembers of the target concept. We will often write the ordered pair $\langle x, c(x) \rangle$ to describe the training example consisting of the instance x and its target concept value $c(x)$. We use the symbol D to denote the set of available training examples.

Given a set of training examples of the target concept c, the problem faced by the learner is to hypothesize, or estimate, c. We use the symbol H to denote the set of *all possible hypotheses* that the learner may consider regarding the identity of the target concept. Usually H is determined by the human designer's choice of hypothesis representation. In general, each hypothesis h in H represents a boolean-valued function defined over X; that is, $h : X \rightarrow \{0, 1\}$. The goal of the learner is to find a hypothesis h such that $h(x) = c(x)$ for all x in X.

2.2.2 The Inductive Learning Hypothesis

Notice that although the learning task is to determine a hypothesis h identical to the target concept c over the entire set of instances X, the only information available about c is its value over the training examples. Therefore, inductive learning algorithms can at best guarantee that the output hypothesis fits the target concept over the training data. Lacking any further information, our assumption is that the best hypothesis regarding unseen instances is the hypothesis that best fits the observed training data. This is the fundamental assumption of inductive learning, and we will have much more to say about it throughout this book. We state it here informally and will revisit and analyze this assumption more formally and more quantitatively in Chapters 5, 6, and 7.

> **The inductive learning hypothesis.** Any hypothesis found to approximate the target function well over a sufficiently large set of training examples will also approximate the target function well over other unobserved examples.

2.3 CONCEPT LEARNING AS SEARCH

Concept learning can be viewed as the task of searching through a large space of hypotheses implicitly defined by the hypothesis representation. The goal of this search is to find the hypothesis that best fits the training examples. It is important to note that by selecting a hypothesis representation, the designer of the learning algorithm implicitly defines the space of all hypotheses that the program can ever represent and therefore can ever learn. Consider, for example, the instances X and hypotheses H in the $EnjoySport$ learning task. Given that the attribute Sky has three possible values, and that $AirTemp$, $Humidity$, $Wind$, $Water$, and $Forecast$ each have two possible values, the instance space X contains exactly

$3 \cdot 2 \cdot 2 \cdot 2 \cdot 2 \cdot 2 = 96$ distinct instances. A similar calculation shows that there are $5 \cdot 4 \cdot 4 \cdot 4 \cdot 4 \cdot 4 = 5120$ *syntactically distinct* hypotheses within H. Notice, however, that every hypothesis containing one or more "Ø" symbols represents the empty set of instances; that is, it classifies every instance as negative. Therefore, the number of *semantically distinct* hypotheses is only $1 + (4 \cdot 3 \cdot 3 \cdot 3 \cdot 3 \cdot 3) = 973$. Our *EnjoySport* example is a very simple learning task, with a relatively small, finite hypothesis space. Most practical learning tasks involve much larger, sometimes infinite, hypothesis spaces.

If we view learning as a search problem, then it is natural that our study of learning algorithms will examine different strategies for searching the hypothesis space. We will be particularly interested in algorithms capable of efficiently searching very large or infinite hypothesis spaces, to find the hypotheses that best fit the training data.

2.3.1 General-to-Specific Ordering of Hypotheses

Many algorithms for concept learning organize the search through the hypothesis space by relying on a very useful structure that exists for any concept learning problem: a general-to-specific ordering of hypotheses. By taking advantage of this naturally occurring structure over the hypothesis space, we can design learning algorithms that exhaustively search even infinite hypothesis spaces without explicitly enumerating every hypothesis. To illustrate the general-to-specific ordering, consider the two hypotheses

$$h_1 = \langle Sunny, ?, ?, Strong, ?, ? \rangle$$

$$h_2 = \langle Sunny, ?, ?, ?, ?, ? \rangle$$

Now consider the sets of instances that are classified positive by h_1 and by h_2. Because h_2 imposes fewer constraints on the instance, it classifies more instances as positive. In fact, any instance classified positive by h_1 will also be classified positive by h_2. Therefore, we say that h_2 is more general than h_1.

This intuitive "more general than" relationship between hypotheses can be defined more precisely as follows. First, for any instance x in X and hypothesis h in H, we say that x *satisfies* h if and only if $h(x) = 1$. We now define the *more_general_than_or_equal_to* relation in terms of the sets of instances that satisfy the two hypotheses: Given hypotheses h_j and h_k, h_j is *more_general_than_or_equal_to* h_k if and only if any instance that satisfies h_k also satisfies h_j.

Definition: Let h_j and h_k be boolean-valued functions defined over X. Then h_j is **more_general_than_or_equal_to** h_k (written $h_j \geq_g h_k$) if and only if

$$(\forall x \in X)[(h_k(x) = 1) \rightarrow (h_j(x) = 1)]$$

We will also find it useful to consider cases where one hypothesis is strictly more general than the other. Therefore, we will say that h_j is (strictly) *more_general_than*

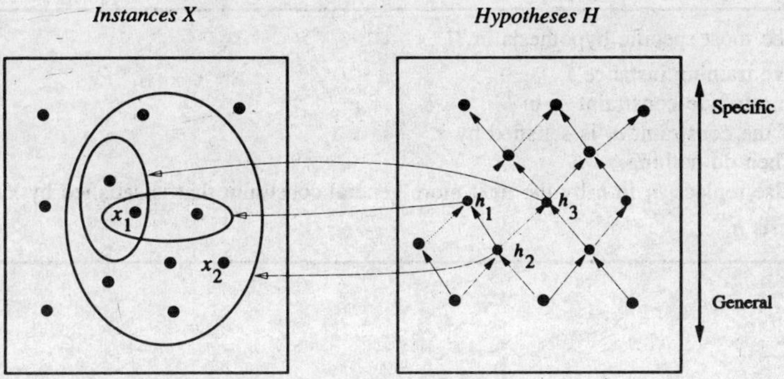

x_1= <*Sunny, Warm, High, Strong, Cool, Same*>
x_2= <*Sunny, Warm, High, Light, Warm, Same*>

h_1= <*Sunny, ?, ?, Strong, ?, ?*>
h_2= <*Sunny, ?, ?, ?, ?, ?*>
h_3= <*Sunny, ?, ?, ?, Cool, ?*>

FIGURE 2.1
Instances, hypotheses, and the *more_general_than* relation. The box on the left represents the set X of all instances, the box on the right the set H of all hypotheses. Each hypothesis corresponds to some subset of X—the subset of instances that it classifies positive. The arrows connecting hypotheses represent the *more_general_than* relation, with the arrow pointing toward the less general hypothesis. Note the subset of instances characterized by h_2 subsumes the subset characterized by h_1, hence h_2 is *more_general_than* h_1.

h_k (written $h_j >_g h_k$) if and only if $(h_j \geq_g h_k) \wedge (h_k \not\geq_g h_j)$. Finally, we will sometimes find the inverse useful and will say that h_j is *more_specific_than* h_k when h_k is *more_general_than* h_j.

To illustrate these definitions, consider the three hypotheses h_1, h_2, and h_3 from our *EnjoySport* example, shown in Figure 2.1. How are these three hypotheses related by the $\geq_g$ relation? As noted earlier, hypothesis h_2 is more general than h_1 because every instance that satisfies h_1 also satisfies h_2. Similarly, h_2 is more general than h_3. Note that neither h_1 nor h_3 is more general than the other; although the instances satisfied by these two hypotheses intersect, neither set subsumes the other. Notice also that the $\geq_g$ and $>_g$ relations are defined independent of the target concept. They depend only on which instances satisfy the two hypotheses and not on the classification of those instances according to the target concept. Formally, the $\geq_g$ relation defines a partial order over the hypothesis space H (the relation is reflexive, antisymmetric, and transitive). Informally, when we say the structure is a partial (as opposed to total) order, we mean there may be pairs of hypotheses such as h_1 and h_3, such that $h_1 \not\geq_g h_3$ and $h_3 \not\geq_g h_1$.

The $\geq_g$ relation is important because it provides a useful structure over the hypothesis space H for *any* concept learning problem. The following sections present concept learning algorithms that take advantage of this partial order to efficiently organize the search for hypotheses that fit the training data.

1. Initialize h to the most specific hypothesis in H
2. For each positive training instance x
   - For each attribute constraint a_i in h
     If the constraint a_i is satisfied by x
     Then do nothing
     Else replace a_i in h by the next more general constraint that is satisfied by x
3. Output hypothesis h

TABLE 2.3
FIND-S Algorithm.

2.4 FIND-S: FINDING A MAXIMALLY SPECIFIC HYPOTHESIS

How can we use the *more_general_than* partial ordering to organize the search for a hypothesis consistent with the observed training examples? One way is to begin with the most specific possible hypothesis in H, then generalize this hypothesis each time it fails to cover an observed positive training example. (We say that a hypothesis "covers" a positive example if it correctly classifies the example as positive.) To be more precise about how the partial ordering is used, consider the FIND-S algorithm defined in Table 2.3.

To illustrate this algorithm, assume the learner is given the sequence of training examples from Table 2.1 for the *EnjoySport* task. The first step of FIND-S is to initialize h to the most specific hypothesis in H

$$h \leftarrow \langle \emptyset, \emptyset, \emptyset, \emptyset, \emptyset, \emptyset \rangle$$

Upon observing the first training example from Table 2.1, which happens to be a positive example, it becomes clear that our hypothesis is too specific. In particular, none of the "Ø" constraints in h are satisfied by this example, so each is replaced by the next more general constraint that fits the example; namely, the attribute values for this training example.

$$h \leftarrow \langle Sunny, Warm, Normal, Strong, Warm, Same \rangle$$

This h is still very specific; it asserts that all instances are negative except for the single positive training example we have observed. Next, the second training example (also positive in this case) forces the algorithm to further generalize h, this time substituting a "?" in place of any attribute value in h that is not satisfied by the new example. The refined hypothesis in this case is

$$h \leftarrow \langle Sunny, Warm, ?, Strong, Warm, Same \rangle$$

Upon encountering the third training example—in this case a negative example—the algorithm makes no change to h. In fact, the FIND-S algorithm simply *ignores every negative example*! While this may at first seem strange, notice that in the current case our hypothesis h is already consistent with the new negative example (i.e., h correctly classifies this example as negative), and hence no revision is needed. In the general case, as long as we assume that the hypothesis space H contains a hypothesis that describes the true target concept c and that the training data contains no errors, then the current hypothesis h can never require a revision in response to a negative example. To see why, recall that the current hypothesis h is the most specific hypothesis in H consistent with the observed positive examples. Because the target concept c is also assumed to be in H and to be consistent with the positive training examples, c must be *more_general_than_or_equal_to* h. But the target concept c will never cover a negative example, thus neither will h (by the definition of *more_general_than*). Therefore, no revision to h will be required in response to any negative example.

To complete our trace of FIND-S, the fourth (positive) example leads to a further generalization of h

$$h \leftarrow \langle Sunny, Warm, ?, Strong, ?, ? \rangle$$

The FIND-S algorithm illustrates one way in which the *more_general_than* partial ordering can be used to organize the search for an acceptable hypothesis. The search moves from hypothesis to hypothesis, searching from the most specific to progressively more general hypotheses along one chain of the partial ordering. Figure 2.2 illustrates this search in terms of the instance and hypothesis spaces. At each step, the hypothesis is generalized only as far as necessary to cover the new positive example. Therefore, at each stage the hypothesis is the most specific hypothesis consistent with the training examples observed up to this point (hence the name FIND-S). The literature on concept learning is

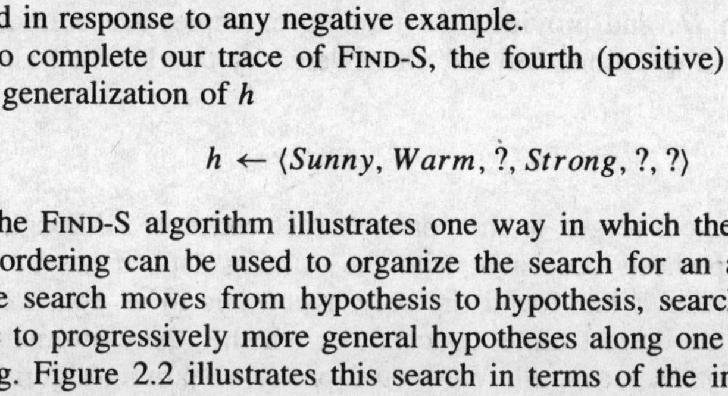

h_0 = <∅, ∅, ∅, ∅, ∅, ∅>

x_1 = <Sunny Warm Normal Strong Warm Same>, + $\quad$ h_1 = <Sunny Warm Normal Strong Warm Same>

x_2 = <Sunny Warm High Strong Warm Same>, + $\quad$ h_2 = <Sunny Warm ? Strong Warm Same>

x_3 = <Rainy Cold High Strong Warm Change>, - $\quad$ h_3 = <Sunny Warm ? Strong Warm Same>

x_4 = <Sunny Warm High Strong Cool Change>, + $\quad$ h_4 = <Sunny Warm ? Strong ? ? >

FIGURE 2.2
The hypothesis space search performed by FIND-S. The search begins (h_0) with the most specific hypothesis in H, then considers increasingly general hypotheses (h_1 through h_4) as mandated by the training examples. In the instance space diagram, positive training examples are denoted by "+," negative by "−," and instances that have not been presented as training examples are denoted by a solid circle.

populated by many different algorithms that utilize this same *more_general_than* partial ordering to organize the search in one fashion or another. A number of such algorithms are discussed in this chapter, and several others are presented in Chapter 10.

The key property of the FIND-S algorithm is that for hypothesis spaces described by conjunctions of attribute constraints (such as H for the *EnjoySport* task), FIND-S is guaranteed to output the most specific hypothesis within H that is consistent with the positive training examples. Its final hypothesis will also be consistent with the negative examples provided the correct target concept is contained in H, and provided the training examples are correct. However, there are several questions still left unanswered by this learning algorithm, such as:

- Has the learner converged to the correct target concept? Although FIND-S will find a hypothesis consistent with the training data, it has no way to determine whether it has found the *only* hypothesis in H consistent with the data (i.e., the correct target concept), or whether there are many other consistent hypotheses as well. We would prefer a learning algorithm that could determine whether it had converged and, if not, at least characterize its uncertainty regarding the true identity of the target concept.

- Why prefer the most specific hypothesis? In case there are multiple hypotheses consistent with the training examples, FIND-S will find the most specific. It is unclear whether we should prefer this hypothesis over, say, the most general, or some other hypothesis of intermediate generality.

- Are the training examples consistent? In most practical learning problems there is some chance that the training examples will contain at least some errors or noise. Such inconsistent sets of training examples can severely mislead FIND-S, given the fact that it ignores negative examples. We would prefer an algorithm that could at least detect when the training data is inconsistent and, preferably, accommodate such errors.

- What if there are several maximally specific consistent hypotheses? In the hypothesis language H for the *EnjoySport* task, there is always a unique, most specific hypothesis consistent with any set of positive examples. However, for other hypothesis spaces (discussed later) there can be several maximally specific hypotheses consistent with the data. In this case, FIND-S must be extended to allow it to backtrack on its choices of how to generalize the hypothesis, to accommodate the possibility that the target concept lies along a different branch of the partial ordering than the branch it has selected. Furthermore, we can define hypothesis spaces for which there is no maximally specific consistent hypothesis, although this is more of a theoretical issue than a practical one (see Exercise 2.7).

2.5 VERSION SPACES AND THE CANDIDATE-ELIMINATION ALGORITHM

This section describes a second approach to concept learning, the CANDIDATE-ELIMINATION algorithm, that addresses several of the limitations of FIND-S. Notice that although FIND-S outputs a hypothesis from H that is consistent with the training examples, this is just one of many hypotheses from H that might fit the training data equally well. The key idea in the CANDIDATE-ELIMINATION algorithm is to output a description of the set of *all hypotheses consistent with the training examples*. Surprisingly, the CANDIDATE-ELIMINATION algorithm computes the description of this set without explicitly enumerating all of its members. This is accomplished by again using the *more_general_than* partial ordering, this time to maintain a compact representation of the set of consistent hypotheses and to incrementally refine this representation as each new training example is encountered.

The CANDIDATE-ELIMINATION algorithm has been applied to problems such as learning regularities in chemical mass spectroscopy (Mitchell 1979) and learning control rules for heuristic search (Mitchell et al. 1983). Nevertheless, practical applications of the CANDIDATE-ELIMINATION and FIND-S algorithms are limited by the fact that they both perform poorly when given noisy training data. More importantly for our purposes here, the CANDIDATE-ELIMINATION algorithm provides a useful conceptual framework for introducing several fundamental issues in machine learning. In the remainder of this chapter we present the algorithm and discuss these issues. Beginning with the next chapter, we will examine learning algorithms that are used more frequently with noisy training data.

2.5.1 Representation

The CANDIDATE-ELIMINATION algorithm finds all describable hypotheses that are consistent with the observed training examples. In order to define this algorithm precisely, we begin with a few basic definitions. First, let us say that a hypothesis is *consistent* with the training examples if it correctly classifies these examples.

> ***Definition***: A hypothesis h is **consistent** with a set of training examples D if and only if $h(x) = c(x)$ for each example $\langle x, c(x)\rangle$ in D.
>
> $$Consistent(h, D) \equiv (\forall \langle x, c(x)\rangle \in D)\ h(x) = c(x)$$

Notice the key difference between this definition of *consistent* and our earlier definition of *satisfies*. An example x is said to *satisfy* hypothesis h when $h(x) = 1$, regardless of whether x is a positive or negative example of the target concept. However, whether such an example is *consistent* with h depends on the target concept, and in particular, whether $h(x) = c(x)$.

The CANDIDATE-ELIMINATION algorithm represents the set of *all* hypotheses consistent with the observed training examples. This subset of all hypotheses is called the *version space* with respect to the hypothesis space H and the training examples D, because it contains all plausible versions of the target concept.

Definition: The **version space**, denoted $VS_{H,D}$, with respect to hypothesis space H and training examples D, is the subset of hypotheses from H consistent with the training examples in D.

$$VS_{H,D} \equiv \{h \in H | Consistent(h, D)\}$$

2.5.2 The LIST-THEN-ELIMINATE Algorithm

One obvious way to represent the version space is simply to list all of its members. This leads to a simple learning algorithm, which we might call the LIST-THEN-ELIMINATE algorithm, defined in Table 2.4.

The LIST-THEN-ELIMINATE algorithm first initializes the version space to contain all hypotheses in H, then eliminates any hypothesis found inconsistent with any training example. The version space of candidate hypotheses thus shrinks as more examples are observed, until ideally just one hypothesis remains that is consistent with all the observed examples. This, presumably, is the desired target concept. If insufficient data is available to narrow the version space to a single hypothesis, then the algorithm can output the entire set of hypotheses consistent with the observed data.

In principle, the LIST-THEN-ELIMINATE algorithm can be applied whenever the hypothesis space H is finite. It has many advantages, including the fact that it is guaranteed to output all hypotheses consistent with the training data. Unfortunately, it requires exhaustively enumerating all hypotheses in H—an unrealistic requirement for all but the most trivial hypothesis spaces.

2.5.3 A More Compact Representation for Version Spaces

The CANDIDATE-ELIMINATION algorithm works on the same principle as the above LIST-THEN-ELIMINATE algorithm. However, it employs a much more compact representation of the version space. In particular, the version space is represented by its most general and least general members. These members form general and specific boundary sets that delimit the version space within the partially ordered hypothesis space.

The LIST-THEN-ELIMINATE Algorithm

1. $VersionSpace \leftarrow$ a list containing every hypothesis in H
2. For each training example, $\langle x, c(x)\rangle$

   remove from $VersionSpace$ any hypothesis h for which $h(x) \neq c(x)$
3. Output the list of hypotheses in $VersionSpace$

TABLE 2.4
The LIST-THEN-ELIMINATE algorithm.

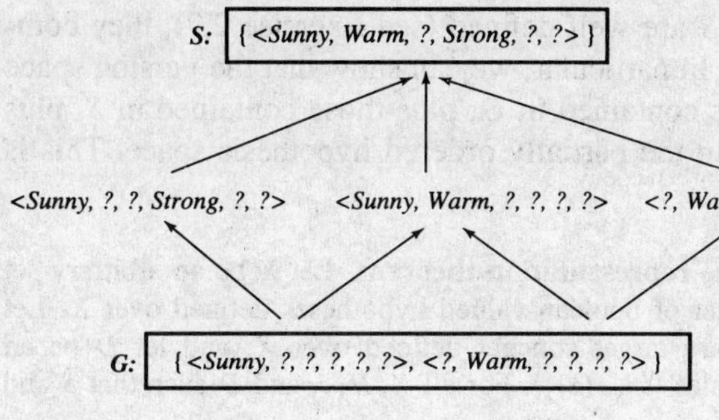

FIGURE 2.3
A version space with its general and specific boundary sets. The version space includes all six hypotheses shown here, but can be represented more simply by S and G. Arrows indicate instances of the *more_general_than* relation. This is the version space for the *EnjoySport* concept learning problem and training examples described in Table 2.1.

To illustrate this representation for version spaces, consider again the *EnjoySport* concept learning problem described in Table 2.2. Recall that given the four training examples from Table 2.1, FIND-S outputs the hypothesis

$$h = \langle Sunny, Warm, ?, Strong, ?, ? \rangle$$

In fact, this is just one of six different hypotheses from H that are consistent with these training examples. All six hypotheses are shown in Figure 2.3. They constitute the version space relative to this set of data and this hypothesis representation. The arrows among these six hypotheses in Figure 2.3 indicate instances of the *more_general_than* relation. The CANDIDATE-ELIMINATION algorithm represents the version space by storing only its most general members (labeled G in Figure 2.3) and its most specific (labeled S in the figure). Given only these two sets S and G, it is possible to enumerate all members of the version space as needed by generating the hypotheses that lie between these two sets in the general-to-specific partial ordering over hypotheses.

It is intuitively plausible that we can represent the version space in terms of its most specific and most general members. Below we define the boundary sets G and S precisely and prove that these sets do in fact represent the version space.

Definition: The **general boundary** G, with respect to hypothesis space H and training data D, is the set of maximally general members of H consistent with D.

$$G \equiv \{g \in H | Consistent(g, D) \wedge (\neg\exists g' \in H)[(g' >_g g) \wedge Consistent(g', D)]\}$$

Definition: The **specific boundary** S, with respect to hypothesis space H and training data D, is the set of minimally general (i.e., maximally specific) members of H consistent with D.

$$S \equiv \{s \in H | Consistent(s, D) \wedge (\neg\exists s' \in H)[(s >_g s') \wedge Consistent(s', D)]\}$$

As long as the sets G and S are well defined (see Exercise 2.7), they completely specify the version space. In particular, we can show that the version space is precisely the set of hypotheses contained in G, plus those contained in S, plus those that lie between G and S in the partially ordered hypothesis space. This is stated precisely in Theorem 2.1.

Theorem 2.1. Version space representation theorem. Let X be an arbitrary set of instances and let H be a set of boolean-valued hypotheses defined over X. Let $c : X \rightarrow \{0, 1\}$ be an arbitrary target concept defined over X, and let D be an arbitrary set of training examples $\{\langle x, c(x)\rangle\}$. For all X, H, c, and D such that S and G are well defined,

$$VS_{H,D} = \{h \in H | (\exists s \in S)(\exists g \in G)(g \geq_g h \geq_g s)\}$$

Proof. To prove the theorem it suffices to show that (1) every h satisfying the right-hand side of the above expression is in $VS_{H,D}$ and (2) every member of $VS_{H,D}$ satisfies the right-hand side of the expression. To show (1) let g be an arbitrary member of G, s be an arbitrary member of S, and h be an arbitrary member of H, such that $g \geq_g h \geq_g s$. Then by the definition of S, s must be satisfied by all positive examples in D. Because $h \geq_g s$, h must also be satisfied by all positive examples in D. Similarly, by the definition of G, g cannot be satisfied by any negative example in D, and because $g \geq_g h$, h cannot be satisfied by any negative example in D. Because h is satisfied by all positive examples in D and by no negative examples in D, h is consistent with D, and therefore h is a member of $VS_{H,D}$. This proves step (1). The argument for (2) is a bit more complex. It can be proven by assuming some h in $VS_{H,D}$ that does not satisfy the right-hand side of the expression, then showing that this leads to an inconsistency. (See Exercise 2.6.) □

2.5.4 Candidate-Elimination Learning Algorithm

The Candidate-Elimination algorithm computes the version space containing all hypotheses from H that are consistent with an observed sequence of training examples. It begins by initializing the version space to the set of all hypotheses in H; that is, by initializing the G boundary set to contain the most general hypothesis in H

$$G_0 \leftarrow \{\langle ?, ?, ?, ?, ?, ? \rangle\}$$

and initializing the S boundary set to contain the most specific (least general) hypothesis

$$S_0 \leftarrow \{\langle \emptyset, \emptyset, \emptyset, \emptyset, \emptyset, \emptyset \rangle\}$$

These two boundary sets delimit the entire hypothesis space, because every other hypothesis in H is both more general than S_0 and more specific than G_0. As each training example is considered, the S and G boundary sets are generalized and specialized, respectively, to eliminate from the version space any hypotheses found inconsistent with the new training example. After all examples have been processed, the computed version space contains all the hypotheses consistent with these examples and only these hypotheses. This algorithm is summarized in Table 2.5.

Initialize *G* to the set of maximally general hypotheses in *H*
Initialize *S* to the set of maximally specific hypotheses in *H*
For each training example *d*, do

- If *d* is a positive example
  - Remove from *G* any hypothesis inconsistent with *d*
  - For each hypothesis *s* in *S* that is not consistent with *d*
    - Remove *s* from *S*
    - Add to *S* all minimal generalizations *h* of *s* such that
      - *h* is consistent with *d*, and some member of *G* is more general than *h*
    - Remove from *S* any hypothesis that is more general than another hypothesis in *S*
- If *d* is a negative example
  - Remove from *S* any hypothesis inconsistent with *d*
  - For each hypothesis *g* in *G* that is not consistent with *d*
    - Remove *g* from *G*
    - Add to *G* all minimal specializations *h* of *g* such that
      - *h* is consistent with *d*, and some member of *S* is more specific than *h*
    - Remove from *G* any hypothesis that is less general than another hypothesis in *G*

TABLE 2.5
CANDIDATE-ELIMINATION algorithm using version spaces. Notice the duality in how positive and negative examples influence *S* and *G*.

Notice that the algorithm is specified in terms of operations such as computing minimal generalizations and specializations of given hypotheses, and identifying nonminimal and nonmaximal hypotheses. The detailed implementation of these operations will depend, of course, on the specific representations for instances and hypotheses. However, the algorithm itself can be applied to any concept learning task and hypothesis space for which these operations are well-defined. In the following example trace of this algorithm, we see how such operations can be implemented for the representations used in the *EnjoySport* example problem.

2.5.5 An Illustrative Example

Figure 2.4 traces the CANDIDATE-ELIMINATION algorithm applied to the first two training examples from Table 2.1. As described above, the boundary sets are first initialized to G_0 and S_0, the most general and most specific hypotheses in H, respectively.

When the first training example is presented (a positive example in this case), the CANDIDATE-ELIMINATION algorithm checks the S boundary and finds that it is overly specific—it fails to cover the positive example. The boundary is therefore revised by moving it to the least more general hypothesis that covers this new example. This revised boundary is shown as S_1 in Figure 2.4. No update of the G boundary is needed in response to this training example because G_0 correctly covers this example. When the second training example (also positive) is observed, it has a similar effect of generalizing S further to S_2, leaving G again unchanged (i.e., $G_2 = G_1 = G_0$). Notice the processing of these first

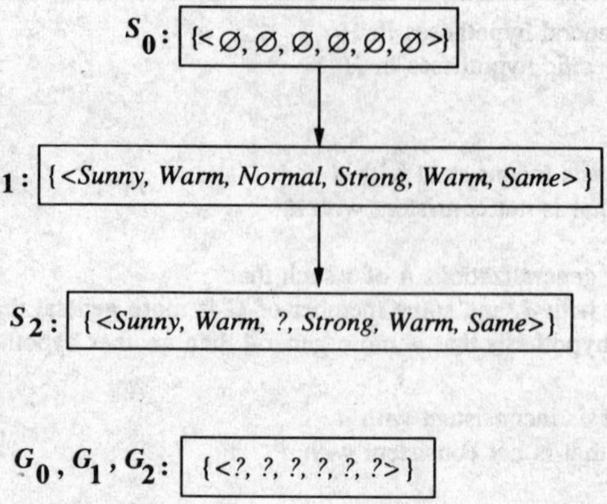

Training examples:

1. *<Sunny, Warm, Normal, Strong, Warm, Same>, Enjoy Sport = Yes*
2. *<Sunny, Warm, High, Strong, Warm, Same>, Enjoy Sport = Yes*

FIGURE 2.4
CANDIDATE-ELIMINATION Trace 1. S_0 and G_0 are the initial boundary sets corresponding to the most specific and most general hypotheses. Training examples 1 and 2 force the S boundary to become more general, as in the FIND-S algorithm. They have no effect on the G boundary.

two positive examples is very similar to the processing performed by the FIND-S algorithm.

As illustrated by these first two steps, positive training examples may force the S boundary of the version space to become increasingly general. Negative training examples play the complimentary role of forcing the G boundary to become increasingly specific. Consider the third training example, shown in Figure 2.5. This negative example reveals that the G boundary of the version space is overly general; that is, the hypothesis in G incorrectly predicts that this new example is a positive example. The hypothesis in the G boundary must therefore be specialized until it correctly classifies this new negative example. As shown in Figure 2.5, there are several alternative minimally more specific hypotheses. All of these become members of the new G_3 boundary set.

Given that there are six attributes that could be specified to specialize G_2, why are there only three new hypotheses in G_3? For example, the hypothesis $h = \langle ?, ?, Normal, ?, ?, ? \rangle$ is a minimal specialization of G_2 that correctly labels the new example as a negative example, but it is not included in G_3. The reason this hypothesis is excluded is that it is inconsistent with the previously encountered positive examples. The algorithm determines this simply by noting that h is not more general than the current specific boundary, S_2. In fact, the S boundary of the version space forms a summary of the previously encountered positive examples that can be used to determine whether any given hypothesis

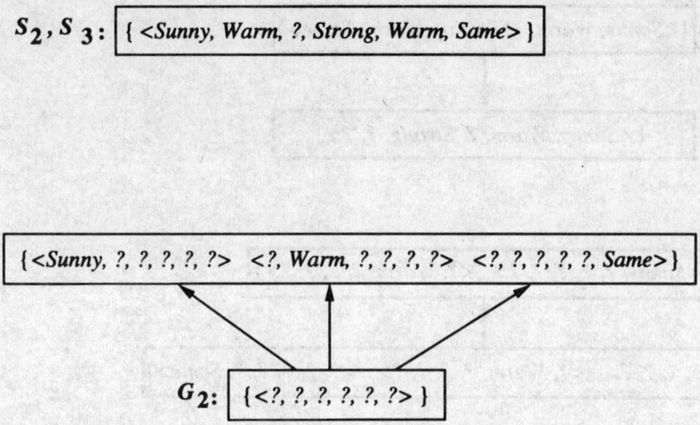

Training Example:

3. *<Rainy, Cold, High, Strong, Warm, Change>, EnjoySport=No*

FIGURE 2.5
CANDIDATE-ELIMINATION Trace 2. Training example 3 is a negative example that forces the G_2 boundary to be specialized to G_3. Note several alternative maximally general hypotheses are included in G_3.

is consistent with these examples. Any hypothesis more general than *S* will, by definition, cover any example that *S* covers and thus will cover any past positive example. In a dual fashion, the *G* boundary summarizes the information from previously encountered negative examples. Any hypothesis more specific than *G* is assured to be consistent with past negative examples. This is true because any such hypothesis, by definition, cannot cover examples that *G* does not cover.

The fourth training example, as shown in Figure 2.6, further generalizes the *S* boundary of the version space. It also results in removing one member of the *G* boundary, because this member fails to cover the new positive example. This last action results from the first step under the condition "If *d* is a positive example" in the algorithm shown in Table 2.5. To understand the rationale for this step, it is useful to consider why the offending hypothesis must be removed from *G*. Notice it cannot be specialized, because specializing it would not make it cover the new example. It also cannot be generalized, because by the definition of *G*, any more general hypothesis will cover at least one negative training example. Therefore, the hypothesis must be dropped from the *G* boundary, thereby removing an entire branch of the partial ordering from the version space of hypotheses remaining under consideration.

After processing these four examples, the boundary sets S_4 and G_4 delimit the version space of *all* hypotheses consistent with the set of incrementally observed training examples. The entire version space, including those hypotheses

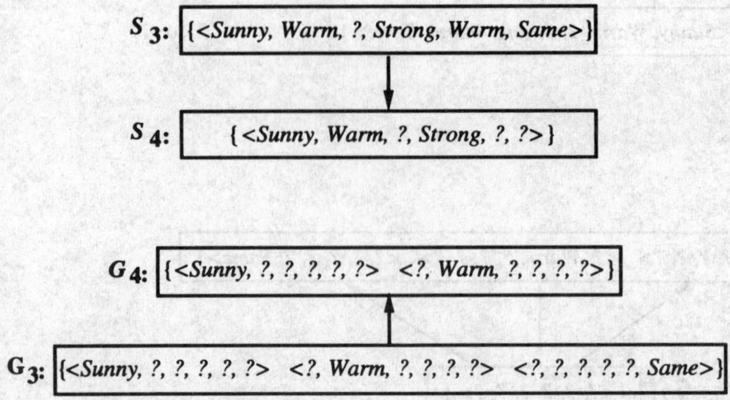

Training Example:

4. *<Sunny, Warm, High, Strong, Cool, Change>, EnjoySport = Yes*

FIGURE 2.6
CANDIDATE-ELIMINATION Trace 3. The positive training example generalizes the S boundary, from S_3 to S_4. One member of G_3 must also be deleted, because it is no longer more general than the S_4 boundary.

bounded by S_4 and G_4, is shown in Figure 2.7. This learned version space is independent of the sequence in which the training examples are presented (because in the end it contains all hypotheses consistent with the set of examples). As further training data is encountered, the S and G boundaries will move monotonically closer to each other, delimiting a smaller and smaller version space of candidate hypotheses.

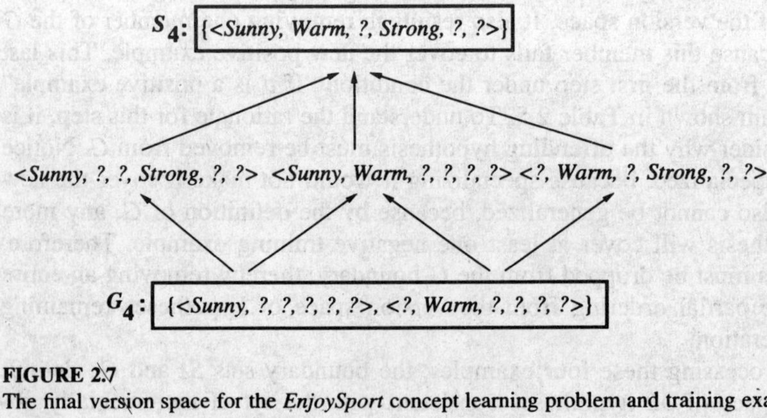

FIGURE 2.7
The final version space for the *EnjoySport* concept learning problem and training examples described earlier.

2.6 REMARKS ON VERSION SPACES AND CANDIDATE-ELIMINATION

2.6.1 Will the CANDIDATE-ELIMINATION Algorithm Converge to the Correct Hypothesis?

The version space learned by the CANDIDATE-ELIMINATION algorithm will converge toward the hypothesis that correctly describes the target concept, provided (1) there are no errors in the training examples, and (2) there is some hypothesis in H that correctly describes the target concept. In fact, as new training examples are observed, the version space can be monitored to determine the remaining ambiguity regarding the true target concept and to determine when sufficient training examples have been observed to unambiguously identify the target concept. The target concept is exactly learned when the S and G boundary sets converge to a single, identical, hypothesis.

What will happen if the training data contains errors? Suppose, for example, that the second training example above is incorrectly presented as a negative example instead of a positive example. Unfortunately, in this case the algorithm is certain to remove the correct target concept from the version space! Because it will remove every hypothesis that is inconsistent with each training example, it will eliminate the true target concept from the version space as soon as this false negative example is encountered. Of course, given sufficient additional training data the learner will eventually detect an inconsistency by noticing that the S and G boundary sets eventually converge to an empty version space. Such an empty version space indicates that there is *no* hypothesis in H consistent with all observed training examples. A similar symptom will appear when the training examples are correct, but the target concept cannot be described in the hypothesis representation (e.g., if the target concept is a disjunction of feature attributes and the hypothesis space supports only conjunctive descriptions). We will consider such eventualities in greater detail later. For now, we consider only the case in which the training examples are correct and the true target concept is present in the hypothesis space.

2.6.2 What Training Example Should the Learner Request Next?

Up to this point we have assumed that training examples are provided to the learner by some external teacher. Suppose instead that the learner is allowed to conduct experiments in which it chooses the next instance, then obtains the correct classification for this instance from an external oracle (e.g., nature or a teacher). This scenario covers situations in which the learner may conduct experiments in nature (e.g., build new bridges and allow nature to classify them as stable or unstable), or in which a teacher is available to provide the correct classification (e.g., propose a new bridge and allow the teacher to suggest whether or not it will be stable). We use the term *query* to refer to such instances constructed by the learner, which are then classified by an external oracle.

Consider again the version space learned from the four training examples of the *EnjoySport* concept and illustrated in Figure 2.3. What would be a good query for the learner to pose at this point? What is a good query strategy in general? Clearly, the learner should attempt to discriminate among the alternative competing hypotheses in its current version space. Therefore, it should choose an instance that would be classified positive by some of these hypotheses, but negative by others. One such instance is

$$\langle Sunny, Warm, Normal, Light, Warm, Same\rangle$$

Note that this instance satisfies three of the six hypotheses in the current version space (Figure 2.3). If the trainer classifies this instance as a positive example, the *S* boundary of the version space can then be generalized. Alternatively, if the trainer indicates that this is a negative example, the *G* boundary can then be specialized. Either way, the learner will succeed in learning more about the true identity of the target concept, shrinking the version space from six hypotheses to half this number.

In general, the optimal query strategy for a concept learner is to generate instances that satisfy exactly half the hypotheses in the current version space. When this is possible, the size of the version space is reduced by half with each new example, and the correct target concept can therefore be found with only $\lceil log_2|VS|\rceil$ experiments. The situation is analogous to playing the game twenty questions, in which the goal is to ask yes-no questions to determine the correct hypothesis. The optimal strategy for playing twenty questions is to ask questions that evenly split the candidate hypotheses into sets that predict yes and no. While we have seen that it is possible to generate an instance that satisfies precisely half the hypotheses in the version space of Figure 2.3, in general it may not be possible to construct an instance that matches precisely half the hypotheses. In such cases, a larger number of queries may be required than $\lceil log_2|VS|\rceil$.

2.6.3 How Can Partially Learned Concepts Be Used?

Suppose that no additional training examples are available beyond the four in our example above, but that the learner is now required to classify new instances that it has not yet observed. Even though the version space of Figure 2.3 still contains multiple hypotheses, indicating that the target concept has not yet been fully learned, it is possible to classify certain examples with the same degree of confidence as if the target concept had been uniquely identified. To illustrate, suppose the learner is asked to classify the four new instances shown in Table 2.6.

Note that although instance *A* was not among the training examples, it is classified as a positive instance by *every* hypothesis in the current version space (shown in Figure 2.3). Because the hypotheses in the version space unanimously agree that this is a positive instance, the learner can classify instance *A* as positive with the same confidence it would have if it had already converged to the single, correct target concept. Regardless of which hypothesis in the version space is eventually found to be the correct target concept, it is already clear that it will classify instance *A* as a positive example. Notice furthermore that we need not enumerate every hypothesis in the version space in order to test whether each

Instance	*Sky*	*AirTemp*	*Humidity*	*Wind*	*Water*	*Forecast*	*EnjoySport*
A	Sunny	Warm	Normal	Strong	Cool	Change	?
B	Rainy	Cold	Normal	Light	Warm	Same	?
C	Sunny	Warm	Normal	Light	Warm	Same	?
D	Sunny	Cold	Normal	Strong	Warm	Same	?

TABLE 2.6
New instances to be classified.

classifies the instance as positive. This condition will be met if and only if the instance satisfies every member of S (why?). The reason is that every other hypothesis in the version space is at least as general as some member of S. By our definition of *more_general_than*, if the new instance satisfies all members of S it must also satisfy each of these more general hypotheses.

Similarly, instance B is classified as a negative instance by every hypothesis in the version space. This instance can therefore be safely classified as negative, given the partially learned concept. An efficient test for this condition is that the instance satisfies none of the members of G (why?).

Instance C presents a different situation. Half of the version space hypotheses classify it as positive and half classify it as negative. Thus, the learner cannot classify this example with confidence until further training examples are available. Notice that instance C is the same instance presented in the previous section as an optimal experimental query for the learner. This is to be expected, because those instances whose classification is most ambiguous are precisely the instances whose true classification would provide the most new information for refining the version space.

Finally, instance D is classified as positive by two of the version space hypotheses and negative by the other four hypotheses. In this case we have less confidence in the classification than in the unambiguous cases of instances A and B. Still, the vote is in favor of a negative classification, and one approach we could take would be to output the majority vote, perhaps with a confidence rating indicating how close the vote was. As we will discuss in Chapter 6, if we assume that all hypotheses in H are equally probable a priori, then such a vote provides the most probable classification of this new instance. Furthermore, the proportion of hypotheses voting positive can be interpreted as the probability that this instance is positive given the training data.

2.7 INDUCTIVE BIAS

As discussed above, the CANDIDATE-ELIMINATION algorithm will converge toward the true target concept provided it is given accurate training examples and provided its initial hypothesis space contains the target concept. What if the target concept is not contained in the hypothesis space? Can we avoid this difficulty by using a hypothesis space that includes every possible hypothesis? How does the size of this hypothesis space influence the ability of the algorithm to generalize to unobserved instances? How does the size of the hypothesis space influence the number of training examples that must be observed? These are fundamental questions for inductive inference in general. Here we examine them in the context of the CANDIDATE-ELIMINATION algorithm. As we shall see, though, the conclusions we draw from this analysis will apply to *any* concept learning system that outputs *any* hypothesis consistent with the training data.

2.7.1 A Biased Hypothesis Space

Suppose we wish to assure that the hypothesis space contains the unknown target concept. The obvious solution is to enrich the hypothesis space to include *every possible* hypothesis. To illustrate, consider again the *EnjoySport* example in which we restricted the hypothesis space to include only conjunctions of attribute values. Because of this restriction, the hypothesis space is unable to represent even simple disjunctive target concepts such as "*Sky* = *Sunny* or *Sky* = *Cloudy*." In fact, given the following three training examples of this disjunctive hypothesis, our algorithm would find that there are zero hypotheses in the version space.

Example	*Sky*	*AirTemp*	*Humidity*	*Wind*	*Water*	*Forecast*	*EnjoySport*
1	Sunny	Warm	Normal	Strong	Cool	Change	Yes
2	Cloudy	Warm	Normal	Strong	Cool	Change	Yes
3	Rainy	Warm	Normal	Strong	Cool	Change	No

To see why there are no hypotheses consistent with these three examples, note that the most specific hypothesis consistent with the first two examples *and representable in the given hypothesis space H* is

$$S_2 : \langle ?, Warm, Normal, Strong, Cool, Change \rangle$$

This hypothesis, although it is the maximally specific hypothesis from H that is consistent with the first two examples, is already overly general: it incorrectly covers the third (negative) training example. The problem is that we have biased the learner to consider only conjunctive hypotheses. In this case we require a more expressive hypothesis space.

2.7.2 An Unbiased Learner

The obvious solution to the problem of assuring that the target concept is in the hypothesis space H is to provide a hypothesis space capable of representing *every teachable concept*; that is, it is capable of representing every possible subset of the instances X. In general, the set of all subsets of a set X is called the *power set* of X.

In the *EnjoySport* learning task, for example, the size of the instance space X of days described by the six available attributes is 96. How many possible concepts can be defined over this set of instances? In other words, how large is the power set of X? In general, the number of distinct subsets that can be defined over a set X containing $|X|$ elements (i.e., the size of the power set of X) is $2^{|X|}$. Thus, there are 2^{96}, or approximately 10^{28} distinct target concepts that could be defined over this instance space and that our learner might be called upon to learn. Recall from Section 2.3 that our conjunctive hypothesis space is able to represent only 973 of these—a very biased hypothesis space indeed!

Let us reformulate the *EnjoySport* learning task in an unbiased way by defining a new hypothesis space H' that can represent every subset of instances; that is, let H' correspond to the power set of X. One way to define such an H' is to allow arbitrary disjunctions, conjunctions, and negations of our earlier hypotheses. For instance, the target concept "*Sky* = *Sunny* or *Sky* = *Cloudy*" could then be described as

$$\langle Sunny, ?, ?, ?, ?, ?\rangle \vee \langle Cloudy, ?, ?, ?, ?, ?\rangle$$

Given this hypothesis space, we can safely use the CANDIDATE-ELIMINATION algorithm without worrying that the target concept might not be expressible. However, while this hypothesis space eliminates any problems of expressibility, it unfortunately raises a new, equally difficult problem: our concept learning algorithm is now completely unable to generalize beyond the observed examples! To see why, suppose we present three positive examples (x_1, x_2, x_3) and two negative examples (x_4, x_5) to the learner. At this point, the S boundary of the version space will contain the hypothesis which is just the disjunction of the positive examples

$$S : \{(x_1 \vee x_2 \vee x_3)\}$$

because this is the most specific possible hypothesis that covers these three examples. Similarly, the G boundary will consist of the hypothesis that rules out only the observed negative examples

$$G : \{\neg(x_4 \vee x_5)\}$$

The problem here is that with this very expressive hypothesis representation, the S boundary will always be simply the disjunction of the observed positive examples, while the G boundary will always be the negated disjunction of the observed negative examples. Therefore, the only examples that will be unambiguously classified by S and G are the observed training examples themselves. In order to converge to a single, final target concept, we will have to present every single instance in X as a training example!

It might at first seem that we could avoid this difficulty by simply using the partially learned version space and by taking a vote among the members of the version space as discussed in Section 2.6.3. Unfortunately, the only instances that will produce a unanimous vote are the previously observed training examples. For all the other instances, taking a vote will be futile: each unobserved instance will be classified positive by *precisely half* the hypotheses in the version space and will be classified negative by the other half (why?). To see the reason, note that when H is the power set of X and x is some previously unobserved instance, then for any hypothesis h in the version space that covers x, there will be another hypothesis h' in the power set that is identical to h except for its classification of x. And of course if h is in the version space, then h' will be as well, because it agrees with h on all the observed training examples.

2.7.3 The Futility of Bias-Free Learning

The above discussion illustrates a fundamental property of inductive inference: *a learner that makes no a priori assumptions regarding the identity of the target concept has no rational basis for classifying any unseen instances.* In fact, the only reason that the CANDIDATE-ELIMINATION algorithm was able to generalize beyond the observed training examples in our original formulation of the *EnjoySport* task is that it was biased by the implicit assumption that the target concept could be represented by a conjunction of attribute values. In cases where this assumption is correct (and the training examples are error-free), its classification of new instances will also be correct. If this assumption is incorrect, however, it is certain that the CANDIDATE-ELIMINATION algorithm will misclassify at least some instances from X.

Because inductive learning requires some form of prior assumptions, or inductive bias, we will find it useful to characterize different learning approaches by the inductive bias† they employ. Let us define this notion of inductive bias more precisely. The key idea we wish to capture here is the policy by which the learner generalizes beyond the observed training data, to infer the classification of new instances. Therefore, consider the general setting in which an arbitrary learning algorithm L is provided an arbitrary set of training data $D_c = \{\langle x, c(x)\rangle\}$ of some arbitrary target concept c. After training, L is asked to classify a new instance x_i. Let $L(x_i, D_c)$ denote the classification (e.g., positive or negative) that L assigns to x_i after learning from the training data D_c. We can describe this inductive inference step performed by L as follows

$$(D_c \wedge x_i) \succ L(x_i, D_c)$$

where the notation $y \succ z$ indicates that z is inductively inferred from y. For example, if we take L to be the CANDIDATE-ELIMINATION algorithm, D_c to be the training data from Table 2.1, and x_i to be the first instance from Table 2.6, then the inductive inference performed in this case concludes that $L(x_i, D_c) = (EnjoySport = yes)$.

Because L is an inductive learning algorithm, the result $L(x_i, D_c)$ that it infers will not in general be provably correct; that is, the classification $L(x_i, D_c)$ need not follow deductively from the training data D_c and the description of the new instance x_i. However, it is interesting to ask what additional assumptions could be added to $D_c \wedge x_i$ so that $L(x_i, D_c)$ would follow deductively. We define the inductive bias of L as this set of additional assumptions. More precisely, we define the

†The term *inductive bias* here is not to be confused with the term *estimation bias* commonly used in statistics. Estimation bias will be discussed in Chapter 5.

inductive bias of L to be the set of assumptions B such that for all new instances x_i

$$(B \wedge D_c \wedge x_i) \vdash L(x_i, D_c)$$

where the notation $y \vdash z$ indicates that z follows deductively from y (i.e., that z is provable from y). Thus, we define the inductive bias of a learner as the set of additional assumptions B sufficient to justify its inductive inferences as deductive inferences. To summarize,

> ***Definition***: Consider a concept learning algorithm L for the set of instances X. Let c be an arbitrary concept defined over X, and let $D_c = \{\langle x, c(x)\rangle\}$ be an arbitrary set of training examples of c. Let $L(x_i, D_c)$ denote the classification assigned to the instance x_i by L after training on the data D_c. The **inductive bias** of L is any minimal set of assertions B such that for any target concept c and corresponding training examples D_c
>
> $$(\forall x_i \in X)[(B \wedge D_c \wedge x_i) \vdash L(x_i, D_c)] \tag{2.1}$$

What, then, is the inductive bias of the CANDIDATE-ELIMINATION algorithm? To answer this, let us specify $L(x_i, D_c)$ exactly for this algorithm: given a set of data D_c, the CANDIDATE-ELIMINATION algorithm will first compute the version space VS_{H,D_c}, then classify the new instance x_i by a vote among hypotheses in this version space. Here let us assume that it will output a classification for x_i only if this vote among version space hypotheses is unanimously positive or negative and that it will not output a classification otherwise. Given this definition of $L(x_i, D_c)$ for the CANDIDATE-ELIMINATION algorithm, what is its inductive bias? It is simply the assumption $c \in H$. Given this assumption, each inductive inference performed by the CANDIDATE-ELIMINATION algorithm can be justified deductively.

To see why the classification $L(x_i, D_c)$ follows deductively from $B = \{c \in H\}$, together with the data D_c and description of the instance x_i, consider the following argument. First, notice that if we assume $c \in H$ then it follows deductively that $c \in VS_{H,D_c}$. This follows from $c \in H$, from the definition of the version space VS_{H,D_c} as the set of all hypotheses in H that are consistent with D_c, and from our definition of $D_c = \{\langle x, c(x)\rangle\}$ as training data consistent with the target concept c. Second, recall that we defined the classification $L(x_i, D_c)$ to be the unanimous vote of all hypotheses in the version space. Thus, if L outputs the classification $L(x_i, D_c)$, it must be the case the every hypothesis in VS_{H,D_c} also produces this classification, including the hypothesis $c \in VS_{H,D_c}$. Therefore $c(x_i) = L(x_i, D_c)$. To summarize, the CANDIDATE-ELIMINATION algorithm defined in this fashion can be characterized by the following bias

> **Inductive bias of CANDIDATE-ELIMINATION algorithm.** The target concept c is contained in the given hypothesis space H.

Figure 2.8 summarizes the situation schematically. The inductive CANDIDATE-ELIMINATION algorithm at the top of the figure takes two inputs: the training examples and a new instance to be classified. At the bottom of the figure, a deductive

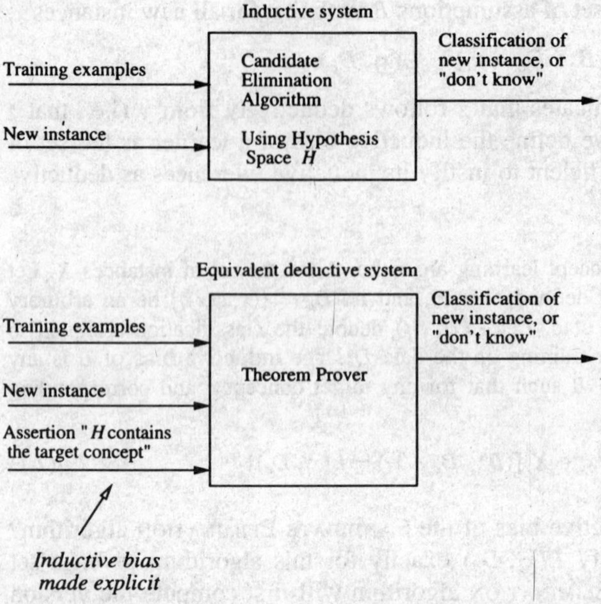

FIGURE 2.8
Modeling inductive systems by equivalent deductive systems. The input-output behavior of the CANDIDATE-ELIMINATION algorithm using a hypothesis space H is identical to that of a deductive theorem prover utilizing the assertion "H contains the target concept." This assertion is therefore called the *inductive bias* of the CANDIDATE-ELIMINATION algorithm. Characterizing inductive systems by their inductive bias allows modeling them by their equivalent deductive systems. This provides a way to compare inductive systems according to their policies for generalizing beyond the observed training data.

theorem prover is given these same two inputs plus the assertion "H contains the target concept." These two systems will in principle produce identical outputs for every possible input set of training examples and every possible new instance in X. Of course the inductive bias that is explicitly input to the theorem prover is only implicit in the code of the CANDIDATE-ELIMINATION algorithm. In a sense, it exists only in the eye of us beholders. Nevertheless, it is a perfectly well-defined set of assertions.

One advantage of viewing inductive inference systems in terms of their inductive bias is that it provides a nonprocedural means of characterizing their policy for generalizing beyond the observed data. A second advantage is that it allows comparison of different learners according to the strength of the inductive bias they employ. Consider, for example, the following three learning algorithms, which are listed from weakest to strongest bias.

1. ROTE-LEARNER: Learning corresponds simply to storing each observed training example in memory. Subsequent instances are classified by looking them

up in memory. If the instance is found in memory, the stored classification is returned. Otherwise, the system refuses to classify the new instance.

2. CANDIDATE-ELIMINATION algorithm: New instances are classified only in the case where all members of the current version space agree on the classification. Otherwise, the system refuses to classify the new instance.
3. FIND-S: This algorithm, described earlier, finds the most specific hypothesis consistent with the training examples. It then uses this hypothesis to classify all subsequent instances.

The ROTE-LEARNER has no inductive bias. The classifications it provides for new instances follow deductively from the observed training examples, with no additional assumptions required. The CANDIDATE-ELIMINATION algorithm has a stronger inductive bias: that the target concept can be represented in its hypothesis space. Because it has a stronger bias, it will classify some instances that the ROTE-LEARNER will not. Of course the correctness of such classifications will depend completely on the correctness of this inductive bias. The FIND-S algorithm has an even stronger inductive bias. In addition to the assumption that the target concept can be described in its hypothesis space, it has an additional inductive bias assumption: that all instances are negative instances unless the opposite is entailed by its other knowledge.†

As we examine other inductive inference methods, it is useful to keep in mind this means of characterizing them and the strength of their inductive bias. More strongly biased methods make more inductive leaps, classifying a greater proportion of unseen instances. Some inductive biases correspond to categorical assumptions that completely rule out certain concepts, such as the bias "the hypothesis space *H* includes the target concept." Other inductive biases merely rank order the hypotheses by stating preferences such as "more specific hypotheses are preferred over more general hypotheses." Some biases are implicit in the learner and are unchangeable by the learner, such as the ones we have considered here. In Chapters 11 and 12 we will see other systems whose bias is made explicit as a set of assertions represented and manipulated by the learner.

2.8 SUMMARY AND FURTHER READING

The main points of this chapter include:

- Concept learning can be cast as a problem of searching through a large predefined space of potential hypotheses.
- The general-to-specific partial ordering of hypotheses, which can be defined for any concept learning problem, provides a useful structure for organizing the search through the hypothesis space.

---

† Notice this last inductive bias assumption involves a kind of default, or nonmonotonic reasoning.

- The FIND-S algorithm utilizes this general-to-specific ordering, performing a specific-to-general search through the hypothesis space along one branch of the partial ordering, to find the most specific hypothesis consistent with the training examples.
- The CANDIDATE-ELIMINATION algorithm utilizes this general-to-specific ordering to compute the version space (the set of all hypotheses consistent with the training data) by incrementally computing the sets of maximally specific (S) and maximally general (G) hypotheses.
- Because the S and G sets delimit the entire set of hypotheses consistent with the data, they provide the learner with a description of its uncertainty regarding the exact identity of the target concept. This version space of alternative hypotheses can be examined to determine whether the learner has converged to the target concept, to determine when the training data are inconsistent, to generate informative queries to further refine the version space, and to determine which unseen instances can be unambiguously classified based on the partially learned concept.
- Version spaces and the CANDIDATE-ELIMINATION algorithm provide a useful conceptual framework for studying concept learning. However, this learning algorithm is not robust to noisy data or to situations in which the unknown target concept is not expressible in the provided hypothesis space. Chapter 10 describes several concept learning algorithms based on the general-to-specific ordering, which are robust to noisy data.
- Inductive learning algorithms are able to classify unseen examples only because of their implicit inductive bias for selecting one consistent hypothesis over another. The bias associated with the CANDIDATE-ELIMINATION algorithm is that the target concept can be found in the provided hypothesis space ($c \in H$). The output hypotheses and classifications of subsequent instances follow *deductively* from this assumption together with the observed training data.
- If the hypothesis space is enriched to the point where there is a hypothesis corresponding to every possible subset of instances (the power set of the instances), this will remove any inductive bias from the CANDIDATE-ELIMINATION algorithm. Unfortunately, this also removes the ability to classify any instance beyond the observed training examples. An unbiased learner cannot make inductive leaps to classify unseen examples.

The idea of concept learning and using the general-to-specific ordering have been studied for quite some time. Bruner et al. (1957) provided an early study of concept learning in humans, and Hunt and Hovland (1963) an early effort to automate it. Winston's (1970) widely known Ph.D. dissertation cast concept learning as a search involving generalization and specialization operators. Plotkin (1970, 1971) provided an early formalization of the *more-general-than* relation, as well as the related notion of θ-subsumption (discussed in Chapter 10). Simon and Lea (1973) give an early account of learning as search through a hypothesis space. Other early concept learning systems include (Popplestone 1969; Michalski 1973; Buchanan 1974; Vere 1975; Hayes-Roth 1974). A very large number of algorithms have since been developed for concept learning based on symbolic representations. Chapter 10 describes several more recent algorithms for concept learning, including algorithms that learn concepts represented in first-order logic, algorithms that are robust to noisy training data, and algorithms whose performance degrades gracefully if the target concept is not representable in the hypothesis space considered by the learner.

Version spaces and the CANDIDATE-ELIMINATION algorithm were introduced by Mitchell (1977, 1982). The application of this algorithm to inferring rules of mass spectroscopy is described in (Mitchell 1979), and its application to learning search control rules is presented in (Mitchell et al. 1983). Haussler (1988) shows that the size of the general boundary can grow exponentially in the number of training examples, even when the hypothesis space consists of simple conjunctions of features. Smith and Rosenbloom (1990) show a simple change to the representation of the G set that can improve complexity in certain cases, and Hirsh (1992) shows that learning can be polynomial in the number of examples in some cases when the G set is not stored at all. Subramanian and Feigenbaum (1986) discuss a method that can generate efficient queries in certain cases by factoring the version space. One of the greatest practical limitations of the CANDIDATE-ELIMINATION algorithm is that it requires noise-free training data. Mitchell (1979) describes an extension that can handle a bounded, predetermined number of misclassified examples, and Hirsh (1990, 1994) describes an elegant extension for handling bounded noise in real-valued attributes that describe the training examples. Hirsh (1990) describes an INCREMENTAL VERSION SPACE MERGING algorithm that generalizes the CANDIDATE-ELIMINATION algorithm to handle situations in which training information can be different types of constraints represented using version spaces. The information from each constraint is represented by a version space and the constraints are then combined by intersecting the version spaces. Sebag (1994, 1996) presents what she calls a disjunctive version space approach to learning disjunctive concepts from noisy data. A separate version space is learned for each positive training example, then new instances are classified by combining the votes of these different version spaces. She reports experiments in several problem domains demonstrating that her approach is competitive with other widely used induction methods such as decision tree learning and k-NEAREST NEIGHBOR.

EXERCISES

2.1. Explain why the size of the hypothesis space in the *EnjoySport* learning task is 973. How would the number of possible instances and possible hypotheses increase with the addition of the attribute *WaterCurrent*, which can take on the values *Light*, *Moderate*, or *Strong*? More generally, how does the number of possible instances and hypotheses grow with the addition of a new attribute A that takes on k possible values?

2.2. Give the sequence of S and G boundary sets computed by the CANDIDATE-ELIMINATION algorithm if it is given the sequence of training examples from Table 2.1 *in reverse order.* Although the final version space will be the same regardless of the sequence of examples (why?), the sets S and G computed at intermediate stages will, of course, depend on this sequence. Can you come up with ideas for ordering the training examples to minimize the sum of the sizes of these intermediate S and G sets for the H used in the *EnjoySport* example?

2.3. Consider again the *EnjoySport* learning task and the hypothesis space H described in Section 2.2. Let us define a new hypothesis space H' that consists of all *pairwise* disjunctions of the hypotheses in H. For example, a typical hypothesis in H' is

$$\langle ?, Cold, High, ?, ?, ? \rangle \vee \langle Sunny, ?, High, ?, ?, Same \rangle$$

Trace the CANDIDATE-ELIMINATION algorithm for the hypothesis space H' given the sequence of training examples from Table 2.1 (i.e., show the sequence of S and G boundary sets.)

2.4. Consider the instance space consisting of integer points in the x, y plane and the set of hypotheses H consisting of rectangles. More precisely, hypotheses are of the form $a \le x \le b, c \le y \le d$, where a, b, c, and d can be any integers.

(*a*) Consider the version space with respect to the set of positive (+) and negative (−) training examples shown below. What is the S boundary of the version space in this case? Write out the hypotheses and draw them in on the diagram.

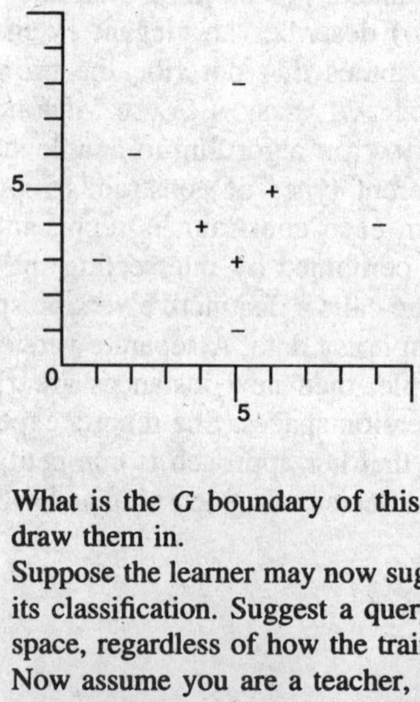

(*b*) What is the G boundary of this version space? Write out the hypotheses and draw them in.

(*c*) Suppose the learner may now suggest a new x, y instance and ask the trainer for its classification. Suggest a query guaranteed to reduce the size of the version space, regardless of how the trainer classifies it. Suggest one that will not.

(*d*) Now assume you are a teacher, attempting to teach a particular target concept (e.g., $3 \le x \le 5, 2 \le y \le 9$). What is the smallest number of training examples you can provide so that the CANDIDATE-ELIMINATION algorithm will perfectly learn the target concept?

2.5. Consider the following sequence of positive and negative training examples describing the concept "pairs of people who live in the same house." Each training example describes an *ordered* pair of people, with each person described by their sex, hair color (black, brown, or blonde), height (tall, medium, or short), and nationality (US, French, German, Irish, Indian, Japanese, or Portuguese).

+ ⟨⟨*male brown tall US*⟩⟨*female black short US*⟩⟩

+ ⟨⟨*male brown short French*⟩⟨*female black short US*⟩⟩

− ⟨⟨*female brown tall German*⟩⟨*female black short Indian*⟩⟩

+ ⟨⟨*male brown tall Irish*⟩⟨*female brown short Irish*⟩⟩

Consider a hypothesis space defined over these instances, in which each hypothesis is represented by a pair of 4-tuples, and where each attribute constraint may be a specific value, "?," or "Ø," just as in the *EnjoySport* hypothesis representation. For example, the hypothesis

⟨⟨*male* ? *tall* ?⟩⟨*female* ? ? *Japanese*⟩⟩

represents the set of all pairs of people where the first is a tall male (of any nationality and hair color), and the second is a Japanese female (of any hair color and height).

(*a*) Provide a hand trace of the CANDIDATE-ELIMINATION algorithm learning from the above training examples and hypothesis language. In particular, show the specific and general boundaries of the version space after it has processed the first training example, then the second training example, etc.

(*b*) How many distinct hypotheses from the given hypothesis space are consistent with the following single positive training example?

+ ⟨⟨*male black short Portuguese*⟩⟨*female blonde tall Indian*⟩⟩

(*c*) Assume the learner has encountered only the positive example from part (*b*), and that it is now allowed to query the trainer by generating any instance and asking the trainer to classify it. Give a specific sequence of queries that assures the learner will converge to the single correct hypothesis, whatever it may be (assuming that the target concept is describable within the given hypothesis language). Give the shortest sequence of queries you can find. How does the length of this sequence relate to your answer to question (*b*)?

(*d*) Note that this hypothesis language cannot express all concepts that can be defined over the instances (i.e., we can define sets of positive and negative examples for which there is no corresponding describable hypothesis). If we were to enrich the language so that it *could* express all concepts that can be defined over the instance language, then how would your answer to (*c*) change?

2.6. Complete the proof of the version space representation theorem (Theorem 2.1).

2.7. Consider a concept learning problem in which each instance is a real number, and in which each hypothesis is an interval over the reals. More precisely, each hypothesis in the hypothesis space H is of the form $a < x < b$, where a and b are any real constants, and x refers to the instance. For example, the hypothesis $4.5 < x < 6.1$ classifies instances between 4.5 and 6.1 as positive, and others as negative. Explain informally why there cannot be a maximally specific consistent hypothesis for any set of positive training examples. Suggest a slight modification to the hypothesis representation so that there will be.

2.8. In this chapter, we commented that given an unbiased hypothesis space (the power set of the instances), the learner would find that each unobserved instance would match exactly half the current members of the version space, regardless of which training examples had been observed. Prove this. In particular, prove that for any instance space X, any set of training examples D, and any instance $x \in X$ not present in D, that if H is the power set of X, then exactly half the hypotheses in $VS_{H,D}$ will classify x as positive and half will classify it as negative.

2.9. Consider a learning problem where each instance is described by a conjunction of n boolean attributes $a_1 \ldots a_n$. Thus, a typical instance would be

$$(a_1 = T) \wedge (a_2 = F) \wedge \ldots \wedge (a_n = T)$$

Now consider a hypothesis space H in which each hypothesis is a *disjunction* of constraints over these attributes. For example, a typical hypothesis would be

$$(a_1 = T) \vee (a_5 = F) \vee (a_7 = T)$$

Propose an algorithm that accepts a sequence of training examples and outputs a consistent hypothesis if one exists. Your algorithm should run in time that is polynomial in n and in the number of training examples.

2.10. Implement the FIND-S algorithm. First verify that it successfully produces the trace in Section 2.4 for the *EnjoySport* example. Now use this program to study the number of random training examples required to exactly learn the target concept. Implement a training example generator that generates random instances, then classifies them according to the target concept:

$$\langle Sunny, Warm, ?, ?, ?, ? \rangle$$

Consider training your FIND-S program on randomly generated examples and measuring the number of examples required before the program's hypothesis is identical to the target concept. Can you predict the average number of examples required? Run the experiment at least 20 times and report the mean number of examples required. How do you expect this number to vary with the number of "?"s in the target concept? How would it vary with the number of attributes used to describe instances and hypotheses?

REFERENCES

Bruner, J. S., Goodnow, J. J., & Austin, G. A. (1957). *A study of thinking*. New York: John Wiley & Sons.

Buchanan, B. G. (1974). Scientific theory formation by computer. In J. C. Simon (Ed.), *Computer Oriented Learning Processes*. Leyden: Noordhoff.

Gunter, C. A., Ngair, T., Panangaden, P., & Subramanian, D. (1991). The common order-theoretic structure of version spaces and ATMS's. *Proceedings of the National Conference on Artificial Intelligence* (pp. 500–505). Anaheim.

Haussler, D. (1988). Quantifying inductive bias: AI learning algorithms and Valiant's learning framework. *Artificial Intelligence*, 36, 177–221.

Hayes-Roth, F. (1974). Schematic classification problems and their solution. *Pattern Recognition*, 6, 105–113.

Hirsh, H. (1990). Incremental version space merging: A general framework for concept learning. Boston: Kluwer.

Hirsh, H. (1991). Theoretical underpinnings of version spaces. *Proceedings of the 12th IJCAI* (pp. 665–670). Sydney.

Hirsh, H. (1994). Generalizing version spaces. *Machine Learning*, 17(1), 5–46.

Hunt, E. G., & Hovland, D. I. (1963). Programming a model of human concept formation. In E. Feigenbaum & J. Feldman (Eds.), *Computers and thought* (pp. 310–325). New York: McGraw Hill.

Michalski, R. S. (1973). AQVAL/1: Computer implementation of a variable valued logic system VL1 and examples of its application to pattern recognition. *Proceedings of the 1st International Joint Conference on Pattern Recognition* (pp. 3–17).

Mitchell, T. M. (1977). Version spaces: A candidate elimination approach to rule learning. *Fifth International Joint Conference on AI* (pp. 305–310). Cambridge, MA: MIT Press.

Mitchell, T. M. (1979). *Version spaces: An approach to concept learning,* (Ph.D. dissertation). Electrical Engineering Dept., Stanford University, Stanford, CA.

Mitchell, T. M. (1982). Generalization as search. *Artificial Intelligence,* 18(2), 203–226.

Mitchell, T. M., Utgoff, P. E., & Banerji, R. (1983). Learning by experimentation: Acquiring and modifying problem-solving heuristics. In Michalski, Carbonell, & Mitchell (Eds.), *Machine Learning* (Vol. 1, pp. 163–190). Tioga Press.

Plotkin, G. D. (1970). A note on inductive generalization. In Meltzer & Michie (Eds.), *Machine Intelligence 5* (pp. 153–163). Edinburgh University Press.

Plotkin, G. D. (1971). A further note on inductive generalization. In Meltzer & Michie (Eds.), *Machine Intelligence 6* (pp. 104–124). Edinburgh University Press.

Popplestone, R. J. (1969). An experiment in automatic induction. In Meltzer & Michie (Eds.), *Machine Intelligence 5* (pp. 204–215). Edinburgh University Press.

Sebag, M. (1994). Using constraints to build version spaces. *Proceedings of the 1994 European Conference on Machine Learning*. Springer-Verlag.

Sebag, M. (1996). Delaying the choice of bias: A disjunctive version space approach. *Proceedings of the 13th International Conference on Machine Learning* (pp. 444–452). San Francisco: Morgan Kaufmann.

Simon, H. A., & Lea, G. (1973). Problem solving and rule induction: A unified view. In Gregg (Ed.), *Knowledge and Cognition* (pp. 105–127). New Jersey: Lawrence Erlbaum Associates.

Smith, B. D., & Rosenbloom, P. (1990). Incremental non-backtracking focusing: A polynomially bounded generalization algorithm for version spaces. *Proceedings of the 1990 National Conference on Artificial Intelligence* (pp. 848–853). Boston.

Subramanian, D., & Feigenbaum, J. (1986). Factorization in experiment generation. *Proceedings of the 1986 National Conference on Artificial Intelligence* (pp. 518–522). Morgan Kaufmann.

Vere, S. A. (1975). Induction of concepts in the predicate calculus. *Fourth International Joint Conference on AI* (pp. 281–287). Tbilisi, USSR.

Winston, P. H. (1970). *Learning structural descriptions from examples,* (Ph.D. dissertation). [MIT Technical Report AI-TR-231].

CHAPTER 3

DECISION TREE LEARNING

Decision tree learning is one of the most widely used and practical methods for inductive inference. It is a method for approximating discrete-valued functions that is robust to noisy data and capable of learning disjunctive expressions. This chapter describes a family of decision tree learning algorithms that includes widely used algorithms such as ID3, ASSISTANT, and C4.5. These decision tree learning methods search a completely expressive hypothesis space and thus avoid the difficulties of restricted hypothesis spaces. Their inductive bias is a preference for small trees over large trees.

3.1 INTRODUCTION

Decision tree learning is a method for approximating discrete-valued target functions, in which the learned function is represented by a decision tree. Learned trees can also be re-represented as sets of if-then rules to improve human readability. These learning methods are among the most popular of inductive inference algorithms and have been successfully applied to a broad range of tasks from learning to diagnose medical cases to learning to assess credit risk of loan applicants.

3.2 DECISION TREE REPRESENTATION

Decision trees classify instances by sorting them down the tree from the root to some leaf node, which provides the classification of the instance. Each node in the tree specifies a test of some *attribute* of the instance, and each branch descending

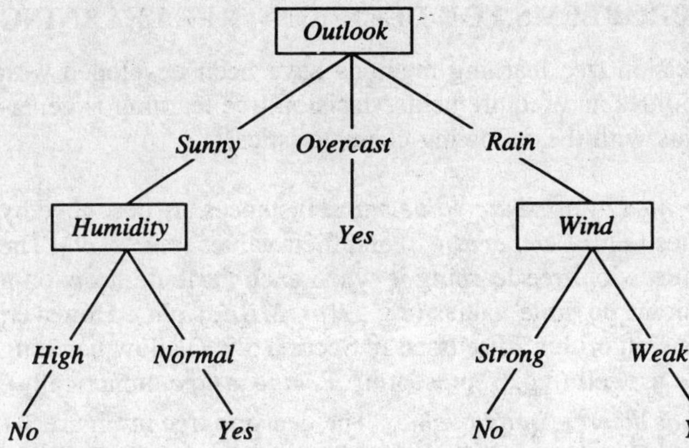

FIGURE 3.1
A decision tree for the concept *PlayTennis*. An example is classified by sorting it through the tree to the appropriate leaf node, then returning the classification associated with this leaf (in this case, *Yes* or *No*). This tree classifies Saturday mornings according to whether or not they are suitable for playing tennis.

from that node corresponds to one of the possible values for this attribute. An instance is classified by starting at the root node of the tree, testing the attribute specified by this node, then moving down the tree branch corresponding to the value of the attribute in the given example. This process is then repeated for the subtree rooted at the new node.

Figure 3.1 illustrates a typical learned decision tree. This decision tree classifies Saturday mornings according to whether they are suitable for playing tennis. For example, the instance

$$\langle Outlook = Sunny,\ Temperature = Hot,\ Humidity = High,\ Wind = Strong\rangle$$

would be sorted down the leftmost branch of this decision tree and would therefore be classified as a negative instance (i.e., the tree predicts that $PlayTennis = no$). This tree and the example used in Table 3.2 to illustrate the ID3 learning algorithm are adapted from (Quinlan 1986).

In general, decision trees represent a disjunction of conjunctions of constraints on the attribute values of instances. Each path from the tree root to a leaf corresponds to a conjunction of attribute tests, and the tree itself to a disjunction of these conjunctions. For example, the decision tree shown in Figure 3.1 corresponds to the expression

$$\begin{aligned} &(Outlook = Sunny \ \wedge \ Humidity = Normal) \\ \vee \quad &(Outlook = Overcast) \\ \vee \quad &(Outlook = Rain \ \wedge \ Wind = Weak) \end{aligned}$$

3.3 APPROPRIATE PROBLEMS FOR DECISION TREE LEARNING

Although a variety of decision tree learning methods have been developed with somewhat differing capabilities and requirements, decision tree learning is generally best suited to problems with the following characteristics:

- *Instances are represented by attribute-value pairs.* Instances are described by a fixed set of attributes (e.g., *Temperature*) and their values (e.g., *Hot*). The easiest situation for decision tree learning is when each attribute takes on a small number of disjoint possible values (e.g., *Hot*, *Mild*, *Cold*). However, extensions to the basic algorithm (discussed in Section 3.7.2) allow handling real-valued attributes as well (e.g., representing *Temperature* numerically).
- *The target function has discrete output values.* The decision tree in Figure 3.1 assigns a boolean classification (e.g., *yes* or *no*) to each example. Decision tree methods easily extend to learning functions with more than two possible output values. A more substantial extension allows learning target functions with real-valued outputs, though the application of decision trees in this setting is less common.
- *Disjunctive descriptions may be required.* As noted above, decision trees naturally represent disjunctive expressions.
- *The training data may contain errors.* Decision tree learning methods are robust to errors, both errors in classifications of the training examples and errors in the attribute values that describe these examples.
- *The training data may contain missing attribute values.* Decision tree methods can be used even when some training examples have unknown values (e.g., if the *Humidity* of the day is known for only some of the training examples). This issue is discussed in Section 3.7.4.

Many practical problems have been found to fit these characteristics. Decision tree learning has therefore been applied to problems such as learning to classify medical patients by their disease, equipment malfunctions by their cause, and loan applicants by their likelihood of defaulting on payments. Such problems, in which the task is to classify examples into one of a discrete set of possible categories, are often referred to as *classification problems*.

The remainder of this chapter is organized as follows. Section 3.4 presents the basic ID3 algorithm for learning decision trees and illustrates its operation in detail. Section 3.5 examines the hypothesis space search performed by this learning algorithm, contrasting it with algorithms from Chapter 2. Section 3.6 characterizes the inductive bias of this decision tree learning algorithm and explores more generally an inductive bias called Occam's razor, which corresponds to a preference for the most simple hypothesis. Section 3.7 discusses the issue of overfitting the training data, as well as strategies such as rule post-pruning to deal with this problem. This section also discusses a number of more advanced topics such as extending the algorithm to accommodate real-valued attributes, training data with unobserved attributes, and attributes with differing costs.

3.4 THE BASIC DECISION TREE LEARNING ALGORITHM

Most algorithms that have been developed for learning decision trees are variations on a core algorithm that employs a top-down, greedy search through the space of possible decision trees. This approach is exemplified by the ID3 algorithm (Quinlan 1986) and its successor C4.5 (Quinlan 1993), which form the primary focus of our discussion here. In this section we present the basic algorithm for decision tree learning, corresponding approximately to the ID3 algorithm. In Section 3.7 we consider a number of extensions to this basic algorithm, including extensions incorporated into C4.5 and other more recent algorithms for decision tree learning.

Our basic algorithm, ID3, learns decision trees by constructing them top-down, beginning with the question "which attribute should be tested at the root of the tree?" To answer this question, each instance attribute is evaluated using a statistical test to determine how well it alone classifies the training examples. The best attribute is selected and used as the test at the root node of the tree. A descendant of the root node is then created for each possible value of this attribute, and the training examples are sorted to the appropriate descendant node (i.e., down the branch corresponding to the example's value for this attribute). The entire process is then repeated using the training examples associated with each descendant node to select the best attribute to test at that point in the tree. This forms a greedy search for an acceptable decision tree, in which the algorithm never backtracks to reconsider earlier choices. A simplified version of the algorithm, specialized to learning boolean-valued functions (i.e., concept learning), is described in Table 3.1.

3.4.1 Which Attribute Is the Best Classifier?

The central choice in the ID3 algorithm is selecting which attribute to test at each node in the tree. We would like to select the attribute that is most useful for classifying examples. What is a good quantitative measure of the worth of an attribute? We will define a statistical property, called *information gain*, that measures how well a given attribute separates the training examples according to their target classification. ID3 uses this information gain measure to select among the candidate attributes at each step while growing the tree.

3.4.1.1 ENTROPY MEASURES HOMOGENEITY OF EXAMPLES

In order to define information gain precisely, we begin by defining a measure commonly used in information theory, called *entropy*, that characterizes the (im)purity of an arbitrary collection of examples. Given a collection S, containing positive and negative examples of some target concept, the entropy of S relative to this boolean classification is

$$Entropy(S) \equiv -p_{\oplus} \log_2 p_{\oplus} - p_{\ominus} \log_2 p_{\ominus} \tag{3.1}$$

ID3(*Examples*, *Target_attribute*, *Attributes*)

Examples are the training examples. Target_attribute is the attribute whose value is to be predicted by the tree. Attributes is a list of other attributes that may be tested by the learned decision tree. Returns a decision tree that correctly classifies the given Examples.

- Create a *Root* node for the tree
- If all *Examples* are positive, Return the single-node tree *Root*, with label = +
- If all *Examples* are negative, Return the single-node tree *Root*, with label = −
- If *Attributes* is empty, Return the single-node tree *Root*, with label = most common value of *Target_attribute* in *Examples*
- Otherwise Begin
    - $A \leftarrow$ the attribute from *Attributes* that best* classifies *Examples*
    - The decision attribute for *Root* $\leftarrow A$
    - For each possible value, v_i, of A,
        - Add a new tree branch below *Root*, corresponding to the test $A = v_i$
        - Let $Examples_{v_i}$ be the subset of *Examples* that have value v_i for A
        - If $Examples_{v_i}$ is empty
            - Then below this new branch add a leaf node with label = most common value of *Target_attribute* in *Examples*
            - Else below this new branch add the subtree ID3($Examples_{v_i}$, *Target_attribute*, *Attributes* − $\{A\}$))
- End
- Return *Root*

---

* The best attribute is the one with highest *information gain*, as defined in Equation (3.4).

TABLE 3.1
Summary of the ID3 algorithm specialized to learning boolean-valued functions. ID3 is a greedy algorithm that grows the tree top-down, at each node selecting the attribute that best classifies the local training examples. This process continues until the tree perfectly classifies the training examples, or until all attributes have been used.

where $p_\oplus$ is the proportion of positive examples in S and $p_\ominus$ is the proportion of negative examples in S. In all calculations involving entropy we define $0 \log 0$ to be 0.

To illustrate, suppose S is a collection of 14 examples of some boolean concept, including 9 positive and 5 negative examples (we adopt the notation [9+, 5−] to summarize such a sample of data). Then the entropy of S relative to this boolean classification is

$$\begin{aligned} Entropy([9+,5-]) &= -(9/14)\log_2(9/14) - (5/14)\log_2(5/14) \\ &= 0.940 \end{aligned} \tag{3.2}$$

Notice that the entropy is 0 if all members of S belong to the same class. For example, if all members are positive ($p_\oplus = 1$), then $p_\ominus$ is 0, and $Entropy(S) = -1 \cdot \log_2(1) - 0 \cdot \log_2 0 = -1 \cdot 0 - 0 \cdot \log_2 0 = 0$. Note the entropy is 1 when the collection contains an equal number of positive and negative examples. If the collection contains unequal numbers of positive and negative examples, the

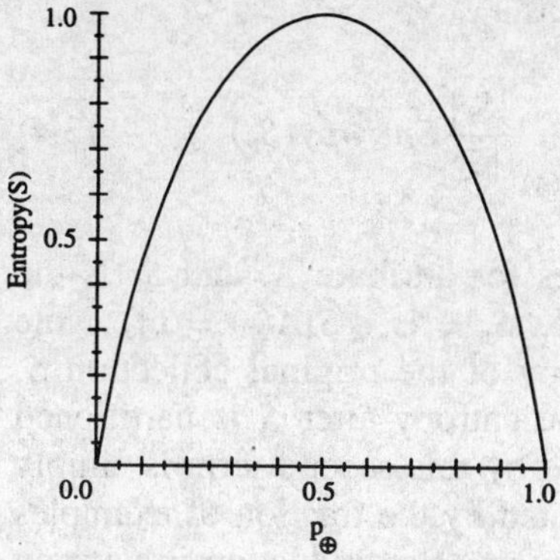

FIGURE 3.2
The entropy function relative to a boolean classification, as the proportion, $p_{\oplus}$, of positive examples varies between 0 and 1.

entropy is between 0 and 1. Figure 3.2 shows the form of the entropy function relative to a boolean classification, as $p_{\oplus}$ varies between 0 and 1.

One interpretation of entropy from information theory is that it specifies the minimum number of bits of information needed to encode the classification of an arbitrary member of S (i.e., a member of S drawn at random with uniform probability). For example, if $p_{\oplus}$ is 1, the receiver knows the drawn example will be positive, so no message need be sent, and the entropy is zero. On the other hand, if $p_{\oplus}$ is 0.5, one bit is required to indicate whether the drawn example is positive or negative. If $p_{\oplus}$ is 0.8, then a collection of messages can be encoded using on average less than 1 bit per message by assigning shorter codes to collections of positive examples and longer codes to less likely negative examples.

Thus far we have discussed entropy in the special case where the target classification is boolean. More generally, if the target attribute can take on c different values, then the entropy of S relative to this c-wise classification is defined as

$$Entropy(S) \equiv \sum_{i=1}^{c} -p_i \log_2 p_i \tag{3.3}$$

where p_i is the proportion of S belonging to class i. Note the logarithm is still base 2 because entropy is a measure of the expected encoding length measured in *bits*. Note also that if the target attribute can take on c possible values, the entropy can be as large as $\log_2 c$.

3.4.1.2 INFORMATION GAIN MEASURES THE EXPECTED REDUCTION IN ENTROPY

Given entropy as a measure of the impurity in a collection of training examples, we can now define a measure of the effectiveness of an attribute in classifying the training data. The measure we will use, called *information gain*, is simply the expected reduction in entropy caused by partitioning the examples according to this attribute. More precisely, the information gain, $Gain(S, A)$ of an attribute A, relative to a collection of examples S, is defined as

$$Gain(S, A) \equiv Entropy(S) - \sum_{v \in Values(A)} \frac{|S_v|}{|S|} Entropy(S_v) \tag{3.4}$$

where $Values(A)$ is the set of all possible values for attribute A, and S_v is the subset of S for which attribute A has value v (i.e., $S_v = \{s \in S | A(s) = v\}$). Note the first term in Equation (3.4) is just the entropy of the original collection S, and the second term is the expected value of the entropy after S is partitioned using attribute A. The expected entropy described by this second term is simply the sum of the entropies of each subset S_v, weighted by the fraction of examples $\frac{|S_v|}{|S|}$ that belong to S_v. $Gain(S, A)$ is therefore the expected reduction in entropy caused by knowing the value of attribute A. Put another way, $Gain(S, A)$ is the information provided about the *target function value*, given the value of some other attribute A. The value of $Gain(S, A)$ is the number of bits saved when encoding the target value of an arbitrary member of S, by knowing the value of attribute A.

For example, suppose S is a collection of training-example days described by attributes including *Wind*, which can have the values *Weak* or *Strong*. As before, assume S is a collection containing 14 examples, [9+, 5−]. Of these 14 examples, suppose 6 of the positive and 2 of the negative examples have *Wind* = *Weak*, and the remainder have *Wind* = *Strong*. The information gain due to sorting the original 14 examples by the attribute *Wind* may then be calculated as

$$\begin{aligned}
Values(Wind) &= Weak, Strong \\
S &= [9+, 5-] \\
S_{Weak} &\leftarrow [6+, 2-] \\
S_{Strong} &\leftarrow [3+, 3-] \\
Gain(S, Wind) &= Entropy(S) - \sum_{v \in \{Weak, Strong\}} \frac{|S_v|}{|S|} Entropy(S_v) \\
&= Entropy(S) - (8/14) Entropy(S_{Weak}) \\
&\quad - (6/14) Entropy(S_{Strong}) \\
&= 0.940 - (8/14)0.811 - (6/14)1.00 \\
&= 0.048
\end{aligned}$$

Information gain is precisely the measure used by ID3 to select the best attribute at each step in growing the tree. The use of information gain to evaluate the relevance of attributes is summarized in Figure 3.3. In this figure the information gain of two different attributes, $Humidity$ and $Wind$, is computed in order to determine which is the better attribute for classifying the training examples shown in Table 3.2.

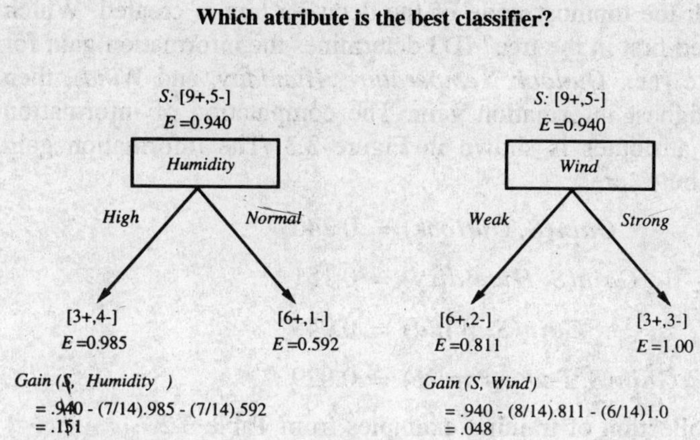

FIGURE 3.3
Humidity provides greater information gain than *Wind*, relative to the target classification. Here, E stands for entropy and S for the original collection of examples. Given an initial collection S of 9 positive and 5 negative examples, $[9+, 5-]$, sorting these by their *Humidity* produces collections of $[3+, 4-]$ $(Humidity = High)$ and $[6+, 1-]$ $(Humidity = Normal)$. The information gained by this partitioning is .151, compared to a gain of only .048 for the attribute *Wind*.

3.4.2 An Illustrative Example

To illustrate the operation of ID3, consider the learning task represented by the training examples of Table 3.2. Here the target attribute *PlayTennis*, which can have values *yes* or *no* for different Saturday mornings, is to be predicted based on other attributes of the morning in question. Consider the first step through

Day	*Outlook*	*Temperature*	*Humidity*	*Wind*	*PlayTennis*
D1	Sunny	Hot	High	Weak	No
D2	Sunny	Hot	High	Strong	No
D3	Overcast	Hot	High	Weak	Yes
D4	Rain	Mild	High	Weak	Yes
D5	Rain	Cool	Normal	Weak	Yes
D6	Rain	Cool	Normal	Strong	No
D7	Overcast	Cool	Normal	Strong	Yes
D8	Sunny	Mild	High	Weak	No
D9	Sunny	Cool	Normal	Weak	Yes
D10	Rain	Mild	Normal	Weak	Yes
D11	Sunny	Mild	Normal	Strong	Yes
D12	Overcast	Mild	High	Strong	Yes
D13	Overcast	Hot	Normal	Weak	Yes
D14	Rain	Mild	High	Strong	No

TABLE 3.2
Training examples for the target concept *PlayTennis*.

the algorithm, in which the topmost node of the decision tree is created. Which attribute should be tested first in the tree? ID3 determines the information gain for each candidate attribute (i.e., *Outlook, Temperature, Humidity*, and *Wind*), then selects the one with highest information gain. The computation of information gain for two of these attributes is shown in Figure 3.3. The information gain values for all four attributes are

$$Gain(S, Outlook) = 0.246$$

$$Gain(S, Humidity) = 0.151$$

$$Gain(S, Wind) = 0.048$$

$$Gain(S, Temperature) = 0.029$$

where *S* denotes the collection of training examples from Table 3.2.

According to the information gain measure, the *Outlook* attribute provides the best prediction of the target attribute, *PlayTennis*, over the training examples. Therefore, *Outlook* is selected as the decision attribute for the root node, and branches are created below the root for each of its possible values (i.e., *Sunny*, *Overcast*, and *Rain*). The resulting partial decision tree is shown in Figure 3.4, along with the training examples sorted to each new descendant node. Note that every example for which *Outlook* = *Overcast* is also a positive example of *PlayTennis*. Therefore, this node of the tree becomes a leaf node with the classification *PlayTennis* = *Yes*. In contrast, the descendants corresponding to *Outlook* = *Sunny* and *Outlook* = *Rain* still have nonzero entropy, and the decision tree will be further elaborated below these nodes.

The process of selecting a new attribute and partitioning the training examples is now repeated for each nonterminal descendant node, this time using only the training examples associated with that node. Attributes that have been incorporated higher in the tree are excluded, so that any given attribute can appear at most once along any path through the tree. This process continues for each new leaf node until either of two conditions is met: (1) every attribute has already been included along this path through the tree, or (2) the training examples associated with this leaf node all have the same target attribute value (i.e., their entropy is zero). Figure 3.4 illustrates the computations of information gain for the next step in growing the decision tree. The final decision tree learned by ID3 from the 14 training examples of Table 3.2 is shown in Figure 3.1.

3.5 HYPOTHESIS SPACE SEARCH IN DECISION TREE LEARNING

As with other inductive learning methods, ID3 can be characterized as searching a space of hypotheses for one that fits the training examples. The hypothesis space searched by ID3 is the set of possible decision trees. ID3 performs a simple-to-complex, hill-climbing search through this hypothesis space, beginning with the empty tree, then considering progressively more elaborate hypotheses in search of a decision tree that correctly classifies the training data. The evaluation function

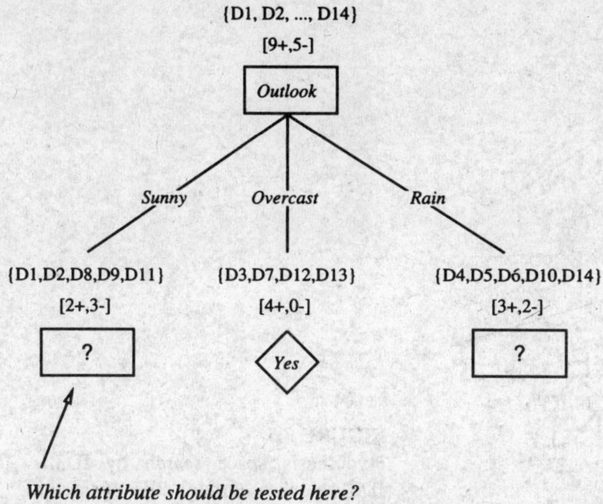

S_{sunny} = {D1,D2,D8,D9,D11}

$Gain\,(S_{sunny}, Humidity) = .970 - (3/5)\,0.0 - (2/5)\,0.0 = .970$

$Gain\,(S_{sunny}, Temperature) = .970 - (2/5)\,0.0 - (2/5)\,1.0 - (1/5)\,0.0 = .570$

$Gain\,(S_{sunny}, Wind) = .970 - (2/5)\,1.0 - (3/5)\,.918 = .019$

FIGURE 3.4
The partially learned decision tree resulting from the first step of ID3. The training examples are sorted to the corresponding descendant nodes. The *Overcast* descendant has only positive examples and therefore becomes a leaf node with classification *Yes*. The other two nodes will be further expanded, by selecting the attribute with highest information gain relative to the new subsets of examples.

that guides this hill-climbing search is the information gain measure. This search is depicted in Figure 3.5.

By viewing ID3 in terms of its search space and search strategy, we can get some insight into its capabilities and limitations.

- ID3's hypothesis space of all decision trees is a *complete* space of finite discrete-valued functions, relative to the available attributes. Because every finite discrete-valued function can be represented by some decision tree, ID3 avoids one of the major risks of methods that search incomplete hypothesis spaces (such as methods that consider only conjunctive hypotheses): that the hypothesis space might not contain the target function.
- ID3 maintains only a single current hypothesis as it searches through the space of decision trees. This contrasts, for example, with the earlier version space CANDIDATE-ELIMINATION method, which maintains the set of *all* hypotheses consistent with the available training examples. By determining only a single hypothesis, ID3 loses the capabilities that follow from

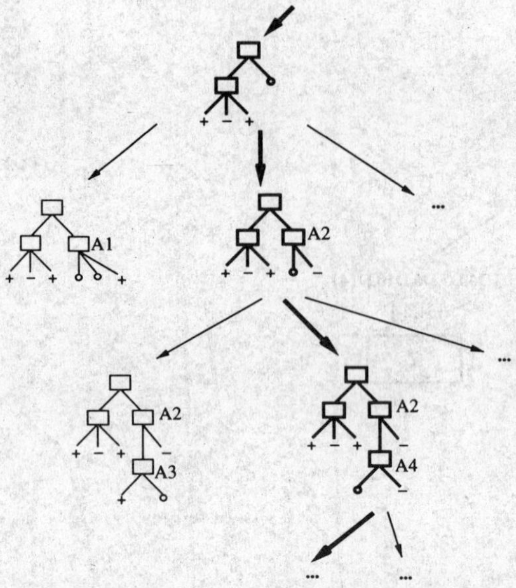

FIGURE 3.5
Hypothesis space search by ID3. ID3 searches through the space of possible decision trees from simplest to increasingly complex, guided by the information gain heuristic.

explicitly representing all consistent hypotheses. For example, it does not have the ability to determine how many alternative decision trees are consistent with the available training data, or to pose new instance queries that optimally resolve among these competing hypotheses.

- ID3 in its pure form performs no backtracking in its search. Once it selects an attribute to test at a particular level in the tree, it never backtracks to reconsider this choice. Therefore, it is susceptible to the usual risks of hill-climbing search without backtracking: converging to locally optimal solutions that are not globally optimal. In the case of ID3, a locally optimal solution corresponds to the decision tree it selects along the single search path it explores. However, this locally optimal solution may be less desirable than trees that would have been encountered along a different branch of the search. Below we discuss an extension that adds a form of backtracking (post-pruning the decision tree).

- ID3 uses all training examples at each step in the search to make statistically based decisions regarding how to refine its current hypothesis. This contrasts with methods that make decisions incrementally, based on individual training examples (e.g., FIND-S or CANDIDATE-ELIMINATION). One advantage of using statistical properties of all the examples (e.g., information gain) is that the resulting search is much less sensitive to errors in individual training examples. ID3 can be easily extended to handle noisy training data by modifying its termination criterion to accept hypotheses that imperfectly fit the training data.

3.6 INDUCTIVE BIAS IN DECISION TREE LEARNING

What is the policy by which ID3 generalizes from observed training examples to classify unseen instances? In other words, what is its inductive bias? Recall from Chapter 2 that inductive bias is the set of assumptions that, together with the training data, deductively justify the classifications assigned by the learner to future instances.

Given a collection of training examples, there are typically many decision trees consistent with these examples. Describing the inductive bias of ID3 therefore consists of describing the basis by which it chooses one of these consistent hypotheses over the others. Which of these decision trees does ID3 choose? It chooses the first acceptable tree it encounters in its simple-to-complex, hill-climbing search through the space of possible trees. Roughly speaking, then, the ID3 search strategy (a) selects in favor of shorter trees over longer ones, and (b) selects trees that place the attributes with highest information gain closest to the root. Because of the subtle interaction between the attribute selection heuristic used by ID3 and the particular training examples it encounters, it is difficult to characterize precisely the inductive bias exhibited by ID3. However, we can approximately characterize its bias as a preference for short decision trees over complex trees.

Approximate inductive bias of ID3: Shorter trees are preferred over larger trees.

In fact, one could imagine an algorithm similar to ID3 that exhibits precisely this inductive bias. Consider an algorithm that begins with the empty tree and searches *breadth first* through progressively more complex trees, first considering all trees of depth 1, then all trees of depth 2, etc. Once it finds a decision tree consistent with the training data, it returns the smallest consistent tree at that search depth (e.g., the tree with the fewest nodes). Let us call this breadth-first search algorithm BFS-ID3. BFS-ID3 finds a shortest decision tree and thus exhibits precisely the bias "shorter trees are preferred over longer trees." ID3 can be viewed as an efficient approximation to BFS-ID3, using a greedy heuristic search to attempt to find the shortest tree without conducting the entire breadth-first search through the hypothesis space.

Because ID3 uses the information gain heuristic and a hill climbing strategy, it exhibits a more complex bias than BFS-ID3. In particular, it does not always find the shortest consistent tree, and it is biased to favor trees that place attributes with high information gain closest to the root.

A closer approximation to the inductive bias of ID3: Shorter trees are preferred over longer trees. Trees that place high information gain attributes close to the root are preferred over those that do not.

3.6.1 Restriction Biases and Preference Biases

There is an interesting difference between the types of inductive bias exhibited by ID3 and by the CANDIDATE-ELIMINATION algorithm discussed in Chapter 2.

Consider the difference between the hypothesis space search in these two approaches:

- ID3 searches a *complete* hypothesis space (i.e., one capable of expressing any finite discrete-valued function). It searches *incompletely* through this space, from simple to complex hypotheses, until its termination condition is met (e.g., until it finds a hypothesis consistent with the data). Its inductive bias is solely a consequence of the ordering of hypotheses by its search strategy. Its hypothesis space introduces no additional bias.
- The version space CANDIDATE-ELIMINATION algorithm searches an *incomplete* hypothesis space (i.e., one that can express only a subset of the potentially teachable concepts). It searches this space *completely*, finding every hypothesis consistent with the training data. Its inductive bias is solely a consequence of the expressive power of its hypothesis representation. Its search strategy introduces no additional bias.

In brief, the inductive bias of ID3 follows from its *search strategy*, whereas the inductive bias of the CANDIDATE-ELIMINATION algorithm follows from the definition of its *search space*.

The inductive bias of ID3 is thus a *preference* for certain hypotheses over others (e.g., for shorter hypotheses), with no hard restriction on the hypotheses that can be eventually enumerated. This form of bias is typically called a *preference bias* (or, alternatively, a *search bias*). In contrast, the bias of the CANDIDATE-ELIMINATION algorithm is in the form of a categorical *restriction* on the set of hypotheses considered. This form of bias is typically called a *restriction bias* (or, alternatively, a *language bias*).

Given that some form of inductive bias is required in order to generalize beyond the training data (see Chapter 2), which type of inductive bias shall we prefer; a preference bias or restriction bias?

Typically, a preference bias is more desirable than a restriction bias, because it allows the learner to work within a complete hypothesis space that is assured to contain the unknown target function. In contrast, a restriction bias that strictly limits the set of potential hypotheses is generally less desirable, because it introduces the possibility of excluding the unknown target function altogether.

Whereas ID3 exhibits a purely preference bias and CANDIDATE-ELIMINATION a purely restriction bias, some learning systems combine both. Consider, for example, the program described in Chapter 1 for learning a numerical evaluation function for game playing. In this case, the learned evaluation function is represented by a linear combination of a fixed set of board features, and the learning algorithm adjusts the parameters of this linear combination to best fit the available training data. In this case, the decision to use a linear function to represent the evaluation function introduces a restriction bias (nonlinear evaluation functions cannot be represented in this form). At the same time, the choice of a particular parameter tuning method (the LMS algorithm in this case) introduces a preference bias stemming from the ordered search through the space of all possible parameter values.

3.6.2 Why Prefer Short Hypotheses?

Is ID3's inductive bias favoring shorter decision trees a sound basis for generalizing beyond the training data? Philosophers and others have debated this question for centuries, and the debate remains unresolved to this day. William of Occam was one of the first to discuss† the question, around the year 1320, so this bias often goes by the name of Occam's razor.

Occam's razor: Prefer the simplest hypothesis that fits the data.

Of course giving an inductive bias a name does not justify it. Why should one prefer simpler hypotheses? Notice that scientists sometimes appear to follow this inductive bias. Physicists, for example, prefer simple explanations for the motions of the planets, over more complex explanations. Why? One argument is that because there are fewer short hypotheses than long ones (based on straightforward combinatorial arguments), it is less likely that one will find a short hypothesis that coincidentally fits the training data. In contrast there are often many very complex hypotheses that fit the current training data but fail to generalize correctly to subsequent data. Consider decision tree hypotheses, for example. There are many more 500-node decision trees than 5-node decision trees. Given a small set of 20 training examples, we might expect to be able to find many 500-node decision trees consistent with these, whereas we would be more surprised if a 5-node decision tree could perfectly fit this data. We might therefore believe the 5-node tree is less likely to be a statistical coincidence and prefer this hypothesis over the 500-node hypothesis.

Upon closer examination, it turns out there is a major difficulty with the above argument. By the same reasoning we could have argued that one should prefer decision trees containing exactly 17 leaf nodes with 11 nonleaf nodes, that use the decision attribute A_1 at the root, and test attributes A_2 through A_{11}, in numerical order. There are relatively few such trees, and we might argue (by the same reasoning as above) that our a priori chance of finding one consistent with an arbitrary set of data is therefore small. The difficulty here is that there are very many small sets of hypotheses that one can define—most of them rather arcane. Why should we believe that the small set of hypotheses consisting of decision trees with *short descriptions* should be any more relevant than the multitude of other small sets of hypotheses that we might define?

A second problem with the above argument for Occam's razor is that the size of a hypothesis is determined by the particular representation used *internally* by the learner. Two learners using different internal representations could therefore arrive at different hypotheses, both justifying their contradictory conclusions by Occam's razor! For example, the function represented by the learned decision tree in Figure 3.1 could be represented as a tree with just one decision node, by a learner that uses the boolean attribute XYZ, where we define the attribute XYZ to

† Apparently while shaving.

be true for instances that are classified positive by the decision tree in Figure 3.1 and false otherwise. Thus, two learners, both applying Occam's razor, would generalize in different ways if one used the XYZ attribute to describe its examples and the other used only the attributes *Outlook, Temperature, Humidity*, and *Wind*.

This last argument shows that Occam's razor will produce two different hypotheses from the same training examples when it is applied by two learners that perceive these examples in terms of different internal representations. On this basis we might be tempted to reject Occam's razor altogether. However, consider the following scenario that examines the question of which internal representations might arise from a process of evolution and natural selection. Imagine a population of artificial learning agents created by a simulated evolutionary process involving reproduction, mutation, and natural selection of these agents. Let us assume that this evolutionary process can alter the perceptual systems of these agents from generation to generation, thereby changing the internal attributes by which they perceive their world. For the sake of argument, let us also assume that the learning agents employ a fixed learning algorithm (say ID3) that cannot be altered by evolution. It is reasonable to assume that over time evolution will produce internal representation that make these agents increasingly successful within their environment. Assuming that the success of an agent depends highly on its ability to generalize accurately, we would therefore expect evolution to develop internal representations that work well with whatever learning algorithm and inductive bias is present. If the species of agents employs a learning algorithm whose inductive bias is Occam's razor, then we expect evolution to produce internal representations for which Occam's razor is a successful strategy. The essence of the argument here is that evolution will create internal representations that make the learning algorithm's inductive bias a self-fulfilling prophecy, simply because it can alter the representation easier than it can alter the learning algorithm.

For now, we leave the debate regarding Occam's razor. We will revisit it in Chapter 6, where we discuss the Minimum Description Length principle, a version of Occam's razor that can be interpreted within a Bayesian framework.

3.7 ISSUES IN DECISION TREE LEARNING

Practical issues in learning decision trees include determining how deeply to grow the decision tree, handling continuous attributes, choosing an appropriate attribute selection measure, handling training data with missing attribute values, handing attributes with differing costs, and improving computational efficiency. Below we discuss each of these issues and extensions to the basic ID3 algorithm that address them. ID3 has itself been extended to address most of these issues, with the resulting system renamed C4.5 (Quinlan 1993).

3.7.1 Avoiding Overfitting the Data

The algorithm described in Table 3.1 grows each branch of the tree just deeply enough to perfectly classify the training examples. While this is sometimes a reasonable strategy, in fact it can lead to difficulties when there is noise in the data, or when the number of training examples is too small to produce a representative sample of the true target function. In either of these cases, this simple algorithm can produce trees that *overfit* the training examples.

We will say that a hypothesis overfits the training examples if some other hypothesis that fits the training examples less well actually performs better over the entire distribution of instances (i.e., including instances beyond the training set).

> ***Definition***: Given a hypothesis space H, a hypothesis $h \in H$ is said to **overfit** the training data if there exists some alternative hypothesis $h' \in H$, such that h has smaller error than h' over the training examples, but h' has a smaller error than h over the entire distribution of instances.

Figure 3.6 illustrates the impact of overfitting in a typical application of decision tree learning. In this case, the ID3 algorithm is applied to the task of learning which medical patients have a form of diabetes. The horizontal axis of this plot indicates the total number of nodes in the decision tree, as the tree is being constructed. The vertical axis indicates the accuracy of predictions made by the tree. The solid line shows the accuracy of the decision tree over the training examples, whereas the broken line shows accuracy measured over an independent set of test examples (not included in the training set). Predictably, the accuracy of the tree over the training examples increases monotonically as the tree is grown. However, the accuracy measured over the independent test examples first increases, then decreases. As can be seen, once the tree size exceeds approximately 25 nodes,

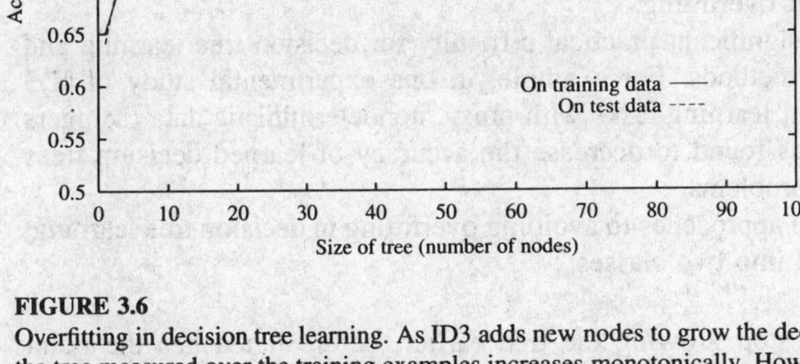

FIGURE 3.6
Overfitting in decision tree learning. As ID3 adds new nodes to grow the decision tree, the accuracy of the tree measured over the training examples increases monotonically. However, when measured over a set of test examples independent of the training examples, accuracy first increases, then decreases. Software and data for experimenting with variations on this plot are available on the World Wide Web at http://www.cs.cmu.edu/~tom/mlbook.html.

further elaboration of the tree decreases its accuracy over the test examples despite increasing its accuracy on the training examples.

How can it be possible for tree h to fit the training examples better than h', but for it to perform more poorly over subsequent examples? One way this can occur is when the training examples contain random errors or noise. To illustrate, consider the effect of adding the following positive training example, incorrectly labeled as negative, to the (otherwise correct) examples in Table 3.2.

$$\langle Outlook = Sunny, Temperature = Hot, Humidity = Normal,$$
$$Wind = Strong, PlayTennis = No\rangle$$

Given the original error-free data, ID3 produces the decision tree shown in Figure 3.1. However, the addition of this incorrect example will now cause ID3 to construct a more complex tree. In particular, the new example will be sorted into the second leaf node from the left in the learned tree of Figure 3.1, along with the previous positive examples D9 and D11. Because the new example is labeled as a negative example, ID3 will search for further refinements to the tree below this node. Of course as long as the new erroneous example differs in some arbitrary way from the other examples affiliated with this node, ID3 will succeed in finding a new decision attribute to separate out this new example from the two previous positive examples at this tree node. The result is that ID3 will output a decision tree (h) that is more complex than the original tree from Figure 3.1 (h'). Of course h will fit the collection of training examples perfectly, whereas the simpler h' will not. However, given that the new decision node is simply a consequence of fitting the noisy training example, we expect h to outperform h' over subsequent data drawn from the same instance distribution.

The above example illustrates how random noise in the training examples can lead to overfitting. In fact, overfitting is possible even when the training data are noise-free, especially when small numbers of examples are associated with leaf nodes. In this case, it is quite possible for coincidental regularities to occur, in which some attribute happens to partition the examples very well, despite being unrelated to the actual target function. Whenever such coincidental regularities exist, there is a risk of overfitting.

Overfitting is a significant practical difficulty for decision tree learning and many other learning methods. For example, in one experimental study of ID3 involving five different learning tasks with noisy, nondeterministic data (Mingers 1989b), overfitting was found to decrease the accuracy of learned decision trees by 10–25% on most problems.

There are several approaches to avoiding overfitting in decision tree learning. These can be grouped into two classes:

- approaches that stop growing the tree earlier, before it reaches the point where it perfectly classifies the training data,
- approaches that allow the tree to overfit the data, and then post-prune the tree.

Although the first of these approaches might seem more direct, the second approach of post-pruning overfit trees has been found to be more successful in practice. This is due to the difficulty in the first approach of estimating precisely when to stop growing the tree.

Regardless of whether the correct tree size is found by stopping early or by post-pruning, a key question is what criterion is to be used to determine the correct final tree size. Approaches include:

- Use a separate set of examples, distinct from the training examples, to evaluate the utility of post-pruning nodes from the tree.
- Use all the available data for training, but apply a statistical test to estimate whether expanding (or pruning) a particular node is likely to produce an improvement beyond the training set. For example, Quinlan (1986) uses a chi-square test to estimate whether further expanding a node is likely to improve performance over the entire instance distribution, or only on the current sample of training data.
- Use an explicit measure of the complexity for encoding the training examples and the decision tree, halting growth of the tree when this encoding size is minimized. This approach, based on a heuristic called the Minimum Description Length principle, is discussed further in Chapter 6, as well as in Quinlan and Rivest (1989) and Mehta et al. (1995).

The first of the above approaches is the most common and is often referred to as a *training and validation set* approach. We discuss the two main variants of this approach below. In this approach, the available data are separated into two sets of examples: a *training set*, which is used to form the learned hypothesis, and a separate *validation set*, which is used to evaluate the accuracy of this hypothesis over subsequent data and, in particular, to evaluate the impact of pruning this hypothesis. The motivation is this: Even though the learner may be misled by random errors and coincidental regularities within the training set, the validation set is unlikely to exhibit the same random fluctuations. Therefore, the validation set can be expected to provide a safety check against overfitting the spurious characteristics of the training set. Of course, it is important that the validation set be large enough to itself provide a statistically significant sample of the instances. One common heuristic is to withhold one-third of the available examples for the validation set, using the other two-thirds for training.

3.7.1.1 REDUCED ERROR PRUNING

How exactly might we use a validation set to prevent overfitting? One approach, called *reduced-error pruning* (Quinlan 1987), is to consider each of the decision nodes in the tree to be candidates for pruning. Pruning a decision node consists of removing the subtree rooted at that node, making it a leaf node, and assigning it the most common classification of the training examples affiliated with that node. Nodes are removed only if the resulting pruned tree performs no worse than the original over the validation set. This has the effect that any leaf node added due to coincidental regularities in the training set is likely to be pruned because these same coincidences are unlikely to occur in the validation set. Nodes are pruned iteratively, always choosing the node whose removal most increases the decision tree accuracy over the validation set. Pruning of nodes continues until further pruning is harmful (i.e., decreases accuracy of the tree over the validation set).

The impact of reduced-error pruning on the accuracy of the decision tree is illustrated in Figure 3.7. As in Figure 3.6, the accuracy of the tree is shown measured over both training examples and test examples. The additional line in Figure 3.7 shows accuracy over the test examples as the tree is pruned. When pruning begins, the tree is at its maximum size and lowest accuracy over the test set. As pruning proceeds, the number of nodes is reduced and accuracy over the test set increases. Here, the available data has been split into three subsets: the training examples, the validation examples used for pruning the tree, and a set of test examples used to provide an unbiased estimate of accuracy over future unseen examples. The plot shows accuracy over the training and test sets. Accuracy over the validation set used for pruning is not shown.

Using a separate set of data to guide pruning is an effective approach provided a large amount of data is available. The major drawback of this approach is that when data is limited, withholding part of it for the validation set reduces even further the number of examples available for training. The following section presents an alternative approach to pruning that has been found useful in many practical situations where data is limited. Many additional techniques have been proposed as well, involving partitioning the available data several different times in

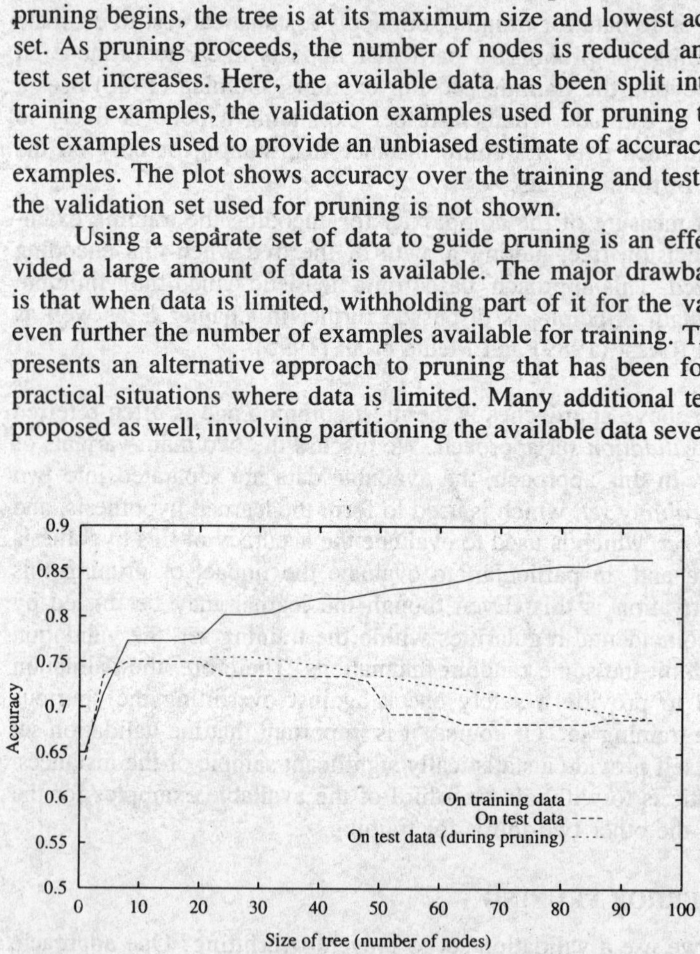

FIGURE 3.7
Effect of reduced-error pruning in decision tree learning. This plot shows the same curves of training and test set accuracy as in Figure 3.6. In addition, it shows the impact of reduced error pruning of the tree produced by ID3. Notice the increase in accuracy over the test set as nodes are pruned from the tree. Here, the validation set used for pruning is distinct from both the training and test sets.

multiple ways, then averaging the results. Empirical evaluations of alternative tree pruning methods are reported by Mingers (1989b) and by Malerba et al. (1995).

3.7.1.2 RULE POST-PRUNING

In practice, one quite successful method for finding high accuracy hypotheses is a technique we shall call *rule post-pruning*. A variant of this pruning method is used by C4.5 (Quinlan 1993), which is an outgrowth of the original ID3 algorithm. Rule post-pruning involves the following steps:

1. Infer the decision tree from the training set, growing the tree until the training data is fit as well as possible and allowing overfitting to occur.
2. Convert the learned tree into an equivalent set of rules by creating one rule for each path from the root node to a leaf node.
3. Prune (generalize) each rule by removing any preconditions that result in improving its estimated accuracy.
4. Sort the pruned rules by their estimated accuracy, and consider them in this sequence when classifying subsequent instances.

To illustrate, consider again the decision tree in Figure 3.1. In rule post-pruning, one rule is generated for each leaf node in the tree. Each attribute test along the path from the root to the leaf becomes a rule antecedent (precondition) and the classification at the leaf node becomes the rule consequent (postcondition). For example, the leftmost path of the tree in Figure 3.1 is translated into the rule

IF $(Outlook = Sunny) \wedge (Humidity = High)$

THEN $PlayTennis = No$

Next, each such rule is pruned by removing any antecedent, or precondition, whose removal does not worsen its estimated accuracy. Given the above rule, for example, rule post-pruning would consider removing the preconditions $(Outlook = Sunny)$ and $(Humidity = High)$. It would select whichever of these pruning steps produced the greatest improvement in estimated rule accuracy, then consider pruning the second precondition as a further pruning step. No pruning step is performed if it reduces the estimated rule accuracy.

As noted above, one method to estimate rule accuracy is to use a validation set of examples disjoint from the training set. Another method, used by C4.5, is to evaluate performance based on the training set itself, using a pessimistic estimate to make up for the fact that the training data gives an estimate biased in favor of the rules. More, precisely, C4.5 calculates its pessimistic estimate by calculating the rule accuracy over the training examples to which it applies, then calculating the standard deviation in this estimated accuracy assuming a binomial distribution. For a given confidence level, the lower-bound estimate is then taken as the measure of rule performance (e.g., for a 95% confidence interval, rule accuracy is pessimistically estimated by the observed accuracy over the training set, minus 1.96 times the estimated standard deviation). The net effect is that for large data sets, the pessimistic estimate is very close to the observed accuracy (e.g., the standard deviation is very small), whereas it grows further from the observed accuracy as the size of the data set decreases. Although this heuristic method is not statistically valid, it has nevertheless been found useful in practice. See Chapter 5 for a discussion of statistically valid approaches to estimating means and confidence intervals.

Why convert the decision tree to rules before pruning? There are three main advantages.

- Converting to rules allows distinguishing among the different contexts in which a decision node is used. Because each distinct path through the decision tree node produces a distinct rule, the pruning decision regarding that attribute test can be made differently for each path. In contrast, if the tree itself were pruned, the only two choices would be to remove the decision node completely, or to retain it in its original form.
- Converting to rules removes the distinction between attribute tests that occur near the root of the tree and those that occur near the leaves. Thus, we avoid messy bookkeeping issues such as how to reorganize the tree if the root node is pruned while retaining part of the subtree below this test.
- Converting to rules improves readability. Rules are often easier for people to understand.

3.7.2 Incorporating Continuous-Valued Attributes

Our initial definition of ID3 is restricted to attributes that take on a discrete set of values. First, the target attribute whose value is predicted by the learned tree must be discrete valued. Second, the attributes tested in the decision nodes of the tree must also be discrete valued. This second restriction can easily be removed so that continuous-valued decision attributes can be incorporated into the learned tree. This can be accomplished by dynamically defining new discrete-valued attributes that partition the continuous attribute value into a discrete set of intervals. In particular, for an attribute A that is continuous-valued, the algorithm can dynamically create a new boolean attribute A_c that is true if $A < c$ and false otherwise. The only question is how to select the best value for the threshold c.

As an example, suppose we wish to include the continuous-valued attribute *Temperature* in describing the training example days in the learning task of Table 3.2. Suppose further that the training examples associated with a particular node in the decision tree have the following values for *Temperature* and the target attribute *PlayTennis*.

Temperature:	40	48	60	72	80	90
PlayTennis:	No	No	Yes	Yes	Yes	No

What threshold-based boolean attribute should be defined based on *Temperature*? Clearly, we would like to pick a threshold, c, that produces the greatest information gain. By sorting the examples according to the continuous attribute A, then identifying adjacent examples that differ in their target classification, we can generate a set of candidate thresholds midway between the corresponding values of A. It can be shown that the value of c that maximizes information gain must always lie at such a boundary (Fayyad 1991). These candidate thresholds can then be evaluated by computing the information gain associated with each. In the current example, there are two candidate thresholds, corresponding to the values of $Temperature$ at which the value of $PlayTennis$ changes: (48 + 60)/2, and (80 + 90)/2. The information gain can then be computed for each of the candidate attributes, $Temperature_{>54}$ and $Temperature_{>85}$, and the best can be selected ($Temperature_{>54}$). This dynamically created boolean attribute can then compete with the other discrete-valued candidate attributes available for growing the decision tree. Fayyad and Irani (1993) discuss an extension to this approach that splits the continuous attribute into multiple intervals rather than just two intervals based on a single threshold. Utgoff and Brodley (1991) and Murthy et al. (1994) discuss approaches that define features by thresholding linear combinations of several continuous-valued attributes.

3.7.3 Alternative Measures for Selecting Attributes

There is a natural bias in the information gain measure that favors attributes with many values over those with few values. As an extreme example, consider the attribute *Date*, which has a very large number of possible values (e.g., March 4, 1979). If we were to add this attribute to the data in Table 3.2, it would have the highest information gain of any of the attributes. This is because *Date* alone perfectly predicts the target attribute over the training data. Thus, it would be selected as the decision attribute for the root node of the tree and lead to a (quite broad) tree of depth one, which perfectly classifies the training data. Of course, this decision tree would fare poorly on subsequent examples, because it is not a useful predictor despite the fact that it perfectly separates the training data.

What is wrong with the attribute *Date*? Simply put, it has so many possible values that it is bound to separate the training examples into very small subsets. Because of this, it will have a very high information gain relative to the training examples, despite being a very poor predictor of the target function over unseen instances.

One way to avoid this difficulty is to select decision attributes based on some measure other than information gain. One alternative measure that has been used successfully is the *gain ratio* (Quinlan 1986). The gain ratio measure penalizes attributes such as *Date* by incorporating a term, called *split information*, that is sensitive to how broadly and uniformly the attribute splits the data:

$$SplitInformation(S, A) \equiv -\sum_{i=1}^{c} \frac{|S_i|}{|S|} \log_2 \frac{|S_i|}{|S|} \tag{3.5}$$

where S_1 through S_c are the c subsets of examples resulting from partitioning S by the c-valued attribute A. Note that *SplitInformation* is actually the entropy of S with respect to the values of attribute A. This is in contrast to our previous uses of entropy, in which we considered only the entropy of S with respect to the target attribute whose value is to be predicted by the learned tree.

The *GainRatio* measure is defined in terms of the earlier *Gain* measure, as well as this *SplitInformation*, as follows

$$GainRatio(S, A) \equiv \frac{Gain(S, A)}{SplitInformation(S, A)} \tag{3.6}$$

Notice that the *SplitInformation* term discourages the selection of attributes with many uniformly distributed values. For example, consider a collection of n examples that are completely separated by attribute A (e.g., *Date*). In this case, the *SplitInformation* value will be $\log_2 n$. In contrast, a boolean attribute B that splits the same n examples exactly in half will have *SplitInformation* of 1. If attributes A and B produce the same information gain, then clearly B will score higher according to the *GainRatio* measure.

One practical issue that arises in using *GainRatio* in place of *Gain* to select attributes is that the denominator can be zero or very small when $|S_i| \approx |S|$ for one of the S_i. This either makes the *GainRatio* undefined or very large for attributes that happen to have the same value for nearly all members of S. To avoid selecting attributes purely on this basis, we can adopt some heuristic such as first calculating the *Gain* of each attribute, then applying the *GainRatio* test only considering those attributes with above average *Gain* (Quinlan 1986).

An alternative to the *GainRatio*, designed to directly address the above difficulty, is a distance-based measure introduced by Lopez de Mantaras (1991). This measure is based on defining a distance metric between partitions of the data. Each attribute is evaluated based on the distance between the data partition it creates and the perfect partition (i.e., the partition that perfectly classifies the training data). The attribute whose partition is closest to the perfect partition is chosen. Lopez de Mantaras (1991) defines this distance measure, proves that it is not biased toward attributes with large numbers of values, and reports experimental studies indicating that the predictive accuracy of the induced trees is not significantly different from that obtained with the *Gain* and *GainRatio* measures. However, this distance measure avoids the practical difficulties associated with the *GainRatio* measure, and in his experiments it produces significantly smaller trees in the case of data sets whose attributes have very different numbers of values.

A variety of other selection measures have been proposed as well (e.g., see Breiman et al. 1984; Mingers 1989a; Kearns and Mansour 1996; Dietterich et al. 1996). Mingers (1989a) provides an experimental analysis of the relative effectiveness of several selection measures over a variety of problems. He reports significant differences in the sizes of the unpruned trees produced by the different selection measures. However, in his experimental domains the choice of attribute selection measure appears to have a smaller impact on final accuracy than does the extent and method of post-pruning.

3.7.4 Handling Training Examples with Missing Attribute Values

In certain cases, the available data may be missing values for some attributes. For example, in a medical domain in which we wish to predict patient outcome based on various laboratory tests, it may be that the lab test *Blood-Test-Result* is available only for a subset of the patients. In such cases, it is common to estimate the missing attribute value based on other examples for which this attribute has a known value.

Consider the situation in which $Gain(S, A)$ is to be calculated at node n in the decision tree to evaluate whether the attribute A is the best attribute to test at this decision node. Suppose that $\langle x, c(x) \rangle$ is one of the training examples in S and that the value $A(x)$ is unknown.

One strategy for dealing with the missing attribute value is to assign it the value that is most common among training examples at node n. Alternatively, we might assign it the most common value among examples at node n that have the classification $c(x)$. The elaborated training example using this estimated value for $A(x)$ can then be used directly by the existing decision tree learning algorithm. This strategy is examined by Mingers (1989a).

A second, more complex procedure is to assign a probability to each of the possible values of A rather than simply assigning the most common value to $A(x)$. These probabilities can be estimated again based on the observed frequencies of the various values for A among the examples at node n. For example, given a boolean attribute A, if node n contains six known examples with $A = 1$ and four with $A = 0$, then we would say the probability that $A(x) = 1$ is 0.6, and the probability that $A(x) = 0$ is 0.4. A fractional 0.6 of instance x is now distributed down the branch for $A = 1$, and a fractional 0.4 of x down the other tree branch. These fractional examples are used for the purpose of computing information $Gain$ and can be further subdivided at subsequent branches of the tree if a second missing attribute value must be tested. This same fractioning of examples can also be applied after learning, to classify new instances whose attribute values are unknown. In this case, the classification of the new instance is simply the most probable classification, computed by summing the weights of the instance fragments classified in different ways at the leaf nodes of the tree. This method for handling missing attribute values is used in C4.5 (Quinlan 1993).

3.7.5 Handling Attributes with Differing Costs

In some learning tasks the instance attributes may have associated costs. For example, in learning to classify medical diseases we might describe patients in terms of attributes such as *Temperature*, *BiopsyResult*, *Pulse*, *BloodTestResults*, etc. These attributes vary significantly in their costs, both in terms of monetary cost and cost to patient comfort. In such tasks, we would prefer decision trees that use low-cost attributes where possible, relying on high-cost attributes only when needed to produce reliable classifications.

ID3 can be modified to take into account attribute costs by introducing a cost term into the attribute selection measure. For example, we might divide the $Gain$

by the cost of the attribute, so that lower-cost attributes would be preferred. While such cost-sensitive measures do not guarantee finding an optimal cost-sensitive decision tree, they do bias the search in favor of low-cost attributes.

Tan and Schlimmer (1990) and Tan (1993) describe one such approach and apply it to a robot perception task in which the robot must learn to classify different objects according to how they can be grasped by the robot's manipulator. In this case the attributes correspond to different sensor readings obtained by a movable sonar on the robot. Attribute cost is measured by the number of seconds required to obtain the attribute value by positioning and operating the sonar. They demonstrate that more efficient recognition strategies are learned, without sacrificing classification accuracy, by replacing the information gain attribute selection measure by the following measure

$$\frac{Gain^2(S, A)}{Cost(A)}$$

Nunez (1988) describes a related approach and its application to learning medical diagnosis rules. Here the attributes are different symptoms and laboratory tests with differing costs. His system uses a somewhat different attribute selection measure

$$\frac{2^{Gain(S,A)} - 1}{(Cost(A) + 1)^w}$$

where $w \in [0, 1]$ is a constant that determines the relative importance of cost versus information gain. Nunez (1991) presents an empirical comparison of these two approaches over a range of tasks.

3.8 SUMMARY AND FURTHER READING

The main points of this chapter include:

- Decision tree learning provides a practical method for concept learning and for learning other discrete-valued functions. The ID3 family of algorithms infers decision trees by growing them from the root downward, greedily selecting the next best attribute for each new decision branch added to the tree.
- ID3 searches a complete hypothesis space (i.e., the space of decision trees can represent any discrete-valued function defined over discrete-valued instances). It thereby avoids the major difficulty associated with approaches that consider only restricted sets of hypotheses: that the target function might not be present in the hypothesis space.
- The inductive bias implicit in ID3 includes a *preference* for smaller trees; that is, its search through the hypothesis space grows the tree only as large as needed in order to classify the available training examples.
- Overfitting the training data is an important issue in decision tree learning. Because the training examples are only a sample of all possible instances,

it is possible to add branches to the tree that improve performance on the training examples while decreasing performance on other instances outside this set. Methods for post-pruning the decision tree are therefore important to avoid overfitting in decision tree learning (and other inductive inference methods that employ a preference bias).

- A large variety of extensions to the basic ID3 algorithm has been developed by different researchers. These include methods for post-pruning trees, handling real-valued attributes, accommodating training examples with missing attribute values, incrementally refining decision trees as new training examples become available, using attribute selection measures other than information gain, and considering costs associated with instance attributes.

Among the earliest work on decision tree learning is Hunt's Concept Learning System (CLS) (Hunt et al. 1966) and Friedman and Breiman's work resulting in the CART system (Friedman 1977; Breiman et al. 1984). Quinlan's ID3 system (Quinlan 1979, 1983) forms the basis for the discussion in this chapter. Other early work on decision tree learning includes ASSISTANT (Kononenko et al. 1984; Cestnik et al. 1987). Implementations of decision tree induction algorithms are now commercially available on many computer platforms.

For further details on decision tree induction, an excellent book by Quinlan (1993) discusses many practical issues and provides executable code for C4.5. Mingers (1989a) and Buntine and Niblett (1992) provide two experimental studies comparing different attribute-selection measures. Mingers (1989b) and Malerba et al. (1995) provide studies of different pruning strategies. Experiments comparing decision tree learning and other learning methods can be found in numerous papers, including (Dietterich et al. 1995; Fisher and McKusick 1989; Quinlan 1988a; Shavlik et al. 1991; Thrun et al. 1991; Weiss and Kapouleas 1989).

EXERCISES

3.1. Give decision trees to represent the following boolean functions:

(*a*) $A \wedge \neg B$

(*b*) $A \vee [B \wedge C]$

(*c*) $A \; XOR \; B$

(*d*) $[A \wedge B] \vee [C \wedge D]$

3.2. Consider the following set of training examples:

Instance	Classification	a_1	a_2
1	+	T	T
2	+	T	T
3	−	T	F
4	+	F	F
5	−	F	T
6	−	F	T

(*a*) What is the entropy of this collection of training examples with respect to the target function classification?

(*b*) What is the information gain of a_2 relative to these training examples?

3.3. True or false: If decision tree D2 is an elaboration of tree D1, then D1 is *more-general-than* D2. Assume D1 and D2 are decision trees representing arbitrary boolean functions, and that D2 is an elaboration of D1 if ID3 could extend D1 into D2. If true, give a proof; if false, a counterexample. (*More-general-than* is defined in Chapter 2.)

3.4. ID3 searches for just one consistent hypothesis, whereas the CANDIDATE-ELIMINATION algorithm finds all consistent hypotheses. Consider the correspondence between these two learning algorithms.

(*a*) Show the decision tree that would be learned by ID3 assuming it is given the four training examples for the *EnjoySport*? target concept shown in Table 2.1 of Chapter 2.

(*b*) What is the relationship between the learned decision tree and the version space (shown in Figure 2.3 of Chapter 2) that is learned from these same examples? Is the learned tree equivalent to one of the members of the version space?

(*c*) Add the following training example, and compute the new decision tree. This time, show the value of the information gain for each candidate attribute at each step in growing the tree.

Sky	*Air-Temp*	*Humidity*	*Wind*	*Water*	*Forecast*	*Enjoy-Sport?*
Sunny	*Warm*	*Normal*	*Weak*	*Warm*	*Same*	*No*

(*d*) Suppose we wish to design a learner that (like ID3) searches a space of decision tree hypotheses and (like CANDIDATE-ELIMINATION) finds all hypotheses consistent with the data. In short, we wish to apply the CANDIDATE-ELIMINATION algorithm to searching the space of decision tree hypotheses. Show the *S* and *G* sets that result from the first training example from Table 2.1. Note *S* must contain the most specific decision trees consistent with the data, whereas *G* must contain the most general. Show how the *S* and *G* sets are refined by the second training example (you may omit syntactically distinct trees that describe the same concept). What difficulties do you foresee in applying CANDIDATE-ELIMINATION to a decision tree hypothesis space?

REFERENCES

Breiman, L., Friedman, J. H., Olshen, R. A., & Stone, P. J. (1984). *Classification and regression trees.* Belmont, CA: Wadsworth International Group.

Brodley, C. E., & Utgoff, P. E. (1995). Multivariate decision trees. *Machine Learning*, 19, 45–77.

Buntine, W., & Niblett, T. (1992). A further comparison of splitting rules for decision-tree induction. *Machine Learning*, 8, 75–86.

Cestnik, B., Kononenko, I., & Bratko, I. (1987). ASSISTANT-86: A knowledge-elicitation tool for sophisticated users. In I. Bratko & N. Lavrač (Eds.), *Progress in machine learning*. Bled, Yugoslavia: Sigma Press.

Dietterich, T. G., Hild, H., & Bakiri, G. (1995). A comparison of ID3 and BACKPROPAGATION for English text-to-speech mapping. *Machine Learning*, 18(1), 51–80.

Dietterich, T. G., Kearns, M., & Mansour, Y. (1996). Applying the weak learning framework to understand and improve C4.5. *Proceedings of the 13th International Conference on Machine Learning* (pp. 96–104). San Francisco: Morgan Kaufmann.

Fayyad, U. M. (1991). *On the induction of decision trees for multiple concept learning*, (Ph.D. dissertation). EECS Department, University of Michigan.

Fayyad, U. M., & Irani, K. B. (1992). On the handling of continuous-valued attributes in decision tree generation. *Machine Learning*, 8, 87–102.

Fayyad, U. M., & Irani, K. B. (1993). Multi-interval discretization of continuous-valued attributes for classification learning. In R. Bajcsy (Ed.), *Proceedings of the 13th International Joint Conference on Artificial Intelligence* (pp. 1022–1027). Morgan-Kaufmann.

Fayyad, U. M., Weir, N., & Djorgovski, S. (1993). SKICAT: A machine learning system for automated cataloging of large scale sky surveys. *Proceedings of the Tenth International Conference on Machine Learning* (pp. 112–119). Amherst, MA: Morgan Kaufmann.

Fisher, D. H., and McKusick, K. B. (1989). An empirical comparison of ID3 and back-propagation. *Proceedings of the Eleventh International Joint Conference on AI* (pp. 788–793). Morgan Kaufmann.

Friedman, J. H. (1977). A recursive partitioning decision rule for non-parametric classification. *IEEE Transactions on Computers* (pp. 404–408).

Hunt, E. B. (1975). *Artificial Intelligence*. New York: Academic Press.

Hunt, E. B., Marin, J., & Stone, P. J. (1966). *Experiments in Induction*. New York: Academic Press.

Kearns, M., & Mansour, Y. (1996). On the boosting ability of top-down decision tree learning algorithms. *Proceedings of the 28th ACM Symposium on the Theory of Computing*. New York: ACM Press.

Kononenko, I., Bratko, I., & Roskar, E. (1984). *Experiments in automatic learning of medical diagnostic rules* (Technical report). Jozef Stefan Institute, Ljubljana, Yugoslavia.

Lopez de Mantaras, R. (1991). A distance-based attribute selection measure for decision tree induction. *Machine Learning*, 6(1), 81–92.

Malerba, D., Floriana, E., & Semeraro, G. (1995). A further comparison of simplification methods for decision tree induction. In D. Fisher & H. Lenz (Eds.), *Learning from data: AI and statistics*. Springer-Verlag.

Mehta, M., Rissanen, J., & Agrawal, R. (1995). MDL-based decision tree pruning. *Proceedings of the First International Conference on Knowledge Discovery and Data Mining* (pp. 216–221). Menlo Park, CA: AAAI Press.

Mingers, J. (1989a). An empirical comparison of selection measures for decision-tree induction. *Machine Learning*, 3(4), 319–342.

Mingers, J. (1989b). An empirical comparison of pruning methods for decision-tree induction. *Machine Learning*, 4(2), 227–243.

Murphy, P. M., & Pazzani, M. J. (1994). Exploring the decision forest: An empirical investigation of Occam's razor in decision tree induction. *Journal of Artificial Intelligence Research*, 1, 257–275.

Murthy, S. K., Kasif, S., & Salzberg, S. (1994). A system for induction of oblique decision trees. *Journal of Artificial Intelligence Research*, 2, 1–33.

Nunez, M. (1991). The use of background knowledge in decision tree induction. *Machine Learning*, 6(3), 231–250.

Pagallo, G., & Haussler, D. (1990). Boolean feature discovery in empirical learning. *Machine Learning*, 5, 71–100.

Quinlan, J. R. (1979). Discovering rules by induction from large collections of examples. In D. Michie (Ed.), *Expert systems in the micro electronic age*. Edinburgh Univ. Press.

Quinlan, J. R. (1983). Learning efficient classification procedures and their application to chess end games. In R. S. Michalski, J. G. Carbonell, & T. M. Mitchell (Eds.), *Machine learning: An artificial intelligence approach*. San Mateo, CA: Morgan Kaufmann.

Quinlan, J. R. (1986). Induction of decision trees. *Machine Learning*, 1(1), 81–106.

Quinlan, J. R. (1987). Rule induction with statistical data—a comparison with multiple regression. *Journal of the Operational Research Society*, 38, 347–352.

Quinlan, J.R. (1988). An empirical comparison of genetic and decision-tree classifiers. *Proceedings of the Fifth International Machine Learning Conference* (135–141). San Mateo, CA: Morgan Kaufmann.

Quinlan, J.R. (1988b). Decision trees and multi-valued attributes. In Hayes, Michie, & Richards (Eds.), *Machine Intelligence 11*, (pp. 305–318). Oxford, England: Oxford University Press.

Quinlan, J. R., & Rivest, R. (1989). *Information and Computation*, (80), 227–248.

Quinlan, J. R. (1993). *C4.5: Programs for Machine Learning*. San Mateo, CA: Morgan Kaufmann.

Rissanen, J. (1983). A universal prior for integers and estimation by minimum description length. *Annals of Statistics 11* (2), 416–431.

Rivest, R. L. (1987). Learning decision lists. *Machine Learning*, 2(3), 229–246.

Schaffer, C. (1993). Overfitting avoidance as bias. *Machine Learning, 10*, 113–152.

Shavlik, J. W., Mooney, R. J., & Towell, G. G. (1991). Symbolic and neural learning algorithms: an experimental comparison. *Machine Learning*, 6(2), 111–144.

Tan, M. (1993). Cost-sensitive learning of classification knowledge and its applications in robotics. *Machine Learning*, 13(1), 1–33.

Tan, M., & Schlimmer, J. C. (1990). Two case studies in cost-sensitive concept acquisition. *Proceedings of the AAAI-90*.

Thrun, S. B. et al. (1991). *The Monk's problems: A performance comparison of different learning algorithms*, (Technical report CMU-CS-91-197). Computer Science Department, Carnegie Mellon Univ., Pittsburgh, PA.

Turney, P. D. (1995). Cost-sensitive classification: empirical evaluation of a hybrid genetic decision tree induction algorithm. *Journal of AI Research*, 2, 369–409.

Utgoff, P. E. (1989). Incremental induction of decision trees. *Machine Learning*, 4(2), 161–186.

Utgoff, P. E., & Brodley, C. E. (1991). *Linear machine decision trees*, (COINS Technical Report 91-10). University of Massachusetts, Amherst, MA.

Weiss, S., & Kapouleas, I. (1989). An empirical comparison of pattern recognition, neural nets, and machine learning classification methods. *Proceedings of the Eleventh IJCAI*, (781–787), Morgan Kaufmann.

CHAPTER 4

ARTIFICIAL NEURAL NETWORKS

Artificial neural networks (ANNs) provide a general, practical method for learning real-valued, discrete-valued, and vector-valued functions from examples. Algorithms such as BACKPROPAGATION use gradient descent to tune network parameters to best fit a training set of input-output pairs. ANN learning is robust to errors in the training data and has been successfully applied to problems such as interpreting visual scenes, speech recognition, and learning robot control strategies.

4.1 INTRODUCTION

Neural network learning methods provide a robust approach to approximating real-valued, discrete-valued, and vector-valued target functions. For certain types of problems, such as learning to interpret complex real-world sensor data, artificial neural networks are among the most effective learning methods currently known. For example, the BACKPROPAGATION algorithm described in this chapter has proven surprisingly successful in many practical problems such as learning to recognize handwritten characters (LeCun et al. 1989), learning to recognize spoken words (Lang et al. 1990), and learning to recognize faces (Cottrell 1990). One survey of practical applications is provided by Rumelhart et al. (1994).

4.1.1 Biological Motivation

The study of artificial neural networks (ANNs) has been inspired in part by the observation that biological learning systems are built of very complex webs of interconnected neurons. In rough analogy, artificial neural networks are built out of a densely interconnected set of simple units, where each unit takes a number of real-valued inputs (possibly the outputs of other units) and produces a single real-valued output (which may become the input to many other units).

To develop a feel for this analogy, let us consider a few facts from neurobiology. The human brain, for example, is estimated to contain a densely interconnected network of approximately 10^{11} neurons, each connected, on average, to 10^4 others. Neuron activity is typically excited or inhibited through connections to other neurons. The fastest neuron switching times are known to be on the order of 10^{-3} seconds—quite slow compared to computer switching speeds of 10^{-10} seconds. Yet humans are able to make surprisingly complex decisions, surprisingly quickly. For example, it requires approximately 10^{-1} seconds to visually recognize your mother. Notice the sequence of neuron firings that can take place during this 10^{-1}-second interval cannot possibly be longer than a few hundred steps, given the switching speed of single neurons. This observation has led many to speculate that the information-processing abilities of biological neural systems must follow from highly parallel processes operating on representations that are distributed over many neurons. One motivation for ANN systems is to capture this kind of highly parallel computation based on distributed representations. Most ANN software runs on sequential machines emulating distributed processes, although faster versions of the algorithms have also been implemented on highly parallel machines and on specialized hardware designed specifically for ANN applications.

While ANNs are loosely motivated by biological neural systems, there are many complexities to biological neural systems that are not modeled by ANNs, and many features of the ANNs we discuss here are known to be inconsistent with biological systems. For example, we consider here ANNs whose individual units output a single constant value, whereas biological neurons output a complex time series of spikes.

Historically, two groups of researchers have worked with artificial neural networks. One group has been motivated by the goal of using ANNs to study and model biological learning processes. A second group has been motivated by the goal of obtaining highly effective machine learning algorithms, independent of whether these algorithms mirror biological processes. Within this book our interest fits the latter group, and therefore we will not dwell further on biological modeling. For more information on attempts to model biological systems using ANNs, see, for example, Churchland and Sejnowski (1992); Zornetzer et al. (1994); Gabriel and Moore (1990).

4.2 NEURAL NETWORK REPRESENTATIONS

A prototypical example of ANN learning is provided by Pomerleau's (1993) system ALVINN, which uses a learned ANN to steer an autonomous vehicle driving at normal speeds on public highways. The input to the neural network is a 30×32 grid of pixel intensities obtained from a forward-pointed camera mounted on the vehicle. The network output is the direction in which the vehicle is steered. The ANN is trained to mimic the observed steering commands of a human driving the vehicle for approximately 5 minutes. ALVINN has used its learned networks to successfully drive at speeds up to 70 miles per hour and for distances of 90 miles on public highways (driving in the left lane of a divided public highway, with other vehicles present).

Figure 4.1 illustrates the neural network representation used in one version of the ALVINN system, and illustrates the kind of representation typical of many ANN systems. The network is shown on the left side of the figure, with the input camera image depicted below it. Each node (i.e., circle) in the network diagram corresponds to the output of a single network *unit*, and the lines entering the node from below are its inputs. As can be seen, there are four units that receive inputs directly from all of the 30×32 pixels in the image. These are called "hidden" units because their output is available only within the network and is not available as part of the global network output. Each of these four hidden units computes a single real-valued output based on a weighted combination of its 960 inputs. These hidden unit outputs are then used as inputs to a second layer of 30 "output" units. Each output unit corresponds to a particular steering direction, and the output values of these units determine which steering direction is recommended most strongly.

The diagrams on the right side of the figure depict the learned weight values associated with one of the four hidden units in this ANN. The large matrix of black and white boxes on the lower right depicts the weights from the 30×32 pixel inputs into the hidden unit. Here, a white box indicates a positive weight, a black box a negative weight, and the size of the box indicates the weight magnitude. The smaller rectangular diagram directly above the large matrix shows the weights from this hidden unit to each of the 30 output units.

The network structure of ALVINN is typical of many ANNs. Here the individual units are interconnected in layers that form a directed acyclic graph. In general, ANNs can be graphs with many types of structures—acyclic or cyclic, directed or undirected. This chapter will focus on the most common and practical ANN approaches, which are based on the BACKPROPAGATION algorithm. The BACKPROPAGATION algorithm assumes the network is a fixed structure that corresponds to a directed graph, possibly containing cycles. Learning corresponds to choosing a weight value for each edge in the graph. Although certain types of cycles are allowed, the vast majority of practical applications involve acyclic feed-forward networks, similar to the network structure used by ALVINN.

4.3 APPROPRIATE PROBLEMS FOR NEURAL NETWORK LEARNING

ANN learning is well-suited to problems in which the training data corresponds to noisy, complex sensor data, such as inputs from cameras and microphones.

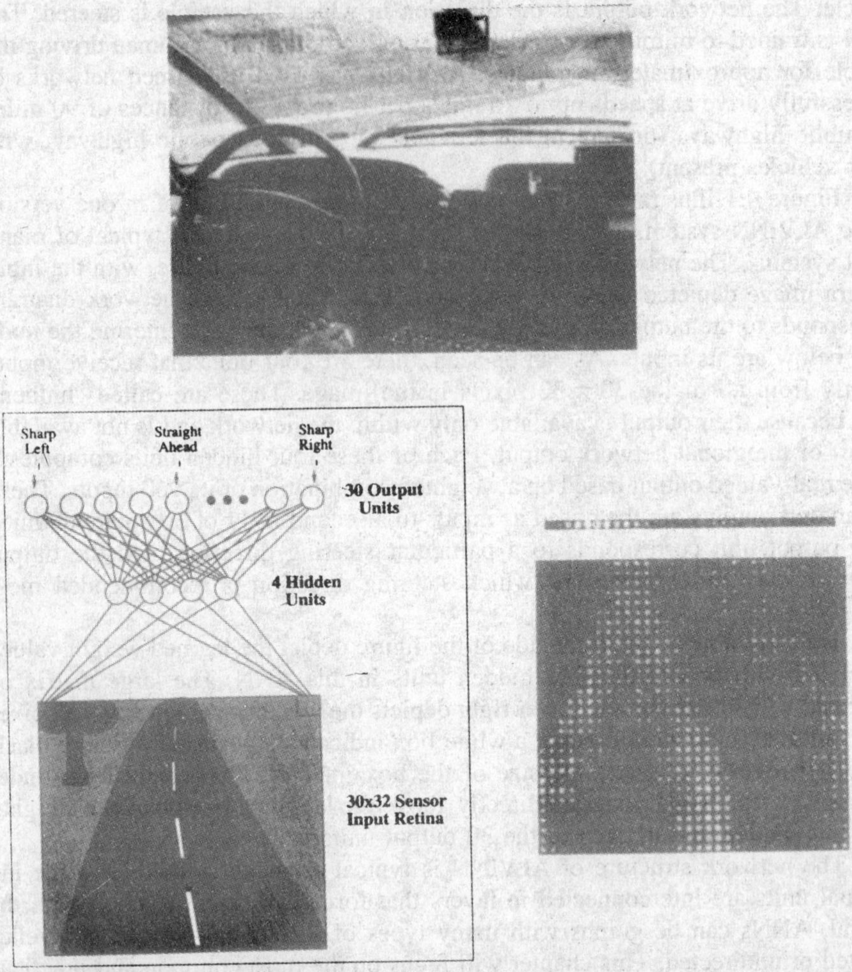

FIGURE 4.1
Neural network learning to steer an autonomous vehicle. The ALVINN system uses BACKPROPAGATION to learn to steer an autonomous vehicle (photo at top) driving at speeds up to 70 miles per hour. The diagram on the left shows how the image of a forward-mounted camera is mapped to 960 neural network inputs, which are fed forward to 4 hidden units, connected to 30 output units. Network outputs encode the commanded steering direction. The figure on the right shows weight values for one of the hidden units in this network. The 30 × 32 weights into the hidden unit are displayed in the large matrix, with white blocks indicating positive and black indicating negative weights. The weights from this hidden unit to the 30 output units are depicted by the smaller rectangular block directly above the large block. As can be seen from these output weights, activation of this particular hidden unit encourages a turn toward the left.

It is also applicable to problems for which more symbolic representations are often used, such as the decision tree learning tasks discussed in Chapter 3. In these cases ANN and decision tree learning often produce results of comparable accuracy. See Shavlik et al. (1991) and Weiss and Kapouleas (1989) for experimental comparisons of decision tree and ANN learning. The BACKPROPAGATION algorithm is the most commonly used ANN learning technique. It is appropriate for problems with the following characteristics:

- *Instances are represented by many attribute-value pairs.* The target function to be learned is defined over instances that can be described by a vector of predefined features, such as the pixel values in the ALVINN example. These input attributes may be highly correlated or independent of one another. Input values can be any real values.
- *The target function output may be discrete-valued, real-valued, or a vector of several real- or discrete-valued attributes.* For example, in the ALVINN system the output is a vector of 30 attributes, each corresponding to a recommendation regarding the steering direction. The value of each output is some real number between 0 and 1, which in this case corresponds to the confidence in predicting the corresponding steering direction. We can also train a single network to output both the steering command and suggested acceleration, simply by concatenating the vectors that encode these two output predictions.
- *The training examples may contain errors.* ANN learning methods are quite robust to noise in the training data.
- *Long training times are acceptable.* Network training algorithms typically require longer training times than, say, decision tree learning algorithms. Training times can range from a few seconds to many hours, depending on factors such as the number of weights in the network, the number of training examples considered, and the settings of various learning algorithm parameters.
- *Fast evaluation of the learned target function may be required.* Although ANN learning times are relatively long, evaluating the learned network, in order to apply it to a subsequent instance, is typically very fast. For example, ALVINN applies its neural network several times per second to continually update its steering command as the vehicle drives forward.
- *The ability of humans to understand the learned target function is not important.* The weights learned by neural networks are often difficult for humans to interpret. Learned neural networks are less easily communicated to humans than learned rules.

The rest of this chapter is organized as follows: We first consider several alternative designs for the primitive units that make up artificial neural networks (perceptrons, linear units, and sigmoid units), along with learning algorithms for training single units. We then present the BACKPROPAGATION algorithm for training multilayer networks of such units and consider several general issues such as the representational capabilities of ANNs, nature of the hypothesis space search, over-fitting problems, and alternatives to the BACKPROPAGATION algorithm. A detailed example is also presented applying BACKPROPAGATION to face recognition, and directions are provided for the reader to obtain the data and code to experiment further with this application.

4.4 PERCEPTRONS

One type of ANN system is based on a unit called a *perceptron*, illustrated in Figure 4.2. A perceptron takes a vector of real-valued inputs, calculates a linear combination of these inputs, then outputs a 1 if the result is greater than some threshold and -1 otherwise. More precisely, given inputs x_1 through x_n, the output $o(x_1, \ldots, x_n)$ computed by the perceptron is

$$o(x_1, \ldots, x_n) = \begin{cases} 1 & \text{if } w_0 + w_1x_1 + w_2x_2 + \cdots + w_nx_n > 0 \\ -1 & \text{otherwise} \end{cases}$$

where each w_i is a real-valued constant, or *weight*, that determines the contribution of input x_i to the perceptron output. Notice the quantity $(-w_0)$ is a threshold that the weighted combination of inputs $w_1x_1 + \cdots + w_nx_n$ must surpass in order for the perceptron to output a 1.

To simplify notation, we imagine an additional constant input $x_0 = 1$, allowing us to write the above inequality as $\sum_{i=0}^{n} w_ix_i > 0$, or in vector form as $\vec{w} \cdot \vec{x} > 0$. For brevity, we will sometimes write the perceptron function as

$$o(\vec{x}) = sgn(\vec{w} \cdot \vec{x})$$

where

$$sgn(y) = \begin{cases} 1 & \text{if } y > 0 \\ -1 & \text{otherwise} \end{cases}$$

Learning a perceptron involves choosing values for the weights $w_0, \ldots, w_n$. Therefore, the space H of candidate hypotheses considered in perceptron learning is the set of all possible real-valued weight vectors.

$$H = \{\vec{w} \mid \vec{w} \in \Re^{(n+1)}\}$$

4.4.1 Representational Power of Perceptrons

We can view the perceptron as representing a hyperplane decision surface in the n-dimensional space of instances (i.e., points). The perceptron outputs a 1 for instances lying on one side of the hyperplane and outputs a -1 for instances lying on the other side, as illustrated in Figure 4.3. The equation for this decision hyperplane is $\vec{w} \cdot \vec{x} = 0$. Of course, some sets of positive and negative examples cannot be separated by any hyperplane. Those that can be separated are called *linearly separable* sets of examples.

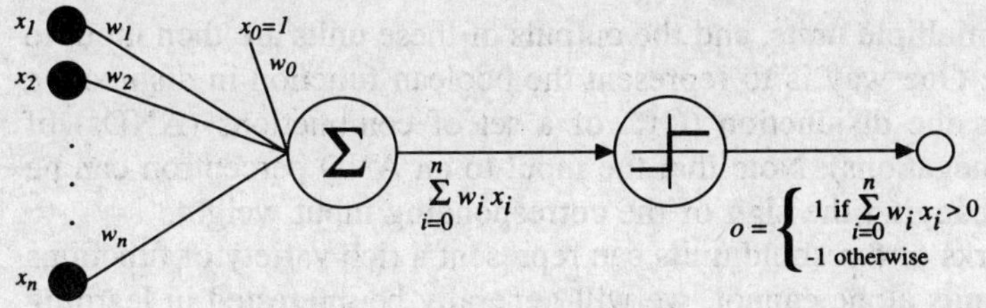

FIGURE 4.2
A perceptron.

A single perceptron can be used to represent many boolean functions. For example, if we assume boolean values of 1 (true) and -1 (false), then one way to use a two-input perceptron to implement the AND function is to set the weights $w_0 = -.8$, and $w_1 = w_2 = .5$. This perceptron can be made to represent the OR function instead by altering the threshold to $w_0 = -.3$. In fact, AND and OR can be viewed as special cases of m-of-n functions: that is, functions where at least m of the n inputs to the perceptron must be true. The OR function corresponds to $m = 1$ and the AND function to $m = n$. Any m-of-n function is easily represented using a perceptron by setting all input weights to the same value (e.g., 0.5) and then setting the threshold w_0 accordingly.

Perceptrons can represent all of the primitive boolean functions AND, OR, NAND ($\neg$ AND), and NOR ($\neg$ OR). Unfortunately, however, some boolean functions cannot be represented by a single perceptron, such as the XOR function whose value is 1 if and only if $x_1 \neq x_2$. Note the set of linearly nonseparable training examples shown in Figure 4.3(b) corresponds to this XOR function.

The ability of perceptrons to represent AND, OR, NAND, and NOR is important because *every* boolean function can be represented by some network of interconnected units based on these primitives. In fact, every boolean function can be represented by some network of perceptrons only two levels deep, in which

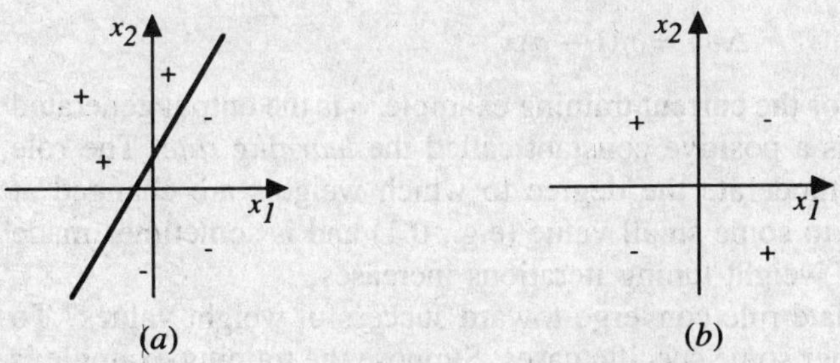

FIGURE 4.3
The decision surface represented by a two-input perceptron. (a) A set of training examples and the decision surface of a perceptron that classifies them correctly. (b) A set of training examples that is not linearly separable (i.e., that cannot be correctly classified by any straight line). x_1 and x_2 are the perceptron inputs. Positive examples are indicated by "+", negative by "$-$".

the inputs are fed to multiple units, and the outputs of these units are then input to a second, final stage. One way is to represent the boolean function in disjunctive normal form (i.e., as the disjunction (OR) of a set of conjunctions (ANDs) of the inputs and their negations). Note that the input to an AND perceptron can be negated simply by changing the sign of the corresponding input weight.

Because networks of threshold units can represent a rich variety of functions and because single units alone cannot, we will generally be interested in learning multilayer networks of threshold units.

4.4.2 The Perceptron Training Rule

Although we are interested in learning networks of many interconnected units, let us begin by understanding how to learn the weights for a single perceptron. Here the precise learning problem is to determine a weight vector that causes the perceptron to produce the correct ± 1 output for each of the given training examples.

Several algorithms are known to solve this learning problem. Here we consider two: the perceptron rule and the delta rule (a variant of the LMS rule used in Chapter 1 for learning evaluation functions). These two algorithms are guaranteed to converge to somewhat different acceptable hypotheses, under somewhat different conditions. They are important to ANNs because they provide the basis for learning networks of many units.

One way to learn an acceptable weight vector is to begin with random weights, then iteratively apply the perceptron to each training example, modifying the perceptron weights whenever it misclassifies an example. This process is repeated, iterating through the training examples as many times as needed until the perceptron classifies all training examples correctly. Weights are modified at each step according to the *perceptron training rule*, which revises the weight w_i associated with input x_i according to the rule

$$w_i \leftarrow w_i + \Delta w_i$$

where

$$\Delta w_i = \eta(t - o)x_i$$

Here t is the target output for the current training example, o is the output generated by the perceptron, and η is a positive constant called the *learning rate*. The role of the learning rate is to moderate the degree to which weights are changed at each step. It is usually set to some small value (e.g., 0.1) and is sometimes made to decay as the number of weight-tuning iterations increases.

Why should this update rule converge toward successful weight values? To get an intuitive feel, consider some specific cases. Suppose the training example is correctly classified already by the perceptron. In this case, $(t - o)$ is zero, making Δw_i zero, so that no weights are updated. Suppose the perceptron outputs a -1, when the target output is $+1$. To make the perceptron output a $+1$ instead of -1 in this case, the weights must be altered to increase the value of $\vec{w} \cdot \vec{x}$. For example, if $x_i > 0$, then increasing w_i will bring the perceptron closer to correctly classifying this example. Notice the training rule will increase w_i in this case, because $(t-o)$, η, and x_i are all positive. For example, if $x_i = .8$, $\eta = 0.1, t = 1$, and $o = -1$, then the weight update will be $\Delta w_i = \eta(t-o)x_i = 0.1(1-(-1))0.8 = 0.16$. On the other hand, if $t = -1$ and $o = 1$, then weights associated with positive x_i will be decreased rather than increased.

In fact, the above learning procedure can be proven to converge within a finite number of applications of the perceptron training rule to a weight vector that correctly classifies all training examples, *provided the training examples are linearly separable* and provided a sufficiently small η is used (see Minsky and Papert 1969). If the data are not linearly separable, convergence is not assured.

4.4.3 Gradient Descent and the Delta Rule

Although the perceptron rule finds a successful weight vector when the training examples are linearly separable, it can fail to converge if the examples are not linearly separable. A second training rule, called the *delta rule*, is designed to overcome this difficulty. If the training examples are not linearly separable, the delta rule converges toward a best-fit approximation to the target concept.

The key idea behind the delta rule is to use *gradient descent* to search the hypothesis space of possible weight vectors to find the weights that best fit the training examples. This rule is important because gradient descent provides the basis for the BACKPROPAGATION algorithm, which can learn networks with many interconnected units. It is also important because gradient descent can serve as the basis for learning algorithms that must search through hypothesis spaces containing many different types of continuously parameterized hypotheses.

The delta training rule is best understood by considering the task of training an *unthresholded* perceptron; that is, a *linear unit* for which the output o is given by

$$o(\vec{x}) = \vec{w} \cdot \vec{x} \tag{4.1}$$

Thus, a linear unit corresponds to the first stage of a perceptron, without the threshold.

In order to derive a weight learning rule for linear units, let us begin by specifying a measure for the *training error* of a hypothesis (weight vector), relative to the training examples. Although there are many ways to define this error, one common measure that will turn out to be especially convenient is

$$E(\vec{w}) \equiv \frac{1}{2} \sum_{d \in D} (t_d - o_d)^2 \tag{4.2}$$

where D is the set of training examples, t_d is the target output for training example d, and o_d is the output of the linear unit for training example d. By this definition, $E(\vec{w})$ is simply half the squared difference between the target output t_d and the linear unit output o_d, summed over all training examples. Here we characterize E as a function of $\vec{w}$ because the linear unit output o depends on this weight vector. Of course E also depends on the particular set of training examples, but we assume these are fixed during training, so we do not bother to write E as an explicit function of these. Chapter 6 provides a Bayesian justification for choosing this particular definition of E. In particular, there we show that under certain conditions the hypothesis that minimizes E is also the most probable hypothesis in H given the training data.

4.4.3.1 VISUALIZING THE HYPOTHESIS SPACE

To understand the gradient descent algorithm, it is helpful to visualize the entire hypothesis space of possible weight vectors and their associated E values, as illustrated in Figure 4.4. Here the axes w_0 and w_1 represent possible values for the two weights of a simple linear unit. The w_0, w_1 plane therefore represents the entire hypothesis space. The vertical axis indicates the error E relative to some fixed set of training examples. The error surface shown in the figure thus summarizes the desirability of every weight vector in the hypothesis space (we desire a hypothesis with minimum error). Given the way in which we chose to define E, for linear units this error surface must always be parabolic with a single global minimum. The specific parabola will depend, of course, on the particular set of training examples.

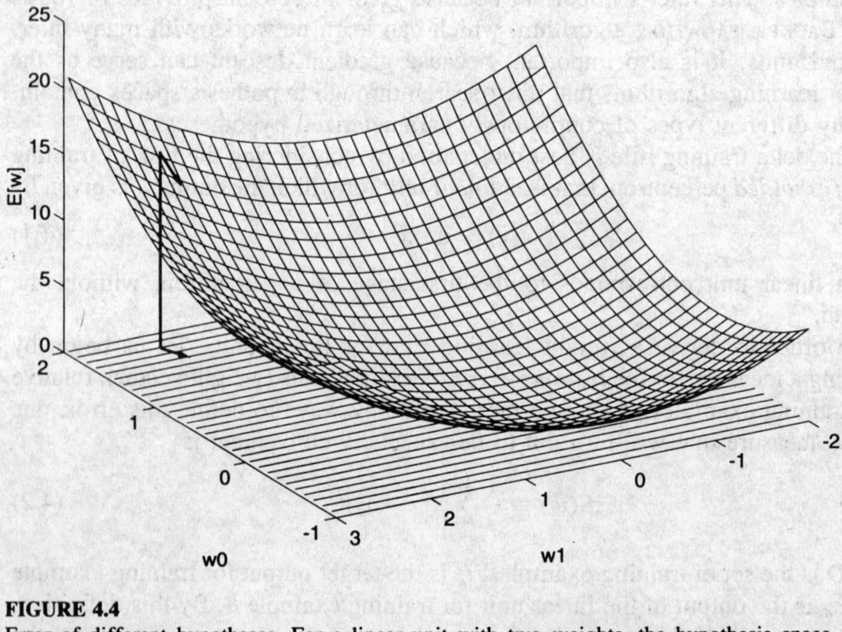

FIGURE 4.4
Error of different hypotheses. For a linear unit with two weights, the hypothesis space H is the w_0, w_1 plane. The vertical axis indicates the error of the corresponding weight vector hypothesis, relative to a fixed set of training examples. The arrow shows the negated gradient at one particular point, indicating the direction in the w_0, w_1 plane producing steepest descent along the error surface.

Gradient descent search determines a weight vector that minimizes E by starting with an arbitrary initial weight vector, then repeatedly modifying it in small steps. At each step, the weight vector is altered in the direction that produces the steepest descent along the error surface depicted in Figure 4.4. This process continues until the global minimum error is reached.

4.4.3.2 DERIVATION OF THE GRADIENT DESCENT RULE

How can we calculate the direction of steepest descent along the error surface? This direction can be found by computing the derivative of E with respect to each component of the vector $\vec{w}$. This vector derivative is called the *gradient* of E with respect to $\vec{w}$, written $\nabla E(\vec{w})$.

$$\nabla E(\vec{w}) \equiv \left[\frac{\partial E}{\partial w_0}, \frac{\partial E}{\partial w_1}, \cdots, \frac{\partial E}{\partial w_n}\right] \tag{4.3}$$

Notice $\nabla E(\vec{w})$ is itself a vector, whose components are the partial derivatives of E with respect to each of the w_i. *When interpreted as a vector in weight space, the gradient specifies the direction that produces the steepest increase in* E. The negative of this vector therefore gives the direction of steepest decrease. For example, the arrow in Figure 4.4 shows the negated gradient $-\nabla E(\vec{w})$ for a particular point in the w_0, w_1 plane.

Since the gradient specifies the direction of steepest increase of E, the training rule for gradient descent is

$$\vec{w} \leftarrow \vec{w} + \Delta\vec{w}$$

where

$$\Delta\vec{w} = -\eta\nabla E(\vec{w}) \tag{4.4}$$

Here η is a positive constant called the learning rate, which determines the step size in the gradient descent search. The negative sign is present because we want to move the weight vector in the direction that *decreases* E. This training rule can also be written in its component form

$$w_i \leftarrow w_i + \Delta w_i$$

where

$$\Delta w_i = -\eta\frac{\partial E}{\partial w_i} \tag{4.5}$$

which makes it clear that steepest descent is achieved by altering each component w_i of $\vec{w}$ in proportion to $\frac{\partial E}{\partial w_i}$.

To construct a practical algorithm for iteratively updating weights according to Equation (4.5), we need an efficient way of calculating the gradient at each step. Fortunately, this is not difficult. The vector of $\frac{\partial E}{\partial w_i}$ derivatives that form the gradient can be obtained by differentiating E from Equation (4.2), as

$$\begin{aligned}
\frac{\partial E}{\partial w_i} &= \frac{\partial}{\partial w_i}\frac{1}{2}\sum_{d\in D}(t_d - o_d)^2 \\
&= \frac{1}{2}\sum_{d\in D}\frac{\partial}{\partial w_i}(t_d - o_d)^2 \\
&= \frac{1}{2}\sum_{d\in D}2(t_d - o_d)\frac{\partial}{\partial w_i}(t_d - o_d) \\
&= \sum_{d\in D}(t_d - o_d)\frac{\partial}{\partial w_i}(t_d - \vec{w}\cdot\vec{x_d})
\end{aligned}$$

$$\frac{\partial E}{\partial w_i} = \sum_{d\in D}(t_d - o_d)(-x_{id}) \tag{4.6}$$

where x_{id} denotes the single input component x_i for training example d. We now have an equation that gives $\frac{\partial E}{\partial w_i}$ in terms of the linear unit inputs x_{id}, outputs t_d, and target values t_d associated with the training examples. Substituting Equation (4.6) into Equation (4.5) yields the weight update rule for gradient descent

$$\Delta w_i = \eta\sum_{d\in D}(t_d - o_d)\, x_{id} \tag{4.7}$$

To summarize, the gradient descent algorithm for training linear units is as follows: Pick an initial random weight vector. Apply the linear unit to all training examples, then compute Δw_i for each weight according to Equation (4.7). Update each weight w_i by adding Δw_i, then repeat this process. This algorithm is given in Table 4.1. Because the error surface contains only a single global minimum, this algorithm will converge to a weight vector with minimum error, regardless of whether the training examples are linearly separable, given a sufficiently small learning rate η is used. If η is too large, the gradient descent search runs the risk of overstepping the minimum in the error surface rather than settling into it. For this reason, one common modification to the algorithm is to gradually reduce the value of η as the number of gradient descent steps grows.

4.4.3.3 STOCHASTIC APPROXIMATION TO GRADIENT DESCENT

Gradient descent is an important general paradigm for learning. It is a strategy for searching through a large or infinite hypothesis space that can be applied whenever (1) the hypothesis space contains continuously parameterized hypotheses (e.g., the weights in a linear unit), and (2) the error can be differentiated with respect to these hypothesis parameters. The key practical difficulties in applying gradient descent are (1) converging to a local minimum can sometimes be quite slow (i.e., it can require many thousands of gradient descent steps), and (2) if there are multiple local minima in the error surface, then there is no guarantee that the procedure will find the global minimum.

GRADIENT-DESCENT(*training_examples*, η)

Each training example is a pair of the form $\langle \vec{x}, t \rangle$, where $\vec{x}$ is the vector of input values, and t is the target output value. η is the learning rate (e.g., .05).

- Initialize each w_i to some small random value
- Until the termination condition is met, Do
  - Initialize each Δw_i to zero.
  - For each $\langle \vec{x}, t \rangle$ in *training_examples*, Do
    - Input the instance $\vec{x}$ to the unit and compute the output o
    - For each linear unit weight w_i, Do

$$\Delta w_i \leftarrow \Delta w_i + \eta(t - o)x_i \tag{T4.1}$$

  - For each linear unit weight w_i, Do

$$w_i \leftarrow w_i + \Delta w_i \tag{T4.2}$$

TABLE 4.1

GRADIENT DESCENT algorithm for training a linear unit. To implement the stochastic approximation to gradient descent, Equation (T4.2) is deleted, and Equation (T4.1) replaced by $w_i \leftarrow w_i + \eta(t - o)x_i$.

One common variation on gradient descent intended to alleviate these difficulties is called *incremental gradient descent*, or alternatively *stochastic gradient descent*. Whereas the gradient descent training rule presented in Equation (4.7) computes weight updates after summing over *all* the training examples in D, the idea behind stochastic gradient descent is to approximate this gradient descent search by updating weights incrementally, following the calculation of the error for *each* individual example. The modified training rule is like the training rule given by Equation (4.7) except that as we iterate through each training example we update the weight according to

$$\Delta w_i = \eta(t - o)\ x_i \tag{4.10}$$

where t, o, and x_i are the target value, unit output, and ith input for the training example in question. To modify the gradient descent algorithm of Table 4.1 to implement this stochastic approximation, Equation (T4.2) is simply deleted and Equation (T4.1) replaced by $w_i \leftarrow w_i + \eta(t - o)\ x_i$. One way to view this stochastic gradient descent is to consider a distinct error function $E_d(\vec{w})$ defined for each individual training example d as follows

$$E_d(\vec{w}) = \frac{1}{2}(t_d - o_d)^2 \tag{4.11}$$

where t_d and o_d are the target value and the unit output value for training example d. Stochastic gradient descent iterates over the training examples d in D, at each iteration altering the weights according to the gradient with respect to $E_d(\vec{w})$. The sequence of these weight updates, when iterated over all training examples, provides a reasonable approximation to descending the gradient with respect to our original error function $E(\vec{w})$. By making the value of η (the gradient descent step size) sufficiently small, stochastic gradient descent can be made to approximate true gradient descent arbitrarily closely. The key differences between standard gradient descent and stochastic gradient descent are:

- In standard gradient descent, the error is summed over all examples before updating weights, whereas in stochastic gradient descent weights are updated upon examining each training example.
- Summing over multiple examples in standard gradient descent requires more computation per weight update step. On the other hand, because it uses the true gradient, standard gradient descent is often used with a larger step size per weight update than stochastic gradient descent.
- In cases where there are multiple local minima with respect to $E(\vec{w})$, stochastic gradient descent can sometimes avoid falling into these local minima because it uses the various $\nabla E_d(\vec{w})$ rather than $\nabla E(\vec{w})$ to guide its search.

Both stochastic and standard gradient descent methods are commonly used in practice.

The training rule in Equation (4.10) is known as the *delta rule*, or sometimes the LMS (least-mean-square) rule, Adaline rule, or Widrow-Hoff rule (after its inventors). In Chapter 1 we referred to it as the LMS weight-update rule when describing its use for learning an evaluation function for game playing. Notice the delta rule in Equation (4.10) is similar to the perceptron training rule in Equation (4.4.2). In fact, the two expressions appear to be identical. However, the rules are different because in the delta rule o refers to the linear unit output $o(\vec{x}) = \vec{w} \cdot \vec{x}$, whereas for the perceptron rule o refers to the thresholded output $o(\vec{x}) = sgn(\vec{w} \cdot \vec{x})$.

Although we have presented the delta rule as a method for learning weights for unthresholded linear units, it can easily be used to train thresholded perceptron units, as well. Suppose that $o = \vec{w} \cdot \vec{x}$ is the unthresholded linear unit output as above, and $o' = sgn(\vec{w} \cdot \vec{x})$ is the result of thresholding o as in the perceptron. Now if we wish to train a perceptron to fit training examples with target values of ± 1 for o', we can use these same target values and examples to train o instead, using the delta rule. Clearly, if the unthresholded output o can be trained to fit these values perfectly, then the threshold output o' will fit them as well (because $sgn(1) = 1$, and $sgn(-1) = -1$). Even when the target values cannot be fit perfectly, the thresholded o' value will correctly fit the ± 1 target value whenever the linear unit output o has the correct sign. Notice, however, that while this procedure will learn weights that minimize the error in the linear unit output o, these weights will not necessarily minimize the number of training examples misclassified by the thresholded output o'.

4.4.4 Remarks

We have considered two similar algorithms for iteratively learning perceptron weights. The key difference between these algorithms is that the perceptron training rule updates weights based on the error in the *thresholded* perceptron output, whereas the delta rule updates weights based on the error in the *unthresholded* linear combination of inputs.

The difference between these two training rules is reflected in different convergence properties. The perceptron training rule converges after a finite number of iterations to a hypothesis that perfectly classifies the training data, *provided the training examples are linearly separable*. The delta rule converges only asymptotically toward the minimum error hypothesis, possibly requiring unbounded time, but converges *regardless of whether the training data are linearly separable*. A detailed presentation of the convergence proofs can be found in Hertz et al. (1991).

A third possible algorithm for learning the weight vector is linear programming. Linear programming is a general, efficient method for solving sets of linear inequalities. Notice each training example corresponds to an inequality of the form $\vec{w} \cdot \vec{x} > 0$ or $\vec{w} \cdot \vec{x} \leq 0$, and their solution is the desired weight vector. Unfortunately, this approach yields a solution only when the training examples are linearly separable; however, Duda and Hart (1973, p. 168) suggest a more subtle formulation that accommodates the nonseparable case. In any case, the approach of linear programming does not scale to training multilayer networks, which is our primary concern. In contrast, the gradient descent approach, on which the delta rule is based, can be easily extended to multilayer networks, as shown in the following section.

4.5 MULTILAYER NETWORKS AND THE BACKPROPAGATION ALGORITHM

As noted in Section 4.4.1, single perceptrons can only express linear decision surfaces. In contrast, the kind of multilayer networks learned by the BACKPROPAGATION algorithm are capable of expressing a rich variety of nonlinear decision surfaces. For example, a typical multilayer network and decision surface is depicted in Figure 4.5. Here the speech recognition task involves distinguishing among 10 possible vowels, all spoken in the context of "h_d" (i.e., "hid," "had," "head," "hood," etc.). The input speech signal is represented by two numerical parameters obtained from a spectral analysis of the sound, allowing us to easily visualize the decision surface over the two-dimensional instance space. As shown in the figure, it is possible for the multilayer network to represent highly nonlinear decision surfaces that are much more expressive than the linear decision surfaces of single units shown earlier in Figure 4.3.

This section discusses how to learn such multilayer networks using a gradient descent algorithm similar to that discussed in the previous section.

4.5.1 A Differentiable Threshold Unit

What type of unit shall we use as the basis for constructing multilayer networks? At first we might be tempted to choose the linear units discussed in the previous

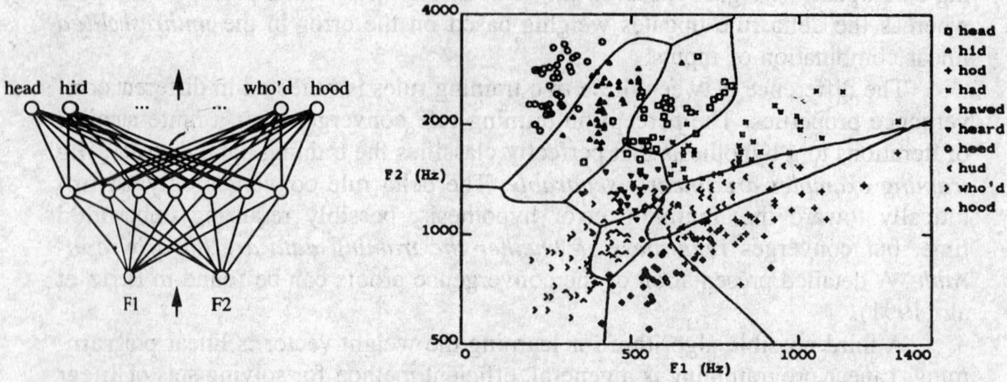

FIGURE 4.5
Decision regions of a multilayer feedforward network. The network shown here was trained to recognize 1 of 10 vowel sounds occurring in the context "h_d" (e.g., "had," "hid"). The network input consists of two parameters, F1 and F2, obtained from a spectral analysis of the sound. The 10 network outputs correspond to the 10 possible vowel sounds. The network prediction is the output whose value is highest. The plot on the right illustrates the highly nonlinear decision surface represented by the learned network. Points shown on the plot are test examples distinct from the examples used to train the network. (Reprinted by permission from Haung and Lippmann (1988).)

section, for which we have already derived a gradient descent learning rule. However, multiple layers of cascaded linear units still produce only linear functions, and we prefer networks capable of representing highly nonlinear functions. The perceptron unit is another possible choice, but its discontinuous threshold makes it undifferentiable and hence unsuitable for gradient descent. What we need is a unit whose output is a nonlinear function of its inputs, but whose output is also a differentiable function of its inputs. One solution is the *sigmoid unit*—a unit very much like a perceptron, but based on a smoothed, differentiable threshold function.

The sigmoid unit is illustrated in Figure 4.6. Like the perceptron, the sigmoid unit first computes a linear combination of its inputs, then applies a threshold to the result. In the case of the sigmoid unit, however, the threshold output is a

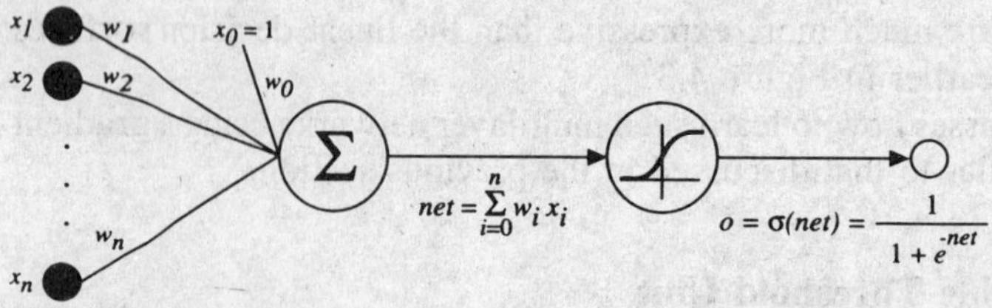

FIGURE 4.6
The sigmoid threshold unit.

continuous function of its input. More precisely, the sigmoid unit computes its output o as

$$o = \sigma(\vec{w} \cdot \vec{x})$$

where

$$\sigma(y) = \frac{1}{1 + e^{-y}} \tag{4.12}$$

σ is often called the sigmoid function or, alternatively, the logistic function. Note its output ranges between 0 and 1, increasing monotonically with its input (see the threshold function plot in Figure 4.6.). Because it maps a very large input domain to a small range of outputs, it is often referred to as the *squashing function* of the unit. The sigmoid function has the useful property that its derivative is easily expressed in terms of its output [in particular, $\frac{d\sigma(y)}{dy} = \sigma(y) \cdot (1 - \sigma(y))$]. As we shall see, the gradient descent learning rule makes use of this derivative. Other differentiable functions with easily calculated derivatives are sometimes used in place of σ. For example, the term e^{-y} in the sigmoid function definition is sometimes replaced by $e^{-k \cdot y}$ where k is some positive constant that determines the steepness of the threshold. The function $tanh$ is also sometimes used in place of the sigmoid function (see Exercise 4.8).

4.5.2 The BACKPROPAGATION Algorithm

The BACKPROPAGATION algorithm learns the weights for a multilayer network, given a network with a fixed set of units and interconnections. It employs gradient descent to attempt to minimize the squared error between the network output values and the target values for these outputs. This section presents the BACKPROPAGATION algorithm, and the following section gives the derivation for the gradient descent weight update rule used by BACKPROPAGATION.

Because we are considering networks with multiple output units rather than single units as before, we begin by redefining E to sum the errors over all of the network output units

$$E(\vec{w}) \equiv \frac{1}{2} \sum_{d \in D} \sum_{k \in outputs} (t_{kd} - o_{kd})^2 \tag{4.13}$$

where $outputs$ is the set of output units in the network, and t_{kd} and o_{kd} are the target and output values associated with the kth output unit and training example d.

The learning problem faced by BACKPROPAGATION is to search a large hypothesis space defined by all possible weight values for all the units in the network. The situation can be visualized in terms of an error surface similar to that shown for linear units in Figure 4.4. The error in that diagram is replaced by our new definition of E, and the other dimensions of the space correspond now to all of the weights associated with all of the units in the network. As in the case of training a single unit, gradient descent can be used to attempt to find a hypothesis to minimize E.

BACKPROPAGATION(*training_examples*, η, n_{in}, n_{out}, n_{hidden})

Each training example is a pair of the form $\langle \vec{x}, \vec{t} \rangle$, where $\vec{x}$ is the vector of network input values, and $\vec{t}$ is the vector of target network output values.

η is the learning rate (e.g., .05). n_{in} is the number of network inputs, n_{hidden} the number of units in the hidden layer, and n_{out} the number of output units.

The input from unit i into unit j is denoted x_{ji}, and the weight from unit i to unit j is denoted w_{ji}.

- Create a feed-forward network with n_{in} inputs, n_{hidden} hidden units, and n_{out} output units.
- Initialize all network weights to small random numbers (e.g., between $-.05$ and .05).
- Until the termination condition is met, Do
  - For each $\langle \vec{x}, \vec{t} \rangle$ in *training_examples*, Do

    Propagate the input forward through the network:

    1. Input the instance $\vec{x}$ to the network and compute the output o_u of every unit u in the network.

    Propagate the errors backward through the network:

    2. For each network output unit k, calculate its error term δ_k

    $$\delta_k \leftarrow o_k(1 - o_k)(t_k - o_k) \tag{T4.3}$$

    3. For each hidden unit h, calculate its error term δ_h

    $$\delta_h \leftarrow o_h(1 - o_h) \sum_{k \in outputs} w_{kh} \delta_k \tag{T4.4}$$

    4. Update each network weight w_{ji}

    $$w_{ji} \leftarrow w_{ji} + \Delta w_{ji}$$

    where

    $$\Delta w_{ji} = \eta \, \delta_j \, x_{ji} \tag{T4.5}$$

TABLE 4.2
The stochastic gradient descent version of the BACKPROPAGATION algorithm for feedforward networks containing two layers of sigmoid units.

One major difference in the case of multilayer networks is that the error surface can have multiple local minima, in contrast to the single-minimum parabolic error surface shown in Figure 4.4. Unfortunately, this means that gradient descent is guaranteed only to converge toward some local minimum, and not necessarily the global minimum error. Despite this obstacle, in practice BACKPROPAGATION has been found to produce excellent results in many real-world applications.

The BACKPROPAGATION algorithm is presented in Table 4.2. The algorithm as described here applies to layered feedforward networks containing two layers of sigmoid units, with units at each layer connected to all units from the preceding layer. This is the incremental, or stochastic, gradient descent version of BACKPROPAGATION. The notation used here is the same as that used in earlier sections, with the following extensions:

- An index (e.g., an integer) is assigned to each node in the network, where a "node" is either an input to the network or the output of some unit in the network.
- x_{ji} denotes the input from node i to unit j, and w_{ji} denotes the corresponding weight.
- δ_n denotes the error term associated with unit n. It plays a role analogous to the quantity $(t - o)$ in our earlier discussion of the delta training rule. As we shall see later, $\delta_n = -\frac{\partial E}{\partial net_n}$.

Notice the algorithm in Table 4.2 begins by constructing a network with the desired number of hidden and output units and initializing all network weights to small random values. Given this fixed network structure, the main loop of the algorithm then repeatedly iterates over the training examples. For each training example, it applies the network to the example, calculates the error of the network output for this example, computes the gradient with respect to the error on this example, then updates all weights in the network. This gradient descent step is iterated (often thousands of times, using the same training examples multiple times) until the network performs acceptably well.

The gradient descent weight-update rule (Equation [T4.5] in Table 4.2) is similar to the delta training rule (Equation [4.10]). Like the delta rule, it updates each weight in proportion to the learning rate η, the input value x_{ji} to which the weight is applied, and the error in the output of the unit. The only difference is that the error $(t - o)$ in the delta rule is replaced by a more complex error term, δ_j. The exact form of δ_j follows from the derivation of the weight-tuning rule given in Section 4.5.3. To understand it intuitively, first consider how δ_k is computed for each network *output* unit k (Equation [T4.3] in the algorithm). δ_k is simply the familiar $(t_k - o_k)$ from the delta rule, multiplied by the factor $o_k(1 - o_k)$, which is the derivative of the sigmoid squashing function. The δ_h value for each *hidden* unit h has a similar form (Equation [T4.4] in the algorithm). However, since training examples provide target values t_k *only* for network outputs, no target values are directly available to indicate the error of hidden units' values. Instead, the error term for hidden unit h is calculated by summing the error terms δ_k for each output unit influenced by h, weighting each of the δ_k's by w_{kh}, the weight from hidden unit h to output unit k. This weight characterizes the degree to which hidden unit h is "responsible for" the error in output unit k.

The algorithm in Table 4.2 updates weights incrementally, following the presentation of each training example. This corresponds to a stochastic approximation to gradient descent. To obtain the true gradient of E one would sum the $\delta_j x_{ji}$ values over all training examples before altering weight values.

The weight-update loop in BACKPROPAGATION may be iterated thousands of times in a typical application. A variety of termination conditions can be used to halt the procedure. One may choose to halt after a fixed number of iterations through the loop, or once the error on the training examples falls below some threshold, or once the error on a separate validation set of examples meets some criterion. The choice of termination criterion is an important one, because too few iterations can fail to reduce error sufficiently, and too many can lead to overfitting the training data. This issue is discussed in greater detail in Section 4.6.5.

4.5.2.1 ADDING MOMENTUM

Because BACKPROPAGATION is such a widely used algorithm, many variations have been developed. Perhaps the most common is to alter the weight-update rule in Equation (T4.5) in the algorithm by making the weight update on the nth iteration depend partially on the update that occurred during the $(n-1)$th iteration, as follows:

$$\Delta w_{ji}(n) = \eta\, \delta_j\, x_{ji} + \alpha \Delta w_{ji}(n-1) \tag{4.18}$$

Here $\Delta w_{ji}(n)$ is the weight update performed during the nth iteration through the main loop of the algorithm, and $0 \leq \alpha < 1$ is a constant called the *momentum*. Notice the first term on the right of this equation is just the weight-update rule of Equation (T4.5) in the BACKPROPAGATION algorithm. The second term on the right is new and is called the momentum term. To see the effect of this momentum term, consider that the gradient descent search trajectory is analogous to that of a (momentumless) ball rolling down the error surface. The effect of α is to add momentum that tends to keep the ball rolling in the same direction from one iteration to the next. This can sometimes have the effect of keeping the ball rolling through small local minima in the error surface, or along flat regions in the surface where the ball would stop if there were no momentum. It also has the effect of gradually increasing the step size of the search in regions where the gradient is unchanging, thereby speeding convergence.

4.5.2.2 LEARNING IN ARBITRARY ACYCLIC NETWORKS

The definition of BACKPROPAGATION presented in Table 4.2 applies only to two-layer networks. However, the algorithm given there easily generalizes to feedforward networks of arbitrary depth. The weight update rule seen in Equation (T4.5) is retained, and the only change is to the procedure for computing δ values. In general, the δ_r value for a unit r in layer m is computed from the δ values at the next deeper layer $m+1$ according to

$$\delta_r = o_r\,(1 - o_r) \sum_{s \in layer\, m+1} w_{sr}\, \delta_s \tag{4.19}$$

Notice this is identical to Step 3 in the algorithm of Table 4.2, so all we are really saying here is that this step may be repeated for any number of hidden layers in the network.

It is equally straightforward to generalize the algorithm to any directed acyclic graph, regardless of whether the network units are arranged in uniform layers as we have assumed up to now. In the case that they are not, the rule for calculating δ for any internal unit (i.e., any unit that is not an output) is

$$\delta_r = o_r\,(1 - o_r) \sum_{s \in Downstream(r)} w_{sr}\, \delta_s \tag{4.20}$$

where $Downstream(r)$ is the set of units immediately downstream from unit r in the network: that is, all units whose inputs include the output of unit r. It is this general form of the weight-update rule that we derive in Section 4.5.3.

4.5.3 Derivation of the BACKPROPAGATION Rule

This section presents the derivation of the BACKPROPAGATION weight-tuning rule. It may be skipped on a first reading, without loss of continuity.

The specific problem we address here is deriving the stochastic gradient descent rule implemented by the algorithm in Table 4.2. Recall from Equation (4.11) that stochastic gradient descent involves iterating through the training examples one at a time, for each training example d descending the gradient of the error E_d with respect to this single example. In other words, for each training example d every weight w_{ji} is updated by adding to it Δw_{ji}

$$\Delta w_{ji} = -\eta \frac{\partial E_d}{\partial w_{ji}} \tag{4.21}$$

where E_d is the error on training example d, summed over all output units in the network

$$E_d(\vec{w}) \equiv \frac{1}{2} \sum_{k \in outputs} (t_k - o_k)^2$$

Here *outputs* is the set of output units in the network, t_k is the target value of unit k for training example d, and o_k is the output of unit k given training example d.

The derivation of the stochastic gradient descent rule is conceptually straightforward, but requires keeping track of a number of subscripts and variables. We will follow the notation shown in Figure 4.6, adding a subscript j to denote to the jth unit of the network as follows:

- x_{ji} = the ith input to unit j
- w_{ji} = the weight associated with the ith input to unit j
- $net_j = \sum_i w_{ji} x_{ji}$ (the weighted sum of inputs for unit j)
- o_j = the output computed by unit j
- t_j = the target output for unit j
- σ = the sigmoid function
- $outputs$ = the set of units in the final layer of the network
- $Downstream(j)$ = the set of units whose immediate inputs include the output of unit j

We now derive an expression for $\frac{\partial E_d}{\partial w_{ji}}$ in order to implement the stochastic gradient descent rule seen in Equation (4.21). To begin, notice that weight w_{ji} can influence the rest of the network only through net_j. Therefore, we can use the chain rule to write

$$\frac{\partial E_d}{\partial w_{ji}} = \frac{\partial E_d}{\partial net_j} \frac{\partial net_j}{\partial w_{ji}}$$
$$= \frac{\partial E_d}{\partial net_j} x_{ji} \tag{4.22}$$

Given Equation (4.22), our remaining task is to derive a convenient expression for $\frac{\partial E_d}{\partial net_j}$. We consider two cases in turn: the case where unit j is an output unit for the network, and the case where j is an internal unit.

Case 1: Training Rule for Output Unit Weights. Just as w_{ji} can influence the rest of the network only through net_j, net_j can influence the network only through o_j. Therefore, we can invoke the chain rule again to write

$$\frac{\partial E_d}{\partial net_j} = \frac{\partial E_d}{\partial o_j} \frac{\partial o_j}{\partial net_j} \tag{4.23}$$

To begin, consider just the first term in Equation (4.23)

$$\frac{\partial E_d}{\partial o_j} = \frac{\partial}{\partial o_j} \frac{1}{2} \sum_{k \in outputs} (t_k - o_k)^2$$

The derivatives $\frac{\partial}{\partial o_j}(t_k - o_k)^2$ will be zero for all output units k except when $k = j$. We therefore drop the summation over output units and simply set $k = j$.

$$\frac{\partial E_d}{\partial o_j} = \frac{\partial}{\partial o_j} \frac{1}{2}(t_j - o_j)^2$$
$$= \frac{1}{2} 2(t_j - o_j) \frac{\partial (t_j - o_j)}{\partial o_j}$$
$$= -(t_j - o_j) \tag{4.24}$$

Next consider the second term in Equation (4.23). Since $o_j = \sigma(net_j)$, the derivative $\frac{\partial o_j}{\partial net_j}$ is just the derivative of the sigmoid function, which we have already noted is equal to $\sigma(net_j)(1 - \sigma(net_j))$. Therefore,

$$\frac{\partial o_j}{\partial net_j} = \frac{\partial \sigma(net_j)}{\partial net_j}$$
$$= o_j(1 - o_j) \tag{4.25}$$

Substituting expressions (4.24) and (4.25) into (4.23), we obtain

$$\frac{\partial E_d}{\partial net_j} = -(t_j - o_j)\; o_j(1 - o_j) \tag{4.26}$$

and combining this with Equations (4.21) and (4.22), we have the stochastic gradient descent rule for output units

$$\Delta w_{ji} = -\eta \frac{\partial E_d}{\partial w_{ji}} = \eta \ (t_j - o_j) \ o_j(1 - o_j) x_{ji} \tag{4.27}$$

Note this training rule is exactly the weight update rule implemented by Equations (T4.3) and (T4.5) in the algorithm of Table 4.2. Furthermore, we can see now that δ_k in Equation (T4.3) is equal to the quantity $-\frac{\partial E_d}{\partial net_k}$. In the remainder of this section we will use δ_i to denote the quantity $-\frac{\partial E_d}{\partial net_i}$ for an arbitrary unit i.

Case 2: Training Rule for Hidden Unit Weights. In the case where j is an internal, or hidden unit in the network, the derivation of the training rule for w_{ji} must take into account the indirect ways in which w_{ji} can influence the network outputs and hence E_d. For this reason, we will find it useful to refer to the set of all units immediately downstream of unit j in the network (i.e., all units whose direct inputs include the output of unit j). We denote this set of units by $Downstream(j)$. Notice that net_j can influence the network outputs (and therefore E_d) only through the units in $Downstream(j)$. Therefore, we can write

$$\begin{aligned}
\frac{\partial E_d}{\partial net_j} &= \sum_{k \in Downstream(j)} \frac{\partial E_d}{\partial net_k} \frac{\partial net_k}{\partial net_j} \\
&= \sum_{k \in Downstream(j)} -\delta_k \frac{\partial net_k}{\partial net_j} \\
&= \sum_{k \in Downstream(j)} -\delta_k \frac{\partial net_k}{\partial o_j} \frac{\partial o_j}{\partial net_j} \\
&= \sum_{k \in Downstream(j)} -\delta_k \ w_{kj} \frac{\partial o_j}{\partial net_j} \\
&= \sum_{k \in Downstream(j)} -\delta_k \ w_{kj} \ o_j(1 - o_j)
\end{aligned} \tag{4.28}$$

Rearranging terms and using δ_j to denote $-\frac{\partial E_d}{\partial net_j}$, we have

$$\delta_j = o_j(1 - o_j) \sum_{k \in Downstream(j)} \delta_k \ w_{kj}$$

and

$$\Delta w_{ji} = \eta \ \delta_j \ x_{ji}$$

which is precisely the general rule from Equation (4.20) for updating internal unit weights in arbitrary acyclic directed graphs. Notice Equation (T4.4) from Table 4.2 is just a special case of this rule, in which $Downstream(j) = outputs$.

4.6 REMARKS ON THE BACKPROPAGATION ALGORITHM

4.6.1 Convergence and Local Minima

As shown above, the BACKPROPAGATION algorithm implements a gradient descent search through the space of possible network weights, iteratively reducing the error E between the training example target values and the network outputs. Because the error surface for multilayer networks may contain many different local minima, gradient descent can become trapped in any of these. As a result, BACKPROPAGATION over multilayer networks is only guaranteed to converge toward some local minimum in E and not necessarily to the global minimum error.

Despite the lack of assured convergence to the global minimum error, BACKPROPAGATION is a highly effective function approximation method in practice. In many practical applications the problem of local minima has not been found to be as severe as one might fear. To develop some intuition here, consider that networks with large numbers of weights correspond to error surfaces in very high dimensional spaces (one dimension per weight). When gradient descent falls into a local minimum with respect to one of these weights, it will not necessarily be in a local minimum with respect to the other weights. In fact, the more weights in the network, the more dimensions that might provide "escape routes" for gradient descent to fall away from the local minimum with respect to this single weight.

A second perspective on local minima can be gained by considering the manner in which network weights evolve as the number of training iterations increases. Notice that if network weights are initialized to values near zero, then during early gradient descent steps the network will represent a very smooth function that is approximately linear in its inputs. This is because the sigmoid threshold function itself is approximately linear when the weights are close to zero (see the plot of the sigmoid function in Figure 4.6). Only after the weights have had time to grow will they reach a point where they can represent highly nonlinear network functions. One might expect more local minima to exist in the region of the weight space that represents these more complex functions. One hopes that by the time the weights reach this point they have already moved close enough to the global minimum that even local minima in this region are acceptable.

Despite the above comments, gradient descent over the complex error surfaces represented by ANNs is still poorly understood, and no methods are known to predict with certainty when local minima will cause difficulties. Common heuristics to attempt to alleviate the problem of local minima include:

- Add a momentum term to the weight-update rule as described in Equation (4.18). Momentum can sometimes carry the gradient descent procedure through narrow local minima (though in principle it can also carry it through narrow global minima into other local minima!).
- Use stochastic gradient descent rather than true gradient descent. As discussed in Section 4.4.3.3, the stochastic approximation to gradient descent effectively descends a different error surface for each training example, re-

lying on the average of these to approximate the gradient with respect to the full training set. These different error surfaces typically will have different local minima, making it less likely that the process will get stuck in any one of them.

- Train multiple networks using the same data, but initializing each network with different random weights. If the different training efforts lead to different local minima, then the network with the best performance over a separate validation data set can be selected. Alternatively, all networks can be retained and treated as a "committee" of networks whose output is the (possibly weighted) average of the individual network outputs.

4.6.2 Representational Power of Feedforward Networks

What set of functions can be represented by feedforward networks? Of course the answer depends on the width and depth of the networks. Although much is still unknown about which function classes can be described by which types of networks, three quite general results are known:

- *Boolean functions.* Every boolean function can be represented exactly by some network with two layers of units, although the number of hidden units required grows exponentially in the worst case with the number of network inputs. To see how this can be done, consider the following general scheme for representing an arbitrary boolean function: For each possible input vector, create a distinct hidden unit and set its weights so that it activates if and only if this specific vector is input to the network. This produces a hidden layer that will always have exactly one unit active. Now implement the output unit as an OR gate that activates just for the desired input patterns.
- *Continuous functions.* Every bounded continuous function can be approximated with arbitrarily small error (under a finite norm) by a network with two layers of units (Cybenko 1989; Hornik et al. 1989). The theorem in this case applies to networks that use sigmoid units at the hidden layer and (unthresholded) linear units at the output layer. The number of hidden units required depends on the function to be approximated.
- *Arbitrary functions.* Any function can be approximated to arbitrary accuracy by a network with three layers of units (Cybenko 1988). Again, the output layer uses linear units, the two hidden layers use sigmoid units, and the number of units required at each layer is not known in general. The proof of this involves showing that any function can be approximated by a linear combination of many localized functions that have value 0 everywhere except for some small region, and then showing that two layers of sigmoid units are sufficient to produce good local approximations.

These results show that limited depth feedforward networks provide a very expressive hypothesis space for BACKPROPAGATION. However, it is important to keep in mind that the network weight vectors reachable by gradient descent from the initial weight values may not include all possible weight vectors. Hertz et al. (1991) provide a more detailed discussion of the above results.

4.6.3 Hypothesis Space Search and Inductive Bias

It is interesting to compare the hypothesis space search of BACKPROPAGATION to the search performed by other learning algorithms. For BACKPROPAGATION, every possible assignment of network weights represents a syntactically distinct hypothesis that in principle can be considered by the learner. In other words, the hypothesis space is the n-dimensional Euclidean space of the n network weights. Notice this hypothesis space is *continuous*, in contrast to the hypothesis spaces of decision tree learning and other methods based on discrete representations. The fact that it is continuous, together with the fact that E is differentiable with respect to the continuous parameters of the hypothesis, results in a well-defined error gradient that provides a very useful structure for organizing the search for the best hypothesis. This structure is quite different from the general-to-specific ordering used to organize the search for symbolic concept learning algorithms, or the simple-to-complex ordering over decision trees used by the ID3 and C4.5 algorithms.

What is the inductive bias by which BACKPROPAGATION generalizes beyond the observed data? It is difficult to characterize precisely the inductive bias of BACKPROPAGATION learning, because it depends on the interplay between the gradient descent search and the way in which the weight space spans the space of representable functions. However, one can roughly characterize it as *smooth interpolation between data points*. Given two positive training examples with no negative examples between them, BACKPROPAGATION will tend to label points in between as positive examples as well. This can be seen, for example, in the decision surface illustrated in Figure 4.5, in which the specific sample of training examples gives rise to smoothly varying decision regions.

4.6.4 Hidden Layer Representations

One intriguing property of BACKPROPAGATION is its ability to discover useful intermediate representations at the hidden unit layers inside the network. Because training examples constrain only the network inputs and outputs, the weight-tuning procedure is free to set weights that define whatever hidden unit representation is most effective at minimizing the squared error E. This can lead BACKPROPAGATION to define new hidden layer features that are not explicit in the input representation, but which capture properties of the input instances that are most relevant to learning the target function.

Consider, for example, the network shown in Figure 4.7. Here, the eight network inputs are connected to three hidden units, which are in turn connected to the eight output units. Because of this structure, the three hidden units will be forced to re-represent the eight input values in some way that captures their

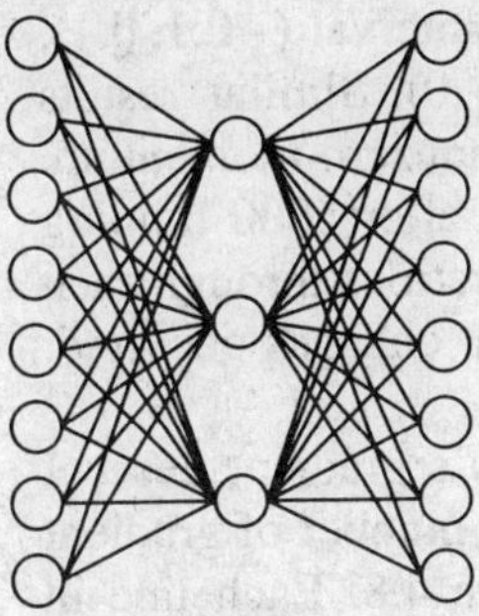

Input		Hidden Values				Output
10000000	→	.89	.04	.08	→	10000000
01000000	→	.15	.99	.99	→	01000000
00100000	→	.01	.97	.27	→	00100000
00010000	→	.99	.97	.71	→	00010000
00001000	→	.03	.05	.02	→	00001000
00000100	→	.01	.11	.88	→	00000100
00000010	→	.80	.01	.98	→	00000010
00000001	→	.60	.94	.01	→	00000001

FIGURE 4.7
Learned Hidden Layer Representation. This $8 \times 3 \times 8$ network was trained to learn the identity function, using the eight training examples shown. After 5000 training epochs, the three hidden unit values encode the eight distinct inputs using the encoding shown on the right. Notice if the encoded values are rounded to zero or one, the result is the standard binary encoding for eight distinct values.

relevant features, so that this hidden layer representation can be used by the output units to compute the correct target values.

Consider training the network shown in Figure 4.7 to learn the simple target function $f(\vec{x}) = \vec{x}$, where $\vec{x}$ is a vector containing seven 0's and a single 1. The network must learn to reproduce the eight inputs at the corresponding eight output units. Although this is a simple function, the network in this case is constrained to use only three hidden units. Therefore, the essential information from all eight input units must be captured by the three learned hidden units.

When BACKPROPAGATION is applied to this task, using each of the eight possible vectors as training examples, it successfully learns the target function. What hidden layer representation is created by the gradient descent BACKPROPAGATION algorithm? By examining the hidden unit values generated by the learned network for each of the eight possible input vectors, it is easy to see that the learned encoding is similar to the familiar standard binary encoding of eight values using three bits (e.g., $000, 001, 010, \ldots, 111$). The exact values of the hidden units for one typical run of BACKPROPAGATION are shown in Figure 4.7.

This ability of multilayer networks to automatically discover useful representations at the hidden layers is a key feature of ANN learning. In contrast to learning methods that are constrained to use only predefined features provided by the human designer, this provides an important degree of flexibility that allows the learner to invent features not explicitly introduced by the human designer. Of course these invented features must still be computable as sigmoid unit functions of the provided network inputs. Note when more layers of units are used in the network, more complex features can be invented. Another example of hidden layer features is provided in the face recognition application discussed in Section 4.7.

In order to develop a better intuition for the operation of BACKPROPAGATION in this example, let us examine the operation of the gradient descent procedure in greater detail†. The network in Figure 4.7 was trained using the algorithm shown in Table 4.2, with initial weights set to random values in the interval $(-0.1, 0.1)$, learning rate $\eta = 0.3$, and no weight momentum (i.e., $\alpha = 0$). Similar results were obtained by using other learning rates and by including nonzero momentum. The hidden unit encoding shown in Figure 4.7 was obtained after 5000 training iterations through the outer loop of the algorithm (i.e., 5000 iterations through each of the eight training examples). Most of the interesting weight changes occurred, however, during the first 2500 iterations.

We can directly observe the effect of BACKPROPAGATION's gradient descent search by plotting the squared output error as a function of the number of gradient descent search steps. This is shown in the top plot of Figure 4.8. Each line in this plot shows the squared output error summed over all training examples, for one of the eight network outputs. The horizontal axis indicates the number of iterations through the outermost loop of the BACKPROPAGATION algorithm. As this plot indicates, the sum of squared errors for each output decreases as the gradient descent procedure proceeds, more quickly for some output units and less quickly for others.

The evolution of the hidden layer representation can be seen in the second plot of Figure 4.8. This plot shows the three hidden unit values computed by the learned network for one of the possible inputs (in particular, 01000000). Again, the horizontal axis indicates the number of training iterations. As this plot indicates, the network passes through a number of different encodings before converging to the final encoding given in Figure 4.7.

Finally, the evolution of individual weights within the network is illustrated in the third plot of Figure 4.8. This plots displays the evolution of weights connecting the eight input units (and the constant 1 bias input) to one of the three hidden units. Notice that significant changes in the weight values for this hidden unit coincide with significant changes in the hidden layer encoding and output squared errors. The weight that converges to a value near zero in this case is the bias weight w_0.

4.6.5 Generalization, Overfitting, and Stopping Criterion

In the description of the BACKPROPAGATION algorithm in Table 4.2, the termination condition for the algorithm has been left unspecified. What is an appropriate condition for terminating the weight update loop? One obvious choice is to continue training until the error E on the training examples falls below some predetermined threshold. In fact, this is a poor strategy because BACKPROPAGATION is susceptible to overfitting the training examples at the cost of decreasing generalization accuracy over other unseen examples.

To see the dangers of minimizing the error over the training data, consider how the error E varies with the number of weight iterations. Figure 4.9 shows

---

† The source code to reproduce this example is available at http://www.cs.cmu.edu/~tom/mlbook.html.

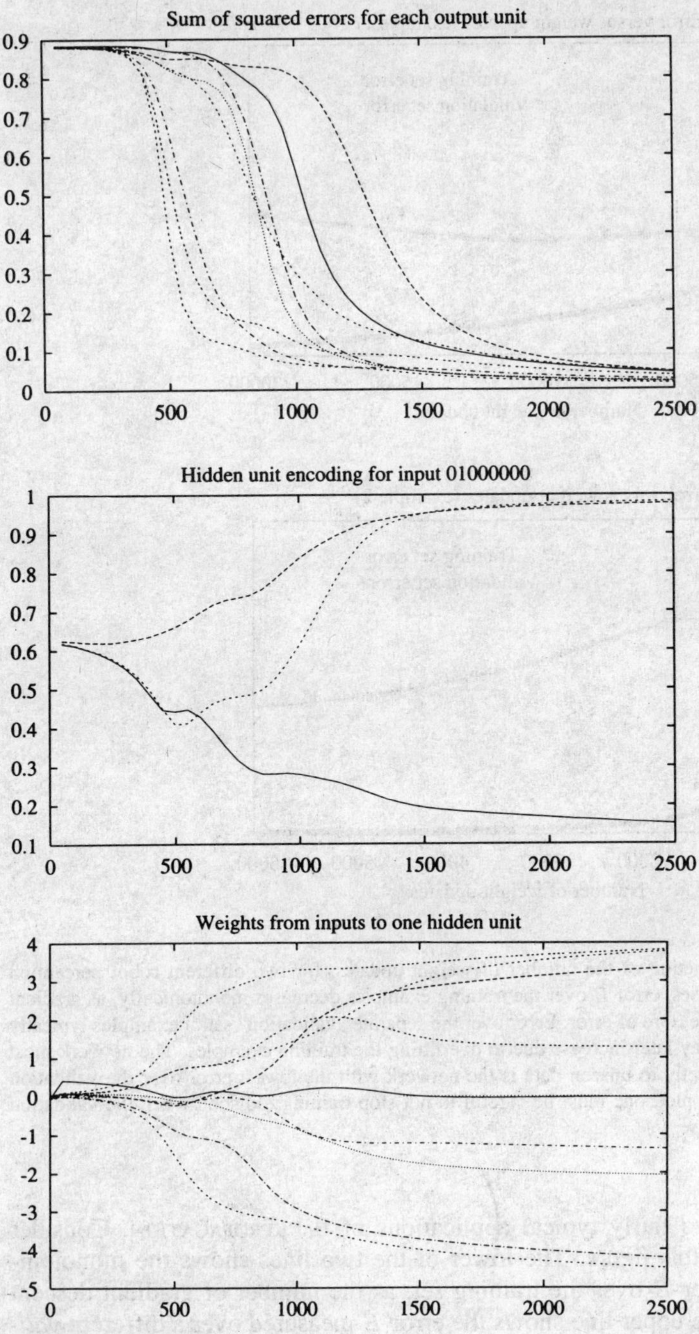

FIGURE 4.8
Learning the 8 × 3 × 8 Network. The top plot shows the evolving sum of squared errors for each of the eight output units, as the number of training iterations (epochs) increases. The middle plot shows the evolving hidden layer representation for the input string "01000000." The bottom plot shows the evolving weights for one of the three hidden units.

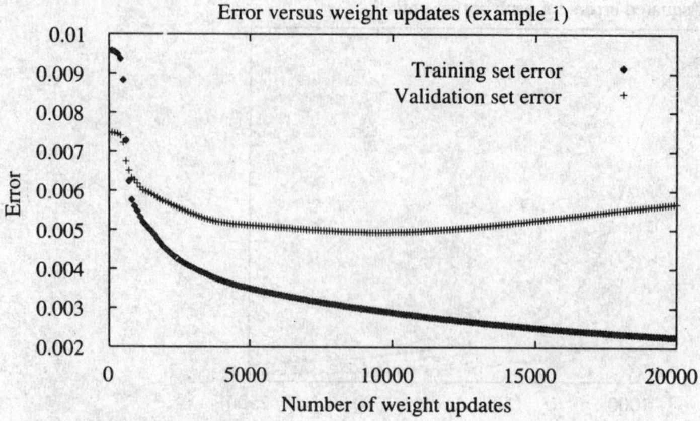

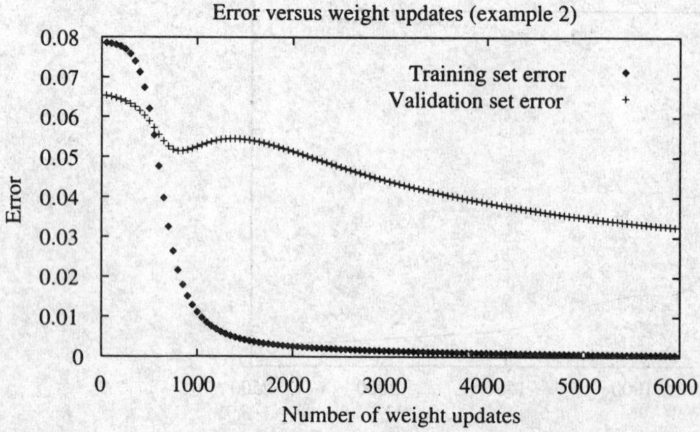

FIGURE 4.9
Plots of error E as a function of the number of weight updates, for two different robot perception tasks. In both learning cases, error E over the training examples decreases monotonically, as gradient descent minimizes this measure of error. Error over the separate "validation" set of examples typically decreases at first, then may later increase due to overfitting the training examples. The network most likely to generalize correctly to unseen data is the network with the lowest error over the validation set. Notice in the second plot, one must be careful to not stop training too soon when the validation set error begins to increase.

this variation for two fairly typical applications of BACKPROPAGATION. Consider first the top plot in this figure. The lower of the two lines shows the monotonically decreasing error E over the training set, as the number of gradient descent iterations grows. The upper line shows the error E measured over a different *validation set* of examples, distinct from the training examples. This line measures the *generalization accuracy* of the network—the accuracy with which it fits examples beyond the training data.

Notice the generalization accuracy measured over the validation examples first decreases, then increases, even as the error over the training examples continues to decrease. How can this occur? This occurs because the weights are being tuned to fit idiosyncrasies of the training examples that are not representative of the general distribution of examples. The large number of weight parameters in ANNs provides many degrees of freedom for fitting such idiosyncrasies.

Why does overfitting tend to occur during later iterations, but not during earlier iterations? Consider that network weights are initialized to small random values. With weights of nearly identical value, only very smooth decision surfaces are describable. As training proceeds, some weights begin to grow in order to reduce the error over the training data, and the complexity of the learned decision surface increases. Thus, the effective complexity of the hypotheses that can be reached by BACKPROPAGATION increases with the number of weight-tuning iterations. Given enough weight-tuning iterations, BACKPROPAGATION will often be able to create overly complex decision surfaces that fit noise in the training data or unrepresentative characteristics of the particular training sample. This overfitting problem is analogous to the overfitting problem in decision tree learning (see Chapter 3).

Several techniques are available to address the overfitting problem for BACKPROPAGATION learning. One approach, known as *weight decay*, is to decrease each weight by some small factor during each iteration. This is equivalent to modifying the definition of E to include a penalty term corresponding to the total magnitude of the network weights. The motivation for this approach is to keep weight values small, to bias learning against complex decision surfaces.

One of the most successful methods for overcoming the overfitting problem is to simply provide a set of validation data to the algorithm in addition to the training data. The algorithm monitors the error with respect to this validation set, while using the training set to drive the gradient descent search. In essence, this allows the algorithm itself to plot the two curves shown in Figure 4.9. How many weight-tuning iterations should the algorithm perform? Clearly, it should use the number of iterations that produces the lowest error *over the validation set,* since this is the best indicator of network performance over unseen examples. In typical implementations of this approach, two copies of the network weights are kept: one copy for training and a separate copy of the best-performing weights thus far, measured by their error over the validation set. Once the trained weights reach a significantly higher error over the validation set than the stored weights, training is terminated and the stored weights are returned as the final hypothesis. When this procedure is applied in the case of the top plot of Figure 4.9, it outputs the network weights obtained after 9100 iterations. The second plot in Figure 4.9 shows that it is not always obvious when the lowest error on the validation set has been reached. In this plot, the validation set error decreases, then increases, then decreases again. Care must be taken to avoid the mistaken conclusion that the network has reached its lowest validation set error at iteration 850.

In general, the issue of overfitting and how to overcome it is a subtle one. The above cross-validation approach works best when extra data are available to provide a validation set. Unfortunately, however, the problem of overfitting is most severe for small training sets. In these cases, a k-fold cross-validation approach is sometimes used, in which cross validation is performed k different times, each time using a different partitioning of the data into training and validation sets, and the results are then averaged. In one version of this approach, the m available examples are partitioned into k disjoint subsets, each of size m/k. The cross-validation procedure is then run k times, each time using a different one of these subsets as the validation set and combining the other subsets for the training set. Thus, each example is used in the validation set for one of the experiments and in the training set for the other $k - 1$ experiments. On each experiment the above cross-validation approach is used to determine the number of iterations i that yield the best performance on the validation set. The mean $\bar{i}$ of these estimates for i is then calculated, and a final run of BACKPROPAGATION is performed *training on all n examples* for $\bar{i}$ iterations, with no validation set. This procedure is closely related to the procedure for comparing two learning methods based on limited data, described in Chapter 5.

4.7 AN ILLUSTRATIVE EXAMPLE: FACE RECOGNITION

To illustrate some of the practical design choices involved in applying BACKPROPAGATION, this section discusses applying it to a learning task involving face recognition. All image data and code used to produce the examples described in this section are available at World Wide Web site http://www.cs.cmu.edu/~tom/mlbook.html, along with complete documentation on how to use the code. Why not try it yourself?

4.7.1 The Task

The learning task here involves classifying camera images of faces of various people in various poses. Images of 20 different people were collected, including approximately 32 images per person, varying the person's expression (happy, sad, angry, neutral), the direction in which they were looking (left, right, straight ahead, up), and whether or not they were wearing sunglasses. As can be seen from the example images in Figure 4.10, there is also variation in the background behind the person, the clothing worn by the person, and the position of the person's face within the image. In total, 624 greyscale images were collected, each with a resolution of 120×128, with each image pixel described by a greyscale intensity value between 0 (black) and 255 (white).

A variety of target functions can be learned from this image data. For example, given an image as input we could train an ANN to output the identity of the person, the direction in which the person is facing, the gender of the person, whether or not they are wearing sunglasses, etc. All of these target functions can be learned to high accuracy from this image data, and the reader is encouraged to try out these experiments. In the remainder of this section we consider one particular task: learning the direction in which the person is facing (to their left, right, straight ahead, or upward).

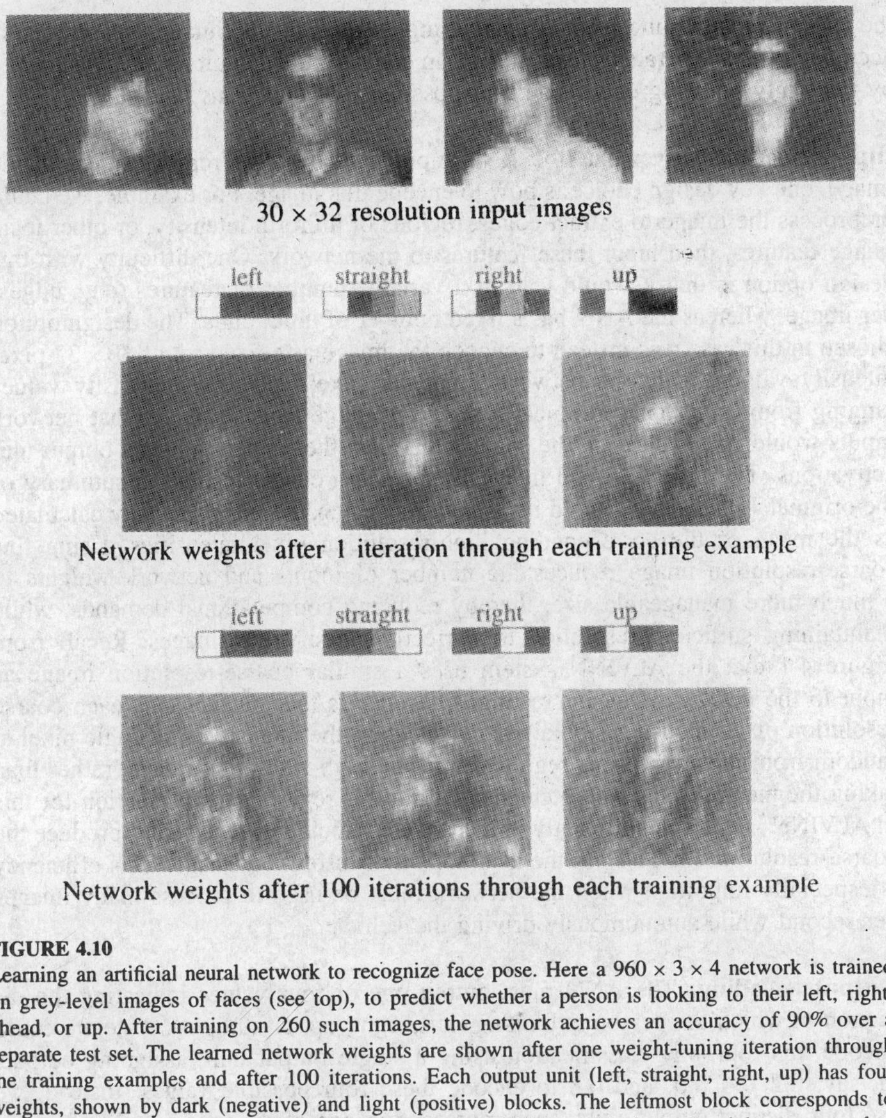

FIGURE 4.10
Learning an artificial neural network to recognize face pose. Here a 960 × 3 × 4 network is trained on grey-level images of faces (see top), to predict whether a person is looking to their left, right, ahead, or up. After training on 260 such images, the network achieves an accuracy of 90% over a separate test set. The learned network weights are shown after one weight-tuning iteration through the training examples and after 100 iterations. Each output unit (left, straight, right, up) has four weights, shown by dark (negative) and light (positive) blocks. The leftmost block corresponds to the weight w_0, which determines the unit threshold, and the three blocks to the right correspond to weights on inputs from the three hidden units. The weights from the image pixels into each hidden unit are also shown, with each weight plotted in the position of the corresponding image pixel.

4.7.2 Design Choices

In applying BACKPROPAGATION to any given task, a number of design choices must be made. We summarize these choices below for our task of learning the direction in which a person is facing. Although no attempt was made to determine the precise optimal design choices for this task, the design described here learns the target function quite well. After training on a set of 260 images, classification accuracy over a separate test set is 90%. In contrast, the default accuracy achieved by randomly guessing one of the four possible face directions is 25%.

Input encoding. Given that the ANN input is to be some representation of the image, one key design choice is how to encode this image. For example, we could preprocess the image to extract edges, regions of uniform intensity, or other local image features, then input these features to the network. One difficulty with this design option is that it would lead to a variable number of features (e.g., edges) per image, whereas the ANN has a fixed number of input units. The design option chosen in this case was instead to encode the image as a fixed set of 30×32 pixel intensity values, with one network input per pixel. The pixel intensity values ranging from 0 to 255 were linearly scaled to range from 0 to 1 so that network inputs would have values in the same interval as the hidden unit and output unit activations. The 30×32 pixel image is, in fact, a coarse resolution summary of the original 120×128 captured image, with each coarse pixel intensity calculated as the mean of the corresponding high-resolution pixel intensities. Using this coarse-resolution image reduces the number of inputs and network weights to a much more manageable size, thereby reducing computational demands, while maintaining sufficient resolution to correctly classify the images. Recall from Figure 4.1 that the ALVINN system uses a similar coarse-resolution image as input to the network. One interesting difference is that in ALVINN, each coarse resolution pixel intensity is obtained by selecting the intensity of a single pixel at random from the appropriate region within the high-resolution image, rather than taking the mean of all pixel intensities within this region. The motivation for this in ALVINN is that it significantly reduces the computation required to produce the coarse-resolution image from the available high-resolution image. This efficiency is especially important when the network must be used to process many images per second while autonomously driving the vehicle.

Output encoding. The ANN must output one of four values indicating the direction in which the person is looking (left, right, up, or straight). Note we could encode this four-way classification using a single output unit, assigning outputs of, say, 0.2, 0.4, 0.6, and 0.8 to encode these four possible values. Instead, we use four distinct output units, each representing one of the four possible face directions, with the highest-valued output taken as the network prediction. This is often called a *1-of-n* output encoding. There are two motivations for choosing the 1-of-n output encoding over the single unit option. First, it provides more degrees of freedom to the network for representing the target function (i.e., there are n times as many weights available in the output layer of units). Second, in the 1-of-n encoding the difference between the highest-valued output and the second-highest can be used as a measure of the confidence in the network prediction (ambiguous classifications may result in near or exact ties). A further design choice here is "what should be the target values for these four output units?" One obvious choice would be to use the four target values $\langle 1, 0, 0, 0\rangle$ to encode a face looking to the left, $\langle 0, 1, 0, 0 \rangle$ to encode a face looking straight, etc. Instead of 0 and 1 values, we use values of 0.1 and 0.9, so that $\langle 0.9, 0.1, 0.1, 0.1 \rangle$ is the target output vector for a face looking to the left. The reason for avoiding target values of 0 and 1 is that sigmoid units cannot produce these output values given finite weights. If we attempt to train the network to fit target values of exactly 0 and 1, gradient descent will force the weights to grow without bound. On the other hand, values of 0.1 and 0.9 are achievable using a sigmoid unit with finite weights.

Network graph structure. As described earlier, BACKPROPAGATION can be applied to any acyclic directed graph of sigmoid units. Therefore, another design choice we face is how many units to include in the network and how to interconnect them. The most common network structure is a layered network with feedforward connections from every unit in one layer to every unit in the next. In the current design we chose this standard structure, using two layers of sigmoid units (one hidden layer and one output layer). It is common to use one or two layers of sigmoid units and, occasionally, three layers. It is not common to use more layers than this because training times become very long and because networks with three layers of sigmoid units can already express a rich variety of target functions (see Section 4.6.2). Given our choice of a layered feedforward network with one hidden layer, how many hidden units should we include? In the results reported in Figure 4.10, only three hidden units were used, yielding a test set accuracy of 90%. In other experiments 30 hidden units were used, yielding a test set accuracy one to two percent higher. Although the generalization accuracy varied only a small amount between these two experiments, the second experiment required significantly more training time. Using 260 training images, the training time was approximately 1 hour on a Sun Sparc5 workstation for the 30 hidden unit network, compared to approximately 5 minutes for the 3 hidden unit network. In many applications it has been found that some minimum number of hidden units is required in order to learn the target function accurately and that extra hidden units above this number do not dramatically affect generalization accuracy, provided cross-validation methods are used to determine how many gradient descent iterations should be performed. If such methods are not used, then increasing the number of hidden units often increases the tendency to overfit the training data, thereby reducing generalization accuracy.

Other learning algorithm parameters. In these learning experiments the learning rate η was set to 0.3, and the momentum α was set to 0.3. Lower values for both parameters produced roughly equivalent generalization accuracy, but longer training times. If these values are set too high, training fails to converge to a network with acceptable error over the training set. Full gradient descent was used in all these experiments (in contrast to the stochastic approximation to gradient descent in the algorithm of Table 4.2). Network weights in the output units were initialized to small random values. However, input unit weights were initialized to zero, because this yields much more intelligible visualizations of the learned weights (see Figure 4.10), without any noticeable impact on generalization accuracy. The number of training iterations was selected by partitioning the available data into a training set and a separate validation set. Gradient descent was used to minimize the error over the training set, and after every 50 gradient descent steps the performance of the network was evaluated over the validation set. The final selected network was the one with the highest accuracy over the validation set. See Section 4.6.5 for an explanation and justification of this procedure. The final reported accuracy (e.g., 90% for the network in Figure 4.10) was measured over yet a third set of test examples that were not used in any way to influence training.

4.7.3 Learned Hidden Representations

It is interesting to examine the learned weight values for the 2899 weights in the network. Figure 4.10 depicts the values of each of these weights after one iteration through the weight update for all training examples, and again after 100 iterations.

To understand this diagram, consider first the four rectangular blocks just below the face images in the figure. Each of these rectangles depicts the weights for one of the four output units in the network (encoding left, straight, right, and up). The four squares within each rectangle indicate the four weights associated with this output unit—the weight w_0, which determines the unit threshold (on the left), followed by the three weights connecting the three hidden units to this output. The brightness of the square indicates the weight value, with bright white indicating a large positive weight, dark black indicating a large negative weight, and intermediate shades of grey indicating intermediate weight values. For example, the output unit labeled "up" has a near zero w_0 threshold weight, a large positive weight from the first hidden unit, and a large negative weight from the second hidden unit.

The weights of the hidden units are shown directly below those for the output units. Recall that each hidden unit receives an input from each of the 30×32 image pixels. The 30×32 weights associated with these inputs are displayed so that each weight is in the position of the corresponding image pixel (with the w_0 threshold weight superimposed in the top left of the array). Interestingly, one can see that the weights have taken on values that are especially sensitive to features in the region of the image in which the face and body typically appear.

The values of the network weights after 100 gradient descent iterations through each training example are shown at the bottom of the figure. Notice the leftmost hidden unit has very different weights than it had after the first iteration, and the other two hidden units have changed as well. It is possible to understand to some degree the encoding in this final set of weights. For example, consider the output unit that indicates a person is looking to his right. This unit has a strong positive weight from the second hidden unit and a strong negative weight from the third hidden unit. Examining the weights of these two hidden units, it is easy to see that if the person's face is turned to his right (i.e., our left), then his bright skin will roughly align with strong positive weights in this hidden unit, and his dark hair will roughly align with negative weights, resulting in this unit outputting a large value. The same image will cause the third hidden unit to output a value close to zero, as the bright face will tend to align with the large negative weights in this case.

4.8 ADVANCED TOPICS IN ARTIFICIAL NEURAL NETWORKS

4.8.1 Alternative Error Functions

As noted earlier, gradient descent can be performed for any function E that is differentiable with respect to the parameterized hypothesis space. While the basic BACKPROPAGATION algorithm defines E in terms of the sum of squared errors of the network, other definitions have been suggested in order to incorporate other constraints into the weight-tuning rule. For each new definition of E a new weight-tuning rule for gradient descent must be derived. Examples of alternative definitions of E include

- Adding a penalty term for weight magnitude. As discussed above, we can add a term to E that increases with the magnitude of the weight vector. This causes the gradient descent search to seek weight vectors with small magnitudes, thereby reducing the risk of overfitting. One way to do this is to redefine E as

$$E(\vec{w}) \equiv \frac{1}{2}\sum_{d\in D}\sum_{k\in outputs}(t_{kd}-o_{kd})^2+\gamma\sum_{i,j}w_{ji}^2$$

  which yields a weight update rule identical to the BACKPROPAGATION rule, except that each weight is multiplied by the constant $(1-2\gamma\eta)$ upon each iteration. Thus, choosing this definition of E is equivalent to using a weight decay strategy (see Exercise 4.10.)

- Adding a term for errors in the *slope*, or derivative of the target function. In some cases, training information may be available regarding desired derivatives of the target function, as well as desired values. For example, Simard et al. (1992) describe an application to character recognition in which certain training derivatives are used to constrain the network to learn character recognition functions that are invariant of translation within the image. Mitchell and Thrun (1993) describe methods for calculating training derivatives based on the learner's prior knowledge. In both of these systems (described in Chapter 12), the error function is modified to add a term measuring the discrepancy between these training derivatives and the actual derivatives of the learned network. One example of such an error function is

$$E(\vec{w}) \equiv \frac{1}{2}\sum_{d\in D}\sum_{k\in outputs}\left[(t_{kd}-o_{kd})^2+\mu\sum_{j\in inputs}\left(\frac{\partial t_{kd}}{\partial x_d^j}-\frac{\partial o_{kd}}{\partial x_d^j}\right)^2\right]$$

  Here x_d^j denotes the value of the jth input unit for training example d. Thus, $\frac{\partial t_{kd}}{\partial x_d^j}$ is the training derivative describing how the target output value

t_{kd} should vary with a change in the input x_d^j. Similarly, $\frac{\partial o_{kd}}{\partial x_d^j}$ denotes the corresponding derivative of the actual learned network. The constant μ determines the relative weight placed on fitting the training values versus the training derivatives.

- Minimizing the *cross entropy* of the network with respect to the target values. Consider learning a probabilistic function, such as predicting whether a loan applicant will pay back a loan based on attributes such as the applicant's age and bank balance. Although the training examples exhibit only boolean target values (either a 1 or 0, depending on whether this applicant paid back the loan), the underlying target function might be best modeled by outputting the *probability* that the given applicant will repay the loan, rather than attempting to output the actual 1 and 0 value for each input instance. Given such situations in which we wish for the network to output probability estimates, it can be shown that the best (i.e., maximum likelihood) probability estimates are given by the network that minimizes the cross entropy, defined as

$$-\sum_{d \in D} t_d \log o_d + (1 - t_d) \log(1 - o_d)$$

  Here o_d is the probability estimate output by the network for training example d, and t_d is the 1 or 0 target value for training example d. Chapter 6 discusses when and why the most probable network hypothesis is the one that minimizes this cross entropy and derives the corresponding gradient descent weight-tuning rule for sigmoid units. That chapter also describes other conditions under which the most probable hypothesis is the one that minimizes the sum of squared errors.

- Altering the effective error function can also be accomplished by weight sharing, or "tying together" weights associated with different units or inputs. The idea here is that different network weights are forced to take on identical values, usually to enforce some constraint known in advance to the human designer. For example, Waibel et al. (1989) and Lang et al. (1990) describe an application of neural networks to speech recognition, in which the network inputs are the speech frequency components at different times within a 144 millisecond time window. One assumption that can be made in this application is that the frequency components that identify a specific sound (e.g., "eee") should be independent of the exact time that the sound occurs within the 144 millisecond window. To enforce this constraint, the various units that receive input from different portions of the time window are forced to share weights. The net effect is to constrain the space of potential hypotheses, thereby reducing the risk of overfitting and improving the chances for accurately generalizing to unseen situations. Such weight sharing is typically implemented by first updating each of the shared weights separately within each unit that uses the weight, then replacing each instance of the shared weight by the mean of their values. The result of this procedure is that shared weights effectively adapt to a different error function than do the unshared weights.

4.8.2 Alternative Error Minimization Procedures

While gradient descent is one of the most general search methods for finding a hypothesis to minimize the error function, it is not always the most efficient. It is not uncommon for BACKPROPAGATION to require tens of thousands of iterations through the weight update loop when training complex networks. For this reason, a number of alternative weight optimization algorithms have been proposed and explored. To see some of the other possibilities, it is helpful to think of a weight-update method as involving two decisions: choosing a direction in which to alter the current weight vector and choosing a distance to move. In BACKPROPAGATION, the direction is chosen by taking the negative of the gradient, and the distance is determined by the learning rate constant η.

One optimization method, known as *line search*, involves a different approach to choosing the distance for the weight update. In particular, once a line is chosen that specifies the direction of the update, the update distance is chosen by finding the minimum of the error function along this line. Notice this can result in a very large or very small weight update, depending on the position of the point along the line that minimizes error. A second method, that builds on the idea of line search, is called the *conjugate gradient* method. Here, a sequence of line searches is performed to search for a minimum in the error surface. On the first step in this sequence, the direction chosen is the negative of the gradient. On each subsequent step, a new direction is chosen so that the component of the error gradient that has just been made zero, remains zero.

While alternative error-minimization methods sometimes lead to improved efficiency in training the network, methods such as conjugate gradient tend to have no significant impact on the generalization error of the final network. The only likely impact on the final error is that different error-minimization procedures may fall into different local minima. Bishop (1996) contains a general discussion of several parameter optimization methods for training networks.

4.8.3 Recurrent Networks

Up to this point we have considered only network topologies that correspond to acyclic directed graphs. Recurrent networks are artificial neural networks that apply to time series data and that use outputs of network units at time t as the input to other units at time $t + 1$. In this way, they support a form of directed cycles in the network. To illustrate, consider the time series prediction task of predicting the next day's stock market average $y(t + 1)$ based on the current day's economic indicators $x(t)$. Given a time series of such data, one obvious approach is to train a feedforward network to predict $y(t + 1)$ as its output, based on the input values $x(t)$. Such a network is shown in Figure 4.11(a).

One limitation of such a network is that the prediction of $y(t + 1)$ depends only on $x(t)$ and cannot capture possible dependencies of $y(t + 1)$ on earlier values of x. This might be necessary, for example, if tomorrow's stock market average $y(t + 1)$ depends on the difference between today's economic indicator values $x(t)$ and yesterday's values $x(t - 1)$. Of course we could remedy this difficulty

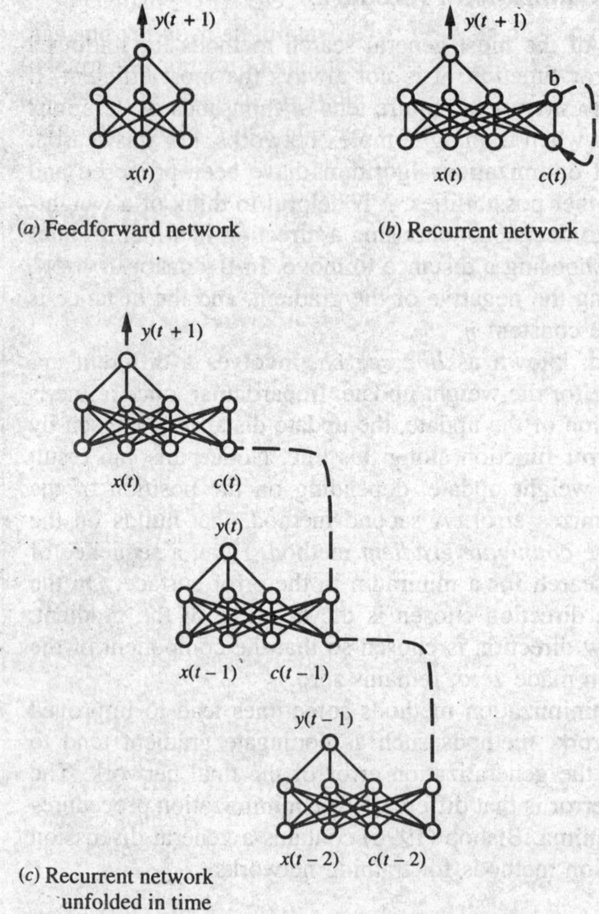

FIGURE 4.11
Recurrent networks.

by making both $x(t)$ and $x(t-1)$ inputs to the feedforward network. However, if we wish the network to consider an arbitrary window of time in the past when predicting $y(t+1)$, then a different solution is required. The recurrent network shown in Figure 4.11(*b*) provides one such solution. Here, we have added a new unit b to the hidden layer, and new input unit $c(t)$. The value of $c(t)$ is defined as the value of unit b at time $t-1$; that is, the input value $c(t)$ to the network at one time step is simply copied from the value of unit b on the previous time step. Notice this implements a recurrence relation, in which b represents information about the history of network inputs. Because b depends on both $x(t)$ and on $c(t)$, it is possible for b to summarize information from earlier values of x that are arbitrarily distant in time. Many other network topologies also can be used to represent recurrence relations. For example, we could have inserted several layers of units between the input and unit b, and we could have added several context units in parallel where we added the single units b and c.

How can such recurrent networks be trained? There are several variants of recurrent networks, and several training methods have been proposed (see, for example, Jordan 1986; Elman 1990; Mozer 1995; Williams and Zipser 1995). Interestingly, recurrent networks such as the one shown in Figure 4.11(b) can be trained using a simple variant of BACKPROPAGATION. To understand how, consider Figure 4.11(c), which shows the data flow of the recurrent network "unfolded" in time. Here we have made several copies of the recurrent network, replacing the feedback loop by connections between the various copies. Notice that this large unfolded network contains no cycles. Therefore, the weights in the unfolded network can be trained directly using BACKPROPAGATION. Of course in practice we wish to keep only one copy of the recurrent network and one set of weights. Therefore, after training the unfolded network, the final weight w_{ji} in the recurrent network can be taken to be the mean value of the corresponding w_{ji} weights in the various copies. Mozer (1995) describes this training process in greater detail. In practice, recurrent networks are more difficult to train than networks with no feedback loops and do not generalize as reliably. However, they remain important due to their increased representational power.

4.8.4 Dynamically Modifying Network Structure

Up to this point we have considered neural network learning as a problem of adjusting weights within a fixed graph structure. A variety of methods have been proposed to dynamically grow or shrink the number of network units and interconnections in an attempt to improve generalization accuracy and training efficiency.

One idea is to begin with a network containing no hidden units, then grow the network as needed by adding hidden units until the training error is reduced to some acceptable level. The CASCADE-CORRELATION algorithm (Fahlman and Lebiere 1990) is one such algorithm. CASCADE-CORRELATION begins by constructing a network with no hidden units. In the case of our face-direction learning task, for example, it would construct a network containing only the four output units completely connected to the 30×32 input nodes. After this network is trained for some time, we may well find that there remains a significant residual error due to the fact that the target function cannot be perfectly represented by a network with this single-layer structure. In this case, the algorithm adds a hidden unit, choosing its weight values to maximize the correlation between the hidden unit value and the residual error of the overall network. The new unit is now installed into the network, with its weight values held fixed, and a new connection from this new unit is added to each output unit. The process is now repeated. The original weights are retrained (holding the hidden unit weights fixed), the residual error is checked, and a second hidden unit added if the residual error is still above threshold. Whenever a new hidden unit is added, its inputs include all of the original network inputs plus the outputs of any existing hidden units. The network is grown in this fashion, accumulating hidden units until the network residual error is reduced to some acceptable level. Fahlman and Lebiere (1990) report cases in which CASCADE-CORRELATION significantly reduces training times, due to the fact that only a single layer of units is trained at each step. One practical difficulty is that because the algorithm can add units indefinitely, it is quite easy for it to overfit the training data, and precautions to avoid overfitting must be taken.

A second idea for dynamically altering network structure is to take the opposite approach. Instead of beginning with the simplest possible network and adding complexity, we begin with a complex network and prune it as we find that certain connections are inessential. One way to decide whether a particular weight is inessential is to see whether its value is close to zero. A second way, which appears to be more successful in practice, is to consider the effect that a small variation in the weight has on the error E. The effect on E of varying w (i.e., $\frac{\partial E}{\partial w}$) can be taken as a measure of the salience of the connection. LeCun et al. (1990) describe a process in which a network is trained, the least salient connections removed, and this process iterated until some termination condition is met. They refer to this as the "optimal brain damage" approach, because at each step the algorithm attempts to remove the least useful connections. They report that in a character recognition application this approach reduced the number of weights in a large network by a factor of 4, with a slight improvement in generalization accuracy and a significant improvement in subsequent training efficiency.

In general, techniques for dynamically modifying network structure have met with mixed success. It remains to be seen whether they can reliably improve on the generalization accuracy of BACKPROPAGATION. However, they have been shown in some cases to provide significant improvements in training times.

4.9 SUMMARY AND FURTHER READING

Main points of this chapter include:

- Artificial neural network learning provides a practical method for learning real-valued and vector-valued functions over continuous and discrete-valued attributes, in a way that is robust to noise in the training data. The BACKPROPAGATION algorithm is the most common network learning method and has been successfully applied to a variety of learning tasks, such as handwriting recognition and robot control.
- The hypothesis space considered by the BACKPROPAGATION algorithm is the space of all functions that can be represented by assigning weights to the given, fixed network of interconnected units. Feedforward networks containing three layers of units are able to approximate *any* function to arbitrary accuracy, given a sufficient (potentially very large) number of units in each layer. Even networks of practical size are capable of representing a rich space of highly nonlinear functions, making feedforward networks a good choice for learning discrete and continuous functions whose general form is unknown in advance.

- BACKPROPAGATION searches the space of possible hypotheses using gradient descent to iteratively reduce the error in the network fit to the training examples. Gradient descent converges to a local minimum in the training error with respect to the network weights. More generally, gradient descent is a potentially useful method for searching many continuously parameterized hypothesis spaces where the training error is a differentiable function of hypothesis parameters.
- One of the most intriguing properties of BACKPROPAGATION is its ability to invent new features that are not explicit in the input to the network. In particular, the internal (hidden) layers of multilayer networks learn to represent intermediate features that are useful for learning the target function and that are only implicit in the network inputs. This capability is illustrated, for example, by the ability of the $8 \times 3 \times 8$ network in Section 4.6.4 to invent the boolean encoding of digits from 1 to 8 and by the image features represented by the hidden layer in the face-recognition application of Section 4.7.
- Overfitting the training data is an important issue in ANN learning. Overfitting results in networks that generalize poorly to new data despite excellent performance over the training data. Cross-validation methods can be used to estimate an appropriate stopping point for gradient descent search and thus to minimize the risk of overfitting.
- Although BACKPROPAGATION is the most common ANN learning algorithm, many others have been proposed, including algorithms for more specialized tasks. For example, recurrent neural network methods train networks containing directed cycles, and algorithms such as CASCADE CORRELATION alter the network structure as well as the network weights.

Additional information on ANN learning can be found in several other chapters in this book. A Bayesian justification for choosing to minimize the sum of squared errors is given in Chapter 6, along with a justification for minimizing the cross-entropy instead of the sum of squared errors in other cases. Theoretical results characterizing the number of training examples needed to reliably learn boolean functions and the Vapnik-Chervonenkis dimension of certain types of networks can be found in Chapter 7. A discussion of overfitting and how to avoid it can be found in Chapter 5. Methods for using prior knowledge to improve the generalization accuracy of ANN learning are discussed in Chapter 12.

Work on artificial neural networks dates back to the very early days of computer science. McCulloch and Pitts (1943) proposed a model of a neuron that corresponds to the perceptron, and a good deal of work through the 1960s explored variations of this model. During the early 1960s Widrow and Hoff (1960) explored perceptron networks (which they called "adelines") and the delta rule, and Rosenblatt (1962) proved the convergence of the perceptron training rule. However, by the late 1960s it became clear that single-layer perceptron networks had limited representational capabilities, and no effective algorithms were known for training multilayer networks. Minsky and Papert (1969) showed that even simple functions such as XOR could not be represented or learned with single-layer perceptron networks, and work on ANNs receded during the 1970s.

During the mid-1980s work on ANNs experienced a resurgence, caused in large part by the invention of BACKPROPAGATION and related algorithms for training multilayer networks (Rumelhart and McClelland 1986; Parker 1985). These ideas can be traced to related earlier work (e.g., Werbos 1975). Since the 1980s, BACKPROPAGATION has become a widely used learning method, and many other ANN approaches have been actively explored. The advent of inexpensive computers during this same period has allowed experimenting with computationally intensive algorithms that could not be thoroughly explored during the 1960s.

A number of textbooks are devoted to the topic of neural network learning. An early but still useful book on parameter learning methods for pattern recognition is Duda and Hart (1973). The text by Widrow and Stearns (1985) covers perceptrons and related single-layer networks and their applications. Rumelhart and McClelland (1986) produced an edited collection of papers that helped generate the increased interest in these methods beginning in the mid-1980s. Recent books on neural network learning include Bishop (1996); Chauvin and Rumelhart (1995); Freeman and Skapina (1991); Fu (1994); Hecht-Nielsen (1990); and Hertz et al. (1991).

EXERCISES

4.1. What are the values of weights w_0, w_1, and w_2 for the perceptron whose decision surface is illustrated in Figure 4.3? Assume the surface crosses the x_1 axis at -1, and the x_2 axis at 2.

4.2. Design a two-input perceptron that implements the boolean function $A \wedge \neg B$. Design a two-layer network of perceptrons that implements $A\ XOR\ B$.

4.3. Consider two perceptrons defined by the threshold expression $w_0 + w_1x_1 + w_2x_2 > 0$. Perceptron A has weight values

$$w_0 = 1,\ w_1 = 2,\ w_2 = 1$$

and perceptron B has the weight values

$$w_0 = 0,\ w_1 = 2,\ w_2 = 1$$

True or false? Perceptron A is *more_general_than* perceptron B. (*more_general_than* is defined in Chapter 2.)

4.4. Implement the delta training rule for a two-input linear unit. Train it to fit the target concept $-2 + x_1 + 2x_2 > 0$. Plot the error E as a function of the number of training iterations. Plot the decision surface after 5, 10, 50, 100, ..., iterations.

(*a*) Try this using various constant values for η and using a decaying learning rate of η_0/i for the ith iteration. Which works better?

(*b*) Try incremental and batch learning. Which converges more quickly? Consider both number of weight updates and total execution time.

4.5. Derive a gradient descent training rule for a single unit with output o, where

$$o = w_0 + w_1x_1 + w_1x_1^2 + \ldots + w_nx_n + w_nx_n^2$$

4.6. Explain informally why the delta training rule in Equation (4.10) is only an approximation to the true gradient descent rule of Equation (4.7).

4.7. Consider a two-layer feedforward ANN with two inputs a and b, one hidden unit c, and one output unit d. This network has five weights ($w_{ca}, w_{cb}, w_{c0}, w_{dc}, w_{d0}$), where w_{x0} represents the threshold weight for unit x. Initialize these weights to the values (.1, .1, .1, .1, .1), then give their values after each of the first two training iterations of the BACKPROPAGATION algorithm. Assume learning rate $\eta = .3$, momentum $\alpha = 0.9$, incremental weight updates, and the following training examples:

a	b	d
1	0	1
0	1	0

4.8. Revise the BACKPROPAGATION algorithm in Table 4.2 so that it operates on units using the squashing function $tanh$ in place of the sigmoid function. That is, assume the output of a single unit is $o = tanh(\vec{w} \cdot \vec{x})$. Give the weight update rule for output layer weights and hidden layer weights. Hint: $tanh'(x) = 1 - tanh^2(x)$.

4.9. Recall the $8 \times 3 \times 8$ network described in Figure 4.7. Consider trying to train a $8 \times 1 \times 8$ network for the same task; that is, a network with just one hidden unit. Notice the eight training examples in Figure 4.7 could be represented by eight distinct values for the single hidden unit (e.g., 0.1, 0.2, ..., 0.8). Could a network with just one hidden unit therefore learn the identity function defined over these training examples? Hint: Consider questions such as "do there exist values for the hidden unit weights that can create the hidden unit encoding suggested above?" "do there exist values for the output unit weights that could correctly decode this encoding of the input?" and "is gradient descent likely to find such weights?"

4.10. Consider the alternative error function described in Section 4.8.1

$$E(\vec{w}) \equiv \frac{1}{2} \sum_{d \in D} \sum_{k \in outputs} (t_{kd} - o_{kd})^2 + \gamma \sum_{i,j} w_{ji}^2$$

Derive the gradient descent update rule for this definition of E. Show that it can be implemented by multiplying each weight by some constant before performing the standard gradient descent update given in Table 4.2.

4.11. Apply BACKPROPAGATION to the task of face recognition. See World Wide Web URL http://www.cs.cmu.edu/~tom/book.html for details, including face-image data, BACKPROPAGATION code, and specific tasks.

4.12. Consider deriving a gradient descent algorithm to learn target concepts corresponding to rectangles in the x, y plane. Describe each hypothesis by the x and y coordinates of the lower-left and upper-right corners of the rectangle – llx, lly, urx, and ury respectively. An instance $\langle x, y \rangle$ is labeled positive by hypothesis $\langle llx, lly, urx, ury \rangle$ if and only if the point $\langle x, y \rangle$ lies inside the corresponding rectangle. Define error E as in the chapter. Can you devise a gradient descent algorithm to learn such rectangle hypotheses? Notice that E is not a continuous function of llx, lly, urx, and ury, just as in the case of perceptron learning. (Hint: Consider the two solutions used for perceptrons: (1) changing the classification rule to make output predictions *continuous* functions of the inputs, and (2) defining an alternative error—such as distance to the rectangle center—as in using the delta rule to train perceptrons.) Does your algorithm converge to the minimum error hypothesis when the positive and negative examples are separable by a rectangle? When they are not? Do you have problems with local minima? How does your algorithm compare to symbolic methods for learning conjunctions of feature constraints?

REFERENCES

Bishop, C. M. (1996). *Neural networks for pattern recognition*. Oxford, England: Oxford University Press.

Chauvin, Y., & Rumelhart, D. (1995). BACKPROPAGATION*: Theory, architectures, and applications* (edited collection). Hillsdale, NJ: Lawrence Erlbaum Assoc.

Churchland, P. S., & Sejnowski, T. J. (1992). *The computational brain*. Cambridge, MA: The MIT Press.

Cybenko, G. (1988). Continuous valued neural networks with two hidden layers are sufficient (Technical Report). Department of Computer Science, Tufts University, Medford, MA.

Cybenko, G. (1989). Approximation by superpositions of a sigmoidal function. *Mathematics of Control, Signals, and Systems*, 2, 303–314.

Cottrell, G. W. (1990). Extracting features from faces using compression networks: Face, identity, emotion and gender recognition using holons. In D. Touretzky (Ed.), *Connection Models: Proceedings of the 1990 Summer School*. San Mateo, CA: Morgan Kaufmann.

Dietterich, T. G., Hild, H., & Bakiri, G. (1995). A comparison of ID3 and BACKPROPAGATION for English text-to-speech mapping. *Machine Learning*, 18(1), 51–80.

Duda, R., & Hart, P. (1973). *Pattern classification and scene analysis*. New York: John Wiley & Sons.

Elman, J. L. (1990). Finding structure in time. *Cognitive Science*, 14, 179–211.

Fahlman, S., & Lebiere, C. (1990). *The* CASCADE-CORRELATION *learning architecture* (Technical Report CMU-CS-90-100). Computer Science Department, Carnegie Mellon University, Pittsburgh, PA.

Freeman, J. A., & Skapura, D. M. (1991). *Neural networks*. Reading, MA: Addison Wesley.

Fu, L. (1994). *Neural networks in computer intelligence*. New York: McGraw Hill.

Gabriel, M. & Moore, J. (1990). *Learning and computational neuroscience: Foundations of adaptive networks* (edited collection). Cambridge, MA: The MIT Press.

Hecht-Nielsen, R. (1990). *Neurocomputing*. Reading, MA: Addison Wesley.

Hertz, J., Krogh, A., & Palmer, R.G. (1991). *Introduction to the theory of neural computation*. Reading, MA: Addison Wesley.

Hornick, K., Stinchcombe, M., & White, H. (1989). Multilayer feedforward networks are universal approximators. *Neural Networks*, 2, 359–366.

Huang, W. Y., & Lippmann, R. P. (1988). Neural net and traditional classifiers. In Anderson (Ed.), *Neural Information Processing Systems* (pp. 387–396).

Jordan, M. (1986). Attractor dynamics and parallelism in a connectionist sequential machine. *Proceedings of the Eighth Annual Conference of the Cognitive Science Society* (pp. 531–546).

Kohonen, T. (1984). *Self-organization and associative memory*. Berlin: Springer-Verlag.

Lang, K. J., Waibel, A. H., & Hinton, G. E. (1990). A time-delay neural network architecture for isolated word recognition. *Neural Networks*, 3, 33–43.

LeCun, Y., Boser, B., Denker, J. S., Henderson, D., Howard, R. E., Hubbard, W., & Jackel, L.D. (1989). BACKPROPAGATION applied to handwritten zip code recognition. *Neural Computation*, 1(4).

LeCun, Y., Denker, J. S., & Solla, S. A. (1990). Optimal brain damage. In D. Touretzky (Ed.), *Advances in Neural Information Processing Systems* (Vol. 2, pp. 598–605). San Mateo, CA: Morgan Kaufmann.

Manke, S., Finke, M. & Waibel, A. (1995). NPEN++: a writer independent, large vocabulary on-line cursive handwriting recognition system. *Proceedings of the International Conference on Document Analysis and Recognition*. Montreal, Canada: IEEE Computer Society.

McCulloch, W. S., & Pitts, W. (1943). A logical calculus of the ideas immanent in nervous activity. *Bulletin of Mathematical Biophysics*, 5, 115–133.

Mitchell, T. M., & Thrun, S. B. (1993). Explanation-based neural network learning for robot control. In Hanson, Cowan, & Giles (Eds.), *Advances in neural information processing systems 5* (pp. 287–294). San Francisco: Morgan Kaufmann.

Mozer, M. (1995). A focused BACKPROPAGATION algorithm for temporal pattern recognition. In Y. Chauvin & D. Rumelhart (Eds.), *Backpropagation: Theory, architectures, and applications* (pp. 137–169). Hillsdale, NJ: Lawrence Erlbaum Associates.

Minsky, M., & Papert, S. (1969). *Perceptrons*. Cambridge, MA: MIT Press.

Nilsson, N. J. (1965). *Learning machines*. New York: McGraw Hill.

Parker, D. (1985). *Learning logic* (MIT Technical Report TR-47). MIT Center for Research in Computational Economics and Management Science.

Pomerleau, D. A. (1993). Knowledge-based training of artificial neural networks for autonomous robot driving. In J. Connell & S. Mahadevan (Eds.), *Robot Learning* (pp. 19–43). Boston: Kluwer Academic Publishers.

Rosenblatt, F. (1959). The perceptron: a probabilistic model for information storage and organization in the brain. *Psychological Review*, 65, 386–408.

Rosenblatt, F. (1962). *Principles of neurodynamics*. New York: Spartan Books.

Rumelhart, D. E., & McClelland, J. L. (1986). *Parallel distributed processing: exploration in the microstructure of cognition* (Vols. 1 & 2). Cambridge, MA: MIT Press.

Rumelhart, D., Widrow, B., & Lehr, M. (1994). The basic ideas in neural networks. *Communications of the ACM*, 37(3), 87–92.

Shavlik, J. W., Mooney, R. J., & Towell, G. G. (1991). Symbolic and neural learning algorithms: An experimental comparison. *Machine Learning*, 6(2), 111–144.

Simard, P. S., Victorri, B., LeCun, Y., & Denker, J. (1992). Tangent prop—A formalism for specifying selected invariances in an adaptive network. In Moody, et al. (Eds.), *Advances in Neural Information Processing Systems 4* (pp. 895–903). San Francisco: Morgan Kaufmann.

Waibel, A., Hanazawa, T., Hinton, G., Shikano, K., & Lang, K. (1989). Phoneme recognition using time-delay neural networks. *IEEE Transactions on Acoustics, Speech and Signal Processing*.

Weiss, S., & Kapouleas, I. (1989). An empirical comparison of pattern recognition, neural nets, and machine learning classification methods. *Proceedings of the Eleventh IJCAI* (pp. 781–787). San Francisco: Morgan Kaufmann.

Werbos, P. (1975). Beyond regression: *New tools for prediction and analysis in the behavioral sciences* (Ph.D. dissertation). Harvard University.

Widrow, B., & Hoff, M. E. (1960). Adaptive switching circuits. *IRE WESCON Convention Record*, 4, 96–104.

Widrow, B., & Stearns, S. D. (1985). *Adaptive signal processing*. Signal Processing Series. Englewood Cliffs, NJ: Prentice Hall.

Williams, R., & Zipser, D. (1995). Gradient-based learning algorithms for recurrent networks and their computational complexity. In Y. Chauvin & D. Rumelhart (Eds.), *Backpropagation: Theory, architectures, and applications* (pp. 433–486). Hillsdale, NJ: Lawrence Erlbaum Associates.

Zornetzer, S. F., Davis, J. L., & Lau, C. (1994). *An introduction to neural and electronic networks* (edited collection) (2nd ed.). New York: Academic Press.

CHAPTER 5

EVALUATING HYPOTHESES

Empirically evaluating the accuracy of hypotheses is fundamental to machine learning. This chapter presents an introduction to statistical methods for estimating hypothesis accuracy, focusing on three questions. First, given the observed accuracy of a hypothesis over a limited sample of data, how well does this estimate its accuracy over additional examples? Second, given that one hypothesis outperforms another over some sample of data, how probable is it that this hypothesis is more accurate in general? Third, when data is limited what is the best way to use this data to both learn a hypothesis and estimate its accuracy? Because limited samples of data might misrepresent the general distribution of data, estimating true accuracy from such samples can be misleading. Statistical methods, together with assumptions about the underlying distributions of data, allow one to bound the difference between observed accuracy over the sample of available data and the true accuracy over the entire distribution of data.

5.1 MOTIVATION

In many cases it is important to evaluate the performance of learned hypotheses as precisely as possible. One reason is simply to understand whether to use the hypothesis. For instance, when learning from a limited-size database indicating the effectiveness of different medical treatments, it is important to understand as precisely as possible the accuracy of the learned hypotheses. A second reason is that evaluating hypotheses is an integral component of many learning methods. For example, in post-pruning decision trees to avoid overfitting, we must evaluate the impact of possible pruning steps on the accuracy of the resulting decision tree. Therefore it is important to understand the likely errors inherent in estimating the accuracy of the pruned and unpruned tree.

Estimating the accuracy of a hypothesis is relatively straightforward when data is plentiful. However, when we must learn a hypothesis and estimate its future accuracy given only a limited set of data, two key difficulties arise:

- *Bias in the estimate.* First, the observed accuracy of the learned hypothesis over the training examples is often a poor estimator of its accuracy over future examples. Because the learned hypothesis was derived from these examples, they will typically provide an optimistically biased estimate of hypothesis accuracy over future examples. This is especially likely when the learner considers a very rich hypothesis space, enabling it to overfit the training examples. To obtain an unbiased estimate of future accuracy, we typically test the hypothesis on some set of test examples chosen independently of the training examples and the hypothesis.
- *Variance in the estimate.* Second, even if the hypothesis accuracy is measured over an unbiased set of test examples independent of the training examples, the measured accuracy can still vary from the true accuracy, depending on the makeup of the particular set of test examples. The smaller the set of test examples, the greater the expected variance.

This chapter discusses methods for evaluating learned hypotheses, methods for comparing the accuracy of two hypotheses, and methods for comparing the accuracy of two learning algorithms when only limited data is available. Much of the discussion centers on basic principles from statistics and sampling theory, though the chapter assumes no special background in statistics on the part of the reader. The literature on statistical tests for hypotheses is very large. This chapter provides an introductory overview that focuses only on the issues most directly relevant to learning, evaluating, and comparing hypotheses.

5.2 ESTIMATING HYPOTHESIS ACCURACY

When evaluating a learned hypothesis we are most often interested in estimating the accuracy with which it will classify future instances. At the same time, we would like to know the probable error in this accuracy estimate (i.e., what error bars to associate with this estimate).

Throughout this chapter we consider the following setting for the learning problem. There is some space of possible instances X (e.g., the set of all people) over which various target functions may be defined (e.g., people who plan to purchase new skis this year). We assume that different instances in X may be encountered with different frequencies. A convenient way to model this is to assume there is some unknown probability distribution $\mathcal{D}$ that defines the probability of encountering each instance in X (e.g., $\mathcal{D}$ might assign a higher probability to encountering 19-year-old people than 109-year-old people). Notice $\mathcal{D}$ says nothing about whether x is a positive or negative example; it only determines the probability that x will be encountered. The learning task is to learn the target concept or target function f by considering a space H of possible hypotheses. Training examples of the target function f are provided to the learner by a trainer who draws each instance independently, according to the distribution $\mathcal{D}$, and who then forwards the instance x along with its correct target value $f(x)$ to the learner.

To illustrate, consider learning the target function "people who plan to purchase new skis this year," given a sample of training data collected by surveying people as they arrive at a ski resort. In this case the instance space X is the space of all people, who might be described by attributes such as their age, occupation, how many times they skied last year, etc. The distribution $\mathcal{D}$ specifies for each person x the probability that x will be encountered as the next person arriving at the ski resort. The target function $f : X \rightarrow \{0, 1\}$ classifies each person according to whether or not they plan to purchase skis this year.

Within this general setting we are interested in the following two questions:

1. Given a hypothesis h and a data sample containing n examples drawn at random according to the distribution $\mathcal{D}$, what is the best estimate of the accuracy of h over future instances drawn from the same distribution?
2. What is the probable error in this accuracy estimate?

5.2.1 Sample Error and True Error

To answer these questions, we need to distinguish carefully between two notions of accuracy or, equivalently, error. One is the error rate of the hypothesis over the sample of data that is available. The other is the error rate of the hypothesis over the entire unknown distribution $\mathcal{D}$ of examples. We will call these the *sample error* and the *true error* respectively.

The *sample error* of a hypothesis with respect to some sample S of instances drawn from X is the fraction of S that it misclassifies:

Definition: The **sample error** (denoted $error_S(h)$) of hypothesis h with respect to target function f and data sample S is

$$error_S(h) \equiv \frac{1}{n} \sum_{x \in S} \delta(f(x), h(x))$$

Where n is the number of examples in S, and the quantity $\delta(f(x), h(x))$ is 1 if $f(x) \neq h(x)$, and 0 otherwise.

The *true error* of a hypothesis is the probability that it will misclassify a single randomly drawn instance from the distribution $\mathcal{D}$.

Definition: The **true error** (denoted $error_{\mathcal{D}}(h)$) of hypothesis h with respect to target function f and distribution $\mathcal{D}$, is the probability that h will misclassify an instance drawn at random according to $\mathcal{D}$.

$$error_{\mathcal{D}}(h) \equiv \Pr_{x \in \mathcal{D}} [f(x) \neq h(x)]$$

Here the notation $\Pr_{x \in \mathcal{D}}$ denotes that the probability is taken over the instance distribution $\mathcal{D}$.

What we usually wish to know is the true error $error_{\mathcal{D}}(h)$ of the hypothesis, because this is the error we can expect when applying the hypothesis to future examples. All we can measure, however, is the sample error $error_S(h)$ of the hypothesis for the data sample S that we happen to have in hand. The main question considered in this section is "How good an estimate of $error_{\mathcal{D}}(h)$ is provided by $error_S(h)$?"

5.2.2 Confidence Intervals for Discrete-Valued Hypotheses

Here we give an answer to the question "How good an estimate of $error_{\mathcal{D}}(h)$ is provided by $error_S(h)$?" for the case in which h is a discrete-valued hypothesis. More specifically, suppose we wish to estimate the true error for some discrete-valued hypothesis h, based on its observed sample error over a sample S, where

- the sample S contains n examples drawn independent of one another, and independent of h, according to the probability distribution $\mathcal{D}$
- $n \geq 30$
- hypothesis h commits r errors over these n examples (i.e., $error_S(h) = r/n$).

Under these conditions, statistical theory allows us to make the following assertions:

1. Given no other information, the most probable value of $error_{\mathcal{D}}(h)$ is $error_S(h)$
2. With approximately 95% probability, the true error $error_{\mathcal{D}}(h)$ lies in the interval

$$error_S(h) \pm 1.96\sqrt{\frac{error_S(h)(1 - error_S(h))}{n}}$$

To illustrate, suppose the data sample S contains $n = 40$ examples and that hypothesis h commits $r = 12$ errors over this data. In this case, the sample error $error_S(h) = 12/40 = .30$. Given no other information, the best estimate of the true error $error_{\mathcal{D}}(h)$ is the observed sample error .30. However, we do not expect this to be a perfect estimate of the true error. If we were to collect a second sample S' containing 40 new randomly drawn examples, we might expect the sample error $error_{S'}(h)$ to vary slightly from the sample error $error_S(h)$. We expect a difference due to the random differences in the makeup of S and S'. In fact, if we repeated this experiment over and over, each time drawing a new sample S_i containing 40 new examples, we would find that for approximately 95% of these experiments, the calculated interval would contain the true error. For this reason, we call this interval the 95% confidence interval estimate for $error_{\mathcal{D}}(h)$. In the current example, where $r = 12$ and $n = 40$, the 95% confidence interval is, according to the above expression, $0.30 \pm (1.96 \cdot .07) = 0.30 \pm .14$.

Confidence level $N\%$:	50%	68%	80%	90%	95%	98%	99%
Constant z_N:	0.67	1.00	1.28	1.64	1.96	2.33	2.58

TABLE 5.1
Values of z_N for two-sided $N\%$ confidence intervals.

The above expression for the 95% confidence interval can be generalized to any desired confidence level. The constant 1.96 is used in case we desire a 95% confidence interval. A different constant, z_N, is used to calculate the $N\%$ confidence interval. The general expression for approximate $N\%$ confidence intervals for $error_{\mathcal{D}}(h)$ is

$$error_S(h) \pm z_N \sqrt{\frac{error_S(h)(1 - error_S(h))}{n}} \tag{5.1}$$

where the constant z_N is chosen depending on the desired confidence level, using the values of z_N given in Table 5.1.

Thus, just as we could calculate the 95% confidence interval for $error_{\mathcal{D}}(h)$ to be $0.30 \pm (1.96 \cdot .07)$ (when $r = 12$, $n = 40$), we can calculate the 68% confidence interval in this case to be $0.30 \pm (1.0 \cdot .07)$. Note it makes intuitive sense that the 68% confidence interval is smaller than the 95% confidence interval, because we have reduced the probability with which we demand that $error_{\mathcal{D}}(h)$ fall into the interval.

Equation (5.1) describes how to calculate the confidence intervals, or error bars, for estimates of $error_{\mathcal{D}}(h)$ that are based on $error_S(h)$. In using this expression, it is important to keep in mind that this applies only to discrete-valued hypotheses, that it assumes the sample S is drawn at random using the same distribution from which future data will be drawn, and that it assumes the data is independent of the hypothesis being tested. We should also keep in mind that the expression provides only an approximate confidence interval, though the approximation is quite good when the sample contains at least 30 examples, and $error_S(h)$ is not too close to 0 or 1. A more accurate rule of thumb is that the above approximation works well when

$$n\ error_S(h)(1 - error_S(h)) \geq 5$$

Above we summarized the procedure for calculating confidence intervals for discrete-valued hypotheses. The following section presents the underlying statistical justification for this procedure.

5.3 BASICS OF SAMPLING THEORY

This section introduces basic notions from statistics and sampling theory, including probability distributions, expected value, variance, Binomial and Normal distributions, and two-sided and one-sided intervals. A basic familiarity with these

- A *random variable* can be viewed as the name of an experiment with a probabilistic outcome. Its value is the outcome of the experiment.
- A *probability distribution* for a random variable Y specifies the probability $\Pr(Y = y_i)$ that Y will take on the value y_i, for each possible value y_i.
- The *expected value*, or *mean*, of a random variable Y is $E[Y] = \sum_i y_i \Pr(Y = y_i)$. The symbol μ_Y is commonly used to represent E[Y].
- The *variance* of a random variable is $Var(Y) = E[(Y - \mu_Y)^2]$. The variance characterizes the width or dispersion of the distribution about its mean.
- The *standard deviation* of Y is $\sqrt{Var(Y)}$. The symbol σ_Y is often used used to represent the standard deviation of Y.
- The *Binomial distribution* gives the probability of observing r heads in a series of n independent coin tosses, if the probability of heads in a single toss is p.
- The *Normal distribution* is a bell-shaped probability distribution that covers many natural phenomena.
- The *Central Limit Theorem* is a theorem stating that the sum of a large number of independent, identically distributed random variables approximately follows a Normal distribution.
- An *estimator* is a random variable Y used to estimate some parameter p of an underlying population.
- The *estimation bias* of Y as an estimator for p is the quantity $(E[Y] - p)$. An unbiased estimator is one for which the bias is zero.
- A N% *confidence interval* estimate for parameter p is an interval that includes p with probability N%.

TABLE 5.2
Basic definitions and facts from statistics.

concepts is important to understanding how to evaluate hypotheses and learning algorithms. Even more important, these same notions provide an important conceptual framework for understanding machine learning issues such as overfitting and the relationship between successful generalization and the number of training examples considered. The reader who is already familiar with these notions may skip or skim this section without loss of continuity. The key concepts introduced in this section are summarized in Table 5.2.

5.3.1 Error Estimation and Estimating Binomial Proportions

Precisely how does the deviation between sample error and true error depend on the size of the data sample? This question is an instance of a well-studied problem in statistics: the problem of estimating the proportion of a population that exhibits some property, given the observed proportion over some random sample of the population. In our case, the property of interest is that h misclassifies the example.

The key to answering this question is to note that when we measure the sample error we are performing an experiment with a random outcome. We first collect a random sample S of n independently drawn instances from the distribution $\mathcal{D}$, and then measure the sample error $error_S(h)$. As noted in the previous section, if we were to repeat this experiment many times, each time drawing a different random sample S_i of size n, we would expect to observe different values for the various $error_{S_i}(h)$, depending on random differences in the makeup of the various S_i. We say in such cases that $error_{S_i}(h)$, the outcome of the ith such experiment, is a *random variable*. In general, one can think of a random variable as the name of an experiment with a random outcome. The value of the random variable is the observed outcome of the random experiment.

Imagine that we were to run k such random experiments, measuring the random variables $error_{S_1}(h), error_{S_2}(h) \ldots error_{S_k}(h)$. Imagine further that we then plotted a histogram displaying the frequency with which we observed each possible error value. As we allowed k to grow, the histogram would approach the form of the distribution shown in Table 5.3. This table describes a particular probability distribution called the *Binomial distribution*.

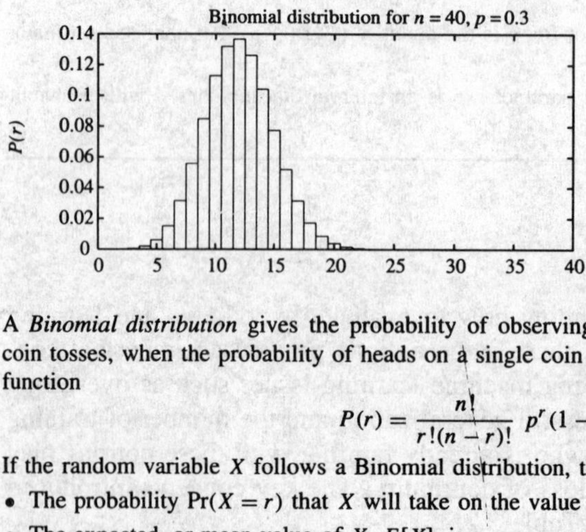

A *Binomial distribution* gives the probability of observing r heads in a sample of n independent coin tosses, when the probability of heads on a single coin toss is p. It is defined by the probability function

$$P(r) = \frac{n!}{r!(n-r)!} p^r (1-p)^{n-r}$$

If the random variable X follows a Binomial distribution, then:

- The probability $\Pr(X = r)$ that X will take on the value r is given by $P(r)$
- The expected, or mean value of X, $E[X]$, is

$$E[X] = np$$

- The variance of X, $Var(X)$, is

$$Var(X) = np(1-p)$$

- The standard deviation of X, σ_X, is

$$\sigma_X = \sqrt{np(1-p)}$$

For sufficiently large values of n the Binomial distribution is closely approximated by a Normal distribution (see Table 5.4) with the same mean and variance. Most statisticians recommend using the Normal approximation only when $np(1-p) \geq 5$.

TABLE 5.3
The Binomial distribution.

5.3.2 The Binomial Distribution

A good way to understand the Binomial distribution is to consider the following problem. You are given a worn and bent coin and asked to estimate the probability that the coin will turn up heads when tossed. Let us call this unknown probability of heads p. You toss the coin n times and record the number of times r that it turns up heads. A reasonable estimate of p is r/n. Note that if the experiment were rerun, generating a new set of n coin tosses, we might expect the number of heads r to vary somewhat from the value measured in the first experiment, yielding a somewhat different estimate for p. The Binomial distribution describes for each possible value of r (i.e., from 0 to n), the probability of observing exactly r heads given a sample of n independent tosses of a coin whose true probability of heads is p.

Interestingly, estimating p from a random sample of coin tosses is equivalent to estimating $error_{\mathcal{D}}(h)$ from testing h on a random sample of instances. A single toss of the coin corresponds to drawing a single random instance from $\mathcal{D}$ and determining whether it is misclassified by h. The probability p that a single random coin toss will turn up heads corresponds to the probability that a single instance drawn at random will be misclassified (i.e., p corresponds to $error_{\mathcal{D}}(h)$). The number r of heads observed over a sample of n coin tosses corresponds to the number of misclassifications observed over n randomly drawn instances. Thus r/n corresponds to $error_S(h)$. The problem of estimating p for coins is identical to the problem of estimating $error_{\mathcal{D}}(h)$ for hypotheses. The Binomial distribution gives the general form of the probability distribution for the random variable r, whether it represents the number of heads in n coin tosses or the number of hypothesis errors in a sample of n examples. The detailed form of the Binomial distribution depends on the specific sample size n and the specific probability p or $error_{\mathcal{D}}(h)$.

The general setting to which the Binomial distribution applies is:

1. There is a base, or underlying, experiment (e.g., toss of the coin) whose outcome can be described by a random variable, say Y. The random variable Y can take on two possible values (e.g., $Y = 1$ if heads, $Y = 0$ if tails).
2. The probability that $Y = 1$ on any single trial of the underlying experiment is given by some constant p, independent of the outcome of any other experiment. The probability that $Y = 0$ is therefore $(1 - p)$. Typically, p is not known in advance, and the problem is to estimate it.
3. A series of n independent trials of the underlying experiment is performed (e.g., n independent coin tosses), producing the sequence of independent, identically distributed random variables $Y_1, Y_2, \ldots, Y_n$. Let R denote the number of trials for which $Y_i = 1$ in this series of n experiments

$$R \equiv \sum_{i=1}^{n} Y_i$$

4. The probability that the random variable R will take on a specific value r (e.g., the probability of observing exactly r heads) is given by the Binomial distribution

$$\Pr(R = r) = \frac{n!}{r!(n-r)!} p^r (1-p)^{n-r} \tag{5.2}$$

A plot of this probability distribution is shown in Table 5.3.

The Binomial distribution characterizes the probability of observing r heads from n coin flip experiments, as well as the probability of observing r errors in a data sample containing n randomly drawn instances.

5.3.3 Mean and Variance

Two properties of a random variable that are often of interest are its expected value (also called its mean value) and its variance. The expected value is the average of the values taken on by repeatedly sampling the random variable. More precisely

Definition: Consider a random variable Y that takes on the possible values $y_1, \ldots y_n$. The **expected value** of Y, $E[Y]$, is

$$E[Y] \equiv \sum_{i=1}^{n} y_i \Pr(Y = y_i) \tag{5.3}$$

For example, if Y takes on the value 1 with probability .7 and the value 2 with probability .3, then its expected value is $(1 \cdot 0.7 + 2 \cdot 0.3 = 1.3)$. In case the random variable Y is governed by a Binomial distribution, then it can be shown that

$$E[Y] = np \tag{5.4}$$

where n and p are the parameters of the Binomial distribution defined in Equation (5.2).

A second property, the variance, captures the "width" or "spread" of the probability distribution; that is, it captures how far the random variable is expected to vary from its mean value.

Definition: The **variance** of a random variable Y, $Var[Y]$, is

$$Var[Y] \equiv E[(Y - E[Y])^2] \tag{5.5}$$

The variance describes the expected squared error in using a single observation of Y to estimate its mean $E[Y]$. The square root of the variance is called the *standard deviation* of Y, denoted σ_Y.

Definition: The **standard deviation** of a random variable Y, σ_Y, is

$$\sigma_Y \equiv \sqrt{E[(Y - E[Y])^2]} \tag{5.6}$$

In case the random variable Y is governed by a Binomial distribution, then the variance and standard deviation are given by

$$Var[Y] = np(1-p)$$

$$\sigma_Y = \sqrt{np(1-p)} \tag{5.7}$$

5.3.4 Estimators, Bias, and Variance

Now that we have shown that the random variable $error_S(h)$ obeys a Binomial distribution, we return to our primary question: What is the likely difference between $error_S(h)$ and the true error $error_{\mathcal{D}}(h)$?

Let us describe $error_S(h)$ and $error_{\mathcal{D}}(h)$ using the terms in Equation (5.2) defining the Binomial distribution. We then have

$$error_S(h) = \frac{r}{n}$$

$$error_{\mathcal{D}}(h) = p$$

where n is the number of instances in the sample S, r is the number of instances from S misclassified by h, and p is the probability of misclassifying a single instance drawn from $\mathcal{D}$.

Statisticians call $error_S(h)$ an *estimator* for the true error $error_{\mathcal{D}}(h)$. In general, an estimator is any random variable used to estimate some parameter of the underlying population from which the sample is drawn. An obvious question to ask about any estimator is whether on average it gives the right estimate. We define the *estimation bias* to be the difference between the expected value of the estimator and the true value of the parameter.

Definition: The **estimation bias** of an estimator Y for an arbitrary parameter p is

$$E[Y] - p$$

If the estimation bias is zero, we say that Y is an *unbiased estimator* for p. Notice this will be the case if the average of many random values of Y generated by repeated random experiments (i.e., $E[Y]$) converges toward p.

Is $error_S(h)$ an unbiased estimator for $error_{\mathcal{D}}(h)$? Yes, because for a Binomial distribution the expected value of r is equal to np (Equation [5.4]). It follows, given that n is a constant, that the expected value of r/n is p.

Two quick remarks are in order regarding the estimation bias. First, when we mentioned at the beginning of this chapter that testing the hypothesis on the training examples provides an optimistically biased estimate of hypothesis error, it is exactly this notion of estimation bias to which we were referring. In order for $error_S(h)$ to give an unbiased estimate of $error_{\mathcal{D}}(h)$, the hypothesis h and sample S must be chosen independently. Second, this notion of *estimation bias* should not be confused with the *inductive bias* of a learner introduced in Chapter 2. The estimation bias is a numerical quantity, whereas the inductive bias is a set of assertions.

A second important property of any estimator is its variance. Given a choice among alternative unbiased estimators, it makes sense to choose the one with least variance. By our definition of variance, this choice will yield the smallest expected squared error between the estimate and the true value of the parameter.

To illustrate these concepts, suppose we test a hypothesis and find that it commits $r = 12$ errors on a sample of $n = 40$ randomly drawn test examples. Then an unbiased estimate for $error_{\mathcal{D}}(h)$ is given by $error_S(h) = r/n = 0.3$. The variance in this estimate arises completely from the variance in r, because n is a constant. Because r is Binomially distributed, its variance is given by Equation (5.7) as $np(1-p)$. Unfortunately p is unknown, but we can substitute our estimate r/n for p. This yields an estimated variance in r of $40 \cdot 0.3(1 - 0.3) = 8.4$, or a corresponding standard deviation of $\sqrt{8.4} \approx 2.9$. This implies that the standard deviation in $error_S(h) = r/n$ is approximately $2.9/40 = .07$. To summarize, $error_S(h)$ in this case is observed to be 0.30, with a standard deviation of approximately 0.07. (See Exercise 5.1.)

In general, given r errors in a sample of n independently drawn test examples, the standard deviation for $error_S(h)$ is given by

$$\sigma_{error_S(h)} = \frac{\sigma_r}{n} = \sqrt{\frac{p(1-p)}{n}} \tag{5.8}$$

which can be approximated by substituting $r/n = error_S(h)$ for p

$$\sigma_{error_S(h)} \approx \sqrt{\frac{error_S(h)(1 - error_S(h))}{n}} \tag{5.9}$$

5.3.5 Confidence Intervals

One common way to describe the uncertainty associated with an estimate is to give an interval within which the true value is expected to fall, along with the probability with which it is expected to fall into this interval. Such estimates are called *confidence interval* estimates.

> ***Definition:*** An $N\%$ **confidence interval** for some parameter p is an interval that is expected with probability $N\%$ to contain p.

For example, if we observe $r = 12$ errors in a sample of $n = 40$ independently drawn examples, we can say with approximately 95% probability that the interval 0.30 ± 0.14 contains the true error $error_{\mathcal{D}}(h)$.

How can we derive confidence intervals for $error_{\mathcal{D}}(h)$? The answer lies in the fact that we know the Binomial probability distribution governing the estimator $error_S(h)$. The mean value of this distribution is $error_{\mathcal{D}}(h)$, and the standard deviation is given by Equation (5.9). Therefore, to derive a 95% confidence interval, we need only find the interval centered around the mean value $error_{\mathcal{D}}(h)$, which is wide enough to contain 95% of the total probability under this distribution. This provides an interval surrounding $error_{\mathcal{D}}(h)$ into which $error_S(h)$ must fall 95% of the time. Equivalently, it provides the size of the interval surrounding $error_S(h)$ into which $error_{\mathcal{D}}(h)$ must fall 95% of the time.

For a given value of N how can we find the size of the interval that contains N% of the probability mass? Unfortunately, for the Binomial distribution this calculation can be quite tedious. Fortunately, however, an easily calculated and very good approximation can be found in most cases, based on the fact that for sufficiently large sample sizes the Binomial distribution can be closely approximated by the Normal distribution. The Normal distribution, summarized in Table 5.4, is perhaps the most well-studied probability distribution in statistics. As illustrated in Table 5.4, it is a bell-shaped distribution fully specified by its

---

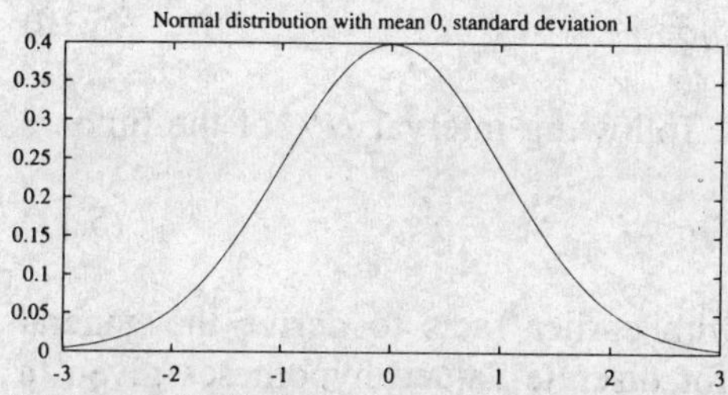

A Normal distribution (also called a gaussian distribution) is a bell-shaped distribution defined by the probability density function

$$p(x) = \frac{1}{\sqrt{2\pi\sigma^2}} e^{-\frac{1}{2}(\frac{x-\mu}{\sigma})^2}$$

A Normal distribution is fully determined by two parameters in the above formula: μ and σ.

If the random variable X follows a normal distribution, then:

- The probability that X will fall into the interval (a, b) is given by

$$\int_a^b p(x)dx$$

- The expected, or mean value of X, $E[X]$, is

$$E[X] = \mu$$

- The variance of X, $Var(X)$, is

$$Var(X) = \sigma^2$$

- The standard deviation of X, σ_X, is

$$\sigma_X = \sigma$$

The Central Limit Theorem (Section 5.4.1) states that the sum of a large number of independent, identically distributed random variables follows a distribution that is approximately Normal.

TABLE 5.4
The Normal or gaussian distribution.

mean μ and standard deviation σ. For large n, any Binomial distribution is very closely approximated by a Normal distribution with the same mean and variance.

One reason that we prefer to work with the Normal distribution is that most statistics references give tables specifying the size of the interval about the mean that contains $N\%$ of the probability mass under the Normal distribution. This is precisely the information needed to calculate our $N\%$ confidence interval. In fact, Table 5.1 is such a table. The constant z_N given in Table 5.1 defines the width of the smallest interval about the mean that includes $N\%$ of the total probability mass under the bell-shaped Normal distribution. More precisely, z_N gives half the width of the interval (i.e., the distance from the mean in either direction) measured in standard deviations. Figure 5.1(*a*) illustrates such an interval for $z_{.80}$.

To summarize, if a random variable Y obeys a Normal distribution with mean μ and standard deviation σ, then the measured random value y of Y will fall into the following interval $N\%$ of the time

$$\mu \pm z_N \sigma \tag{5.10}$$

Equivalently, the mean μ will fall into the following interval $N\%$ of the time

$$y \pm z_N \sigma \tag{5.11}$$

We can easily combine this fact with earlier facts to derive the general expression for $N\%$ confidence intervals for discrete-valued hypotheses given in Equation (5.1). First, we know that $error_S(h)$ follows a Binomial distribution with mean value $error_{\mathcal{D}}(h)$ and standard deviation as given in Equation (5.9). Second, we know that for sufficiently large sample size n, this Binomial distribution is well approximated by a Normal distribution. Third, Equation (5.11) tells us how to find the $N\%$ confidence interval for estimating the mean value of a Normal distribution. Therefore, substituting the mean and standard deviation of $error_S(h)$ into Equation (5.11) yields the expression from Equation (5.1) for $N\%$ confidence

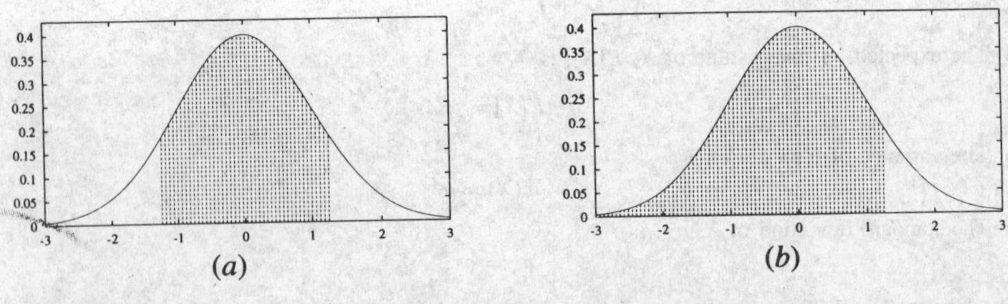

FIGURE 5.1
A Normal distribution with mean 0, standard deviation 1. (*a*) With 80% confidence, the value of the random variable will lie in the two-sided interval $[-1.28, 1.28]$. Note $z_{.80} = 1.28$. With 10% confidence it will lie to the right of this interval, and with 10% confidence it will lie to the left. (*b*) With 90% confidence, it will lie in the one-sided interval $[-\infty, 1.28]$.

intervals for discrete-valued hypotheses

$$error_S(h) \pm z_N \sqrt{\frac{error_S(h)(1 - error_S(h))}{n}}$$

Recall that two approximations were involved in deriving this expression, namely:

1. in estimating the standard deviation σ of $error_S(h)$, we have approximated $error_{\mathcal{D}}(h)$ by $error_S(h)$ [i.e., in going from Equation (5.8) to (5.9)], and
2. the Binomial distribution has been approximated by the Normal distribution.

The common rule of thumb in statistics is that these two approximations are very good as long as $n \geq 30$, or when $np(1-p) \geq 5$. For smaller values of n it is wise to use a table giving exact values for the Binomial distribution.

5.3.6 Two-Sided and One-Sided Bounds

Notice that the above confidence interval is a *two-sided* bound; that is, it bounds the estimated quantity from above and from below. In some cases, we will be interested only in a *one-sided* bound. For example, we might be interested in the question "What is the probability that $error_{\mathcal{D}}(h)$ is at most U?" This kind of one-sided question is natural when we are only interested in bounding the maximum error of h and do not mind if the true error is much smaller than estimated.

There is an easy modification to the above procedure for finding such one-sided error bounds. It follows from the fact that the Normal distribution is symmetric about its mean. Because of this fact, any two-sided confidence interval based on a Normal distribution can be converted to a corresponding one-sided interval with twice the confidence (see Figure 5.1(b)). That is, a $100(1-\alpha)\%$ confidence interval with lower bound L and upper bound U implies a $100(1-\alpha/2)\%$ confidence interval with lower bound L and no upper bound. It also implies a $100(1-\alpha/2)\%$ confidence interval with upper bound U and no lower bound. Here α corresponds to the probability that the correct value lies outside the stated interval. In other words, α is the probability that the value will fall into the *unshaded* region in Figure 5.1(a), and $\alpha/2$ is the probability that it will fall into the unshaded region in Figure 5.1(b).

To illustrate, consider again the example in which h commits $r = 12$ errors over a sample of $n = 40$ independently drawn examples. As discussed above, this leads to a (two-sided) 95% confidence interval of 0.30 ± 0.14. In this case, $100(1-\alpha) = 95\%$, so $\alpha = 0.05$. Thus, we can apply the above rule to say with $100(1-\alpha/2) = 97.5\%$ confidence that $error_{\mathcal{D}}(h)$ is at most $0.30 + 0.14 = 0.44$, making no assertion about the lower bound on $error_{\mathcal{D}}(h)$. Thus, we have a one-sided error bound on $error_{\mathcal{D}}(h)$ with double the confidence that we had in the corresponding two-sided bound (see Exercise 5.3).

5.4 A GENERAL APPROACH FOR DERIVING CONFIDENCE INTERVALS

The previous section described in detail how to derive confidence interval estimates for one particular case: estimating $error_{\mathcal{D}}(h)$ for a discrete-valued hypothesis h, based on a sample of n independently drawn instances. The approach described there illustrates a general approach followed in many estimation problems. In particular, we can see this as a problem of estimating the mean (expected value) of a population based on the mean of a randomly drawn sample of size n. The general process includes the following steps:

1. Identify the underlying population parameter p to be estimated, for example, $error_{\mathcal{D}}(h)$.
2. Define the estimator Y (e.g., $error_S(h)$). It is desirable to choose a minimum-variance, unbiased estimator.
3. Determine the probability distribution $\mathcal{D}_Y$ that governs the estimator Y, including its mean and variance.
4. Determine the $N\%$ confidence interval by finding thresholds L and U such that $N\%$ of the mass in the probability distribution $\mathcal{D}_Y$ falls between L and U.

In later sections of this chapter we apply this general approach to several other estimation problems common in machine learning. First, however, let us discuss a fundamental result from estimation theory called the *Central Limit Theorem*.

5.4.1 Central Limit Theorem

One essential fact that simplifies attempts to derive confidence intervals is the Central Limit Theorem. Consider again our general setting, in which we observe the values of n independently drawn random variables $Y_1 \ldots Y_n$ that obey the same unknown underlying probability distribution (e.g., n tosses of the same coin). Let μ denote the mean of the unknown distribution governing each of the Y_i and let σ denote the standard deviation. We say that these variables Y_i are *independent, identically distributed* random variables, because they describe independent experiments, each obeying the same underlying probability distribution. In an attempt to estimate the mean μ of the distribution governing the Y_i, we calculate the sample mean $\bar{Y}_n \equiv \frac{1}{n}\sum_{i=1}^{n} Y_i$ (e.g., the fraction of heads among the n coin tosses). The Central Limit Theorem states that the probability distribution governing $\bar{Y}_n$ approaches a Normal distribution as $n \rightarrow \infty$, *regardless of the distribution that governs the underlying random variables* Y_i. Furthermore, the mean of the distribution governing $\bar{Y}_n$ approaches μ and the standard deviation approaches $\frac{\sigma}{\sqrt{n}}$. More precisely,

Theorem 5.1. Central Limit Theorem. Consider a set of independent, identically distributed random variables $Y_1 \ldots Y_n$ governed by an arbitrary probability distribution with mean μ and finite variance σ^2. Define the sample mean, $\bar{Y}_n \equiv \frac{1}{n}\sum_{i=1}^{n} Y_i$.

Then as $n \to \infty$, the distribution governing

$$\frac{\bar{Y}_n - \mu}{\frac{\sigma}{\sqrt{n}}}$$

approaches a Normal distribution, with zero mean and standard deviation equal to 1.

This is a quite surprising fact, because it states that we know the form of the distribution that governs the sample mean $\bar{Y}$ even when we do not know the form of the underlying distribution that governs the individual Y_i that are being observed! Furthermore, the Central Limit Theorem describes how the mean and variance of $\bar{Y}$ can be used to determine the mean and variance of the individual Y_i.

The Central Limit Theorem is a very useful fact, because it implies that whenever we define an estimator that is the mean of some sample (e.g., $error_S(h)$ is the mean error), the distribution governing this estimator can be approximated by a Normal distribution for sufficiently large n. If we also know the variance for this (approximately) Normal distribution, then we can use Equation (5.11) to compute confidence intervals. A common rule of thumb is that we can use the Normal approximation when $n \geq 30$. Recall that in the preceding section we used such a Normal distribution to approximate the Binomial distribution that more precisely describes $error_S(h)$.

5.5 DIFFERENCE IN ERROR OF TWO HYPOTHESES

Consider the case where we have two hypotheses h_1 and h_2 for some discrete-valued target function. Hypothesis h_1 has been tested on a sample S_1 containing n_1 randomly drawn examples, and h_2 has been tested on an independent sample S_2 containing n_2 examples drawn from the same distribution. Suppose we wish to estimate the difference d between the true errors of these two hypotheses.

$$d \equiv error_{\mathcal{D}}(h_1) - error_{\mathcal{D}}(h_2)$$

We will use the generic four-step procedure described at the beginning of Section 5.4 to derive a confidence interval estimate for d. Having identified d as the parameter to be estimated, we next define an estimator. The obvious choice for an estimator in this case is the difference between the sample errors, which we denote by $\hat{d}$

$$\hat{d} \equiv error_{S_1}(h_1) - error_{S_2}(h_2)$$

Although we will not prove it here, it can be shown that $\hat{d}$ gives an unbiased estimate of d; that is $E[\hat{d}\ ] = d$.

What is the probability distribution governing the random variable $\hat{d}$? From earlier sections, we know that for large n_1 and n_2 (e.g., both ≥ 30), both $error_{S_1}(h_1)$ and $error_{S_2}(h_2)$ follow distributions that are approximately Normal. Because the difference of two Normal distributions is also a Normal distribution, $\hat{d}$ will also follow a distribution that is approximately Normal, with mean d. It can also be shown that the variance of this distribution is the sum of the variances of $error_{S_1}(h_1)$ and $error_{S_2}(h_2)$. Using Equation (5.9) to obtain the approximate variance of each of these distributions, we have

$$\sigma_{\hat{d}}^2 \approx \frac{error_{S_1}(h_1)(1 - error_{S_1}(h_1))}{n_1} + \frac{error_{S_2}(h_2)(1 - error_{S_2}(h_2))}{n_2} \tag{5.12}$$

Now that we have determined the probability distribution that governs the estimator $\hat{d}$, it is straightforward to derive confidence intervals that characterize the likely error in employing $\hat{d}$ to estimate d. For a random variable $\hat{d}$ obeying a Normal distribution with mean d and variance σ^2, the N% confidence interval estimate for d is $\hat{d} \pm z_N \sigma$. Using the approximate variance $\sigma_{\hat{d}}^2$ given above, this approximate $N\%$ confidence interval estimate for d is

$$\hat{d} \pm z_N \sqrt{\frac{error_{S_1}(h_1)(1 - error_{S_1}(h_1))}{n_1} + \frac{error_{S_2}(h_2)(1 - error_{S_2}(h_2))}{n_2}} \tag{5.13}$$

where z_N is the same constant described in Table 5.1. The above expression gives the general two-sided confidence interval for estimating the difference between errors of two hypotheses. In some situations we might be interested in one-sided bounds—either bounding the largest possible difference in errors or the smallest, with some confidence level. One-sided confidence intervals can be obtained by modifying the above expression as described in Section 5.3.6.

Although the above analysis considers the case in which h_1 and h_2 are tested on independent data samples, it is often acceptable to use the confidence interval seen in Equation (5.13) in the setting where h_1 and h_2 are tested on a single sample S (where S is still independent of h_1 and h_2). In this later case, we redefine $\hat{d}$ as

$$\hat{d} \equiv error_S(h_1) - error_S(h_2)$$

The variance in this new $\hat{d}$ will usually be smaller than the variance given by Equation (5.12), when we set S_1 and S_2 to S. This is because using a single sample S eliminates the variance due to random differences in the compositions of S_1 and S_2. In this case, the confidence interval given by Equation (5.13) will generally be an overly conservative, but still correct, interval.

5.5.1 Hypothesis Testing

In some cases we are interested in the probability that some specific conjecture is true, rather than in confidence intervals for some parameter. Suppose, for example, that we are interested in the question "what is the probability that $error_{\mathcal{D}}(h_1) > error_{\mathcal{D}}(h_2)$?" Following the setting in the previous section, suppose we measure the sample errors for h_1 and h_2 using two independent samples S_1 and S_2 of size 100 and find that $error_{S_1}(h_1) = .30$ and $error_{S_2}(h_2) = .20$, hence the observed difference is $\hat{d} = .10$. Of course, due to random variation in the data sample, we might observe this difference in the sample errors even when $error_{\mathcal{D}}(h_1) \leq error_{\mathcal{D}}(h_2)$. What is the probability that $error_{\mathcal{D}}(h_1) > error_{\mathcal{D}}(h_2)$, given the observed difference in sample errors $\hat{d} = .10$ in this case? Equivalently, what is the probability that $d > 0$, given that we observed $\hat{d} = .10$?

Note the probability $\Pr(d > 0)$ is equal to the probability that $\hat{d}$ has not overestimated d by more than .10. Put another way, this is the probability that $\hat{d}$ falls into the one-sided interval $\hat{d} < d + .10$. Since d is the mean of the distribution governing $\hat{d}$, we can equivalently express this one-sided interval as $\hat{d} < \mu_{\hat{d}} + .10$.

To summarize, the probability $\Pr(d > 0)$ equals the probability that $\hat{d}$ falls into the one-sided interval $\hat{d} < \mu_{\hat{d}} + .10$. Since we already calculated the approximate distribution governing $\hat{d}$ in the previous section, we can determine the probability that $\hat{d}$ falls into this one-sided interval by calculating the probability mass of the $\hat{d}$ distribution within this interval.

Let us begin this calculation by re-expressing the interval $\hat{d} < \mu_{\hat{d}} + .10$ in terms of the number of standard deviations it allows deviating from the mean. Using Equation (5.12) we find that $\sigma_{\hat{d}} \approx .061$, so we can re-express the interval as approximately

$$\hat{d} < \mu_{\hat{d}} + 1.64\sigma_{\hat{d}}$$

What is the confidence level associated with this one-sided interval for a Normal distribution? Consulting Table 5.1, we find that 1.64 standard deviations about the mean corresponds to a two-sided interval with confidence level 90%. Therefore, the one-sided interval will have an associated confidence level of 95%.

Therefore, given the observed $\hat{d} = .10$, the probability that $error_{\mathcal{D}}(h_1) > error_{\mathcal{D}}(h_2)$ is approximately .95. In the terminology of the statistics literature, we say that we accept the hypothesis that "$error_{\mathcal{D}}(h_1) > error_{\mathcal{D}}(h_2)$" with confidence 0.95. Alternatively, we may state that we reject the opposite hypothesis (often called the null hypothesis) at a $(1 - 0.95) = .05$ level of significance.

5.6 COMPARING LEARNING ALGORITHMS

Often we are interested in comparing the performance of two learning algorithms L_A and L_B, rather than two specific hypotheses. What is an appropriate test for comparing learning algorithms, and how can we determine whether an observed difference between the algorithms is statistically significant? Although there is active debate within the machine-learning research community regarding the best method for comparison, we present here one reasonable approach. A discussion of alternative methods is given by Dietterich (1996).

As usual, we begin by specifying the parameter we wish to estimate. Suppose we wish to determine which of L_A and L_B is the better learning method on average for learning some particular target function f. A reasonable way to define "on average" is to consider the relative performance of these two algorithms averaged over all the training sets of size n that might be drawn from the underlying instance distribution $\mathcal{D}$. In other words, we wish to estimate the expected value of the difference in their errors

$$\underset{S \subset \mathcal{D}}{E} [error_{\mathcal{D}}(L_A(S)) - error_{\mathcal{D}}(L_B(S))] \tag{5.14}$$

where $L(S)$ denotes the hypothesis output by learning method L when given the sample S of training data and where the subscript $S \subset \mathcal{D}$ indicates that the expected value is taken over samples S drawn according to the underlying instance distribution $\mathcal{D}$. The above expression describes the expected value of the difference in errors between learning methods L_A and L_B.

Of course in practice we have only a limited sample D_0 of data when comparing learning methods. In such cases, one obvious approach to estimating the above quantity is to divide D_0 into a training set S_0 and a disjoint test set T_0. The training data can be used to train both L_A and L_B, and the test data can be used to compare the accuracy of the two learned hypotheses. In other words, we measure the quantity

$$error_{T_0}(L_A(S_0)) - error_{T_0}(L_B(S_0)) \tag{5.15}$$

Notice two key differences between this estimator and the quantity in Equation (5.14). First, we are using $error_{T_0}(h)$ to approximate $error_{\mathcal{D}}(h)$. Second, we are only measuring the difference in errors for one training set S_0 rather than taking the expected value of this difference over all samples S that might be drawn from the distribution $\mathcal{D}$.

One way to improve on the estimator given by Equation (5.15) is to repeatedly partition the data D_0 into disjoint training and test sets and to take the mean of the test set errors for these different experiments. This leads to the procedure shown in Table 5.5 for estimating the difference between errors of two learning methods, based on a fixed sample D_0 of available data. This procedure first partitions the data into k disjoint subsets of equal size, where this size is at least 30. It then trains and tests the learning algorithms k times, using each of the k subsets in turn as the test set, and using all remaining data as the training set. In this way, the learning algorithms are tested on k independent test sets, and the mean difference in errors $\bar{\delta}$ is returned as an estimate of the difference between the two learning algorithms.

The quantity $\bar{\delta}$ returned by the procedure of Table 5.5 can be taken as an estimate of the desired quantity from Equation 5.14. More appropriately, we can view $\bar{\delta}$ as an estimate of the quantity

$$\underset{S \subset D_0}{E} [error_{\mathcal{D}}(L_A(S)) - error_{\mathcal{D}}(L_B(S))] \tag{5.16}$$

where S represents a random sample of size $\frac{k-1}{k}|D_0|$ drawn uniformly from D_0. The only difference between this expression and our original expression in Equation (5.14) is that this new expression takes the expected value over subsets of the available data D_0, rather than over subsets drawn from the full instance distribution $\mathcal{D}$.

1. Partition the available data D_0 into k disjoint subsets $T_1, T_2, \ldots, T_k$ of equal size, where this size is at least 30.
2. For i from 1 to k, do
   use T_i for the test set, and the remaining data for training set S_i
   - $S_i \leftarrow \{D_0 - T_i\}$
   - $h_A \leftarrow L_A(S_i)$
   - $h_B \leftarrow L_B(S_i)$
   - $\delta_i \leftarrow error_{T_i}(h_A) - error_{T_i}(h_B)$
3. Return the value $\bar{\delta}$, where

$$\bar{\delta} \equiv \frac{1}{k} \sum_{i=1}^{k} \delta_i \tag{T5.1}$$

TABLE 5.5
A procedure to estimate the difference in error between two learning methods L_A and L_B. Approximate confidence intervals for this estimate are given in the text.

The approximate $N\%$ confidence interval for estimating the quantity in Equation (5.16) using $\bar{\delta}$ is given by

$$\bar{\delta} \pm t_{N,k-1}\ s_{\bar{\delta}} \tag{5.17}$$

where $t_{N,k-1}$ is a constant that plays a role analogous to that of z_N in our earlier confidence interval expressions, and where $s_{\bar{\delta}}$ is an estimate of the standard deviation of the distribution governing $\bar{\delta}$. In particular, $s_{\bar{\delta}}$ is defined as

$$s_{\bar{\delta}} \equiv \sqrt{\frac{1}{k(k-1)} \sum_{i=1}^{k} (\delta_i - \bar{\delta})^2} \tag{5.18}$$

Notice the constant $t_{N,k-1}$ in Equation (5.17) has two subscripts. The first specifies the desired confidence level, as it did for our earlier constant z_N. The second parameter, called the number of *degrees of freedom* and usually denoted by ν, is related to the number of independent random events that go into producing the value for the random variable $\bar{\delta}$. In the current setting, the number of degrees of freedom is $k - 1$. Selected values for the parameter t are given in Table 5.6. Notice that as $k \rightarrow \infty$, the value of $t_{N,k-1}$ approaches the constant z_N.

Note the procedure described here for comparing two learning methods involves testing the two learned hypotheses on identical test sets. This contrasts with the method described in Section 5.5 for comparing hypotheses that have been evaluated using two independent test sets. Tests where the hypotheses are evaluated over identical samples are called *paired tests*. Paired tests typically produce tighter confidence intervals because any differences in observed errors in a paired test are due to differences between the hypotheses. In contrast, when the hypotheses are tested on separate data samples, differences in the two sample errors might be partially attributable to differences in the makeup of the two samples.

	Confidence level N			
	90%	95%	98%	99%
$\nu = 2$	2.92	4.30	6.96	9.92
$\nu = 5$	2.02	2.57	3.36	4.03
$\nu = 10$	1.81	2.23	2.76	3.17
$\nu = 20$	1.72	2.09	2.53	2.84
$\nu = 30$	1.70	2.04	2.46	2.75
$\nu = 120$	1.66	1.98	2.36	2.62
$\nu = \infty$	1.64	1.96	2.33	2.58

TABLE 5.6
Values of $t_{N,\nu}$ for two-sided confidence intervals. As $\nu \rightarrow \infty$, $t_{N,\nu}$ approaches z_N.

5.6.1 Paired *t* Tests

Above we described one procedure for comparing two learning methods given a fixed set of data. This section discusses the statistical justification for this procedure, and for the confidence interval defined by Equations (5.17) and (5.18). It can be skipped or skimmed on a first reading without loss of continuity.

The best way to understand the justification for the confidence interval estimate given by Equation (5.17) is to consider the following estimation problem:

- We are given the observed values of a set of independent, identically distributed random variables $Y_1, Y_2, \ldots, Y_k$.
- We wish to estimate the mean μ of the probability distribution governing these Y_i.
- The estimator we will use is the sample mean $\bar{Y}$

$$\bar{Y} \equiv \frac{1}{k}\sum_{i=1}^{k} Y_i$$

This problem of estimating the distribution mean μ based on the sample mean $\bar{Y}$ is quite general. For example, it covers the problem discussed earlier of using $error_S(h)$ to estimate $error_{\mathcal{D}}(h)$. (In that problem, the Y_i are 1 or 0 to indicate whether h commits an error on an individual example from S, and $error_{\mathcal{D}}(h)$ is the mean μ of the underlying distribution.) The t test, described by Equations (5.17) and (5.18), applies to a special case of this problem—the case in which the individual Y_i follow a Normal distribution.

Now consider the following idealization of the method in Table 5.5 for comparing learning methods. Assume that instead of having a fixed sample of data D_0, we can request new training examples drawn according to the underlying instance distribution. In particular, in this idealized method we modify the procedure of Table 5.5 so that on each iteration through the loop it generates a new random training set S_i and new random test set T_i by drawing from this underlying instance distribution instead of drawing from the fixed sample D_0. This idealized method perfectly fits the form of the above estimation problem. In particular, the δ_i measured by the procedure now correspond to the independent, identically distributed random variables Y_i. The mean μ of their distribution corresponds to the expected difference in error between the two learning methods [i.e., Equation (5.14)]. The sample mean $\bar{Y}$ is the quantity $\bar{\delta}$ computed by this idealized version of the method. We wish to answer the question "how good an estimate of μ is provided by $\bar{\delta}$?"

First, note that the size of the test sets T_i has been chosen to contain at least 30 examples. Because of this, the individual δ_i will each follow an approximately Normal distribution (due to the Central Limit Theorem). Hence, we have a special case in which the Y_i are governed by an approximately Normal distribution. It can be shown in general that when the individual Y_i each follow a Normal distribution, then the sample mean $\bar{Y}$ follows a Normal distribution as well. Given that $\bar{Y}$ is Normally distributed, we might consider using the earlier expression for confidence intervals (Equation [5.11]) that applies to estimators governed by Normal distributions. Unfortunately, that equation requires that we know the standard deviation of this distribution, which we do not.

The t test applies to precisely these situations, in which the task is to estimate the sample mean of a collection of independent, identically and Normally distributed random variables. In this case, we can use the confidence interval given by Equations (5.17) and (5.18), which can be restated using our current notation as

$$\mu = \bar{Y} \pm t_{N,k-1}\, s_{\bar{Y}}$$

where $s_{\bar{Y}}$ is the estimated standard deviation of the sample mean

$$s_{\bar{Y}} \equiv \sqrt{\frac{1}{k(k-1)}\sum_{i=1}^{k}(Y_i - \bar{Y})^2}$$

and where $t_{N,k-1}$ is a constant analogous to our earlier z_N. In fact, the constant $t_{N,k-1}$ characterizes the area under a probability distribution known as the t distribution, just as the constant z_N characterizes the area under a Normal distribution. The t distribution is a bell-shaped distribution similar to the Normal distribution, but wider and shorter to reflect the greater variance introduced by using $s_{\bar{Y}}$ to approximate the true standard deviation $\sigma_{\bar{Y}}$. The t distribution approaches the Normal distribution (and therefore $t_{N,k-1}$ approaches z_N) as k approaches infinity. This is intuitively satisfying because we expect $s_{\bar{Y}}$ to converge toward the true standard deviation $\sigma_{\bar{Y}}$ as the sample size k grows, and because we can use z_N when the standard deviation is known exactly.

5.6.2 Practical Considerations

Note the above discussion justifies the use of the confidence interval estimate given by Equation (5.17) in the case where we wish to use the sample mean $\bar{Y}$ to estimate the mean of a sample containing k independent, identically and Normally distributed random variables. This fits the idealized method described above, in which we assume unlimited access to examples of the target function. In practice, given a limited set of data D_0 and the more practical method described by Table 5.5, this justification does not strictly apply. In practice, the problem is that the only way to generate new δ_i is to resample D_0, dividing it into training and test sets in different ways. The δ_i are not independent of one another in this case, because they are based on overlapping sets of training examples drawn from the limited subset D_0 of data, rather than from the full distribution $\mathcal{D}$.

When only a limited sample of data D_0 is available, several methods can be used to resample D_0. Table 5.5 describes a k-fold method in which D_0 is partitioned into k disjoint, equal-sized subsets. In this k-fold approach, each example from D_0 is used exactly once in a test set, and $k - 1$ times in a training set. A second popular approach is to randomly choose a test set of at least 30 examples from D_0, use the remaining examples for training, then repeat this process as many times as desired. This randomized method has the advantage that it can be repeated an indefinite number of times, to shrink the confidence interval to the desired width. In contrast, the k-fold method is limited by the total number of examples, by the use of each example only once in a test set, and by our desire to use samples of size at least 30. However, the randomized method has the disadvantage that the test sets no longer qualify as being independently drawn with respect to the underlying instance distribution $\mathcal{D}$. In contrast, the test sets generated by k-fold cross validation are independent because each instance is included in only one test set.

To summarize, no single procedure for comparing learning methods based on limited data satisfies all the constraints we would like. It is wise to keep in mind that statistical models rarely fit perfectly the practical constraints in testing learning algorithms when available data is limited. Nevertheless, they do provide approximate confidence intervals that can be of great help in interpreting experimental comparisons of learning methods.

5.7 SUMMARY AND FURTHER READING

The main points of this chapter include:

- Statistical theory provides a basis for estimating the true error ($error_{\mathcal{D}}(h)$) of a hypothesis h, based on its observed error ($error_S(h)$) over a sample S of data. For example, if h is a discrete-valued hypothesis and the data sample S contains $n \geq 30$ examples drawn independently of h and of one another, then the $N\%$ confidence interval for $error_{\mathcal{D}}(h)$ is approximately

$$error_S(h) \pm z_N \sqrt{\frac{error_S(h)(1 - error_S(h))}{n}}$$

  where values for z_N are given in Table 5.1.
- In general, the problem of estimating confidence intervals is approached by identifying the parameter to be estimated (e.g., $error_{\mathcal{D}}(h)$) and an estimator

(e.g., $error_S(h)$) for this quantity. Because the estimator is a random variable (e.g., $error_S(h)$ depends on the random sample S), it can be characterized by the probability distribution that governs its value. Confidence intervals can then be calculated by determining the interval that contains the desired probability mass under this distribution.

- One possible cause of errors in estimating hypothesis accuracy is *estimation bias*. If Y is an estimator for some parameter p, the estimation bias of Y is the difference between p and the expected value of Y. For example, if S is the training data used to formulate hypothesis h, then $error_S(h)$ gives an optimistically biased estimate of the true error $error_{\mathcal{D}}(h)$.
- A second cause of estimation error is *variance* in the estimate. Even with an unbiased estimator, the observed value of the estimator is likely to vary from one experiment to another. The variance σ^2 of the distribution governing the estimator characterizes how widely this estimate is likely to vary from the correct value. This variance decreases as the size of the data sample is increased.
- Comparing the relative effectiveness of two learning algorithms is an estimation problem that is relatively easy when data and time are unlimited, but more difficult when these resources are limited. One possible approach described in this chapter is to run the learning algorithms on different subsets of the available data, testing the learned hypotheses on the remaining data, then averaging the results of these experiments.
- In most cases considered here, deriving confidence intervals involves making a number of assumptions and approximations. For example, the above confidence interval for $error_{\mathcal{D}}(h)$ involved approximating a Binomial distribution by a Normal distribution, approximating the variance of this distribution, and assuming instances are generated by a fixed, unchanging probability distribution. While intervals based on such approximations are only approximate confidence intervals, they nevertheless provide useful guidance for designing and interpreting experimental results in machine learning.

The key statistical definitions presented in this chapter are summarized in Table 5.2.

An ocean of literature exists on the topic of statistical methods for estimating means and testing significance of hypotheses. While this chapter introduces the basic concepts, more detailed treatments of these issues can be found in many books and articles. Billingsley et al. (1986) provide a very readable introduction to statistics that elaborates on the issues discussed here. Other texts on statistics include DeGroot (1986); Casella and Berger (1990). Duda and Hart (1973) provide a treatment of these issues in the context of numerical pattern recognition.

Segre et al. (1991, 1996), Etzioni and Etzioni (1994), and Gordon and Segre (1996) discuss statistical significance tests for evaluating learning algorithms whose performance is measured by their ability to improve computational efficiency.

Geman et al. (1992) discuss the tradeoff involved in attempting to minimize bias and variance simultaneously. There is ongoing debate regarding the best way to learn and compare hypotheses from limited data. For example, Dietterich (1996) discusses the risks of applying the paired-difference t test repeatedly to different train-test splits of the data.

EXERCISES

5.1. Suppose you test a hypothesis h and find that it commits $r = 300$ errors on a sample S of $n = 1000$ randomly drawn test examples. What is the standard deviation in $error_S(h)$? How does this compare to the standard deviation in the example at the end of Section 5.3.4?

5.2. Consider a learned hypothesis, h, for some boolean concept. When h is tested on a set of 100 examples, it classifies 83 correctly. What is the standard deviation and the 95% confidence interval for the true error rate for $Error_{\mathcal{D}}(h)$?

5.3. Suppose hypothesis h commits $r = 10$ errors over a sample of $n = 65$ independently drawn examples. What is the 90% confidence interval (two-sided) for the true error rate? What is the 95% one-sided interval (i.e., what is the upper bound U such that $error_{\mathcal{D}}(h) \leq U$ with 95% confidence)? What is the 90% one-sided interval?

5.4. You are about to test a hypothesis h whose $error_{\mathcal{D}}(h)$ is known to be in the range between 0.2 and 0.6. What is the minimum number of examples you must collect to assure that the width of the two-sided 95% confidence interval will be smaller than 0.1?

5.5. Give general expressions for the upper and lower one-sided $N\%$ confidence intervals for the difference in errors between two hypotheses tested on different samples of data. Hint: Modify the expression given in Section 5.5.

5.6. Explain why the confidence interval estimate given in Equation (5.17) applies to estimating the quantity in Equation (5.16), and not the quantity in Equation (5.14).

REFERENCES

Billingsley, P., Croft, D. J., Huntsberger, D. V., & Watson, C. J. (1986). *Statistical inference for management and economics*. Boston: Allyn and Bacon, Inc.

Casella, G., & Berger, R. L. (1990). *Statistical inference*. Pacific Grove, CA: Wadsworth and Brooks/Cole.

DeGroot, M. H. (1986). *Probability and statistics*. (2d ed.) Reading, MA: Addison Wesley.

Dietterich, T. G. (1996). *Proper statistical tests for comparing supervised classification learning algorithms* (Technical Report). Department of Computer Science, Oregon State University, Corvallis, OR.

Dietterich, T. G., & Kong, E. B. (1995). *Machine learning bias, statistical bias, and statistical variance of decision tree algorithms* (Technical Report). Department of Computer Science, Oregon State University, Corvallis, OR.

Duda, R., & Hart, P. (1973). *Pattern classification and scene analysis*. New York: John Wiley & Sons.

Efron, B., & Tibshirani, R. (1991). Statistical data analysis in the computer age. *Science*, 253, 390–395.

Etzioni, O., & Etzioni, R. (1994). Statistical methods for analyzing speedup learning experiments. *Machine Learning*, 14, 333–347.

Geman, S., Bienenstock, E., & Doursat, R. (1992). Neural networks and the bias/variance dilemma. *Neural Computation*, 4, 1–58.

Gordon, G., & Segre, A.M. (1996). Nonparametric statistical methods for experimental evaluations of speedup learning. *Proceedings of the Thirteenth International Conference on Machine Learning*, Bari, Italy.

Maisel, L. (1971). *Probability, statistics, and random processes*. Simon and Schuster Tech Outlines. New York: Simon and Schuster.

Segre, A., Elkan, C., & Russell, A. (1991). A critical look at experimental evaluations of EBL. *Machine Learning*, 6(2).

Segre, A.M, Gordon G., & Elkan, C. P. (1996). Exploratory analysis of speedup learning data using expectation maximization. *Artificial Intelligence*, 85, 301–319.

Speigel, M. R. (1991). *Theory and problems of probability and statistics*. Schaum's Outline Series. New York: McGraw Hill.

Thompson, M.L., & Zucchini, W. (1989). On the statistical analysis of ROC curves. *Statistics in Medicine*, 8, 1277–1290.

White, A. P., & Liu, W. Z. (1994). Bias in information-based measures in decision tree induction. *Machine Learning*, 15, 321–329.

CHAPTER 6

BAYESIAN LEARNING

Bayesian reasoning provides a probabilistic approach to inference. It is based on the assumption that the quantities of interest are governed by probability distributions and that optimal decisions can be made by reasoning about these probabilities together with observed data. It is important to machine learning because it provides a quantitative approach to weighing the evidence supporting alternative hypotheses. Bayesian reasoning provides the basis for learning algorithms that directly manipulate probabilities, as well as a framework for analyzing the operation of other algorithms that do not explicitly manipulate probabilities.

6.1 INTRODUCTION

Bayesian learning methods are relevant to our study of machine learning for two different reasons. First, Bayesian learning algorithms that calculate explicit probabilities for hypotheses, such as the naive Bayes classifier, are among the most practical approaches to certain types of learning problems. For example, Michie et al. (1994) provide a detailed study comparing the naive Bayes classifier to other learning algorithms, including decision tree and neural network algorithms. These researchers show that the naive Bayes classifier is competitive with these other learning algorithms in many cases and that in some cases it outperforms these other methods. In this chapter we describe the naive Bayes classifier and provide a detailed example of its use. In particular, we discuss its application to the problem of learning to classify text documents such as electronic news articles.

For such learning tasks, the naive Bayes classifier is among the most effective algorithms known.

The second reason that Bayesian methods are important to our study of machine learning is that they provide a useful perspective for understanding many learning algorithms that do not explicitly manipulate probabilities. For example, in this chapter we analyze algorithms such as the FIND-S and CANDIDATE-ELIMINATION algorithms of Chapter 2 to determine conditions under which they output the most probable hypothesis given the training data. We also use a Bayesian analysis to justify a key design choice in neural network learning algorithms: choosing to minimize the sum of squared errors when searching the space of possible neural networks. We also derive an alternative error function, cross entropy, that is more appropriate than sum of squared errors when learning target functions that predict probabilities. We use a Bayesian perspective to analyze the inductive bias of decision tree learning algorithms that favor short decision trees and examine the closely related Minimum Description Length principle. A basic familiarity with Bayesian methods is important to understanding and characterizing the operation of many algorithms in machine learning.

Features of Bayesian learning methods include:

- Each observed training example can incrementally decrease or increase the estimated probability that a hypothesis is correct. This provides a more flexible approach to learning than algorithms that completely eliminate a hypothesis if it is found to be inconsistent with any single example.
- Prior knowledge can be combined with observed data to determine the final probability of a hypothesis. In Bayesian learning, prior knowledge is provided by asserting (1) a prior probability for each candidate hypothesis, and (2) a probability distribution over observed data for each possible hypothesis.
- Bayesian methods can accommodate hypotheses that make probabilistic predictions (e.g., hypotheses such as "this pneumonia patient has a 93% chance of complete recovery").
- New instances can be classified by combining the predictions of multiple hypotheses, weighted by their probabilities.
- Even in cases where Bayesian methods prove computationally intractable, they can provide a standard of optimal decision making against which other practical methods can be measured.

One practical difficulty in applying Bayesian methods is that they typically require initial knowledge of many probabilities. When these probabilities are not known in advance they are often estimated based on background knowledge, previously available data, and assumptions about the form of the underlying distributions. A second practical difficulty is the significant computational cost required to determine the Bayes optimal hypothesis in the general case (linear in the number of candidate hypotheses). In certain specialized situations, this computational cost can be significantly reduced.

The remainder of this chapter is organized as follows. Section 6.2 introduces Bayes theorem and defines maximum likelihood and maximum a posteriori probability hypotheses. The four subsequent sections then apply this probabilistic framework to analyze several issues and learning algorithms discussed in earlier chapters. For example, we show that several previously described algorithms output maximum likelihood hypotheses, under certain assumptions. The remaining sections then introduce a number of learning algorithms that explicitly manipulate probabilities. These include the Bayes optimal classifier, Gibbs algorithm, and naive Bayes classifier. Finally, we discuss Bayesian belief networks, a relatively recent approach to learning based on probabilistic reasoning, and the EM algorithm, a widely used algorithm for learning in the presence of unobserved variables.

6.2 BAYES THEOREM

In machine learning we are often interested in determining the best hypothesis from some space H, given the observed training data D. One way to specify what we mean by the *best* hypothesis is to say that we demand the *most probable* hypothesis, given the data D plus any initial knowledge about the prior probabilities of the various hypotheses in H. Bayes theorem provides a direct method for calculating such probabilities. More precisely, Bayes theorem provides a way to calculate the probability of a hypothesis based on its prior probability, the probabilities of observing various data given the hypothesis, and the observed data itself.

To define Bayes theorem precisely, let us first introduce a little notation. We shall write $P(h)$ to denote the initial probability that hypothesis h holds, before we have observed the training data. $P(h)$ is often called the *prior probability* of h and may reflect any background knowledge we have about the chance that h is a correct hypothesis. If we have no such prior knowledge, then we might simply assign the same prior probability to each candidate hypothesis. Similarly, we will write $P(D)$ to denote the prior probability that training data D will be observed (i.e., the probability of D given no knowledge about which hypothesis holds). Next, we will write $P(D|h)$ to denote the probability of observing data D given some world in which hypothesis h holds. More generally, we write $P(x|y)$ to denote the probability of x given y. In machine learning problems we are interested in the probability $P(h|D)$ that h holds given the observed training data D. $P(h|D)$ is called the *posterior probability* of h, because it reflects our confidence that h holds after we have seen the training data D. Notice the posterior probability $P(h|D)$ reflects the influence of the training data D, in contrast to the prior probability $P(h)$, which is independent of D.

Bayes theorem is the cornerstone of Bayesian learning methods because it provides a way to calculate the posterior probability $P(h|D)$, from the prior probability $P(h)$, together with $P(D)$ and $P(D|h)$.

Bayes theorem:

$$P(h|D) = \frac{P(D|h)P(h)}{P(D)} \tag{6.1}$$

As one might intuitively expect, $P(h|D)$ increases with $P(h)$ and with $P(D|h)$ according to Bayes theorem. It is also reasonable to see that $P(h|D)$ decreases as $P(D)$ increases, because the more probable it is that D will be observed independent of h, the less evidence D provides in support of h.

In many learning scenarios, the learner considers some set of candidate hypotheses H and is interested in finding the most probable hypothesis $h \in H$ given the observed data D (or at least one of the maximally probable if there are several). Any such maximally probable hypothesis is called a *maximum a posteriori* (MAP) hypothesis. We can determine the MAP hypotheses by using Bayes theorem to calculate the posterior probability of each candidate hypothesis. More precisely, we will say that h_{MAP} is a MAP hypothesis provided

$$\begin{aligned} h_{MAP} &\equiv \underset{h \in H}{\operatorname{argmax}}\, P(h|D) \\ &= \underset{h \in H}{\operatorname{argmax}}\, \frac{P(D|h)\,P(h)}{P(D)} \\ &= \underset{h \in H}{\operatorname{argmax}}\, P(D|h)\,P(h) \end{aligned} \tag{6.2}$$

Notice in the final step above we dropped the term $P(D)$ because it is a constant independent of h.

In some cases, we will assume that every hypothesis in H is equally probable a priori ($P(h_i) = P(h_j)$ for all h_i and h_j in H). In this case we can further simplify Equation (6.2) and need only consider the term $P(D|h)$ to find the most probable hypothesis. $P(D|h)$ is often called the *likelihood* of the data D given h, and any hypothesis that maximizes $P(D|h)$ is called a *maximum likelihood* (ML) hypothesis, h_{ML}.

$$h_{ML} \equiv \underset{h \in H}{\operatorname{argmax}}\, P(D|h) \tag{6.3}$$

In order to make clear the connection to machine learning problems, we introduced Bayes theorem above by referring to the data D as training examples of some target function and referring to H as the space of candidate target functions. In fact, Bayes theorem is much more general than suggested by this discussion. It can be applied equally well to any set H of mutually exclusive propositions whose probabilities sum to one (e.g., "the sky is blue," and "the sky is not blue"). In this chapter, we will at times consider cases where H is a hypothesis space containing possible target functions and the data D are training examples. At other times we will consider cases where H is some other set of mutually exclusive propositions, and D is some other kind of data.

6.2.1 An Example

To illustrate Bayes rule, consider a medical diagnosis problem in which there are two alternative hypotheses: (1) that the patient has a particular form of cancer, and (2) that the patient does not. The available data is from a particular laboratory test with two possible outcomes: $\oplus$ (positive) and $\ominus$ (negative). We have prior knowledge that over the entire population of people only .008 have this disease. Furthermore, the lab test is only an imperfect indicator of the disease. The test returns a correct positive result in only 98% of the cases in which the disease is actually present and a correct negative result in only 97% of the cases in which the disease is not present. In other cases, the test returns the opposite result. The above situation can be summarized by the following probabilities:

$$P(cancer) = .008, \qquad P(\neg cancer) = .992$$
$$P(\oplus|cancer) = .98, \qquad P(\ominus|cancer) = .02$$
$$P(\oplus|\neg cancer) = .03, \qquad P(\ominus|\neg cancer) = .97$$

Suppose we now observe a new patient for whom the lab test returns a positive result. Should we diagnose the patient as having cancer or not? The maximum a posteriori hypothesis can be found using Equation (6.2):

$$P(\oplus|cancer)P(cancer) = (.98).008 = .0078$$
$$P(\oplus|\neg cancer)P(\neg cancer) = (.03).992 = .0298$$

Thus, $h_{MAP} = \neg cancer$. The exact posterior probabilities can also be determined by normalizing the above quantities so that they sum to 1 (e.g., $P(cancer|\oplus) = \frac{.0078}{.0078+.0298} = .21$). This step is warranted because Bayes theorem states that the posterior probabilities are just the above quantities divided by the probability of the data, $P(\oplus)$. Although $P(\oplus)$ was not provided directly as part of the problem statement, we can calculate it in this fashion because we know that $P(cancer|\oplus)$ and $P(\neg cancer|\oplus)$ must sum to 1 (i.e., either the patient has cancer or they do not). Notice that while the posterior probability of *cancer* is significantly higher than its prior probability, the most probable hypothesis is still that the patient does not have cancer.

As this example illustrates, the result of Bayesian inference depends strongly on the prior probabilities, which must be available in order to apply the method directly. Note also that in this example the hypotheses are not completely accepted or rejected, but rather become more or less probable as more data is observed.

Basic formulas for calculating probabilities are summarized in Table 6.1.

6.3 BAYES THEOREM AND CONCEPT LEARNING

What is the relationship between Bayes theorem and the problem of concept learning? Since Bayes theorem provides a principled way to calculate the posterior probability of each hypothesis given the training data, we can use it as the basis for a straightforward learning algorithm that calculates the probability for each possible hypothesis, then outputs the most probable. This section considers such a brute-force Bayesian concept learning algorithm, then compares it to concept learning algorithms we considered in Chapter 2. As we shall see, one interesting result of this comparison is that under certain conditions several algorithms discussed in earlier chapters output the same hypotheses as this brute-force Bayesian

- *Product rule*: probability $P(A \wedge B)$ of a conjunction of two events A and B

$$P(A \wedge B) = P(A|B)P(B) = P(B|A)P(A)$$

- *Sum rule*: probability of a disjunction of two events A and B

$$P(A \vee B) = P(A) + P(B) - P(A \wedge B)$$

- *Bayes theorem*: the posterior probability $P(h|D)$ of h given D

$$P(h|D) = \frac{P(D|h)P(h)}{P(D)}$$

- *Theorem of total probability*: if events $A_1, \ldots, A_n$ are mutually exclusive with $\sum_{i=1}^{n} P(A_i) = 1$, then

$$P(B) = \sum_{i=1}^{n} P(B|A_i)P(A_i)$$

TABLE 6.1
Summary of basic probability formulas.

algorithm, despite the fact that they do not explicitly manipulate probabilities and are considerably more efficient.

6.3.1 Brute-Force Bayes Concept Learning

Consider the concept learning problem first introduced in Chapter 2. In particular, assume the learner considers some finite hypothesis space H defined over the instance space X, in which the task is to learn some target concept $c : X \rightarrow \{0, 1\}$. As usual, we assume that the learner is given some sequence of training examples $\langle\langle x_1, d_1\rangle \ldots \langle x_m, d_m\rangle\rangle$ where x_i is some instance from X and where d_i is the target value of x_i (i.e., $d_i = c(x_i)$). To simplify the discussion in this section, we assume the sequence of instances $\langle x_1 \ldots x_m\rangle$ is held fixed, so that the training data D can be written simply as the sequence of target values $D = \langle d_1 \ldots d_m\rangle$. It can be shown (see Exercise 6.4) that this simplification does not alter the main conclusions of this section.

We can design a straightforward concept learning algorithm to output the maximum a posteriori hypothesis, based on Bayes theorem, as follows:

BRUTE-FORCE MAP LEARNING algorithm

1. For each hypothesis h in H, calculate the posterior probability

$$P(h|D) = \frac{P(D|h)P(h)}{P(D)}$$

2. Output the hypothesis h_{MAP} with the highest posterior probability

$$h_{MAP} = \underset{h \in H}{\operatorname{argmax}} \; P(h|D)$$

This algorithm may require significant computation, because it applies Bayes theorem to each hypothesis in H to calculate $P(h|D)$. While this may prove impractical for large hypothesis spaces, the algorithm is still of interest because it provides a standard against which we may judge the performance of other concept learning algorithms.

In order specify a learning problem for the BRUTE-FORCE MAP LEARNING algorithm we must specify what values are to be used for $P(h)$ and for $P(D|h)$ (as we shall see, $P(D)$ will be determined once we choose the other two). We may choose the probability distributions $P(h)$ and $P(D|h)$ in any way we wish, to describe our prior knowledge about the learning task. Here let us choose them to be consistent with the following assumptions:

1. The training data D is noise free (i.e., $d_i = c(x_i)$).
2. The target concept c is contained in the hypothesis space H.
3. We have no a priori reason to believe that any hypothesis is more probable than any other.

Given these assumptions, what values should we specify for $P(h)$? Given no prior knowledge that one hypothesis is more likely than another, it is reasonable to assign the same prior probability to every hypothesis h in H. Furthermore, because we assume the target concept is contained in H we should require that these prior probabilities sum to 1. Together these constraints imply that we should choose

$$P(h) = \frac{1}{|H|} \quad \text{for all } h \text{ in } H$$

What choice shall we make for $P(D|h)$? $P(D|h)$ is the probability of observing the target values $D = \langle d_1 \dots d_m \rangle$ for the fixed set of instances $\langle x_1 \dots x_m \rangle$, given a world in which hypothesis h holds (i.e., given a world in which h is the correct description of the target concept c). Since we assume noise-free training data, the probability of observing classification d_i given h is just 1 if $d_i = h(x_i)$ and 0 if $d_i \neq h(x_i)$. Therefore,

$$P(D|h) = \begin{cases} 1 \text{ if } d_i = h(x_i) \text{ for all } d_i \text{ in } D \\ 0 \text{ otherwise} \end{cases} \tag{6.4}$$

In other words, the probability of data D given hypothesis h is 1 if D is consistent with h, and 0 otherwise.

Given these choices for $P(h)$ and for $P(D|h)$ we now have a fully-defined problem for the above BRUTE-FORCE MAP LEARNING algorithm. Let us consider the first step of this algorithm, which uses Bayes theorem to compute the posterior probability $P(h|D)$ of each hypothesis h given the observed training data D.

Recalling Bayes theorem, we have

$$P(h|D) = \frac{P(D|h)P(h)}{P(D)}$$

First consider the case where h is inconsistent with the training data D. Since Equation (6.4) defines $P(D|h)$ to be 0 when h is inconsistent with D, we have

$$P(h|D) = \frac{0 \cdot P(h)}{P(D)} = 0 \text{ if } h \text{ is inconsistent with } D$$

The posterior probability of a hypothesis inconsistent with D is zero.

Now consider the case where h is consistent with D. Since Equation (6.4) defines $P(D|h)$ to be 1 when h is consistent with D, we have

$$\begin{aligned} P(h|D) &= \frac{1 \cdot \frac{1}{|H|}}{P(D)} \\ &= \frac{1 \cdot \frac{1}{|H|}}{\frac{|VS_{H,D}|}{|H|}} \\ &= \frac{1}{|VS_{H,D}|} \text{ if } h \text{ is consistent with } D \end{aligned}$$

where $VS_{H,D}$ is the subset of hypotheses from H that are consistent with D (i.e., $VS_{H,D}$ is the version space of H with respect to D as defined in Chapter 2). It is easy to verify that $P(D) = \frac{|VS_{H,D}|}{|H|}$ above, because the sum over all hypotheses of $P(h|D)$ must be one and because the number of hypotheses from H consistent with D is by definition $|VS_{H,D}|$. Alternatively, we can derive $P(D)$ from the theorem of total probability (see Table 6.1) and the fact that the hypotheses are mutually exclusive (i.e., $(\forall i \neq j)(P(h_i \wedge h_j) = 0)$)

$$\begin{aligned} P(D) &= \sum_{h_i \in H} P(D|h_i)P(h_i) \\ &= \sum_{h_i \in VS_{H,D}} 1 \cdot \frac{1}{|H|} + \sum_{h_i \notin VS_{H,D}} 0 \cdot \frac{1}{|H|} \\ &= \sum_{h_i \in VS_{H,D}} 1 \cdot \frac{1}{|H|} \\ &= \frac{|VS_{H,D}|}{|H|} \end{aligned}$$

To summarize, Bayes theorem implies that the posterior probability $P(h|D)$ under our assumed $P(h)$ and $P(D|h)$ is

$$P(h|D) = \begin{cases} \frac{1}{|VS_{H,D}|} & \text{if } h \text{ is consistent with } D \\ 0 & \text{otherwise} \end{cases} \tag{6.5}$$

where $|VS_{H,D}|$ is the number of hypotheses from H consistent with D. The evolution of probabilities associated with hypotheses is depicted schematically in Figure 6.1. Initially (Figure 6.1*a*) all hypotheses have the same probability. As training data accumulates (Figures 6.1*b* and 6.1*c*), the posterior probability for inconsistent hypotheses becomes zero while the total probability summing to one is shared equally among the remaining consistent hypotheses.

The above analysis implies that under our choice for $P(h)$ and $P(D|h)$, every *consistent* hypothesis has posterior probability $(1/|VS_{H,D}|)$, and every inconsistent hypothesis has posterior probability 0. Every consistent hypothesis is, therefore, a MAP hypothesis.

6.3.2 MAP Hypotheses and Consistent Learners

The above analysis shows that in the given setting, every hypothesis consistent with D is a MAP hypothesis. This statement translates directly into an interesting statement about a general class of learners that we might call *consistent learners*. We will say that a learning algorithm is a *consistent learner* provided it outputs a hypothesis that commits zero errors over the training examples. Given the above analysis, we can conclude that *every consistent learner outputs a MAP hypothesis, if we assume a uniform prior probability distribution over H (i.e., $P(h_i) = P(h_j)$ for all i, j), and if we assume deterministic, noise-free training data (i.e., $P(D|h) = 1$ if D and h are consistent, and 0 otherwise).*

Consider, for example, the concept learning algorithm FIND-S discussed in Chapter 2. FIND-S searches the hypothesis space H from specific to general hypotheses, outputting a maximally specific consistent hypothesis (i.e., a maximally specific member of the version space). Because FIND-S outputs a consistent hypothesis, we know that it will output a MAP hypothesis under the probability distributions $P(h)$ and $P(D|h)$ defined above. Of course FIND-S does not explicitly manipulate probabilities at all—it simply outputs a maximally specific member

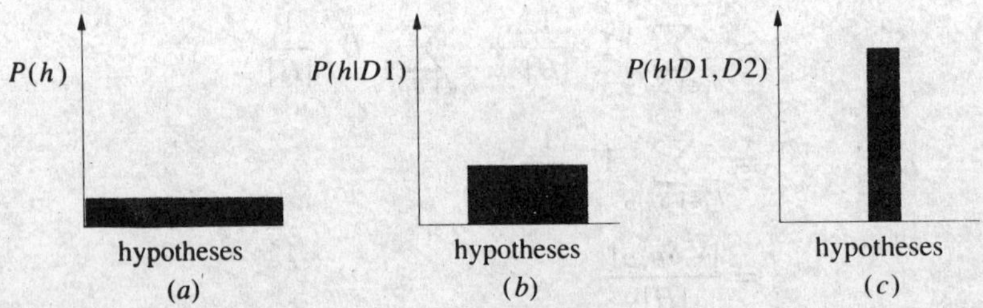

FIGURE 6.1
Evolution of posterior probabilities $P(h|D)$ with increasing training data. (*a*) Uniform priors assign equal probability to each hypothesis. As training data increases first to $D1$ (*b*), then to $D1 \wedge D2$ (*c*), the posterior probability of inconsistent hypotheses becomes zero, while posterior probabilities increase for hypotheses remaining in the version space.

of the version space. However, by identifying distributions for $P(h)$ and $P(D|h)$ under which its output hypotheses will be MAP hypotheses, we have a useful way of characterizing the behavior of FIND-S.

Are there other probability distributions for $P(h)$ and $P(D|h)$ under which FIND-S outputs MAP hypotheses? Yes. Because FIND-S outputs a *maximally specific* hypothesis from the version space, its output hypothesis will be a MAP hypothesis relative to any prior probability distribution that favors more specific hypotheses. More precisely, suppose $\mathcal{H}$ is any probability distribution $P(h)$ over H that assigns $P(h_1) \geq P(h_2)$ if h_1 is more specific than h_2. Then it can be shown that FIND-S outputs a MAP hypothesis assuming the prior distribution $\mathcal{H}$ and the same distribution $P(D|h)$ discussed above.

To summarize the above discussion, the Bayesian framework allows one way to characterize the behavior of learning algorithms (e.g., FIND-S), even when the learning algorithm does not explicitly manipulate probabilities. By identifying probability distributions $P(h)$ and $P(D|h)$ under which the algorithm outputs optimal (i.e., MAP) hypotheses, we can characterize the implicit assumptions under which this algorithm behaves optimally.

Using the Bayesian perspective to characterize learning algorithms in this way is similar in spirit to characterizing the inductive bias of the learner. Recall that in Chapter 2 we defined the inductive bias of a learning algorithm to be the set of assumptions B sufficient to *deductively* justify the inductive inference performed by the learner. For example, we described the inductive bias of the CANDIDATE-ELIMINATION algorithm as the assumption that the target concept c is included in the hypothesis space H. Furthermore, we showed there that the output of this learning algorithm follows deductively from its inputs plus this implicit inductive bias assumption. The above Bayesian interpretation provides an alternative way to characterize the assumptions implicit in learning algorithms. Here, instead of modeling the inductive inference method by an equivalent deductive system, we model it by an equivalent *probabilistic reasoning* system based on Bayes theorem. And here the implicit assumptions that we attribute to the learner are assumptions of the form "the prior probabilities over H are given by the distribution $P(h)$, and the strength of data in rejecting or accepting a hypothesis is given by $P(D|h)$." The definitions of $P(h)$ and $P(D|h)$ given in this section characterize the implicit assumptions of the CANDIDATE-ELIMINATION and FIND-S algorithms. A probabilistic reasoning system based on Bayes theorem will exhibit input-output behavior equivalent to these algorithms, provided it is given these assumed probability distributions.

The discussion throughout this section corresponds to a special case of Bayesian reasoning, because we considered the case where $P(D|h)$ takes on values of only 0 and 1, reflecting the deterministic predictions of hypotheses and the assumption of noise-free training data. As we shall see in the next section, we can also model learning from noisy training data, by allowing $P(D|h)$ to take on values other than 0 and 1, and by introducing into $P(D|h)$ additional assumptions about the probability distributions that govern the noise.

6.4 MAXIMUM LIKELIHOOD AND LEAST-SQUARED ERROR HYPOTHESES

As illustrated in the above section, Bayesian analysis can sometimes be used to show that a particular learning algorithm outputs MAP hypotheses even though it may not explicitly use Bayes rule or calculate probabilities in any form.

In this section we consider the problem of learning a continuous-valued target function—a problem faced by many learning approaches such as neural network learning, linear regression, and polynomial curve fitting. A straightforward Bayesian analysis will show that *under certain assumptions any learning algorithm that minimizes the squared error between the output hypothesis predictions and the training data will output a maximum likelihood hypothesis.* The significance of this result is that it provides a Bayesian justification (under certain assumptions) for many neural network and other curve fitting methods that attempt to minimize the sum of squared errors over the training data.

Consider the following problem setting. Learner L considers an instance space X and a hypothesis space H consisting of some class of real-valued functions defined over X (i.e., each h in H is a function of the form $h : X \rightarrow \Re$, where $\Re$ represents the set of real numbers). The problem faced by L is to learn an unknown target function $f : X \rightarrow \Re$ drawn from H. A set of m training examples is provided, where the target value of each example is corrupted by random noise drawn according to a Normal probability distribution. More precisely, each training example is a pair of the form $\langle x_i, d_i \rangle$ where $d_i = f(x_i) + e_i$. Here $f(x_i)$ is the noise-free value of the target function and e_i is a random variable representing the noise. It is assumed that the values of the e_i are drawn independently and that they are distributed according to a Normal distribution with zero mean. The task of the learner is to output a maximum likelihood hypothesis, or, equivalently, a MAP hypothesis assuming all hypotheses are equally probable a priori.

A simple example of such a problem is learning a linear function, though our analysis applies to learning arbitrary real-valued functions. Figure 6.2 illustrates

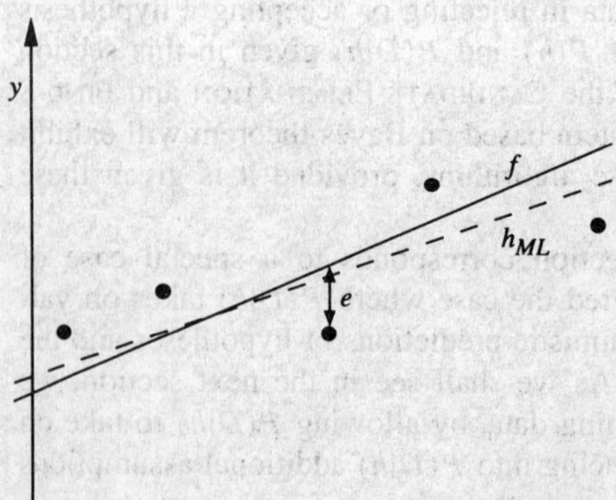

FIGURE 6.2
Learning a real-valued function. The target function f corresponds to the solid line. The training examples $\langle x_i, d_i \rangle$ are assumed to have Normally distributed noise e_i with zero mean added to the true target value $f(x_i)$. The dashed line corresponds to the linear function that minimizes the sum of squared errors. Therefore, it is the maximum likelihood hypothesis h_{ML}, given these five training examples.

a linear target function f depicted by the solid line, and a set of noisy training examples of this target function. The dashed line corresponds to the hypothesis h_{ML} with least-squared training error, hence the maximum likelihood hypothesis. Notice that the maximum likelihood hypothesis is not necessarily identical to the correct hypothesis, f, because it is inferred from only a limited sample of noisy training data.

Before showing why a hypothesis that minimizes the sum of squared errors in this setting is also a maximum likelihood hypothesis, let us quickly review two basic concepts from probability theory: probability densities and Normal distributions. First, in order to discuss probabilities over continuous variables such as e, we must introduce probability *densities*. The reason, roughly, is that we wish for the total probability over all possible values of the random variable to sum to one. In the case of continuous variables we cannot achieve this by assigning a finite probability to each of the infinite set of possible values for the random variable. Instead, we speak of a probability *density* for continuous variables such as e and require that the integral of this probability density over all possible values be one. In general we will use lower case p to refer to the probability density function, to distinguish it from a finite probability P (which we will sometimes refer to as a probability *mass*). The probability density $p(x_0)$ is the limit as ϵ goes to zero, of $\frac{1}{\epsilon}$ times the probability that x will take on a value in the interval $[x_0, x_0 + \epsilon)$.

Probability density function:

$$p(x_0) \equiv \lim_{\epsilon \to 0} \frac{1}{\epsilon} P(x_0 \le x < x_0 + \epsilon)$$

Second, we stated that the random noise variable e is generated by a Normal probability distribution. A Normal distribution is a smooth, bell-shaped distribution that can be completely characterized by its mean μ and its standard deviation σ. See Table 5.4 for a precise definition.

Given this background we now return to the main issue: showing that the least-squared error hypothesis is, in fact, the maximum likelihood hypothesis within our problem setting. We will show this by deriving the maximum likelihood hypothesis starting with our earlier definition Equation (6.3), but using lower case p to refer to the probability density

$$h_{ML} = \underset{h \in H}{\operatorname{argmax}}\, p(D|h)$$

As before, we assume a fixed set of training instances $\langle x_1 \dots x_m \rangle$ and therefore consider the data D to be the corresponding sequence of target values $D = \langle d_1 \dots d_m \rangle$. Here $d_i = f(x_i) + e_i$. Assuming the training examples are mutually independent given h, we can write $P(D|h)$ as the product of the various $p(d_i|h)$

$$h_{ML} = \underset{h \in H}{\operatorname{argmax}} \prod_{i=1}^{m} p(d_i|h)$$

Given that the noise e_i obeys a Normal distribution with zero mean and unknown variance σ^2, each d_i must also obey a Normal distribution with variance σ^2 centered around the true target value $f(x_i)$ rather than zero. Therefore $p(d_i|h)$ can be written as a Normal distribution with variance σ^2 and mean $\mu = f(x_i)$. Let us write the formula for this Normal distribution to describe $p(d_i|h)$, beginning with the general formula for a Normal distribution from Table 5.4 and substituting the appropriate μ and σ^2. Because we are writing the expression for the probability of d_i given that h is the correct description of the target function f, we will also substitute $\mu = f(x_i) = h(x_i)$, yielding

$$h_{ML} = \underset{h \in H}{\operatorname{argmax}} \prod_{i=1}^{m} \frac{1}{\sqrt{2\pi\sigma^2}} e^{-\frac{1}{2\sigma^2}(d_i - \mu)^2}$$

$$= \underset{h \in H}{\operatorname{argmax}} \prod_{i=1}^{m} \frac{1}{\sqrt{2\pi\sigma^2}} e^{-\frac{1}{2\sigma^2}(d_i - h(x_i))^2}$$

We now apply a transformation that is common in maximum likelihood calculations: Rather than maximizing the above complicated expression we shall choose to maximize its (less complicated) logarithm. This is justified because $\ln p$ is a monotonic function of p. Therefore maximizing $\ln p$ also maximizes p.

$$h_{ML} = \underset{h \in H}{\operatorname{argmax}} \sum_{i=1}^{m} \ln \frac{1}{\sqrt{2\pi\sigma^2}} - \frac{1}{2\sigma^2}(d_i - h(x_i))^2$$

The first term in this expression is a constant independent of h, and can therefore be discarded, yielding

$$h_{ML} = \underset{h \in H}{\operatorname{argmax}} \sum_{i=1}^{m} -\frac{1}{2\sigma^2}(d_i - h(x_i))^2$$

Maximizing this negative quantity is equivalent to minimizing the corresponding positive quantity.

$$h_{ML} = \underset{h \in H}{\operatorname{argmin}} \sum_{i=1}^{m} \frac{1}{2\sigma^2}(d_i - h(x_i))^2$$

Finally, we can again discard constants that are independent of h.

$$h_{ML} = \underset{h \in H}{\operatorname{argmin}} \sum_{i=1}^{m} (d_i - h(x_i))^2 \tag{6.6}$$

Thus, Equation (6.6) shows that the maximum likelihood hypothesis h_{ML} is the one that minimizes the sum of the squared errors between the observed training values d_i and the hypothesis predictions $h(x_i)$. This holds under the assumption that the observed training values d_i are generated by adding random noise to the true target value, where this random noise is drawn independently for each example from a Normal distribution with zero mean. As the above derivation makes clear, the squared error term $(d_i - h(x_i))^2$ follows directly from the exponent in the definition of the Normal distribution. Similar derivations can be performed starting with other assumed noise distributions, producing different results.

Notice the structure of the above derivation involves selecting the hypothesis that maximizes the logarithm of the likelihood ($\ln p(D|h)$) in order to determine the most probable hypothesis. As noted earlier, this yields the same result as maximizing the likelihood $p(D|h)$. This approach of working with the log likelihood is common to many Bayesian analyses, because it is often more mathematically tractable than working directly with the likelihood. Of course, as noted earlier, the maximum likelihood hypothesis might not be the MAP hypothesis, but if one assumes uniform prior probabilities over the hypotheses then it is.

Why is it reasonable to choose the Normal distribution to characterize noise? One reason, it must be admitted, is that it allows for a mathematically straightforward analysis. A second reason is that the smooth, bell-shaped distribution is a good approximation to many types of noise in physical systems. In fact, the Central Limit Theorem discussed in Chapter 5 shows that the sum of a sufficiently large number of independent, identically distributed random variables itself obeys a Normal distribution, regardless of the distributions of the individual variables. This implies that noise generated by the sum of very many independent, but identically distributed factors will itself be Normally distributed. Of course, in reality, different components that contribute to noise might not follow identical distributions, in which case this theorem will not necessarily justify our choice.

Minimizing the sum of squared errors is a common approach in many neural network, curve fitting, and other approaches to approximating real-valued functions. Chapter 4 describes gradient descent methods that seek the least-squared error hypothesis in neural network learning.

Before leaving our discussion of the relationship between the maximum likelihood hypothesis and the least-squared error hypothesis, it is important to note some limitations of this problem setting. The above analysis considers noise only in the *target value* of the training example and does not consider noise in the *attributes describing the instances themselves.* For example, if the problem is to learn to predict the weight of someone based on that person's age and height, then the above analysis assumes noise in measurements of weight, but perfect measurements of age and height. The analysis becomes significantly more complex as these simplifying assumptions are removed.

6.5 MAXIMUM LIKELIHOOD HYPOTHESES FOR PREDICTING PROBABILITIES

In the problem setting of the previous section we determined that the maximum likelihood hypothesis is the one that minimizes the sum of squared errors over the training examples. In this section we derive an analogous criterion for a second setting that is common in neural network learning: learning to predict probabilities.

Consider the setting in which we wish to learn a nondeterministic (probabilistic) function $f : X \rightarrow \{0, 1\}$, which has two discrete output values. For example, the instance space X might represent medical patients in terms of their symptoms, and the target function $f(x)$ might be 1 if the patient survives the disease and 0 if not. Alternatively, X might represent loan applicants in terms of their past credit history, and $f(x)$ might be 1 if the applicant successfully repays their next loan and 0 if not. In both of these cases we might well expect f to be probabilistic. For example, among a collection of patients exhibiting the same set of observable symptoms, we might find that 92% survive, and 8% do not. This unpredictability could arise from our inability to observe all the important distinguishing features of the patients, or from some genuinely probabilistic mechanism in the evolution of the disease. Whatever the source of the problem, the effect is that we have a target function $f(x)$ whose output is a probabilistic function of the input.

Given this problem setting, we might wish to learn a neural network (or other real-valued function approximator) whose output is the *probability* that $f(x) = 1$. In other words, we seek to learn the target function, $f' : X \rightarrow [0, 1]$, such that $f'(x) = P(f(x) = 1)$. In the above medical patient example, if x is one of those indistinguishable patients of which 92% survive, then $f'(x) = 0.92$ whereas the probabilistic function $f(x)$ will be equal to 1 in 92% of cases and equal to 0 in the remaining 8%.

How can we learn f' using, say, a neural network? One obvious, brute-force way would be to first collect the observed frequencies of 1's and 0's for each possible value of x and to then train the neural network to output the target frequency for each x. As we shall see below, we can instead train a neural network directly from the observed training examples of f, yet still derive a maximum likelihood hypothesis for f'.

What criterion should we optimize in order to find a maximum likelihood hypothesis for f' in this setting? To answer this question we must first obtain an expression for $P(D|h)$. Let us assume the training data D is of the form $D = \{\langle x_1, d_1 \rangle \ldots \langle x_m, d_m \rangle\}$, where d_i is the observed 0 or 1 value for $f(x_i)$.

Recall that in the maximum likelihood, least-squared error analysis of the previous section, we made the simplifying assumption that the instances $\langle x_1 \ldots x_m \rangle$ were fixed. This enabled us to characterize the data by considering only the target values d_i. Although we could make a similar simplifying assumption in this case, let us avoid it here in order to demonstrate that it has no impact on the final outcome. Thus treating both x_i and d_i as random variables, and assuming that each training example is drawn independently, we can write $P(D|h)$ as

$$P(D|h) = \prod_{i=1}^{m} P(x_i, d_i|h) \tag{6.7}$$

It is reasonable to assume, furthermore, that the probability of encountering any particular instance x_i is independent of the hypothesis h. For example, the probability that our training set contains a particular *patient* x_i is independent of our hypothesis about survival rates (though of course the *survival* d_i of the patient does depend strongly on h). When x is independent of h we can rewrite the above expression (applying the product rule from Table 6.1) as

$$P(D|h) = \prod_{i=1}^{m} P(x_i, d_i|h) = \prod_{i=1}^{m} P(d_i|h, x_i)P(x_i) \tag{6.8}$$

Now what is the probability $P(d_i|h, x_i)$ of observing $d_i = 1$ for a single instance x_i, given a world in which hypothesis h holds? Recall that h is our hypothesis regarding the target function, which computes this very probability. Therefore, $P(d_i = 1|h, x_i) = h(x_i)$, and in general

$$P(d_i|h, x_i) = \begin{cases} h(x_i) & \text{if } d_i = 1 \\ (1 - h(x_i)) & \text{if } d_i = 0 \end{cases} \tag{6.9}$$

In order to substitute this into the Equation (6.8) for $P(D|h)$, let us first re-express it in a more mathematically manipulable form, as

$$P(d_i|h, x_i) = h(x_i)^{d_i}(1 - h(x_i))^{1-d_i} \tag{6.10}$$

It is easy to verify that the expressions in Equations (6.9) and (6.10) are equivalent. Notice that when $d_i = 1$, the second term from Equation (6.10), $(1 - h(x_i))^{1-d_i}$, becomes equal to 1. Hence $P(d_i = 1|h, x_i) = h(x_i)$, which is equivalent to the first case in Equation (6.9). A similar analysis shows that the two equations are also equivalent when $d_i = 0$.

We can use Equation (6.10) to substitute for $P(d_i|h, x_i)$ in Equation (6.8) to obtain

$$P(D|h) = \prod_{i=1}^{m} h(x_i)^{d_i}(1 - h(x_i))^{1-d_i} P(x_i) \tag{6.11}$$

Now we write an expression for the maximum likelihood hypothesis

$$h_{ML} = \underset{h \in H}{\operatorname{argmax}} \prod_{i=1}^{m} h(x_i)^{d_i}(1 - h(x_i))^{1-d_i} P(x_i)$$

The last term is a constant independent of h, so it can be dropped

$$h_{ML} = \underset{h \in H}{\operatorname{argmax}} \prod_{i=1}^{m} h(x_i)^{d_i}(1 - h(x_i))^{1-d_i} \tag{6.12}$$

The expression on the right side of Equation (6.12) can be seen as a generalization of the *Binomial distribution* described in Table 5.3. The expression in Equation (6.12) describes the probability that flipping each of m distinct coins will produce the outcome $\langle d_1 \ldots d_m \rangle$, assuming that each coin x_i has probability $h(x_i)$ of producing a heads. Note the Binomial distribution described in Table 5.3 is similar, but makes the additional assumption that the coins have identical probabilities of turning up heads (i.e., that $h(x_i) = h(x_j), \forall i, j$). In both cases we assume the outcomes of the coin flips are mutually independent—an assumption that fits our current setting.

As in earlier cases, we will find it easier to work with the log of the likelihood, yielding

$$h_{ML} = \underset{h \in H}{\operatorname{argmax}} \sum_{i=1}^{m} d_i \ln h(x_i) + (1 - d_i) \ln(1 - h(x_i)) \tag{6.13}$$

Equation (6.13) describes the quantity that must be maximized in order to obtain the maximum likelihood hypothesis in our current problem setting. This result is analogous to our earlier result showing that minimizing the sum of squared errors produces the maximum likelihood hypothesis in the earlier problem setting. Note the similarity between Equation (6.13) and the general form of the entropy function, $-\sum_i p_i \log p_i$, discussed in Chapter 3. Because of this similarity, the negation of the above quantity is sometimes called the *cross entropy*.

6.5.1 Gradient Search to Maximize Likelihood in a Neural Net

Above we showed that maximizing the quantity in Equation (6.13) yields the maximum likelihood hypothesis. Let us use $G(h, D)$ to denote this quantity. In this section we derive a weight-training rule for neural network learning that seeks to maximize $G(h, D)$ using gradient ascent.

As discussed in Chapter 4, the gradient of $G(h, D)$ is given by the vector of partial derivatives of $G(h, D)$ with respect to the various network weights that define the hypothesis h represented by the learned network (see Chapter 4 for a general discussion of gradient-descent search and for details of the terminology that we reuse here). In this case, the partial derivative of $G(h, D)$ with respect to weight w_{jk} from input k to unit j is

$$\begin{aligned}
\frac{\partial G(h, D)}{\partial w_{jk}} &= \sum_{i=1}^{m} \frac{\partial G(h, D)}{\partial h(x_i)} \frac{\partial h(x_i)}{\partial w_{jk}} \\
&= \sum_{i=1}^{m} \frac{\partial (d_i \ln h(x_i) + (1 - d_i) \ln(1 - h(x_i)))}{\partial h(x_i)} \frac{\partial h(x_i)}{\partial w_{jk}} \\
&= \sum_{i=1}^{m} \frac{d_i - h(x_i)}{h(x_i)(1 - h(x_i))} \frac{\partial h(x_i)}{\partial w_{jk}} \qquad (6.14)
\end{aligned}$$

To keep our analysis simple, suppose our neural network is constructed from a single layer of sigmoid units. In this case we have

$$\frac{\partial h(x_i)}{\partial w_{jk}} = \sigma'(x_i) x_{ijk} = h(x_i)(1 - h(x_i)) x_{ijk}$$

where x_{ijk} is the kth input to unit j for the ith training example, and $\sigma'(x)$ is the derivative of the sigmoid squashing function (again, see Chapter 4). Finally, substituting this expression into Equation (6.14), we obtain a simple expression for the derivatives that constitute the gradient

$$\frac{\partial G(h, D)}{\partial w_{jk}} = \sum_{i=1}^{m} (d_i - h(x_i))\ x_{ijk}$$

Because we seek to maximize rather than minimize $P(D|h)$, we perform gradient ascent rather than gradient descent search. On each iteration of the search the weight vector is adjusted in the direction of the gradient, using the weight-update rule

$$w_{jk} \leftarrow w_{jk} + \Delta w_{jk}$$

where

$$\Delta w_{jk} = \eta \sum_{i=1}^{m} (d_i - h(x_i))\ x_{ijk} \tag{6.15}$$

and where η is a small positive constant that determines the step size of the gradient ascent search.

It is interesting to compare this weight-update rule to the weight-update rule used by the BACKPROPAGATION algorithm to minimize the sum of squared errors between predicted and observed network outputs. The BACKPROPAGATION update rule for output unit weights (see Chapter 4), re-expressed using our current notation, is

$$w_{jk} \leftarrow w_{jk} + \Delta w_{jk}$$

where

$$\Delta w_{jk} = \eta \sum_{i=1}^{m} h(x_i)(1 - h(x_i))(d_i - h(x_i))\ x_{ijk}$$

Notice this is similar to the rule given in Equation (6.15) except for the extra term $h(x_i)(1 - h(x_i))$, which is the derivative of the sigmoid function.

To summarize, these two weight update rules converge toward maximum likelihood hypotheses in two different settings. The rule that minimizes sum of squared error seeks the maximum likelihood hypothesis under the assumption that the training data can be modeled by Normally distributed noise added to the target function value. The rule that minimizes cross entropy seeks the maximum likelihood hypothesis under the assumption that the observed boolean value is a probabilistic function of the input instance.

6.6 MINIMUM DESCRIPTION LENGTH PRINCIPLE

Recall from Chapter 3 the discussion of Occam's razor, a popular inductive bias that can be summarized as "choose the shortest explanation for the observed data." In that chapter we discussed several arguments in the long-standing debate regarding Occam's razor. Here we consider a Bayesian perspective on this issue and a closely related principle called the Minimum Description Length (MDL) principle.

The Minimum Description Length principle is motivated by interpreting the definition of h_{MAP} in the light of basic concepts from information theory. Consider again the now familiar definition of h_{MAP}.

$$h_{MAP} = \underset{h \in H}{\operatorname{argmax}} \; P(D|h)P(h)$$

which can be equivalently expressed in terms of maximizing the $\log_2$

$$h_{MAP} = \underset{h \in H}{\operatorname{argmax}} \; \log_2 P(D|h) + \log_2 P(h)$$

or alternatively, minimizing the negative of this quantity

$$h_{MAP} = \underset{h \in H}{\operatorname{argmin}} \; -\log_2 P(D|h) - \log_2 P(h) \tag{6.16}$$

Somewhat surprisingly, Equation (6.16) can be interpreted as a statement that short hypotheses are preferred, assuming a particular representation scheme for encoding hypotheses and data. To explain this, let us introduce a basic result from information theory: Consider the problem of designing a code to transmit messages drawn at random, where the probability of encountering message i is p_i. We are interested here in the most compact code; that is, we are interested in the code that minimizes the expected number of bits we must transmit in order to encode a message drawn at random. Clearly, to minimize the expected code length we should assign shorter codes to messages that are more probable. Shannon and Weaver (1949) showed that the optimal code (i.e., the code that minimizes the expected message length) assigns $-\log_2 p_i$ bits† to encode message i. We will refer to the number of bits required to encode message i using code C as the *description length of message i with respect to C*, which we denote by $L_C(i)$.

Let us interpret Equation (6.16) in light of the above result from coding theory.

- $-\log_2 P(h)$ is the description length of h under the optimal encoding for the hypothesis space H. In other words, this is the size of the description of hypothesis h using this optimal representation. In our notation, $L_{C_H}(h) = -\log_2 P(h)$, where C_H is the optimal code for hypothesis space H.
- $-\log_2 P(D|h)$ is the description length of the training data D given hypothesis h, under its optimal encoding. In our notation, $L_{C_{D|h}}(D|h) = -\log_2 P(D|h)$, where $C_{D|h}$ is the optimal code for describing data D assuming that both the sender and receiver know the hypothesis h.

†Notice the expected length for transmitting one message is therefore $\sum_i -p_i \log_2 p_i$, the formula for the *entropy* (see Chapter 3) of the set of possible messages.

- Therefore we can rewrite Equation (6.16) to show that h_{MAP} is the hypothesis h that minimizes the sum given by the description length of the hypothesis plus the description length of the data given the hypothesis.

$$h_{MAP} = \underset{h}{\text{argmin}}\, L_{C_H}(h) + L_{C_{D|h}}(D|h)$$

where C_H and $C_{D|h}$ are the optimal encodings for H and for D given h, respectively.

The Minimum Description Length (MDL) principle recommends choosing the hypothesis that minimizes the sum of these two description lengths. Of course to apply this principle in practice we must choose specific encodings or representations appropriate for the given learning task. Assuming we use the codes C_1 and C_2 to represent the hypothesis and the data given the hypothesis, we can state the MDL principle as

Minimum Description Length principle: Choose h_{MDL} where

$$h_{MDL} = \underset{h \in H}{\text{argmin}}\, L_{C_1}(h) + L_{C_2}(D|h) \tag{6.17}$$

The above analysis shows that if we choose C_1 to be the optimal encoding of hypotheses C_H, and if we choose C_2 to be the optimal encoding $C_{D|h}$, then $h_{MDL} = h_{MAP}$.

Intuitively, we can think of the MDL principle as recommending the shortest method for re-encoding the training data, where we count both the size of the hypothesis and any additional cost of encoding the data given this hypothesis.

Let us consider an example. Suppose we wish to apply the MDL principle to the problem of learning decision trees from some training data. What should we choose for the representations C_1 and C_2 of hypotheses and data? For C_1 we might naturally choose some obvious encoding of decision trees, in which the description length grows with the number of nodes in the tree and with the number of edges. How shall we choose the encoding C_2 of the data given a particular decision tree hypothesis? To keep things simple, suppose that the sequence of instances $\langle x_1 \ldots x_m \rangle$ is already known to both the transmitter and receiver, so that we need only transmit the classifications $\langle f(x_1) \ldots f(x_m) \rangle$. (Note the cost of transmitting the instances themselves is independent of the correct hypothesis, so it does not affect the selection of h_{MDL} in any case.) Now if the training classifications $\langle f(x_1) \ldots f(x_m) \rangle$ are identical to the predictions of the hypothesis, then there is no need to transmit any information about these examples (the receiver can compute these values once it has received the hypothesis). The description length of the classifications given the hypothesis in this case is, therefore, zero. In the case where some examples are misclassified by h, then for each misclassification we need to transmit a message that identifies which example is misclassified (which can be done using at most $\log_2 m$ bits) as well as its correct classification (which can be done using at most $\log_2 k$ bits, where k is the number of possible classifications). The hypothesis h_{MDL} under the encodings C_1 and C_2 is just the one that minimizes the sum of these description lengths.

Thus the MDL principle provides a way of trading off hypothesis complexity for the number of errors committed by the hypothesis. It might select a shorter hypothesis that makes a few errors over a longer hypothesis that perfectly classifies the training data. Viewed in this light, it provides one method for dealing with the issue of *overfitting* the data.

Quinlan and Rivest (1989) describe experiments applying the MDL principle to choose the best size for a decision tree. They report that the MDL-based method produced learned trees whose accuracy was comparable to that of the standard tree-pruning methods discussed in Chapter 3. Mehta et al. (1995) describe an alternative MDL-based approach to decision tree pruning, and describe experiments in which an MDL-based approach produced results comparable to standard tree-pruning methods.

What shall we conclude from this analysis of the Minimum Description Length principle? Does this prove once and for all that short hypotheses are best? No. What we have shown is only that *if* a representation of hypotheses is chosen so that the size of hypothesis h is $-\log_2 P(h)$, and *if* a representation for exceptions is chosen so that the encoding length of D given h is equal to $-\log_2 P(D|h)$, *then* the MDL principle produces MAP hypotheses. However, to show that we have such a representation we must know all the prior probabilities $P(h)$, as well as the $P(D|h)$. There is no reason to believe that the MDL hypothesis relative to *arbitrary* encodings C_1 and C_2 should be preferred. As a practical matter it might sometimes be easier for a human designer to specify a representation that captures knowledge about the relative probabilities of hypotheses than it is to fully specify the probability of each hypothesis. Descriptions in the literature on the application of MDL to practical learning problems often include arguments providing some form of justification for the encodings chosen for C_1 and C_2.

6.7 BAYES OPTIMAL CLASSIFIER

So far we have considered the question "what is the most probable *hypothesis* given the training data?" In fact, the question that is often of most significance is the closely related question "what is the most probable *classification* of the new instance given the training data?" Although it may seem that this second question can be answered by simply applying the MAP hypothesis to the new instance, in fact it is possible to do better.

To develop some intuitions consider a hypothesis space containing three hypotheses, h_1, h_2, and h_3. Suppose that the posterior probabilities of these hypotheses given the training data are .4, .3, and .3 respectively. Thus, h_1 is the MAP hypothesis. Suppose a new instance x is encountered, which is classified positive by h_1, but negative by h_2 and h_3. Taking all hypotheses into account, the probability that x is positive is .4 (the probability associated with h_1), and the probability that it is negative is therefore .6. The most probable classification (negative) in this case is different from the classification generated by the MAP hypothesis.

In general, the most probable classification of the new instance is obtained by combining the predictions of all hypotheses, weighted by their posterior probabilities. If the possible classification of the new example can take on any value v_j from some set V, then the probability $P(v_j|D)$ that the correct classification for the new instance is v_j, is just

$$P(v_j|D) = \sum_{h_i \in H} P(v_j|h_i)P(h_i|D)$$

The optimal classification of the new instance is the value v_j, for which $P(v_j|D)$ is maximum.

Bayes optimal classification:

$$\underset{v_j \in V}{\operatorname{argmax}} \sum_{h_i \in H} P(v_j|h_i)P(h_i|D) \tag{6.18}$$

To illustrate in terms of the above example, the set of possible classifications of the new instance is $V = \{\oplus, \ominus\}$, and

$$P(h_1|D) = .4,\ \ P(\ominus|h_1) = 0,\ \ P(\oplus|h_1) = 1$$
$$P(h_2|D) = .3,\ \ P(\ominus|h_2) = 1,\ \ P(\oplus|h_2) = 0$$
$$P(h_3|D) = .3,\ \ P(\ominus|h_3) = 1,\ \ P(\oplus|h_3) = 0$$

therefore

$$\sum_{h_i \in H} P(\oplus|h_i)P(h_i|D) = .4$$
$$\sum_{h_i \in H} P(\ominus|h_i)P(h_i|D) = .6$$

and

$$\underset{v_j \in \{\oplus, \ominus\}}{\operatorname{argmax}} \sum_{h_i \in H} P(v_j|h_i)P(h_i|D) = \ominus$$

Any system that classifies new instances according to Equation (6.18) is called a *Bayes optimal classifier*, or Bayes optimal learner. No other classification method using the same hypothesis space and same prior knowledge can outperform this method on average. This method maximizes the probability that the new instance is classified correctly, given the available data, hypothesis space, and prior probabilities over the hypotheses.

For example, in learning boolean concepts using version spaces as in the earlier section, the Bayes optimal classification of a new instance is obtained by taking a weighted vote among all members of the version space, with each candidate hypothesis weighted by its posterior probability.

Note one curious property of the Bayes optimal classifier is that the predictions it makes can correspond to a hypothesis not contained in H! Imagine using Equation (6.18) to classify every instance in X. The labeling of instances defined in this way need not correspond to the instance labeling of any single hypothesis h from H. One way to view this situation is to think of the Bayes optimal classifier as effectively considering a hypothesis space H' different from the space of hypotheses H to which Bayes theorem is being applied. In particular, H' effectively includes hypotheses that perform comparisons between linear combinations of predictions from multiple hypotheses in H.

6.8 GIBBS ALGORITHM

Although the Bayes optimal classifier obtains the best performance that can be achieved from the given training data, it can be quite costly to apply. The expense is due to the fact that it computes the posterior probability for every hypothesis in H and then combines the predictions of each hypothesis to classify each new instance.

An alternative, less optimal method is the Gibbs algorithm (see Opper and Haussler 1991), defined as follows:

1. Choose a hypothesis h from H at random, according to the posterior probability distribution over H.
2. Use h to predict the classification of the next instance x.

Given a new instance to classify, the Gibbs algorithm simply applies a hypothesis drawn at random according to the current posterior probability distribution. Surprisingly, it can be shown that under certain conditions the expected misclassification error for the Gibbs algorithm is at most twice the expected error of the Bayes optimal classifier (Haussler et al. 1994). More precisely, the expected value is taken over target concepts drawn at random according to the prior probability distribution assumed by the learner. Under this condition, the expected value of the error of the Gibbs algorithm is at worst twice the expected value of the error of the Bayes optimal classifier.

This result has an interesting implication for the concept learning problem described earlier. In particular, it implies that if the learner assumes a uniform prior over H, and if target concepts are in fact drawn from such a distribution when presented to the learner, *then classifying the next instance according to a hypothesis drawn at random from the current version space (according to a uniform distribution), will have expected error at most twice that of the Bayes optimal classifier.* Again, we have an example where a Bayesian analysis of a non-Bayesian algorithm yields insight into the performance of that algorithm.

6.9 NAIVE BAYES CLASSIFIER

One highly practical Bayesian learning method is the naive Bayes learner, often called the *naive Bayes classifier*. In some domains its performance has been shown to be comparable to that of neural network and decision tree learning. This section introduces the naive Bayes classifier; the next section applies it to the practical problem of learning to classify natural language text documents.

The naive Bayes classifier applies to learning tasks where each instance x is described by a conjunction of attribute values and where the target function $f(x)$ can take on any value from some finite set V. A set of training examples of the target function is provided, and a new instance is presented, described by the tuple of attribute values $\langle a_1, a_2 \ldots a_n \rangle$. The learner is asked to predict the target value, or classification, for this new instance.

The Bayesian approach to classifying the new instance is to assign the most probable target value, v_{MAP}, given the attribute values $\langle a_1, a_2 \ldots a_n \rangle$ that describe the instance.

$$v_{MAP} = \underset{v_j \in V}{\operatorname{argmax}} P(v_j | a_1, a_2 \ldots a_n)$$

We can use Bayes theorem to rewrite this expression as

$$\begin{aligned} v_{MAP} &= \underset{v_j \in V}{\operatorname{argmax}} \frac{P(a_1, a_2 \ldots a_n | v_j) P(v_j)}{P(a_1, a_2 \ldots a_n)} \\ &= \underset{v_j \in V}{\operatorname{argmax}} P(a_1, a_2 \ldots a_n | v_j) P(v_j) \end{aligned} \tag{6.19}$$

Now we could attempt to estimate the two terms in Equation (6.19) based on the training data. It is easy to estimate each of the $P(v_j)$ simply by counting the frequency with which each target value v_j occurs in the training data. However, estimating the different $P(a_1, a_2 \ldots a_n | v_j)$ terms in this fashion is not feasible unless we have a very, very large set of training data. The problem is that the number of these terms is equal to the number of possible instances times the number of possible target values. Therefore, we need to see every instance in the instance space many times in order to obtain reliable estimates.

The naive Bayes classifier is based on the simplifying assumption that the attribute values are conditionally independent given the target value. In other words, the assumption is that given the target value of the instance, the probability of observing the conjunction $a_1, a_2 \ldots a_n$ is just the product of the probabilities for the individual attributes: $P(a_1, a_2 \ldots a_n | v_j) = \prod_i P(a_i | v_j)$. Substituting this into Equation (6.19), we have the approach used by the naive Bayes classifier.

Naive Bayes classifier:

$$v_{NB} = \underset{v_j \in V}{\operatorname{argmax}} P(v_j) \prod_i P(a_i | v_j) \tag{6.20}$$

where v_{NB} denotes the target value output by the naive Bayes classifier. Notice that in a naive Bayes classifier the number of distinct $P(a_i | v_j)$ terms that must be estimated from the training data is just the number of distinct attribute values times the number of distinct target values—a much smaller number than if we were to estimate the $P(a_1, a_2 \ldots a_n|v_j)$ terms as first contemplated.

To summarize, the naive Bayes learning method involves a learning step in which the various $P(v_j)$ and $P(a_i|v_j)$ terms are estimated, based on their frequencies over the training data. The set of these estimates corresponds to the learned hypothesis. This hypothesis is then used to classify each new instance by applying the rule in Equation (6.20). Whenever the naive Bayes assumption of conditional independence is satisfied, this naive Bayes classification v_{NB} is identical to the MAP classification.

One interesting difference between the naive Bayes learning method and other learning methods we have considered is that there is no explicit search through the space of possible hypotheses (in this case, the space of possible hypotheses is the space of possible values that can be assigned to the various $P(v_j)$ and $P(a_i|v_j)$ terms). Instead, the hypothesis is formed without searching, simply by counting the frequency of various data combinations within the training examples.

6.9.1 An Illustrative Example

Let us apply the naive Bayes classifier to a concept learning problem we considered during our discussion of decision tree learning: classifying days according to whether someone will play tennis. Table 3.2 from Chapter 3 provides a set of 14 training examples of the target concept $PlayTennis$, where each day is described by the attributes *Outlook, Temperature, Humidity*, and *Wind*. Here we use the naive Bayes classifier and the training data from this table to classify the following novel instance:

$$\langle Outlook = sunny, Temperature = cool, Humidity = high, Wind = strong\rangle$$

Our task is to predict the target value (*yes* or *no*) of the target concept $PlayTennis$ for this new instance. Instantiating Equation (6.20) to fit the current task, the target value v_{NB} is given by

$$\begin{aligned} v_{NB} &= \underset{v_j \in \{yes,no\}}{\operatorname{argmax}} P(v_j) \prod_i P(a_i|v_j) \\ &= \underset{v_j \in \{yes,no\}}{\operatorname{argmax}} P(v_j) \quad P(Outlook = sunny|v_j) P(Temperature = cool|v_j) \\ &\qquad\qquad P(Humidity = high|v_j) P(Wind = strong|v_j) \qquad (6.21) \end{aligned}$$

Notice in the final expression that a_i has been instantiated using the particular attribute values of the new instance. To calculate v_{NB} we now require 10 probabilities that can be estimated from the training data. First, the probabilities of the different target values can easily be estimated based on their frequencies over the 14 training examples

$$P(PlayTennis = yes) = 9/14 = .64$$

$$P(PlayTennis = no) = 5/14 = .36$$

Similarly, we can estimate the conditional probabilities. For example, those for $Wind = strong$ are

$$P(Wind = strong|PlayTennis = yes) = 3/9 = .33$$
$$P(Wind = strong|PlayTennis = no) = 3/5 = .60$$

Using these probability estimates and similar estimates for the remaining attribute values, we calculate v_{NB} according to Equation (6.21) as follows (now omitting attribute names for brevity)

$$P(yes)\ P(sunny|yes)\ P(cool|yes)\ P(high|yes)\ P(strong|yes) = .0053$$
$$P(no)\ P(sunny|no)\ P(cool|no)\ P(high|no)\ P(strong|no) = .0206$$

Thus, the naive Bayes classifier assigns the target value $PlayTennis = no$ to this new instance, based on the probability estimates learned from the training data. Furthermore, by normalizing the above quantities to sum to one we can calculate the conditional probability that the target value is *no*, given the observed attribute values. For the current example, this probability is $\frac{.0206}{.0206+.0053} = .795$.

6.9.1.1 ESTIMATING PROBABILITIES

Up to this point we have estimated probabilities by the fraction of times the event is observed to occur over the total number of opportunities. For example, in the above case we estimated $P(Wind = strong|PlayTennis = no)$ by the fraction $\frac{n_c}{n}$ where $n = 5$ is the total number of training examples for which $PlayTennis = no$, and $n_c = 3$ is the number of these for which $Wind = strong$.

While this observed fraction provides a good estimate of the probability in many cases, it provides poor estimates when n_c is very small. To see the difficulty, imagine that, in fact, the value of $P(Wind = strong|PlayTennis = no)$ is .08 and that we have a sample containing only 5 examples for which $PlayTennis = no$. Then the most probable value for n_c is 0. This raises two difficulties. First, $\frac{n_c}{n}$ produces a biased underestimate of the probability. Second, when this probability estimate is zero, this probability term will dominate the Bayes classifier if the future query contains $Wind = strong$. The reason is that the quantity calculated in Equation (6.20) requires multiplying all the other probability terms by this zero value.

To avoid this difficulty we can adopt a Bayesian approach to estimating the probability, using the *m*-estimate defined as follows.

***m*-estimate of probability:**

$$\frac{n_c + mp}{n + m} \tag{6.22}$$

Here, n_c and n are defined as before, p is our prior estimate of the probability we wish to determine, and m is a constant called the *equivalent sample size,* which determines how heavily to weight p relative to the observed data. A typical method for choosing p in the absence of other information is to assume uniform priors; that is, if an attribute has k possible values we set $p = \frac{1}{k}$. For example, in estimating $P(Wind = strong|PlayTennis = no)$ we note the attribute $Wind$ has two possible values, so uniform priors would correspond to choosing $p = .5$. Note that if m is zero, the m-estimate is equivalent to the simple fraction $\frac{n_c}{n}$. If both n and m are nonzero, then the observed fraction $\frac{n_c}{n}$ and prior p will be combined according to the weight m. The reason m is called the equivalent sample size is that Equation (6.22) can be interpreted as augmenting the n actual observations by an additional m virtual samples distributed according to p.

6.10 AN EXAMPLE: LEARNING TO CLASSIFY TEXT

To illustrate the practical importance of Bayesian learning methods, consider learning problems in which the instances are text documents. For example, we might wish to learn the target concept "electronic news articles that I find interesting," or "pages on the World Wide Web that discuss machine learning topics." In both cases, if a computer could learn the target concept accurately, it could automatically filter the large volume of online text documents to present only the most relevant documents to the user.

We present here a general algorithm for learning to classify text, based on the naive Bayes classifier. Interestingly, probabilistic approaches such as the one described here are among the most effective algorithms currently known for learning to classify text documents. Examples of such systems are described by Lewis (1991), Lang (1995), and Joachims (1996).

The naive Bayes algorithm that we shall present applies in the following general setting. Consider an instance space X consisting of all possible *text documents* (i.e., all possible strings of words and punctuation of all possible lengths). We are given training examples of some unknown target function $f(x)$, which can take on any value from some finite set V. The task is to learn from these training examples to predict the target value for subsequent text documents. For illustration, we will consider the target function classifying documents as interesting or uninteresting to a particular person, using the target values $like$ and $dislike$ to indicate these two classes.

The two main design issues involved in applying the naive Bayes classifier to such text classification problems are first to decide how to represent an arbitrary text document in terms of attribute values, and second to decide how to estimate the probabilities required by the naive Bayes classifier.

Our approach to representing arbitrary text documents is disturbingly simple: Given a text document, such as this paragraph, we define an attribute for each word position in the document and define the value of that attribute to be the English word found in that position. Thus, the current paragraph would be described by 111 attribute values, corresponding to the 111 word positions. The value of the first attribute is the word "our," the value of the second attribute is the word "approach," and so on. Notice that long text documents will require a larger number of attributes than short documents. As we shall see, this will not cause us any trouble.

Given this representation for text documents, we can now apply the naive Bayes classifier. For the sake of concreteness, let us assume we are given a set of 700 training documents that a friend has classified as *dislike* and another 300 she has classified as *like*. We are now given a new document and asked to classify it. Again, for concreteness let us assume the new text document is the preceding paragraph. In this case, we instantiate Equation (6.20) to calculate the naive Bayes classification as

$$\begin{aligned} v_{NB} &= \underset{v_j \in \{like, dislike\}}{\operatorname{argmax}} \; P(v_j) \prod_{i=1}^{111} P(a_i|v_j) \\ &= \underset{v_j \in \{like, dislike\}}{\operatorname{argmax}} \; P(v_j) \; P(a_1 = \text{“}our\text{”}|v_j) P(a_2 = \text{“}approach\text{”}|v_j) \\ &\qquad \ldots \; P(a_{111} = \text{“}trouble\text{”}|v_j) \end{aligned}$$

To summarize, the naive Bayes classification v_{NB} is the classification that maximizes the probability of observing the words that were actually found in the document, subject to the usual naive Bayes independence assumption. The independence assumption $P(a_1, \ldots a_{111}|v_j) = \prod_1^{111} P(a_i|v_j)$ states in this setting that the word probabilities for one text position are independent of the words that occur in other positions, given the document classification v_j. Note this assumption is clearly incorrect. For example, the probability of observing the word "learning" in some position may be greater if the preceding word is "machine." Despite the obvious inaccuracy of this independence assumption, we have little choice but to make it—without it, the number of probability terms that must be computed is prohibitive. Fortunately, in practice the naive Bayes learner performs remarkably well in many text classification problems despite the incorrectness of this independence assumption. Domingos and Pazzani (1996) provide an interesting analysis of this fortunate phenomenon.

To calculate v_{NB} using the above expression, we require estimates for the probability terms $P(v_j)$ and $P(a_i = w_k|v_j)$ (here we introduce w_k to indicate the kth word in the English vocabulary). The first of these can easily be estimated based on the fraction of each class in the training data ($P(like) = .3$ and $P(dislike) = .7$ in the current example). As usual, estimating the class conditional probabilities (e.g., $P(a_1 = \text{“}our\text{”}|dislike)$) is more problematic because we must estimate one such probability term for each combination of text position, English word, and target value. Unfortunately, there are approximately 50,000 distinct words in the English vocabulary, 2 possible target values, and 111 text positions in the current example, so we must estimate $2 \cdot 111 \cdot 50,000 \approx 10$ million such terms from the training data.

Fortunately, we can make an additional reasonable assumption that reduces the number of probabilities that must be estimated. In particular, we shall assume the probability of encountering a specific word w_k (e.g., "chocolate") is independent of the specific word position being considered (e.g., a_{23} versus a_{95}). More formally, this amounts to assuming that the attributes are independent and identically distributed, given the target classification; that is, $P(a_i = w_k|v_j) =$

$P(a_m = w_k|v_j)$ for all i, j, k, m. Therefore, we estimate the entire set of probabilities $P(a_1 = w_k|v_j), P(a_2 = w_k|v_j) \ldots$ by the single position-independent probability $P(w_k|v_j)$, which we will use regardless of the word position. The net effect is that we now require only $2 \cdot 50,000$ distinct terms of the form $P(w_k|v_j)$. This is still a large number, but manageable. Notice in cases where training data is limited, the primary advantage of making this assumption is that it increases the number of examples available to estimate each of the required probabilities, thereby increasing the reliability of the estimates.

To complete the design of our learning algorithm, we must still choose a method for estimating the probability terms. We adopt the m-estimate—Equation (6.22)—with uniform priors and with m equal to the size of the word vocabulary. Thus, the estimate for $P(w_k|v_j)$ will be

$$\frac{n_k + 1}{n + |Vocabulary|}$$

where n is the total number of word positions in all training examples whose target value is v_j, n_k is the number of times word w_k is found among these n word positions, and $|Vocabulary|$ is the total number of distinct words (and other tokens) found within the training data.

To summarize, the final algorithm uses a naive Bayes classifier together with the assumption that the probability of word occurrence is independent of position within the text. The final algorithm is shown in Table 6.2. Notice the algorithm is quite simple. During learning, the procedure LEARN_NAIVE_BAYES_TEXT examines all training documents to extract the vocabulary of all words and tokens that appear in the text, then counts their frequencies among the different target classes to obtain the necessary probability estimates. Later, given a new document to be classified, the procedure CLASSIFY_NAIVE_BAYES_TEXT uses these probability estimates to calculate v_{NB} according to Equation (6.20). Note that any words appearing in the new document that were not observed in the training set are simply ignored by CLASSIFY_NAIVE_BAYES_TEXT. Code for this algorithm, as well as training data sets, are available on the World Wide Web at http://www.cs.cmu.edu/~tom/book.html.

6.10.1 Experimental Results

How effective is the learning algorithm of Table 6.2? In one experiment (see Joachims 1996), a minor variant of this algorithm was applied to the problem of classifying usenet news articles. The target classification for an article in this case was the name of the usenet newsgroup in which the article appeared. One can think of the task as creating a newsgroup posting service that learns to assign documents to the appropriate newsgroup. In the experiment described by Joachims (1996), 20 electronic newsgroups were considered (listed in Table 6.3). Then 1,000 articles were collected from each newsgroup, forming a data set of 20,000 documents. The naive Bayes algorithm was then applied using two-thirds of these 20,000 documents as training examples, and performance was measured

LEARN_NAIVE_BAYES_TEXT(*Examples*, *V*)

Examples is a set of text documents along with their target values. V is the set of all possible target values. This function learns the probability terms $P(w_k|v_j)$, describing the probability that a randomly drawn word from a document in class v_j will be the English word w_k. It also learns the class prior probabilities $P(v_j)$.

1. collect all words, punctuation, and other tokens that occur in Examples

- *Vocabulary* ← the set of all distinct words and other tokens occurring in any text document from *Examples*

2. calculate the required $P(v_j)$ and $P(w_k|v_j)$ probability terms

- For each target value v_j in V do
  - $docs_j$ ← the subset of documents from *Examples* for which the target value is v_j
  - $P(v_j) \leftarrow \frac{|docs_j|}{|Examples|}$
  - $Text_j$ ← a single document created by concatenating all members of $docs_j$
  - n ← total number of distinct word positions in $Text_j$
  - for each word w_k in *Vocabulary*
    - n_k ← number of times word w_k occurs in $Text_j$
    - $P(w_k|v_j) \leftarrow \frac{n_k+1}{n+|Vocabulary|}$

CLASSIFY_NAIVE_BAYES_TEXT(*Doc*)

Return the estimated target value for the document Doc. a_i denotes the word found in the ith position within Doc.

- *positions* ← all word positions in *Doc* that contain tokens found in *Vocabulary*
- Return v_{NB}, where

$$v_{NB} = \underset{v_j \in V}{\operatorname{argmax}} P(v_j) \prod_{i \in positions} P(a_i|v_j)$$

TABLE 6.2
Naive Bayes algorithms for learning and classifying text. In addition to the usual naive Bayes assumptions, these algorithms assume the probability of a word occurring is independent of its position within the text.

over the remaining third. Given 20 possible newsgroups, we would expect random guessing to achieve a classification accuracy of approximately 5%. The accuracy achieved by the program was 89%. The algorithm used in these experiments was exactly the algorithm of Table 6.2, with one exception: Only a subset of the words occurring in the documents were included as the value of the *Vocabulary* variable in the algorithm. In particular, the 100 most frequent words were removed (these include words such as "the" and "of"), and any word occurring fewer than three times was also removed. The resulting vocabulary contained approximately 38,500 words.

Similarly impressive results have been achieved by others applying similar statistical learning approaches to text classification. For example, Lang (1995) describes another variant of the naive Bayes algorithm and its application to learning the target concept "usenet articles that I find interesting." He describes the NEWSWEEDER system—a program for reading netnews that allows the user to rate articles as he or she reads them. NEWSWEEDER then uses these rated articles as

comp.graphics	misc.forsale	soc.religion.christian	sci.space
comp.os.ms-windows.misc	rec.autos	talk.politics.guns	sci.crypt
comp.sys.ibm.pc.hardware	rec.motorcycles	talk.politics.mideast	sci.electronics
comp.sys.mac.hardware	rec.sport.baseball	talk.politics.misc	sci.med
comp.windows.x	rec.sport.hockey	talk.religion.misc	
		alt.atheism	

TABLE 6.3
Twenty usenet newsgroups used in the text classification experiment. After training on 667 articles from each newsgroup, a naive Bayes classifier achieved an accuracy of 89% predicting to which newsgroup subsequent articles belonged. Random guessing would produce an accuracy of only 5%.

training examples to learn to predict which subsequent articles will be of interest to the user, so that it can bring these to the user's attention. Lang (1995) reports experiments in which NEWSWEEDER used its learned profile of user interests to suggest the most highly rated new articles each day. By presenting the user with the top 10% of its automatically rated new articles each day, it created a pool of articles containing three to four times as many interesting articles as the general pool of articles read by the user. For example, for one user the fraction of articles rated "interesting" was 16% overall, but was 59% among the articles recommended by NEWSWEEDER.

Several other, non-Bayesian, statistical text learning algorithms are common, many based on similarity metrics initially developed for information retrieval (e.g., see Rocchio 1971; Salton 1991). Additional text learning algorithms are described in Hearst and Hirsh (1996).

6.11 BAYESIAN BELIEF NETWORKS

As discussed in the previous two sections, the naive Bayes classifier makes significant use of the assumption that the values of the attributes $a_1 \ldots a_n$ are conditionally independent given the target value v. This assumption dramatically reduces the complexity of learning the target function. When it is met, the naive Bayes classifier outputs the optimal Bayes classification. However, in many cases this conditional independence assumption is clearly overly restrictive.

A Bayesian belief network describes the probability distribution governing a set of variables by specifying a set of conditional independence assumptions along with a set of conditional probabilities. In contrast to the naive Bayes classifier, which assumes that *all* the variables are conditionally independent given the value of the target variable, Bayesian belief networks allow stating conditional independence assumptions that apply to *subsets* of the variables. Thus, Bayesian belief networks provide an intermediate approach that is less constraining than the global assumption of conditional independence made by the naive Bayes classifier, but more tractable than avoiding conditional independence assumptions altogether. Bayesian belief networks are an active focus of current research, and a variety of algorithms have been proposed for learning them and for using them for inference.

In this section we introduce the key concepts and the representation of Bayesian belief networks. More detailed treatments are given by Pearl (1988), Russell and Norvig (1995), Heckerman et al. (1995), and Jensen (1996).

In general, a Bayesian belief network describes the probability distribution over a set of variables. Consider an arbitrary set of random variables $Y_1 \ldots Y_n$, where each variable Y_i can take on the set of possible values $V(Y_i)$. We define the *joint space* of the set of variables Y to be the cross product $V(Y_1) \times V(Y_2) \times \ldots V(Y_n)$. In other words, each item in the joint space corresponds to one of the possible assignments of values to the tuple of variables $\langle Y_1 \ldots Y_n \rangle$. The probability distribution over this joint space is called the *joint probability distribution*. The joint probability distribution specifies the probability for each of the possible variable bindings for the tuple $\langle Y_1 \ldots Y_n \rangle$. A Bayesian belief network describes the joint probability distribution for a set of variables.

6.11.1 Conditional Independence

Let us begin our discussion of Bayesian belief networks by defining precisely the notion of conditional independence. Let X, Y, and Z be three discrete-valued random variables. We say that X is *conditionally independent* of Y given Z if the probability distribution governing X is independent of the value of Y given a value for Z; that is, if

$$(\forall x_i, y_j, z_k)\ P(X = x_i | Y = y_j, Z = z_k) = P(X = x_i | Z = z_k)$$

where $x_i \in V(X)$, $y_j \in V(Y)$, and $z_k \in V(Z)$. We commonly write the above expression in abbreviated form as $P(X|Y, Z) = P(X|Z)$. This definition of conditional independence can be extended to sets of variables as well. We say that the set of variables $X_1 \ldots X_l$ is conditionally independent of the set of variables $Y_1 \ldots Y_m$ given the set of variables $Z_1 \ldots Z_n$ if

$$P(X_1 \ldots X_l | Y_1 \ldots Y_m, Z_1 \ldots Z_n) = P(X_1 \ldots X_l | Z_1 \ldots Z_n)$$

Note the correspondence between this definition and our use of conditional independence in the definition of the naive Bayes classifier. The naive Bayes classifier assumes that the instance attribute A_1 is conditionally independent of instance attribute A_2 given the target value V. This allows the naive Bayes classifier to calculate $P(A_1, A_2|V)$ in Equation (6.20) as follows

$$P(A_1, A_2|V) = P(A_1|A_2, V)P(A_2|V) \tag{6.23}$$

$$= P(A_1|V)P(A_2|V) \tag{6.24}$$

Equation (6.23) is just the general form of the product rule of probability from Table 6.1. Equation (6.24) follows because if A_1 is conditionally independent of A_2 given V, then by our definition of conditional independence $P(A_1|A_2, V) = P(A_1|V)$.

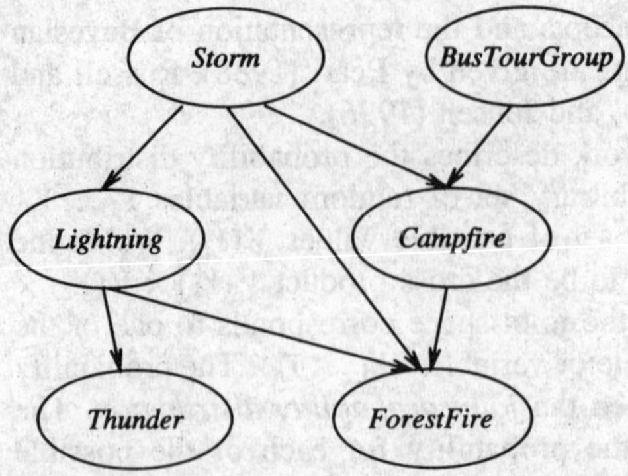

	S,B	S,¬B	¬S,B	¬S,¬B
C	0.4	0.1	0.8	0.2
¬C	0.6	0.9	0.2	0.8

FIGURE 6.3
A Bayesian belief network. The network on the left represents a set of conditional independence assumptions. In particular, each node is asserted to be conditionally independent of its nondescendants, given its immediate parents. Associated with each node is a conditional probability table, which specifies the conditional distribution for the variable given its immediate parents in the graph. The conditional probability table for the *Campfire* node is shown at the right, where *Campfire* is abbreviated to *C*, *Storm* abbreviated to *S*, and *BusTourGroup* abbreviated to *B*.

6.11.2 Representation

A *Bayesian belief network* (Bayesian network for short) represents the joint probability distribution for a set of variables. For example, the Bayesian network in Figure 6.3 represents the joint probability distribution over the boolean variables *Storm, Lightning, Thunder, ForestFire, Campfire*, and *BusTourGroup*. In general, a Bayesian network represents the joint probability distribution by specifying a set of conditional independence assumptions (represented by a directed acyclic graph), together with sets of local conditional probabilities. Each variable in the joint space is represented by a node in the Bayesian network. For each variable two types of information are specified. First, the network arcs represent the assertion that the variable is conditionally independent of its nondescendants in the network given its immediate predecessors in the network. We say X is a *descendant* of Y if there is a directed path from Y to X. Second, a conditional probability table is given for each variable, describing the probability distribution for that variable given the values of its immediate predecessors. The joint probability for any desired assignment of values $\langle y_1, \ldots, y_n \rangle$ to the tuple of network variables $\langle Y_1 \ldots Y_n \rangle$ can be computed by the formula

$$P(y_1, \ldots, y_n) = \prod_{i=1}^{n} P(y_i | Parents(Y_i))$$

where $Parents(Y_i)$ denotes the set of immediate predecessors of Y_i in the network. Note the values of $P(y_i | Parents(Y_i))$ are precisely the values stored in the conditional probability table associated with node Y_i.

To illustrate, the Bayesian network in Figure 6.3 represents the joint probability distribution over the boolean variables *Storm, Lightning, Thunder, Forest-*

Fire, *Campfire*, and *BusTourGroup*. Consider the node *Campfire*. The network nodes and arcs represent the assertion that *Campfire* is conditionally independent of its nondescendants *Lightning* and *Thunder*, given its immediate parents *Storm* and *BusTourGroup*. This means that once we know the value of the variables *Storm* and *BusTourGroup*, the variables *Lightning* and *Thunder* provide no additional information about *Campfire*. The right side of the figure shows the conditional probability table associated with the variable *Campfire*. The top left entry in this table, for example, expresses the assertion that

$$P(Campfire = True|Storm = True, BusTourGroup = True) = 0.4$$

Note this table provides only the conditional probabilities of *Campfire* given its parent variables *Storm* and *BusTourGroup*. The set of local conditional probability tables for all the variables, together with the set of conditional independence assumptions described by the network, describe the full joint probability distribution for the network.

One attractive feature of Bayesian belief networks is that they allow a convenient way to represent causal knowledge such as the fact that *Lightning* causes *Thunder*. In the terminology of conditional independence, we express this by stating that *Thunder* is conditionally independent of other variables in the network, given the value of *Lightning*. Note this conditional independence assumption is implied by the arcs in the Bayesian network of Figure 6.3.

6.11.3 Inference

We might wish to use a Bayesian network to infer the value of some target variable (e.g., *ForestFire*) given the observed values of the other variables. Of course, given that we are dealing with random variables it will not generally be correct to assign the target variable a single determined value. What we really wish to infer is the probability distribution for the target variable, which specifies the probability that it will take on each of its possible values given the observed values of the other variables. This inference step can be straightforward if values for all of the other variables in the network are known exactly. In the more general case we may wish to infer the probability distribution for some variable (e.g., *ForestFire*) given observed values for only a subset of the other variables (e.g., *Thunder* and *BusTourGroup* may be the only observed values available). In general, a Bayesian network can be used to compute the probability distribution for any subset of network variables given the values or distributions for any subset of the remaining variables.

Exact inference of probabilities in general for an arbitrary Bayesian network is known to be NP-hard (Cooper 1990). Numerous methods have been proposed for probabilistic inference in Bayesian networks, including exact inference methods and approximate inference methods that sacrifice precision to gain efficiency. For example, Monte Carlo methods provide approximate solutions by randomly sampling the distributions of the unobserved variables (Pradham and Dagum 1996). In theory, even approximate inference of probabilities in Bayesian networks can be NP-hard (Dagum and Luby 1993). Fortunately, in practice approximate methods have been shown to be useful in many cases. Discussions of inference methods for Bayesian networks are provided by Russell and Norvig (1995) and by Jensen (1996).

6.11.4 Learning Bayesian Belief Networks

Can we devise effective algorithms for learning Bayesian belief networks from training data? This question is a focus of much current research. Several different settings for this learning problem can be considered. First, the network structure might be given in advance, or it might have to be inferred from the training data. Second, all the network variables might be directly observable in each training example, or some might be unobservable.

In the case where the network structure is given in advance and the variables are fully observable in the training examples, learning the conditional probability tables is straightforward. We simply estimate the conditional probability table entries just as we would for a naive Bayes classifier.

In the case where the network structure is given but only some of the variable values are observable in the training data, the learning problem is more difficult. This problem is somewhat analogous to learning the weights for the hidden units in an artificial neural network, where the input and output node values are given but the hidden unit values are left unspecified by the training examples. In fact, Russell et al. (1995) propose a similar gradient ascent procedure that learns the entries in the conditional probability tables. This gradient ascent procedure searches through a space of hypotheses that corresponds to the set of all possible entries for the conditional probability tables. The objective function that is maximized during gradient ascent is the probability $P(D|h)$ of the observed training data D given the hypothesis h. By definition, this corresponds to searching for the maximum likelihood hypothesis for the table entries.

6.11.5 Gradient Ascent Training of Bayesian Networks

The gradient ascent rule given by Russell et al. (1995) maximizes $P(D|h)$ by following the gradient of $\ln P(D|h)$ with respect to the parameters that define the conditional probability tables of the Bayesian network. Let w_{ijk} denote a single entry in one of the conditional probability tables. In particular, let w_{ijk} denote the conditional probability that the network variable Y_i will take on the value y_{ij} given that its immediate parents U_i take on the values given by u_{ik}. For example, if w_{ijk} is the top right entry in the conditional probability table in Figure 6.3, then Y_i is the variable *Campfire*, U_i is the tuple of its parents $\langle Storm, BusTourGroup\rangle$, $y_{ij} = True$, and $u_{ik} = \langle False, False\rangle$. The gradient of $\ln P(D|h)$ is given by the derivatives $\frac{\partial \ln P(D|h)}{\partial w_{ijk}}$ for each of the w_{ijk}. As we show below, each of these derivatives can be calculated as

$$\frac{\partial \ln P(D|h)}{\partial w_{ij}} = \sum_{d \in D} \frac{P(Y_i = y_{ij}, U_i = u_{ik}|d)}{w_{ijk}} \tag{6.25}$$

For example, to calculate the derivative of $\ln P(D|h)$ with respect to the upper-rightmost entry in the table of Figure 6.3 we will have to calculate the quantity $P(Campfire = True, Storm = False, BusTourGroup = False|d)$ for each training example d in D. When these variables are unobservable for the training example d, this required probability can be calculated from the observed variables in d using standard Bayesian network inference. In fact, these required quantities are easily derived from the calculations performed during most Bayesian network inference, so learning can be performed at little additional cost whenever the Bayesian network is used for inference and new evidence is subsequently obtained.

Below we derive Equation (6.25) following Russell et al. (1995). The remainder of this section may be skipped on a first reading without loss of continuity. To simplify notation, in this derivation we will write the abbreviation $P_h(D)$ to represent $P(D|h)$. Thus, our problem is to derive the gradient defined by the set of derivatives $\frac{\partial P_h(D)}{\partial w_{ijk}}$ for all i, j, and k. Assuming the training examples d in the data set D are drawn independently, we write this derivative as

$$\begin{aligned}\frac{\partial \ln P_h(D)}{\partial w_{ijk}} &= \frac{\partial}{\partial w_{ijk}} \ln \prod_{d \in D} P_h(d) \\ &= \sum_{d \in D} \frac{\partial \ln P_h(d)}{\partial w_{ijk}} \\ &= \sum_{d \in D} \frac{1}{P_h(d)} \frac{\partial P_h(d)}{\partial w_{ijk}}\end{aligned}$$

This last step makes use of the general equality $\frac{\partial \ln f(x)}{\partial x} = \frac{1}{f(x)} \frac{\partial f(x)}{\partial x}$. We can now introduce the values of the variables Y_i and $U_i = Parents(Y_i)$, by summing over their possible values $y_{ij'}$ and $u_{ik'}$.

$$\begin{aligned}\frac{\partial \ln P_h(D)}{\partial w_{ijk}} &= \sum_{d \in D} \frac{1}{P_h(d)} \frac{\partial}{\partial w_{ijk}} \sum_{j',k'} P_h(d|y_{ij'}, u_{ik'}) P_h(y_{ij'}, u_{ik'}) \\ &= \sum_{d \in D} \frac{1}{P_h(d)} \frac{\partial}{\partial w_{ijk}} \sum_{j',k'} P_h(d|y_{ij'}, u_{ik'}) P_h(y_{ij'}|u_{ik'}) P_h(u_{ik'})\end{aligned}$$

This last step follows from the product rule of probability, Table 6.1. Now consider the rightmost sum in the final expression above. Given that $w_{ijk} \equiv P_h(y_{ij}|u_{ik})$, the only term in this sum for which $\frac{\partial}{\partial w_{ijk}}$ is nonzero is the term for which $j' = j$ and $i' = i$. Therefore

$$\begin{aligned}\frac{\partial \ln P_h(D)}{\partial w_{ijk}} &= \sum_{d \in D} \frac{1}{P_h(d)} \frac{\partial}{\partial w_{ijk}} P_h(d|y_{ij}, u_{ik}) P_h(y_{ij}|u_{ik}) P_h(u_{ik}) \\ &= \sum_{d \in D} \frac{1}{P_h(d)} \frac{\partial}{\partial w_{ijk}} P_h(d|y_{ij}, u_{ik}) w_{ijk} P_h(u_{ik}) \\ &= \sum_{d \in D} \frac{1}{P_h(d)} P_h(d|y_{ij}, u_{ik}) P_h(u_{ik})\end{aligned}$$

Applying Bayes theorem to rewrite $P_h(d|y_{ij}, u_{ik})$, we have

$$\begin{aligned}
\frac{\partial \ln P_h(D)}{\partial w_{ijk}} &= \sum_{d \in D} \frac{1}{P_h(d)} \frac{P_h(y_{ij}, u_{ik}|d) P_h(d) P_h(u_{ik})}{P_h(y_{ij}, u_{ik})} \\
&= \sum_{d \in D} \frac{P_h(y_{ij}, u_{ik}|d) P_h(u_{ik})}{P_h(y_{ij}, u_{ik})} \\
&= \sum_{d \in D} \frac{P_h(y_{ij}, u_{ik}|d)}{P_h(y_{ij}|u_{ik})} \\
&= \sum_{d \in D} \frac{P_h(y_{ij}, u_{ik}|d)}{w_{ijk}} \qquad (6.26)
\end{aligned}$$

Thus, we have derived the gradient given in Equation (6.25). There is one more item that must be considered before we can state the gradient ascent training procedure. In particular, we require that as the weights w_{ijk} are updated they must remain valid probabilities in the interval [0,1]. We also require that the sum $\sum_j w_{ijk}$ remains 1 for all i, k. These constraints can be satisfied by updating weights in a two-step process. First we update each w_{ijk} by gradient ascent

$$w_{ijk} \leftarrow w_{ijk} + \eta \sum_{d \in D} \frac{P_h(y_{ij}, u_{ik}|d)}{w_{ijk}}$$

where η is a small constant called the learning rate. Second, we renormalize the weights w_{ijk} to assure that the above constraints are satisfied. As discussed by Russell et al., this process will converge to a locally maximum likelihood hypothesis for the conditional probabilities in the Bayesian network.

As in other gradient-based approaches, this algorithm is guaranteed only to find some local optimum solution. An alternative to gradient ascent is the EM algorithm discussed in Section 6.12, which also finds locally maximum likelihood solutions.

6.11.6 Learning the Structure of Bayesian Networks

Learning Bayesian networks when the network structure is not known in advance is also difficult. Cooper and Herskovits (1992) present a Bayesian scoring metric for choosing among alternative networks. They also present a heuristic search algorithm called K2 for learning network structure when the data is fully observable. Like most algorithms for learning the structure of Bayesian networks, K2 performs a greedy search that trades off network complexity for accuracy over the training data. In one experiment K2 was given a set of 3,000 training examples generated at random from a manually constructed Bayesian network containing 37 nodes and 46 arcs. This particular network described potential anesthesia problems in a hospital operating room. In addition to the data, the program was also given an initial ordering over the 37 variables that was consistent with the partial ordering of variable dependencies in the actual network. The program succeeded in reconstructing the correct Bayesian network structure almost exactly, with the exception of one incorrectly deleted arc and one incorrectly added arc.

Constraint-based approaches to learning Bayesian network structure have also been developed (e.g., Spirtes et al. 1993). These approaches infer independence and dependence relationships from the data, and then use these relationships to construct Bayesian networks. Surveys of current approaches to learning Bayesian networks are provided by Heckerman (1995) and Buntine (1994).

6.12 THE EM ALGORITHM

In many practical learning settings, only a subset of the relevant instance features might be observable. For example, in training or using the Bayesian belief network of Figure 6.3, we might have data where only a subset of the network variables *Storm, Lightning, Thunder, ForestFire, Campfire*, and *BusTourGroup* have been observed. Many approaches have been proposed to handle the problem of learning in the presence of unobserved variables. As we saw in Chapter 3, if some variable is sometimes observed and sometimes not, then we can use the cases for which it has been observed to learn to predict its values when it is not. In this section we describe the EM algorithm (Dempster et al. 1977), a widely used approach to learning in the presence of unobserved variables. The EM algorithm can be used even for variables whose value is never directly observed, provided the general form of the probability distribution governing these variables is known. The EM algorithm has been used to train Bayesian belief networks (see Heckerman 1995) as well as radial basis function networks discussed in Section 8.4. The EM algorithm is also the basis for many unsupervised clustering algorithms (e.g., Cheeseman et al. 1988), and it is the basis for the widely used Baum-Welch forward-backward algorithm for learning Partially Observable Markov Models (Rabiner 1989).

6.12.1 Estimating Means of *k* Gaussians

The easiest way to introduce the EM algorithm is via an example. Consider a problem in which the data D is a set of instances generated by a probability distribution that is a mixture of k distinct Normal distributions. This problem setting is illustrated in Figure 6.4 for the case where $k = 2$ and where the instances are the points shown along the x axis. Each instance is generated using a two-step process. First, one of the k Normal distributions is selected at random. Second, a single random instance x_i is generated according to this selected distribution. This process is repeated to generate a set of data points as shown in the figure. To simplify our discussion, we consider the special case where the selection of the single Normal distribution at each step is based on choosing each with uniform probability, where each of the k Normal distributions has the same variance σ^2, and where σ^2 is known. The learning task is to output a hypothesis $h = \langle \mu_1, \dots \mu_k \rangle$ that describes the means of each of the k distributions. We would like to find

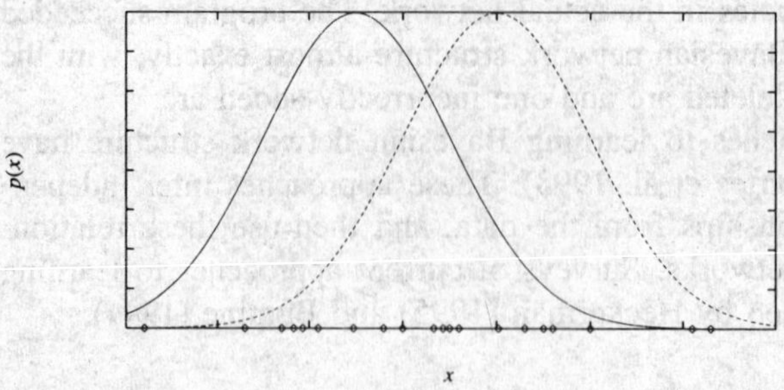

FIGURE 6.4
Instances generated by a mixture of two Normal distributions with identical variance σ. The instances are shown by the points along the x axis. If the means of the Normal distributions are unknown, the EM algorithm can be used to search for their maximum likelihood estimates.

a maximum likelihood hypothesis for these means; that is, a hypothesis h that maximizes $p(D|h)$.

Note it is easy to calculate the maximum likelihood hypothesis for the mean of a single Normal distribution given the observed data instances $x_1, x_2, \ldots, x_m$ drawn from this single distribution. This problem of finding the mean of a single distribution is just a special case of the problem discussed in Section 6.4, Equation (6.6), where we showed that the maximum likelihood hypothesis is the one that minimizes the sum of squared errors over the m training instances. Restating Equation (6.6) using our current notation, we have

$$\mu_{ML} = \underset{\mu}{\operatorname{argmin}} \sum_{i=1}^{m} (x_i - \mu)^2 \tag{6.27}$$

In this case, the sum of squared errors is minimized by the sample mean

$$\mu_{ML} = \frac{1}{m} \sum_{i=1}^{m} x_i \tag{6.28}$$

Our problem here, however, involves a mixture of k different Normal distributions, and we cannot observe which instances were generated by which distribution. Thus, we have a prototypical example of a problem involving hidden variables. In the example of Figure 6.4, we can think of the full description of each instance as the triple $\langle x_i, z_{i1}, z_{i2} \rangle$, where x_i is the observed value of the ith instance and where z_{i1} and z_{i2} indicate which of the two Normal distributions was used to generate the value x_i. In particular, z_{ij} has the value 1 if x_i was created by the jth Normal distribution and 0 otherwise. Here x_i is the observed variable in the description of the instance, and z_{i1} and z_{i2} are hidden variables. If the values of z_{i1} and z_{i2} were observed, we could use Equation (6.27) to solve for the means μ_1 and μ_2. Because they are not, we will instead use the EM algorithm.

Applied to our k-means problem the EM algorithm searches for a maximum likelihood hypothesis by repeatedly re-estimating the expected values of the hidden variables z_{ij} given its current hypothesis $\langle \mu_1 \ldots \mu_k \rangle$, then recalculating the maximum likelihood hypothesis using these expected values for the hidden variables. We will first describe this instance of the EM algorithm, and later state the EM algorithm in its general form.

Applied to the problem of estimating the two means for Figure 6.4, the EM algorithm first initializes the hypothesis to $h = \langle \mu_1, \mu_2 \rangle$, where μ_1 and μ_2 are arbitrary initial values. It then iteratively re-estimates h by repeating the following two steps until the procedure converges to a stationary value for h.

Step 1: Calculate the expected value $E[z_{ij}]$ of each hidden variable z_{ij}, assuming the current hypothesis $h = \langle \mu_1, \mu_2 \rangle$ holds.

Step 2: Calculate a new maximum likelihood hypothesis $h' = \langle \mu'_1, \mu'_2 \rangle$, assuming the value taken on by each hidden variable z_{ij} is its expected value $E[z_{ij}]$ calculated in Step 1. Then replace the hypothesis $h = \langle \mu_1, \mu_2 \rangle$ by the new hypothesis $h' = \langle \mu'_1, \mu'_2 \rangle$ and iterate.

Let us examine how both of these steps can be implemented in practice. Step 1 must calculate the expected value of each z_{ij}. This $E[z_{ij}]$ is just the probability that instance x_i was generated by the jth Normal distribution

$$E[z_{ij}] = \frac{p(x = x_i | \mu = \mu_j)}{\sum_{n=1}^{2} p(x = x_i | \mu = \mu_n)}$$

$$= \frac{e^{-\frac{1}{2\sigma^2}(x_i - \mu_j)^2}}{\sum_{n=1}^{2} e^{-\frac{1}{2\sigma^2}(x_i - \mu_n)^2}}$$

Thus the first step is implemented by substituting the current values $\langle \mu_1, \mu_2 \rangle$ and the observed x_i into the above expression.

In the second step we use the $E[z_{ij}]$ calculated during Step 1 to derive a new maximum likelihood hypothesis $h' = \langle \mu'_1, \mu'_2 \rangle$. As we will discuss later, the maximum likelihood hypothesis in this case is given by

$$\mu_j \leftarrow \frac{1}{m} \sum_{i=1}^{m} E[z_{ij}] \; x_i$$

Note this expression is similar to the sample mean from Equation (6.28) that is used to estimate μ for a single Normal distribution. Our new expression is just the weighted sample mean for μ_j, with each instance weighted by the expectation $E[z_{ij}]$ that it was generated by the jth Normal distribution.

The above algorithm for estimating the means of a mixture of k Normal distributions illustrates the essence of the EM approach: The current hypothesis is used to estimate the unobserved variables, and the expected values of these variables are then used to calculate an improved hypothesis. It can be proved that on each iteration through this loop, the EM algorithm increases the likelihood $P(D|h)$ unless it is at a local maximum. The algorithm thus converges to a local maximum likelihood hypothesis for $\langle \mu_1, \mu_2 \rangle$.

6.12.2 General Statement of EM Algorithm

Above we described an EM algorithm for the problem of estimating means of a mixture of Normal distributions. More generally, the EM algorithm can be applied in many settings where we wish to estimate some set of parameters θ that describe an underlying probability distribution, given only the observed portion of the full data produced by this distribution. In the above two-means example the parameters of interest were $\theta = \langle \mu_1, \mu_2 \rangle$, and the full data were the triples $\langle x_i, z_{i1}, z_{i2} \rangle$ of which only the x_i were observed. In general let $X = \{x_1, \ldots, x_m\}$ denote the observed data in a set of m independently drawn instances, let $Z = \{z_1, \ldots, z_m\}$ denote the unobserved data in these same instances, and let $Y = X \cup Z$ denote the full data. Note the unobserved Z can be treated as a random variable whose probability distribution depends on the unknown parameters θ and on the observed data X. Similarly, Y is a random variable because it is defined in terms of the random variable Z. In the remainder of this section we describe the general form of the EM algorithm. We use h to denote the current hypothesized values of the parameters θ, and h' to denote the revised hypothesis that is estimated on each iteration of the EM algorithm.

The EM algorithm searches for the maximum likelihood hypothesis h' by seeking the h' that maximizes $E[\ln P(Y|h')]$. This expected value is taken over the probability distribution governing Y, which is determined by the unknown parameters θ. Let us consider exactly what this expression signifies. First, $P(Y|h')$ is the likelihood of the full data Y given hypothesis h'. It is reasonable that we wish to find a h' that maximizes some function of this quantity. Second, maximizing the logarithm of this quantity $\ln P(Y|h')$ also maximizes $P(Y|h')$, as we have discussed on several occasions already. Third, we introduce the expected value $E[\ln P(Y|h')]$ because the full data Y is itself a random variable. Given that the full data Y is a combination of the observed data X and unobserved data Z, we must average over the possible values of the unobserved Z, weighting each according to its probability. In other words we take the expected value $E[\ln P(Y|h')]$ over the probability distribution governing the random variable Y. The distribution governing Y is determined by the completely known values for X, plus the distribution governing Z.

What is the probability distribution governing Y? In general we will not know this distribution because it is determined by the parameters θ that we are trying to estimate. Therefore, the EM algorithm uses its current hypothesis h in place of the actual parameters θ to estimate the distribution governing Y. Let us define a function $Q(h'|h)$ that gives $E[\ln P(Y|h')]$ as a function of h', under the assumption that $\theta = h$ and given the observed portion X of the full data Y.

$$Q(h'|h) = E[\ln p(Y|h')|h, X]$$

We write this function Q in the form $Q(h'|h)$ to indicate that it is defined in part by the assumption that the current hypothesis h is equal to θ. In its general form, the EM algorithm repeats the following two steps until convergence:

Step 1: *Estimation (E) step:* Calculate $Q(h'|h)$ using the current hypothesis h and the observed data X to estimate the probability distribution over Y.

$$Q(h'|h) \leftarrow E[\ln P(Y|h')|h, X]$$

Step 2: *Maximization (M) step:* Replace hypothesis h by the hypothesis h' that maximizes this Q function.

$$h \leftarrow \underset{h'}{\operatorname{argmax}}\, Q(h'|h)$$

When the function Q is continuous, the EM algorithm converges to a stationary point of the likelihood function $P(Y|h')$. When this likelihood function has a single maximum, EM will converge to this global maximum likelihood estimate for h'. Otherwise, it is guaranteed only to converge to a local maximum. In this respect, EM shares some of the same limitations as other optimization methods such as gradient descent, line search, and conjugate gradient discussed in Chapter 4.

6.12.3 Derivation of the k Means Algorithm

To illustrate the general EM algorithm, let us use it to derive the algorithm given in Section 6.12.1 for estimating the means of a mixture of k Normal distributions. As discussed above, the k-means problem is to estimate the parameters $\theta = \langle \mu_1 \ldots \mu_k \rangle$ that define the means of the k Normal distributions. We are given the observed data $X = \{\langle x_i \rangle\}$. The hidden variables $Z = \{\langle z_{i1}, \ldots, z_{ik} \rangle\}$ in this case indicate which of the k Normal distributions was used to generate x_i.

To apply EM we must derive an expression for $Q(h|h')$ that applies to our k-means problem. First, let us derive an expression for $\ln p(Y|h')$. Note the probability $p(y_i|h')$ of a single instance $y_i = \langle x_i, z_{i1}, \ldots z_{ik} \rangle$ of the full data can be written

$$p(y_i|h') = p(x_i, z_{i1}, \ldots, z_{ik}|h') = \frac{1}{\sqrt{2\pi\sigma^2}} e^{-\frac{1}{2\sigma^2} \sum_{j=1}^{k} z_{ij}(x_i - \mu_j')^2}$$

To verify this note that only one of the z_{ij} can have the value 1, and all others must be 0. Therefore, this expression gives the probability distribution for x_i generated by the selected Normal distribution. Given this probability for a single instance $p(y_i|h')$, the logarithm of the probability $\ln P(Y|h')$ for all m instances in the data is

$$\begin{aligned}
\ln P(Y|h') &= \ln \prod_{i=1}^{m} p(y_i|h') \\
&= \sum_{i=1}^{m} \ln p(y_i|h') \\
&= \sum_{i=1}^{m} \left(\ln \frac{1}{\sqrt{2\pi\sigma^2}} - \frac{1}{2\sigma^2} \sum_{j=1}^{k} z_{ij}(x_i - \mu_j')^2 \right)
\end{aligned}$$

Finally we must take the expected value of this $\ln P(Y|h')$ over the probability distribution governing Y or, equivalently, over the distribution governing the unobserved components z_{ij} of Y. Note the above expression for $\ln P(Y|h')$ is a linear function of these z_{ij}. In general, for any function $f(z)$ that is a *linear* function of z, the following equality holds

$$E[f(z)] = f(E[z])$$

This general fact about linear functions allows us to write

$$\begin{aligned} E[\ln P(Y|h')] &= E\left[\sum_{i=1}^{m}\left(\ln \frac{1}{\sqrt{2\pi\sigma^2}} - \frac{1}{2\sigma^2}\sum_{j=1}^{k} z_{ij}(x_i - \mu_j')^2\right)\right] \\ &= \sum_{i=1}^{m}\left(\ln \frac{1}{\sqrt{2\pi\sigma^2}} - \frac{1}{2\sigma^2}\sum_{j=1}^{k} E[z_{ij}](x_i - \mu_j')^2\right) \end{aligned}$$

To summarize, the function $Q(h'|h)$ for the k means problem is

$$Q(h'|h) = \sum_{i=1}^{m}\left(\ln \frac{1}{\sqrt{2\pi\sigma^2}} - \frac{1}{2\sigma^2}\sum_{j=1}^{k} E[z_{ij}](x_i - \mu_j')^2\right)$$

where $h' = \langle \mu_1', \ldots, \mu_k' \rangle$ and where $E[z_{ij}]$ is calculated based on the current hypothesis h and observed data X. As discussed earlier

$$E[z_{ij}] = \frac{e^{-\frac{1}{2\sigma^2}(x_i - \mu_j)^2}}{\sum_{n=1}^{k} e^{-\frac{1}{2\sigma^2}(x_i - \mu_n)^2}} \tag{6.29}$$

Thus, the first (estimation) step of the EM algorithm defines the Q function based on the estimated $E[z_{ij}]$ terms. The second (maximization) step then finds the values $\mu_1', \ldots, \mu_k'$ that maximize this Q function. In the current case

$$\begin{aligned} \underset{h'}{\operatorname{argmax}}\, Q(h'|h) &= \underset{h'}{\operatorname{argmax}} \sum_{i=1}^{m}\left(\ln \frac{1}{\sqrt{2\pi\sigma^2}} - \frac{1}{2\sigma^2}\sum_{j=1}^{k} E[z_{ij}](x_i - \mu_j')^2\right) \\ &= \underset{h'}{\operatorname{argmin}} \sum_{i=1}^{m}\sum_{j=1}^{k} E[z_{ij}](x_i - \mu_j')^2 \end{aligned} \tag{6.30}$$

Thus, the maximum likelihood hypothesis here minimizes a weighted sum of squared errors, where the contribution of each instance x_i to the error that defines μ_j' is weighted by $E[z_{ij}]$. The quantity given by Equation (6.30) is minimized by setting each μ_j' to the weighted sample mean

$$\mu_j \leftarrow \frac{1}{m}\sum_{i=1}^{m} E[z_{ij}]\ x_i \tag{6.31}$$

Note that Equations (6.29) and (6.31) define the two steps in the k-means algorithm described in Section 6.12.1.

6.13 SUMMARY AND FURTHER READING

The main points of this chapter include:

- Bayesian methods provide the basis for probabilistic learning methods that accommodate (and require) knowledge about the prior probabilities of alternative hypotheses and about the probability of observing various data given the hypothesis. Bayesian methods allow assigning a posterior probability to each candidate hypothesis, based on these assumed priors and the observed data.
- Bayesian methods can be used to determine the most probable hypothesis given the data—the maximum a posteriori (MAP) hypothesis. This is the optimal hypothesis in the sense that no other hypothesis is more likely.
- The Bayes optimal classifier combines the predictions of all alternative hypotheses, weighted by their posterior probabilities, to calculate the most probable classification of each new instance.
- The naive Bayes classifier is a Bayesian learning method that has been found to be useful in many practical applications. It is called "naive" because it incorporates the simplifying assumption that attribute values are conditionally independent, given the classification of the instance. When this assumption is met, the naive Bayes classifier outputs the MAP classification. Even when this assumption is not met, as in the case of learning to classify text, the naive Bayes classifier is often quite effective. Bayesian belief networks provide a more expressive representation for sets of conditional independence assumptions among subsets of the attributes.
- The framework of Bayesian reasoning can provide a useful basis for analyzing certain learning methods that do not directly apply Bayes theorem. For example, under certain conditions it can be shown that minimizing the squared error when learning a real-valued target function corresponds to computing the maximum likelihood hypothesis.
- The Minimum Description Length principle recommends choosing the hypothesis that minimizes the description length of the hypothesis plus the description length of the data given the hypothesis. Bayes theorem and basic results from information theory can be used to provide a rationale for this principle.
- In many practical learning tasks, some of the relevant instance variables may be unobservable. The EM algorithm provides a quite general approach to learning in the presence of unobservable variables. This algorithm begins with an arbitrary initial hypothesis. It then repeatedly calculates the expected values of the hidden variables (assuming the current hypothesis is correct), and then recalculates the maximum likelihood hypothesis (assuming the hidden variables have the expected values calculated by the first step). This procedure converges to a local maximum likelihood hypothesis, along with estimated values for the hidden variables.

There are many good introductory texts on probability and statistics, such as Casella and Berger (1990). Several quick-reference books (e.g., Maisel 1971; Speigel 1991) also provide excellent treatments of the basic notions of probability and statistics relevant to machine learning.

Many of the basic notions of Bayesian classifiers and least-squared error classifiers are discussed by Duda and Hart (1973). Domingos and Pazzani (1996) provide an analysis of conditions under which naive Bayes will output optimal classifications, even when its independence assumption is violated (the key here is that there are conditions under which it will output optimal classifications even when the associated posterior probability estimates are incorrect).

Cestnik (1990) provides a discussion of using the m-estimate to estimate probabilities.

Experimental results comparing various Bayesian approaches to decision tree learning and other algorithms can be found in Michie et al. (1994). Chauvin and Rumelhart (1995) provide a Bayesian analysis of neural network learning based on the BACKPROPAGATION algorithm.

A discussion of the Minimum Description Length principle can be found in Rissanen (1983, 1989). Quinlan and Rivest (1989) describe its use in avoiding overfitting in decision trees.

EXERCISES

6.1. Consider again the example application of Bayes rule in Section 6.2.1. Suppose the doctor decides to order a second laboratory test for the same patient, and suppose the second test returns a positive result as well. What are the posterior probabilities of *cancer* and $\neg$*cancer* following these two tests? Assume that the two tests are independent.

6.2. In the example of Section 6.2.1 we computed the posterior probability of cancer by normalizing the quantities $P(+|cancer) \cdot P(cancer)$ and $P(+|\neg cancer) \cdot P(\neg cancer)$ so that they summed to one. Use Bayes theorem and the theorem of total probability (see Table 6.1) to prove that this method is valid (i.e., that normalizing in this way yields the correct value for $P(cancer|+)$).

6.3. Consider the concept learning algorithm $FindG$, which outputs a maximally general consistent hypothesis (e.g., some maximally general member of the version space).

(*a*) Give a distribution for $P(h)$ and $P(D|h)$ under which $FindG$ is guaranteed to output a MAP hypothesis.

(*b*) Give a distribution for $P(h)$ and $P(D|h)$ under which $FindG$ is not guaranteed to output a MAP hypothesis.

(*c*) Give a distribution for $P(h)$ and $P(D|h)$ under which $FindG$ is guaranteed to output a ML hypothesis but not a MAP hypothesis.

6.4. In the analysis of concept learning in Section 6.3 we assumed that the sequence of instances $\langle x_1 \ldots x_m \rangle$ was held fixed. Therefore, in deriving an expression for $P(D|h)$ we needed only consider the probability of observing the sequence of target values $\langle d_1 \ldots d_m \rangle$ for this fixed instance sequence. Consider the more general setting in which the instances are not held fixed, but are drawn independently from some probability distribution defined over the instance space X. The data D must now be described as the set of ordered pairs $\{\langle x_i, d_i \rangle\}$, and $P(D|h)$ must now reflect the probability of encountering the specific instance x_1, as well as the probability of the observed target value d_i. Show that Equation (6.5) holds even under this more general setting. Hint: Consider the analysis of Section 6.5.

6.5. Consider the Minimum Description Length principle applied to the hypothesis space H consisting of conjunctions of up to n boolean attributes (e.g., $Sunny \wedge Warm$). Assume each hypothesis is encoded simply by listing the attributes present in the hypothesis, where the number of bits needed to encode any one of the n boolean attributes is $\log_2 n$. Suppose the encoding of an example given the hypothesis uses zero bits if the example is consistent with the hypothesis and uses $\log_2 m$ bits otherwise (to indicate which of the m examples was misclassified—the correct classification can be inferred to be the opposite of that predicted by the hypothesis).

(*a*) Write down the expression for the quantity to be minimized according to the Minimum Description Length principle.

(*b*) Is it possible to construct a set of training data such that a consistent hypothesis exists, but MDL chooses a less consistent hypothesis? If so, give such a training set. If not, explain why not.

(*c*) Give probability distributions for $P(h)$ and $P(D|h)$ such that the above MDL algorithm outputs MAP hypotheses.

6.6. Draw the Bayesian belief network that represents the conditional independence assumptions of the naive Bayes classifier for the *PlayTennis* problem of Section 6.9.1. Give the conditional probability table associated with the node *Wind*.

REFERENCES

Buntine W. L. (1994). Operations for learning with graphical models. *Journal of Artificial Intelligence Research*, 2, 159–225. http://www.cs.washington.edu/research/jair/home.html.

Casella, G., & Berger, R. L. (1990). *Statistical inference*. Pacific Grove, CA: Wadsworth & Brooks/Cole.

Cestnik, B. (1990). Estimating probabilities: A crucial task in machine learning. *Proceedings of the Ninth European Conference on Artificial Intelligence* (pp. 147–149). London: Pitman.

Chauvin, Y., & Rumelhart, D. (1995). *Backpropagation: Theory, architectures, and applications*, (edited collection). Hillsdale, NJ: Lawrence Erlbaum Assoc.

Cheeseman, P., Kelly, J., Self, M., Stutz, J., Taylor, W., & Freeman, D. (1988). AUTOCLASS: A bayesian classification system. *Proceedings of AAAI 1988* (pp. 607–611).

Cooper, G. (1990). Computational complexity of probabilistic inference using Bayesian belief networks (research note). *Artificial Intelligence*, 42, 393–405.

Cooper, G., & Herskovits, E. (1992). A Bayesian method for the induction of probabilistic networks from data. *Machine Learning*, 9, 309–347.

Dagum, P., & Luby, M. (1993). Approximating probabilistic reasoning in Bayesian belief networks is NP-hard. *Artificial Intelligence*, 60(1), 141–153.

Dempster, A. P., Laird, N. M., & Rubin, D. B. (1977). Maximum likelihood from incomplete data via the EM algorithm. *Journal of the Royal Statistical Society*, Series B, 39(1), 1–38.

Domingos, P., & Pazzani, M. (1996). Beyond independence: Conditions for the optimality of the simple Bayesian classifier. *Proceedings of the 13th International Conference on Machine Learning* (pp. 105–112).

Duda, R. O., & Hart, P. E. (1973). *Pattern classification and scene analysis*. New York: John Wiley & Sons.

Hearst, M., & Hirsh, H. (Eds.) (1996). Papers from the AAAI Spring Symposium on Machine Learning in Information Access, Stanford, March 25–27. http://www.parc.xerox.com/istl/projects/mlia/

Heckerman, D., Geiger, D., & Chickering, D. (1995) Learning Bayesian networks: The combination of knowledge and statistical data. *Machine Learning*, 20, 197. Kluwer Academic Publishers.

Jensen, F. V. (1996). *An introduction to Bayesian networks*. New York: Springer Verlag.

Joachims, T. (1996). *A probabilistic analysis of the Rocchio algorithm with TFIDF for text categorization*, (Computer Science Technical Report CMU-CS-96-118). Carnegie Mellon University.

Lang, K. (1995). Newsweeder: Learning to filter netnews. In Prieditis and Russell (Eds.), *Proceedings of the 12th International Conference on Machine Learning* (pp. 331–339). San Francisco: Morgan Kaufmann Publishers.

Lewis, D. (1991). *Representation and learning in information retrieval*, (Ph.D. thesis), (COINS Technical Report 91-93). Dept. of Computer and Information Science, University of Massachusetts.

Madigan, D., & Rafferty, A. (1994). Model selection and accounting for model uncertainty in graphical models using Occam's window. *Journal of the American Statistical Association*, 89, 1535–1546.

Maisel, L. (1971). *Probability, statistics, and random processes*. Simon and Schuster Tech Outlines. New York: Simon and Schuster.

Mehta, M., Rissanen, J., & Agrawal, R. (1995). MDL-based decision tree pruning. In U. M. Fayyard and R. Uthurusamy (Eds.), *Proceedings of the First International Conference on Knowledge Discovery and Data Mining*. Menlo Park, CA: AAAI Press.

Michie, D., Spiegelhalter, D. J., & Taylor, C. C. (1994). *Machine learning, neural and statistical classification*, (edited collection). New York: Ellis Horwood.

Opper, M., & Haussler, D. (1991). Generalization performance of Bayes optimal prediction algorithm for learning a perception. *Physics Review Letters*, 66, 2677–2681.

Pearl, J. (1988). *Probabilistic reasoning in intelligent systems: Networks of plausible inference*. San Mateo, CA: Morgan-Kaufmann.

Pradham, M., & Dagum, P. (1996). Optimal Monte Carlo estimation of belief network inference. In *Proceedings of the Conference on Uncertainty in Artificial Intelligence* (pp. 446–453).

Quinlan, J. R., & Rivest, R. (1989). Inferring decision trees using the minimum description length principle. *Information and Computation*, 80, 227–248.

Rabiner, L. R. (1989). A tutorial on hidden Markov models and selected applications in speech recognition. *Proceedings of the IEEE*, 77(2), 257–286.

Rissanen, J. (1983). A universal prior for integers and estimation by minimum description length. *The Annals of Statistics*, 11(2), 416–431.

Rissanen, J., (1989). *Stochastic complexity in statistical inquiry*. New Jersey: World Scientific Pub.

Rissanen, J. (1991). *Information theory and neural nets*. IBM Research Report RJ 8438 (76446), IBM Thomas J. Watson Research Center, Yorktown Heights, NY.

Rocchio, J. (1971). Relevance feedback in information retrieval. In *The SMART retrieval system: Experiments in automatic document processing*, (Chap. 14, pp. 313–323). Englewood Cliffs, NJ: Prentice-Hall.

Russell, S., & Norvig, P. (1995). *Artificial intelligence: A modern approach*. Englewood Cliffs, NJ: Prentice-Hall.

Russell, S., Binder, J., Koller, D., & Kanazawa, K. (1995). Local learning in probabilistic networks with hidden variables. *Proceedings of the 14th International Joint Conference on Artificial Intelligence*, Montreal. San Francisco: Morgan Kaufmann.

Salton, G. (1991). Developments in automatic text retrieval. *Science*, 253, 974–979.

Shannon, C. E., & Weaver, W. (1949). *The mathematical theory of communication*. Urbana: University of Illinois Press.

Speigel, M. R. (1991). *Theory and problems of probability and statistics*. Schaum's Outline Series. New York: McGraw Hill.

Spirtes, P., Glymour, C., & Scheines, R. (1993). *Causation, prediction, and search*. New York: Springer Verlag. http://hss.cmu.edu/html/departments/philosophy/TETRAD.BOOK/book.html

CHAPTER 7

COMPUTATIONAL LEARNING THEORY

This chapter presents a theoretical characterization of the difficulty of several types of machine learning problems and the capabilities of several types of machine learning algorithms. This theory seeks to answer questions such as "Under what conditions is successful learning possible and impossible?" and "Under what conditions is a particular learning algorithm assured of learning successfully?" Two specific frameworks for analyzing learning algorithms are considered. Within the probably approximately correct (PAC) framework, we identify classes of hypotheses that can and cannot be learned from a polynomial number of training examples and we define a natural measure of complexity for hypothesis spaces that allows bounding the number of training examples required for inductive learning. Within the mistake bound framework, we examine the number of training errors that will be made by a learner before it determines the correct hypothesis.

7.1 INTRODUCTION

When studying machine learning it is natural to wonder what general laws may govern machine (and nonmachine) learners. Is it possible to identify classes of learning problems that are inherently difficult or easy, independent of the learning algorithm? Can one characterize the number of training examples necessary or sufficient to assure successful learning? How is this number affected if the learner is allowed to pose queries to the trainer, versus observing a random sample of training examples? Can one characterize the number of mistakes that a learner will make before learning the target function? Can one characterize the inherent computational complexity of classes of learning problems?

Although general answers to all these questions are not yet known, fragments of a computational theory of learning have begun to emerge. This chapter presents key results from this theory, providing answers to these questions within particular problem settings. We focus here on the problem of inductively learning an unknown target function, given only training examples of this target function and a space of candidate hypotheses. Within this setting, we will be chiefly concerned with questions such as how many training examples are sufficient to successfully learn the target function, and how many mistakes will the learner make before succeeding. As we shall see, it is possible to set quantitative bounds on these measures, depending on attributes of the learning problem such as:

- the size or complexity of the hypothesis space considered by the learner
- the accuracy to which the target concept must be approximated
- the probability that the learner will output a successful hypothesis
- the manner in which training examples are presented to the learner

For the most part, we will focus not on individual learning algorithms, but rather on broad classes of learning algorithms characterized by the hypothesis spaces they consider, the presentation of training examples, etc. Our goal is to answer questions such as:

- *Sample complexity.* How many training examples are needed for a learner to converge (with high probability) to a successful hypothesis?
- *Computational complexity.* How much computational effort is needed for a learner to converge (with high probability) to a successful hypothesis?
- *Mistake bound.* How many training examples will the learner misclassify before converging to a successful hypothesis?

Note there are many specific settings in which we could pursue such questions. For example, there are various ways to specify what it means for the learner to be "successful." We might specify that to succeed, the learner must output a hypothesis identical to the target concept. Alternatively, we might simply require that it output a hypothesis that agrees with the target concept most of the time, or that it usually output such a hypothesis. Similarly, we must specify how training examples are to be obtained by the learner. We might specify that training examples are presented by a helpful teacher, or obtained by the learner performing experiments, or simply generated at random according to some process outside the learner's control. As we might expect, the answers to the above questions depend on the particular setting, or learning model, we have in mind.

The remainder of this chapter is organized as follows. Section 7.2 introduces the probably approximately correct (PAC) learning setting. Section 7.3 then analyzes the sample complexity and computational complexity for several learning problems within this PAC setting. Section 7.4 introduces an important measure of hypothesis space complexity called the VC-dimension and extends our PAC analysis to problems in which the hypothesis space is infinite. Section 7.5 introduces the mistake-bound model and provides a bound on the number of mistakes made by several learning algorithms discussed in earlier chapters. Finally, we introduce the WEIGHTED-MAJORITY algorithm, a practical algorithm for combining the predictions of multiple competing learning algorithms, along with a theoretical mistake bound for this algorithm.

7.2 PROBABLY LEARNING AN APPROXIMATELY CORRECT HYPOTHESIS

In this section we consider a particular setting for the learning problem, called the *probably approximately correct* (PAC) learning model. We begin by specifying the problem setting that defines the PAC learning model, then consider the questions of how many training examples and how much computation are required in order to learn various classes of target functions within this PAC model. For the sake of simplicity, we restrict the discussion to the case of learning boolean-valued concepts from noise-free training data. However, many of the results can be extended to the more general scenario of learning real-valued target functions (see, for example, Natarajan 1991), and some can be extended to learning from certain types of noisy data (see, for example, Laird 1988; Kearns and Vazirani 1994).

7.2.1 The Problem Setting

As in earlier chapters, let X refer to the set of all possible instances over which target functions may be defined. For example, X might represent the set of all people, each described by the attributes *age* (e.g., *young* or *old*) and *height* (*short* or *tall*). Let C refer to some set of target concepts that our learner might be called upon to learn. Each target concept c in C corresponds to some subset of X, or equivalently to some boolean-valued function $c : X \rightarrow \{0, 1\}$. For example, one target concept c in C might be the concept "people who are skiers." If x is a positive example of c, then we will write $c(x) = 1$; if x is a negative example, $c(x) = 0$.

We assume instances are generated at random from X according to some probability distribution $\mathcal{D}$. For example, $\mathcal{D}$ might be the distribution of instances generated by observing people who walk out of the largest sports store in Switzerland. In general, $\mathcal{D}$ may be any distribution, and it will not generally be known to the learner. All that we require of $\mathcal{D}$ is that it be stationary; that is, that the distribution not change over time. Training examples are generated by drawing an instance x at random according to $\mathcal{D}$, then presenting x along with its target value, $c(x)$, to the learner.

The learner L considers some set H of possible hypotheses when attempting to learn the target concept. For example, H might be the set of all hypotheses describable by conjunctions of the attributes *age* and *height*. After observing a sequence of training examples of the target concept c, L must output some hypothesis h from H, which is its estimate of c. To be fair, we evaluate the success of L by the performance of h over new instances drawn randomly from X according to $\mathcal{D}$, the same probability distribution used to generate the training data.

Within this setting, we are interested in characterizing the performance of various learners L using various hypothesis spaces H, when learning individual target concepts drawn from various classes C. Because we demand that L be general enough to learn any target concept from C regardless of the distribution of training examples, we will often be interested in worst-case analyses over all possible target concepts from C and all possible instance distributions $\mathcal{D}$.

7.2.2 Error of a Hypothesis

Because we are interested in how closely the learner's output hypothesis h approximates the actual target concept c, let us begin by defining the *true error* of a hypothesis h with respect to target concept c and instance distribution $\mathcal{D}$. Informally, the true error of h is just the error rate we expect when applying h to future instances drawn according to the probability distribution $\mathcal{D}$. In fact, we already defined the true error of h in Chapter 5. For convenience, we restate the definition here using c to represent the boolean target function.

> ***Definition:*** The **true error** (denoted $error_{\mathcal{D}}(h)$) of hypothesis h with respect to target concept c and distribution $\mathcal{D}$ is the probability that h will misclassify an instance drawn at random according to $\mathcal{D}$.
>
> $$error_{\mathcal{D}}(h) \equiv \Pr_{x \in \mathcal{D}} [c(x) \neq h(x)]$$

Here the notation $\Pr_{x \in \mathcal{D}}$ indicates that the probability is taken over the instance distribution $\mathcal{D}$.

Figure 7.1 shows this definition of error in graphical form. The concepts c and h are depicted by the sets of instances within X that they label as positive. The error of h with respect to c is the probability that a randomly drawn instance will fall into the region where h and c disagree (i.e., their set difference). Note we have chosen to define error over the *entire distribution* of instances—not simply over the training examples—because this is the true error we expect to encounter when actually using the learned hypothesis h on subsequent instances drawn from $\mathcal{D}$.

Note that error depends strongly on the unknown probability distribution $\mathcal{D}$. For example, if $\mathcal{D}$ is a uniform probability distribution that assigns the same probability to every instance in X, then the error for the hypothesis in Figure 7.1 will be the fraction of the total instance space that falls into the region where h and c disagree. However, the same h and c will have a much higher error if $\mathcal{D}$ happens to assign very high probability to instances for which h and c disagree. In the extreme, if $\mathcal{D}$ happens to assign zero probability to the instances for which

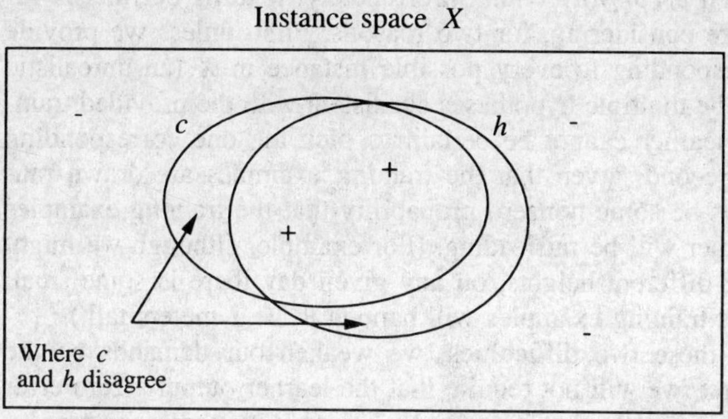

FIGURE 7.1
The error of hypothesis h with respect to target concept c. The error of h with respect to c is the probability that a randomly drawn instance will fall into the region where h and c disagree on its classification. The $+$ and $-$ points indicate positive and negative training examples. Note h has a nonzero error with respect to c despite the fact that h and c agree on all five training examples observed thus far.

$h(x) = c(x)$, then the error for the h in Figure 7.1 will be 1, despite the fact the h and c agree on a very large number of (zero probability) instances.

Finally, note that the error of h with respect to c is not directly observable to the learner. L can only observe the performance of h over the *training examples*, and it must choose its output hypothesis on this basis only. We will use the term *training error* to refer to the fraction of training examples misclassified by h, in contrast to the *true error* defined above. Much of our analysis of the complexity of learning centers around the question "how probable is it that the observed *training error* for h gives a misleading estimate of the *true* $error_{\mathcal{D}}(h)$?"

Notice the close relationship between this question and the questions considered in Chapter 5. Recall that in Chapter 5 we defined the *sample error* of h with respect to a set S of examples to be the fraction of S misclassified by h. The training error defined above is just the sample error when S is the set of training examples. In Chapter 5 we determined the probability that the sample error will provide a misleading estimate of the true error, under the assumption that the data sample S is drawn independent of h. However, when S is the set of training data, the learned hypothesis h depends very much on S! Therefore, in this chapter we provide an analysis that addresses this important special case.

7.2.3 PAC Learnability

Our aim is to characterize classes of target concepts that can be reliably learned from a reasonable number of randomly drawn training examples and a reasonable amount of computation.

What kinds of statements about learnability should we guess hold true? We might try to characterize the number of training examples needed to learn a hypothesis h for which $error_{\mathcal{D}}(h) = 0$. Unfortunately, it turns out this is futile in the setting we are considering, for two reasons. First, unless we provide training examples corresponding to every possible instance in X (an unrealistic assumption), there may be multiple hypotheses consistent with the provided training examples, and the learner cannot be certain to pick the one corresponding to the target concept. Second, given that the training examples are drawn randomly, there will always be some nonzero probability that the training examples encountered by the learner will be misleading. (For example, although we might frequently see skiers of different heights, on any given day there is some small chance that all observed training examples will happen to be 2 meters tall.)

To accommodate these two difficulties, we weaken our demands on the learner in two ways. First, we will not require that the learner output a zero error hypothesis—we will require only that its error be bounded by some constant, ϵ, that can be made arbitrarily small. Second, we will not require that the learner succeed for *every* sequence of randomly drawn training examples—we will require only that its probability of failure be bounded by some constant, δ, that can be made arbitrarily small. In short, we require only that the learner *probably* learn a hypothesis that is *approximately correct*—hence the term probably approximately correct learning, or PAC learning for short.

Consider some class C of possible target concepts and a learner L using hypothesis space H. Loosely speaking, we will say that the concept class C is PAC-learnable by L using H if, for any target concept c in C, L will with probability $(1 - \delta)$ output a hypothesis h with $error_{\mathcal{D}}(h) < \epsilon$, after observing a reasonable number of training examples and performing a reasonable amount of computation. More precisely,

> ***Definition:*** Consider a concept class C defined over a set of instances X of length n and a learner L using hypothesis space H. C is **PAC-learnable** by L using H if for all $c \in C$, distributions $\mathcal{D}$ over X, ϵ such that $0 < \epsilon < 1/2$, and δ such that $0 < \delta < 1/2$, learner L will with probability at least $(1 - \delta)$ output a hypothesis $h \in H$ such that $error_{\mathcal{D}}(h) \leq \epsilon$, in time that is polynomial in $1/\epsilon$, $1/\delta$, n, and $size(c)$.

Our definition requires two things from L. First, L must, with arbitrarily high probability $(1 - \delta)$, output a hypothesis having arbitrarily low error (ϵ). Second, it must do so efficiently—in time that grows at most polynomially with $1/\epsilon$ and $1/\delta$, which define the strength of our demands on the output hypothesis, and with n and $size(c)$ that define the inherent complexity of the underlying instance space X and concept class C. Here, n is the size of instances in X. For example, if instances in X are conjunctions of k boolean features, then $n = k$. The second space parameter, $size(c)$, is the encoding length of c in C, assuming some representation for C. For example, if concepts in C are conjunctions of up to k boolean features, each described by listing the indices of the features in the conjunction, then $size(c)$ is the number of boolean features actually used to describe c.

Our definition of PAC learning may at first appear to be concerned only with the computational resources required for learning, whereas in practice we are usually more concerned with the number of training examples required. However, the two are very closely related: If L requires some minimum processing time per training example, then for C to be PAC-learnable by L, *L must learn from a polynomial number of training examples.* In fact, a typical approach to showing that some class C of target concepts is PAC-learnable, is to first show that each target concept in C can be learned from a polynomial number of training examples and then show that the processing time per example is also polynomially bounded.

Before moving on, we should point out a restrictive assumption implicit in our definition of PAC-learnable. This definition implicitly assumes that the learner's hypothesis space H contains a hypothesis with arbitrarily small error for every target concept in C. This follows from the requirement in the above definition that the learner succeed when the error bound ϵ is arbitrarily close to zero. Of course this is difficult to assure if one does not know C in advance (what is C for a program that must learn to recognize faces from images?), unless H is taken to be the power set of X. As pointed out in Chapter 2, such an unbiased H will not support accurate generalization from a reasonable number of training examples. Nevertheless, the results based on the PAC learning model provide useful insights regarding the relative complexity of different learning problems and regarding the rate at which generalization accuracy improves with additional training examples. Furthermore, in Section 7.3.1 we will lift this restrictive assumption, to consider the case in which the learner makes no prior assumption about the form of the target concept.

7.3 SAMPLE COMPLEXITY FOR FINITE HYPOTHESIS SPACES

As noted above, PAC-learnability is largely determined by the number of training examples required by the learner. The growth in the number of required training examples with problem size, called the *sample complexity* of the learning problem, is the characteristic that is usually of greatest interest. The reason is that in most practical settings the factor that most limits success of the learner is the limited availability of training data.

Here we present a general bound on the sample complexity for a very broad class of learners, called *consistent learners*. A learner is *consistent* if it outputs hypotheses that perfectly fit the training data, whenever possible. It is quite reasonable to ask that a learning algorithm be consistent, given that we typically prefer a hypothesis that fits the training data over one that does not. Note that many of the learning algorithms discussed in earlier chapters, including all the learning algorithms described in Chapter 2, are consistent learners.

Can we derive a bound on the number of training examples required by *any* consistent learner, independent of the specific algorithm it uses to derive a consistent hypothesis? The answer is yes. To accomplish this, it is useful to recall the definition of version space from Chapter 2. There we defined the version space, $VS_{H,D}$, to be the set of all hypotheses $h \in H$ that correctly classify the training examples D.

$$VS_{H,D} = \{h \in H | (\forall \langle x, c(x) \rangle \in D) \; (h(x) = c(x))\}$$

The significance of the version space here is that *every consistent learner outputs a hypothesis belonging to the version space*, regardless of the instance space X, hypothesis space H, or training data D. The reason is simply that by definition the version space $VS_{H,D}$ contains every consistent hypothesis in H. Therefore, *to bound the number of examples needed by any consistent learner, we need only bound the number of examples needed to assure that the version space contains no unacceptable hypotheses.* The following definition, after Haussler (1988), states this condition precisely.

> ***Definition:*** Consider a hypothesis space H, target concept c, instance distribution $\mathcal{D}$, and set of training examples D of c. The version space $VS_{H,D}$ is said to be **ϵ-exhausted** with respect to c and $\mathcal{D}$, if every hypothesis h in $VS_{H,D}$ has error less than ϵ with respect to c and $\mathcal{D}$.
>
> $$(\forall h \in VS_{H,D})\ error_{\mathcal{D}}(h) < \epsilon$$

This definition is illustrated in Figure 7.2. The version space is ϵ-exhausted just in the case that all the hypotheses consistent with the observed training examples (i.e., those with zero training error) happen to have true error less than ϵ. Of course from the learner's viewpoint all that can be known is that these hypotheses fit the training data equally well—they all have zero training error. Only an observer who knew the identity of the target concept could determine with certainty whether the version space is ϵ-exhausted. Surprisingly, a probabilistic argument allows us to bound the probability that the version space will be ϵ-exhausted after a given number of training examples, even without knowing the identity of the target concept or the distribution from which training examples

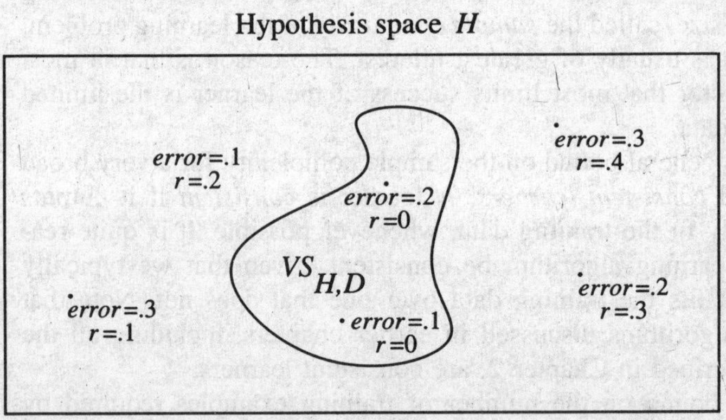

FIGURE 7.2
Exhausting the version space. The version space $VS_{H,D}$ is the subset of hypotheses $h \in H$, which have zero training error (denoted by $r = 0$ in the figure). Of course the true $error_{\mathcal{D}}(h)$ (denoted by *error* in the figure) may be nonzero, even for hypotheses that commit zero errors over the training data. The version space is said to be ϵ-exhausted when all hypotheses h remaining in $VS_{H,D}$ have $error_{\mathcal{D}}(h) < \epsilon$.

are drawn. Haussler (1988) provides such a bound, in the form of the following theorem.

Theorem 7.1. **ϵ-exhausting the version space.** If the hypothesis space H is finite, and D is a sequence of $m \geq 1$ independent randomly drawn examples of some target concept c, then for any $0 \leq \epsilon \leq 1$, the probability that the version space $VS_{H,D}$ is not ϵ-exhausted (with respect to c) is less than or equal to

$$|H|e^{-\epsilon m}$$

Proof. Let $h_1, h_2, \ldots h_k$ be all the hypotheses in H that have true error greater than ϵ with respect to c. We fail to ϵ-exhaust the version space if and only if at least one of these k hypotheses happens to be consistent with all m independent random training examples. The probability that any single hypothesis having true error greater than ϵ would be consistent with one randomly drawn example is at most $(1-\epsilon)$. Therefore the probability that this hypothesis will be consistent with m independently drawn examples is at most $(1-\epsilon)^m$. Given that we have k hypotheses with error greater than ϵ, the probability that at least one of these will be consistent with all m training examples is at most

$$k(1-\epsilon)^m$$

And since $k \leq |H|$, this is at most $|H|(1-\epsilon)^m$. Finally, we use a general inequality stating that if $0 \leq \epsilon \leq 1$ then $(1-\epsilon) \leq e^{-\epsilon}$. Thus,

$$k(1-\epsilon)^m \leq |H|(1-\epsilon)^m \leq |H|e^{-\epsilon m}$$

which proves the theorem. □

We have just proved an upper bound on the probability that the version space is not ϵ-exhausted, based on the number of training examples m, the allowed error ϵ, and the size of H. Put another way, this bounds the probability that m training examples will fail to eliminate all "bad" hypotheses (i.e., hypotheses with true error greater than ϵ), for any consistent learner using hypothesis space H.

Let us use this result to determine the number of training examples required to reduce this probability of failure below some desired level δ.

$$|H|e^{-\epsilon m} \leq \delta \tag{7.1}$$

Rearranging terms to solve for m, we find

$$m \geq \frac{1}{\epsilon}(\ln|H| + \ln(1/\delta)) \tag{7.2}$$

To summarize, the inequality shown in Equation (7.2) provides a general bound on the number of training examples sufficient for *any consistent learner* to successfully learn any target concept in H, for any desired values of δ and ϵ. This number m of training examples is sufficient to assure that any consistent hypothesis will be probably (with probability $(1-\delta)$) approximately (within error ϵ) correct. Notice m grows linearly in $1/\epsilon$ and logarithmically in $1/\delta$. It also grows logarithmically in the size of the hypothesis space H.

Note that the above bound can be a substantial overestimate. For example, although the probability of failing to exhaust the version space must lie in the interval [0, 1], the bound given by the theorem grows linearly with $|H|$. For sufficiently large hypothesis spaces, this bound can easily be greater than one. As a result, the bound given by the inequality in Equation (7.2) can substantially overestimate the number of training examples required. The weakness of this bound is mainly due to the $|H|$ term, which arises in the proof when summing the probability that a single hypothesis could be unacceptable, over all possible hypotheses. In fact, a much tighter bound is possible in many cases, as well as a bound that covers infinitely large hypothesis spaces. This will be the subject of Section 7.4.

7.3.1 Agnostic Learning and Inconsistent Hypotheses

Equation (7.2) is important because it tells us how many training examples suffice to ensure (with probability $(1-\delta)$) that every hypothesis in H having zero training error will have a true error of at most ϵ. Unfortunately, if H does not contain the target concept c, then a zero-error hypothesis cannot always be found. In this case, the most we might ask of our learner is to output the hypothesis from H that has the *minimum* error over the training examples. A learner that makes no assumption that the target concept is representable by H and that simply finds the hypothesis with minimum training error, is often called an *agnostic* learner, because it makes no prior commitment about whether or not $C \subseteq H$.

Although Equation (7.2) is based on the assumption that the learner outputs a zero-error hypothesis, a similar bound can be found for this more general case in which the learner entertains hypotheses with nonzero training error. To state this precisely, let D denote the particular set of training examples available to the learner, in contrast to $\mathcal{D}$, which denotes the probability distribution over the entire set of instances. Let $error_D(h)$ denote the training error of hypothesis h. In particular, $error_D(h)$ is defined as the fraction of the training examples in D that are misclassified by h. Note the $error_D(h)$ over the particular sample of training data D may differ from the true error $error_{\mathcal{D}}(h)$ over the entire probability distribution $\mathcal{D}$. Now let h_{best} denote the hypothesis from H having lowest training error over the training examples. How many training examples suffice to ensure (with high probability) that its true error $error_{\mathcal{D}}(h_{best})$ will be no more than $\epsilon + error_D(h_{best})$? Notice the question considered in the previous section is just a special case of this question, when $error_D(h_{best})$ happens to be zero.

This question can be answered (see Exercise 7.3) using an argument analogous to the proof of Theorem 7.1. It is useful here to invoke the general Hoeffding bounds (sometimes called the additive Chernoff bounds). The Hoeffding bounds characterize the deviation between the true probability of some event and its observed frequency over m independent trials. More precisely, these bounds apply to experiments involving m distinct Bernoulli trials (e.g., m independent flips of a coin with some probability of turning up heads). This is exactly analogous to the setting we consider when estimating the error of a hypothesis in Chapter 5: The probability of the coin being heads corresponds to the probability that the hypothesis will misclassify a randomly drawn instance. The m independent coin flips correspond to the m independently drawn instances. The frequency of heads over the m examples corresponds to the frequency of misclassifications over the m instances.

The Hoeffding bounds state that if the training error $error_D(h)$ is measured over the set D containing m randomly drawn examples, then

$$\Pr[error_{\mathcal{D}}(h) > error_D(h) + \epsilon] \leq e^{-2m\epsilon^2}$$

This gives us a bound on the probability that an arbitrarily chosen single hypothesis has a very misleading training error. To assure that the *best* hypothesis found by L has an error bounded in this way, we must consider the probability that any one of the $|H|$ hypotheses could have a large error

$$\Pr[(\exists h \in H)(error_{\mathcal{D}}(h) > error_D(h) + \epsilon)] \leq |H|e^{-2m\epsilon^2}$$

If we call this probability δ, and ask how many examples m suffice to hold δ to some desired value, we now obtain

$$m \geq \frac{1}{2\epsilon^2}(\ln|H| + \ln(1/\delta)) \tag{7.3}$$

This is the generalization of Equation (7.2) to the case in which the learner still picks the best hypothesis $h \in H$, but where the best hypothesis may have nonzero training error. Notice that m depends logarithmically on H and on $1/\delta$, as it did in the more restrictive case of Equation (7.2). However, in this less restrictive situation m now grows as the square of $1/\epsilon$, rather than linearly with $1/\epsilon$.

7.3.2 Conjunctions of Boolean Literals Are PAC-Learnable

Now that we have a bound indicating the number of training examples sufficient to probably approximately learn the target concept, we can use it to determine the sample complexity and PAC-learnability of some specific concept classes.

Consider the class C of target concepts described by conjunctions of boolean literals. A boolean *literal* is any boolean variable (e.g., Old), or its negation (e.g., $\neg Old$). Thus, conjunctions of boolean literals include target concepts such as "$Old \wedge \neg Tall$". Is C PAC-learnable? We can show that the answer is yes by first showing that any consistent learner will require only a polynomial number of training examples to learn any c in C, and then suggesting a specific algorithm that uses polynomial time per training example.

Consider any consistent learner L using a hypothesis space H identical to C. We can use Equation (7.2) to compute the number m of random training examples sufficient to ensure that L will, with probability $(1 - \delta)$, output a hypothesis with maximum error ϵ. To accomplish this, we need only determine the size $|H|$ of the hypothesis space.

Now consider the hypothesis space H defined by conjunctions of literals based on n boolean variables. The size $|H|$ of this hypothesis space is 3^n. To see this, consider the fact that there are only three possibilities for each variable in any given hypothesis: Include the variable as a literal in the hypothesis, include its negation as a literal, or ignore it. Given n such variables, there are 3^n distinct hypotheses.

Substituting $|H| = 3^n$ into Equation (7.2) gives the following bound for the sample complexity of learning conjunctions of up to n boolean literals.

$$m \geq \frac{1}{\epsilon}(n \ln 3 + \ln(1/\delta)) \tag{7.4}$$

For example, if a consistent learner attempts to learn a target concept described by conjunctions of up to 10 boolean literals, and we desire a 95% probability that it will learn a hypothesis with error less than .1, then it suffices to present m randomly drawn training examples, where $m = \frac{1}{.1}(10 \ln 3 + \ln(1/.05)) = 140$.

Notice that m grows linearly in the number of literals n, linearly in $1/\epsilon$, and logarithmically in $1/\delta$. What about the overall computational effort? That will depend, of course, on the specific learning algorithm. However, as long as our learning algorithm requires no more than polynomial computation per training example, and no more than a polynomial number of training examples, then the total computation required will be polynomial as well.

In the case of learning conjunctions of boolean literals, one algorithm that meets this requirement has already been presented in Chapter 2. It is the FIND-S algorithm, which incrementally computes the most specific hypothesis consistent with the training examples. For each new positive training example, this algorithm computes the intersection of the literals shared by the current hypothesis and the new training example, using time linear in n. Therefore, the FIND-S algorithm PAC-learns the concept class of conjunctions of n boolean literals with negations.

Theorem 7.2. PAC-learnability of boolean conjunctions. The class C of conjunctions of boolean literals is PAC-learnable by the FIND-S algorithm using $H = C$.

Proof. Equation (7.4) shows that the sample complexity for this concept class is polynomial in n, $1/\delta$, and $1/\epsilon$, and independent of $size(c)$. To incrementally process each training example, the FIND-S algorithm requires effort linear in n and independent of $1/\delta$, $1/\epsilon$, and $size(c)$. Therefore, this concept class is PAC-learnable by the FIND-S algorithm. □

7.3.3 PAC-Learnability of Other Concept Classes

As we just saw, Equation (7.2) provides a general basis for bounding the sample complexity for learning target concepts in some given class C. Above we applied it to the class of conjunctions of boolean literals. It can also be used to show that many other concept classes have polynomial sample complexity (e.g., see Exercise 7.2).

7.3.3.1 UNBIASED LEARNERS

Not all concept classes have polynomially bounded sample complexity according to the bound of Equation (7.2). For example, consider the *unbiased* concept class

C that contains every teachable concept relative to X. The set C of all definable target concepts corresponds to the power set of X—the set of all subsets of X—which contains $|C| = 2^{|X|}$ concepts. Suppose that instances in X are defined by n boolean features. In this case, there will be $|X| = 2^n$ distinct instances, and therefore $|C| = 2^{|X|} = 2^{2^n}$ distinct concepts. Of course to learn such an unbiased concept class, the learner must itself use an unbiased hypothesis space $H = C$. Substituting $|H| = 2^{2^n}$ into Equation (7.2) gives the sample complexity for learning the unbiased concept class relative to X.

$$m \geq \frac{1}{\epsilon}(2^n \ln 2 + \ln(1/\delta)) \tag{7.5}$$

Thus, this unbiased class of target concepts has exponential sample complexity under the PAC model, according to Equation (7.2). Although Equations (7.2) and (7.5) are not tight upper bounds, it can in fact be proven that the sample complexity for the unbiased concept class is exponential in n.

7.3.3.2 K-TERM DNF AND K-CNF CONCEPTS

It is also possible to find concept classes that have polynomial sample complexity, but nevertheless cannot be learned in polynomial time. One interesting example is the concept class C of k-term disjunctive normal form (k-term DNF) expressions. k-term DNF expressions are of the form $T_1 \vee T_2 \vee \cdots \vee T_k$, where each term T_i is a conjunction of n boolean attributes and their negations. Assuming $H = C$, it is easy to show that $|H|$ is at most $k3^n$ (because there are only k terms, times 3^n possibilities for each term). Note $k3^n$ is an overestimate of H, because it is double counting the cases where $T_i = T_j$ and where T_i is *more_general_than* T_j. Still, we can use this upper bound on $|H|$ to obtain an upper bound on the sample complexity, substituting this into Equation (7.2).

$$m \geq \frac{1}{\epsilon}(n \ln 3 + \ln k + \ln(1/\delta)) \tag{7.6}$$

which indicates that the sample complexity of k-term DNF is polynomial in $1/\epsilon$, $1/\delta$, n, and k. Despite having polynomial sample complexity, the computational complexity is not polynomial, because this learning problem can be shown to be equivalent to other problems that are known to be unsolvable in polynomial time (unless $RP \neq NP$). Thus, although k-term DNF has polynomial sample complexity, it does not have polynomial computational complexity for a learner using $H = C$.

The surprising fact about k-term DNF is that although it is not PAC-learnable, there is a strictly larger concept class that is! This is possible because the larger concept class has polynomial computation complexity per example and still has polynomial sample complexity. This larger class is the class of k-CNF expressions: conjunctions of arbitrary length of the form $T_1 \wedge T_2 \wedge \cdots \wedge T_j$, where each T_i is a disjunction of up to k boolean attributes. It is straightforward to show that k-CNF subsumes k-DNF, because any k-term DNF expression can easily be rewritten as a k-CNF expression (but not vice versa). Although k-CNF is more expressive than k-term DNF, it has both polynomial sample complexity and polynomial time complexity. Hence, the concept class k-term DNF is PAC learnable by an efficient algorithm using $H = k$-CNF. See Kearns and Vazirani (1994) for a more detailed discussion.

7.4 SAMPLE COMPLEXITY FOR INFINITE HYPOTHESIS SPACES

In the above section we showed that sample complexity for PAC learning grows as the logarithm of the size of the hypothesis space. While Equation (7.2) is quite useful, there are two drawbacks to characterizing sample complexity in terms of $|H|$. First, it can lead to quite weak bounds (recall that the bound on δ can be significantly greater than 1 for large $|H|$). Second, in the case of infinite hypothesis spaces we cannot apply Equation (7.2) at all!

Here we consider a second measure of the complexity of H, called the Vapnik-Chervonenkis dimension of H (VC dimension, or $VC(H)$, for short). As we shall see, we can state bounds on sample complexity that use $VC(H)$ rather than $|H|$. In many cases, the sample complexity bounds based on $VC(H)$ will be tighter than those from Equation (7.2). In addition, these bounds allow us to characterize the sample complexity of many infinite hypothesis spaces, and can be shown to be fairly tight.

7.4.1 Shattering a Set of Instances

The VC dimension measures the complexity of the hypothesis space H, not by the number of distinct hypotheses $|H|$, but instead by the number of distinct instances from X that can be completely discriminated using H.

To make this notion more precise, we first define the notion of *shattering* a set of instances. Consider some subset of instances $S \subseteq X$. For example, Figure 7.3 shows a subset of three instances from X. Each hypothesis h from H imposes some dichotomy on S; that is, h partitions S into the two subsets $\{x \in S | h(x) = 1\}$ and $\{x \in S | h(x) = 0\}$. Given some instance set S, there are $2^{|S|}$ possible dichotomies, though H may be unable to represent some of these. We say that H shatters S if every possible dichotomy of S can be represented by some hypothesis from H.

> ***Definition:*** A set of instances S is **shattered** by hypothesis space H if and only if for every dichotomy of S there exists some hypothesis in H consistent with this dichotomy.

Figure 7.3 illustrates a set S of three instances that is shattered by the hypothesis space. Notice that each of the 2^3 dichotomies of these three instances is covered by some hypothesis.

Note that if a set of instances is not shattered by a hypothesis space, then there must be some concept (dichotomy) that can be defined over the instances, but that cannot be represented by the hypothesis space. The ability of H to shatter

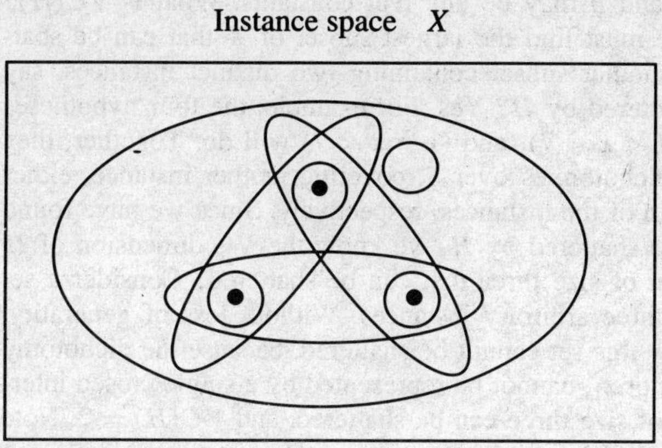

FIGURE 7.3
A set of three instances shattered by eight hypotheses. For every possible dichotomy of the instances, there exists a corresponding hypothesis.

a set of instances is thus a measure of its capacity to represent target concepts defined over these instances.

7.4.2 The Vapnik-Chervonenkis Dimension

The ability to shatter a set of instances is closely related to the inductive bias of a hypothesis space. Recall from Chapter 2 that an unbiased hypothesis space is one capable of representing every possible concept (dichotomy) definable over the instance space X. Put briefly, an unbiased hypothesis space H is one that shatters the instance space X. What if H cannot shatter X, but can shatter some large subset S of X? Intuitively, it seems reasonable to say that the larger the subset of X that can be shattered, the more expressive H. The VC dimension of H is precisely this measure.

> ***Definition:*** The **Vapnik-Chervonenkis dimension**, $VC(H)$, of hypothesis space H defined over instance space X is the size of the largest finite subset of X shattered by H. If arbitrarily large finite sets of X can be shattered by H, then $VC(H) \equiv \infty$.

Note that for any finite H, $VC(H) \leq \log_2 |H|$. To see this, suppose that $VC(H) = d$. Then H will require 2^d distinct hypotheses to shatter d instances. Hence, $2^d \leq |H|$, and $d = VC(H) \leq \log_2 |H|$.

7.4.2.1 ILLUSTRATIVE EXAMPLES

In order to develop an intuitive feeling for $VC(H)$, consider a few example hypothesis spaces. To get started, suppose the instance space X is the set of real numbers $X = \Re$ (e.g., describing the *height* of people), and H the set of intervals on the real number line. In other words, H is the set of hypotheses of the form $a < x < b$, where a and b may be any real constants. What is $VC(H)$? To answer this question, we must find the largest subset of X that can be shattered by H. Consider a particular subset containing two distinct instances, say $S = \{3.1, 5.7\}$. Can S be shattered by H? Yes. For example, the four hypotheses $(1 < x < 2)$, $(1 < x < 4)$, $(4 < x < 7)$, and $(1 < x < 7)$ will do. Together, they represent each of the four dichotomies over S, covering neither instance, either one of the instances, and both of the instances, respectively. Since we have found a set of size two that can be shattered by H, we know the VC dimension of H is at least two. Is there a set of size three that can be shattered? Consider a set $S = \{x_0, x_1, x_2\}$ containing three arbitrary instances. Without loss of generality, assume $x_0 < x_1 < x_2$. Clearly this set cannot be shattered, because the dichotomy that includes x_0 and x_2, but not x_1, cannot be represented by a single closed interval. Therefore, *no* subset S of size three can be shattered, and $VC(H) = 2$. Note here that H is infinite, but $VC(H)$ finite.

Next consider the set X of instances corresponding to points on the x, y plane (see Figure 7.4). Let H be the set of all linear decision surfaces in the plane. In other words, H is the hypothesis space corresponding to a single perceptron unit with two inputs (see Chapter 4 for a general discussion of perceptrons). What is the VC dimension of this H? It is easy to see that any two distinct points in the plane can be shattered by H, because we can find four linear surfaces that include neither, either, or both points. What about sets of three points? As long as the points are not colinear, we will be able to find 2^3 linear surfaces that shatter them. Of course three colinear points cannot be shattered (for the same reason that the three points on the real line could not be shattered in the previous example). What is $VC(H)$ in this case—two or three? It is at least three. The definition of VC dimension indicates that if we find *any* set of instances of size d that can be shattered, then $VC(H) \geq d$. To show that $VC(H) < d$, we must show that no set of size d can be shattered. In this example, no sets of size four can be shattered, so $VC(H) = 3$. More generally, it can be shown that the VC dimension of linear decision surfaces in an r dimensional space (i.e., the VC dimension of a perceptron with r inputs) is $r + 1$.

As one final example, suppose each instance in X is described by the conjunction of exactly three boolean literals, and suppose that each hypothesis in H is described by the conjunction of up to three boolean literals. What is $VC(H)$? We

FIGURE 7.4
The VC dimension for linear decision surfaces in the x, y plane is 3. (a) A set of three points that can be shattered using linear decision surfaces. (b) A set of three that cannot be shattered.

can show that it is at least 3, as follows. Represent each instance by a 3-bit string corresponding to the values of each of its three literals l_1, l_2, and l_3. Consider the following set of three instances:

instance$_1$: 100
instance$_2$: 010
instance$_3$: 001

This set of three instances can be shattered by H, because a hypothesis can be constructed for any desired dichotomy as follows: If the dichotomy is to exclude $instance_i$, add the literal $\neg l_i$ to the hypothesis. For example, suppose we wish to include $instance_2$, but exclude $instance_1$ and $instance_3$. Then we use the hypothesis $\neg l_1 \wedge \neg l_3$. This argument easily extends from three features to n. Thus, the VC dimension for conjunctions of n boolean literals is at least n. In fact, it is exactly n, though showing this is more difficult, because it requires demonstrating that no set of $n+1$ instances can be shattered.

7.4.3 Sample Complexity and the VC Dimension

Earlier we considered the question "How many randomly drawn training examples suffice to probably approximately learn any target concept in C?" (i.e., how many examples suffice to ϵ-exhaust the version space with probability $(1-\delta)$?). Using $VC(H)$ as a measure for the complexity of H, it is possible to derive an alternative answer to this question, analogous to the earlier bound of Equation (7.2). This new bound (see Blumer et al. 1989) is

$$m \geq \frac{1}{\epsilon}(4\log_2(2/\delta) + 8VC(H)\log_2(13/\epsilon)) \tag{7.7}$$

Note that just as in the bound from Equation (7.2), the number of required training examples m grows logarithmically in $1/\delta$. It now grows log times linear in $1/\epsilon$, rather than linearly. Significantly, the $\ln|H|$ term in the earlier bound has now been replaced by the alternative measure of hypothesis space complexity, $VC(H)$ (recall $VC(H) \leq \log_2|H|$).

Equation (7.7) provides an upper bound on the number of training examples sufficient to probably approximately learn any target concept in C, for any desired ϵ and δ. It is also possible to obtain a lower bound, as summarized in the following theorem (see Ehrenfeucht et al. 1989).

Theorem 7.3. Lower bound on sample complexity. Consider any concept class C such that $VC(C) \geq 2$, any learner L, and any $0 < \epsilon < \frac{1}{8}$, and $0 < \delta < \frac{1}{100}$. Then there exists a distribution $\mathcal{D}$ and target concept in C such that if L observes fewer examples than

$$\max\left[\frac{1}{\epsilon}\log(1/\delta), \frac{VC(C)-1}{32\epsilon}\right]$$

then with probability at least δ, L outputs a hypothesis h having $error_{\mathcal{D}}(h) > \epsilon$.

This theorem states that if the number of training examples is too few, then no learner can PAC-learn every target concept in any nontrivial C. Thus, this theorem provides a lower bound on the number of training examples *necessary* for successful learning, complementing the earlier upper bound that gives a *sufficient* number. Notice this lower bound is determined by the complexity of the concept class C, whereas our earlier upper bounds were determined by H. (Why?)†

This lower bound shows that the upper bound of the inequality in Equation (7.7) is fairly tight. Both bounds are logarithmic in $1/\delta$ and linear in $VC(H)$. The only difference in the order of these two bounds is the extra $\log(1/\epsilon)$ dependence in the upper bound.

7.4.4 VC Dimension for Neural Networks

Given the discussion of artificial neural network learning in Chapter 4, it is interesting to consider how we might calculate the VC dimension of a network of interconnected units such as the feedforward networks trained by the BACKPROPAGATION procedure. This section presents a general result that allows computing the VC dimension of layered acyclic networks, based on the structure of the network and the VC dimension of its individual units. This VC dimension can then be used to bound the number of training examples sufficient to probably approximately correctly learn a feedforward network to desired values of ϵ and δ. This section may be skipped on a first reading without loss of continuity.

Consider a network, G, of units, which forms a layered directed acyclic graph. A *directed acyclic* graph is one for which the edges have a direction (e.g., the units have inputs and outputs), and in which there are no directed cycles. A *layered* graph is one whose nodes can be partitioned into layers such that all directed edges from nodes at layer l go to nodes at layer $l+1$. The layered feedforward neural networks discussed throughout Chapter 4 are examples of such layered directed acyclic graphs.

It turns out that we can bound the VC dimension of such networks based on their graph structure and the VC dimension of the primitive units from which they are constructed. To formalize this, we must first define a few more terms. Let n be the number of inputs to the network G, and let us assume that there is just one output node. Let each internal unit N_i of G (i.e., each node that is not an input) have at most r inputs and implement a boolean-valued function $c_i : \Re^r \rightarrow \{0, 1\}$ from some function class C. For example, if the internal nodes are perceptrons, then C will be the class of linear threshold functions defined over $\Re^r$.

We can now define the *G-composition of C* to be the class of all functions that can be implemented by the network G assuming individual units in G take on functions from the class C. In brief, the G-composition of C is the hypothesis space representable by the network G.

---

†Hint: If we were to substitute H for C in the lower bound, this would result in a tighter bound on m in the case $H \supset C$.

The following theorem bounds the VC dimension of the G-composition of C, based on the VC dimension of C and the structure of G.

> **Theorem 7.4. VC-dimension of directed acyclic layered networks.** (See Kearns and Vazirani 1994.) Let G be a layered directed acyclic graph with n input nodes and $s \geq 2$ internal nodes, each having at most r inputs. Let C be a concept class over $\Re^r$ of VC dimension d, corresponding to the set of functions that can be described by each of the s internal nodes. Let C_G be the G-composition of C, corresponding to the set of functions that can be represented by G. Then $VC(C_G) \leq 2ds \log(es)$, where e is the base of the natural logarithm.

Note this bound on the VC dimension of the network G grows linearly with the VC dimension d of its individual units and log times linear in s, the number of threshold units in the network.

Suppose we consider acyclic layered networks whose individual nodes are perceptrons. Recall from Chapter 4 that an r input perceptron uses linear decision surfaces to represent boolean functions over $\Re^r$. As noted in Section 7.4.2.1, the VC dimension of linear decision surfaces over $\Re^r$ is $r + 1$. Therefore, a single perceptron with r inputs has VC dimension $r + 1$. We can use this fact, together with the above theorem, to bound the VC dimension of acyclic layered networks containing s perceptrons, each with r inputs, as

$$VC(C_G^{perceptrons}) \leq 2(r + 1)s \log(es)$$

We can now bound the number m of training examples sufficient to learn (with probability at least $(1 - \delta)$) any target concept from $C_G^{perceptrons}$ to within error ϵ. Substituting the above expression for the network VC dimension into Equation (7.7), we have

$$m \geq \frac{1}{\epsilon}(4 \log(2/\delta) + 8VC(H) \log(13/\epsilon))$$

$$\geq \frac{1}{\epsilon}(4 \log(2/\delta) + 16(r + 1)s \log(es) \log(13/\epsilon)) \qquad (7.8)$$

As illustrated by this perceptron network example, the above theorem is interesting because it provides a general method for bounding the VC dimension of layered, acyclic networks of units, based on the network structure and the VC dimension of the individual units. Unfortunately the above result does not directly apply to networks trained using BACKPROPAGATION, for two reasons. First, this result applies to networks of perceptrons rather than networks of *sigmoid units* to which the BACKPROPAGATION algorithm applies. Nevertheless, notice that the VC dimension of sigmoid units will be at least as great as that of perceptrons, because a sigmoid unit can approximate a perceptron to arbitrary accuracy by using sufficiently large weights. Therefore, the above bound on m will be at least as large for acyclic layered networks of sigmoid units. The second shortcoming of the above result is that it fails to account for the fact that BACKPROPAGATION trains a network by beginning with near-zero weights, then iteratively modifying these weights until an acceptable hypothesis is found. Thus, BACKPROPAGATION with a cross-validation stopping criterion exhibits an inductive bias in favor of networks with small weights. This inductive bias, which reduces the effective VC dimension, is not captured by the above analysis.

7.5 THE MISTAKE BOUND MODEL OF LEARNING

While we have focused thus far on the PAC learning model, computational learning theory considers a variety of different settings and questions. Different learning settings that have been studied vary by how the training examples are generated (e.g., passive observation of random examples, active querying by the learner), noise in the data (e.g., noisy or error-free), the definition of success (e.g., the target concept must be learned exactly, or only probably and approximately), assumptions made by the learner (e.g., regarding the distribution of instances and whether $C \subseteq H$), and the measure according to which the learner is evaluated (e.g., number of training examples, number of mistakes, total time).

In this section we consider the *mistake bound* model of learning, in which the learner is evaluated by the total number of mistakes it makes before it converges to the correct hypothesis. As in the PAC setting, we assume the learner receives a sequence of training examples. However, here we demand that upon receiving each example x, the learner must predict the target value $c(x)$, before it is shown the correct target value by the trainer. The question considered is "How many *mistakes* will the learner make in its predictions before it learns the target concept?" This question is significant in practical settings where learning must be done while the system is in actual use, rather than during some off-line training stage. For example, if the system is to learn to predict which credit card purchases should be approved and which are fraudulent, based on data collected during use, then we are interested in minimizing the total number of mistakes it will make before converging to the correct target function. Here the total number of mistakes can be even more important than the total number of training examples.

This mistake bound learning problem may be studied in various specific settings. For example, we might count the number of mistakes made before PAC learning the target concept. In the examples below, we consider instead the number of mistakes made before learning the target concept *exactly*. Learning the target concept exactly means converging to a hypothesis such that $(\forall x) h(x) = c(x)$.

7.5.1 Mistake Bound for the FIND-S Algorithm

To illustrate, consider again the hypothesis space H consisting of conjunctions of up to n boolean literals $l_1 \ldots l_n$ and their negations (e.g., $Rich \wedge \neg Handsome$). Recall the FIND-S algorithm from Chapter 2, which incrementally computes the maximally specific hypothesis consistent with the training examples. A straightforward implementation of FIND-S for the hypothesis space H is as follows:

FIND-S:

- Initialize h to the most specific hypothesis $l_1 \wedge \neg l_1 \wedge l_2 \wedge \neg l_2 \ldots l_n \wedge \neg l_n$
- For each positive training instance x
  - Remove from h any literal that is not satisfied by x
- Output hypothesis h.

FIND-S converges in the limit to a hypothesis that makes no errors, provided $C \subseteq H$ and provided the training data is noise-free. FIND-S begins with the most specific hypothesis (which classifies every instance a negative example), then incrementally generalizes this hypothesis as needed to cover observed positive training examples. For the hypothesis representation used here, this generalization step consists of deleting unsatisfied literals.

Can we prove a bound on the total number of mistakes that FIND-S will make before exactly learning the target concept c? The answer is yes. To see this, note first that if $c \in H$, then FIND-S can never mistakenly classify a negative example as positive. The reason is that its current hypothesis h is always at least as specific as the target concept c. Therefore, to calculate the number of mistakes it will make, we need only count the number of mistakes it will make misclassifying truly positive examples as negative. How many such mistakes can occur before FIND-S learns c exactly? Consider the first positive example encountered by FIND-S. The learner will certainly make a mistake classifying this example, because its initial hypothesis labels every instance negative. However, the result will be that half of the $2n$ terms in its initial hypothesis will be eliminated, leaving only n terms. For each subsequent positive example that is mistakenly classified by the current hypothesis, at least one more of the remaining n terms must be eliminated from the hypothesis. Therefore, the total number of mistakes can be at most $n+1$. This number of mistakes will be required in the worst case, corresponding to learning the most general possible target concept $(\forall x)c(x) = 1$ and corresponding to a worst case sequence of instances that removes only one literal per mistake.

7.5.2 Mistake Bound for the HALVING Algorithm

As a second example, consider an algorithm that learns by maintaining a description of the version space, incrementally refining the version space as each new training example is encountered. The CANDIDATE-ELIMINATION algorithm and the LIST-THEN-ELIMINATE algorithm from Chapter 2 are examples of such algorithms. In this section we derive a worst-case bound on the number of mistakes that will be made by such a learner, for any finite hypothesis space H, assuming again that the target concept must be learned exactly.

To analyze the number of mistakes made while learning we must first specify precisely how the learner will make predictions given a new instance x. Let us assume this prediction is made by taking a majority vote among the hypotheses in the current version space. If the majority of version space hypotheses classify the new instance as positive, then this prediction is output by the learner. Otherwise a negative prediction is output.

This combination of learning the version space, together with using a majority vote to make subsequent predictions, is often called the HALVING algorithm. What is the maximum number of mistakes that can be made by the HALVING algorithm, for an arbitrary finite H, before it exactly learns the target concept? Notice that learning the target concept "exactly" corresponds to reaching a state where the version space contains only a single hypothesis (as usual, we assume the target concept c is in H).

To derive the mistake bound, note that the only time the HALVING algorithm can make a mistake is when the majority of hypotheses in its current version space incorrectly classify the new example. In this case, once the correct classification is revealed to the learner, the version space will be reduced to at most half its current size (i.e., only those hypotheses that voted with the minority will be retained). Given that each mistake reduces the size of the version space by at least half, and given that the initial version space contains only $|H|$ members, the maximum number of mistakes possible before the version space contains just one member is $\log_2 |H|$. In fact one can show the bound is $\lfloor \log_2 |H| \rfloor$. Consider, for example, the case in which $|H| = 7$. The first mistake must reduce $|H|$ to at most 3, and the second mistake will then reduce it to 1.

Note that $\lfloor \log_2 |H| \rfloor$ is a worst-case bound, and that it is possible for the HALVING algorithm to learn the target concept exactly without making any mistakes at all! This can occur because even when the majority vote is correct, the algorithm will remove the incorrect, minority hypotheses. If this occurs over the entire training sequence, then the version space may be reduced to a single member while making no mistakes along the way.

One interesting extension to the HALVING algorithm is to allow the hypotheses to vote with different weights. Chapter 6 describes the Bayes optimal classifier, which takes such a weighted vote among hypotheses. In the Bayes optimal classifier, the weight assigned to each hypothesis is the estimated posterior probability that it describes the target concept, given the training data. Later in this section we describe a different algorithm based on weighted voting, called the WEIGHTED-MAJORITY algorithm.

7.5.3 Optimal Mistake Bounds

The above analyses give worst-case mistake bounds for two specific algorithms: FIND-S and CANDIDATE-ELIMINATION. It is interesting to ask what is the optimal mistake bound for an arbitrary concept class C, assuming $H = C$. By optimal mistake bound we mean the lowest worst-case mistake bound over all possible learning algorithms. To be more precise, for any learning algorithm A and any target concept c, let $M_A(c)$ denote the maximum over all possible sequences of training examples of the number of mistakes made by A to exactly learn c. Now for any nonempty concept class C, let $M_A(C) \equiv \max_{c \in C} M_A(c)$. Note that above we showed $M_{Find-S}(C) = n + 1$ when C is the concept class described by up to n boolean literals. We also showed $M_{Halving}(C) \leq log_2(|C|)$ for any concept class C.

We define the optimal mistake bound for a concept class C below.

Definition: Let C be an arbitrary nonempty concept class. The **optimal mistake bound** for C, denoted $Opt(C)$, is the minimum over all possible learning algorithms A of $M_A(C)$.

$$Opt(C) \equiv \min_{A \in learning\ algorithms} M_A(C)$$

Speaking informally, this definition states that $Opt(C)$ is the number of mistakes made for the hardest target concept in C, using the hardest training sequence, by the best algorithm. Littlestone (1987) shows that for any concept class C, there is an interesting relationship among the optimal mistake bound for C, the bound of the HALVING algorithm, and the VC dimension of C, namely

$$VC(C) \leq Opt(C) \leq M_{Halving}(C) \leq log_2(|C|)$$

Furthermore, there exist concept classes for which the four quantities above are exactly equal. One such concept class is the powerset C_P of any finite set of instances X. In this case, $VC(C_P) = |X| = \log_2(|C_P|)$, so all four quantities must be equal. Littlestone (1987) provides examples of other concept classes for which $VC(C)$ is strictly less than $Opt(C)$ and for which $Opt(C)$ is strictly less than $M_{Halving}(C)$.

7.5.4 WEIGHTED-MAJORITY Algorithm

In this section we consider a generalization of the HALVING algorithm called the WEIGHTED-MAJORITY algorithm. The WEIGHTED-MAJORITY algorithm makes predictions by taking a weighted vote among a pool of prediction algorithms and learns by altering the weight associated with each prediction algorithm. These prediction algorithms can be taken to be the alternative hypotheses in H, or they can be taken to be alternative learning algorithms that themselves vary over time. All that we require of a prediction algorithm is that it predict the value of the target concept, given an instance. One interesting property of the WEIGHTED-MAJORITY algorithm is that it is able to accommodate inconsistent training data. This is because it does not eliminate a hypothesis that is found to be inconsistent with some training example, but rather reduces its weight. A second interesting property is that we can bound the number of mistakes made by WEIGHTED-MAJORITY in terms of the number of mistakes committed by the best of the pool of prediction algorithms.

The WEIGHTED-MAJORITY algorithm begins by assigning a weight of 1 to each prediction algorithm, then considers the training examples. Whenever a prediction algorithm misclassifies a new training example its weight is decreased by multiplying it by some number β, where $0 \leq \beta < 1$. The exact definition of the WEIGHTED-MAJORITY algorithm is given in Table 7.1.

Notice if $\beta = 0$ then WEIGHTED-MAJORITY is identical to the HALVING algorithm. On the other hand, if we choose some other value for β, no prediction

---

a_i denotes the ith prediction algorithm in the pool A of algorithms. w_i denotes the weight associated with a_i.

- For all i initialize $w_i \leftarrow 1$
- For each training example $\langle x, c(x)\rangle$
  - Initialize q_0 and q_1 to 0
  - For each prediction algorithm a_i
    - If $a_i(x) = 0$ then $q_0 \leftarrow q_0 + w_i$
      If $a_i(x) = 1$ then $q_1 \leftarrow q_1 + w_i$
  - If $q_1 > q_0$ then predict $c(x) = 1$
    If $q_0 > q_1$ then predict $c(x) = 0$
    If $q_1 = q_0$ then predict 0 or 1 at random for $c(x)$
  - For each prediction algorithm a_i in A do
    If $a_i(x) \neq c(x)$ then $w_i \leftarrow \beta w_i$

TABLE 7.1
WEIGHTED-MAJORITY algorithm.

algorithm will ever be eliminated completely. If an algorithm misclassifies a training example, it will simply receive a smaller vote in the future.

We now show that the number of mistakes committed by the WEIGHTED-MAJORITY algorithm can be bounded in terms of the number of mistakes made by the best prediction algorithm in the voting pool.

Theorem 7.5. Relative mistake bound for WEIGHTED-MAJORITY. Let D be any sequence of training examples, let A be any set of n prediction algorithms, and let k be the minimum number of mistakes made by any algorithm in A for the training sequence D. Then the number of mistakes over D made by the WEIGHTED-MAJORITY algorithm using $\beta = \frac{1}{2}$ is at most

$$2.4(k + \log_2 n)$$

Proof. We prove the theorem by comparing the final weight of the best prediction algorithm to the sum of weights over all algorithms. Let a_j denote an algorithm from A that commits the optimal number k of mistakes. The final weight w_j associated with a_j will be $(\frac{1}{2})^k$, because its initial weight is 1 and it is multiplied by $\frac{1}{2}$ for each mistake. Now consider the sum $W = \sum_{i=1}^{n} w_i$ of the weights associated with all n algorithms in A. W is initially n. For each mistake made by WEIGHTED-MAJORITY, W is reduced to at most $\frac{3}{4}W$. This is the case because the algorithms voting in the weighted majority must hold at least half of the total weight W, and this portion of W will be reduced by a factor of $\frac{1}{2}$. Let M denote the total number of mistakes committed by WEIGHTED-MAJORITY for the training sequence D. Then the final total weight W is at most $n(\frac{3}{4})^M$. Because the final weight w_j cannot be greater than the final total weight, we have

$$\left(\frac{1}{2}\right)^k \leq n\left(\frac{3}{4}\right)^M$$

Rearranging terms yields

$$M \leq \frac{(k + \log_2 n)}{-\log_2\left(\frac{3}{4}\right)} \leq 2.4(k + \log_2 n)$$

which proves the theorem. □

To summarize, the above theorem states that the number of mistakes made by the WEIGHTED-MAJORITY algorithm will never be greater than a constant factor times the number of mistakes made by the best member of the pool, plus a term that grows only logarithmically in the size of the pool.

This theorem is generalized by Littlestone and Warmuth (1991), who show that for an arbitrary $0 \leq \beta < 1$ the above bound is

$$\frac{k \log_2 \frac{1}{\beta} + \log_2 n}{\log_2 \frac{2}{1+\beta}}$$

7.6 SUMMARY AND FURTHER READING

The main points of this chapter include:

- The probably approximately correct (PAC) model considers algorithms that learn target concepts from some concept class C, using training examples drawn at random according to an unknown, but fixed, probability distribution. It requires that the learner probably (with probability at least $[1 - \delta]$) learn a hypothesis that is approximately (within error ϵ) correct, given computational effort and training examples that grow only polynomially with $1/\epsilon$, $1/\delta$, the size of the instances, and the size of the target concept.
- Within the setting of the PAC learning model, any consistent learner using a finite hypothesis space H where $C \subseteq H$ will, with probability $(1 - \delta)$, output a hypothesis within error ϵ of the target concept, after observing m randomly drawn training examples, as long as

$$m \geq \frac{1}{\epsilon}(\ln(1/\delta) + \ln|H|)$$

  This gives a bound on the number of training examples sufficient for successful learning under the PAC model.
- One constraining assumption of the PAC learning model is that the learner knows in advance some restricted concept class C that contains the target concept to be learned. In contrast, the *agnostic learning* model considers the more general setting in which the learner makes no assumption about the class from which the target concept is drawn. Instead, the learner outputs the hypothesis from H that has the least error (possibly nonzero) over the training data. Under this less restrictive agnostic learning model, the learner is assured with probability $(1 - \delta)$ to output a hypothesis within error ϵ of the

best possible hypothesis in H, after observing m randomly drawn training examples, provided

$$m \geq \frac{1}{2\epsilon^2}(\ln(1/\delta) + \ln|H|)$$

- The number of training examples required for successful learning is strongly influenced by the complexity of the hypothesis space considered by the learner. One useful measure of the complexity of a hypothesis space H is its Vapnik-Chervonenkis dimension, $VC(H)$. $VC(H)$ is the size of the largest subset of instances that can be shattered (split in all possible ways) by H.
- An alternative upper bound on the number of training examples sufficient for successful learning under the PAC model, stated in terms of $VC(H)$ is

$$m \geq \frac{1}{\epsilon}(4\log_2(2/\delta) + 8VC(H)\log_2(13/\epsilon))$$

A lower bound is

$$m \geq \max\left[\frac{1}{\epsilon}\log(1/\delta), \frac{VC(C) - 1}{32\epsilon}\right]$$

- An alternative learning model, called the *mistake bound model*, is used to analyze the number of training examples a learner will misclassify before it exactly learns the target concept. For example, the HALVING algorithm will make at most $\lfloor \log_2 |H| \rfloor$ mistakes before exactly learning any target concept drawn from H. For an arbitrary concept class C, the best worst-case algorithm will make $Opt(C)$ mistakes, where

$$VC(C) \leq Opt(C) \leq \log_2(|C|)$$

- The WEIGHTED-MAJORITY algorithm combines the weighted votes of multiple prediction algorithms to classify new instances. It learns weights for each of these prediction algorithms based on errors made over a sequence of examples. Interestingly, the number of mistakes made by WEIGHTED-MAJORITY can be bounded in terms of the number of mistakes made by the best prediction algorithm in the pool.

Much early work on computational learning theory dealt with the question of whether the learner could identify the target concept in the limit, given an indefinitely long sequence of training examples. The identification in the limit model was introduced by Gold (1967). A good overview of results in this area is (Angluin 1992). Vapnik (1982) examines in detail the problem of uniform convergence, and the closely related PAC-learning model was introduced by Valiant (1984). The discussion in this chapter of ϵ-exhausting the version space is based on Haussler's (1988) exposition. A useful collection of results under the PAC model can be found in Blumer et al. (1989). Kearns and Vazirani (1994) provide an excellent exposition of many results from computational learning theory. Earlier texts in this area include Anthony and Biggs (1992) and Natarajan (1991).

Current research on computational learning theory covers a broad range of learning models and learning algorithms. Much of this research can be found in the proceedings of the annual conference on Computational Learning Theory (COLT). Several special issues of the journal *Machine Learning* have also been devoted to this topic.

EXERCISES

7.1. Consider training a two-input perceptron. Give an upper bound on the number of training examples sufficient to assure with 90% confidence that the learned perceptron will have true error of at most 5%. Does this bound seem realistic?

7.2. Consider the class C of concepts of the form $(a \leq x \leq b) \wedge (c \leq y \leq d)$, where a, b, c, and d are integers in the interval (0, 99). Note each concept in this class corresponds to a rectangle with integer-valued boundaries on a portion of the x, y plane. Hint: Given a region in the plane bounded by the points $(0, 0)$ and $(n-1, n-1)$, the number of distinct rectangles with integer-valued boundaries within this region is $(\frac{n(n+1)}{2})^2$.

(*a*) Give an upper bound on the number of randomly drawn training examples sufficient to assure that for any target concept c in C, any consistent learner using $H = C$ will, with probability 95%, output a hypothesis with error at most .15.

(*b*) Now suppose the rectangle boundaries a, b, c, and d take on *real* values instead of integer values. Update your answer to the first part of this question.

7.3. In this chapter we derived an expression for the number of training examples sufficient to ensure that every hypothesis will have true error no worse than ϵ plus its observed training error $error_D(h)$. In particular, we used Hoeffding bounds to derive Equation (7.3). Derive an alternative expression for the number of training examples sufficient to ensure that every hypothesis will have true error no worse than $(1+\gamma)error_D(h)$. You can use the general Chernoff bounds to derive such a result.

Chernoff bounds: Suppose $X_1, \ldots, X_m$ are the outcomes of m independent coin flips (Bernoulli trials), where the probability of heads on any single trial is $\Pr[X_i = 1] = p$ and the probability of tails is $\Pr[X_i = 0] = 1 - p$. Define $S = X_1 + X_2 + \cdots + X_m$ to be the sum of the outcomes of these m trials. The expected value of S/m is $E[S/m] = p$. The Chernoff bounds govern the probability that S/m will differ from p by some factor $0 \leq \gamma \leq 1$.

$$\Pr[S/m > (1+\gamma)p] \leq e^{-mp\gamma^2/3}$$

$$\Pr[S/m < (1-\gamma)p] \leq e^{-mp\gamma^2/2}$$

7.4. Consider a learning problem in which $X = \Re$ is the set of real numbers, and $C = H$ is the set of intervals over the reals, $H = \{(a < x < b) \mid a, b \in \Re\}$. What is the probability that a hypothesis consistent with m examples of this target concept will have error at least ϵ? Solve this using the VC dimension. Can you find a second way to solve this, based on first principles and ignoring the VC dimension?

7.5. Consider the space of instances X corresponding to all points in the x, y plane. Give the VC dimension of the following hypothesis spaces:

(*a*) $H_r =$ the set of all rectangles in the x, y plane. That is, $H = \{((a < x < b) \wedge (c < y < d)) | a, b, c, d \in \Re\}$.

(*b*) $H_c =$ circles in the x, y plane. Points inside the circle are classified as positive examples

(*c*) H_t =triangles in the x, y plane. Points inside the triangle are classified as positive examples

7.6. Write a consistent learner for H_r from Exercise 7.5. Generate a variety of target concept rectangles at random, corresponding to different rectangles in the plane. Generate random examples of each of these target concepts, based on a uniform distribution of instances within the rectangle from $\langle 0, 0 \rangle$ to $\langle 100, 100 \rangle$. Plot the generalization error as a function of the number of training examples, m. On the same graph, plot the theoretical relationship between ϵ and m, for $\delta = .95$. Does theory fit experiment?

7.7. Consider the hypothesis class H_{rd2} of "regular, depth-2 decision trees" over n Boolean variables. A "regular, depth-2 decision tree" is a depth-2 decision tree (a tree with four leaves, all distance 2 from the root) in which the left and right child of the root are *required to contain the same variable*. For instance, the following tree is in H_{rd2}.

```
          x3
         /  \
      x1      x1
     /  \    /  \
    +    -  -    +
```

(*a*) As a function of n, how many syntactically distinct trees are there in H_{rd2}?

(*b*) Give an upper bound for the number of examples needed in the PAC model to learn H_{rd2} with error ϵ and confidence δ.

(*c*) Consider the following WEIGHTED-MAJORITY algorithm, for the class H_{rd2}. You begin with all hypotheses in H_{rd2} assigned an initial weight equal to 1. Every time you see a new example, you predict based on a weighted majority vote over all hypotheses in H_{rd2}. Then, instead of eliminating the inconsistent trees, you cut down their weight by a factor of 2. How many mistakes will this procedure make at most, as a function of n and the number of mistakes of the best tree in H_{rd2}?

7.8. This question considers the relationship between the PAC analysis considered in this chapter and the evaluation of hypotheses discussed in Chapter 5. Consider a learning task in which instances are described by n boolean variables (e.g., $x_1 \wedge \bar{x_2} \wedge x_3 \ldots \bar{x_n}$) and are drawn according to a fixed but unknown probability distribution $\mathcal{D}$. The target concept is known to be describable by a conjunction of boolean attributes and their negations (e.g., $x_2 \wedge \bar{x_5}$), and the learning algorithm uses this concept class as its hypothesis space H. A consistent learner is provided a set of 100 training examples drawn according to $\mathcal{D}$. It outputs a hypothesis h from H that is consistent with all 100 examples (i.e., the error of h over these training examples is zero).

(*a*) We are interested in the true error of h, that is, the probability that it will misclassify future instances drawn randomly according to $\mathcal{D}$. Based on the above information, can you give an interval into which this true error will fall with at least 95% probability? If so, state it and justify it briefly. If not, explain the difficulty.

(*b*) You now draw a new set of 100 instances, drawn independently according to the same distribution $\mathcal{D}$. You find that h misclassifies 30 of these 100 new examples. Can you give an interval into which this true error will fall with approximately 95% probability? (Ignore the performance over the earlier training data for this part.) If so, state it and justify it briefly. If not, explain the difficulty.

(*c*) It may seem a bit odd that h misclassifies 30% of the new examples even though it perfectly classified the training examples. Is this event more likely for large n or small n? Justify your answer in a sentence.

REFERENCES

Angluin, D. (1992). Computational learning theory: Survey and selected bibliography. *Proceedings of the Twenty-Fourth Annual ACM Symposium on Theory of Computing* (pp. 351–369). ACM Press.

Angluin, D., Frazier, M., & Pitt, L. (1992). Learning conjunctions of horn clauses. *Machine Learning*, 9, 147–164.

Anthony, M., & Biggs, N. (1992). *Computational learning theory: An introduction*. Cambridge, England: Cambridge University Press.

Blumer, A., Ehrenfeucht, A., Haussler, D., & Warmuth, M. (1989). Learnability and the Vapnik-Chervonenkis dimension. *Journal of the ACM*, 36(4) (October), 929–965.

Ehrenfeucht, A., Haussler, D., Kearns, M., & Valiant, L. (1989). A general lower bound on the number of examples needed for learning. *Information and Computation*, 82, 247–261.

Gold, E. M. (1967). Language identification in the limit. *Information and Control*, 10, 447–474.

Goldman, S. (Ed.). (1995). Special issue on computational learning theory. *Machine Learning*, 18(2/3), February.

Haussler, D. (1988). Quantifying inductive bias: AI learning algorithms and Valiant's learning framework. *Artificial Intelligence*, 36, 177–221.

Kearns, M. J., & Vazirani, U. V. (1994). *An introduction to computational learning theory*. Cambridge, MA: MIT Press.

Laird, P. (1988). *Learning from good and bad data*. Dordrecht: Kluwer Academic Publishers.

Li, M., & Valiant, L. G. (Eds.). (1994). Special issue on computational learning theory. *Machine Learning*, 14(1).

Littlestone, N. (1987). Learning quickly when irrelevant attributes abound: A new linear-threshold algorithm. *Machine Learning*, 2, 285–318.

Littlestone, N., & Warmuth, M. (1991). *The weighted majority algorithm* (Technical report UCSC-CRL-91-28). Univ. of California Santa Cruz, Computer Engineering and Information Sciences Dept., Santa Cruz, CA.

Littlestone, N., & Warmuth, M. (1994). The weighted majority algorithm. *Information and Computation* (108), 212–261.

Pitt, L. (Ed.). (1990). Special issue on computational learning theory. *Machine Learning*, 5(2).

Natarajan, B. K. (1991). *Machine learning: A theoretical approach*. San Mateo, CA: Morgan Kaufmann.

Valiant, L. (1984). A theory of the learnable. *Communications of the ACM*, 27(11), 1134–1142.

Vapnik, V. N. (1982). *Estimation of dependences based on empirical data*. New York: Springer-Verlag.

Vapnik, V. N., & Chervonenkis, A. (1971). On the uniform convergence of relative frequencies of events to their probabilities. *Theory of Probability and Its Applications*, 16, 264–280.

CHAPTER 8

INSTANCE-BASED LEARNING

In contrast to learning methods that construct a general, explicit description of the target function when training examples are provided, instance-based learning methods simply store the training examples. Generalizing beyond these examples is postponed until a new instance must be classified. Each time a new query instance is encountered, its relationship to the previously stored examples is examined in order to assign a target function value for the new instance. Instance-based learning includes nearest neighbor and locally weighted regression methods that assume instances can be represented as points in a Euclidean space. It also includes case-based reasoning methods that use more complex, symbolic representations for instances. Instance-based methods are sometimes referred to as "lazy" learning methods because they delay processing until a new instance must be classified. A key advantage of this kind of delayed, or lazy, learning is that instead of estimating the target function once for the entire instance space, these methods can estimate it locally and differently for each new instance to be classified.

8.1 INTRODUCTION

Instance-based learning methods such as nearest neighbor and locally weighted regression are conceptually straightforward approaches to approximating real-valued or discrete-valued target functions. Learning in these algorithms consists of simply storing the presented training data. When a new query instance is encountered, a set of similar related instances is retrieved from memory and used to classify the new query instance. One key difference between these approaches and the methods discussed in other chapters is that instance-based approaches can construct a different approximation to the target function for each distinct query instance that must be classified. In fact, many techniques construct only a local approximation to the target function that applies in the neighborhood of the new query instance, and never construct an approximation designed to perform well over the entire instance space. This has significant advantages when the target function is very complex, but can still be described by a collection of less complex local approximations.

Instance-based methods can also use more complex, symbolic representations for instances. In case-based learning, instances are represented in this fashion and the process for identifying "neighboring" instances is elaborated accordingly. Case-based reasoning has been applied to tasks such as storing and reusing past experience at a help desk, reasoning about legal cases by referring to previous cases, and solving complex scheduling problems by reusing relevant portions of previously solved problems.

One disadvantage of instance-based approaches is that the cost of classifying new instances can be high. This is due to the fact that nearly all computation takes place at classification time rather than when the training examples are first encountered. Therefore, techniques for efficiently indexing training examples are a significant practical issue in reducing the computation required at query time. A second disadvantage to many instance-based approaches, especially nearest-neighbor approaches, is that they typically consider *all* attributes of the instances when attempting to retrieve similar training examples from memory. If the target concept depends on only a few of the many available attributes, then the instances that are truly most "similar" may well be a large distance apart.

In the next section we introduce the k-NEAREST NEIGHBOR learning algorithm, including several variants of this widely-used approach. The subsequent section discusses locally weighted regression, a learning method that constructs local approximations to the target function and that can be viewed as a generalization of k-NEAREST NEIGHBOR algorithms. We then describe radial basis function networks, which provide an interesting bridge between instance-based and neural network learning algorithms. The next section discusses case-based reasoning, an instance-based approach that employs symbolic representations and knowledge-based inference. This section includes an example application of case-based reasoning to a problem in engineering design. Finally, we discuss the fundamental differences in capabilities that distinguish lazy learning methods discussed in this chapter from eager learning methods discussed in the other chapters of this book.

8.2 k-NEAREST NEIGHBOR LEARNING

The most basic instance-based method is the k-NEAREST NEIGHBOR algorithm. This algorithm assumes all instances correspond to points in the n-dimensional space $\Re^n$. The nearest neighbors of an instance are defined in terms of the standard

Euclidean distance. More precisely, let an arbitrary instance x be described by the feature vector

$$\langle a_1(x), a_2(x), \ldots a_n(x)\rangle$$

where $a_r(x)$ denotes the value of the rth attribute of instance x. Then the distance between two instances x_i and x_j is defined to be $d(x_i, x_j)$, where

$$d(x_i, x_j) \equiv \sqrt{\sum_{r=1}^{n} (a_r(x_i) - a_r(x_j))^2}$$

In nearest-neighbor learning the target function may be either discrete-valued or real-valued. Let us first consider learning discrete-valued target functions of the form $f : \Re^n \to V$, where V is the finite set $\{v_1, \ldots v_s\}$. The k-NEAREST NEIGHBOR algorithm for approximating a discrete-valued target function is given in Table 8.1. As shown there, the value $\hat{f}(x_q)$ returned by this algorithm as its estimate of $f(x_q)$ is just the most common value of f among the k training examples nearest to x_q. If we choose $k = 1$, then the 1-NEAREST NEIGHBOR algorithm assigns to $\hat{f}(x_q)$ the value $f(x_i)$ where x_i is the training instance nearest to x_q. For larger values of k, the algorithm assigns the most common value among the k nearest training examples.

Figure 8.1 illustrates the operation of the k-NEAREST NEIGHBOR algorithm for the case where the instances are points in a two-dimensional space and where the target function is boolean valued. The positive and negative training examples are shown by "+" and "−" respectively. A query point x_q is shown as well. Note the 1-NEAREST NEIGHBOR algorithm classifies x_q as a positive example in this figure, whereas the 5-NEAREST NEIGHBOR algorithm classifies it as a negative example.

What is the nature of the hypothesis space H implicitly considered by the k-NEAREST NEIGHBOR algorithm? Note the k-NEAREST NEIGHBOR algorithm never forms an explicit general hypothesis $\hat{f}$ regarding the target function f. It simply computes the classification of each new query instance as needed. Nevertheless,

---

Training algorithm:

- For each training example $\langle x, f(x)\rangle$, add the example to the list *training_examples*

Classification algorithm:

- Given a query instance x_q to be classified,
  - Let $x_1 \ldots x_k$ denote the k instances from *training_examples* that are nearest to x_q
  - Return

$$\hat{f}(x_q) \leftarrow \underset{v \in V}{\operatorname{argmax}} \sum_{i=1}^{k} \delta(v, f(x_i))$$

where $\delta(a, b) = 1$ if $a = b$ and where $\delta(a, b) = 0$ otherwise.

TABLE 8.1
The k-NEAREST NEIGHBOR algorithm for approximating a discrete-valued function $f : \Re^n \to V$.

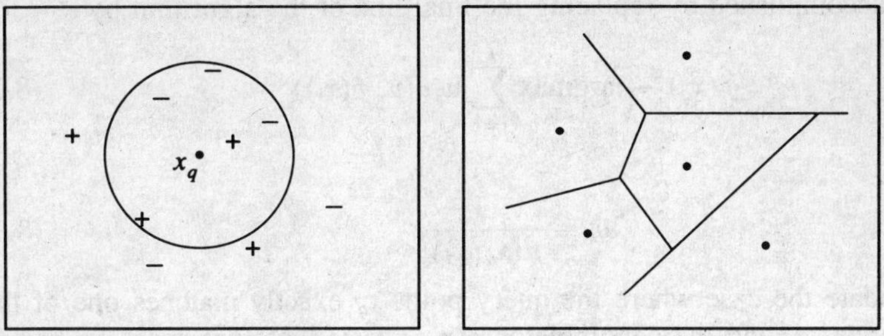

FIGURE 8.1
k-NEAREST NEIGHBOR. A set of positive and negative training examples is shown on the left, along with a query instance x_q to be classified. The 1-NEAREST NEIGHBOR algorithm classifies x_q positive, whereas 5-NEAREST NEIGHBOR classifies it as negative. On the right is the decision surface induced by the 1-NEAREST NEIGHBOR algorithm for a typical set of training examples. The convex polygon surrounding each training example indicates the region of instance space closest to that point (i.e., the instances for which the 1-NEAREST NEIGHBOR algorithm will assign the classification belonging to that training example).

we can still ask what the implicit general function is, or what classifications would be assigned if we were to hold the training examples constant and query the algorithm with every possible instance in X. The diagram on the right side of Figure 8.1 shows the shape of this decision surface induced by 1-NEAREST NEIGHBOR over the entire instance space. The decision surface is a combination of convex polyhedra surrounding each of the training examples. For every training example, the polyhedron indicates the set of query points whose classification will be completely determined by that training example. Query points outside the polyhedron are closer to some other training example. This kind of diagram is often called the *Voronoi diagram* of the set of training examples.

The k-NEAREST NEIGHBOR algorithm is easily adapted to approximating continuous-valued target functions. To accomplish this, we have the algorithm calculate the mean value of the k nearest training examples rather than calculate their most common value. More precisely, to approximate a real-valued target function $f : \Re^n \rightarrow \Re$ we replace the final line of the above algorithm by the line

$$\hat{f}(x_q) \leftarrow \frac{\sum_{i=1}^{k} f(x_i)}{k} \tag{8.1}$$

8.2.1 Distance-Weighted NEAREST NEIGHBOR Algorithm

One obvious refinement to the k-NEAREST NEIGHBOR algorithm is to weight the contribution of each of the k neighbors according to their distance to the query point x_q, giving greater weight to closer neighbors. For example, in the algorithm of Table 8.1, which approximates discrete-valued target functions, we might weight the vote of each neighbor according to the inverse square of its distance from x_q.

This can be accomplished by replacing the final line of the algorithm by

$$\hat{f}(x_q) \leftarrow \underset{v \in V}{\operatorname{argmax}} \sum_{i=1}^{k} w_i \delta(v, f(x_i)) \tag{8.2}$$

where

$$w_i \equiv \frac{1}{d(x_q, x_i)^2} \tag{8.3}$$

To accommodate the case where the query point x_q exactly matches one of the training instances x_i and the denominator $d(x_q, x_i)^2$ is therefore zero, we assign $\hat{f}(x_q)$ to be $f(x_i)$ in this case. If there are several such training examples, we assign the majority classification among them.

We can distance-weight the instances for real-valued target functions in a similar fashion, replacing the final line of the algorithm in this case by

$$\hat{f}(x_q) \leftarrow \frac{\sum_{i=1}^{k} w_i f(x_i)}{\sum_{i=1}^{k} w_i} \tag{8.4}$$

where w_i is as defined in Equation (8.3). Note the denominator in Equation (8.4) is a constant that normalizes the contributions of the various weights (e.g., it assures that if $f(x_i) = c$ for all training examples, then $\hat{f}(x_q) \leftarrow c$ as well).

Note all of the above variants of the k-NEAREST NEIGHBOR algorithm consider only the k nearest neighbors to classify the query point. Once we add distance weighting, there is really no harm in allowing all training examples to have an influence on the classification of the x_q, because very distant examples will have very little effect on $\hat{f}(x_q)$. The only disadvantage of considering all examples is that our classifier will run more slowly. If all training examples are considered when classifying a new query instance, we call the algorithm a *global* method. If only the nearest training examples are considered, we call it a *local* method. When the rule in Equation (8.4) is applied as a global method, using all training examples, it is known as Shepard's method (Shepard 1968).

8.2.2 Remarks on k-NEAREST NEIGHBOR Algorithm

The distance-weighted k-NEAREST NEIGHBOR algorithm is a highly effective inductive inference method for many practical problems. It is robust to noisy training data and quite effective when it is provided a sufficiently large set of training data. Note that by taking the weighted average of the k neighbors nearest to the query point, it can smooth out the impact of isolated noisy training examples.

What is the inductive bias of k-NEAREST NEIGHBOR? The basis for classifying new query points is easily understood based on the diagrams in Figure 8.1. The inductive bias corresponds to an assumption that the classification of an instance x_q will be most similar to the classification of other instances that are nearby in Euclidean distance.

One practical issue in applying k-NEAREST NEIGHBOR algorithms is that the distance between instances is calculated based on *all* attributes of the instance (i.e., on all axes in the Euclidean space containing the instances). This lies in contrast to methods such as rule and decision tree learning systems that select only a subset of the instance attributes when forming the hypothesis. To see the effect of this policy, consider applying k-NEAREST NEIGHBOR to a problem in which each instance is described by 20 attributes, but where only 2 of these attributes are relevant to determining the classification for the particular target function. In this case, instances that have identical values for the 2 relevant attributes may nevertheless be distant from one another in the 20-dimensional instance space. As a result, the similarity metric used by k-NEAREST NEIGHBOR—depending on all 20 attributes—will be misleading. The distance between neighbors will be dominated by the large number of irrelevant attributes. This difficulty, which arises when many irrelevant attributes are present, is sometimes referred to as the *curse of dimensionality*. Nearest-neighbor approaches are especially sensitive to this problem.

One interesting approach to overcoming this problem is to weight each attribute differently when calculating the distance between two instances. This corresponds to stretching the axes in the Euclidean space, shortening the axes that correspond to less relevant attributes, and lengthening the axes that correspond to more relevant attributes. The amount by which each axis should be stretched can be determined automatically using a cross-validation approach. To see how, first note that we wish to stretch (multiply) the jth axis by some factor z_j, where the values $z_1 \ldots z_n$ are chosen to minimize the true classification error of the learning algorithm. Second, note that this true error can be estimated using cross-validation. Hence, one algorithm is to select a random subset of the available data to use as training examples, then determine the values of $z_1 \ldots z_n$ that lead to the minimum error in classifying the remaining examples. By repeating this process multiple times the estimate for these weighting factors can be made more accurate. This process of stretching the axes in order to optimize the performance of k-NEAREST NEIGHBOR provides a mechanism for suppressing the impact of irrelevant attributes.

An even more drastic alternative is to completely eliminate the least relevant attributes from the instance space. This is equivalent to setting some of the z_i scaling factors to zero. Moore and Lee (1994) discuss efficient cross-validation methods for selecting relevant subsets of the attributes for k-NEAREST NEIGHBOR algorithms. In particular, they explore methods based on leave-one-out cross-validation, in which the set of m training instances is repeatedly divided into a training set of size $m-1$ and test set of size 1, in all possible ways. This leave-one-out approach is easily implemented in k-NEAREST NEIGHBOR algorithms because no additional training effort is required each time the training set is redefined. Note both of the above approaches can be seen as stretching each axis by some constant factor. Alternatively, we could stretch each axis by a value that varies over the instance space. However, as we increase the number of degrees of freedom available to the algorithm for redefining its distance metric in such a fashion, we also increase the risk of overfitting. Therefore, the approach of locally stretching the axes is much less common.

One additional practical issue in applying k-NEAREST NEIGHBOR is efficient memory indexing. Because this algorithm delays all processing until a new query is received, significant computation can be required to process each new query. Various methods have been developed for indexing the stored training examples so that the nearest neighbors can be identified more efficiently at some additional cost in memory. One such indexing method is the *kd*-tree (Bentley 1975; Friedman et al. 1977), in which instances are stored at the leaves of a tree, with nearby instances stored at the same or nearby nodes. The internal nodes of the tree sort the new query x_q to the relevant leaf by testing selected attributes of x_q.

8.2.3 A Note on Terminology

Much of the literature on nearest-neighbor methods and weighted local regression uses a terminology that has arisen from the field of statistical pattern recognition. In reading that literature, it is useful to know the following terms:

- *Regression* means approximating a real-valued target function.
- *Residual* is the error $\hat{f}(x) - f(x)$ in approximating the target function.
- *Kernel function* is the function of distance that is used to determine the weight of each training example. In other words, the kernel function is the function K such that $w_i = K(d(x_i, x_q))$.

8.3 LOCALLY WEIGHTED REGRESSION

The nearest-neighbor approaches described in the previous section can be thought of as approximating the target function $f(x)$ at the single query point $x = x_q$. Locally weighted regression is a generalization of this approach. It constructs an explicit approximation to f over a local region surrounding x_q. Locally weighted regression uses nearby or distance-weighted training examples to form this local approximation to f. For example, we might approximate the target function in the neighborhood surrounding x_q using a linear function, a quadratic function, a multilayer neural network, or some other functional form. The phrase "locally weighted regression" is called *local* because the function is approximated based only on data near the query point, *weighted* because the contribution of each training example is weighted by its distance from the query point, and *regression* because this is the term used widely in the statistical learning community for the problem of approximating real-valued functions.

Given a new query instance x_q, the general approach in locally weighted regression is to construct an approximation $\hat{f}$ that fits the training examples in the neighborhood surrounding x_q. This approximation is then used to calculate the value $\hat{f}(x_q)$, which is output as the estimated target value for the query instance. The description of $\hat{f}$ may then be deleted, because a different local approximation will be calculated for each distinct query instance.

8.3.1 Locally Weighted Linear Regression

Let us consider the case of locally weighted regression in which the target function f is approximated near x_q using a linear function of the form

$$\hat{f}(x) = w_0 + w_1 a_1(x) + \cdots + w_n a_n(x)$$

As before, $a_i(x)$ denotes the value of the ith attribute of the instance x.

Recall that in Chapter 4 we discussed methods such as gradient descent to find the coefficients $w_0 \ldots w_n$ to minimize the error in fitting such linear functions to a given set of training examples. In that chapter we were interested in a global approximation to the target function. Therefore, we derived methods to choose weights that minimize the squared error summed over the set D of training examples

$$E \equiv \frac{1}{2} \sum_{x \in D} (f(x) - \hat{f}(x))^2 \tag{8.5}$$

which led us to the gradient descent training rule

$$\Delta w_j = \eta \sum_{x \in D} (f(x) - \hat{f}(x)) a_j(x) \tag{8.6}$$

where η is a constant learning rate, and where the training rule has been re-expressed from the notation of Chapter 4 to fit our current notation (i.e., $t \rightarrow f(x)$, $o \rightarrow \hat{f}(x)$, and $x_j \rightarrow a_j(x)$).

How shall we modify this procedure to derive a local approximation rather than a global one? The simple way is to redefine the error criterion E to emphasize fitting the local training examples. Three possible criteria are given below. Note we write the error $E(x_q)$ to emphasize the fact that now the error is being defined as a function of the query point x_q.

1. Minimize the squared error over just the k nearest neighbors:

$$E_1(x_q) \equiv \frac{1}{2} \sum_{x \in \ k \ nearest \ nbrs \ of \ x_q} (f(x) - \hat{f}(x))^2$$

2. Minimize the squared error over the entire set D of training examples, while weighting the error of each training example by some decreasing function K of its distance from x_q:

$$E_2(x_q) \equiv \frac{1}{2} \sum_{x \in D} (f(x) - \hat{f}(x))^2 \ K(d(x_q, x))$$

3. Combine 1 and 2:

$$E_3(x_q) \equiv \frac{1}{2} \sum_{x \in \ k \ nearest \ nbrs \ of \ x_q} (f(x) - \hat{f}(x))^2 \ K(d(x_q, x))$$

Criterion two is perhaps the most esthetically pleasing because it allows every training example to have an impact on the classification of x_q. However, this approach requires computation that grows linearly with the number of training examples. Criterion three is a good approximation to criterion two and has the advantage that computational cost is independent of the total number of training examples; its cost depends only on the number k of neighbors considered.

If we choose criterion three above and rederive the gradient descent rule using the same style of argument as in Chapter 4, we obtain the following training rule (see Exercise 8.1):

$$\Delta w_j = \eta \sum_{x \in \ k \ nearest \ nbrs \ of \ x_q} K(d(x_q, x)) \ (f(x) - \hat{f}(x)) \ a_j(x) \tag{8.7}$$

Notice the only differences between this new rule and the rule given by Equation (8.6) are that the contribution of instance x to the weight update is now multiplied by the distance penalty $K(d(x_q, x))$, and that the error is summed over only the k nearest training examples. In fact, if we are fitting a linear function to a fixed set of training examples, then methods much more efficient than gradient descent are available to directly solve for the desired coefficients $w_0 \ldots w_n$. Atkeson et al. (1997a) and Bishop (1995) survey several such methods.

8.3.2 Remarks on Locally Weighted Regression

Above we considered using a linear function to approximate f in the neighborhood of the query instance x_q. The literature on locally weighted regression contains a broad range of alternative methods for distance weighting the training examples, and a range of methods for locally approximating the target function. In most cases, the target function is approximated by a constant, linear, or quadratic function. More complex functional forms are not often found because (1) the cost of fitting more complex functions for each query instance is prohibitively high, and (2) these simple approximations model the target function quite well over a sufficiently small subregion of the instance space.

8.4 RADIAL BASIS FUNCTIONS

One approach to function approximation that is closely related to distance-weighted regression and also to artificial neural networks is learning with radial basis functions (Powell 1987; Broomhead and Lowe 1988; Moody and Darken 1989). In this approach, the learned hypothesis is a function of the form

$$\hat{f}(x) = w_0 + \sum_{u=1}^{k} w_u K_u(d(x_u, x)) \tag{8.8}$$

where each x_u is an instance from X and where the kernel function $K_u(d(x_u, x))$ is defined so that it decreases as the distance $d(x_u, x)$ increases. Here k is a user-provided constant that specifies the number of kernel functions to be included. Even though $\hat{f}(x)$ is a global approximation to $f(x)$, the contribution from each of the $K_u(d(x_u, x))$ terms is localized to a region nearby the point x_u. It is common to choose each function $K_u(d(x_u, x))$ to be a Gaussian function (see Table 5.4) centered at the point x_u with some variance σ_u^2.

$$K_u(d(x_u, x)) = e^{\frac{1}{2\sigma_u^2}d^2(x_u, x)}$$

We will restrict our discussion here to this common Gaussian kernel function. As shown by Hartman et al. (1990), the functional form of Equation (8.8) can approximate any function with arbitrarily small error, provided a sufficiently large number k of such Gaussian kernels and provided the width σ^2 of each kernel can be separately specified.

The function given by Equation (8.8) can be viewed as describing a two-layer network where the first layer of units computes the values of the various $K_u(d(x_u, x))$ and where the second layer computes a linear combination of these first-layer unit values. An example radial basis function (RBF) network is illustrated in Figure 8.2.

Given a set of training examples of the target function, RBF networks are typically trained in a two-stage process. First, the number k of hidden units is determined and each hidden unit u is defined by choosing the values of x_u and σ_u^2 that define its kernel function $K_u(d(x_u, x))$. Second, the weights w_u are trained to maximize the fit of the network to the training data, using the global error criterion given by Equation (8.5). Because the kernel functions are held fixed during this second stage, the linear weight values w_u can be trained very efficiently.

Several alternative methods have been proposed for choosing an appropriate number of hidden units or, equivalently, kernel functions. One approach is to allocate a Gaussian kernel function for each training example $\langle x_i, f(x_i)\rangle$, centering this Gaussian at the point x_i. Each of these kernels may be assigned the same width σ^2. Given this approach, the RBF network learns a global approximation to the target function in which each training example $\langle x_i, f(x_i)\rangle$ can influence the value of $\hat{f}$ only in the neighborhood of x_i. One advantage of this choice of kernel functions is that it allows the RBF network to fit the training data exactly. That is, for any set of m training examples the weights $w_0 \ldots w_m$ for combining the m Gaussian kernel functions can be set so that $\hat{f}(x_i) = f(x_i)$ for each training example $\langle x_i, f(x_i)\rangle$.

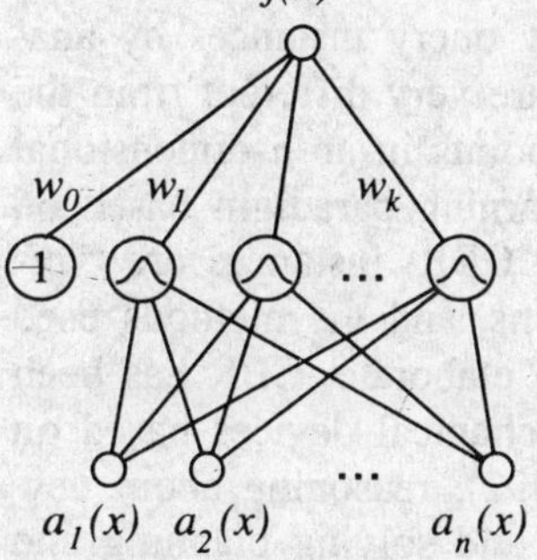

FIGURE 8.2
A radial basis function network. Each hidden unit produces an activation determined by a Gaussian function centered at some instance x_u. Therefore, its activation will be close to zero unless the input x is near x_u. The output unit produces a linear combination of the hidden unit activations. Although the network shown here has just one output, multiple output units can also be included.

A second approach is to choose a set of kernel functions that is smaller than the number of training examples. This approach can be much more efficient than the first approach, especially when the number of training examples is large. The set of kernel functions may be distributed with centers spaced uniformly throughout the instance space X. Alternatively, we may wish to distribute the centers nonuniformly, especially if the instances themselves are found to be distributed nonuniformly over X. In this later case, we can pick kernel function centers by randomly selecting a subset of the training instances, thereby sampling the underlying distribution of instances. Alternatively, we may identify prototypical clusters of instances, then add a kernel function centered at each cluster. The placement of the kernel functions in this fashion can be accomplished using unsupervised clustering algorithms that fit the training instances (but not their target values) to a mixture of Gaussians. The EM algorithm discussed in Section 6.12.1 provides one algorithm for choosing the means of a mixture of k Gaussians to best fit the observed instances. In the case of the EM algorithm, the means are chosen to maximize the probability of observing the instances x_i, given the k estimated means. Note the target function value $f(x_i)$ of the instance does not enter into the calculation of kernel centers by unsupervised clustering methods. The only role of the target values $f(x_i)$ in this case is to determine the output layer weights w_u.

To summarize, radial basis function networks provide a global approximation to the target function, represented by a linear combination of many local kernel functions. The value for any given kernel function is non-negligible only when the input x falls into the region defined by its particular center and width. Thus, the network can be viewed as a smooth linear combination of many local approximations to the target function. One key advantage to RBF networks is that they can be trained much more efficiently than feedforward networks trained with BACKPROPAGATION. This follows from the fact that the input layer and the output layer of an RBF are trained separately.

8.5 CASE-BASED REASONING

Instance-based methods such as k-NEAREST NEIGHBOR and locally weighted regression share three key properties. First, they are *lazy* learning methods in that they defer the decision of how to generalize beyond the training data until a new query instance is observed. Second, they classify new query instances by analyzing similar instances while ignoring instances that are very different from the query. Third, they represent instances as real-valued points in an n-dimensional Euclidean space. Case-based reasoning (CBR) is a learning paradigm based on the first two of these principles, but not the third. In CBR, instances are typically represented using more rich symbolic descriptions, and the methods used to retrieve similar instances are correspondingly more elaborate. CBR has been applied to problems such as conceptual design of mechanical devices based on a stored library of previous designs (Sycara et al. 1992), reasoning about new legal cases based on previous rulings (Ashley 1990), and solving planning and scheduling problems by reusing and combining portions of previous solutions to similar problems (Veloso 1992).

Let us consider a prototypical example of a case-based reasoning system to ground our discussion. The CADET system (Sycara et al. 1992) employs case-based reasoning to assist in the conceptual design of simple mechanical devices such as water faucets. It uses a library containing approximately 75 previous designs and design fragments to suggest conceptual designs to meet the specifications of new design problems. Each instance stored in memory (e.g., a water pipe) is represented by describing both its structure and its qualitative function. New design problems are then presented by specifying the desired function and requesting the corresponding structure. This problem setting is illustrated in Figure 8.3. The top half of the figure shows the description of a typical stored case called a T-junction pipe. Its function is represented in terms of the qualitative relationships among the waterflow levels and temperatures at its inputs and outputs. In the functional description at its right, an arrow with a "+" label indicates that the variable at the arrowhead increases with the variable at its tail. For example, the output waterflow Q_3 increases with increasing input waterflow Q_1. Similarly,

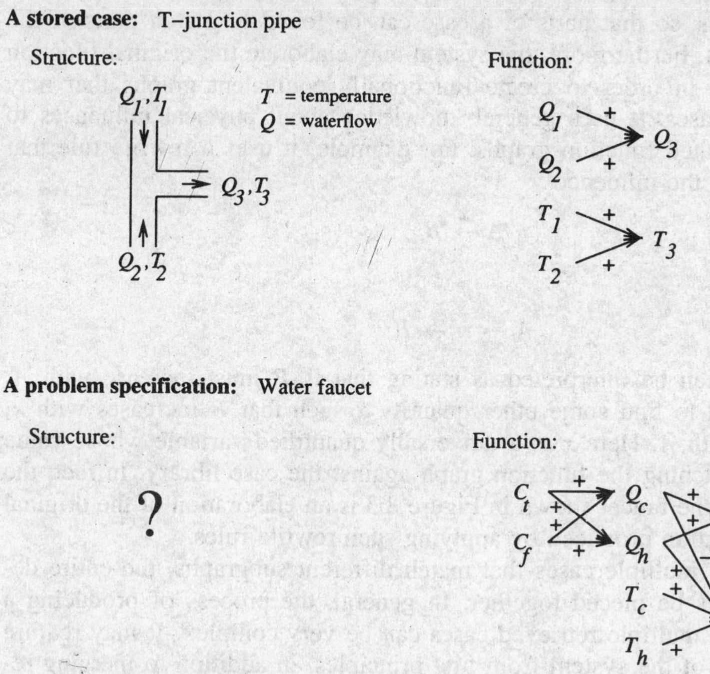

FIGURE 8.3
A stored case and a new problem. The top half of the figure describes a typical design fragment in the case library of CADET. The function is represented by the graph of qualitative dependencies among the T-junction variables (described in the text). The bottom half of the figure shows a typical design problem.

a "–" label indicates that the variable at the head decreases with the variable at the tail. The bottom half of this figure depicts a new design problem described by its desired function. This particular function describes the required behavior of one type of water faucet. Here Q_c refers to the flow of cold water into the faucet, Q_h to the input flow of hot water, and Q_m to the single mixed flow out of the faucet. Similarly, T_c, T_h, and T_m refer to the temperatures of the cold water, hot water, and mixed water respectively. The variable C_t denotes the control signal for temperature that is input to the faucet, and C_f denotes the control signal for waterflow. Note the description of the desired function specifies that these controls C_t and C_f are to influence the water flows Q_c and Q_h, thereby indirectly influencing the faucet output flow Q_m and temperature T_m.

Given this functional specification for the new design problem, CADET searches its library for stored cases whose functional descriptions match the design problem. If an exact match is found, indicating that some stored case implements exactly the desired function, then this case can be returned as a suggested solution to the design problem. If no exact match occurs, CADET may find cases that match various subgraphs of the desired functional specification. In Figure 8.3, for example, the T-junction function matches a subgraph of the water faucet function graph. More generally, CADET searches for subgraph isomorphisms between the two function graphs, so that parts of a case can be found to match parts of the design specification. Furthermore, the system may elaborate the original function specification graph in order to create functionally equivalent graphs that may match still more cases. It uses general knowledge about physical influences to create these elaborated function graphs. For example, it uses a rewrite rule that allows it to rewrite the influence

$$A \stackrel{+}{\rightarrow} B$$

as

$$A \stackrel{+}{\rightarrow} x \stackrel{+}{\rightarrow} B$$

This rewrite rule can be interpreted as stating that if B must increase with A, then it is sufficient to find some other quantity x such that B increases with x, and x increases with A. Here x is a universally quantified variable whose value is bound when matching the function graph against the case library. In fact, the function graph for the faucet shown in Figure 8.3 is an elaboration of the original functional specification produced by applying such rewrite rules.

By retrieving multiple cases that match different subgraphs, the entire design can sometimes be pieced together. In general, the process of producing a final solution from multiple retrieved cases can be very complex. It may require designing portions of the system from first principles, in addition to merging retrieved portions from stored cases. It may also require backtracking on earlier choices of design subgoals and, therefore, rejecting cases that were previously retrieved. CADET has very limited capabilities for combining and adapting multiple retrieved cases to form the final design and relies heavily on the user for this adaptation stage of the process. As described by Sycara et al. (1992), CADET is a research prototype system intended to explore the potential role of case-based reasoning in conceptual design. It does not have the range of analysis algorithms needed to refine these abstract conceptual designs into final designs.

It is instructive to examine the correspondence between the problem setting of CADET and the general setting for instance-based methods such as k-NEAREST NEIGHBOR. In CADET each stored training example describes a function graph along with the structure that implements it. New queries correspond to new function graphs. Thus, we can map the CADET problem into our standard notation by defining the space of instances X to be the space of all function graphs. The target function f maps function graphs to the structures that implement them. Each stored training example $\langle x, f(x) \rangle$ is a pair that describes some function graph x and the structure $f(x)$ that implements x. The system must learn from the training example cases to output the structure $f(x_q)$ that successfully implements the input function graph query x_q.

The above sketch of the CADET system illustrates several generic properties of case-based reasoning systems that distinguish them from approaches such as k-NEAREST NEIGHBOR.

- Instances or cases may be represented by rich symbolic descriptions, such as the function graphs used in CADET. This may require a similarity metric different from Euclidean distance, such as the size of the largest shared subgraph between two function graphs.
- Multiple retrieved cases may be combined to form the solution to the new problem. This is similar to the k-NEAREST NEIGHBOR approach, in that multiple similar cases are used to construct a response for the new query. However, the process for combining these multiple retrieved cases can be very different, relying on knowledge-based reasoning rather than statistical methods.
- There may be a tight coupling between case retrieval, knowledge-based reasoning, and problem solving. One simple example of this is found in CADET, which uses generic knowledge about influences to rewrite function graphs during its attempt to find matching cases. Other systems have been developed that more fully integrate case-based reasoning into general search-based problem-solving systems. Two examples are ANAPRON (Golding and Rosenbloom 1991) and PRODIGY/ANALOGY (Veloso 1992).

To summarize, case-based reasoning is an instance-based learning method in which instances (cases) may be rich relational descriptions and in which the retrieval and combination of cases to solve the current query may rely on knowledge-based reasoning and search-intensive problem-solving methods. One current research issue in case-based reasoning is to develop improved methods for indexing cases. The central issue here is that syntactic similarity measures (e.g., subgraph isomorphism between function graphs) provide only an approximate indication of the relevance of a particular case to a particular problem. When the CBR system attempts to reuse the retrieved cases it may uncover difficulties that were not captured by this syntactic similarity measure. For example, in CADET the multiple retrieved design fragments may turn out to be incompatible with one another, making it impossible to combine them into a consistent final design. When this occurs in general, the CBR system may backtrack and search for additional cases, adapt the existing cases, or resort to other problem-solving methods. Importantly, when such difficulties are detected they also provide training data for improving the similarity metric or, equivalently, the indexing structure for the case library. In particular, if a case is retrieved based on the similarity metric, but found to be irrelevant based on further analysis, then the similarity metric should be refined to reject this case for similar subsequent queries.

8.6 REMARKS ON LAZY AND EAGER LEARNING

In this chapter we considered three *lazy* learning methods: the *k*-NEAREST NEIGHBOR algorithm, locally weighted regression, and case-based reasoning. We call these methods lazy because they defer the decision of how to generalize beyond the training data until each new query instance is encountered. We also discussed one *eager* learning method: the method for learning radial basis function networks. We call this method eager because it generalizes beyond the training data before observing the new query, committing at training time to the network structure and weights that define its approximation to the target function. In this same sense, every other algorithm discussed elsewhere in this book (e.g., BACKPROPAGATION, C4.5) is an eager learning algorithm.

Are there important differences in what can be achieved by lazy versus eager learning? Let us distinguish between two kinds of differences: differences in computation time and differences in the classifications produced for new queries. There are obviously differences in computation time between eager and lazy methods. For example, lazy methods will generally require less computation during training, but more computation when they must predict the target value for a new query.

The more fundamental question is whether there are essential differences in the inductive bias that can be achieved by lazy versus eager methods. The key difference between lazy and eager methods in this regard is

- Lazy methods may consider the query instance x_q when deciding how to generalize beyond the training data D.
- Eager methods cannot. By the time they observe the query instance x_q they have already chosen their (global) approximation to the target function.

Does this distinction affect the generalization accuracy of the learner? It does if we require that the lazy and eager learner employ the same hypothesis space H. To illustrate, consider the hypothesis space consisting of linear functions. The locally weighted linear regression algorithm discussed earlier is a lazy learning method based on this hypothesis space. For each new query x_q it generalizes from the training data by choosing a new hypothesis based on the training examples near x_q. In contrast, an eager learner that uses the same hypothesis space of linear functions must choose its approximation before the queries are observed. The eager learner must therefore commit to a single linear function hypothesis that covers the entire instance space and all future queries. The lazy method effectively uses a richer hypothesis space because it uses many different local linear functions to form its implicit global approximation to the target function. Note this same situation holds for other learners and hypothesis spaces as well. A lazy version of BACKPROPAGATION, for example, could learn a different neural network for each distinct query point, compared to the eager version of BACKPROPAGATION discussed in Chapter 4.

The key point in the above paragraph is that a lazy learner has the option of (implicitly) representing the target function by a combination of many local approximations, whereas an eager learner must commit at training time to a single global approximation. The distinction between eager and lazy learning is thus related to the distinction between global and local approximations to the target function.

Can we create eager methods that use multiple local approximations to achieve the same effects as lazy local methods? Radial basis function networks can be seen as one attempt to achieve this. The RBF learning methods we discussed are eager methods that commit to a global approximation to the target function at training time. However, an RBF network represents this global function as a linear combination of multiple local kernel functions. Nevertheless, because RBF learning methods must commit to the hypothesis before the query point is known, the local approximations they create are not specifically targeted to the query point to the same degree as in a lazy learning method. Instead, RBF networks are built eagerly from local approximations centered around the training examples, or around clusters of training examples, but not around the unknown future query points.

To summarize, lazy methods have the option of selecting a different hypothesis or local approximation to the target function for each query instance. Eager methods using the same hypothesis space are more restricted because they must commit to a single hypothesis that covers the entire instance space. Eager methods can, of course, employ hypothesis spaces that combine multiple local approximations, as in RBF networks. However, even these combined local approximations do not give eager methods the full ability of lazy methods to customize to unknown future query instances.

8.7 SUMMARY AND FURTHER READING

The main points of this chapter include:

- Instance-based learning methods differ from other approaches to function approximation because they delay processing of training examples until they must label a new query instance. As a result, they need not form an explicit hypothesis of the entire target function over the entire instance space, independent of the query instance. Instead, they may form a different local approximation to the target function for each query instance.

- Advantages of instance-based methods include the ability to model complex target functions by a collection of less complex local approximations and the fact that information present in the training examples is never lost (because the examples themselves are stored explicitly). The main practical difficulties include efficiency of labeling new instances (all processing is done at query time rather than in advance), difficulties in determining an appropriate distance metric for retrieving "related" instances (especially when examples are represented by complex symbolic descriptions), and the negative impact of irrelevant features on the distance metric.
- k-NEAREST NEIGHBOR is an instance-based algorithm for approximating real-valued or discrete-valued target functions, assuming instances correspond to points in an n-dimensional Euclidean space. The target function value for a new query is estimated from the known values of the k nearest training examples.
- Locally weighted regression methods are a generalization of k-NEAREST NEIGHBOR in which an explicit local approximation to the target function is constructed for each query instance. The local approximation to the target function may be based on a variety of functional forms such as constant, linear, or quadratic functions or on spatially localized kernel functions.
- Radial basis function (RBF) networks are a type of artificial neural network constructed from spatially localized kernel functions. These can be seen as a blend of instance-based approaches (spatially localized influence of each kernel function) and neural network approaches (a global approximation to the target function is formed at training time rather than a local approximation at query time). Radial basis function networks have been used successfully in applications such as interpreting visual scenes, in which the assumption of spatially local influences is well-justified.
- Case-based reasoning is an instance-based approach in which instances are represented by complex logical descriptions rather than points in a Euclidean space. Given these complex symbolic descriptions of instances, a rich variety of methods have been proposed for mapping from the training examples to target function values for new instances. Case-based reasoning methods have been used in applications such as modeling legal reasoning and for guiding searches in complex manufacturing and transportation planning problems.

The k-NEAREST NEIGHBOR algorithm is one of the most thoroughly analyzed algorithms in machine learning, due in part to its age and in part to its simplicity. Cover and Hart (1967) present early theoretical results, and Duda and Hart (1973) provide a good overview. Bishop (1995) provides a discussion of k-NEAREST NEIGHBOR and its relation to estimating probability densities. An excellent current survey of methods for locally weighted regression is given by Atkeson et al. (1997). The application of these methods to robot control is surveyed by Atkeson et al. (1997b).

A thorough discussion of radial basis functions is provided by Bishop (1995). Other treatments are given by Powell (1987) and Poggio and Girosi (1990). See Section 6.12 of this book for a discussion of the EM algorithm and its application to selecting the means of a mixture of Gaussians.

Kolodner (1993) provides a general introduction to case-based reasoning. Other general surveys and collections describing recent research are given by Aamodt et al. (1994), Aha et al. (1991), Haton et al. (1995), Riesbeck and Schank (1989), Schank et al. (1994), Veloso and Aamodt (1995), Watson (1995), and Wess et al. (1994).

EXERCISES

8.1. Derive the gradient descent rule for a distance-weighted local linear approximation to the target function, given by Equation (8.1).

8.2. Consider the following alternative method for accounting for distance in weighted local regression. Create a virtual set of training examples D' as follows: For each training example $\langle x, f(x)\rangle$ in the original data set D, create some (possibly fractional) number of copies of $\langle x, f(x)\rangle$ in D', where the number of copies is $K(d(x_q, x))$. Now train a linear approximation to minimize the error criterion

$$E_4 \equiv \frac{1}{2} \sum_{x \in D'} (f(x) - \hat{f}(x))^2$$

The idea here is to make more copies of training examples that are near the query instance, and fewer of those that are distant. Derive the gradient descent rule for this criterion. Express the rule in the form of a sum over members of D rather than D', and compare it with the rules given by Equations (8.6) and (8.7).

8.3. Suggest a lazy version of the eager decision tree learning algorithm ID3 (see Chapter 3). What are the advantages and disadvantages of your lazy algorithm compared to the original eager algorithm?

REFERENCES

Aamodt, A., & Plazas, E. (1994). Case-based reasoning: Foundational issues, methodological variations, and system approaches. *AI Communications*, 7(1), 39–52.

Aha, D., & Kibler, D. (1989). Noise-tolerant instance-based learning algorithms. *Proceedings of the IJCAI-89* (794–799).

Aha, D., Kibler, D., & Albert, M. (1991). Instance-based learning algorithms. *Machine Learning*, 6, 37–66.

Ashley, K. D. (1990). *Modeling legal argument: Reasoning with cases and hypotheticals*. Cambridge, MA: MIT Press.

Atkeson, C. G., Schaal, S. A., & Moore, A. W. (1997a). Locally weighted learning. *AI Review*, (to appear).

Atkeson, C. G., Moore, A. W., & Schaal, S. A. (1997b). Locally weighted learning for control. *AI Review*, (to appear).

Bareiss, E. R., Porter, B., & Weir, C. C. (1988). PROTOS: An exemplar-based learning apprentice. *International Journal of Man-Machine Studies*, 29, 549–561.

Bentley, J. L. (1975). Multidimensional binary search trees used for associative searching. *Communications of the ACM*, 18(9), 509–517.

Bishop, C. M. (1995). *Neural networks for pattern recognition*. Oxford, England: Oxford University Press.

Bisio, R., & Malabocchia, F. (1995). Cost estimation of software projects through case-based reasoning. In M. Veloso and A. Aamodt (Eds.), *Lecture Notes in Artificial Intelligence* (pp. 11–22). Berlin: Springer-Verlag.

Broomhead, D. S., & Lowe, D. (1988). Multivariable functional interpolation and adaptive networks. *Complex Systems*, 2, 321–355.

Cover, T., & Hart, P. (1967). Nearest neighbor pattern classification. *IEEE Transactions on Information Theory*, 13, 21–27.

Duda, R., & Hart, P. (1973). *Pattern classification and scene analysis*. New York: John Wiley & Sons.

Franke, R. (1982). Scattered data interpolation: Tests of some methods. *Mathematics of Computation*, 38, 181–200.

Friedman, J., Bentley, J., & Finkel, R. (1977). An algorithm for finding best matches in logarithmic expected time. *ACM Transactions on Mathematical Software*, 3(3), 209–226.

Golding, A., & Rosenbloom, P. (1991). Improving rule-based systems through case-based reasoning. *Proceedings of the Ninth National Conference on Artificial Intelligence* (pp. 22–27). Cambridge: AAAI Press/The MIT Press.

Hartman, E. J., Keller, J. D., & Kowalski, J. M. (1990). Layered neural networks with Gaussian hidden units as universal approximations. *Neural Computation*, 2(2), 210–215.

Haton, J.-P., Keane, M., & Manago, M. (Eds.). (1995). *Advances in case-based reasoning: Second European workshop*. Berlin: Springer-Verlag.

Kolodner, J. L. (1993). *Case-Based Reasoning*. San Francisco: Morgan Kaufmann.

Moody, J. E., & Darken, C. J. (1989). Fast learning in networks of locally-tuned processing units. *Neural Computation*, 1(2), 281–294.

Moore, A. W., & Lee, M. S. (1994). Efficient algorithms for minimizing cross validation error. *Proceedings of the 11th International Conference on Machine Learning*. San Francisco: Morgan Kaufmann.

Poggio, T., & Girosi, F. (1990). Networks for approximation and learning. *Proceedings of the IEEE*, 78(9), 1481–1497.

Powell, M. J. D. (1987). Radial basis functions for multivariable interpolation: A review. In Mason, J., & Cox, M. (Eds.). *Algorithms for approximation* (pp. 143–167). Oxford: Clarendon Press.

Riesbeck, C., & Schank, R. (1989). *Inside case-based reasoning*. Hillsdale, NJ: Lawrence Erlbaum.

Schank, R. (1982). *Dynamic Memory*. Cambridge, England: Cambridge University Press.

Schank, R., Riesbeck, C., & Kass, A. (1994). *Inside case-based explanation*. Hillsdale, NJ: Lawrence Erlbaum.

Shepard, D. (1968). A two-dimensional interpolation function for irregularly spaced data. *Proceedings of the 23rd National Conference of the ACM* (pp. 517–523).

Stanfill, C., & Waltz, D. (1986). Toward memory-based reasoning. *Communications of the ACM*, 29(12), 1213–1228.

Sycara, K., Guttal, R., Koning, J., Narasimhan, S., & Navinchandra, D. (1992). CADET: A case-based synthesis tool for engineering design. *International Journal of Expert Systems*, 4(2), 157–188.

Veloso, M. M. (1992). *Planning and learning by analogical reasoning*. Berlin: Springer-Verlag.

Veloso, M. M., & Aamodt, A. (Eds.). (1995). *Case-based reasoning research and development*. Lecture Notes in Artificial Intelligence. Berlin: Springer-Verlag.

Watson, I. (Ed.). (1995). *Progress in case-based reasoning: First United Kingdom workshop*. Berlin: Springer-Verlag.

Wess, S., Althoff, K., & Richter, M. (Eds.). (1994). *Topics in case-based reasoning*. Berlin: Springer-Verlag.

CHAPTER 9

GENETIC ALGORITHMS

Genetic algorithms provide an approach to learning that is based loosely on simulated evolution. Hypotheses are often described by bit strings whose interpretation depends on the application, though hypotheses may also be described by symbolic expressions or even computer programs. The search for an appropriate hypothesis begins with a population, or collection, of initial hypotheses. Members of the current population give rise to the next generation population by means of operations such as random mutation and crossover, which are patterned after processes in biological evolution. At each step, the hypotheses in the current population are evaluated relative to a given measure of fitness, with the most fit hypotheses selected probabilistically as seeds for producing the next generation. Genetic algorithms have been applied successfully to a variety of learning tasks and to other optimization problems. For example, they have been used to learn collections of rules for robot control and to optimize the topology and learning parameters for artificial neural networks. This chapter covers both genetic algorithms, in which hypotheses are typically described by bit strings, and genetic programming, in which hypotheses are described by computer programs.

9.1 MOTIVATION

Genetic algorithms (GAs) provide a learning method motivated by an analogy to biological evolution. Rather than search from general-to-specific hypotheses, or from simple-to-complex, GAs generate successor hypotheses by repeatedly mutating and recombining parts of the best currently known hypotheses. At each step, a collection of hypotheses called the current *population* is updated by replacing some fraction of the population by offspring of the most fit current hypotheses. The process forms a generate-and-test beam-search of hypotheses, in which variants of the best current hypotheses are most likely to be considered next. The popularity of GAs is motivated by a number of factors including:

- Evolution is known to be a successful, robust method for adaptation within biological systems.
- GAs can search spaces of hypotheses containing complex interacting parts, where the impact of each part on overall hypothesis fitness may be difficult to model.
- Genetic algorithms are easily parallelized and can take advantage of the decreasing costs of powerful computer hardware.

This chapter describes the genetic algorithm approach, illustrates its use, and examines the nature of its hypothesis space search. We also describe a variant called genetic programming, in which entire computer programs are evolved to certain fitness criteria. Genetic algorithms and genetic programming are two of the more popular approaches in a field that is sometimes called evolutionary computation. In the final section we touch on selected topics in the study of biological evolution, including the Baldwin effect, which describes an interesting interplay between the learning capabilities of single individuals and the rate of evolution of the entire population.

9.2 GENETIC ALGORITHMS

The problem addressed by GAs is to search a space of candidate hypotheses to identify the best hypothesis. In GAs the "best hypothesis" is defined as the one that optimizes a predefined numerical measure for the problem at hand, called the hypothesis *fitness*. For example, if the learning task is the problem of approximating an unknown function given training examples of its input and output, then fitness could be defined as the accuracy of the hypothesis over this training data. If the task is to learn a strategy for playing chess, fitness could be defined as the number of games won by the individual when playing against other individuals in the current population.

Although different implementations of genetic algorithms vary in their details, they typically share the following structure: The algorithm operates by iteratively updating a pool of hypotheses, called the population. On each iteration, all members of the population are evaluated according to the fitness function. A new population is then generated by probabilistically selecting the most fit individuals from the current population. Some of these selected individuals are carried forward into the next generation population intact. Others are used as the basis for creating new offspring individuals by applying genetic operations such as crossover and mutation.

GA(*Fitness*, *Fitness_threshold*, p, r, m)

Fitness: A function that assigns an evaluation score, given a hypothesis.

Fitness_threshold: A threshold specifying the termination criterion.

p: The number of hypotheses to be included in the population.

r: The fraction of the population to be replaced by Crossover at each step.

m: The mutation rate.

- *Initialize population:* $P \leftarrow$ Generate p hypotheses at random
- *Evaluate:* For each h in P, compute $Fitness(h)$
- While $[\max_h Fitness(h)] < Fitness\_threshold$ do

Create a new generation, P_S:

1. *Select:* Probabilistically select $(1-r)p$ members of P to add to P_S. The probability $\Pr(h_i)$ of selecting hypothesis h_i from P is given by

$$\Pr(h_i) = \frac{Fitness(h_i)}{\sum_{j=1}^{p} Fitness(h_j)}$$

2. *Crossover:* Probabilistically select $\frac{r \cdot p}{2}$ pairs of hypotheses from P, according to $\Pr(h_i)$ given above. For each pair, $\langle h_1, h_2 \rangle$, produce two offspring by applying the Crossover operator. Add all offspring to P_s.
3. *Mutate:* Choose m percent of the members of P_s with uniform probability. For each, invert one randomly selected bit in its representation.
4. *Update:* $P \leftarrow P_s$.
5. *Evaluate:* for each h in P, compute $Fitness(h)$

- Return the hypothesis from P that has the highest fitness.

TABLE 9.1
A prototypical genetic algorithm. A population containing p hypotheses is maintained. On each iteration, the successor population P_S is formed by probabilistically selecting current hypotheses according to their fitness and by adding new hypotheses. New hypotheses are created by applying a crossover operator to pairs of most fit hypotheses and by creating single point mutations in the resulting generation of hypotheses. This process is iterated until sufficiently fit hypotheses are discovered. Typical crossover and mutation operators are defined in a subsequent table.

A prototypical genetic algorithm is described in Table 9.1. The inputs to this algorithm include the fitness function for ranking candidate hypotheses, a threshold defining an acceptable level of fitness for terminating the algorithm, the size of the population to be maintained, and parameters that determine how successor populations are to be generated: the fraction of the population to be replaced at each generation and the mutation rate.

Notice in this algorithm each iteration through the main loop produces a new generation of hypotheses based on the current population. First, a certain number of hypotheses from the current population are selected for inclusion in the next generation. These are selected *probabilistically*, where the probability of selecting hypothesis h_i is given by

$$\Pr(h_i) = \frac{Fitness(h_i)}{\sum_{j=1}^{p} Fitness(h_j)} \tag{9.1}$$

Thus, the probability that a hypothesis will be selected is proportional to its own fitness and is inversely proportional to the fitness of the other competing hypotheses in the current population.

Once these members of the current generation have been selected for inclusion in the next generation population, additional members are generated using a crossover operation. Crossover, defined in detail in the next section, takes two parent hypotheses from the current generation and creates two offspring hypotheses by recombining portions of both parents. The parent hypotheses are chosen probabilistically from the current population, again using the probability function given by Equation (9.1). After new members have been created by this crossover operation, the new generation population now contains the desired number of members. At this point, a certain fraction m of these members are chosen at random, and random mutations all performed to alter these members.

This GA algorithm thus performs a randomized, parallel beam search for hypotheses that perform well according to the fitness function. In the following subsections, we describe in more detail the representation of hypotheses and genetic operators used in this algorithm.

9.2.1 Representing Hypotheses

Hypotheses in GAs are often represented by bit strings, so that they can be easily manipulated by genetic operators such as mutation and crossover. The hypotheses represented by these bit strings can be quite complex. For example, sets of if-then rules can easily be represented in this way, by choosing an encoding of rules that allocates specific substrings for each rule precondition and postcondition. Examples of such rule representations in GA systems are described by Holland (1986); Grefenstette (1988); and DeJong et al. (1993).

To see how if-then rules can be encoded by bit strings, first consider how we might use a bit string to describe a constraint on the value of a single attribute. To pick an example, consider the attribute *Outlook*, which can take on any of the three values *Sunny*, *Overcast*, or *Rain*. One obvious way to represent a constraint on *Outlook* is to use a bit string of length three, in which each bit position corresponds to one of its three possible values. Placing a 1 in some position indicates that the attribute is allowed to take on the corresponding value. For example, the string 010 represents the constraint that *Outlook* must take on the second of these values, or $Outlook = Overcast$. Similarly, the string 011 represents the more general constraint that allows two possible values, or $(Outlook = Overcast \vee Rain)$. Note 111 represents the most general possible constraint, indicating that we don't care which of its possible values the attribute takes on.

Given this method for representing constraints on a single attribute, conjunctions of constraints on multiple attributes can easily be represented by concatenating the corresponding bit strings. For example, consider a second attribute, *Wind*, that can take on the value *Strong* or *Weak*. A rule precondition such as

$$(Outlook = Overcast \vee Rain) \wedge (Wind = Strong)$$

can then be represented by the following bit string of length five:

Outlook	*Wind*
011	10

Rule postconditions (such as $PlayTennis = yes$) can be represented in a similar fashion. Thus, an entire rule can be described by concatenating the bit strings describing the rule preconditions, together with the bit string describing the rule postcondition. For example, the rule

$$\text{IF } Wind = Strong \text{ THEN } PlayTennis = yes$$

would be represented by the string

Outlook	*Wind*	*PlayTennis*
111	10	10

where the first three bits describe the "don't care" constraint on $Outlook$, the next two bits describe the constraint on $Wind$, and the final two bits describe the rule postcondition (here we assume $PlayTennis$ can take on the values Yes or No). Note the bit string representing the rule contains a substring for each attribute in the hypothesis space, even if that attribute is not constrained by the rule preconditions. This yields a fixed length bit-string representation for rules, in which substrings at specific locations describe constraints on specific attributes. Given this representation for single rules, we can represent sets of rules by similarly concatenating the bit string representations of the individual rules.

In designing a bit string encoding for some hypothesis space, it is useful to arrange for every syntactically legal bit string to represent a well-defined hypothesis. To illustrate, note in the rule encoding in the above paragraph the bit string 111 10 11 represents a rule whose postcondition does not constrain the target attribute $PlayTennis$. If we wish to avoid considering this hypothesis, we may employ a different encoding (e.g., allocate just one bit to the $PlayTennis$ postcondition to indicate whether the value is Yes or No), alter the genetic operators so that they explicitly avoid constructing such bit strings, or simply assign a very low fitness to such bit strings.

In some GAs, hypotheses are represented by symbolic descriptions rather than bit strings. For example, in Section 9.5 we discuss a genetic algorithm that encodes hypotheses as computer programs.

9.2.2 Genetic Operators

The generation of successors in a GA is determined by a set of operators that recombine and mutate selected members of the current population. Typical GA operators for manipulating bit string hypotheses are illustrated in Table 9.1. These operators correspond to idealized versions of the genetic operations found in biological evolution. The two most common operators are *crossover* and *mutation*.

The *crossover operator* produces two new offspring from two parent strings, by copying selected bits from each parent. The bit at position *i* in each offspring is copied from the bit at position *i* in one of the two parents. The choice of which parent contributes the bit for position *i* is determined by an additional string called the *crossover mask*. To illustrate, consider the *single-point crossover* operator at the top of Table 9.2. Consider the topmost of the two offspring in this case. This offspring takes its first five bits from the first parent and its remaining six bits from the second parent, because the crossover mask 11111000000 specifies these choices for each of the bit positions. The second offspring uses the same crossover mask, but switches the roles of the two parents. Therefore, it contains the bits that were not used by the first offspring. In single-point crossover, the crossover mask is always constructed so that it begins with a string containing *n* contiguous 1s, followed by the necessary number of 0s to complete the string. This results in offspring in which the first *n* bits are contributed by one parent and the remaining bits by the second parent. Each time the single-point crossover operator is applied,

	Initial strings	*Crossover Mask*	*Offspring*
Single-point crossover:			
	11101001000	11111000000	11101010101
	00001010101		00001001000
Two-point crossover:			
	11101001000	00111110000	11001011000
	00001010101		00101000101
Uniform crossover:			
	11101001000	10011010011	10001000100
	00001010101		01101011001
Point mutation:			
	11101001000	→	11101011000

TABLE 9.2
Common operators for genetic algorithms. These operators form offspring of hypotheses represented by bit strings. The crossover operators create two descendants from two parents, using the crossover mask to determine which parent contributes which bits. Mutation creates a single descendant from a single parent by changing the value of a randomly chosen bit.

the crossover point n is chosen at random, and the crossover mask is then created and applied.

In *two-point crossover*, offspring are created by substituting intermediate segments of one parent into the middle of the second parent string. Put another way, the crossover mask is a string beginning with n_0 zeros, followed by a contiguous string of n_1 ones, followed by the necessary number of zeros to complete the string. Each time the two-point crossover operator is applied, a mask is generated by randomly choosing the integers n_0 and n_1. For instance, in the example shown in Table 9.2 the offspring are created using a mask for which $n_0 = 2$ and $n_1 = 5$. Again, the two offspring are created by switching the roles played by the two parents.

Uniform crossover combines bits sampled uniformly from the two parents, as illustrated in Table 9.2. In this case the crossover mask is generated as a random bit string with each bit chosen at random and independent of the others.

In addition to recombination operators that produce offspring by combining parts of two parents, a second type of operator produces offspring from a single parent. In particular, the *mutation* operator produces small random changes to the bit string by choosing a single bit at random, then changing its value. Mutation is often performed after crossover has been applied as in our prototypical algorithm from Table 9.1.

Some GA systems employ additional operators, especially operators that are specialized to the particular hypothesis representation used by the system. For example, Grefenstette et al. (1991) describe a system that learns sets of rules for robot control. It uses mutation and crossover, together with an operator for specializing rules. Janikow (1993) describes a system that learns sets of rules using operators that generalize and specialize rules in a variety of directed ways (e.g., by explicitly replacing the condition on an attribute by "don't care").

9.2.3 Fitness Function and Selection

The fitness function defines the criterion for ranking potential hypotheses and for probabilistically selecting them for inclusion in the next generation population. If the task is to learn classification rules, then the fitness function typically has a component that scores the classification accuracy of the rule over a set of provided training examples. Often other criteria may be included as well, such as the complexity or generality of the rule. More generally, when the bit-string hypothesis is interpreted as a complex procedure (e.g., when the bit string represents a collection of if-then rules that will be chained together to control a robotic device), the fitness function may measure the overall performance of the resulting procedure rather than performance of individual rules.

In our prototypical GA shown in Table 9.1, the probability that a hypothesis will be selected is given by the ratio of its fitness to the fitness of other members of the current population as seen in Equation (9.1). This method is sometimes often called *fitness proportionate selection*, or roulette wheel selection. Other methods for using fitness to select hypotheses have also been proposed. For example, in *tournament selection*, two hypotheses are first chosen at random from the current population. With some predefined probability p the more fit of these two is then selected, and with probability $(1 - p)$ the less fit hypothesis is selected. Tournament selection often yields a more diverse population than fitness proportionate selection (Goldberg and Deb 1991). In another method called *rank selection*, the hypotheses in the current population are first sorted by fitness. The probability that a hypothesis will be selected is then proportional to its rank in this sorted list, rather than its fitness.

9.3 AN ILLUSTRATIVE EXAMPLE

A genetic algorithm can be viewed as a general optimization method that searches a large space of candidate objects seeking one that performs best according to the fitness function. Although not guaranteed to find an optimal object, GAs often succeed in finding an object with high fitness. GAs have been applied to a number of optimization problems outside machine learning, including problems such as circuit layout and job-shop scheduling. Within machine learning, they have been applied both to function-approximation problems and to tasks such as choosing the network topology for artificial neural network learning systems.

To illustrate the use of GAs for concept learning, we briefly summarize the GABIL system described by DeJong et al. (1993). GABIL uses a GA to learn boolean concepts represented by a disjunctive set of propositional rules. In experiments over several concept learning problems, GABIL was found to be roughly comparable in generalization accuracy to other learning algorithms such as the decision tree learning algorithm C4.5 and the rule learning system AQ14. The learning tasks in this study included both artificial learning tasks designed to explore the systems' generalization accuracy and the real world problem of breast cancer diagnosis.

The algorithm used by GABIL is exactly the algorithm described in Table 9.1. In experiments reported by DeJong et al. (1993), the parameter r, which determines the fraction of the parent population replaced by crossover, was set to 0.6. The parameter m, which determines the mutation rate, was set to 0.001. These are typical settings for these parameters. The population size p was varied from 100 to 1000, depending on the specific learning task.

The specific instantiation of the GA algorithm in GABIL can be summarized as follows:

- **Representation.** Each hypothesis in GABIL corresponds to a disjunctive set of propositional rules, encoded as described in Section 9.2.1. In particular, the hypothesis space of rule preconditions consists of a conjunction of constraints on a fixed set of attributes, as described in that earlier section. To represent a set of rules, the bit-string representations of individual rules are concatenated. To illustrate, consider a hypothesis space in which rule preconditions are conjunctions of constraints over two boolean attributes, a_1 and a_2. The rule postcondition is described by a single bit that indicates the predicted value of the target attribute c. Thus, the hypothesis consisting of the two rules

$$\text{IF } a_1 = T \wedge a_2 = F \text{ THEN } c = T; \quad \text{IF } a_2 = T \text{ THEN } c = F$$

would be represented by the string

$$\begin{array}{cccccc} a_1 & a_2 & c & a_1 & a_2 & c \\ 10 & 01 & 1 & 11 & 10 & 0 \end{array}$$

Note the length of the bit string grows with the number of rules in the hypothesis. This variable bit-string length requires a slight modification to the crossover operator, as described below.

- **Genetic operators.** GABIL uses the standard mutation operator of Table 9.2, in which a single bit is chosen at random and replaced by its complement. The crossover operator that it uses is a fairly standard extension to the two-point crossover operator described in Table 9.2. In particular, to accommodate the variable-length bit strings that encode rule sets, and to constrain the system so that crossover occurs only between like sections of the bit strings that encode rules, the following approach is taken. To perform a crossover operation on two parents, two crossover points are first chosen at random in the first parent string. Let d_1 (d_2) denote the distance from the leftmost (rightmost) of these two crossover points to the rule boundary immediately to its left. The crossover points in the second parent are now randomly chosen, subject to the constraint that they must have the same d_1 and d_2 value. For example, if the two parent strings are

$$\begin{array}{rcccccc} & a_1 & a_2 & c & a_1 & a_2 & c \\ h_1: & 10 & 01 & 1 & 11 & 10 & 0 \end{array}$$

and

$$\begin{array}{rcccccc} & a_1 & a_2 & c & a_1 & a_2 & c \\ h_2: & 01 & 11 & 0 & 10 & 01 & 0 \end{array}$$

and the crossover points chosen for the first parent are the points following bit positions 1 and 8,

$$\begin{array}{rcccccc} & a_1 & a_2 & c & a_1 & a_2 & c \\ h_1: & 1[0 & 01 & 1 & 11 & 1]0 & 0 \end{array}$$

where "[" and "]" indicate crossover points, then $d_1 = 1$ and $d_2 = 3$. Hence the allowed pairs of crossover points for the second parent include the pairs of bit positions $\langle 1, 3\rangle$, $\langle 1, 8\rangle$, and $\langle 6, 8\rangle$. If the pair $\langle 1, 3\rangle$ happens to be chosen,

$$\begin{array}{rcccccc} & a_1 & a_2 & c & a_1 & a_2 & c \\ h_2: & 0[1 & 1]1 & 0 & 10 & 01 & 0 \end{array}$$

then the two resulting offspring will be

$$h_3: \begin{array}{ccc} a_1 & a_2 & c \\ 11 & 10 & 0 \end{array}$$

and

$$h_4: \begin{array}{ccccccccc} a_1 & a_2 & c & a_1 & a_2 & c & a_1 & a_2 & c \\ 00 & 01 & 1 & 11 & 11 & 0 & 10 & 01 & 0 \end{array}$$

As this example illustrates, this crossover operation enables offspring to contain a different number of rules than their parents, while assuring that all bit strings generated in this fashion represent well-defined rule sets.

- **Fitness function.** The fitness of each hypothesized rule set is based on its classification accuracy over the training data. In particular, the function used to measure fitness is

$$Fitness(h) = (correct(h))^2$$

where $correct(h)$ is the percent of all training examples correctly classified by hypothesis h.

In experiments comparing the behavior of GABIL to decision tree learning algorithms such as C4.5 and ID5R, and to the rule learning algorithm AQ14, DeJong et al. (1993) report roughly comparable performance among these systems, tested on a variety of learning problems. For example, over a set of 12 synthetic problems, GABIL achieved an average generalization accuracy of 92.1 %, whereas the performance of the other systems ranged from 91.2 % to 96.6 %.

9.3.1 Extensions

DeJong et al. (1993) also explore two interesting extensions to the basic design of GABIL. In one set of experiments they explored the addition of two new genetic operators that were motivated by the generalization operators common in many symbolic learning methods. The first of these operators, *AddAlternative*, generalizes the constraint on a specific attribute by changing a 0 to a 1 in the substring corresponding to the attribute. For example, if the constraint on an attribute is represented by the string 10010, this operator might change it to 10110. This operator was applied with probability .01 to selected members of the population on each generation. The second operator, *DropCondition* performs a more drastic generalization step, by replacing all bits for a particular attribute by a 1. This operator corresponds to generalizing the rule by completely dropping the constraint on the attribute, and was applied on each generation with probability .60. The authors report this revised system achieved an average performance of 95.2% over the above set of synthetic learning tasks, compared to 92.1% for the basic GA algorithm.

In the above experiment, the two new operators were applied with the same probability to each hypothesis in the population on each generation. In a second experiment, the bit-string representation for hypotheses was extended to include two bits that determine which of these operators may be applied to the hypothesis. In this extended representation, the bit string for a typical rule set hypothesis would be

a_1	a_2	c	a_1	a_2	c	AA	DC
01	11	0	10	01	0	1	0

where the final two bits indicate in this case that the *AddAlternative* operator may be applied to this bit string, but that the *DropCondition* operator may not. These two new bits define part of the search strategy used by the GA and are themselves altered and evolved using the same crossover and mutation operators that operate on other bits in the string. While the authors report mixed results with this approach (i.e., improved performance on some problems, decreased performance on others), it provides an interesting illustration of how GAs might in principle be used to evolve their own hypothesis search methods.

9.4 HYPOTHESIS SPACE SEARCH

As illustrated above, GAs employ a randomized beam search method to seek a maximally fit hypothesis. This search is quite different from that of other learning methods we have considered in this book. To contrast the hypothesis space search of GAs with that of neural network BACKPROPAGATION, for example, the gradient descent search in BACKPROPAGATION moves smoothly from one hypothesis to a new hypothesis that is very similar. In contrast, the GA search can move much more abruptly, replacing a parent hypothesis by an offspring that may be radically different from the parent. Note the GA search is therefore less likely to fall into the same kind of local minima that can plague gradient descent methods.

One practical difficulty in some GA applications is the problem of *crowding*. Crowding is a phenomena in which some individual that is more highly fit than others in the population quickly reproduces, so that copies of this individual and very similar individuals take over a large fraction of the population. The negative impact of crowding is that it reduces the diversity of the population, thereby slowing further progress by the GA. Several strategies have been explored for reducing crowding. One approach is to alter the selection function, using criteria such as tournament selection or rank selection in place of fitness proportionate roulette wheel selection. A related strategy is "fitness sharing," in which the measured fitness of an individual is reduced by the presence of other, similar individuals in the population. A third approach is to restrict the kinds of individuals allowed to recombine to form offspring. For example, by allowing only the most similar individuals to recombine, we can encourage the formation of clusters of similar individuals, or multiple "subspecies" within the population. A related approach is to spatially distribute individuals and allow only nearby individuals to recombine. Many of these techniques are inspired by the analogy to biological evolution.

9.4.1 Population Evolution and the Schema Theorem

It is interesting to ask whether one can mathematically characterize the evolution over time of the population within a GA. The schema theorem of Holland (1975) provides one such characterization. It is based on the concept of *schemas*, or patterns that describe sets of bit strings. To be precise, a schema is any string composed of 0s, 1s, and *'s. Each schema represents the set of bit strings containing the indicated 0s and 1s, with each "*" interpreted as a "don't care." For example, the schema 0*10 represents the set of bit strings that includes exactly 0010 and 0110.

An individual bit string can be viewed as a representative of each of the different schemas that it matches. For example, the bit string 0010 can be thought of as a representative of 2^4 distinct schemas including 00**, 0*10, ****, etc. Similarly, a population of bit strings can be viewed in terms of the set of schemas that it represents and the number of individuals associated with each of these schema.

The schema theorem characterizes the evolution of the population within a GA in terms of the number of instances representing each schema. Let $m(s,t)$ denote the number of instances of schema s in the population at time t (i.e., during the tth generation). The schema theorem describes the expected value of $m(s, t+1)$ in terms of $m(s,t)$ and other properties of the schema, population, and GA algorithm parameters.

The evolution of the population in the GA depends on the selection step, the recombination step, and the mutation step. Let us start by considering just the effect of the selection step. Let $f(h)$ denote the fitness of the individual bit string h and $\bar{f}(t)$ denote the average fitness of all individuals in the population at time t. Let n be the total number of individuals in the population. Let $h \in s \cap p_t$ indicate that the individual h is both a representative of schema s and a member of the population at time t. Finally, let $\hat{u}(s,t)$ denote the average fitness of instances of schema s in the population at time t.

We are interested in calculating the expected value of $m(s, t+1)$, which we denote $E[m(s, t+1)]$. We can calculate $E[m(s, t+1)]$ using the probability distribution for selection given in Equation (9.1), which can be restated using our current terminology as follows:

$$\begin{aligned} \Pr(h) &= \frac{f(h)}{\sum_{i=1}^{n} f(h_i)} \\ &= \frac{f(h)}{n\bar{f}(t)} \end{aligned}$$

Now if we select one member for the new population according to this probability distribution, then the probability that we will select a representative of schema s is

$$\begin{aligned} \Pr(h \in s) &= \sum_{h \in s \cap p_t} \frac{f(h)}{n\bar{f}(t)} \\ &= \frac{\hat{u}(s,t)}{n\bar{f}(t)} m(s,t) \end{aligned} \tag{9.2}$$

The second step above follows from the fact that by definition,

$$\hat{u}(s,t) = \frac{\sum_{h \in s \cap p_t} f(h)}{m(s,t)}$$

Equation (9.2) gives the probability that a single hypothesis selected by the GA will be an instance of schema s. Therefore, the expected number of instances of s resulting from the n independent selection steps that create the entire new generation is just n times this probability.

$$E[m(s,t+1)] = \frac{\hat{u}(s,t)}{\bar{f}(t)} m(s,t) \tag{9.3}$$

Equation (9.3) states that the expected number of instances of schema s at generation $t+1$ is proportional to the average fitness $\hat{u}(s,t)$ of instances of this schema at time t, and inversely proportional to the average fitness $\bar{f}(t)$ of all members of the population at time t. Thus, we can expect schemas with above average fitness to be represented with increasing frequency on successive generations. If we view the GA as performing a virtual parallel search through the space of possible schemas at the same time it performs its explicit parallel search through the space of individuals, then Equation (9.3) indicates that more fit schemas will grow in influence over time.

While the above analysis considered only the selection step of the GA, the crossover and mutation steps must be considered as well. The schema theorem considers only the possible negative influence of these genetic operators (e.g., random mutation may decrease the number of representatives of s, independent of $\hat{u}(s,t)$), and considers only the case of single-point crossover. The full schema theorem thus provides a lower bound on the expected frequency of schema s, as follows:

$$E[m(s,t+1)] \geq \frac{\hat{u}(s,t)}{\bar{f}(t)} m(s,t) \left(1 - p_c \frac{d(s)}{l-1}\right) (1-p_m)^{o(s)} \tag{9.4}$$

Here, p_c is the probability that the single-point crossover operator will be applied to an arbitrary individual, and p_m is the probability that an arbitrary bit of an arbitrary individual will be mutated by the mutation operator. $o(s)$ is the number of *defined bits* in schema s, where 0 and 1 are defined bits, but * is not. $d(s)$ is the distance between the leftmost and rightmost defined bits in s. Finally, l is the length of the individual bit strings in the population. Notice the leftmost term in Equation (9.4) is identical to the term from Equation (9.3) and describes the effect of the selection step. The middle term describes the effect of the single-point crossover operator—in particular, it describes the probability that an arbitrary individual representing s will still represent s following application of this crossover operator. The rightmost term describes the probability that an arbitrary individual representing schema s will still represent schema s following application of the mutation operator. Note that the effects of single-point crossover and mutation increase with the number of defined bits $o(s)$ in the schema and with the distance $d(s)$ between the defined bits. Thus, the schema theorem can be roughly interpreted as stating that more fit schemas will tend to grow in influence, especially schemas containing a small number of defined bits (i.e., containing a large number of *'s), and especially when these defined bits are near one another within the bit string.

The schema theorem is perhaps the most widely cited characterization of population evolution within a GA. One way in which it is incomplete is that it fails to consider the (presumably) positive effects of crossover and mutation. Numerous more recent theoretical analyses have been proposed, including analyses based on Markov chain models and on statistical mechanics models. See, for example, Whitley and Vose (1995) and Mitchell (1996).

9.5 GENETIC PROGRAMMING

Genetic programming (GP) is a form of evolutionary computation in which the individuals in the evolving population are computer programs rather than bit strings. Koza (1992) describes the basic genetic programming approach and presents a broad range of simple programs that can be successfully learned by GP.

9.5.1 Representing Programs

Programs manipulated by a GP are typically represented by trees corresponding to the parse tree of the program. Each function call is represented by a node in the tree, and the arguments to the function are given by its descendant nodes. For example, Figure 9.1 illustrates this tree representation for the function $\sin(x) + \sqrt{x^2 + y}$. To apply genetic programming to a particular domain, the user must define the primitive functions to be considered (e.g., sin, cos, $\sqrt{\ }$, +, −, exponentials), as well as the terminals (e.g., x, y, constants such as 2). The genetic programming algorithm then uses an evolutionary search to explore the vast space of programs that can be described using these primitives.

As in a genetic algorithm, the prototypical genetic programming algorithm maintains a population of individuals (in this case, program trees). On each iteration, it produces a new generation of individuals using selection, crossover, and mutation. The fitness of a given individual program in the population is typically determined by executing the program on a set of training data. Crossover operations are performed by replacing a randomly chosen subtree of one parent

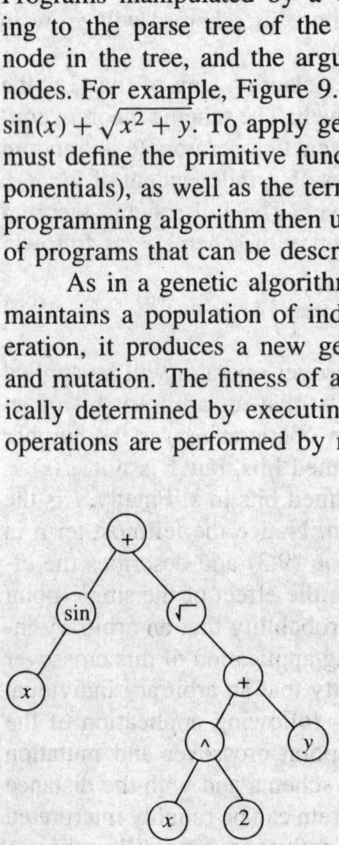

FIGURE 9.1
Program tree representation in genetic programming. Arbitrary programs are represented by their parse trees.

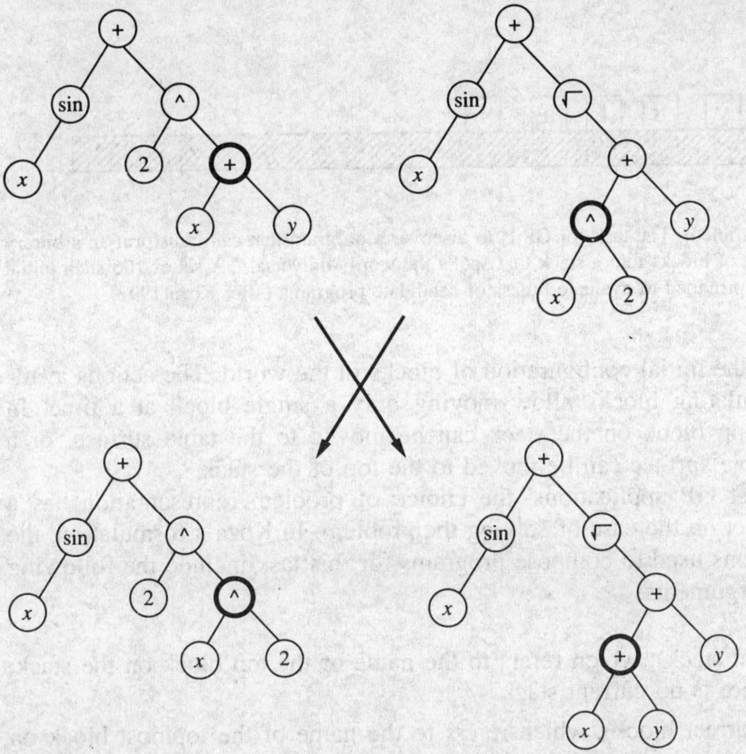

FIGURE 9.2
Crossover operation applied to two parent program trees (top). Crossover points (nodes shown in bold at top) are chosen at random. The subtrees rooted at these crossover points are then exchanged to create children trees (bottom).

program by a subtree from the other parent program. Figure 9.2 illustrates a typical crossover operation.

Koza (1992) describes a set of experiments applying a GP to a number of applications. In his experiments, 10% of the current population, selected probabilistically according to fitness, is retained unchanged in the next generation. The remainder of the new generation is created by applying crossover to pairs of programs from the current generation, again selected probabilistically according to their fitness. The mutation operator was not used in this particular set of experiments.

9.5.2 Illustrative Example

One illustrative example presented by Koza (1992) involves learning an algorithm for stacking the blocks shown in Figure 9.3. The task is to develop a general algorithm for stacking the blocks into a single stack that spells the word "universal,"

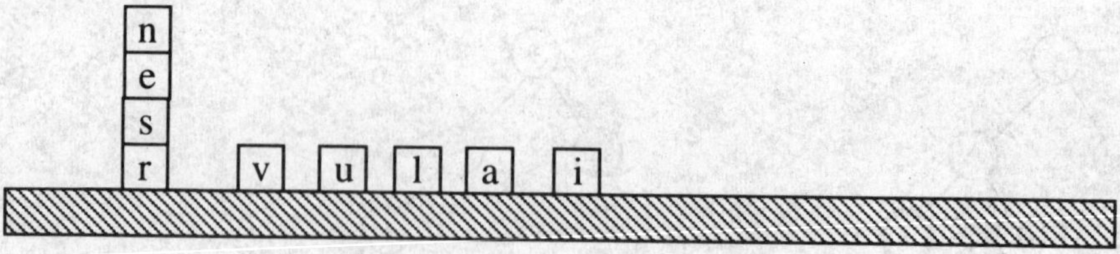

FIGURE 9.3
A block-stacking problem. The task for GP is to discover a program that can transform an arbitrary initial configuration of blocks into a stack that spells the word "universal." A set of 166 such initial configurations was provided to evaluate fitness of candidate programs (after Koza 1992).

independent of the initial configuration of blocks in the world. The actions available for manipulating blocks allow moving only a single block at a time. In particular, the top block on the stack can be moved to the table surface, or a block on the table surface can be moved to the top of the stack.

As in most GP applications, the choice of problem representation has a significant impact on the ease of solving the problem. In Koza's formulation, the primitive functions used to compose programs for this task include the following three terminal arguments:

- CS (current stack), which refers to the name of the top block on the stack, or F if there is no current stack.
- TB (top correct block), which refers to the name of the topmost block on the stack, such that it and those blocks beneath it are in the correct order.
- NN (next necessary), which refers to the name of the next block needed above TB in the stack, in order to spell the word "universal," or F if no more blocks are needed.

As can be seen, this particular choice of terminal arguments provides a natural representation for describing programs for manipulating blocks for this task. Imagine, in contrast, the relative difficulty of the task if we were to instead define the terminal arguments to be the x and y coordinates of each block.

In addition to these terminal arguments, the program language in this application included the following primitive functions:

- (MS x) (move to stack), if block x is on the table, this operator moves x to the top of the stack and returns the value T. Otherwise, it does nothing and returns the value F.
- (MT x) (move to table), if block x is somewhere in the stack, this moves the block at the top of the stack to the table and returns the value T. Otherwise, it returns the value F.
- (EQ x y) (equal), which returns T if x equals y, and returns F otherwise.
- (NOT x), which returns T if $x = F$, and returns F if $x = T$.

- (DU x y) (do until), which executes the expression x repeatedly until expression y returns the value T.

To allow the system to evaluate the fitness of any given program, Koza provided a set of 166 training example problems representing a broad variety of initial block configurations, including problems of differing degrees of difficulty. The fitness of any given program was taken to be the number of these examples solved by the algorithm. The population was initialized to a set of 300 random programs. After 10 generations, the system discovered the following program, which solves all 166 problems.

(EQ (DU (MT CS)(NOT CS)) (DU (MS NN)(NOT NN)))

Notice this program contains a sequence of two DU, or "Do Until" statements. The first repeatedly moves the current top of the stack onto the table, until the stack becomes empty. The second "Do Until" statement then repeatedly moves the next necessary block from the table onto the stack. The role played by the top level EQ expression here is to provide a syntactically legal way to sequence these two "Do Until" loops.

Somewhat surprisingly, after only a few generations, this GP was able to discover a program that solves all 166 training problems. Of course the ability of the system to accomplish this depends strongly on the primitive arguments and functions provided, and on the set of training example cases used to evaluate fitness.

9.5.3 Remarks on Genetic Programming

As illustrated in the above example, genetic programming extends genetic algorithms to the evolution of complete computer programs. Despite the huge size of the hypothesis space it must search, genetic programming has been demonstrated to produce intriguing results in a number of applications. A comparison of GP to other methods for searching through the space of computer programs, such as hillclimbing and simulated annealing, is given by O'Reilly and Oppacher (1994).

While the above example of GP search is fairly simple, Koza et al. (1996) summarize the use of a GP in several more complex tasks such as designing electronic filter circuits and classifying segments of protein molecules. The filter circuit design problem provides an example of a considerably more complex problem. Here, programs are evolved that transform a simple fixed seed circuit into a final circuit design. The primitive functions used by the GP to construct its programs are functions that edit the seed circuit by inserting or deleting circuit components and wiring connections. The fitness of each program is calculated by simulating the circuit it outputs (using the SPICE circuit simulator) to determine how closely this circuit meets the design specifications for the desired filter. More precisely, the fitness score is the sum of the magnitudes of errors between the desired and actual circuit output at 101 different input frequencies. In this case, a population of size 640,000 was maintained, with selection producing 10% of the successor population, crossover producing 89%, and mutation producing 1%. The system was executed on a 64-node parallel processor. Within the first randomly generated population, the circuits produced were so unreasonable that the SPICE simulator could not even simulate the behavior of 98% of the circuits. The percentage of unsimulatable circuits dropped to 84.9% following the first generation, to 75.0% following the second generation, and to an average of 9.6% over succeeding generations. The fitness score of the best circuit in the initial population was 159, compared to a score of 39 after 20 generations and a score of 0.8 after 137 generations. The best circuit, produced after 137 generations, exhibited performance very similar to the desired behavior.

In most cases, the performance of genetic programming depends crucially on the choice of representation and on the choice of fitness function. For this reason, an active area of current research is aimed at the automatic discovery and incorporation of subroutines that improve on the original set of primitive functions, thereby allowing the system to dynamically alter the primitives from which it constructs individuals. See, for example, Koza (1994).

9.6 MODELS OF EVOLUTION AND LEARNING

In many natural systems, individual organisms learn to adapt significantly during their lifetime. At the same time, biological and social processes allow their species to adapt over a time frame of many generations. One interesting question regarding evolutionary systems is "What is the relationship between learning during the lifetime of a single individual, and the longer time frame species-level learning afforded by evolution?"

9.6.1 Lamarckian Evolution

Lamarck was a scientist who, in the late nineteenth century, proposed that evolution over many generations was directly influenced by the experiences of individual organisms during their lifetime. In particular, he proposed that experiences of a single organism directly affected the genetic makeup of their offspring: If an individual learned during its lifetime to avoid some toxic food, it could pass this trait on genetically to its offspring, which therefore would not need to learn the trait. This is an attractive conjecture, because it would presumably allow for more efficient evolutionary progress than a generate-and-test process (like that of GAs and GPs) that ignores the experience gained during an individual's lifetime. Despite the attractiveness of this theory, current scientific evidence overwhelmingly contradicts Lamarck's model. The currently accepted view is that the genetic makeup of an individual is, in fact, unaffected by the lifetime experience of one's biological parents. Despite this apparent biological fact, recent computer studies have shown that Lamarckian processes can sometimes improve the effectiveness of computerized genetic algorithms (see Grefenstette 1991; Ackley and Littman 1994; and Hart and Belew 1995).

9.6.2 Baldwin Effect

Although Lamarckian evolution is not an accepted model of biological evolution, other mechanisms have been suggested by which individual learning can alter the course of evolution. One such mechanism is called the Baldwin effect, after J. M. Baldwin (1896), who first suggested the idea. The Baldwin effect is based on the following observations:

- If a species is evolving in a changing environment, there will be evolutionary pressure to favor individuals with the capability to learn during their lifetime. For example, if a new predator appears in the environment, then individuals capable of learning to avoid the predator will be more successful than individuals who cannot learn. In effect, the ability to learn allows an individual to perform a small local search during its lifetime to maximize its fitness. In contrast, nonlearning individuals whose fitness is fully determined by their genetic makeup will operate at a relative disadvantage.
- Those individuals who are able to learn many traits will rely less strongly on their genetic code to "hard-wire" traits. As a result, these individuals can support a more diverse gene pool, relying on individual learning to overcome the "missing" or "not quite optimized" traits in the genetic code. This more diverse gene pool can, in turn, support more rapid evolutionary adaptation. Thus, the ability of individuals to learn can have an indirect accelerating effect on the rate of evolutionary adaptation for the entire population.

To illustrate, imagine some new change in the environment of some species, such as a new predator. Such a change will selectively favor individuals capable of learning to avoid the predator. As the proportion of such self-improving individuals in the population grows, the population will be able to support a more diverse gene pool, allowing evolutionary processes (even non-Lamarckian generate-and-test processes) to adapt more rapidly. This accelerated adaptation may in turn enable standard evolutionary processes to more quickly evolve a genetic (nonlearned) trait to avoid the predator (e.g., an instinctive fear of this animal). Thus, the Baldwin effect provides an indirect mechanism for individual learning to positively impact the rate of evolutionary progress. By increasing survivability and genetic diversity of the species, individual learning supports more rapid evolutionary progress, thereby increasing the chance that the species will evolve genetic, nonlearned traits that better fit the new environment.

There have been several attempts to develop computational models to study the Baldwin effect. For example, Hinton and Nowlan (1987) experimented with evolving a population of simple neural networks, in which some network weights were fixed during the individual network "lifetime," while others were trainable. The genetic makeup of the individual determined which weights were trainable and which were fixed. In their experiments, when no individual learning was allowed, the population failed to improve its fitness over time. However, when individual learning was allowed, the population quickly improved its fitness. During early generations of evolution the population contained a greater proportion of individuals with many trainable weights. However, as evolution proceeded, the number of fixed, correct network weights tended to increase, as the population evolved toward genetically given weight values and toward less dependence on individual learning of weights. Additional computational studies of the Baldwin effect have been reported by Belew (1990), Harvey (1993), and French and Messinger (1994). An excellent overview of this topic can be found in Mitchell (1996). A special issue of the journal *Evolutionary Computation* on this topic (Turney et al. 1997) contains several articles on the Baldwin effect.

9.7 PARALLELIZING GENETIC ALGORITHMS

GAs are naturally suited to parallel implementation, and a number of approaches to parallelization have been explored. *Coarse grain* approaches to parallelization subdivide the population into somewhat distinct groups of individuals, called *demes*. Each deme is assigned to a different computational node, and a standard GA search is performed at each node. Communication and cross-fertilization between demes occurs on a less frequent basis than within demes. Transfer between demes occurs by a *migration* process, in which individuals from one deme are copied or transferred to other demes. This process is modeled after the kind of cross-fertilization that might occur between physically separated subpopulations of biological species. One benefit of such approaches is that it reduces the crowding problem often encountered in nonparallel GAs, in which the system falls into a local optimum due to the early appearance of a genotype that comes to dominate the entire population. Examples of coarse-grained parallel GAs are described by Tanese (1989) and by Cohoon et al. (1987).

In contrast to coarse-grained parallel implementations of GAs, fine-grained implementations typically assign one processor per individual in the population. Recombination then takes place among neighboring individuals. Several different types of neighborhoods have been proposed, ranging from planar grid to torus. Examples of such systems are described by Spiessens and Manderick (1991). An edited collection of papers on parallel GAs is available in Stender (1993).

9.8 SUMMARY AND FURTHER READING

The main points of this chapter include:

- Genetic algorithms (GAs) conduct a randomized, parallel, hill-climbing search for hypotheses that optimize a predefined fitness function.
- The search performed by GAs is based on an analogy to biological evolution. A diverse population of competing hypotheses is maintained. At each

iteration, the most fit members of the population are selected to produce new offspring that replace the least fit members of the population. Hypotheses are often encoded by strings that are combined by crossover operations, and subjected to random mutations.

- GAs illustrate how learning can be viewed as a special case of optimization. In particular, the learning task is to find the optimal hypothesis, according to the predefined fitness function. This suggests that other optimization techniques such as simulated annealing can also be applied to machine learning problems.
- GAs have most commonly been applied to optimization problems outside machine learning, such as design optimization problems. When applied to learning tasks, GAs are especially suited to tasks in which hypotheses are complex (e.g., sets of rules for robot control, or computer programs), and in which the objective to be optimized may be an indirect function of the hypothesis (e.g., that the set of acquired rules successfully controls a robot).
- Genetic programming is a variant of genetic algorithms in which the hypotheses being manipulated are computer programs rather than bit strings. Operations such as crossover and mutation are generalized to apply to programs rather than bit strings. Genetic programming has been demonstrated to learn programs for tasks such as simulated robot control (Koza 1992) and recognizing objects in visual scenes (Teller and Veloso 1994).

Evolution-based computational approaches have been explored since the early days of computer science (e.g., Box 1957 and Bledsoe 1961). Several different evolutionary approaches were introduced during the 1960s and have been further explored since that time. Evolution strategies, developed by Rechenberg (1965, 1973) to optimize numerical parameters in engineering design, were followed up by Schwefel (1975, 1977, 1995) and others. Evolutionary programming, developed by Folgel, Owens, and Walsh (1966) as a method for evolving finite-state machines, was followed up by numerous researchers (e.g., Fogel and Atmar 1993). Genetic algorithms, introduced by Holland (1962, 1975) included the notion of maintaining a large population of individuals and emphasized crossover as a key operation in such systems. Genetic programming, introduced by Koza (1992), applies the search strategy of genetic algorithms to hypotheses consisting of computer programs. As computer hardware continues to become faster and less expensive, interest in evolutionary approaches continues to grow.

One approach to using GAs to learn sets of rules was developed by K. DeJong and his students at the University of Pittsburgh (e.g., Smith 1980). In this approach, each rule set is one member in the population of competing hypotheses, as in the GABIL system discussed in this chapter. A somewhat different approach was developed at University of Michigan by Holland and his students (Holland 1986), in which each rule is a member of the population, and the population itself is the rule set. A biological perspective on the roles of mutation, inbreeding, cross-breeding, and selection in evolution is provided by Wright (1977).

Mitchell (1996) and Goldberg (1989) are two textbooks devoted to the subject of genetic algorithms. Forrest (1993) provides an overview of the technical issues in GAs, and Goldberg (1994) provides an overview of several recent applications. Koza's (1992) monograph on genetic programming is the standard reference for this extension of genetic algorithms to manipulation of computer programs. The primary conference in which new results are published is the *International Conference on Genetic Algorithms*. Other relevant conferences include the *Conference on Simulation of Adaptive Behavior*, the *International Conference on Artificial Neural Networks and Genetic Algorithms*, and the *IEEE International Conference on Evolutionary Computation*. An annual conference is now held on genetic programming, as well (Koza et al. 1996b). The *Evolutionary Computation Journal* is one source of recent research results in the field. Several special issues of the journal *Machine Learning* have also been devoted to GAs.

EXERCISES

9.1. Design a genetic algorithm to learn conjunctive classification rules for the *PlayTennis* problem described in Chapter 3. Describe precisely the bit-string encoding of hypotheses and a set of crossover operators.

9.2. Implement a simple GA for Exercise 9.1. Experiment with varying population size p, the fraction r of the population replaced at each generation, and the mutation rate m.

9.3. Represent the program discovered by the GP (described in Section 9.5.2) as a tree. Illustrate the operation of the GP crossover operator by applying it using two copies of your tree as the two parents.

9.4. Consider applying GAs to the task of finding an appropriate set of weights for an artificial neural network (in particular, a feedforward network identical to those trained by BACKPROPAGATION (Chapter 4)). Consider a $3 \times 2 \times 1$ layered, feedforward network. Describe an encoding of network weights as a bit string, and describe an appropriate set of crossover operators. Hint: Do not allow all possible crossover operations on bit strings. State one advantage and one disadvantage of using GAs in contrast to BACKPROPAGATION to train network weights.

REFERENCES

Ackley, D., & Littman, M. (1994). A case for Lamarckian evolution. In C. Langton (Ed.), *Artificial life III*. Reading, MA: Addison Wesley.

Back, T. (1996). *Evolutionary algorithms in theory and practice*. Oxford, England: Oxford University Press.

Baldwin, J. M. (1896). A new factor in evolution. *American Naturalist*, 3, 441–451, 536–553. http://www.santafe.edu/sfi/publications/Bookinfo/baldwin.html

Belew, R. (1990). Evolution, learning, and culture: Computational metaphors for adaptive algorithms. *Complex Systems*, 4, 11–49.

Belew, R. K., & Mitchell, M. (Eds.). (1996). *Adaptive individuals in evolving populations: Models and algorithms*. Reading, MA: Addison-Wesley.

Bledsoe, W. (1961). The use of biological concepts in the analytical study of systems. *Proceedings of the ORSA-TIMS National Meeting*, San Francisco.

Booker, L. B., Goldberg, D. E., & Holland, J. H. (1989). Classifier systems and genetic algorithms. *Artificial Intelligence*, 40, 235–282.

Box, G. (1957). Evolutionary operation: A method for increasing industrial productivity. *Journal of the Royal Statistical Society*, 6(2), 81–101.

Cohoon, J. P., Hegde, S. U., Martin, W. N., & Richards, D. (1987). Punctuated equilibria: A parallel genetic algorithm. *Proceedings of the Second International Conference on Genetic Algorithms* (pp. 148–154).

DeJong, K. A. (1975). *An analysis of behavior of a class of genetic adaptive systems* (Ph.D. dissertation). University of Michigan.

DeJong, K. A., Spears, W. M., & Gordon, D. F. (1993). Using genetic algorithms for concept learning. *Machine Learning*, 13, 161–188.

Folgel, L. J., Owens, A. J., & Walsh, M. J. (1966). *Artificial intelligence through simulated evolution*. New York: John Wiley & Sons.

Fogel, L. J., & Atmar, W. (Eds.). (1993). *Proceedings of the Second Annual Conference on Evolutionary Programming*. Evolutionary Programming Society.

Forrest, S. (1993). Genetic algorithms: Principles of natural selection applied to computation. *Science*, 261, 872–878.

French, R., & Messinger A. (1994). Genes, phenes, and the Baldwin effect: Learning and evolution in a simulated population. In R. Brooks and P. Maes (Eds.), *Artificial Life IV*. Cambridge, MA: MIT Press.

Goldberg, D. (1989). *Genetic algorithms in search, optimization, and machine learning*. Reading, MA: Addison-Wesley.

Goldberg, D. (1994). Genetic and evolutionary algorithms come of age. *Communications of the ACM*, 37(3), 113–119.

Green, D. P., & Smith, S. F. (1993). Competition based induction of decision models from examples. *Machine Learning*, 13, 229–257.

Grefenstette, J. J. (1988). Credit assignment in rule discovery systems based on genetic algorithms. *Machine Learning*, 3, 225–245.

Grefenstette, J. J. (1991). Lamarckian learning in multi-agent environments. In R. Belew and L. Booker (Eds.), *Proceedings of the Fourth International Conference on Genetic Algorithms*. San Mateo, CA: Morgan Kaufmann.

Hart, W., & Belew, R. (1995). Optimization with genetic algorithm hybrids that use local search. In R. Below and M. Mitchell (Eds.), *Adaptive individuals in evolving populations: Models and algorithms*. Reading, MA: Addison-Wesley.

Harvey, I. (1993). The puzzle of the persistent question marks: A case study of genetic drift. In Forrest (Ed.), *Proceedings of the Fifth International Conference on Genetic Algorithms*. San Mateo, CA: Morgan Kaufmann.

Hinton, G. E., & Nowlan, S. J. (1987). How learning can guide evolution. *Complex Systems*, 1, 495–502.

Holland, J. H. (1962). Outline for a logical theory of adaptive systems. *Journal of the Association for Computing Machinery*, 3, 297–314.

Holland, J. H. (1975). *Adaptation in natural and artificial systems*. University of Michigan Press (reprinted in 1992 by MIT Press, Cambridge, MA).

Holland, J. H. (1986). Escaping brittleness: The possibilities of general-purpose learning algorithms applied to parallel rule-based systems. In R. Michalski, J. Carbonell, & T. Mitchell (Eds.), *Machine learning: An artificial intelligence approach* (Vol. 2). San Mateo, CA: Morgan Kaufmann.

Holland, J. H. (1989). Searching nonlinear functions for high values. *Applied Mathematics and Computation*, 32, 255–274.

Janikow, C. Z. (1993). A knowledge-intensive GA for supervised learning. *Machine Learning*, 13, 189–228.

Koza, J. (1992). *Genetic programming: On the programming of computers by means of natural selection*. Cambridge, MA: MIT Press.

Koza, J. R. (1994). *Genetic Programming II: Automatic discovery of reusable programs*. Cambridge, MA: The MIT Press.

Koza, J. R., Bennett III, F. H., Andre, D., & Keane, M. A. (1996). Four problems for which a computer program evolved by genetic programming is competitive with human performance. *Proceedings of the 1996 IEEE International Conference on Evolutionary Computation* (pp. 1–10). IEEE Press.

Koza, J. R., Goldberg, D. E., Fogel, D. B., & Riolo, R. L. (Eds.). (1996b). *Genetic programming 1996: Proceedings of the First Annual Conference*. Cambridge, MA: MIT Press.

Machine Learning: Special Issue on Genetic Algorithms (1988) 3:2–3, October.

Machine Learning: Special Issue on Genetic Algorithms (1990) 5:4, October.

Machine Learning: Special Issue on Genetic Algorithms (1993) 13:2,3, November.

Mitchell, M. (1996). *An introduction to genetic algorithms*. Cambridge, MA: MIT Press.

O'Reilly, U-M., & Oppacher, R. (1994). Program search with a hierarchical variable length representation: Genetic programming, simulated annealing, and hill climbing. In Y. Davidor et al. (Eds.), *Parallel problem solving from nature—PPSN III* (Vol. 866) (Lecture notes in computer science). Springer-Verlag.

Rechenberg, I. (1965). *Cybernetic solution path of an experimental problem*. Ministry of aviation, Royal Aircraft Establishment, U.K.

Rechenberg, I. (1973). *Evolutionsstrategie: Optimierung technischer systeme nach prinzipien der biolgischen evolution*. Stuttgart: Frommann-Holzboog.

Schwefel, H. P. (1975). *Evolutionsstrategie und numerische optimierung* (Ph.D. thesis). Technical University of Berlin.

Schwefel, H. P. (1977). *Numerische optimierung von computer-modellen mittels der evolutionsstrategie*. Basel: Birkhauser.

Schwefel, H. P. (1995). *Evolution and optimum seeking*. New York: John Wiley & Sons.

Spiessens, P., & Manderick, B. (1991). A massively parallel genetic algorithm: Implementation and first analysis. *Proceedings of the 4th International Conference on Genetic Algorithms* (pp. 279–286).

Smith, S. (1980). *A learning system based on genetic adaptive algorithms* (Ph.D. dissertation). Computer Science, University of Pittsburgh.

Stender, J. (Ed.) (1993). *Parallel genetic algorithms*. Amsterdam: IOS Publishing.

Tanese, R. (1989). Distributed genetic algorithms. *Proceedings of the 3rd International Conference on Genetic Algorithms* (pp. 434–439).

Teller, A., & Veloso, M. (1994). PADO: A new learning architecture for object recognition. In K. Ikeuchi & M. Veloso (Eds.), *Symbolic visual learning* (pp. 81–116). Oxford, England: Oxford Univ. Press.

Turney, P. D. (1995). Cost-sensitive classification: Empirical evaluation of a hybrid genetic decision tree induction algorithm. *Journal of AI Research*, 2, 369–409. http://www.cs.washington.edu/research/jair/home.html.

Turney, P. D., Whitley, D., & Anderson, R. (1997). *Evolutionary Computation*. Special issue: The Baldwin effect, 4(3). Cambridge, MA: MIT Press. http://www-mitpress.mit.edu/jrnls-catalog/evolution-abstracts/evol.html.

Whitley, L. D., & Vose, M. D. (Eds.). (1995). *Foundations of genetic algorithms 3*. Morgan Kaufmann.

Wright, S. (1977). *Evolution and the genetics of populations*. Vol. 4: *Variability within and among Natural Populations*. Chicago: University of Chicago Press.

Zbignlew, M. (1992). *Genetic algorithms + data structures = evolution programs*. Berlin: Springer-Verlag.

CHAPTER 10

LEARNING SETS OF RULES

One of the most expressive and human readable representations for learned hypotheses is sets of if-then rules. This chapter explores several algorithms for learning such sets of rules. One important special case involves learning sets of rules containing variables, called first-order Horn clauses. Because sets of first-order Horn clauses can be interpreted as programs in the logic programming language PROLOG, learning them is often called inductive logic programming (ILP). This chapter examines several approaches to learning sets of rules, including an approach based on inverting the deductive operators of mechanical theorem provers.

10.1 INTRODUCTION

In many cases it is useful to learn the target function represented as a set of if-then rules that jointly define the function. As shown in Chapter 3, one way to learn sets of rules is to first learn a decision tree, then translate the tree into an equivalent set of rules—one rule for each leaf node in the tree. A second method, illustrated in Chapter 9, is to use a genetic algorithm that encodes each rule set as a bit string and uses genetic search operators to explore this hypothesis space. In this chapter we explore a variety of algorithms that directly learn rule sets and that differ from these algorithms in two key respects. First, they are designed to learn sets of first-order rules that contain variables. This is significant because first-order rules are much more expressive than propositional rules. Second, the algorithms discussed here use sequential covering algorithms that learn one rule at a time to incrementally grow the final set of rules.

As an example of first-order rule sets, consider the following two rules that jointly describe the target concept *Ancestor*. Here we use the predicate $Parent(x, y)$ to indicate that y is the mother or father of x, and the predicate $Ancestor(x, y)$ to indicate that y is an ancestor of x related by an arbitrary number of family generations.

IF	$Parent(x, y)$	THEN	$Ancestor(x, y)$
IF	$Parent(x, z) \wedge Ancestor(z, y)$	THEN	$Ancestor(x, y)$

Note these two rules compactly describe a recursive function that would be very difficult to represent using a decision tree or other propositional representation. One way to see the representational power of first-order rules is to consider the general purpose programming language PROLOG. In PROLOG, programs are sets of first-order rules such as the two shown above (rules of this form are also called *Horn clauses*). In fact, when stated in a slightly different syntax the above rules form a valid PROLOG program for computing the *Ancestor* relation. In this light, a general purpose algorithm capable of learning such rule sets may be viewed as an algorithm for automatically inferring PROLOG programs from examples. In this chapter we explore learning algorithms capable of learning such rules, given appropriate sets of training examples.

In practice, learning systems based on first-order representations have been successfully applied to problems such as learning which chemical bonds fragment in a mass spectrometer (Buchanan 1976; Lindsay 1980), learning which chemical substructures produce mutagenic activity (a property related to carcinogenicity) (Srinivasan et al. 1994), and learning to design finite element meshes to analyze stresses in physical structures (Dolsak and Muggleton 1992). In each of these applications, the hypotheses that must be represented involve relational assertions that can be conveniently expressed using first-order representations, while they are very difficult to describe using propositional representations.

In this chapter we begin by considering algorithms that learn sets of propositional rules; that is, rules without variables. Algorithms for searching the hypothesis space to learn disjunctive sets of rules are most easily understood in this setting. We then consider extensions of these algorithms to learn first-order rules. Two general approaches to inductive logic programming are then considered, and the fundamental relationship between inductive and deductive inference is explored.

10.2 SEQUENTIAL COVERING ALGORITHMS

Here we consider a family of algorithms for learning rule sets based on the strategy of learning one rule, removing the data it covers, then iterating this process. Such algorithms are called *sequential covering* algorithms. To elaborate, imagine we have a subroutine LEARN-ONE-RULE that accepts a set of positive and negative training examples as input, then outputs a single rule that covers many of the positive examples and few of the negative examples. We require that this output rule have high accuracy, but not necessarily high coverage. By high accuracy, we mean the predictions it makes should be correct. By accepting low coverage, we mean it need not make predictions for every training example.

Given this LEARN-ONE-RULE subroutine for learning a single rule, one obvious approach to learning a set of rules is to invoke LEARN-ONE-RULE on all the available training examples, remove any positive examples covered by the rule it learns, then invoke it again to learn a second rule based on the remaining training examples. This procedure can be iterated as many times as desired to learn a disjunctive set of rules that together cover any desired fraction of the positive examples. This is called a *sequential covering* algorithm because it sequentially learns a set of rules that together cover the full set of positive examples. The final set of rules can then be sorted so that more accurate rules will be considered first when a new instance must be classified. A prototypical sequential covering algorithm is described in Table 10.1.

This sequential covering algorithm is one of the most widespread approaches to learning disjunctive sets of rules. It reduces the problem of learning a disjunctive set of rules to a sequence of simpler problems, each requiring that a single conjunctive rule be learned. Because it performs a greedy search, formulating a sequence of rules without backtracking, it is not guaranteed to find the smallest or best set of rules that cover the training examples.

How shall we design LEARN-ONE-RULE to meet the needs of the sequential covering algorithm? We require an algorithm that can formulate a single rule with high accuracy, but that need not cover all of the positive examples. In this section we present a variety of algorithms and describe the main variations that have been explored in the research literature. In this section we consider learning only propositional rules. In later sections, we extend these algorithms to learn first-order Horn clauses.

SEQUENTIAL-COVERING(*Target_attribute*, *Attributes*, *Examples*, *Threshold*)

- *Learned_rules* ← {}
- *Rule* ← LEARN-ONE-RULE(*Target_attribute*, *Attributes*, *Examples*)
- while PERFORMANCE(*Rule*, *Examples*) > *Threshold*, do
    - *Learned_rules* ← *Learned_rules* + *Rule*
    - *Examples* ← *Examples* − {examples correctly classified by *Rule*}
    - *Rule* ← LEARN-ONE-RULE(*Target_attribute*, *Attributes*, *Examples*)
- *Learned_rules* ← sort *Learned_rules* accord to PERFORMANCE over *Examples*
- return *Learned_rules*

TABLE 10.1
The sequential covering algorithm for learning a disjunctive set of rules. LEARN-ONE-RULE must return a single rule that covers at least some of the *Examples*. PERFORMANCE is a user-provided subroutine to evaluate rule quality. This covering algorithm learns rules until it can no longer learn a rule whose performance is above the given *Threshold*.

10.2.1 General to Specific Beam Search

One effective approach to implementing LEARN-ONE-RULE is to organize the hypothesis space search in the same general fashion as the ID3 algorithm, but to follow only the most promising branch in the tree at each step. As illustrated in the search tree of Figure 10.1, the search begins by considering the most general rule precondition possible (the empty test that matches every instance), then greedily adding the attribute test that most improves rule performance measured over the training examples. Once this test has been added, the process is repeated by greedily adding a second attribute test, and so on. Like ID3, this process grows the hypothesis by greedily adding new attribute tests until the hypothesis reaches an acceptable level of performance. Unlike ID3, this implementation of LEARN-ONE-RULE follows only a single descendant at each search step—the attribute-value pair yielding the best performance—rather than growing a subtree that covers all possible values of the selected attribute.

This approach to implementing LEARN-ONE-RULE performs a general-to-specific search through the space of possible rules in search of a rule with high accuracy, though perhaps incomplete coverage of the data. As in decision tree learning, there are many ways to define a measure to select the "best" descendant. To follow the lead of ID3 let us for now define the best descendant as the one whose covered examples have the lowest entropy (recall Equation [3.3]).

The general-to-specific search suggested above for the LEARN-ONE-RULE algorithm is a greedy depth-first search with no backtracking. As with any greedy

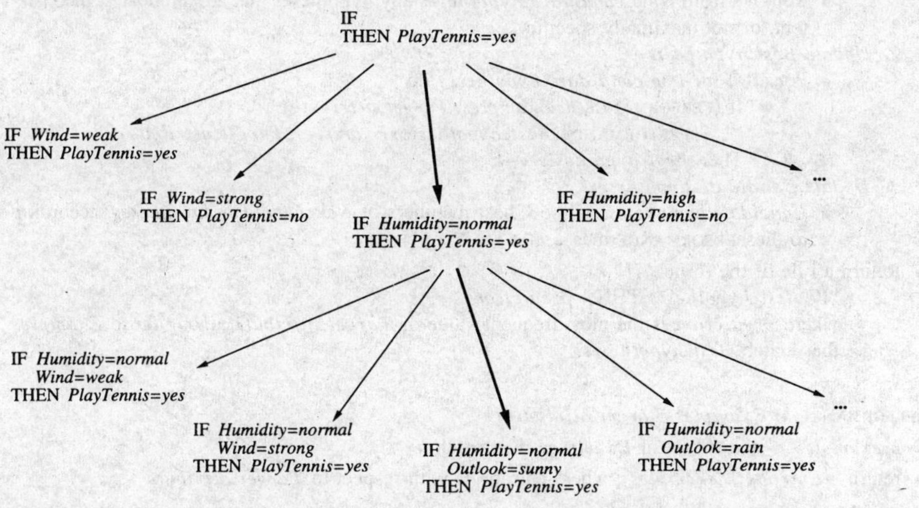

FIGURE 10.1
The search for rule preconditions as LEARN-ONE-RULE proceeds from general to specific. At each step, the preconditions of the best rule are specialized in all possible ways. Rule postconditions are determined by the examples found to satisfy the preconditions. This figure illustrates a beam search of width 1.

search, there is a danger that a suboptimal choice will be made at any step. To reduce this risk, we can extend the algorithm to perform a *beam search*; that is, a search in which the algorithm maintains a list of the k best candidates at each step, rather than a single best candidate. On each search step, descendants (specializations) are generated for each of these k best candidates, and the resulting set is again reduced to the k most promising members. Beam search keeps track of the most promising alternatives to the current top-rated hypothesis, so that all of their successors can be considered at each search step. This general to specific beam search algorithm is used by the CN2 program described by Clark and Niblett (1989). The algorithm is described in Table 10.2.

LEARN-ONE-RULE(*Target_attribute, Attributes, Examples, k*)

Returns a single rule that covers some of the Examples. Conducts a general_to_specific greedy beam search for the best rule, guided by the PERFORMANCE *metric.*

- Initialize *Best_hypothesis* to the most general hypothesis ∅
- Initialize *Candidate_hypotheses* to the set {*Best_hypothesis*}
- While *Candidate_hypotheses* is not empty, Do
  1. *Generate the next more specific candidate_hypotheses*
     - *All_constraints* ← the set of all constraints of the form $(a = v)$, where a is a member of *Attributes*, and v is a value of a that occurs in the current set of *Examples*
     - *New_candidate_hypotheses* ←
       for each h in *Candidate_hypotheses*,
       for each c in *All_constraints*,
         - create a specialization of h by adding the constraint c
     - Remove from *New_candidate_hypotheses* any hypotheses that are duplicates, inconsistent, or not maximally specific
  2. *Update Best_hypothesis*
     - For all h in *New_candidate_hypotheses* do
       - If (PERFORMANCE(h, *Examples, Target_attribute*)
         > PERFORMANCE(*Best_hypothesis, Examples, Target_attribute*))
         Then *Best_hypothesis* ← h
  3. *Update Candidate_hypotheses*
     - *Candidate_hypotheses* ← the k best members of *New_candidate_hypotheses*, according to the PERFORMANCE measure.
- Return a rule of the form
  "IF *Best_hypothesis* THEN *prediction*"
  where *prediction* is the most frequent value of *Target_attribute* among those *Examples* that match *Best_hypothesis*.

PERFORMANCE(h, *Examples, Target_attribute*)

- *h_examples* ← the subset of *Examples* that match h
- return −*Entropy*(*h_examples*), where entropy is with respect to *Target_attribute*

TABLE 10.2
One implementation for LEARN-ONE-RULE is a general-to-specific beam search. The frontier of current hypotheses is represented by the variable *Candidate_hypotheses*. This algorithm is similar to that used by the CN2 program, described by Clark and Niblett (1989).

A few remarks on the LEARN-ONE-RULE algorithm of Table 10.2 are in order. First, note that each hypothesis considered in the main loop of the algorithm is a conjunction of attribute-value constraints. Each of these conjunctive hypotheses corresponds to a candidate set of preconditions for the rule to be learned and is evaluated by the entropy of the examples it covers. The search considers increasingly specific candidate hypotheses until it reaches a maximally specific hypothesis that contains all available attributes. The rule that is output by the algorithm is the rule encountered during the search whose PERFORMANCE is greatest—not necessarily the final hypothesis generated in the search. The postcondition for the output rule is chosen only in the final step of the algorithm, after its precondition (represented by the variable *Best_hypothesis*) has been determined. The algorithm constructs the rule postcondition to predict the value of the target attribute that is most common among the examples covered by the rule precondition. Finally, note that despite the use of beam search to reduce the risk, the greedy search may still produce suboptimal rules. However, even when this occurs the SEQUENTIAL-COVERING algorithm can still learn a collection of rules that together cover the training examples, because it repeatedly calls LEARN-ONE-RULE on the remaining uncovered examples.

10.2.2 Variations

The SEQUENTIAL-COVERING algorithm, together with the LEARN-ONE-RULE algorithm, learns a set of if-then rules that covers the training examples. Many variations on this approach have been explored. For example, in some cases it might be desirable to have the program learn only rules that cover positive examples and to include a "default" that assigns a negative classification to instances not covered by any rule. This approach might be desirable, say, if one is attempting to learn a target concept such as "pregnant women who are likely to have twins." In this case, the fraction of positive examples in the entire population is small, so the rule set will be more compact and intelligible to humans if it identifies only classes of positive examples, with the default classification of all other examples as negative. This approach also corresponds to the "negation-as-failure" strategy of PROLOG, in which any expression that cannot be proven to be true is by default assumed to be false. In order to learn such rules that predict just a single target value, the LEARN-ONE-RULE algorithm can be modified to accept an additional input argument specifying the target value of interest. The general-to-specific beam search is conducted just as before, changing only the PERFORMANCE subroutine that evaluates hypotheses. Note the definition of PERFORMANCE as negative entropy is no longer appropriate in this new setting, because it assigns a maximal score to hypotheses that cover exclusively negative examples, as well as those that cover exclusively positive examples. Using a measure that evaluates the fraction of positive examples covered by the hypothesis would be more appropriate in this case.

Another variation is provided by a family of algorithms called AQ (Michalski 1969, Michalski et al. 1986), that predate the CN2 algorithm on which the above discussion is based. Like CN2, AQ learns a disjunctive set of rules that together cover the target function. However, AQ differs in several ways from the algorithms given here. First, the covering algorithm of AQ differs from the SEQUENTIAL-COVERING algorithm because it explicitly seeks rules that cover a particular target value, learning a disjunctive set of rules for each target value in turn. Second, AQ's algorithm for learning a single rule differs from LEARN-ONE-RULE. While it conducts a general-to-specific beam search for each rule, it uses a single positive example to focus this search. In particular, it considers only those attributes satisfied by the positive example as it searches for progressively more specific hypotheses. Each time it learns a new rule it selects a new positive example from those that are not yet covered, to act as a seed to guide the search for this new disjunct.

10.3 LEARNING RULE SETS: SUMMARY

The SEQUENTIAL-COVERING algorithm described above and the decision tree learning algorithms of Chapter 3 suggest a variety of possible methods for learning sets of rules. This section considers several key dimensions in the design space of such rule learning algorithms.

First, *sequential covering* algorithms learn one rule at a time, removing the covered examples and repeating the process on the remaining examples. In contrast, decision tree algorithms such as ID3 learn the entire set of disjuncts simultaneously as part of the single search for an acceptable decision tree. We might, therefore, call algorithms such as ID3 *simultaneous covering* algorithms, in contrast to sequential covering algorithms such as CN2. Which should we prefer? The key difference occurs in the choice made at the most primitive step in the search. At each search step ID3 chooses among alternative *attributes* by comparing the *partitions* of the data they generate. In contrast, CN2 chooses among alternative *attribute-value* pairs, by comparing the *subsets* of data they cover. One way to see the significance of this difference is to compare the number of distinct choices made by the two algorithms in order to learn the same set of rules. To learn a set of n rules, each containing k attribute-value tests in their preconditions, sequential covering algorithms will perform $n \cdot k$ primitive search steps, making an independent decision to select each precondition of each rule. In contrast, simultaneous covering algorithms will make many fewer independent choices, because each choice of a decision node in the decision tree corresponds to choosing the precondition for the multiple rules associated with that node. In other words, if the decision node tests an attribute that has m possible values, the choice of the decision node corresponds to choosing a precondition for each of the m corresponding rules (see Exercise 10.1). Thus, sequential covering algorithms such as CN2 make a larger number of independent choices than simultaneous covering algorithms such as ID3. Still, the question remains, which should we prefer? The answer may depend on how much training data is available. If data is plentiful, then it may support the larger number of independent decisions required by the sequential covering algorithm, whereas if data is scarce, the "sharing" of decisions regarding preconditions of different rules may be more effective. An additional consideration is the task-specific question of whether it is desirable that different rules test the same attributes. In the simultaneous covering decision tree learning algorithms, they will. In sequential covering algorithms, they need not.

A second dimension along which approaches vary is the direction of the search in LEARN-ONE-RULE. In the algorithm described above, the search is from *general to specific* hypotheses. Other algorithms we have discussed (e.g., FIND-S from Chapter 2) search from *specific to general*. One advantage of general to specific search in this case is that there is a single maximally general hypothesis from which to begin the search, whereas there are very many specific hypotheses in most hypothesis spaces (i.e., one for each possible instance). Given many maximally specific hypotheses, it is unclear which to select as the starting point of the search. One program that conducts a specific-to-general search, called GOLEM (Muggleton and Feng 1990), addresses this issue by choosing several positive examples at random to initialize and to guide the search. The best hypothesis obtained through multiple random choices is then selected.

A third dimension is whether the LEARN-ONE-RULE search is a *generate then test* search through the syntactically legal hypotheses, as it is in our suggested implementation, or whether it is *example-driven* so that individual training examples constrain the generation of hypotheses. Prototypical example-driven search algorithms include the FIND-S and CANDIDATE-ELIMINATION algorithms of Chapter 2, the AQ algorithm, and the CIGOL algorithm discussed later in this chapter. In each of these algorithms, the generation or revision of hypotheses is driven by the analysis of an individual training example, and the result is a revised hypothesis designed to correct performance for this single example. This contrasts to the generate and test search of LEARN-ONE-RULE in Table 10.2, in which successor hypotheses are generated based only on the syntax of the hypothesis representation. The training data is considered only after these candidate hypotheses are generated and is used to choose among the candidates based on their performance over the entire collection of training examples. One important advantage of the generate and test approach is that each choice in the search is based on the hypothesis performance over *many* examples, so that the impact of noisy data is minimized. In contrast, example-driven algorithms that refine the hypothesis based on individual examples are more easily misled by a single noisy training example and are therefore less robust to errors in the training data.

A fourth dimension is whether and how rules are post-pruned. As in decision tree learning, it is possible for LEARN-ONE-RULE to formulate rules that perform very well on the training data, but less well on subsequent data. As in decision tree learning, one way to address this issue is to post-prune each rule after it is learned from the training data. In particular, preconditions can be removed from the rule whenever this leads to improved performance over a set of pruning examples distinct from the training examples. A more detailed discussion of rule post-pruning is provided in Section 3.7.1.2.

A final dimension is the particular definition of rule PERFORMANCE used to guide the search in LEARN-ONE-RULE. Various evaluation functions have been used. Some common evaluation functions include:

- *Relative frequency.* Let n denote the number of examples the rule matches and let n_c denote the number of these that it classifies correctly. The relative frequency estimate of rule performance is

$$\frac{n_c}{n}$$

Relative frequency is used to evaluate rules in the AQ program.

- *m-estimate of accuracy.* This accuracy estimate is biased toward the default accuracy expected of the rule. It is often preferred when data is scarce and the rule must be evaluated based on few examples. As above, let n and n_c denote the number of examples matched and correctly predicted by the rule. Let p be the prior probability that a randomly drawn example from the entire data set will have the classification assigned by the rule (e.g., if 12 out of 100 examples have the value predicted by the rule, then $p = .12$). Finally, let m be the weight, or equivalent number of examples for weighting this prior p. The m-estimate of rule accuracy is

$$\frac{n_c + mp}{n + m}$$

Note if m is set to zero, then the m-estimate becomes the above relative frequency estimate. As m is increased, a larger number of examples is needed to override the prior assumed accuracy p. The m-estimate measure is advocated by Cestnik and Bratko (1991) and has been used in some versions of the CN2 algorithm. It is also used in the naive Bayes classifier discussed in Section 6.9.1.

- *Entropy.* This is the measure used by the PERFORMANCE subroutine in the algorithm of Table 10.2. Let S be the set of examples that match the rule preconditions. Entropy measures the uniformity of the target function values for this set of examples. We take the negative of the entropy so that better rules will have higher scores.

$$-Entropy(S) = \sum_{i=1}^{c} p_i \log_2 p_i$$

where c is the number of distinct values the target function may take on, and where p_i is the proportion of examples from S for which the target function takes on the ith value. This entropy measure, combined with a test for statistical significance, is used in the CN2 algorithm of Clark and Niblett (1989). It is also the basis for the information gain measure used by many decision tree learning algorithms.

10.4 LEARNING FIRST-ORDER RULES

In the previous sections we discussed algorithms for learning sets of propositional (i.e., variable-free) rules. In this section, we consider learning rules that contain variables—in particular, learning first-order Horn theories. Our motivation for considering such rules is that they are much more expressive than propositional rules. Inductive learning of first-order rules or theories is often referred to as *inductive logic programming* (or ILP for short), because this process can be viewed as automatically inferring PROLOG programs from examples. PROLOG is a general purpose, Turing-equivalent programming language in which programs are expressed as collections of Horn clauses.

10.4.1 First-Order Horn Clauses

To see the advantages of first-order representations over propositional (variable-free) representations, consider the task of learning the simple target concept $Daughter(x, y)$, defined over pairs of people x and y. The value of $Daughter(x, y)$ is $True$ when x is the daughter of y, and $False$ otherwise. Suppose each person in the data is described by the attributes $Name$, $Mother$, $Father$, $Male$, $Female$. Hence, each training example will consist of the description of two people in terms of these attributes, along with the value of the target attribute $Daughter$. For example, the following is a positive example in which Sharon is the daughter of Bob:

$$\begin{array}{lll}\langle Name_1 = Sharon, & Mother_1 = Louise, & Father_1 = Bob, \\ Male_1 = False, & Female_1 = True, & \\ Name_2 = Bob, & Mother_2 = Nora, & Father_2 = Victor, \\ Male_2 = True, & Female_2 = False, & Daughter_{1,2} = True\rangle\end{array}$$

where the subscript on each attribute name indicates which of the two persons is being described. Now if we were to collect a number of such training examples for the target concept $Daughter_{1,2}$ and provide them to a propositional rule learner such as CN2 or C4.5, the result would be a collection of very specific rules such as

$$\begin{array}{ll}\text{IF} & (Father_1 = Bob) \wedge (Name_2 = Bob) \wedge (Female_1 = True) \\ \text{THEN} & Daughter_{1,2} = True\end{array}$$

Although it is correct, this rule is so specific that it will rarely, if ever, be useful in classifying future pairs of people. The problem is that propositional representations offer no general way to describe the essential *relations* among the values of the attributes. In contrast, a program using first-order representations could learn the following general rule:

$$\text{IF} \quad Father(y, x) \wedge Female(y), \quad \text{THEN} \quad Daughter(x, y)$$

where x and y are variables that can be bound to any person.

First-order Horn clauses may also refer to variables in the preconditions that do not occur in the postconditions. For example, one rule for *GrandDaughter* might be

IF $Father(y, z) \wedge Mother(z, x) \wedge Female(y)$
THEN $GrandDaughter(x, y)$

Note the variable z in this rule, which refers to the father of y, is not present in the rule postconditions. Whenever such a variable occurs only in the preconditions, it is assumed to be existentially quantified; that is, the rule preconditions are satisfied as long as there exists at least one binding of the variable that satisfies the corresponding literal.

It is also possible to use the same predicates in the rule postconditions and preconditions, enabling the description of recursive rules. For example, the two rules at the beginning of this chapter provide a recursive definition of the concept $Ancestor(x, y)$. ILP learning methods such as those described below have been demonstrated to learn a variety of simple recursive functions, such as the above *Ancestor* function, and functions for sorting the elements of a list, removing a specific element from a list, and appending two lists.

10.4.2 Terminology

Before moving on to algorithms for learning sets of Horn clauses, let us introduce some basic terminology from formal logic. All expressions are composed of *constants* (e.g., *Bob*, *Louise*), *variables* (e.g., x, y), *predicate* symbols (e.g., *Married*, *Greater_Than*), and *function* symbols (e.g., *age*). The difference between predicates and functions is that predicates take on values of *True* or *False*, whereas functions may take on any constant as their value. We will use lowercase symbols for variables and capitalized symbols for constants. Also, we will use lowercase for functions and capitalized symbols for predicates.

From these symbols, we build up expressions as follows: A *term* is any constant, any variable, or any function applied to any term (e.g., *Bob*, x, $age(Bob)$). A *literal* is any predicate or its negation applied to any term (e.g., $Married(Bob, Louise)$, $\neg Greater\_Than(age(Sue), 20)$). If a literal contains a negation ($\neg$) symbol, we call it a *negative literal*, otherwise a *positive literal*.

A *clause* is any disjunction of literals, where all variables are assumed to be universally quantified. A *Horn clause* is a clause containing at most one positive literal, such as

$$H \vee \neg L_1 \vee \ldots \neg L_n$$

where H is the positive literal, and $\neg L_1 \ldots \neg L_n$ are negative literals. Because of the equalities $(B \vee \neg A) = (B \leftarrow A)$ and $\neg(A \wedge B) = (\neg A \vee \neg B)$, the above Horn clause can alternatively be written in the form

$$H \leftarrow (L_1 \wedge \ldots \wedge L_n)$$

- Every well-formed expression is composed of *constants* (e.g., $Mary$, 23, or Joe), *variables* (e.g., x), *predicates* (e.g., $Female$, as in $Female(Mary)$), and *functions* (e.g., age, as in $age(Mary)$).
- A *term* is any constant, any variable, or any function applied to any term. Examples include $Mary$, x, $age(Mary)$, $age(x)$.
- A *literal* is any predicate (or its negation) applied to any set of terms. Examples include $Female(Mary)$, $\neg Female(x)$, $Greater\_than(age(Mary), 20)$.
- A *ground literal* is a literal that does not contain any variables (e.g., $\neg Female(Joe)$).
- A *negative literal* is a literal containing a negated predicate (e.g., $\neg Female(Joe)$).
- A *positive literal* is a literal with no negation sign (e.g., $Female(Mary)$).
- A *clause* is any disjunction of literals $M_1 \vee \ldots M_n$ whose variables are universally quantified.
- A *Horn clause* is an expression of the form

$$H \leftarrow (L_1 \wedge \ldots \wedge L_n)$$

  where $H, L_1 \ldots L_n$ are positive literals. H is called the *head* or *consequent* of the Horn clause. The conjunction of literals $L_1 \wedge L_2 \wedge \ldots \wedge L_n$ is called the *body* or *antecedents* of the Horn clause.
- For any literals A and B, the expression $(A \leftarrow B)$ is equivalent to $(A \vee \neg B)$, and the expression $\neg(A \wedge B)$ is equivalent to $(\neg A \vee \neg B)$. Therefore, a Horn clause can equivalently be written as the disjunction

$$H \vee \neg L_1 \vee \ldots \vee \neg L_n$$

- A *substitution* is any function that replaces variables by terms. For example, the substitution $\{x/3, y/z\}$ replaces the variable x by the term 3 and replaces the variable y by the term z. Given a substitution θ and a literal L we write $L\theta$ to denote the result of applying substitution θ to L.
- A *unifying substitution* for two literals L_1 and L_2 is any substitution θ such that $L_1\theta = L_2\theta$.

TABLE 10.3
Basic definitions from first-order logic.

which is equivalent to the following, using our earlier rule notation

$$\text{IF } L_1 \wedge \ldots \wedge L_n, \text{ THEN } H$$

Whatever the notation, the Horn clause preconditions $L_1 \wedge \ldots \wedge L_n$ are called the clause *body* or, alternatively, the clause *antecedents*. The literal H that forms the postcondition is called the clause *head* or, alternatively, the clause *consequent*. For easy reference, these definitions are summarized in Table 10.3, along with other definitions introduced later in this chapter.

10.5 LEARNING SETS OF FIRST-ORDER RULES: FOIL

A variety of algorithms has been proposed for learning first-order rules, or Horn clauses. In this section we consider a program called FOIL (Quinlan 1990) that employs an approach very similar to the SEQUENTIAL-COVERING and LEARN-ONE-RULE algorithms of the previous section. In fact, the FOIL program is the natural extension of these earlier algorithms to first-order representations. Formally, the hypotheses learned by FOIL are sets of first-order rules, where each rule is similar to a Horn clause with two exceptions. First, the rules learned by FOIL are more restricted than general Horn clauses, because the literals are not permitted to contain function symbols (this reduces the complexity of the hypothesis space search). Second, FOIL rules are more expressive than Horn clauses, because the literals appearing in the body of the rule may be negated. FOIL has been applied to a variety of problem domains. For example, it has been demonstrated to learn a recursive definition of the QUICKSORT algorithm and to learn to discriminate legal from illegal chess positions.

The FOIL algorithm is summarized in Table 10.4. Notice the outer loop corresponds to a variant of the SEQUENTIAL-COVERING algorithm discussed earlier; that is, it learns new rules one at a time, removing the positive examples covered by the latest rule before attempting to learn the next rule. The inner loop corresponds to a variant of our earlier LEARN-ONE-RULE algorithm, extended to accommodate first-order rules. Note also there are a few minor differences between FOIL and these earlier algorithms. In particular, FOIL seeks only rules that predict when the target literal is *True*, whereas our earlier algorithm would seek both rules that predict when it is *True* and rules that predict when it is *False*. Also, FOIL performs a simple hillclimbing search rather than a beam search (equivalently, it uses a beam of width one).

The hypothesis space search performed by FOIL is best understood by viewing it hierarchically. Each iteration through FOIL's outer loop adds a new rule to its disjunctive hypothesis, *Learned_rules*. The effect of each new rule is to gen-

---

FOIL(*Target_predicate*, *Predicates*, *Examples*)

- *Pos* ← those *Examples* for which the *Target_predicate* is *True*
- *Neg* ← those *Examples* for which the *Target_predicate* is *False*
- *Learned_rules* ← {}
- while *Pos*, do

  Learn a NewRule
  - *NewRule* ← the rule that predicts *Target_predicate* with no preconditions
  - *NewRuleNeg* ← *Neg*
  - while *NewRuleNeg*, do

    Add a new literal to specialize NewRule
    - *Candidate_literals* ← generate candidate new literals for *NewRule*, based on *Predicates*
    - *Best_literal* ← $\underset{L \in Candidate\_literals}{\text{argmax}}$ *Foil_Gain*(*L*, *NewRule*)
    - add *Best_literal* to preconditions of *NewRule*
    - *NewRuleNeg* ← subset of *NewRuleNeg* that satisfies *NewRule* preconditions
  - *Learned_rules* ← *Learned_rules* + *NewRule*
  - *Pos* ← *Pos* − {members of *Pos* covered by *NewRule*}
- Return *Learned_rules*

TABLE 10.4
The basic FOIL algorithm. The specific method for generating *Candidate_literals* and the definition of *Foil_Gain* are given in the text. This basic algorithm can be modified slightly to better accommodate noisy data, as described in the text.

eralize the current disjunctive hypothesis (i.e., to increase the number of instances it classifies as positive), by adding a new disjunct. Viewed at this level, the search is a *specific-to-general* search through the space of hypotheses, beginning with the most specific empty disjunction and terminating when the hypothesis is sufficiently general to cover all positive training examples. The inner loop of FOIL performs a finer-grained search to determine the exact definition of each new rule. This inner loop searches a second hypothesis space, consisting of conjunctions of literals, to find a conjunction that will form the preconditions for the new rule. Within this hypothesis space, it conducts a *general-to-specific*, hill-climbing search, beginning with the most general preconditions possible (the empty precondition), then adding literals one at a time to specialize the rule until it avoids all negative examples.

The two most substantial differences between FOIL and our earlier SEQUENTIAL-COVERING and LEARN-ONE-RULE algorithm follow from the requirement that it accommodate first-order rules. These differences are:

1. In its general-to-specific search to learn each new rule, FOIL employs different detailed steps to generate candidate specializations of the rule. This difference follows from the need to accommodate variables in the rule preconditions.
2. FOIL employs a PERFORMANCE measure, $Foil\_Gain$, that differs from the entropy measure shown for LEARN-ONE-RULE in Table 10.2. This difference follows from the need to distinguish between different bindings of the rule variables and from the fact that FOIL seeks only rules that cover positive examples.

The following two subsections consider these two differences in greater detail.

10.5.1 Generating Candidate Specializations in FOIL

To generate candidate specializations of the current rule, FOIL generates a variety of new literals, each of which may be individually added to the rule preconditions. More precisely, suppose the current rule being considered is

$$P(x_1, x_2, \ldots, x_k) \leftarrow L_1 \ldots L_n$$

where $L_1 \ldots L_n$ are literals forming the current rule preconditions and where $P(x_1, x_2, \ldots, x_k)$ is the literal that forms the rule head, or postconditions. FOIL generates candidate specializations of this rule by considering new literals L_{n+1} that fit one of the following forms:

- $Q(v_1, \ldots, v_r)$, where Q is any predicate name occurring in $Predicates$ and where the v_i are either new variables or variables already present in the rule. At least one of the v_i in the created literal must already exist as a variable in the rule.
- $Equal(x_j, x_k)$, where x_j and x_k are variables already present in the rule.

- The negation of either of the above forms of literals.

To illustrate, consider learning rules to predict the target literal $GrandDaughter(x, y)$, where the other predicates used to describe examples are $Father$ and $Female$. The general-to-specific search in FOIL begins with the most general rule

$$GrandDaughter(x, y) \leftarrow$$

which asserts that $GrandDaughter(x, y)$ is true of any x and y. To specialize this initial rule, the above procedure generates the following literals as candidate additions to the rule preconditions: $Equal(x, y)$, $Female(x)$, $Female(y)$, $Father(x, y)$, $Father(y, x)$, $Father(x, z)$, $Father(z, x)$, $Father(y, z)$, $Father(z, y)$, and the negations of each of these literals (e.g., $\neg Equal(x, y)$). Note that z is a new variable here, whereas x and y exist already within the current rule.

Now suppose that among the above literals FOIL greedily selects $Father(y, z)$ as the most promising, leading to the more specific rule

$$GrandDaughter(x, y) \leftarrow Father(y, z)$$

In generating candidate literals to further specialize this rule, FOIL will now consider all of the literals mentioned in the previous step, plus the additional literals $Female(z)$, $Equal(z, x)$, $Equal(z, y)$, $Father(z, w)$, $Father(w, z)$, and their negations. These new literals are considered at this point because the variable z was added to the rule in the previous step. Because of this, FOIL now considers an additional new variable w.

If FOIL at this point were to select the literal $Father(z, x)$ and on the next iteration select the literal $Female(y)$, this would lead to the following rule, which covers only positive examples and hence terminates the search for further specializations of the rule.

$$GrandDaughter(x, y) \leftarrow Father(y, z) \wedge Father(z, x) \wedge Female(y)$$

At this point, FOIL will remove all positive examples covered by this new rule. If additional positive examples remain to be covered, then it will begin yet another general-to-specific search for an additional rule.

10.5.2 Guiding the Search in FOIL

To select the most promising literal from the candidates generated at each step, FOIL considers the performance of the rule over the training data. In doing this, it considers all possible bindings of each variable in the current rule. To illustrate this process, consider again the example in which we seek to learn a set of rules for the target literal $GrandDaughter(x, y)$. For illustration, assume the training data includes the following simple set of assertions, where we use the convention that $P(x, y)$ can be read as "The P of x is y."

$GrandDaughter(Victor, Sharon)$	$Father(Sharon, Bob)$	$Father(Tom, Bob)$
$Female(Sharon)$	$Father(Bob, Victor)$	

Here let us also make the closed world assumption that any literal involving the predicate $GrandDaughter$, $Father$, or $Female$ and the constants $Victor$, $Sharon$, Bob, and Tom that is not listed above can be assumed to be false (i.e., we also implicitly assert $\neg GrandDaughter(Tom, Bob)$, $\neg GrandDaughter(Victor, Victor)$, etc.).

To select the best specialization of the current rule, FOIL considers each distinct way in which the rule variables can bind to constants in the training examples. For example, in the initial step when the rule is

$$GrandDaughter(x, y) \leftarrow$$

the rule variables x and y are not constrained by any preconditions and may therefore bind in any combination to the four constants $Victor$, $Sharon$, Bob, and Tom. We will use the notation $\{x/Bob, y/Sharon\}$ to denote a particular variable binding; that is, a substitution mapping each variable to a constant. Given the four possible constants, there are 16 possible variable bindings for this initial rule. The binding $\{x/Victor, y/Sharon\}$ corresponds to a positive example binding, because the training data includes the assertion $GrandDaughter(Victor, Sharon)$. The other 15 bindings allowed by the rule (e.g., the binding $\{x/Bob, y/Tom\}$) constitute negative evidence for the rule in the current example, because no corresponding assertion can be found in the training data.

At each stage, the rule is evaluated based on these sets of positive and negative variable bindings, with preference given to rules that possess more positive bindings and fewer negative bindings. As new literals are added to the rule, the sets of bindings will change. Note if a literal is added that introduces a new variable, then the bindings for the rule will grow in length (e.g., if $Father(y, z)$ is added to the above rule, then the original binding $\{x/Victor, y/Sharon\}$ will become the more lengthy $\{x/Victor, y/Sharon, z/Bob\}$. Note also that if the new variable can bind to several different constants, then the number of bindings fitting the extended rule can be greater than the number associated with the original rule.

The evaluation function used by FOIL to estimate the utility of adding a new literal is based on the numbers of positive and negative bindings covered before and after adding the new literal. More precisely, consider some rule R, and a candidate literal L that might be added to the body of R. Let R' be the rule created by adding literal L to rule R. The value $Foil\_Gain(L, R)$ of adding L to R is defined as

$$Foil\_Gain(L, R) \equiv t\left(\log_2 \frac{p_1}{p_1 + n_1} - \log_2 \frac{p_0}{p_0 + n_0}\right) \qquad (10.1)$$

where p_0 is the number of positive bindings of rule R, n_0 is the number of negative bindings of R, p_1 is the number of positive bindings of rule R', and n_1 is the number of negative bindings of R'. Finally, t is the number of positive bindings of rule R that are still covered after adding literal L to R. When a new variable is introduced into R by adding L, then any original binding is considered to be covered so long as some binding extending it is present in the bindings of R'.

This *Foil_Gain* function has a straightforward interpretation in terms of information theory. According to information theory, $-\log_2 \frac{p_0}{p_0+n_0}$ is the minimum number of bits needed to encode the classification of an arbitrary positive binding among the bindings covered by rule R. Similarly, $-\log_2 \frac{p_1}{p_1+n_1}$ is the number of bits required if the binding is one of those covered by rule R'. Since t is just the number of positive bindings covered by R that remain covered by R', $Foil\_Gain(L, R)$ can be seen as the reduction due to L in the total number of bits needed to encode the classification of all positive bindings of R.

10.5.3 Learning Recursive Rule Sets

In the above discussion, we ignored the possibility that new literals added to the rule body could refer to the target predicate itself (i.e., the predicate occurring in the rule head). However, if we include the target predicate in the input list of *Predicates*, then FOIL will consider it as well when generating candidate literals. This will allow it to form recursive rules—rules that use the same predicate in the body and the head of the rule. For instance, recall the following rule set that provides a recursive definition of the *Ancestor* relation.

IF $Parent(x, y)$ THEN $Ancestor(x, y)$
IF $Parent(x, z) \wedge Ancestor(z, y)$ THEN $Ancestor(x, y)$

Given an appropriate set of training examples, these two rules can be learned following a trace similar to the one above for *GrandDaughter*. Note the second rule is among the rules that are potentially within reach of FOIL's search, provided *Ancestor* is included in the list *Predicates* that determines which predicates may be considered when generating new literals. Of course whether this particular rule would be learned or not depends on whether these particular literals outscore competing candidates during FOIL's greedy search for increasingly specific rules. Cameron-Jones and Quinlan (1993) discuss several examples in which FOIL has successfully discovered recursive rule sets. They also discuss important subtleties that arise, such as how to avoid learning rule sets that produce infinite recursion.

10.5.4 Summary of FOIL

To summarize, FOIL extends the sequential covering algorithm of CN2 to handle the case of learning first-order rules similar to Horn clauses. To learn each rule FOIL performs a general-to-specific search, at each step adding a single new literal to the rule preconditions. The new literal may refer to variables already mentioned in the rule preconditions or postconditions, and may introduce new variables as well. At each step, it uses the *Foil_Gain* function of Equation (10.1) to select among the candidate new literals. If new literals are allowed to refer to the target predicate, then FOIL can, in principle, learn sets of recursive rules. While this introduces the complexity of avoiding rule sets that result in infinite recursion, FOIL has been demonstrated to successfully learn recursive rule sets in several cases.

In the case of noise-free training data, FOIL may continue adding new literals to the rule until it covers no negative examples. To handle noisy data, the search is continued until some tradeoff occurs between rule accuracy, coverage, and complexity. FOIL uses a minimum description length approach to halt the growth of rules, in which new literals are added only when their description length is shorter than the description length of the training data they explain. The details of this strategy are given in Quinlan (1990). In addition, FOIL post-prunes each rule it learns, using the same rule post-pruning strategy used for decision trees (Chapter 3).

10.6 INDUCTION AS INVERTED DEDUCTION

A second, quite different approach to inductive logic programming is based on the simple observation that induction is just the inverse of deduction! In general, machine learning involves building theories that explain the observed data. Given some data D and some partial background knowledge B, learning can be described as generating a hypothesis h that, together with B, explains D. Put more precisely, assume as usual that the training data D is a set of training examples, each of the form $\langle x_i, f(x_i)\rangle$. Here x_i denotes the ith training instance and $f(x_i)$ denotes its target value. Then learning is the problem of discovering a hypothesis h, such that the classification $f(x_i)$ of each training instance x_i follows deductively from the hypothesis h, the description of x_i, and any other background knowledge B known to the system.

$$(\forall \langle x_i, f(x_i)\rangle \in D)\ (B \wedge h \wedge x_i) \vdash f(x_i) \tag{10.2}$$

The expression $X \vdash Y$ is read "Y follows deductively from X," or alternatively "X entails Y." Expression (10.2) describes the constraint that must be satisfied by the learned hypothesis h; namely, for every training instance x_i, the target classification $f(x_i)$ must follow deductively from B, h, and x_i.

As an example, consider the case where the target concept to be learned is "pairs of people $\langle u, v\rangle$ such that the child of u is v," represented by the predicate $Child(u, v)$. Assume we are given a single positive example $Child(Bob, Sharon)$, where the instance is described by the literals $Male(Bob)$, $Female(Sharon)$, and $Father(Sharon, Bob)$. Furthermore, suppose we have the general background knowledge $Parent(u, v) \leftarrow Father(u, v)$. We can describe this situation in the terms of Equation (10.2) as follows:

$$x_i : Male(Bob), Female(Sharon), Father(Sharon, Bob)$$

$$f(x_i) : \quad Child(Bob, Sharon)$$

$$B : \quad Parent(u, v) \leftarrow Father(u, v)$$

In this case, two of the many hypotheses that satisfy the constraint $(B \wedge h \wedge x_i) \vdash f(x_i)$ are

$$h_1 : Child(u, v) \leftarrow Father(v, u)$$

$$h_2 : Child(u, v) \leftarrow Parent(v, u)$$

Note that the target literal $Child(Bob, Sharon)$ is entailed by $h_1 \wedge x_i$ with no need for the background information B. In the case of hypothesis h_2, however, the situation is different. The target $Child(Bob, Sharon)$ follows from $B \wedge h_2 \wedge x_i$, but not from $h_2 \wedge x_i$ alone. This example illustrates the role of background knowledge in expanding the set of acceptable hypotheses for a given set of training data. It also illustrates how new predicates (e.g., $Parent$) can be introduced into hypotheses (e.g., h_2), even when the predicate is not present in the original description of the instance x_i. This process of augmenting the set of predicates, based on background knowledge, is often referred to as *constructive induction.*

The significance of Equation (10.2) is that it casts the learning problem in the framework of deductive inference and formal logic. In the case of propositional and first-order logics, there exist well-understood algorithms for automated deduction. Interestingly, it is possible to develop inverses of these procedures in order to automate the process of inductive generalization. The insight that induction might be performed by inverting deduction appears to have been first observed by the nineteenth century economist W. S. Jevons, who wrote:

> Induction is, in fact, the inverse operation of deduction, and cannot be conceived to exist without the corresponding operation, so that the question of relative importance cannot arise. Who thinks of asking whether addition or subtraction is the more important process in arithmetic? But at the same time much difference in difficulty may exist between a direct and inverse operation; ... it must be allowed that inductive investigations are of a far higher degree of difficulty and complexity than any questions of deduction.... (Jevons 1874)

In the remainder of this chapter we will explore this view of induction as the inverse of deduction. The general issue we will be interested in here is designing *inverse entailment operators*. An inverse entailment operator, $O(B, D)$ takes the training data $D = \{\langle x_i, f(x_i)\rangle\}$ and background knowledge B as input and produces as output a hypothesis h satisfying Equation (10.2).

$$O(B, D) = h \text{ such that } (\forall \langle x_i, f(x_i)\rangle \in D)\ (B \wedge h \wedge x_i) \vdash f(x_i)$$

Of course there will, in general, be many different hypotheses h that satisfy $(\forall \langle x_i, f(x_i)\rangle \in D)\ (B \wedge h \wedge x_i) \vdash f(x_i)$. One common heuristic in ILP for choosing among such hypotheses is to rely on the heuristic known as the Minimum Description Length principle (see Section 6.6).

There are several attractive features to formulating the learning task as finding a hypothesis h that solves the relation $(\forall \langle x_i, f(x_i)\rangle \in D)\ (B \wedge h \wedge x_i) \vdash f(x_i)$.

- This formulation subsumes the common definition of learning as finding some general concept that matches a given set of training examples (which corresponds to the special case where no background knowledge B is available).
- By incorporating the notion of background information B, this formulation allows a more rich definition of when a hypothesis may be said to "fit" the data. Up until now, we have always determined whether a hypothesis

(e.g., neural network) fits the data based solely on the description of the hypothesis and data, independent of the task domain under study. In contrast, this formulation allows the domain-specific background information B to become part of the definition of "fit." In particular, h fits the training example $\langle x_i, f(x_i)\rangle$ as long as $f(x_i)$ follows deductively from $B \wedge h \wedge x_i$.

- By incorporating background information B, this formulation invites learning methods that use this background information to guide the search for h, rather than merely searching the space of syntactically legal hypotheses. The inverse resolution procedure described in the following section uses background knowledge in this fashion.

At the same time, research on inductive logic programing following this formulation has encountered several practical difficulties.

- The requirement $(\forall\langle x_i, f(x_i)\rangle \in D)\ (B \wedge h \wedge x_i) \vdash f(x_i)$ does not naturally accommodate noisy training data. The problem is that this expression does not allow for the possibility that there may be errors in the observed description of the instance x_i or its target value $f(x_i)$. Such errors can produce an inconsistent set of constraints on h. Unfortunately, most formal logic frameworks completely lose their ability to distinguish between truth and falsehood once they are given inconsistent sets of assertions.
- The language of first-order logic is so expressive, and the number of hypotheses that satisfy $(\forall\langle x_i, f(x_i)\rangle \in D)\ (B \wedge h \wedge x_i) \vdash f(x_i)$ is so large, that the search through the space of hypotheses is intractable in the general case. Much recent work has sought restricted forms of first-order expressions, or additional second-order knowledge, to improve the tractability of the hypothesis space search.
- Despite our intuition that background knowledge B should help constrain the search for a hypothesis, in most ILP systems (including all discussed in this chapter) the complexity of the hypothesis space search *increases* as background knowledge B is increased. (However, see Chapters 11 and 12 for algorithms that use background knowledge to *decrease* rather than increase sample complexity).

In the following section, we examine one quite general inverse entailment operator that constructs hypotheses by inverting a deductive inference rule.

10.7 INVERTING RESOLUTION

A general method for automated deduction is the *resolution rule* introduced by Robinson (1965). The resolution rule is a sound and complete rule for deductive inference in first-order logic. Therefore, it is sensible to ask whether we can invert the resolution rule to form an inverse entailment operator. The answer is yes, and it is just this operator that forms the basis of the CIGOL program introduced by Muggleton and Buntine (1988).

It is easiest to introduce the resolution rule in propositional form, though it is readily extended to first-order representations. Let L be an arbitrary propositional literal, and let P and R be arbitrary propositional clauses. The resolution rule is

$$\frac{\begin{array}{ccc} P & \vee & L \\ \neg L & \vee & R \end{array}}{\begin{array}{ccc} P & \vee & R \end{array}}$$

which should be read as follows: Given the two clauses above the line, conclude the clause below the line. Intuitively, the resolution rule is quite sensible. Given the two assertions $P \vee L$ and $\neg L \vee R$, it is obvious that either L or $\neg L$ must be false. Therefore, either P or R must be true. Thus, the conclusion $P \vee R$ of the resolution rule is intuitively satisfying.

The general form of the propositional resolution operator is described in Table 10.5. Given two clauses C_1 and C_2, the resolution operator first identifies a literal L that occurs as a positive literal in one of these two clauses and as a negative literal in the other. It then draws the conclusion given by the above formula. For example, consider the application of the resolution operator illustrated on the left side of Figure 10.2. Given clauses C_1 and C_2, the first step of the procedure identifies the literal $L = \neg KnowMaterial$, which is present in C_1, and whose negation $\neg(\neg KnowMaterial) = KnowMaterial$ is present in C_2. Thus the conclusion is the clause formed by the union of the literals $C_1 - \{L\} = PassExam$ and $C_2 - \{\neg L\} = \neg Study$. As another example, the result of applying the resolution rule to the clauses $C_1 = A \vee B \vee C \vee \neg D$ and $C_2 = \neg B \vee E \vee F$ is the clause $A \vee C \vee \neg D \vee E \vee F$.

It is easy to invert the resolution operator to form an inverse entailment operator $O(C, C_1)$ that performs inductive inference. In general, the inverse entailment operator must derive one of the initial clauses, C_2, given the resolvent C and the other initial clause C_1. Consider an example in which we are given the resolvent $C = A \vee B$ and the initial clause $C_1 = B \vee D$. How can we derive a clause C_2 such that $C_1 \wedge C_2 \vdash C$? First, note that by the definition of the resolution operator, any literal that occurs in C but not in C_1 must have been present in C_2. In our example, this indicates that C_2 must contain the literal A. Second, the literal

---

1. Given initial clauses C_1 and C_2, find a literal L from clause C_1 such that $\neg L$ occurs in clause C_2.
2. Form the resolvent C by including all literals from C_1 and C_2, except for L and $\neg L$. More precisely, the set of literals occurring in the conclusion C is

$$C = (C_1 - \{L\}) \cup (C_2 - \{\neg L\})$$

where $\cup$ denotes set union, and "$-$" denotes set difference.

TABLE 10.5
Resolution operator (propositional form). Given clauses C_1 and C_2, the resolution operator constructs a clause C such that $C_1 \wedge C_2 \vdash C$.

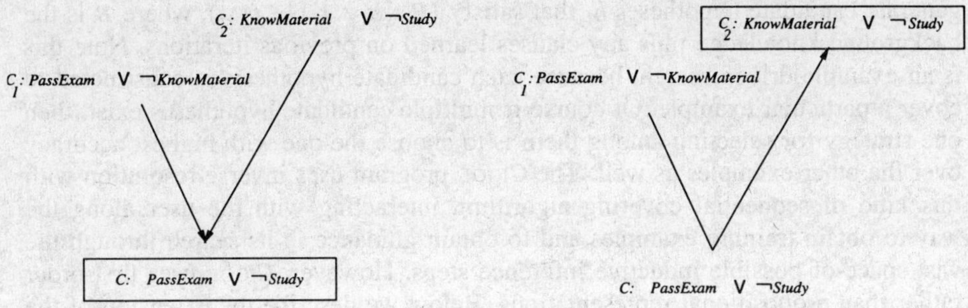

FIGURE 10.2
On the left, an application of the (deductive) resolution rule inferring clause C from the given clauses C_1 and C_2. On the right, an application of its (inductive) inverse, inferring C_2 from C and C_1.

that occurs in C_1 but not in C must be the literal removed by the resolution rule, and therefore its negation must occur in C_2. In our example, this indicates that C_2 must contain the literal $\neg D$. Hence, $C_2 = A \vee \neg D$. The reader can easily verify that applying the resolution rule to C_1 and C_2 does, in fact, produce the desired resolvent C.

Notice there is a second possible solution for C_2 in the above example. In particular, C_2 can also be the more specific clause $A \vee \neg D \vee B$. The difference between this and our first solution is that we have now included in C_2 a literal that occurred in C_1. The general point here is that inverse resolution is not deterministic—in general there may be multiple clauses C_2 such that C_1 and C_2 produce the resolvent C. One heuristic for choosing among the alternatives is to prefer shorter clauses over longer clauses, or equivalently, to assume C_2 shares no literals in common with C_1. If we incorporate this bias toward short clauses, the general statement of this inverse resolution procedure is as shown in Table 10.6.

We can develop rule-learning algorithms based on inverse entailment operators such as inverse resolution. In particular, the learning algorithm can use inverse entailment to construct hypotheses that, together with the background information, entail the training data. One strategy is to use a sequential covering algorithm to iteratively learn a set of Horn clauses in this way. On each iteration, the algorithm selects a training example $\langle x_i, f(x_i)\rangle$ that is not yet covered by previously learned clauses. The inverse resolution rule is then applied to

---

1. Given initial clauses C_1 and C, find a literal L that occurs in clause C_1, but not in clause C.
2. Form the second clause C_2 by including the following literals

$$C_2 = (C - (C_1 - \{L\})) \cup \{\neg L\}$$

TABLE 10.6
Inverse resolution operator (propositional form). Given two clauses C and C_1, this computes a clause C_2 such that $C_1 \wedge C_2 \vdash C$.

generate candidate hypotheses h_i that satisfy $(B \wedge h_i \wedge x_i) \vdash f(x_i)$, where B is the background knowledge plus any clauses learned on previous iterations. Note this is an example-driven search, because each candidate hypothesis is constructed to cover a particular example. Of course if multiple candidate hypotheses exist, then one strategy for selecting among them is to choose the one with highest accuracy over the other examples as well. The CIGOL program uses inverse resolution with this kind of sequential covering algorithm, interacting with the user along the way to obtain training examples and to obtain guidance in its search through the vast space of possible inductive inference steps. However, CIGOL uses first-order rather than propositional representations. Below we describe the extension of the resolution rule required to accommodate first-order representations.

10.7.1 First-Order Resolution

The resolution rule extends easily to first-order expressions. As in the propositional case, it takes two clauses as input and produces a third clause as output. The key difference from the propositional case is that the process is now based on the notion of *unifying* substitutions.

We define a *substitution* to be any mapping of variables to terms. For example, the substitution $\theta = \{x/Bob, y/z\}$ indicates that the variable x is to be replaced by the term Bob, and that the variable y is to be replaced by the term z. We use the notation $W\theta$ to denote the result of applying the substitution θ to some expression W. For example, if L is the literal $Father(x, Bill)$ and θ is the substitution defined above, then $L\theta = Father(Bob, Bill)$.

We say that θ is a *unifying substitution* for two literals L_1 and L_2, provided $L_1\theta = L_2\theta$. For example, if $L_1 = Father(x, y)$, $L_2 = Father(Bill, z)$, and $\theta = \{x/Bill, z/y\}$, then θ is a unifying substitution for L_1 and L_2 because $L_1\theta = L_2\theta = Father(Bill, y)$. The significance of a unifying substitution is this: In the propositional form of resolution, the resolvent of two clauses C_1 and C_2 is found by identifying a literal L that appears in C_1 such that $\neg L$ appears in C_2. In first-order resolution, this generalizes to finding one literal L_1 from clause C_1 and one literal L_2 from C_2, such that some unifying substitution θ can be found for L_1 and $\neg L_2$ (i.e., such that $L_1\theta = \neg L_2\theta$). The resolution rule then constructs the resolvent C according to the equation

$$C = (C_1 - \{L_1\})\theta \cup (C_2 - \{L_2\})\theta \tag{10.3}$$

The general statement of the resolution rule is shown in Table 10.7. To illustrate, suppose $C_1 = White(x) \leftarrow Swan(x)$ and suppose $C_2 = Swan(Fred)$. To apply the resolution rule, we first re-express C_1 in clause form as the equivalent expression $C_1 = White(x) \vee \neg Swan(x)$. The resolution rule can now be applied. In the first step, it finds the literal $L_1 = \neg Swan(x)$ from C_1 and the literal $L_2 = Swan(Fred)$ from C_2. If we choose the unifying substitution $\theta = \{x/Fred\}$ then these two literals satisfy $L_1\theta = \neg L_2\theta = \neg Swan(Fred)$. Therefore, the conclusion C is the union of $(C_1 - \{L_1\})\theta = White(Fred)$ and $(C_2 - \{L_2\})\theta = \emptyset$, or $C = White(Fred)$.

1. Find a literal L_1 from clause C_1, literal L_2 from clause C_2, and substitution θ such that $L_1\theta = \neg L_2\theta$.
2. Form the resolvent C by including all literals from $C_1\theta$ and $C_2\theta$, except for $L_1\theta$ and $\neg L_2\theta$. More precisely, the set of literals occurring in the conclusion C is

$$C = (C_1 - \{L_1\})\theta \cup (C_2 - \{L_2\})\theta$$

TABLE 10.7
Resolution operator (first-order form).

10.7.2 Inverting Resolution: First-Order Case

We can derive the inverse resolution operator analytically, by algebraic manipulation of Equation (10.3) which defines the resolution rule. First, note the unifying substitution θ in Equation (10.3) can be uniquely factored into θ_1 and θ_2, where $\theta = \theta_1\theta_2$, where θ_1 contains all substitutions involving variables from clause C_1, and where θ_2 contains all substitutions involving variables from C_2. This factorization is possible because C_1 and C_2 will always begin with distinct variable names (because they are distinct universally quantified statements). Using this factorization of θ, we can restate Equation (10.3) as

$$C = (C_1 - \{L_1\})\theta_1 \cup (C_2 - \{L_2\})\theta_2$$

Keep in mind that "–" here stands for set difference. Now if we restrict inverse resolution to infer only clauses C_2 that contain no literals in common with C_1 (corresponding to a preference for shortest C_2 clauses), then we can re-express the above as

$$C - (C_1 - \{L_1\})\theta_1 = (C_2 - \{L_2\})\theta_2$$

Finally we use the fact that by definition of the resolution rule $L_2 = \neg L_1\theta_1\theta_2^{-1}$, and solve for C_2 to obtain

Inverse resolution:

$$C_2 = (C - (C_1 - \{L_1\})\theta_1)\theta_2^{-1} \cup \{\neg L_1\theta_1\theta_2^{-1}\} \tag{10.4}$$

Equation (10.4) gives the inverse resolution rule for first-order logic. As in the propositional case, this inverse entailment operator is nondeterministic. In particular, in applying it we may in general find multiple choices for the clause C_1 to be resolved and for the unifying substitutions θ_1 and θ_2. Each set of choices may yield a different solution for C_2.

Figure 10.3 illustrates a multistep application of this inverse resolution rule for a simple example. In this figure, we wish to learn rules for the target predicate $GrandChild(y, x)$, given the training data $D = GrandChild(Bob, Shannon)$ and the background information $B = \{Father(Shannon, Tom), Father(Tom, Bob)\}$. Consider the bottommost step in the inverse resolution tree of Figure 10.3. Here, we set the conclusion C to the training example $GrandChild(Bob, Shannon)$

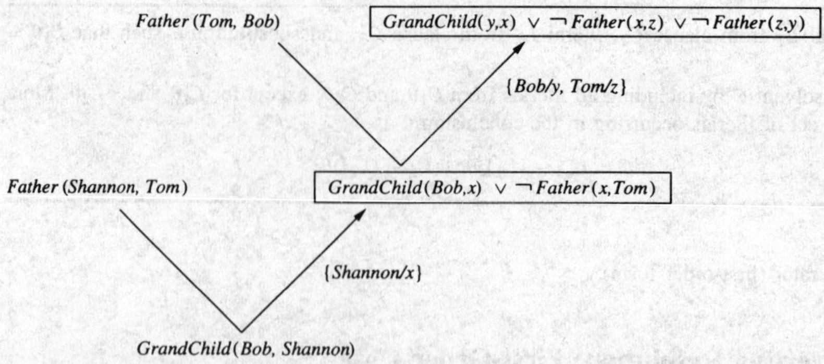

FIGURE 10.3
A multistep inverse resolution. In each case, the boxed clause is the result of the inference step. For each step, C is the clause at the bottom, C_1 the clause to the left, and C_2 the boxed clause to the right. In both inference steps here, θ_1 is the empty substitution {}, and θ_2^{-1} is the substitution shown below C_2. Note the final conclusion (the boxed clause at the top right) is the alternative form of the Horn clause $GrandChild(y, x) \leftarrow Father(x, z) \wedge Father(z, y)$.

and select the clause $C_1 = Father(Shannon, Tom)$ from the background information. To apply the inverse resolution operator we have only one choice for the literal L_1, namely $Father(Shannon, Tom)$. Suppose we choose the inverse substitutions $\theta_1^{-1} = \{\}$ and $\theta_2^{-1} = \{Shannon/x\}$. In this case, the resulting clause C_2 is the union of the clause $(C - (C_1 - \{L_1\})\theta_1)\theta_2^{-1} = (C\theta_1)\theta_2^{-1} = GrandChild(Bob, x)$, and the clause $\{\neg L_1\theta_1\theta_2^{-1}\} = \neg Father(x, Tom)$. Hence the result is the clause $GrandChild(Bob, x) \vee \neg Father(x, Tom)$, or equivalently $(GrandChild(Bob, x) \leftarrow Father(x, Tom))$. Note this general rule, together with C_1 entails the training example $GrandChild(Bob, Shannon)$.

In similar fashion, this inferred clause may now be used as the conclusion C for a second inverse resolution step, as illustrated in Figure 10.3. At each such step, note there are several possible outcomes, depending on the choices for the substitutions. (See Exercise 10.7.) In the example of Figure 10.3, the particular set of choices produces the intuitively satisfying final clause $GrandChild(y, x) \leftarrow Father(x, z) \wedge Father(z, y)$.

10.7.3 Summary of Inverse Resolution

To summarize, inverse resolution provides a general approach to automatically generating hypotheses h that satisfy the constraint $(B \wedge h \wedge x_i) \vdash f(x_i)$. This is accomplished by inverting the general resolution rule given by Equation (10.3). Beginning with the resolution rule and solving for the clause C_2, the inverse resolution rule of Equation (10.4) is easily derived.

Given a set of beginning clauses, multiple hypotheses may be generated by repeated application of this inverse resolution rule. Note the inverse resolution rule has the advantage that it generates *only* hypotheses that satisfy $(B \wedge h \wedge x_i) \vdash f(x_i)$.

In contrast, the generate-and-test search of FOIL generates many hypotheses at each search step, including some that do not satisfy this constraint. FOIL then considers the data D to choose among these hypotheses. Given this difference, we might expect the search based on inverse resolution to be more focused and efficient. However, this will not necessarily be the case. One reason is that the inverse resolution operator can consider only a small fraction of the available data when generating its hypothesis at any given step, whereas FOIL considers all available data to select among its syntactically generated hypotheses. The differences between search strategies that use inverse entailment and those that use generate-and-test search is a subject of ongoing research. Srinivasan et al. (1995) provide one experimental comparison of these two approaches.

10.7.4 Generalization, θ-Subsumption, and Entailment

The previous section pointed out the correspondence between induction and inverse entailment. Given our earlier focus on using the general-to-specific ordering to organize the hypothesis search, it is interesting to consider the relationship between the *more_general_than* relation and inverse entailment. To illuminate this relationship, consider the following definitions.

- *more_general_than*. In Chapter 2, we defined the *more_general_than_or_equal_to* relation ($\geq_g$) as follows: Given two boolean-valued functions $h_j(x)$ and $h_k(x)$, we say that $h_j \geq_g h_k$ if and only if $(\forall x) h_k(x) \rightarrow h_j(x)$. This $\geq_g$ relation is used by many learning algorithms to guide search through the hypothesis space.
- *θ-subsumption*. Consider two clauses C_j and C_k, both of the form $H \vee L_1 \vee \ldots L_n$, where H is a positive literal, and the L_i are arbitrary literals. Clause C_j is said to *θ-subsume* clause C_k if and only if there exists a substitution θ such that $C_j\theta \subseteq C_k$ (where we here describe any clause C by the set of literals in its disjunctive form). This definition is due to Plotkin (1970).
- *Entailment*. Consider two clauses C_j and C_k. Clause C_j is said to *entail* clause C_k (written $C_j \vdash C_k$) if and only if C_k follows deductively from C_j.

What is the relationship among these three definitions? First, let us re-express the definition of $\geq_g$ using the same first-order notation as the other two definitions. If we consider a boolean-valued hypothesis $h(x)$ for some target concept $c(x)$, where $h(x)$ is expressed by a conjunction of literals, then we can re-express the hypothesis as the clause

$$c(x) \leftarrow h(x)$$

Here we follow the usual PROLOG interpretation that x is classified a negative example if it cannot be proven to be a positive example. Hence, we can see that our earlier definition of $\geq_g$ applies to the preconditions, or bodies, of Horn clauses. The implicit postcondition of the Horn clause is the target concept $c(x)$.

What is the relationship between this definition of $\geq_g$ and the definition of θ-subsumption? Note that if $h_1 \geq_g h_2$, then the clause $C_1 : c(x) \leftarrow h_1(x)$ θ-subsumes the clause $C_2 : c(x) \leftarrow h_2(x)$. Furthermore, θ-subsumption can hold even when the clauses have different heads. For example, clause A θ-subsumes clause B in the following case:

$$A: \quad Mother(x, y) \leftarrow Father(x, z) \wedge Spouse(z, y)$$

$$B: Mother(x, Louise) \leftarrow Father(x, Bob) \wedge Spouse(Bob, y) \wedge Female(x)$$

because $A\theta \subseteq B$ if we choose $\theta = \{y/Louise, z/Bob\}$. The key difference here is that $\geq_g$ implicitly assumes two clauses for which the heads are the same, whereas θ-subsumption can hold even for clauses with different heads.

Finally, θ-subsumption is a special case of entailment. That is, if clause A θ-subsumes clause B, then $A \vdash B$. However, we can find clauses A and B such that $A \vdash B$, but where A does not θ-subsume B. One example is the following pair of clauses

$$A: \quad Elephant(father\_of(x)) \leftarrow Elephant(x)$$

$$B: Elephant(father\_of(father\_of(y))) \leftarrow Elephant(y)$$

where $father\_of(x)$ is a function that refers to the individual who is the father of x. Note that although B can be proven from A, there is no substitution θ that allows B to be θ-subsumed by A.

As shown by these examples, our earlier notion of *more_general_than* is a special case of θ-subsumption, which is itself a special case of entailment. Therefore, searching the hypothesis space by generalizing or specializing hypotheses is more limited than searching by using general inverse entailment operators. Unfortunately, in its most general form, inverse entailment produces intractable searches. However, the intermediate notion of θ-subsumption provides one convenient notion that lies midway between our earlier definition of *more_general_than* and entailment.

10.7.5 PROGOL

Although inverse resolution is an intriguing method for generating candidate hypotheses, in practice it can easily lead to a combinatorial explosion of candidate hypotheses. An alternative approach is to use inverse entailment to generate just the single most specific hypothesis that, together with the background information, entails the observed data. This most specific hypothesis can then be used to bound a general-to-specific search through the hypothesis space similar to that used by FOIL, but with the additional constraint that the only hypotheses considered are hypotheses more general than this bound. This approach is employed by the PROGOL system, whose algorithm can be summarized as follows:

1. The user specifies a restricted language of first-order expressions to be used as the hypothesis space H. Restrictions are stated using "mode declarations,"

which enable the user to specify the predicate and function symbols to be considered, and the types and formats of arguments for each.

2. PROGOL uses a sequential covering algorithm to learn a set of expressions from H that cover the data. For each example $\langle x_i, f(x_i)\rangle$ that is not yet covered by these learned expressions, it first searches for the most specific hypothesis h_i within H such that $(B \wedge h_i \wedge x_i) \vdash f(x_i)$. More precisely, it approximates this by calculating the most specific hypothesis among those that entail $f(x_i)$ within k applications of the resolution rule (where k is a user-specified parameter).
3. PROGOL then performs a general-to-specific search of the hypothesis space bounded by the most general possible hypothesis and by the specific bound h_i calculated in step 2. Within this set of hypotheses, it seeks the hypothesis having minimum description length (measured by the number of literals). This part of the search is guided by an A^*-like heuristic that allows pruning without running the risk of pruning away the shortest hypothesis.

The details of the PROGOL algorithm are described by Muggleton (1992, 1995).

10.8 SUMMARY AND FURTHER READING

The main points of this chapter include:

- The sequential covering algorithm learns a disjunctive set of rules by first learning a single accurate rule, then removing the positive examples covered by this rule and iterating the process over the remaining training examples. It provides an efficient, greedy algorithm for learning rule sets, and an alternative to top-down decision tree learning algorithms such as ID3, which can be viewed as simultaneous, rather than sequential covering algorithms.
- In the context of sequential covering algorithms, a variety of methods have been explored for learning a single rule. These methods vary in the search strategy they use for examining the space of possible rule preconditions. One popular approach, exemplified by the CN2 program, is to conduct a general-to-specific beam search, generating and testing progressively more specific rules until a sufficiently accurate rule is found. Alternative approaches search from specific to general hypotheses, use an example-driven search rather than generate and test, and employ different statistical measures of rule accuracy to guide the search.
- Sets of first-order rules (i.e., rules containing variables) provide a highly expressive representation. For example, the programming language PROLOG represents general programs using collections of first-order Horn clauses. The problem of learning first-order Horn clauses is therefore often referred to as the problem of inductive logic programming.
- One approach to learning sets of first-order rules is to extend the sequential covering algorithm of CN2 from propositional to first-order representations.

This approach is exemplified by the FOIL program, which can learn sets of first-order rules, including simple recursive rule sets.

- A second approach to learning first-order rules is based on the observation that induction is the inverse of deduction. In other words, the problem of induction is to find a hypothesis h that satisfies the constraint

$$(\forall \langle x_i, f(x_i) \rangle \in D)\ (B \wedge h \wedge x_i) \vdash f(x_i)$$

where B is general background information, $x_1 \ldots x_n$ are descriptions of the instances in the training data D, and $f(x_1) \ldots f(x_n)$ are the target values of the training instances.

- Following the view of induction as the inverse of deduction, some programs search for hypotheses by using operators that invert the well-known operators for deductive reasoning. For example, CIGOL uses inverse resolution, an operation that is the inverse of the deductive resolution operator commonly used for mechanical theorem proving. PROGOL combines an inverse entailment strategy with a general-to-specific strategy for searching the hypothesis space.

Early work on learning relational descriptions includes Winston's (1970) well-known program for learning network-style descriptions for concepts such as "arch." Banerji's (1964, 1969) work and Michalski's series of AQ programs (e.g., Michalski 1969; Michalski et al. 1986) were among the earliest to explore the use of logical representations in learning. Plotkin's (1970) definition of θ-subsumption provided an early formalization of the relationship between induction and deduction. Vere (1975) also explored learning logical representations, and Buchanan's (1976) META-DENDRAL program learned relational descriptions representing molecular substructures likely to fragment in a mass spectrometer. This program succeeded in discovering useful rules that were subsequently published in the chemistry literature. Mitchell's (1979) CANDIDATE-ELIMINATION version space algorithm was applied to these same relational descriptions of chemical structures.

With the popularity of the PROLOG language in the mid-1980s, researchers began to look more carefully at learning relational descriptions represented by Horn clauses. Early work on learning Horn clauses includes Shapiro's (1983) MIS and Sammut and Banerji's (1986) MARVIN. Quinlan's (1990) FOIL algorithm, discussed here, was quickly followed by a number of algorithms employing a general-to-specific search for first-order rules including MFOIL (Džeroski 1991), FOCL (Pazzani et al. 1991), CLAUDIEN (De Raedt and Bruynooghe 1993), and MARKUS (Grobelnik 1992). The FOCL algorithm is described in Chapter 12.

An alternative line of research on learning Horn clauses by inverse entailment was spurred by Muggleton and Buntine (1988), who built on related ideas by Sammut and Banerji (1986) and Muggleton (1987). More recent work along this line has focused on alternative search strategies and methods for constraining the hypothesis space to make learning more tractable. For example, Kietz and

Wrobel (1992) use rule schemata in their RDT program to restrict the form of expressions that may be considered during learning, and Muggleton and Feng (1992) discuss the restriction of first-order expressions to ij-determinate literals. Cohen (1994) discusses the GRENDEL program, which accepts as input an explicit description of the language for describing the clause body, thereby allowing the user to explicitly constrain the hypothesis space.

Lavrač and Džeroski (1994) provide a very readable textbook on inductive logic programming. Other useful recent monographs and edited collections include (Bergadano and Gunetti 1995; Morik et al. 1993; Muggleton 1992, 1995b). The overview chapter by Wrobel (1996) also provides a good perspective on the field. Bratko and Muggleton (1995) summarize a number of recent applications of ILP to problems of practical importance. A series of annual workshops on ILP provides a good source of recent research papers (e.g., see De Raedt 1996).

EXERCISES

10.1. Consider a sequential covering algorithm such as CN2 and a simultaneous covering algorithm such as ID3. Both algorithms are to be used to learn a target concept defined over instances represented by conjunctions of n boolean attributes. If ID3 learns a balanced decision tree of depth d, it will contain $2^d - 1$ distinct decision nodes, and therefore will have made $2^d - 1$ distinct choices while constructing its output hypothesis. How many rules will be formed if this tree is re-expressed as a disjunctive set of rules? How many preconditions will each rule possess? How many distinct choices would a *sequential* covering algorithm have to make to learn this same set of rules? Which system do you suspect would be more prone to overfitting if both were given the same training data?

10.2. Refine the LEARN-ONE-RULE algorithm of Table 10.2 so that it can learn rules whose preconditions include thresholds on real-valued attributes (e.g., $temperature > 42$). Specify your new algorithm as a set of editing changes to the algorithm of Table 10.2. Hint: Consider how this is accomplished for decision tree learning.

10.3. Refine the LEARN-ONE-RULE algorithm of Table 10.2 so that it can learn rules whose preconditions include constraints such as $nationality \in \{Canadian, Brazilian\}$, where a discrete-valued attribute is allowed to take on any value in some specified set. Your modified program should explore the hypothesis space containing all such subsets. Specify your new algorithm as a set of editing changes to the algorithm of Table 10.2.

10.4. Consider the options for implementing LEARN-ONE-RULE in terms of the possible strategies for searching the hypothesis space. In particular, consider the following attributes of the search

(*a*) generate-and-test versus data-driven
(*b*) general-to-specific versus specific-to-general
(*c*) sequential cover versus simultaneous cover

Discuss the benefits of the choice made by the algorithm in Tables 10.1 and 10.2. For each of these three attributes of the search strategy, discuss the (positive and negative) impact of choosing the alternative option.

10.5. Apply inverse resolution in propositional form to the clauses $C = A \vee B$, $C_1 = A \vee B \vee G$. Give at least two possible results for C_2.

10.6. Apply inverse resolution to the clauses $C = R(B, x) \vee P(x, A)$ and $C_1 = S(B, y) \vee R(z, x)$. Give at least four possible results for C_2. Here A and B are constants, x and y are variables.

10.7. Consider the bottom-most inverse resolution step in Figure 10.3. Derive at least two different outcomes that could result given different choices for the substitutions θ_1 and θ_2. Derive a result for the inverse resolution step if the clause $Father(Tom, Bob)$ is used in place of $Father(Shannon, Tom)$.

10.8. Consider the relationship between the definition of the induction problem in this chapter

$$(\forall \langle x_i, f(x_i) \rangle \in D) \ (B \wedge h \wedge x_i) \vdash f(x_i)$$

and our earlier definition of inductive bias from Chapter 2, Equation 2.1. There we defined the inductive bias, B_{bias}, by the expression

$$(\forall x_i \in X)(B_{bias} \wedge D \wedge x_i) \vdash L(x_i, D)$$

where $L(x_i, D)$ is the classification that the learner assigns to the new instance x_i after learning from the training data D, and where X is the entire instance space. Note the first expression is intended to describe the hypothesis we wish the learner to output, whereas the second expression is intended to describe the learner's policy for generalizing beyond the training data. Invent a learner for which the inductive bias B_{bias} of the learner is identical to the background knowledge B that it is provided.

REFERENCES

Banerji, R. (1964). A language for the description of concepts. *General Systems*, 9, 135–141.

Banerji, R. (1969). *Theory of problem solving—an approach to artificial intelligence*. New York: American Elsevier Publishing Company.

Bergadano, F., & Gunetti, D. (1995). *Inductive logic programming: From machine learning to software engineering*. Cambridge, Ma: MIT Press.

Bratko, I., & Muggleton, S. (1995). Applications of inductive logic programming. *Communications of the ACM*, 38(11), 65–70.

Buchanan, B. G., Smith, D. H., White, W. C., Gritter, R., Feigenbaum, E. A., Lederberg, J., & Djerassi, C. (1976). Applications of artificial intelligence for chemical inference, XXII: Automatic rule formation in mass spectrometry by means of the meta-DENDRAL program. *Journal of the American Chemical Society*, 98, 6168.

Buntine, W. (1986). Generalised subsumption. *Proceedings of the European Conference on Artificial Intelligence*, London.

Buntine, W. (1988). Generalized subsumption and its applications to induction and redundancy. *Artificial Intelligence*, 36, 149–176.

Cameron-Jones, R., & Quinlan, J. R. (1993). Avoiding pitfalls when learning recursive theories. *Proceedings of the Eighth International Workshop on Machine Learning* (pp 389–393). San Mateo, CA: Morgan Kaufmann.

Cestnik, B., & Bratko, I. (1991). On estimating probabilities in tree pruning. *Proceedings of the European Working Session on Machine Learning* (pp. 138–150). Porto, Portugal.

Clark, P., & Niblett, R. (1989). The CN2 induction algorithm. *Machine Learning*, 3, 261–284.

Cohen, W. (1994). Grammatically biased learning: Learning logic programs using an explicit antecedent description language. *Artificial Intelligence*, 68(2), 303–366.

De Raedt, L. (1992). *Interactive theory revision: An inductive logic programming approach*. London: Academic Press.

De Raedt, L., & Bruynooghe, M. (1993). A theory of clausal discovery. *Proceedings of the Thirteenth International Joint Conference on Artificial Intelligence*. San Mateo, CA: Morgan Kaufmann.

De Raedt, L. (Ed.). (1996). *Advances in inductive logic programming: Proceedings of the Fifth International Workshop on Inductive Logic Programming*. Amsterdam: IOS Press.

Dolsak, B., & Muggleton, S. (1992). The application of inductive logic programming to finite element mesh design. In S. Muggleton (Ed.), *Inductive Logic Programming*. London: Academic Press.

Džeroski, S. (1991). *Handling noise in inductive logic programming* (Master's thesis). Electrical Engineering and Computer Science, University of Ljubljana, Ljubljana, Slovenia.

Flener, P. (1994). *Logic program synthesis from incomplete information*. The Kluwer international series in engineering and computer science. Boston: Kluwer Academic Publishers.

Grobelnik, M. (1992). MARKUS: An optimized model inference system. *Proceedings of the Workshop on Logical Approaches to Machine Learning, Tenth European Conference on AI*, Vienna, Austria.

Jevons, W. S. (1874). *The principles of science: A treatise on logic and scientific method*. London: Macmillan.

Kietz, J-U., & Wrobel, S. (1992). Controlling the complexity of learning in logic through syntactic and task-oriented models. In S. Muggleton (Ed.), *Inductive logic programming*. London: Academic Press.

Lavrač, N., & Džeroski, S. (1994). *Inductive logic programming: Techniques and applications*. Ellis Horwood.

Lindsay, R. K., Buchanan, B. G., Feigenbaum, E. A., & Lederberg, J. (1980). *Applications of artificial intelligence for organic chemistry*. New York: McGraw-Hill.

Michalski, R. S., (1969). On the quasi-minimal solution of the general covering problem. *Proceedings of the First International Symposium on Information Processing* (pp. 125–128). Bled, Yugoslavia.

Michalski, R. S., Mozetic, I., Hong, J., and Lavrac, H. (1986). The multi-purpose incremental learning system AQ15 and its testing application to three medical domains. *Proceedings of the Fifth National Conference on AI* (pp. 1041–1045). Philadelphia: Morgan-Kaufmann.

Mitchell, T. M. (1979). *Version spaces: An approach to concept learning* (Ph.D. dissertation). Electrical Engineering Dept., Stanford University, Stanford, CA.

Morik, K., Wrobel, S., Kietz, J.-U., & Emde, W. (1993). *Knowledge acquisition and machine learning: Theory, methods, and applications*. London: Academic Press.

Muggleton, S. (1987). DUCE: An oracle based approach to constructive induction. *Proceedings of the International Joint Conference on AI* (pp. 287–292). San Mateo, CA: Morgan Kaufmann.

Muggleton, S. (1995a). Inverse entailment and PROGOL. *New Generation Computing*, 13, 245–286.

Muggleton, S. (1995b). *Foundations of inductive logic programming*. Englewood Cliffs, NJ: Prentice Hall.

Muggleton, S., & Buntine, W. (1988). Machine invention of first-order predicates by inverting resolution. *Proceedings of the Fifth International Machine Learning Conference* (pp. 339–352). Ann Arbor, Michigan: Morgan Kaufmann.

Muggleton, S., & Feng, C. (1990). Efficient induction of logic programs. *Proceedings of the First Conference on Algorithmic Learning Theory*. Ohmsha, Tokyo.

Muggleton, S., & Feng, C. (1992). Efficient induction of logic programs. In Muggleton (Ed.), *Inductive logic programming*. London: Academic Press.

Muggleton, S. (Ed.). (1992). *Inductive logic programming*. London: Academic Press.

Pazzani, M., Brunk, C., & Silverstein, G. (1991). A knowledge-intensive approach to learning relational concepts. *Proceedings of the Eighth International Workshop on Machine Learning* (pp. 432–436). San Francisco: Morgan Kaufmann.

Plotkin, G. D. (1970). A note on inductive generalization. In B. Meltzer & D. Michie (Eds.), *Machine Intelligence 5* (pp. 153–163). Edinburgh University Press.

Plotkin, G. D. (1971). A further note on inductive generalization. In B. Meltzer & D. Michie (Eds.), *Machine Intelligence 6*. New York: Elsevier.

Quinlan, J. R. (1990). Learning logical definitions from relations. *Machine Learning*, 5, 239–266.

Quinlan, J. R. (1991). *Improved estimates for the accuracy of small disjuncts* (Technical Note). *Machine Learning*, 6(1), 93–98. Boston: Kluwer Academic Publishers.

Rivest R. L. (1987). Learning decision lists. *Machine Learning*, 2(3), 229–246.

Robinson, J. A. (1965). A machine-oriented logic based on the resolution principle. *Journal of the ACM*, 12(1), 23–41.

Sammut, C. A. (1981). Concept learning by experiment. *Seventh International Joint Conference on Artificial Intelligence*, Vancouver.

Sammut, C. A., & Banerji, R. B. (1986). Learning concepts by asking questions. In R. S. Michalski, J. G. Carbonell, & T. M. Mitchell (Eds.), *Machine learning: An artificial intelligence approach* (Vol 2, pp. 167–192). Los Altos, California: Morgan Kaufmann.

Shapiro, E. (1983). *Algorithmic program debugging*. Cambridge MA: MIT Press.

Srinivasan, A., Muggleton, S., & King, R. D. (1995). *Comparing the use of background knowledge by inductive logic programming systems* (PRG Technical report PRG-TR-9-95). Oxford University Computing Laboratory.

Srinivasan, A., Muggleton, S., King, R. D., & Sternberg, M. J. E. (1994). Mutagenesis: ILP experiments in a non-determinate biological domain. *Proceedings of the Fourth Inductive Logic Programming Workshop*.

Vere, S. (1975). Induction of concepts in the predicate calculus. *Proceedings of the Fourth International Joint Conference on Artificial Intelligence* (pp. 351–356).

Winston, P. (1970). *Learning structural descriptions from examples* (Ph.D. dissertation) (MIT Technical Report AI-TR-231).

Wrobel, S. (1994). *Concept formation and knowledge revision*. Boston: Kluwer Academic Publishers.

Wrobel, S. (1996). Inductive logic programming. In G. Brewka (Ed)., *Principles of knowledge representation*. Stanford, CA: CSLI Publications.

CHAPTER 11

ANALYTICAL LEARNING

Inductive learning methods such as neural network and decision tree learning require a certain number of training examples to achieve a given level of generalization accuracy, as reflected in the theoretical bounds and experimental results discussed in earlier chapters. Analytical learning uses prior knowledge and deductive reasoning to augment the information provided by the training examples, so that it is not subject to these same bounds. This chapter considers an analytical learning method called explanation-based learning (EBL). In explanation-based learning, prior knowledge is used to analyze, or explain, how each observed training example satisfies the target concept. This explanation is then used to distinguish the relevant features of the training example from the irrelevant, so that examples can be generalized based on logical rather than statistical reasoning. Explanation-based learning has been successfully applied to learning search control rules for a variety of planning and scheduling tasks. This chapter considers explanation-based learning when the learner's prior knowledge is correct and complete. The next chapter considers combining inductive and analytical learning in situations where prior knowledge is only approximately correct.

11.1 INTRODUCTION

Previous chapters have considered a variety of *inductive* learning methods: that is, methods that generalize from observed training examples by identifying features that empirically distinguish positive from negative training examples. Decision tree learning, neural network learning, inductive logic programming, and genetic algorithms are all examples of inductive methods that operate in this fashion. The key practical limit on these inductive learners is that they perform poorly when insufficient data is available. In fact, as discussed in Chapter 7, theoretical analysis shows that there are fundamental bounds on the accuracy that can be achieved when learning inductively from a given number of training examples.

Can we develop learning methods that are not subject to these fundamental bounds on learning accuracy imposed by the amount of training data available? Yes, if we are willing to reconsider the formulation of the learning problem itself. One way is to develop learning algorithms that accept explicit prior knowledge as an input, in addition to the input training data. Explanation-based learning is one such approach. It uses prior knowledge to analyze, or explain, each training example in order to infer which example features are relevant to the target function and which are irrelevant. These explanations enable it to generalize more accurately than inductive systems that rely on the data alone. As we saw in the previous chapter, inductive logic programming systems such as CIGOL also use prior background knowledge to guide learning. However, they use their background knowledge to infer features that augment the input descriptions of instances, thereby increasing the complexity of the hypothesis space to be searched. In contrast, explanation-based learning uses prior knowledge to *reduce* the complexity of the hypothesis space to be searched, thereby reducing sample complexity and improving generalization accuracy of the learner.

To capture the intuition underlying explanation-based learning, consider the task of learning to play chess. In particular, suppose we would like our chess program to learn to recognize important classes of game positions, such as the target concept "chessboard positions in which black will lose its queen within two moves." Figure 11.1 shows a positive training example of this target concept. Inductive learning methods could, of course, be employed to learn this target concept. However, because the chessboard is fairly complex (there are 32 pieces that may be on any of 64 squares), and because the particular patterns that capture this concept are fairly subtle (involving the relative positions of various pieces on the board), we would have to provide thousands of training examples similar to the one in Figure 11.1 to expect an inductively learned hypothesis to generalize correctly to new situations.

FIGURE 11.1
A positive example of the target concept "chess positions in which black will lose its queen within two moves." Note the white knight is simultaneously attacking both the black king and queen. Black must therefore move its king, enabling white to capture its queen.

What is interesting about this chess-learning task is that humans appear to learn such target concepts from just a handful of training examples! In fact, after considering only the single example shown in Figure 11.1, most people would be willing to suggest a general hypothesis for the target concept, such as "board positions in which the black king and queen are simultaneously attacked," and would not even consider the (equally consistent) hypothesis "board positions in which four white pawns are still in their original locations." How is it that humans can generalize so successfully from just this one example?

The answer appears to be that people rely heavily on explaining, or analyzing, the training example in terms of their prior knowledge about the legal moves of chess. If asked to explain why the training example of Figure 11.1 is a positive example of "positions in which the queen will be lost in two moves," most people would give an explanation similar to the following: "Because white's knight is attacking both the king and queen, black must move out of check, thereby allowing the knight to capture the queen." The importance of such explanations is that they provide the information needed to *rationally* generalize from the details of the training example to a correct general hypothesis. Features of the training example that are mentioned by the explanation (e.g., the position of the white knight, black king, and black queen) are relevant to the target concept and should be included in the general hypothesis. In contrast, features of the example that are not mentioned by the explanation (e.g., the fact that there are six black pawns on the board) can be assumed to be irrelevant details.

What exactly is the prior knowledge needed by a learner to construct the explanation in this chess example? It is simply knowledge about the legal rules of chess: knowledge of which moves are legal for the knight and other pieces, the fact that players must alternate moves in the game, and the fact that to win the game one player must capture his opponent's king. Note that given just this prior knowledge it is possible *in principle* to calculate the optimal chess move for any board position. However, in practice this calculation can be frustratingly complex and despite the fact that we humans ourselves possess this complete, perfect knowledge of chess, we remain unable to play the game optimally. As a result, much of human learning in chess (and in other search-intensive problems such as scheduling and planning) involves a long process of uncovering the consequences of our prior knowledge, guided by specific training examples encountered as we play the game.

This chapter describes learning algorithms that automatically construct and learn from such explanations. In the remainder of this section we define more precisely the analytical learning problem. The next section presents a particular explanation-based learning algorithm called PROLOG-EBG. Subsequent sections then examine the general properties of this algorithm and its relationship to inductive learning algorithms discussed in other chapters. The final section describes the application of explanation-based learning to improving performance at large state-space search problems. In this chapter we consider the special case in which explanations are generated from prior knowledge that is perfectly correct, as it is for us humans in the above chess example. In Chapter 12 we consider the more general case of learning when prior knowledge is only approximately correct.

11.1.1 Inductive and Analytical Learning Problems

The essential difference between analytical and inductive learning methods is that they assume two different formulations of the learning problem:

- In inductive learning, the learner is given a hypothesis space H from which it must select an output hypothesis, and a set of training examples $D = \{\langle x_1, f(x_1)\rangle, \ldots \langle x_n, f(x_n)\rangle\}$ where $f(x_i)$ is the target value for the instance x_i. The desired output of the learner is a hypothesis h from H that is consistent with these training examples.
- In analytical learning, the input to the learner includes the same hypothesis space H and training examples D as for inductive learning. In addition, the learner is provided an additional input: A *domain theory* B consisting of background knowledge that can be used to explain observed training examples. The desired output of the learner is a hypothesis h from H that is consistent with both the training examples D and the domain theory B.

To illustrate, in our chess example each instance x_i would describe a particular chess position, and $f(x_i)$ would be $True$ when x_i is a position for which black will lose its queen within two moves, and $False$ otherwise. We might define the hypothesis space H to consist of sets of Horn clauses (if-then rules) as in Chapter 10, where the predicates used by the rules refer to the positions or relative positions of specific pieces on the board. The domain theory B would consist of a formalization of the rules of chess, describing the legal moves, the fact that players must take turns, and the fact that the game is won when one player captures her opponent's king.

Note in analytical learning, the learner must output a hypothesis that is consistent with *both* the training data and the domain theory. We say that hypothesis h is *consistent* with domain theory B provided B does not entail the negation of h (i.e., $B \nvdash \neg h$). This additional constraint that the output hypothesis must be consistent with B reduces the ambiguity faced by the learner when the data alone cannot resolve among all hypotheses in H. The net effect, provided the domain theory is correct, is to increase the accuracy of the output hypothesis.

Let us introduce in detail a second example of an analytical learning problem—one that we will use for illustration throughout this chapter. Consider an instance space X in which each instance is a pair of physical objects. Each of the two physical objects in the instance is described by the predicates *Color*, *Volume*, *Owner*, *Material*, *Type*, and *Density*, and the relationship between the two objects is described by the predicate *On*. Given this instance space, the task is to learn the target concept "pairs of physical objects, such that one can be stacked safely on the other," denoted by the predicate *SafeToStack(x,y)*. Learning this target concept might be useful, for example, to a robot system that has the task of storing various physical objects within a limited workspace. The full definition of this analytical learning task is given in Table 11.1.

Given:

- Instance space X: Each instance describes a pair of objects represented by the predicates $Type$, $Color$, $Volume$, $Owner$, $Material$, $Density$, and On.
- Hypothesis space H: Each hypothesis is a set of Horn clause rules. The head of each Horn clause is a literal containing the target predicate *SafeToStack*. The body of each Horn clause is a conjunction of literals based on the same predicates used to describe the instances, as well as the predicates $LessThan$, $Equal$, $GreaterThan$, and the functions $plus$, $minus$, and $times$. For example, the following Horn clause is in the hypothesis space:

$$SafeToStack(x, y) \leftarrow Volume(x, vx) \wedge Volume(y, vy) \wedge LessThan(vx, vy)$$

- Target concept: *SafeToStack(x,y)*
- Training Examples: A typical positive example, $SafeToStack(Obj1, Obj2)$, is shown below:

$On(Obj1, Obj2)$	$Owner(Obj1, Fred)$
$Type(Obj1, Box)$	$Owner(Obj2, Louise)$
$Type(Obj2, Endtable)$	$Density(Obj1, 0.3)$
$Color(Obj1, Red)$	$Material(Obj1, Cardboard)$
$Color(Obj2, Blue)$	$Material(Obj2, Wood)$
$Volume(Obj1, 2)$	

- Domain Theory B:
  $SafeToStack(x, y) \leftarrow \neg Fragile(y)$
  $SafeToStack(x, y) \leftarrow Lighter(x, y)$
  $Lighter(x, y) \leftarrow Weight(x, wx) \wedge Weight(y, wy) \wedge LessThan(wx, wy)$
  $Weight(x, w) \leftarrow Volume(x, v) \wedge Density(x, d) \wedge Equal(w, times(v, d))$
  $Weight(x, 5) \leftarrow Type(x, Endtable)$
  $Fragile(x) \leftarrow Material(x, Glass)$
  ...

Determine:

- A hypothesis from H consistent with the training examples and domain theory.

TABLE 11.1
An analytical learning problem: *SafeToStack(x,y)*.

As shown in Table 11.1, we have chosen a hypothesis space H in which each hypothesis is a set of first-order if-then rules, or Horn clauses (throughout this chapter we follow the notation and terminology for first-order Horn clauses summarized in Table 10.3). For instance, the example Horn clause hypothesis shown in the table asserts that it is *SafeToStack* any object x on any object y, if the $Volume$ of x is $LessThan$ the $Volume$ of y (in this Horn clause the variables vx and vy represent the volumes of x and y, respectively). Note the Horn clause hypothesis can refer to any of the predicates used to describe the instances, as well as several additional predicates and functions. A typical positive training example, $SafeToStack(Obj1, Obj2)$, is also shown in the table.

To formulate this task as an analytical learning problem we must also provide a domain theory sufficient to explain why observed positive examples satisfy the target concept. In our earlier chess example, the domain theory corresponded to knowledge of the legal moves in chess, from which we constructed explanations describing why black would lose its queen. In the current example, the domain theory must similarly explain why certain pairs of objects can be safely stacked on one another. The domain theory shown in the table includes assertions such as "it is safe to stack x on y if y is not *Fragile*," and "an object x is *Fragile* if the *Material* from which x is made is *Glass*." Like the learned hypothesis, the domain theory is described by a collection of Horn clauses, enabling the system in principle to incorporate any learned hypotheses into subsequent domain theories. Notice that the domain theory refers to additional predicates such as *Lighter* and *Fragile*, which are not present in the descriptions of the training examples, but which can be inferred from more primitive instance attributes such as *Material*, *Density*, and *Volume*, using other other rules in the domain theory. Finally, notice that the domain theory shown in the table is sufficient to prove that the positive example shown there satisfies the target concept *SafeToStack*.

11.2 LEARNING WITH PERFECT DOMAIN THEORIES: PROLOG-EBG

As stated earlier, in this chapter we consider explanation-based learning from domain theories that are perfect, that is, domain theories that are correct and complete. A domain theory is said to be *correct* if each of its assertions is a truthful statement about the world. A domain theory is said to be *complete* with respect to a given target concept and instance space, if the domain theory covers every positive example in the instance space. Put another way, it is complete if every instance that satisfies the target concept can be proven by the domain theory to satisfy it. Notice our definition of completeness does not require that the domain theory be able to prove that negative examples do not satisfy the target concept. However, if we follow the usual PROLOG convention that unprovable assertions are assumed to be false, then this definition of completeness includes full coverage of both positive and negative examples by the domain theory.

The reader may well ask at this point whether it is reasonable to assume that such perfect domain theories are available to the learner. After all, if the learner had a perfect domain theory, why would it need to learn? There are two responses to this question.

- First, there are cases in which it is feasible to provide a perfect domain theory. Our earlier chess problem provides one such case, in which the legal moves of chess form a perfect domain theory from which the optimal chess playing strategy can (in principle) be inferred. Furthermore, although it is quite easy to write down the legal moves of chess that constitute this domain theory, it is extremely difficult to write down the optimal chess-playing strategy. In such cases, we prefer to provide the domain theory to the learner and rely on the learner to formulate a useful description of the target concept (e.g., "board states in which I am about to lose my queen") by examining and generalizing from specific training examples. Section 11.4 describes the successful application of explanation-based learning with perfect domain theories to automatically improve performance at several search-intensive planning and optimization problems.

- Second, in many other cases it is unreasonable to assume that a perfect domain theory is available. It is difficult to write a perfectly correct and complete theory even for our relatively simple *SafeToStack* problem. A more realistic assumption is that plausible explanations based on imperfect domain theories must be used, rather than exact proofs based on perfect knowledge. Nevertheless, we can begin to understand the role of explanations in learning by considering the ideal case of perfect domain theories. In Chapter 12 we will consider learning from imperfect domain theories.

This section presents an algorithm called PROLOG-EBG (Kedar-Cabelli and McCarty 1987) that is representative of several explanation-based learning algorithms. PROLOG-EBG is a sequential covering algorithm (see Chapter 10). In other words, it operates by learning a single Horn clause rule, removing the positive training examples covered by this rule, then iterating this process on the remaining positive examples until no further positive examples remain uncovered. When given a complete and correct domain theory, PROLOG-EBG is guaranteed to output a hypothesis (set of rules) that is itself correct and that covers the observed positive training examples. For any set of training examples, the hypothesis output by PROLOG-EBG constitutes a set of logically sufficient conditions for the target concept, according to the domain theory. PROLOG-EBG is a refinement of the EBG algorithm introduced by Mitchell et al. (1986) and is similar to the EGGS algorithm described by DeJong and Mooney (1986). The PROLOG-EBG algorithm is summarized in Table 11.2.

11.2.1 An Illustrative Trace

To illustrate, consider again the training example and domain theory shown in Table 11.1. As summarized in Table 11.2, the PROLOG-EBG algorithm is a sequential covering algorithm that considers the training data incrementally. For each new positive training example that is not yet covered by a learned Horn clause, it forms a new Horn clause by: (1) explaining the new positive training example, (2) analyzing this explanation to determine an appropriate generalization, and (3) refining the current hypothesis by adding a new Horn clause rule to cover this positive example, as well as other similar instances. Below we examine each of these three steps in turn.

11.2.1.1 EXPLAIN THE TRAINING EXAMPLE

The first step in processing each novel training example is to construct an explanation in terms of the domain theory, showing how this positive example satisfies the target concept. When the domain theory is correct and complete this explanation constitutes a *proof* that the training example satisfies the target concept. When dealing with imperfect prior knowledge, the notion of explanation must be extended to allow for plausible, approximate arguments rather than perfect proofs.

PROLOG-EBG(*TargetConcept*, *TrainingExamples*, *DomainTheory*)

- *LearnedRules* ← {}
- *Pos* ← the positive examples from *TrainingExamples*
- for each *PositiveExample* in *Pos* that is not covered by *LearnedRules*, do
  1. *Explain:*
     - *Explanation* ← an explanation (proof) in terms of the *DomainTheory* that *PositiveExample* satisfies the *TargetConcept*
  2. *Analyze:*
     - *SufficientConditions* ← the most general set of features of *PositiveExample* sufficient to satisfy the *TargetConcept* according to the *Explanation*.
  3. *Refine:*
     - *LearnedRules* ← *LearnedRules* + *NewHornClause*, where *NewHornClause* is of the form

       TargetConcept ← *SufficientConditions*
- Return *LearnedRules*

TABLE 11.2
The explanation-based learning algorithm PROLOG-EBG. For each positive example that is not yet covered by the set of learned Horn clauses (*LearnedRules*), a new Horn clause is created. This new Horn clause is created by (1) explaining the training example in terms of the domain theory, (2) analyzing this explanation to determine the relevant features of the example, then (3) constructing a new Horn clause that concludes the target concept when this set of features is satisfied.

The explanation for the current training example is shown in Figure 11.2. Note the bottom of this figure depicts in graphical form the positive training example *SafeToStack*(*Obj1*, *Obj2*) from Table 11.1. The top of the figure depicts the explanation constructed for this training example. Notice the explanation, or proof, states that it is *SafeToStack Obj1* on *Obj2* because *Obj1* is *Lighter* than *Obj2*. Furthermore, *Obj1* is known to be *Lighter*, because its *Weight* can be inferred from its *Density* and *Volume*, and because the *Weight* of *Obj2* can be inferred from the default weight of an *Endtable*. The specific Horn clauses that underlie this explanation are shown in the domain theory of Table 11.1. Notice that the explanation mentions only a small fraction of the known attributes of *Obj1* and *Obj2* (i.e., those attributes corresponding to the shaded region in the figure).

While only a single explanation is possible for the training example and domain theory shown here, in general there may be multiple possible explanations. In such cases, any or all of the explanations may be used. While each may give rise to a somewhat different generalization of the training example, all will be justified by the given domain theory. In the case of PROLOG-EBG, the explanation is generated using a backward chaining search as performed by PROLOG. PROLOG-EBG, like PROLOG, halts once it finds the first valid proof.

11.2.1.2 ANALYZE THE EXPLANATION

The key question faced in generalizing the training example is "of the many features that happen to be true of the current training example, which ones are gen-

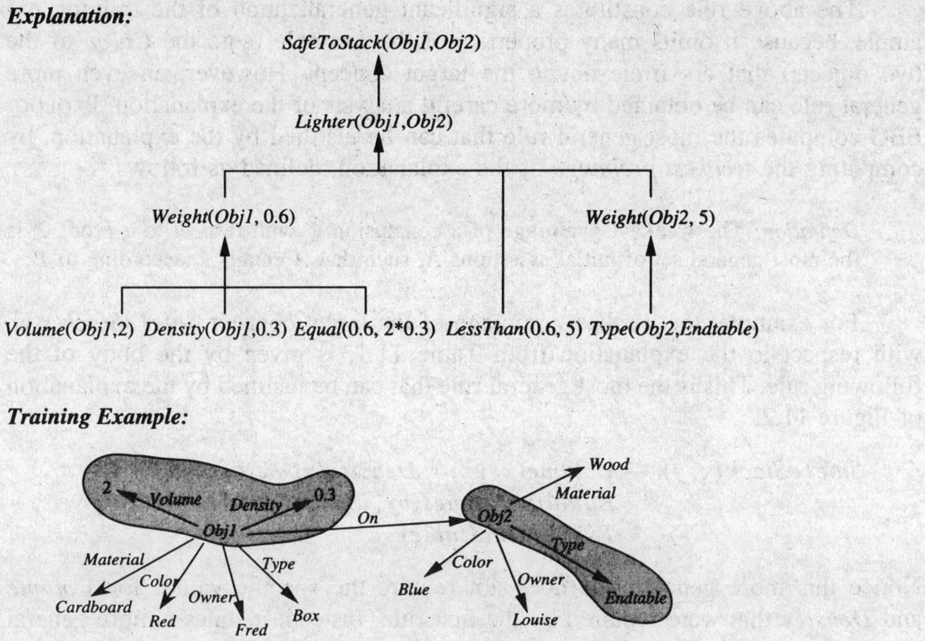

FIGURE 11.2
Explanation of a training example. The network at the bottom depicts graphically the training example *SafeToStack*(*Obj1*, *Obj2*) described in Table 11.1. The top portion of the figure depicts the explanation of how this example satisfies the target concept, *SafeToStack*. The shaded region of the training example indicates the example attributes used in the explanation. The other, irrelevant, example attributes will be dropped from the generalized hypothesis formed from this analysis.

erally relevant to the target concept?" The explanation constructed by the learner provides a direct answer to this question: precisely those features mentioned in the explanation. For example, the explanation of Figure 11.2 refers to the $Density$ of $Obj1$, but not to its $Owner$. Therefore, the hypothesis for *SafeToStack(x,y)* should include $Density(x, 0.3)$, but not $Owner(x, Fred)$. By collecting just the features mentioned in the leaf nodes of the explanation in Figure 11.2 and substituting variables x and y for $Obj1$ and $Obj2$, we can form a general rule that is justified by the domain theory:

$$SafeToStack(x, y) \leftarrow Volume(x, 2) \wedge Density(x, 0.3) \wedge Type(y, Endtable)$$

The body of the above rule includes each leaf node in the proof tree, except for the leaf nodes "$Equal(0.6, times(2, 0.3))$" and "$LessThan(0.6, 5)$." We omit these two because they are by definition always satisfied, independent of x and y.

Along with this learned rule, the program can also provide its justification: The explanation of the training example forms a proof for the correctness of this rule. Although this explanation was formed to cover the observed training example, the same explanation will apply to any instance that matches this general rule,

The above rule constitutes a significant generalization of the training example, because it omits many properties of the example (e.g., the *Color* of the two objects) that are irrelevant to the target concept. However, an even more general rule can be obtained by more careful analysis of the explanation. PROLOG-EBG computes the most general rule that can be justified by the explanation, by computing the *weakest preimage* of the explanation, defined as follows:

Definition: The **weakest preimage** of a conclusion C with respect to a proof P is the most general set of initial assertions A, such that A entails C according to P.

For example, the weakest preimage of the target concept *SafeToStack(x,y)*, with respect to the explanation from Table 11.1, is given by the body of the following rule. This is the most general rule that can be justified by the explanation of Figure 11.2:

$$\begin{aligned} SafeToStack(x, y) \leftarrow\ & Volume(x, vx) \wedge Density(x, dx) \wedge \\ & Equal(wx, times(vx, dx)) \wedge LessThan(wx, 5) \wedge \\ & Type(y, Endtable) \end{aligned}$$

Notice this more general rule does not require the specific values for *Volume* and *Density* that were required by the first rule. Instead, it states a more general constraint on the values of these attributes.

PROLOG-EBG computes the weakest preimage of the target concept with respect to the explanation, using a general procedure called *regression* (Waldinger 1977). The regression procedure operates on a domain theory represented by an arbitrary set of Horn clauses. It works iteratively backward through the explanation, first computing the weakest preimage of the target concept with respect to the final proof step in the explanation, then computing the weakest preimage of the resulting expressions with respect to the preceding step, and so on. The procedure terminates when it has iterated over all steps in the explanation, yielding the weakest precondition of the target concept with respect to the literals at the leaf nodes of the explanation.

A trace of this regression process is illustrated in Figure 11.3. In this figure, the explanation from Figure 11.2 is redrawn in standard (nonitalic) font. The frontier of regressed expressions created at each step by the regression procedure is shown underlined in italics. The process begins at the root of the tree, with the frontier initialized to the general target concept *SafeToStack(x,y)*. The first step is to compute the weakest preimage of this frontier expression with respect to the final (top-most) inference rule in the explanation. The rule in this case is $SafeToStack(x, y) \leftarrow Lighter(x, y)$, so the resulting weakest preimage is $Lighter(x, y)$. The process now continues by regressing the new frontier, $\{Lighter(x, y)\}$, through the next Horn clause in the explanation, resulting in the regressed expressions $\{Weight(x, wx), LessThan(wx, wy), Weight(y, wy)\}$. This indicates that the explanation will hold for any x and y such that the weight wx of x is less than the weight wy of y. The regression of this frontier back to the leaf nodes of the explanation continues in this step-by-step fashion, finally

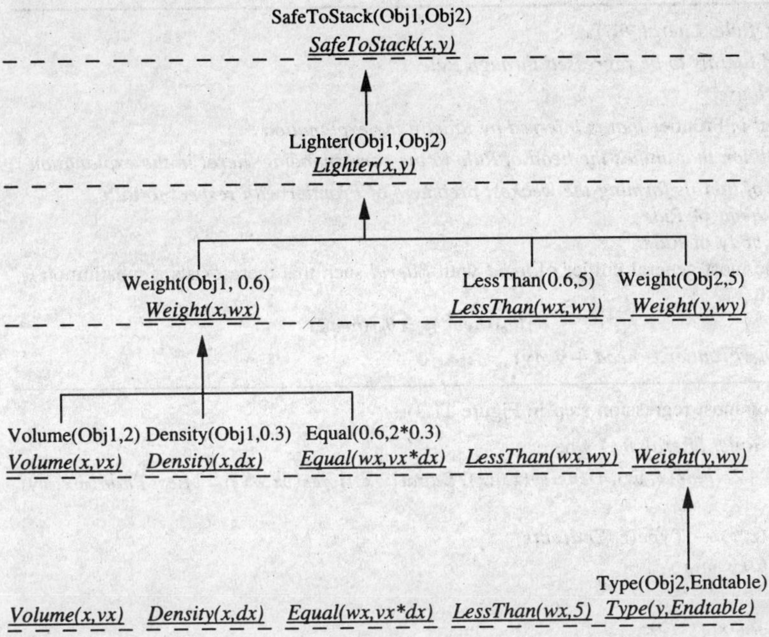

FIGURE 11.3
Computing the weakest preimage of *SafeToStack*(*Obj*1, *Obj*2) with respect to the explanation. The target concept is regressed from the root (conclusion) of the explanation, down to the leaves. At each step (indicated by the dashed lines) the current frontier set of literals (underlined in italics) is regressed backward over one rule in the explanation. When this process is completed, the conjunction of resulting literals constitutes the weakest preimage of the target concept with respect to the explanation. This weakest preimage is shown by the italicized literals at the bottom of the figure.

resulting in a set of generalized literals for the leaf nodes of the tree. This final set of literals, shown at the bottom of Figure 11.3, forms the body of the final rule.

The heart of the regression procedure is the algorithm that at each step regresses the current frontier of expressions through a single Horn clause from the domain theory. This algorithm is described and illustrated in Table 11.3. The illustrated example in this table corresponds to the bottommost single regression step of Figure 11.3. As shown in the table, the REGRESS algorithm operates by finding a substitution that unifies the head of the Horn clause rule with the corresponding literal in the frontier, replacing this expression in the frontier by the rule body, then applying a unifying substitution to the entire frontier.

The final Horn clause rule output by PROLOG-EBG is formulated as follows: The clause body is defined to be the weakest preconditions calculated by the above procedure. The clause head is the target concept itself, with each substitution from each regression step (i.e., the substitution θ_{hl} in Table 11.3) applied to it. This substitution is necessary in order to keep consistent variable names between the head and body of the created clause, and to specialize the clause head when the

---

REGRESS(*Frontier, Rule, Literal,* θ_{hi})

Frontier: Set of literals to be regressed through Rule

Rule: A Horn clause

Literal: A literal in Frontier *that is inferred by Rule in the explanation*

θ_{hi}: *The substitution that unifies the head of Rule to the corresponding literal in the explanation*

Returns the set of literals forming the weakest preimage of Frontier with respect to Rule

- *head* ← *head* of *Rule*
- *body* ← *body* of *Rule*
- θ_{hl} ← the most general unifier of *head* with *Literal* such that there exists a substitution θ_{li} for which

$$\theta_{li}(\theta_{hl}(head)) = \theta_{hi}(head)$$

- Return $\theta_{hl}(Frontier - head + body)$

Example (the bottommost regression step in Figure 11.3):

REGRESS(*Frontier, Rule, Literal,* θ_{hi}) where

Frontier = {*Volume*(*x*, *vs*), *Density*(*x*, *dx*), *Equal*(*wx*, *times*(*vx*, *dx*)), *LessThan*(*wx*, *wy*), *Weight*(*y*, *wy*)}

Rule = *Weight*(*z*, 5) ← *Type*(*z*, *Endtable*)

Literal = *Weight*(*y*, *wy*)

$\theta_{hi} = \{z/Obj2\}$

- *head* ← *Weight*(*z*, 5)
- *body* ← *Type*(*z*, *Endtable*)
- $\theta_{hl} \leftarrow \{z/y, wy/5\}$, where $\theta_{li} = \{y/Obj2\}$
- Return {*Volume*(*x*, *vs*), *Density*(*x*, *dx*), *Equal*(*wx*, *times*(*vx*, *dx*)), *LessThan*(*wx*, 5), *Type*(*y*, *Endtable*)}

TABLE 11.3

Algorithm for regressing a set of literals through a single Horn clause. The set of literals given by *Frontier* is regressed through *Rule*. *Literal* is the member of *Frontier* inferred by *Rule* in the explanation. The substitution θ_{hi} gives the binding of variables from the head of *Rule* to the corresponding literal in the explanation. The algorithm first computes a substitution θ_{hl} that unifies the *Rule* head to *Literal*, in a way that is consistent with the substitution θ_{hi}. It then applies this substitution θ_{hl} to construct the preimage of *Frontier* with respect to *Rule*. The symbols "+" and "−" in the algorithm denote set union and set difference. The notation $\{z/y\}$ denotes the substitution of y in place of z. An example trace is given.

explanation applies to only a special case of the target concept. As noted earlier, for the current example the final rule is

$$\begin{aligned} SafeToStack(x, y) \leftarrow\ & Volume(x, vx) \wedge Density(x, dx) \wedge \\ & Equal(wx, times(vx, dx)) \wedge LessThan(wx, 5) \wedge \\ & Type(y, Endtable) \end{aligned}$$

11.2.1.3 REFINE THE CURRENT HYPOTHESIS

The current hypothesis at each stage consists of the set of Horn clauses learned thus far. At each stage, the sequential covering algorithm picks a new positive example that is not yet covered by the current Horn clauses, explains this new example, and formulates a new rule according to the procedure described above. Notice only positive examples are covered in the algorithm as we have defined it, and the learned set of Horn clause rules predicts only positive examples. A new instance is classified as negative if the current rules fail to predict that it is positive. This is in keeping with the standard negation-as-failure approach used in Horn clause inference systems such as PROLOG.

11.3 REMARKS ON EXPLANATION-BASED LEARNING

As we saw in the above example, PROLOG-EBG conducts a detailed analysis of individual training examples to determine how best to generalize from the specific example to a general Horn clause hypothesis. The following are the key properties of this algorithm.

- Unlike inductive methods, PROLOG-EBG produces *justified* general hypotheses by using prior knowledge to analyze individual examples.
- The explanation of how the example satisfies the target concept determines which example attributes are relevant: those mentioned by the explanation.
- The further analysis of the explanation, regressing the target concept to determine its weakest preimage with respect to the explanation, allows deriving more general constraints on the values of the relevant features.
- Each learned Horn clause corresponds to a sufficient condition for satisfying the target concept. The set of learned Horn clauses covers the positive training examples encountered by the learner, as well as other instances that share the same explanations.
- The generality of the learned Horn clauses will depend on the formulation of the domain theory and on the sequence in which training examples are considered.
- PROLOG-EBG implicitly assumes that the domain theory is correct and complete. If the domain theory is incorrect or incomplete, the resulting learned concept may also be incorrect.

There are several related perspectives on explanation-based learning that help to understand its capabilities and limitations.

- *EBL as theory-guided generalization of examples.* EBL uses its given domain theory to generalize *rationally* from examples, distinguishing the relevant example attributes from the irrelevant, thereby allowing it to avoid the bounds on sample complexity that apply to purely inductive learning. This is the perspective implicit in the above description of the PROLOG-EBG algorithm.
- *EBL as example-guided reformulation of theories.* The PROLOG-EBG algorithm can be viewed as a method for reformulating the domain theory into a more operational form. In particular, the original domain theory is reformulated by creating rules that (a) follow deductively from the domain theory,

and (b) classify the observed training examples in a single inference step. Thus, the learned rules can be seen as a reformulation of the domain theory into a set of special-case rules capable of classifying instances of the target concept in a single inference step.

- *EBL as "just" restating what the learner already "knows."* In one sense, the learner in our *SafeToStack* example begins with full knowledge of the *SafeToStack* concept. That is, if its initial domain theory is sufficient to explain any observed training examples, then it is also sufficient to predict their classification in advance. In what sense, then, does this qualify as learning? One answer is that in many tasks the difference between what one knows *in principle* and what one can efficiently compute *in practice* may be great, and in such cases this kind of "knowledge reformulation" can be an important form of learning. In playing chess, for example, the rules of the game constitute a perfect domain theory, sufficient in principle to play perfect chess. Despite this fact, people still require considerable experience to learn how to play chess well. This is precisely a situation in which a complete, perfect domain theory is already known to the (human) learner, and further learning is "simply" a matter of reformulating this knowledge into a form in which it can be used more effectively to select appropriate moves. A beginning course in Newtonian physics exhibits the same property—the basic laws of physics are easily stated, but students nevertheless spend a large part of a semester working out the consequences so they have this knowledge in more operational form and need not derive every problem solution from first principles come the final exam. PROLOG-EBG performs this type of reformulation of knowledge—its learned rules map directly from observable instance features to the classification relative to the target concept, in a way that is consistent with the underlying domain theory. Whereas it may require many inference steps and considerable search to classify an arbitrary instance using the original domain theory, the learned rules classify the observed instances in a single inference step.

Thus, in its pure form EBL involves reformulating the domain theory to produce general rules that classify examples in a single inference step. This kind of knowledge reformulation is sometimes referred to as *knowledge compilation*, indicating that the transformation is an efficiency improving one that does not alter the correctness of the system's knowledge.

11.3.1 Discovering New Features

One interesting capability of PROLOG-EBG is its ability to formulate new features that are not explicit in the description of the training examples, but that are needed to describe the general rule underlying the training example. This capability is illustrated by the algorithm trace and the learned rule in the previous section. In particular, the learned rule asserts that the essential constraint on the $Volume$ and $Density$ of x is that their product is less than 5. In fact, the training examples contain no description of such a product, or of the value it should take on. Instead, this constraint is formulated automatically by the learner.

Notice this learned "feature" is similar in kind to the types of features represented by the hidden units of neural networks; that is, this feature is one of a very large set of potential features that can be computed from the available instance attributes. Like the BACKPROPAGATION algorithm, PROLOG-EBG automatically formulates such features in its attempt to fit the training data. However, unlike the statistical process that derives hidden unit features in neural networks from many training examples, PROLOG-EBG employs an analytical process to derive new features based on analysis of single training examples. Above, PROLOG-EBG derives the feature $Volume \cdot Density > 5$ analytically from the particular instantiation of the domain theory used to explain a single training example. For example, the notion that the product of $Volume$ and $Density$ is important arises from the domain theory rule that defines $Weight$. The notion that this product should be less than 5 arises from two other domain theory rules that assert that $Obj1$ should be $Lighter$ than the $Endtable$, and that the $Weight$ of the $Endtable$ is 5. Thus, it is the particular composition and instantiation of these primitive terms from the domain theory that gives rise to defining this new feature.

The issue of automatically learning useful features to augment the instance representation is an important issue for machine learning. The analytical derivation of new features in explanation-based learning and the inductive derivation of new features in the hidden layer of neural networks provide two distinct approaches. Because they rely on different sources of information (statistical regularities over many examples versus analysis of single examples using the domain theory), it may be useful to explore new methods that combine both sources.

11.3.2 Deductive Learning

In its pure form, PROLOG-EBG is a deductive, rather than inductive, learning process. That is, by calculating the weakest preimage of the explanation it produces a hypothesis h that follows deductively from the domain theory B, while covering the training data D. To be more precise, PROLOG-EBG outputs a hypothesis h that satisfies the following two constraints:

$$(\forall \langle x_i, f(x_i) \rangle \in D) \ \ (h \wedge x_i) \vdash f(x_i) \tag{11.1}$$

$$D \wedge B \vdash h \tag{11.2}$$

where the training data D consists of a set of training examples in which x_i is the ith training instance and $f(x_i)$ is its target value (f is the target function). Notice the first of these constraints is simply a formalization of the usual requirement in machine learning, that the hypothesis h correctly predict the target value $f(x_i)$ for each instance x_i in the training data.† Of course there will, in general, be many

† Here we include PROLOG-style negation-by-failure in our definition of entailment ($\vdash$), so that examples are entailed to be negative examples if they cannot be proven to be positive.

alternative hypotheses that satisfy this first constraint. The second constraint describes the impact of the domain theory in PROLOG-EBL: The output hypothesis is further constrained so that it must follow from the domain theory and the data. This second constraint reduces the ambiguity faced by the learner when it must choose a hypothesis. Thus, the impact of the domain theory is to reduce the effective size of the hypothesis space and hence reduce the sample complexity of learning.

Using similar notation, we can state the type of knowledge that is required by PROLOG-EBG for its domain theory. In particular, PROLOG-EBG assumes the domain theory B entails the classifications of the instances in the training data:

$$(\forall \langle x_i, f(x_i) \rangle \in D) \quad (B \wedge x_i) \vdash f(x_i) \tag{11.3}$$

This constraint on the domain theory B assures that an explanation can be constructed for each positive example.

It is interesting to compare the PROLOG-EBG learning setting to the setting for inductive logic programming (ILP) discussed in Chapter 10. In that chapter, we discussed a generalization of the usual inductive learning task, in which background knowledge B' is provided to the learner. We will use B' rather than B to denote the background knowledge used by ILP, because it does not typically satisfy the constraint given by Equation (11.3). ILP is an inductive learning system, whereas PROLOG-EBG is deductive. ILP uses its background knowledge B' to enlarge the set of hypotheses to be considered, whereas PROLOG-EBG uses its domain theory B to reduce the set of acceptable hypotheses. As stated in Equation (10.2), ILP systems output a hypothesis h that satisfies the following constraint:

$$(\forall \langle x_i, f(x_i) \rangle \in D) \quad (B' \wedge h \wedge x_i) \vdash f(x_i)$$

Note the relationship between this expression and the constraints on h imposed by PROLOG-EBG (given by Equations (11.1) and (11.2)). This ILP constraint on h is a weakened form of the constraint given by Equation (11.1)—the ILP constraint requires only that $(B' \wedge h \wedge x_i) \vdash f(x_i)$, whereas the PROLOG-EBG constraint requires the more strict $(h \wedge x_i) \vdash f(x_i)$. Note also that ILP imposes no constraint corresponding to the PROLOG-EBG constraint of Equation (11.2).

11.3.3 Inductive Bias in Explanation-Based Learning

Recall from Chapter 2 that the inductive bias of a learning algorithm is a set of assertions that, together with the training examples, deductively entail subsequent predictions made by the learner. The importance of inductive bias is that it characterizes how the learner generalizes beyond the observed training examples.

What is the inductive bias of PROLOG-EBG? In PROLOG-EBG the output hypothesis h follows deductively from $D \wedge B$, as described by Equation (11.2). Therefore, the domain theory B is a set of assertions which, together with the training examples, entail the output hypothesis. Given that predictions of the learner follow from this hypothesis h, it appears that the inductive bias of PROLOG-EBG is simply the domain theory B input to the learner. In fact, this is the case except for one additional detail that must be considered: There are many alternative sets of Horn clauses entailed by the domain theory. The remaining component of the inductive bias is therefore the basis by which PROLOG-EBG chooses among these alternative sets of Horn clauses. As we saw above, PROLOG-EBG employs a sequential covering algorithm that continues to formulate additional Horn clauses until all positive training examples have been covered. Furthermore, each individual Horn clause is the most general clause (weakest preimage) licensed by the explanation of the current training example. Therefore, among the sets of Horn clauses entailed by the domain theory, we can characterize the bias of PROLOG-EBG as a preference for small sets of maximally general Horn clauses. In fact, the greedy algorithm of PROLOG-EBG is only a heuristic approximation to the exhaustive search algorithm that would be required to find the truly shortest set of maximally general Horn clauses. Nevertheless, the inductive bias of PROLOG-EBG can be approximately characterized in this fashion.

> **Approximate inductive bias of PROLOG-EBG:** The domain theory B, plus a preference for small sets of maximally general Horn clauses.

The most important point here is that the inductive bias of PROLOG-EBG—the policy by which it generalizes beyond the training data—is largely determined by the input domain theory. This lies in stark contrast to most of the other learning algorithms we have discussed (e.g., neural networks, decision tree learning), in which the inductive bias is a fixed property of the learning algorithm, typically determined by the syntax of its hypothesis representation. Why is it important that the inductive bias be an input parameter rather than a fixed property of the learner? Because, as we have discussed in Chapter 2 and elsewhere, there is no universally effective inductive bias and because bias-free learning is futile. Therefore, any attempt to develop a general-purpose learning method must at minimum allow the inductive bias to vary with the learning problem at hand. On a more practical level, in many tasks it is quite natural to input domain-specific knowledge (e.g., the knowledge about *Weight* in the *SafeToStack* example) to influence how the learner will generalize beyond the training data. In contrast, it is less natural to "implement" an appropriate bias by restricting the syntactic form of the hypotheses (e.g., prefer short decision trees). Finally, if we consider the larger issue of how an autonomous agent may improve its learning capabilities over time, then it is attractive to have a learning algorithm whose generalization capabilities improve as it acquires more knowledge of its domain.

11.3.4 Knowledge Level Learning

As pointed out in Equation (11.2), the hypothesis h output by PROLOG-EBG follows deductively from the domain theory B and training data D. In fact, by examining the PROLOG-EBG algorithm it is easy to see that h follows directly from B alone, independent of D. One way to see this is to imagine an algorithm that we might call LEMMA-ENUMERATOR. The LEMMA-ENUMERATOR algorithm simply enumerates all proof trees that conclude the target concept based on assertions in the domain theory B. For each such proof tree, LEMMA-ENUMERATOR calculates the weakest preimage and constructs a Horn clause, in the same fashion as PROLOG-EBG. The only difference between LEMMA-ENUMERATOR and PROLOG-EBG is that LEMMA-ENUMERATOR ignores the training data and enumerates all proof trees.

Notice LEMMA-ENUMERATOR will output a superset of the Horn clauses output by PROLOG-EBG. Given this fact, several questions arise. First, if its hypotheses follow from the domain theory alone, then what is the role of training data in PROLOG-EBG? The answer is that training examples focus the PROLOG-EBG algorithm on generating rules that cover the distribution of instances that occur in practice. In our original chess example, for instance, the set of all possible lemmas is huge, whereas the set of chess positions that occur in normal play is only a small fraction of those that are syntactically possible. Therefore, by focusing only on training examples encountered in practice, the program is likely to develop a smaller, more relevant set of rules than if it attempted to enumerate all possible lemmas about chess.

The second question that arises is whether PROLOG-EBG can ever learn a hypothesis that goes beyond the knowledge that is already implicit in the domain theory. Put another way, will it ever learn to classify an instance that could not be classified by the original domain theory (assuming a theorem prover with unbounded computational resources)? Unfortunately, it will not. If $B \vdash h$, then any classification entailed by h will also be entailed by B. Is this an inherent limitation of analytical or deductive learning methods? No, it is not, as illustrated by the following example.

To produce an instance of deductive learning in which the learned hypothesis h entails conclusions that are not entailed by B, we must create an example where $B \nvdash h$ but where $D \wedge B \vdash h$ (recall the constraint given by Equation (11.2)). One interesting case is when B contains assertions such as "If x satisfies the target concept, then so will $g(x)$." Taken alone, this assertion does not entail the classification of any instances. However, once we observe a positive example, it allows generalizing deductively to other unseen instances. For example, consider learning the *PlayTennis* target concept, describing the days on which our friend Ross would like to play tennis. Imagine that each day is described only by the single attribute *Humidity*, and the domain theory B includes the single assertion "If Ross likes to play tennis when the humidity is x, then he will also like to play tennis when the humidity is lower than x," which can be stated more formally as

$$(\forall x) \quad \text{IF } ((PlayTennis = Yes) \leftarrow (Humidity = x))$$
$$\text{THEN } ((PlayTennis = Yes) \leftarrow (Humidity \leq x))$$

Note that this domain theory does not entail any conclusions regarding which instances are positive or negative instances of *PlayTennis*. However, once the learner observes a positive example day for which $Humidity = .30$, the domain theory together with this positive example entails the following general hypothesis h:

$$(PlayTennis = Yes) \leftarrow (Humidity \leq .30)$$

To summarize, this example illustrates a situation where $B \nvdash h$, but where $B \wedge D \vdash h$. The learned hypothesis in this case entails predictions that are not entailed by the domain theory alone. The phrase *knowledge-level learning* is sometimes used to refer to this type of learning, in which the learned hypothesis entails predictions that go beyond those entailed by the domain theory. The set of all predictions entailed by a set of assertions Y is often called the *deductive closure* of Y. The key distinction here is that in knowledge-level learning the deductive closure of B is a proper subset of the deductive closure of $B + h$.

A second example of knowledge-level analytical learning is provided by considering a type of assertions known as *determinations*, which have been explored in detail by Russell (1989) and others. Determinations assert that some attribute of the instance is fully determined by certain other attributes, without specifying the exact nature of the dependence. For example, consider learning the target concept "people who speak Portuguese," and imagine we are given as a domain theory the single determination assertion "the language spoken by a person is determined by their nationality." Taken alone, this domain theory does not enable us to classify any instances as positive or negative. However, if we observe that "Joe, a 23-year-old left-handed Brazilian, speaks Portuguese," then we can conclude from this positive example and the domain theory that "all Brazilians speak Portuguese."

Both of these examples illustrate how deductive learning can produce output hypotheses that are not entailed by the domain theory alone. In both of these cases, the output hypothesis h satisfies $B \wedge D \vdash h$, but does not satisfy $B \vdash h$. In both cases, the learner *deduces* a justified hypothesis that does not follow from either the domain theory alone or the training data alone.

11.4 EXPLANATION-BASED LEARNING OF SEARCH CONTROL KNOWLEDGE

As noted above, the practical applicability of the PROLOG-EBG algorithm is restricted by its requirement that the domain theory be correct and complete. One important class of learning problems where this requirement is easily satisfied is learning to speed up complex search programs. In fact, the largest scale attempts to apply explanation-based learning have addressed the problem of learning to control search, or what is sometimes called "speedup" learning. For example, playing games such as chess involves searching through a vast space of possible moves and board positions to find the best move. Many practical scheduling and optimization problems are easily formulated as large search problems, in which the task is to find some move toward the goal state. In such problems the definitions of the legal search operators, together with the definition of the search objective, provide a complete and correct domain theory for learning search control knowledge.

Exactly how should we formulate the problem of learning search control so that we can apply explanation-based learning? Consider a general search problem where S is the set of possible search states, O is a set of legal search operators that transform one search state into another, and G is a predicate defined over S that indicates which states are goal states. The problem in general is to find a sequence of operators that will transform an arbitrary initial state s_i to some final state s_f that satisfies the goal predicate G. One way to formulate the learning problem is to have our system learn a separate target concept for each of the operators in O. In particular, for each operator o in O it might attempt to learn the target concept "the set of states for which o leads toward a goal state." Of course the exact choice of which target concepts to learn depends on the internal structure of problem solver that must use this learned knowledge. For example, if the problem solver is a means-ends planning system that works by establishing and solving subgoals, then we might instead wish to learn target concepts such as "the set of planning states in which subgoals of type A should be solved before subgoals of type B."

One system that employs explanation-based learning to improve its search is PRODIGY (Carbonell et al. 1990). PRODIGY is a domain-independent planning system that accepts the definition of a problem domain in terms of the state space S and operators O. It then solves problems of the form "find a sequence of operators that leads from initial state s_i to a state that satisfies goal predicate G." PRODIGY uses a means-ends planner that decomposes problems into subgoals, solves them, then combines their solutions into a solution for the full problem. Thus, during its search for problem solutions PRODIGY repeatedly faces questions such as "Which subgoal should be solved next?" and "Which operator should be considered for solving this subgoal?" Minton (1988) describes the integration of explanation-based learning into PRODIGY by defining a set of target concepts appropriate for these kinds of control decisions that it repeatedly confronts. For example, one target concept is "the set of states in which subgoal A should be solved before subgoal B." An example of a rule learned by PRODIGY for this target concept in a simple block-stacking problem domain is

IF	One subgoal to be solved is $On(x, y)$, and
	One subgoal to be solved is $On(y, z)$
THEN	Solve the subgoal $On(y, z)$ before $On(x, y)$

To understand this rule, consider again the simple block stacking problem illustrated in Figure 9.3. In the problem illustrated by that figure, the goal is to stack the blocks so that they spell the word "universal." PRODIGY would decompose this problem into several subgoals to be achieved, including $On(U, N)$, $On(N, I)$, etc. Notice the above rule matches the subgoals $On(U, N)$ and $On(N, I)$, and recommends solving the subproblem $On(N, I)$ before solving $On(U, N)$. The justification for this rule (and the explanation used by PRODIGY to learn the rule) is that if we solve the subgoals in the reverse sequence, we will encounter a conflict in which we must undo the solution to the $On(U, N)$ subgoal in order to achieve the other subgoal $On(N, I)$. PRODIGY learns by first encountering such a conflict, then explaining to itself the reason for this conflict and creating a rule such as the one above. The net effect is that PRODIGY uses domain-independent knowledge about possible subgoal conflicts, together with domain-specific knowledge of specific operators (e.g., the fact that the robot can pick up only one block at a time), to learn useful domain-specific planning rules such as the one illustrated above.

The use of explanation-based learning to acquire control knowledge for PRODIGY has been demonstrated in a variety of problem domains including the simple block-stacking problem above, as well as more complex scheduling and planning problems. Minton (1988) reports experiments in three problem domains, in which the learned control rules improve problem-solving efficiency by a factor of two to four. Furthermore, the performance of these learned rules is comparable to that of handwritten rules across these three problem domains. Minton also describes a number of extensions to the basic explanation-based learning procedure that improve its effectiveness for learning control knowledge. These include methods for simplifying learned rules and for removing learned rules whose benefits are smaller than their cost.

A second example of a general problem-solving architecture that incorporates a form of explanation-based learning is the SOAR system (Laird et al. 1986; Newell 1990). SOAR supports a broad variety of problem-solving strategies that subsumes PRODIGY's means-ends planning strategy. Like PRODIGY, however, SOAR learns by explaining situations in which its current search strategy leads to inefficiencies. When it encounters a search choice for which it does not have a definite answer (e.g., which operator to apply next) SOAR reflects on this search impasse, using weak methods such as generate-and-test to determine the correct course of action. The reasoning used to resolve this impasse can be interpreted as an explanation for how to resolve similar impasses in the future. SOAR uses a variant of explanation-based learning called *chunking* to extract the general conditions under which the same explanation applies. SOAR has been applied in a great number of problem domains and has also been proposed as a psychologically plausible model of human learning processes (see Newell 1990).

PRODIGY and SOAR demonstrate that explanation-based learning methods can be successfully applied to acquire search control knowledge in a variety of problem domains. Nevertheless, many or most heuristic search programs still use numerical evaluation functions similar to the one described in Chapter 1, rather than rules acquired by explanation-based learning. What is the reason for this? In fact, there are significant practical problems with applying EBL to learning search control. First, in many cases the number of control rules that must be learned is very large (e.g., many thousands of rules). As the system learns more and more control rules to improve its search, it must pay a larger and larger cost at each step to match this set of rules against the current search state. Note this problem is not specific to explanation-based learning; it will occur for any system that represents its learned knowledge by a growing set of rules. Efficient algorithms for matching rules can alleviate this problem, but not eliminate it completely. Minton (1988) discusses strategies for empirically estimating the computational cost and benefit of each rule, learning rules only when the estimated benefits outweigh the estimated costs and deleting rules later found to have negative utility. He describes how using this kind of *utility analysis* to determine what should be learned and what should be forgotten significantly enhances the effectiveness of explanation-based learning in PRODIGY. For example, in a series of robot block-stacking problems, PRODIGY encountered 328 opportunities for learning a new rule, but chose to exploit only 69 of these, and eventually reduced the learned rules to a set of 19, once low-utility rules were eliminated. Tambe et al. (1990) and Doorenbos (1993) discuss how to identify types of rules that will be particularly costly to match, as well as methods for re-expressing such rules in more efficient forms and methods for optimizing rule-matching algorithms. Doorenbos (1993) describes how these methods enabled SOAR to efficiently match a set of 100,000 learned rules in one problem domain, without a significant increase in the cost of matching rules per state.

A second practical problem with applying explanation-based learning to learning search control is that in many cases it is intractable even to construct the explanations for the desired target concept. For example, in chess we might wish to learn a target concept such as "states for which operator *A* leads toward the optimal solution." Unfortunately, to prove or explain why *A* leads toward the optimal solution requires explaining that every alternative operator leads to a less optimal outcome. This typically requires effort exponential in the search depth. Chien (1993) and Tadepalli (1990) explore methods for "lazy" or "incremental" explanation, in which heuristics are used to produce partial and approximate, but tractable, explanations. Rules are extracted from these imperfect explanations as though the explanations were perfect. Of course these learned rules may be incorrect due to the incomplete explanations. The system accommodates this by monitoring the performance of the rule on subsequent cases. If the rule subsequently makes an error, then the original explanation is incrementally elaborated to cover the new case, and a more refined rule is extracted from this incrementally improved explanation.

Many additional research efforts have explored the use of explanation-based learning for improving the efficiency of search-based problem solvers (for example, Mitchell 1981; Silver 1983; Shavlik 1990; Mahadevan et al. 1993; Gervasio and DeJong 1994; DeJong 1994). Bennett and DeJong (1996) explore explanation-based learning for robot planning problems where the system has an imperfect domain theory that describes its world and actions. Dietterich and Flann (1995) explore the integration of explanation-based learning with reinforcement learning methods discussed in Chapter 13. Mitchell and Thrun (1993) describe the application of an explanation-based neural network learning method (see the EBNN algorithm discussed in Chapter 12) to reinforcement learning problems.

11.5 SUMMARY AND FURTHER READING

The main points of this chapter include:

- In contrast to purely inductive learning methods that seek a hypothesis to fit the training data, purely analytical learning methods seek a hypothesis that fits the learner's prior knowledge and covers the training examples. Humans often make use of prior knowledge to guide the formation of new hypotheses. This chapter examines purely analytical learning methods. The next chapter examines combined inductive-analytical learning.

- Explanation-based learning is a form of analytical learning in which the learner processes each novel training example by (1) explaining the observed target value for this example in terms of the domain theory, (2) analyzing this explanation to determine the general conditions under which the explanation holds, and (3) refining its hypothesis to incorporate these general conditions.
- PROLOG-EBG is an explanation-based learning algorithm that uses first-order Horn clauses to represent both its domain theory and its learned hypotheses. In PROLOG-EBG an explanation is a PROLOG proof, and the hypothesis extracted from the explanation is the weakest preimage of this proof. As a result, the hypotheses output by PROLOG-EBG follow deductively from its domain theory.
- Analytical learning methods such as PROLOG-EBG construct useful intermediate features as a side effect of analyzing individual training examples. This analytical approach to feature generation complements the statistically based generation of intermediate features (eg., hidden unit features) in inductive methods such as BACKPROPAGATION.
- Although PROLOG-EBG does not produce hypotheses that extend the deductive closure of its domain theory, other deductive learning procedures can. For example, a domain theory containing determination assertions (e.g., "nationality determines language") can be used together with observed data to deductively infer hypotheses that go beyond the deductive closure of the domain theory.
- One important class of problems for which a correct and complete domain theory can be found is the class of large state-space search problems. Systems such as PRODIGY and SOAR have demonstrated the utility of explanation-based learning methods for automatically acquiring effective search control knowledge that speeds up problem solving in subsequent cases.
- Despite the apparent usefulness of explanation-based learning methods in humans, purely deductive implementations such as PROLOG-EBG suffer the disadvantage that the output hypothesis is only as correct as the domain theory. In the next chapter we examine approaches that combine inductive and analytical learning methods in order to learn effectively from imperfect domain theories and limited training data.

The roots of analytical learning methods can be traced to early work by Fikes et al. (1972) on learning macro-operators through analysis of operators in ABSTRIPS and to somewhat later work by Soloway (1977) on the use of explicit prior knowledge in learning. Explanation-based learning methods similar to those discussed in this chapter first appeared in a number of systems developed during the early 1980s, including DeJong (1981); Mitchell (1981); Winston et al.

(1983); and Silver (1983). DeJong and Mooney (1986) and Mitchell et al. (1986) provided general descriptions of the explanation-based learning paradigm, which helped spur a burst of research on this topic during the late 1980s. A collection of research on explanation-based learning performed at the University of Illinois is described by DeJong (1993), including algorithms that modify the structure of the explanation in order to correctly generalize iterative and temporal explanations. More recent research has focused on extending explanation-based methods to accommodate imperfect domain theories and to incorporate inductive together with analytical learning (see Chapter 12). An edited collection exploring the role of goals and prior knowledge in human and machine learning is provided by Ram and Leake (1995), and a recent overview of explanation-based learning is given by DeJong (1997).

The most serious attempts to employ explanation-based learning with perfect domain theories have been in the area of learning search control, or "speedup" learning. The SOAR system described by Laird et al. (1986) and the PRODIGY system described by Carbonell et al. (1990) are among the most developed systems that use explanation-based learning methods for learning in problem solving. Rosenbloom and Laird (1986) discuss the close relationship between SOAR's learning method (called "chunking") and other explanation-based learning methods. More recently, Dietterich and Flann (1995) have explored the combination of explanation-based learning with reinforcement learning methods for learning search control.

While our primary purpose here is to study machine learning algorithms, it is interesting to note that experimental studies of human learning provide support for the conjecture that human learning is based on explanations. For example, Ahn et al. (1987) and Qin et al. (1992) summarize evidence supporting the conjecture that humans employ explanation-based learning processes. Wisniewski and Medin (1995) describe experimental studies of human learning that suggest a rich interplay between prior knowledge and observed data to influence the learning process. Kotovsky and Baillargeon (1994) describe experiments that suggest even 11-month-old infants build on prior knowledge as they learn.

The analysis performed in explanation-based learning is similar to certain kinds of program optimization methods used for PROLOG programs, such as partial evaluation; van Harmelen and Bundy (1988) provide one discussion of the relationship.

EXERCISES

11.1. Consider the problem of learning the target concept "pairs of people who live in the same house," denoted by the predicate $HouseMates(x, y)$. Below is a positive example of the concept.

$HouseMates(Joe, Sue)$

$Person(Joe)$	$Person(Sue)$
$Sex(Joe, Male)$	$Sex(Sue, Female)$
$HairColor(Joe, Black)$	$HairColor(Sue, Brown)$

$Height(Joe, Short)$	$Height(Sue, Short)$
$Nationality(Joe, US)$	$Nationality(Sue, US)$
$Mother(Joe, Mary)$	$Mother(Sue, Mary)$
$Age(Joe, 8)$	$Age(Sue, 6)$

The following domain theory is helpful for acquiring the $HouseMates$ concept:

$$HouseMates(x, y) \leftarrow InSameFamily(x, y)$$
$$HouseMates(x, y) \leftarrow FraternityBrothers(x, y)$$
$$InSameFamily(x, y) \leftarrow Married(x, y)$$
$$InSameFamily(x, y) \leftarrow Youngster(x) \wedge Youngster(y) \wedge SameMother(x, y)$$
$$SameMother(x, y) \leftarrow Mother(x, z) \wedge Mother(y, z)$$
$$Youngster(x) \leftarrow Age(x, a) \wedge LessThan(a, 10)$$

Apply the PROLOG-EBG algorithm to the task of generalizing from the above instance, using the above domain theory. In particular,

(*a*) Show a hand-trace of the PROLOG-EBG algorithm applied to this problem; that is, show the explanation generated for the training instance, show the result of regressing the target concept through this explanation, and show the resulting Horn clause rule.

(*b*) Suppose that the target concept is "people who live with Joe" instead of "pairs of people who live together." Write down this target concept in terms of the above formalism. Assuming the same training instance and domain theory as before, what Horn clause rule will PROLOG-EBG produce for this new target concept?

11.2. As noted in Section 11.3.1, PROLOG-EBG can construct useful new features that are not explicit features of the instances, but that are defined in terms of the explicit features and that are useful for describing the appropriate generalization. These features are derived as a side effect of analyzing the training example explanation. A second method for deriving useful features is the BACKPROPAGATION algorithm for multilayer neural networks, in which new features are learned by the hidden units based on the statistical properties of a large number of examples. Can you suggest a way in which one might combine these analytical and inductive approaches to generating new features? (Warning: This is an open research problem.)

REFERENCES

Ahn, W., Mooney, R. J., Brewer, W. F., & DeJong, G. F. (1987). Schema acquisition from one example: Psychological evidence for explanation-based learning. *Ninth Annual Conference of the Cognitive Science Society* (pp. 50–57). Hillsdale, NJ: Lawrence Erlbaum Associates.

Bennett, S. W., & DeJong, G. F. (1996). Real-world robotics: Learning to plan for robust execution. *Machine Learning*, 23, 121.

Carbonell, J., Knoblock, C., & Minton, S. (1990). PRODIGY: An integrated architecture for planning and learning. In K. VanLehn (Ed.), *Architectures for Intelligence*. Hillsdale, NJ: Lawrence Erlbaum Associates.

Chien, S. (1993). NONMON: Learning with recoverable simplifications. In G. DeJong (Ed.), *Investigating explanation-based learning* (pp. 410–434). Boston, MA: Kluwer Academic Publishers.

Davies, T. R., and Russell, S. J. (1987). A logical approach to reasoning by analogy. *Proceedings of the 10th International Joint Conference on Artificial Intelligence* (pp. 264–270). San Mateo, CA: Morgan Kaufmann.

DeJong, G. (1981). Generalizations based on explanations. *Proceedings of the Seventh International Joint Conference on Artificial Intelligence* (pp. 67–70).

DeJong, G., & Mooney, R. (1986). Explanation-based learning: An alternative view. *Machine Learning*, 1(2), 145–176.

DeJong, G. (Ed.). (1993). *Investigating explanation-based learning*. Boston, MA: Kluwer Academic Publishers.

DeJong, G. (1994). Learning to plan in continuous domains. *Artificial Intelligence*, 64(1), 71–141.

DeJong, G. (1997). Explanation-based learning. In A. Tucker (Ed.), *The Computer Science and Engineering Handbook* (pp. 499–520). Boca Raton, FL: CRC Press.

Dietterich, T. G., Flann, N. S. (1995). Explanation-based learning and reinforcement learning: A unified view. *Proceedings of the 12th International Conference on Machine Learning* (pp. 176–184). San Mateo, CA: Morgan Kaufmann.

Doorenbos, R. E. (1993). Matching 100,000 learned rules. *Proceedings of the Eleventh National Conference on Artificial Intelligence* (pp. 290–296). AAAI Press/MIT Press.

Fikes, R., Hart, P., & Nilsson, N. (1972). Learning and executing generalized robot plans. *Artificial Intelligence*, 3(4), 251–288.

Fisher, D., Subramanian, D., & Tadepalli, P. (1992). An overview of current research on knowledge compilation and speedup learning. *Proceedings of the Second International Workshop on Knowledge Compilation and Speedup Learning*.

Flann, N. S., & Dietterich, T. G. (1989). A study of explanation-based methods for inductive learning. *Machine Learning*, 4, 187–226.

Gervasio, M. T., & DeJong, G. F. (1994). An incremental learning approach to completable planning. *Proceedings of the Eleventh International Conference on Machine Learning*, New Brunswick, NJ. San Mateo, CA: Morgan Kaufmann.

van Harmelen, F., & Bundy, A. (1988). Explanation-based generalisation = partial evaluation. *Artificial Intelligence*, 36(3), 401–412.

Kedar-Cabelli, S., & McCarty, T. (1987). Explanation-based generalization as resolution theorem proving. *Proceedings of the Fourth International Workshop on Machine Learning* (pp. 383–389). San Francisco: Morgan Kaufmann.

Kotovsky, L., & Baillargeon, R. (1994). Calibration-based reasoning about collision events in 11-month-old infants. *Cognition*, 51, 107–129.

Laird, J. E., Rosenbloom, P. S., & Newell, A. (1986). Chunking in SOAR: The anatomy of a general learning mechanism. *Machine Learning*, 1, 11.

Mahadevan, S., Mitchell, T., Mostow, D. J., Steinberg, L., & Tadepalli, P. (1993). An apprentice-based approach to knowledge acquisition. In S. Mahadevan, T. Mitchell, D. J. Mostow, L. Steinberg, & P. Tadepalli (Eds.), *Artificial Intelligence*, 64(1), 1–52.

Minton, S. (1988). *Learning search control knowledge: An explanation-based approach*. Boston, MA: Kluwer Academic Publishers.

Minton, S., Carbonell, J., Knoblock, C., Kuokka, D., Etzioni, O., & Gil, Y. (1989). Explanation-based learning: A problem solving perspective. *Artificial Intelligence*, 40, 63–118.

Minton, S. (1990). Quantitative results concerning the utility of explanation-based learning. *Artificial Intelligence*, 42, 363–391.

Mitchell, T. M. (1981). *Toward combining empirical and analytical methods for inferring heuristics* (Technical Report LCSR-TR-27), Rutgers Computer Science Department. (Also reprinted in A. Elithorn & R. Banerji (Eds), *Artificial and Human Intelligence*. North-Holland, 1984.)

Mitchell, T. M. (1983). Learning and problem-solving. *Proceedings of the Eighth International Joint Conference on Artificial Intelligence*. San Francisco: Morgan Kaufmann.

Mitchell, T. M., Keller, R., & Kedar-Cabelli, S. (1986). Explanation-based generalization: A unifying view. *Machine Learning*, 1(1), 47–80.

Mitchell, T. M. (1990). Becoming increasingly reactive. *Proceedings of the Eighth National Conference on Artificial Intelligence*. Menlo Park, CA: AAAI Press.

Mitchell, T. M., & Thrun, S. B. (1993). Explanation-based neural network learning for robot control. In S. Hanson et al. (Eds.), *Advances in neural information processing systems 5* (pp. 287–294). San Mateo, CA: Morgan-Kaufmann Press.

Newell, A. (1990). *Unified theories of cognition*. Cambridge, MA: Harvard University Press.

Qin, Y., Mitchell, T., & Simon, H. (1992). Using explanation-based generalization to simulate human learning from examples and learning by doing. *Proceedings of the Florida AI Research Symposium* (pp. 235–239).

Ram, A., & Leake, D. B. (Eds.). (1995). *Goal-driven learning*. Cambridge, MA: MIT Press.

Rosenbloom, P., & Laird, J. (1986). Mapping explanation-based generalization onto SOAR. *Fifth National Conference on Artificial Intelligence* (pp. 561–567). AAAI Press.

Russell, S. (1989). *The use of knowledge in analogy and induction*. San Francisco: Morgan Kaufmann.

Shavlik, J. W. (1990). Acquiring recursive and iterative concepts with explanation-based learning. *Machine Learning*, 5, 39.

Silver, B. (1983). Learning equation solving methods from worked examples. *Proceedings of the 1983 International Workshop on Machine Learning* (pp. 99–104). CS Department, University of Illinois at Urbana-Champaign.

Silver, B. (1986). Precondition analysis: Learning control information. In R. Michalski et al. (Eds.), *Machine Learning: An AI approach* (pp. 647–670). San Mateo, CA: Morgan Kaufmann.

Soloway, E. (1977). *Knowledge directed learning using multiple levels of description* (Ph.D. thesis). University of Massachusetts, Amherst.

Tadepalli, P. (1990). *Tractable learning and planning in games* (Technical report ML-TR-31) (Ph.D. dissertation). Rutgers University Computer Science Department.

Tambe, M., Newell, A., & Rosenbloom, P. S. (1990). The problem of expensive chunks and its solution by restricting expressiveness. *Machine Learning*, 5(4), 299–348.

Waldinger, R. (1977). Achieving several goals simultaneously. In E. Elcock & D. Michie (Eds.), *Machine Intelligence 8*. London: Ellis Horwood Ltd.

Winston, P., Binford, T., Katz, B., & Lowry, M. (1983). Learning physical descriptions from functional definitions, examples, and precedents. *Proceedings of the National Conference on Artificial Intelligence* (pp. 433–439). San Mateo, CA: Morgan Kaufmann.

Wisniewski, E. J., & Medin, D. L. (1995). Harpoons and long sticks: The interaction of theory and similarity in rule induction. In A. Ram & D. B. Leake (Eds.), *Goal-driven learning* (pp. 177–210). Cambridge, MA: MIT Press.

CHAPTER 12

COMBINING INDUCTIVE AND ANALYTICAL LEARNING

Purely inductive learning methods formulate general hypotheses by finding empirical regularities over the training examples. Purely analytical methods use prior knowledge to derive general hypotheses deductively. This chapter considers methods that combine inductive and analytical mechanisms to obtain the benefits of both approaches: better generalization accuracy when prior knowledge is available and reliance on observed training data to overcome shortcomings in prior knowledge. The resulting combined methods outperform both purely inductive and purely analytical learning methods. This chapter considers inductive-analytical learning methods based on both symbolic and artificial neural network representations.

12.1 MOTIVATION

In previous chapters we have seen two paradigms for machine learning: inductive learning and analytical learning. Inductive methods, such as decision tree induction and neural network BACKPROPAGATION, seek general hypotheses that fit the observed training data. Analytical methods, such as PROLOG-EBG, seek general hypotheses that fit prior knowledge while covering the observed data. These two learning paradigms are based on fundamentally different justifications for learned hypotheses and offer complementary advantages and disadvantages. Combining them offers the possibility of more powerful learning methods.

Purely analytical learning methods offer the advantage of generalizing more accurately from less data by using prior knowledge to guide learning. However, they can be misled when given incorrect or insufficient prior knowledge. Purely inductive methods offer the advantage that they require no explicit prior knowledge and learn regularities based solely on the training data. However, they can fail when given insufficient training data, and can be misled by the implicit inductive bias they must adopt in order to generalize beyond the observed data. Table 12.1 summarizes these complementary advantages and pitfalls of inductive and analytical learning methods. This chapter considers the question of how to combine the two into a single algorithm that captures the best aspects of both.

The difference between inductive and analytical learning methods can be seen in the nature of the *justifications* that can be given for their learned hypotheses. Hypotheses output by purely analytical learning methods such as PROLOG-EBG carry a *logical* justification; the output hypothesis follows deductively from the domain theory and training examples. Hypotheses output by purely inductive learning methods such as BACKPROPAGATION carry a *statistical* justification; the output hypothesis follows from statistical arguments that the training sample is sufficiently large that it is probably representative of the underlying distribution of examples. This statistical justification for induction is clearly articulated in the PAC-learning results discussed in Chapter 7.

Given that analytical methods provide logically justified hypotheses and inductive methods provide statistically justified hypotheses, it is easy to see why combining them would be useful: Logical justifications are only as compelling as the assumptions, or prior knowledge, on which they are built. They are suspect or powerless if prior knowledge is incorrect or unavailable. Statistical justifications are only as compelling as the data and statistical assumptions on which they rest. They are suspect or powerless when assumptions about the underlying distributions cannot be trusted or when data is scarce. In short, the two approaches work well for different types of problems. By combining them we can hope to devise a more general learning approach that covers a more broad range of learning tasks.

Figure 12.1 summarizes a spectrum of learning problems that varies by the availability of prior knowledge and training data. At one extreme, a large volume

	Inductive learning	**Analytical learning**
Goal:	Hypothesis fits data	Hypothesis fits domain theory
Justification:	Statistical inference	Deductive inference
Advantages:	Requires little prior knowledge	Learns from scarce data
Pitfalls:	Scarce data, incorrect bias	Imperfect domain theory

TABLE 12.1
Comparison of purely analytical and purely inductive learning.

Inductive learning ⟷ Analytical learning

Plentiful data
No prior knowledge

Perfect prior knowledge
Scarce data

FIGURE 12.1
A spectrum of learning tasks. At the left extreme, no prior knowledge is available, and purely inductive learning methods with high sample complexity are therefore necessary. At the rightmost extreme, a perfect domain theory is available, enabling the use of purely analytical methods such as PROLOG-EBG. Most practical problems lie somewhere between these two extremes.

of training data is available, but no prior knowledge. At the other extreme, strong prior knowledge is available, but little training data. Most practical learning problems lie somewhere between these two extremes of the spectrum. For example, in analyzing a database of medical records to learn "symptoms for which treatment x is more effective than treatment y," one often begins with approximate prior knowledge (e.g., a qualitative model of the cause-effect mechanisms underlying the disease) that suggests the patient's temperature is more likely to be relevant than the patient's middle initial. Similarly, in analyzing a stock market database to learn the target concept "companies whose stock value will double over the next 10 months," one might have approximate knowledge of economic causes and effects, suggesting that the gross revenue of the company is more likely to be relevant than the color of the company logo. In both of these settings, our own prior knowledge is incomplete, but is clearly useful in helping discriminate relevant features from irrelevant.

The question considered in this chapter is "What kinds of learning algorithms can we devise that make use of approximate prior knowledge, together with available data, to form general hypotheses?" Notice that even when using a purely inductive learning algorithm, one has the opportunity to make design choices based on prior knowledge of the particular learning task. For example, when applying BACKPROPAGATION to a problem such as speech recognition, one must choose the encoding of input and output data, the error function to be minimized during gradient descent, the number of hidden units, the topology of the network, the learning rate and momentum, etc. In making these choices, human designers have the opportunity to embed task-specific knowledge into the learning algorithm. The result, however, is a purely inductive instantiation of BACKPROPAGATION, *specialized* by the designer's choices to the task of speech recognition. Our interest here lies in something different. We are interested in systems that take prior knowledge as an *explicit input* to the learner, in the same sense that the training data is an explicit input, so that they remain general purpose algorithms, even while taking advantage of domain-specific knowledge. In brief, our interest here lies in *domain-independent algorithms that employ explicitly input domain-dependent knowledge.*

What criteria should we use to compare alternative approaches to combining inductive and analytical learning? Given that the learner will generally not know the quality of the domain theory or the training data in advance, we are interested in general methods that can operate robustly over the entire spectrum of problems of Figure 12.1. Some specific properties we would like from such a learning method include:

- Given no domain theory, it should learn at least as effectively as purely inductive methods.
- Given a perfect domain theory, it should learn at least as effectively as purely analytical methods.
- Given an imperfect domain theory and imperfect training data, it should combine the two to outperform either purely inductive or purely analytical methods.
- It should accommodate an unknown level of error in the training data.
- It should accommodate an unknown level of error in the domain theory.

Notice this list of desirable properties is quite ambitious. For example, accommodating errors in the training data is problematic even for statistically based induction without at least some prior knowledge or assumption regarding the distribution of errors. Combining inductive and analytical learning is an area of active current research. While the above list is a fair summary of what we would like our algorithms to accomplish, we do not yet have algorithms that satisfy all these constraints in a fully general fashion.

The next section provides a more detailed discussion of the combined inductive-analytical learning problem. Subsequent sections describe three different approaches to combining approximate prior knowledge with available training data to guide the learner's search for an appropriate hypothesis. Each of these three approaches has been demonstrated to outperform purely inductive methods in multiple task domains. For ease of comparison, we use a single example problem to illustrate all three approaches.

12.2 INDUCTIVE-ANALYTICAL APPROACHES TO LEARNING

12.2.1 The Learning Problem

To summarize, the learning problem considered in this chapter is

Given:

- A set of training examples D, possibly containing errors
- A domain theory B, possibly containing errors
- A space of candidate hypotheses H

Determine:

- A hypothesis that best fits the training examples and domain theory

What precisely shall we mean by "the hypothesis that best fits the training examples and domain theory?" In particular, shall we prefer hypotheses that fit the data a little better at the expense of fitting the theory less well, or vice versa? We can be more precise by defining measures of hypothesis error with respect to the data and with respect to the domain theory, then phrasing the question in terms of these errors. Recall from Chapter 5 that $error_D(h)$ is defined to be the proportion of examples from D that are misclassified by h. Let us define the error $error_B(h)$ of h with respect to a domain theory B to be the probability that h will disagree with B on the classification of a randomly drawn instance. We can attempt to characterize the desired output hypothesis in terms of these errors. For example, we could require the hypothesis that minimizes some combined measure of these errors, such as

$$\underset{h \in H}{\operatorname{argmin}}\ k_D error_D(h) + k_B error_B(h)$$

While this appears reasonable at first glance, it is not clear what values to assign to k_D and k_B to specify the relative importance of fitting the data versus fitting the theory. If we have a very poor theory and a great deal of reliable data, it will be best to weight $error_D(h)$ more heavily. Given a strong theory and a small sample of very noisy data, the best results would be obtained by weighting $error_B(h)$ more heavily. Of course if the learner does not know in advance the quality of the domain theory or training data, it will be unclear how it should weight these two error components.

An alternative perspective on the question of how to weight prior knowledge and data is the Bayesian perspective. Recall from Chapter 6 that Bayes theorem describes how to compute the posterior probability $P(h|D)$ of hypothesis h given observed training data D. In particular, Bayes theorem computes this posterior probability based on the observed data D, together with prior knowledge in the form of $P(h)$, $P(D)$, and $P(D|h)$. Thus we can think of $P(h)$, $P(D)$, and $P(D|h)$ as a form of background knowledge or domain theory, and we can think of Bayes theorem as a method for weighting this domain theory, together with the observed data D, to assign a posterior probability $P(h|D)$ to h. The Bayesian view is that one should simply choose the hypothesis whose posterior probability is greatest, and that Bayes theorem provides the proper method for weighting the contribution of this prior knowledge and observed data. Unfortunately, Bayes theorem implicitly assumes *perfect* knowledge about the probability distributions $P(h)$, $P(D)$, and $P(D|h)$. When these quantities are only imperfectly known, Bayes theorem alone does not prescribe how to combine them with the observed data. (One possible approach in such cases is to assume prior probability distributions over $P(h)$, $P(D)$, and $P(D|h)$ themselves, then calculate the expected value of the posterior $P(h|D)$. However, this requires additional knowledge about the priors over $P(h)$, $P(D)$, and $P(D|h)$, so it does not really solve the general problem.)

We will revisit the question of what we mean by "best" fit to the hypothesis and data as we examine specific algorithms. For now, we will simply say that the learning problem is to minimize some combined measure of the error of the hypothesis over the data and the domain theory.

12.2.2 Hypothesis Space Search

How can the domain theory and training data best be combined to constrain the search for an acceptable hypothesis? This remains an open question in machine learning. This chapter surveys a variety of approaches that have been proposed, many of which consist of extensions to inductive methods we have already studied (e.g., BACKPROPAGATION, FOIL).

One way to understand the range of possible approaches is to return to our view of learning as a task of searching through the space of alternative hypotheses. We can characterize most learning methods as search algorithms by describing the hypothesis space H they search, the initial hypothesis h_0 at which they begin their search, the set of search operators O that define individual search steps, and the goal criterion G that specifies the search objective. In this chapter we explore three different methods for using prior knowledge to alter the search performed by purely inductive methods.

- *Use prior knowledge to derive an initial hypothesis from which to begin the search.* In this approach the domain theory B is used to construct an initial hypothesis h_0 that is consistent with B. A standard inductive method is then applied, starting with the initial hypothesis h_0. For example, the KBANN system described below learns artificial neural networks in this way. It uses prior knowledge to design the interconnections and weights for an initial network, so that this initial network is perfectly consistent with the given domain theory. This initial network hypothesis is then refined inductively using the BACKPROPAGATION algorithm and available data. Beginning the search at a hypothesis consistent with the domain theory makes it more likely that the final output hypothesis will better fit this theory.

- *Use prior knowledge to alter the objective of the hypothesis space search.* In this approach, the goal criterion G is modified to require that the output hypothesis fits the domain theory as well as the training examples. For example, the EBNN system described below learns neural networks in this way. Whereas inductive learning of neural networks performs gradient descent search to minimize the squared error of the network over the training data, EBNN performs gradient descent to optimize a different criterion. This modified criterion includes an additional term that measures the error of the learned network relative to the domain theory.

- *Use prior knowledge to alter the available search steps.* In this approach, the set of search operators O is altered by the domain theory. For example, the FOCL system described below learns sets of Horn clauses in this way. It is based on the inductive system FOIL, which conducts a greedy search through the space of possible Horn clauses, at each step revising its current hypothesis by adding a single new literal. FOCL uses the domain theory to expand the set of alternatives available when revising the hypothesis, allowing the addition of multiple literals in a single search step when warranted by the domain theory. In this way, FOCL allows single-step moves through the hypothesis space that would correspond to many steps using the original inductive algorithm. These "macro-moves" can dramatically alter the course of the search, so that the final hypothesis found consistent with the data is different from the one that would be found using only the inductive search steps.

The following sections describe each of these approaches in turn.

12.3 USING PRIOR KNOWLEDGE TO INITIALIZE THE HYPOTHESIS

One approach to using prior knowledge is to initialize the hypothesis to perfectly fit the domain theory, then inductively refine this initial hypothesis as needed to fit the training data. This approach is used by the KBANN (Knowledge-Based Artificial Neural Network) algorithm to learn artificial neural networks. In KBANN an initial network is first constructed so that for every possible instance, the classification assigned by the network is identical to that assigned by the domain theory. The BACKPROPAGATION algorithm is then employed to adjust the weights of this initial network as needed to fit the training examples.

It is easy to see the motivation for this technique: if the domain theory is correct, the initial hypothesis will correctly classify all the training examples and there will be no need to revise it. However, if the initial hypothesis is found to imperfectly classify the training examples, then it will be refined inductively to improve its fit to the training examples. Recall that in the purely inductive BACKPROPAGATION algorithm, weights are typically initialized to small random values. The intuition behind KBANN is that even if the domain theory is only approximately correct, initializing the network to fit this domain theory will give a better starting approximation to the target function than initializing the network to random initial weights. This should lead, in turn, to better generalization accuracy for the final hypothesis.

This *initialize-the-hypothesis* approach to using the domain theory has been explored by several researchers, including Shavlik and Towell (1989), Towell and Shavlik (1994), Fu (1989, 1993), and Pratt (1993a, 1993b). We will use the KBANN algorithm described in Shavlik and Towell (1989) to illustrate this approach.

12.3.1 The KBANN Algorithm

The KBANN algorithm exemplifies the initialize-the-hypothesis approach to using domain theories. It assumes a domain theory represented by a set of propositional, nonrecursive Horn clauses. A Horn clause is propositional if it contains no variables. The input and output of KBANN are as follows:

KBANN(*Domain_Theory*, *Training_Examples*)
Domain_Theory: Set of propositional, nonrecursive Horn clauses.
Training_Examples: Set of ⟨input output⟩ pairs of the target function.

Analytical step: Create an initial network equivalent to the domain theory.

1. For each instance attribute create a network input.
2. For each Horn clause in the *Domain_Theory*, create a network unit as follows:
   - Connect the inputs of this unit to the attributes tested by the clause antecedents.
   - For each non-negated antecedent of the clause, assign a weight of W to the corresponding sigmoid unit input.
   - For each negated antecedent of the clause, assign a weight of $-W$ to the corresponding sigmoid unit input.
   - Set the threshold weight w_0 for this unit to $-(n - .5)W$, where n is the number of non-negated antecedents of the clause.
3. Add additional connections among the network units, connecting each network unit at depth i from the input layer to all network units at depth $i + 1$. Assign random near-zero weights to these additional connections.

Inductive step: Refine the initial network.

4. Apply the BACKPROPAGATION algorithm to adjust the initial network weights to fit the *Training_Examples*.

TABLE 12.2
The KBANN algorithm. The domain theory is translated into an equivalent neural network (steps 1–3), which is inductively refined using the BACKPROPAGATION algorithm (step 4). A typical value for the constant W is 4.0.

Given:

- A set of training examples
- A domain theory consisting of nonrecursive, propositional Horn clauses

Determine:

- An artificial neural network that fits the training examples, biased by the domain theory

The two stages of the KBANN algorithm are first to create an artificial neural network that perfectly fits the domain theory and second to use the BACKPROPAGATION algorithm to refine this initial network to fit the training examples. The details of this algorithm, including the algorithm for creating the initial network, are given in Table 12.2 and illustrated in Section 12.3.2.

12.3.2 An Illustrative Example

To illustrate the operation of KBANN, consider the simple learning problem summarized in Table 12.3, adapted from Towell and Shavlik (1989). Here each instance describes a physical object in terms of the material from which it is made, whether it is light, etc. The task is to learn the target concept *Cup* defined over such physical objects. Table 12.3 describes a set of training examples and a domain theory for the *Cup* target concept. Notice the domain theory defines a *Cup*

Domain theory:

Cup ← *Stable, Liftable, OpenVessel*
Stable ← *BottomIsFlat*
Liftable ← *Graspable, Light*
Graspable ← *HasHandle*
OpenVessel ← *HasConcavity, ConcavityPointsUp*

Training examples:

	Cups				*Non-Cups*					
BottomIsFlat	✓	✓	✓	✓	✓	✓	✓			✓
ConcavityPointsUp	✓	✓	✓	✓	✓		✓	✓		
Expensive	✓		✓				✓		✓	
Fragile	✓	✓			✓	✓		✓		✓
HandleOnTop					✓		✓			
HandleOnSide	✓			✓					✓	
HasConcavity	✓	✓	✓	✓	✓		✓	✓	✓	✓
HasHandle	✓			✓	✓		✓		✓	
Light	✓	✓	✓	✓	✓	✓	✓		✓	
MadeOfCeramic	✓				✓		✓	✓		
MadeOfPaper				✓					✓	
MadeOfStyrofoam		✓	✓			✓				✓

TABLE 12.3
The *Cup* learning task. An approximate domain theory and a set of training examples for the target concept *Cup*.

as an object that is *Stable*, *Liftable*, and an *OpenVessel*. The domain theory also defines each of these three attributes in terms of more primitive attributes, terminating in the primitive, operational attributes that describe the instances. Note the domain theory is not perfectly consistent with the training examples. For example, the domain theory fails to classify the second and third training examples as positive examples. Nevertheless, the domain theory forms a useful approximation to the target concept. KBANN uses the domain theory and training examples together to learn the target concept more accurately than it could from either alone.

In the first stage of the KBANN algorithm (steps 1–3 in the algorithm), an initial network is constructed that is consistent with the domain theory. For example, the network constructed from the *Cup* domain theory is shown in Figure 12.2. In general the network is constructed by creating a sigmoid threshold unit for each Horn clause in the domain theory. KBANN follows the convention that a sigmoid output value greater than 0.5 is interpreted as *True* and a value below 0.5 as *False*. Each unit is therefore constructed so that its output will be greater than 0.5 just in those cases where the corresponding Horn clause applies. For each antecedent to the Horn clause, an input is created to the corresponding sigmoid unit. The weights of the sigmoid unit are then set so that it computes the logical AND of its inputs. In particular, for each input corresponding to a non-negated antecedent,

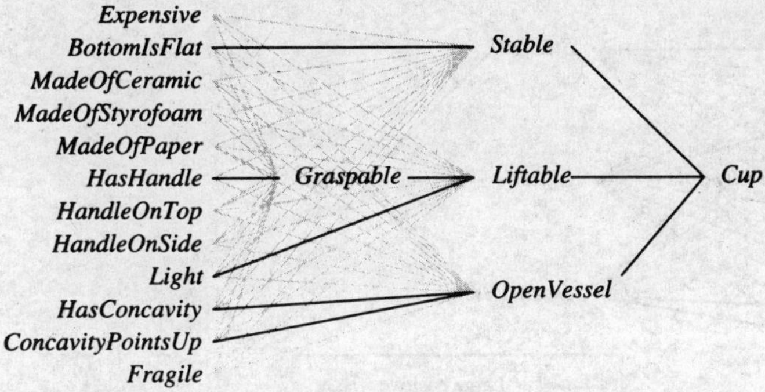

FIGURE 12.2
A neural network equivalent to the domain theory. This network, created in the first stage of the KBANN algorithm, produces output classifications identical to those of the given domain theory clauses. Dark lines indicate connections with weight W and correspond to antecedents of clauses from the domain theory. Light lines indicate connections with weights of approximately zero.

the weight is set to some positive constant W. For each input corresponding to a negated antecedent, the weight is set to $-W$. The threshold weight of the unit, w_0 is then set to $-(n-.5)W$, where n is the number of non-negated antecedents. When unit input values are 1 or 0, this assures that their weighted sum plus w_0 will be positive (and the sigmoid output will therefore be greater than 0.5) if and only if all clause antecedents are satisfied. Note for sigmoid units at the second and subsequent layers, unit inputs will not necessarily be 1 and 0 and the above argument may not apply. However, if a sufficiently large value is chosen for W, this KBANN algorithm can correctly encode the domain theory for arbitrarily deep networks. Towell and Shavlik (1994) report using $W = 4.0$ in many of their experiments.

Each sigmoid unit input is connected to the appropriate network input or to the output of another sigmoid unit, to mirror the graph of dependencies among the corresponding attributes in the domain theory. As a final step many additional inputs are added to each threshold unit, with their weights set approximately to zero. The role of these additional connections is to enable the network to inductively learn additional dependencies beyond those suggested by the given domain theory. The solid lines in the network of Figure 12.2 indicate unit inputs with weights of W, whereas the lightly shaded lines indicate connections with initial weights near zero. It is easy to verify that for sufficiently large values of W this network will output values identical to the predictions of the domain theory.

The second stage of KBANN (step 4 in the algorithm of Table 12.2) uses the training examples and the BACKPROPAGATION algorithm to refine the initial network weights. Of course if the domain theory and training examples contain no errors, the initial network will already fit the training data. In the *Cup* example, however, the domain theory and training data are inconsistent, and this step therefore alters the initial network weights. The resulting trained network is summarized in Figure 12.3, with dark solid lines indicating the largest positive weights, dashed lines indicating the largest negative weights, and light lines

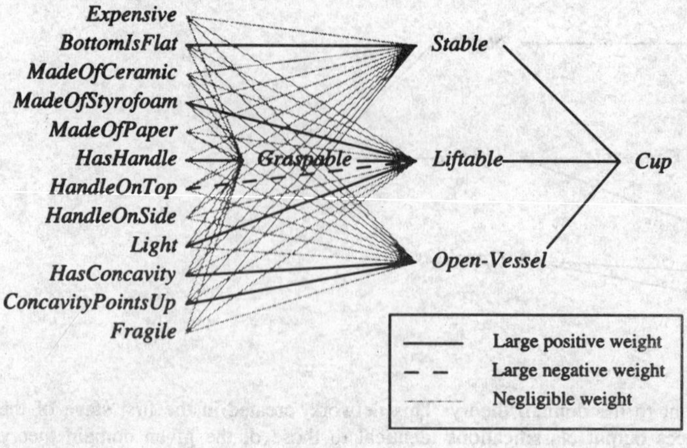

FIGURE 12.3
Result of inductively refining the initial network. KBANN uses the training examples to modify the network weights derived from the domain theory. Notice the new dependency of *Liftable* on *MadeOfStyrofoam* and *HandleOnTop*.

indicating negligible weights. Although the initial network misclassifies several training examples from Table 12.3, the refined network of Figure 12.3 perfectly classifies all of these training examples.

It is interesting to compare the final, inductively refined network weights to the initial weights derived from the domain theory. As can be seen in Figure 12.3, significant new dependencies were discovered during the inductive step, including the dependency of the *Liftable* unit on the feature *MadeOfStyrofoam*. It is important to keep in mind that while the unit labeled *Liftable* was initially defined by the given Horn clause for *Liftable*, the subsequent weight changes performed by BACKPROPAGATION may have dramatically changed the meaning of this hidden unit. After training of the network, this unit may take on a very different meaning unrelated to the initial notion of *Liftable*.

12.3.3 Remarks

To summarize, KBANN analytically creates a network equivalent to the given domain theory, then inductively refines this initial hypothesis to better fit the training data. In doing so, it modifies the network weights as needed to overcome inconsistencies between the domain theory and observed data.

The chief benefit of KBANN over purely inductive BACKPROPAGATION (beginning with random initial weights) is that it typically generalizes more accurately than BACKPROPAGATION when given an approximately correct domain theory, especially when training data is scarce. KBANN and other initialize-the-hypothesis approaches have been demonstrated to outperform purely inductive systems in several practical problems. For example, Towell et al. (1990) describe the application of KBANN to a molecular genetics problem. Here the task was to learn to recognize DNA segments called promoter regions, which influence gene activity. In this experiment KBANN was given an initial domain theory obtained from a molecular geneticist, and a set of 53 positive and 53 negative training examples of promoter regions. Performance was evaluated using a leave-one-out strategy in which the system was run 106 different times. On each iteration KBANN was trained using 105 of the 106 examples and tested on the remaining example. The results of these 106 experiments were accumulated to provide an estimate of the true error rate. KBANN obtained an error rate of 4/106, compared to an error rate of 8/106 using standard BACKPROPAGATION. A variant of the KBANN approach was applied by Fu (1993), who reports an error rate of 2/106 on the same data. Thus, the impact of prior knowledge in these experiments was to reduce significantly the error rate. The training data for this experiment is available at World Wide Web site http://www.ics.uci.edu/~mlearn/MLRepository.html.

Both Fu (1993) and Towell et al. (1990) report that Horn clauses extracted from the final trained network provided a refined domain theory that better fit the observed data. Although it is sometimes possible to map from the learned network weights back to a refined set of Horn clauses, in the general case this is problematic because some weight settings have no direct Horn clause analog. Craven and Shavlik (1994) and Craven (1996) describe alternative methods for extracting symbolic rules from learned networks.

To understand the significance of KBANN it is useful to consider how its hypothesis search differs from that of the purely inductive BACKPROPAGATION algorithm. The hypothesis space search conducted by both algorithms is depicted schematically in Figure 12.4. As shown there, the key difference is the initial hypothesis from which weight tuning is performed. In the case that multiple hypotheses (weight vectors) can be found that fit the data—a condition that will be especially likely when training data is scarce—KBANN is likely to converge to a hypothesis that generalizes beyond the data in a way that is more similar to the domain theory predictions. On the other hand, the particular hypothesis to which BACKPROPAGATION converges will more likely be a hypothesis with small weights, corresponding roughly to a generalization bias of smoothly interpolating between training examples. In brief, KBANN uses a domain-specific theory to bias generalization, whereas BACKPROPAGATION uses a domain-independent syntactic bias toward small weight values. Note in this summary we have ignored the effect of local minima on the search.

Limitations of KBANN include the fact that it can accommodate only propositional domain theories; that is, collections of variable-free Horn clauses. It is also possible for KBANN to be misled when given highly inaccurate domain theories, so that its generalization accuracy can deteriorate below the level of BACKPROPAGATION. Nevertheless, it and related algorithms have been shown to be useful for several practical problems.

KBANN illustrates the initialize-the-hypothesis approach to combining analytical and inductive learning. Other examples of this approach include Fu (1993); Gallant (1988); Bradshaw et al. (1989); Yang and Bhargava (1990); Lacher et al. (1991). These approaches vary in the exact technique for constructing the initial

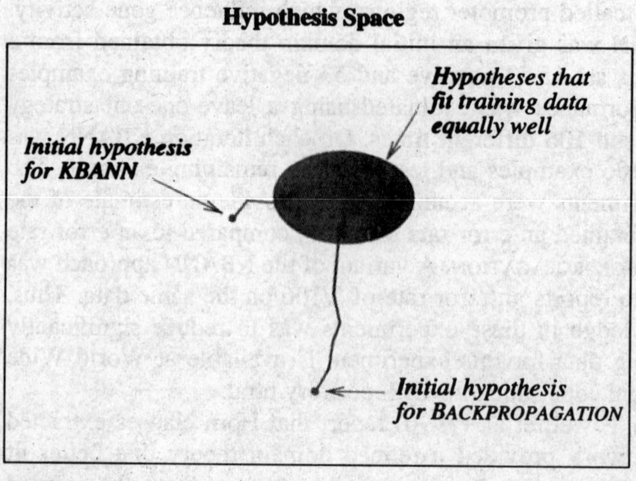

FIGURE 12.4
Hypothesis space search in KBANN. KBANN initializes the network to fit the domain theory, whereas BACKPROPAGATION initializes the network to small random weights. Both then refine the weights iteratively using the same gradient descent rule. When multiple hypotheses can be found that fit the training data (shaded region), KBANN and BACKPROPAGATION are likely to find different hypotheses due to their different starting points.

network, the application of BACKPROPAGATION to weight tuning, and in methods for extracting symbolic descriptions from the refined network. Pratt (1993a, 1993b) describes an initialize-the-hypothesis approach in which the prior knowledge is provided by a previously learned neural network for a related task, rather than a manually provided symbolic domain theory. Methods for training the values of Bayesian belief networks, as discussed in Section 6.11, can also be viewed as using prior knowledge to initialize the hypothesis. Here the prior knowledge corresponds to a set of conditional independence assumptions that determine the graph structure of the Bayes net, whose conditional probability tables are then induced from the training data.

12.4 USING PRIOR KNOWLEDGE TO ALTER THE SEARCH OBJECTIVE

The above approach begins the gradient descent search with a hypothesis that perfectly fits the domain theory, then perturbs this hypothesis as needed to maximize the fit to the training data. An alternative way of using prior knowledge is to incorporate it into the error criterion minimized by gradient descent, so that the network must fit a combined function of the training data and domain theory. In this section, we consider using prior knowledge in this fashion. In particular, we consider prior knowledge in the form of known derivatives of the target function. Certain types of prior knowledge can be expressed quite naturally in this form. For example, in training a neural network to recognize handwritten characters we can specify certain derivatives of the target function in order to express our prior knowledge that "the identity of the character is independent of small translations and rotations of the image."

Below we describe the TANGENTPROP algorithm, which trains a neural network to fit both training values and training derivatives. Section 12.4.4 then describes how these training derivatives can be obtained from a domain theory similar to the one used in the *Cup* example of Section 12.3. In particular, it discusses how the EBNN algorithm constructs explanations of individual training examples in order to extract training derivatives for use by TANGENTPROP. TANGENTPROP and EBNN have been demonstrated to outperform purely inductive methods in a variety of domains, including character and object recognition, and robot perception and control tasks.

12.4.1 The TANGENTPROP Algorithm

TANGENTPROP (Simard et al. 1992) accommodates domain knowledge expressed as derivatives of the target function with respect to transformations of its inputs. Consider a learning task involving an instance space X and target function f. Up to now we have assumed that each training example consists of a pair $\langle x_i, f(x_i)\rangle$ that describes some instance x_i and its training value $f(x_i)$. The TANGENTPROP algorithm assumes various training derivatives of the target function are also provided. For example, if each instance x_i is described by a single real value, then each training example may be of the form $\langle x_i, f(x_i), \frac{\partial f(x)}{\partial x}|_{x_i}\rangle$. Here $\frac{\partial f(x)}{\partial x}|_{x_i}$ denotes the derivative of the target function f with respect to x, evaluated at the point $x = x_i$.

To develop an intuition for the benefits of providing training derivatives as well as training values during learning, consider the simple learning task depicted in Figure 12.5. The task is to learn the target function f shown in the leftmost plot of the figure, based on the three training examples shown: $\langle x_1, f(x_1)\rangle$, $\langle x_2, f(x_2)\rangle$, and $\langle x_3, f(x_3)\rangle$. Given these three training examples, the BACKPROPAGATION algorithm can be expected to hypothesize a smooth function, such as the function g depicted in the middle plot of the figure. The rightmost plot shows the effect of

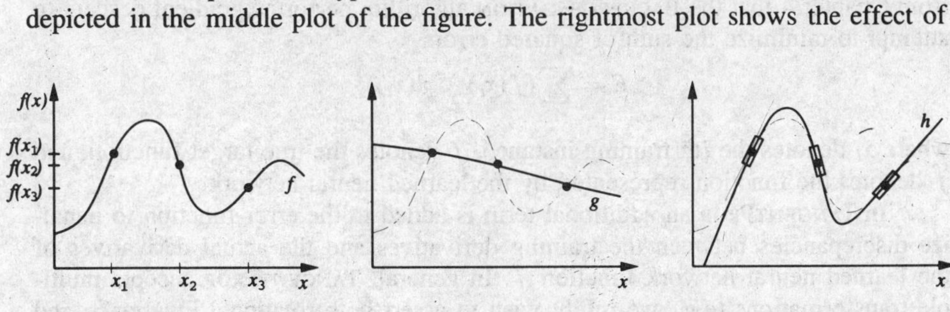

FIGURE 12.5
Fitting values and derivatives with TANGENTPROP. Let f be the target function for which three examples $\langle x_1, f(x_1)\rangle$, $\langle x_2, f(x_2)\rangle$, and $\langle x_3, f(x_3)\rangle$ are known. Based on these points the learner might generate the hypothesis g. If the derivatives are also known, the learner can generalize more accurately h.

providing training derivatives, or slopes, as additional information for each training example (e.g., $\langle x_1, f(x_1), \frac{\partial f(x)}{\partial x}|_{x_1}\rangle$). By fitting both the training values $f(x_i)$ and these training derivatives $\frac{\partial f(x)}{\partial x}|_{x_i}$, the learner has a better chance to correctly generalize from the sparse training data. To summarize, the impact of including the training derivatives is to override the usual syntactic inductive bias of BACKPROPAGATION that favors a smooth interpolation between points, replacing it by explicit input information about required derivatives. The resulting hypothesis h shown in the rightmost plot of the figure provides a much more accurate estimate of the true target function f.

In the above example, we considered only simple kinds of derivatives of the target function. In fact, TANGENTPROP can accept training derivatives with respect to various transformations of the input x. Consider, for example, the task of learning to recognize handwritten characters. In particular, assume the input x corresponds to an image containing a single handwritten character, and the task is to correctly classify the character. In this task, we might be interested in informing the learner that "the target function is invariant to small rotations of the character within the image." In order to express this prior knowledge to the learner, we first define a transformation $s(\alpha, x)$, which rotates the image x by α degrees. Now we can express our assertion about rotational invariance by stating that for each training instance x_i, the derivative of the target function with respect to this transformation is zero (i.e., that rotating the input image does not alter the value of the target function). In other words, we can assert the following training derivative for every training instance x_i

$$\frac{\partial f(s(\alpha, x_i))}{\partial \alpha} = 0$$

where f is the target function and $s(\alpha, x_i)$ is the image resulting from applying the transformation s to the image x_i.

How are such training derivatives used by TANGENTPROP to constrain the weights of the neural network? In TANGENTPROP these training derivatives are incorporated into the error function that is minimized by gradient descent. Recall from Chapter 4 that the BACKPROPAGATION algorithm performs gradient descent to attempt to minimize the sum of squared errors

$$E = \sum_i (f(x_i) - \hat{f}(x_i))^2$$

where x_i denotes the ith training instance, f denotes the true target function, and $\hat{f}$ denotes the function represented by the learned neural network.

In TANGENTPROP an additional term is added to the error function to penalize discrepancies between the training derivatives and the actual derivatives of the learned neural network function $\hat{f}$. In general, TANGENTPROP accepts multiple transformations (e.g., we might wish to assert both rotational invariance and translational invariance of the character identity). Each transformation must be of the form $s_j(\alpha, x)$ where α is a continuous parameter, where s_j is differentiable, and where $s_j(0, x) = x$ (e.g., for rotation of zero degrees the transformation is the identity function). For each such transformation, $s_j(\alpha, x)$, TANGENT-

PROP considers the squared error between the specified training derivative and the actual derivative of the learned neural network. The modified error function is

$$E = \sum_i \left[(f(x_i) - \hat{f}(x_i))^2 + \mu \sum_j \left(\frac{\partial f(s_j(\alpha, x_i))}{\partial \alpha} - \frac{\partial \hat{f}(s_j(\alpha, x_i))}{\partial \alpha} \right)^2_{\alpha=0} \right] \quad (12.1)$$

where μ is a constant provided by the user to determine the relative importance of fitting training values versus fitting training derivatives. Notice the first term in this definition of E is the original squared error of the network versus training *values*, and the second term is the squared error in the network versus training *derivatives*.

Simard et al. (1992) give the gradient descent rule for minimizing this extended error function E. It can be derived in a fashion analogous to the derivation given in Chapter 4 for the simpler BACKPROPAGATION rule.

12.4.2 An Illustrative Example

Simard et al. (1992) present results comparing the generalization accuracy of TANGENTPROP and purely inductive BACKPROPAGATION for the problem of recognizing handwritten characters. More specifically, the task in this case is to label images containing a single digit between 0 and 9. In one experiment, both TANGENTPROP and BACKPROPAGATION were trained using training sets of varying size, then evaluated based on their performance over a separate test set of 160 examples. The prior knowledge given to TANGENTPROP was the fact that the classification of the digit is invariant of vertical and horizontal translation of the image (i.e., that the derivative of the target function was 0 with respect to these transformations). The results, shown in Table 12.4, demonstrate the ability of TANGENTPROP using this prior knowledge to generalize more accurately than purely inductive BACKPROPAGATION.

Training set size	Percent error on test set	
	TANGENTPROP	BACKPROPAGATION
10	34	48
20	17	33
40	7	18
80	4	10
160	0	3
320	0	0

TABLE 12.4
Generalization accuracy for TANGENTPROP and BACKPROPAGATION, for handwritten digit recognition. TANGENTPROP generalizes more accurately due to its prior knowledge that the identity of the digit is invariant of translation. These results are from Simard et al. (1992).

12.4.3 Remarks

To summarize, TANGENTPROP uses prior knowledge in the form of desired derivatives of the target function with respect to transformations of its inputs. It combines this prior knowledge with observed training data, by minimizing an objective function that measures both the network's error with respect to the training example values (fitting the data) and its error with respect to the desired derivatives (fitting the prior knowledge). The value of μ determines the degree to which the network will fit one or the other of these two components in the total error. The behavior of the algorithm is sensitive to μ, which must be chosen by the designer.

Although TANGENTPROP succeeds in combining prior knowledge with training data to guide learning of neural networks, it is not robust to errors in the prior knowledge. Consider what will happen when prior knowledge is incorrect, that is, when the training derivatives input to the learner do not correctly reflect the derivatives of the true target function. In this case the algorithm will attempt to fit incorrect derivatives. It may therefore generalize less accurately than if it ignored this prior knowledge altogether and used the purely inductive BACKPROPAGATION algorithm. If we knew in advance the degree of error in the training derivatives, we might use this information to select the constant μ that determines the relative importance of fitting training values and fitting training derivatives. However, this information is unlikely to be known in advance. In the next section we discuss the EBNN algorithm, which automatically selects values for μ on an example-by-example basis in order to address the possibility of incorrect prior knowledge.

It is interesting to compare the search through hypothesis space (weight space) performed by TANGENTPROP, KBANN, and BACKPROPAGATION. TANGENTPROP incorporates prior knowledge to influence the hypothesis search by altering the objective function to be minimized by gradient descent. This corresponds to altering the goal of the hypothesis space search, as illustrated in Figure 12.6. Like BACKPROPAGATION (but unlike KBANN), TANGENTPROP begins the search with an initial network of small random weights. However, the gradient descent training rule produces different weight updates than BACKPROPAGATION, resulting in a different final hypothesis. As shown in the figure, the set of hypotheses that minimizes the TANGENTPROP objective may differ from the set that minimizes the BACKPROPAGATION objective. Importantly, if the training examples and prior knowledge are both correct, and the target function can be accurately represented by the ANN, then the set of weight vectors that satisfy the TANGENTPROP objective will be a subset of those satisfying the weaker BACKPROPAGATION objective. The difference between these two sets of final hypotheses is the set of incorrect hypotheses that will be considered by BACKPROPAGATION, but ruled out by TANGENTPROP due to its prior knowledge.

Note one alternative to fitting the training derivatives of the target function is to simply synthesize additional training examples near the observed training examples, using the known training derivatives to estimate training values for these nearby instances. For example, one could take a training image in the above character recognition task, translate it a small amount, and assert that the trans-

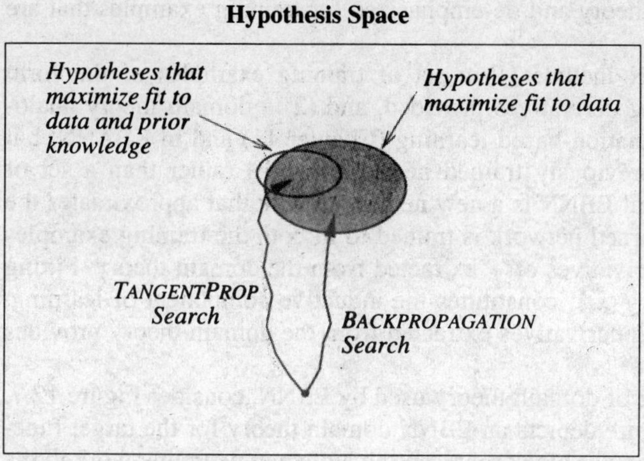

FIGURE 12.6
Hypothesis space search in TANGENTPROP. TANGENTPROP initializes the network to small random weights, just as in BACKPROPAGATION. However, it uses a different error function to drive the gradient descent search. The error used by TANGENTPROP includes both the error in predicting training *values* and in predicting the training *derivatives* provided as prior knowledge.

lated image belonged to the same class as the original example. We might expect that fitting these synthesized examples using BACKPROPAGATION would produce results similar to fitting the original training examples and derivatives using TANGENTPROP. Simard et al. (1992) report experiments showing similar generalization error in the two cases, but report that TANGENTPROP converges considerably more efficiently. It is interesting to note that the ALVINN system, which learns to steer an autonomous vehicle (see Chapter 4), uses a very similar approach to synthesize additional training examples. It uses prior knowledge of how the desired steering direction changes with horizontal translation of the camera image to create multiple synthetic training examples to augment each observed training example.

12.4.4 The EBNN Algorithm

The EBNN (Explanation-Based Neural Network learning) algorithm (Mitchell and Thrun 1993a; Thrun 1996) builds on the TANGENTPROP algorithm in two significant ways. First, instead of relying on the user to provide training derivatives, EBNN computes training derivatives itself for each observed training example. These training derivatives are calculated by explaining each training example in terms of a given domain theory, then extracting training derivatives from this explanation. Second, EBNN addresses the issue of how to weight the relative importance of the inductive and analytical components of learning (i.e., how to select the parameter μ in Equation [12.1]). The value of μ is chosen independently for each training example, based on a heuristic that considers how accurately the domain theory predicts the training value for this particular example. Thus, the analytical component of learning is emphasized for those training examples that are correctly explained by the domain theory and de-emphasized for training examples that are poorly explained.

The inputs to EBNN include (1) a set of training examples of the form $\langle x_i, f(x_i)\rangle$ with no training derivatives provided, and (2) a domain theory analogous to that used in explanation-based learning (Chapter 11) and in KBANN, but represented by a set of previously trained neural networks rather than a set of Horn clauses. The output of EBNN is a new neural network that approximates the target function f. This learned network is trained to fit both the training examples $\langle x_i, f(x_i)\rangle$ and training derivatives of f extracted from the domain theory. Fitting the training examples $\langle x_i, f(x_i)\rangle$ constitutes the inductive component of learning, whereas fitting the training derivatives extracted from the domain theory provides the analytical component.

To illustrate the type of domain theory used by EBNN, consider Figure 12.7. The top portion of this figure depicts an EBNN domain theory for the target function Cup, with each rectangular block representing a distinct neural network in the domain theory. Notice in this example there is one network for each of the Horn clauses in the symbolic domain theory of Table 12.3. For example, the network labeled *Graspable* takes as input the description of an instance and produces as output a value indicating whether the object is graspable (EBNN typically represents true propositions by the value 0.8 and false propositions by the value 0.2). This network is analogous to the Horn clause for *Graspable* given in Table 12.3. Some networks take the outputs of other networks as their inputs (e.g., the rightmost network labeled Cup takes its inputs from the outputs of the *Stable*, *Liftable*, and $OpenVessel$ networks). Thus, the networks that make up the domain theory can be chained together to infer the target function value for the input instance, just as Horn clauses might be chained together for this purpose. In general, these domain theory networks may be provided to the learner by some external source, or they may be the result of previous learning by the same system. EBNN makes use of these domain theory networks to learn the new target function. It does not alter the domain theory networks during this process.

The goal of EBNN is to learn a new neural network to describe the target function. We will refer to this new network as the *target network*. In the example of Figure 12.7, the target network Cup_{target} shown at the bottom of the figure takes as input the description of an arbitrary instance and outputs a value indicating whether the object is a Cup.

EBNN learns the target network by invoking the TANGENTPROP algorithm described in the previous section. Recall that TANGENTPROP trains a network to fit both training values and training derivatives. EBNN passes along to TANGENTPROP the training values $\langle x_i, f(x_i)\rangle$ that it receives as input. In addition, EBNN provides TANGENTPROP with derivatives that it calculates from the domain theory. To see how EBNN calculates these training derivatives, consider again Figure 12.7. The top portion of this figure shows the domain theory prediction of the target function value for a particular training instance, x_i. EBNN calculates the derivative of this prediction with respect to each feature of the input instance. For the example in the figure, the instance x_i is described by features such as $MadeOfStyrofoam = 0.2$

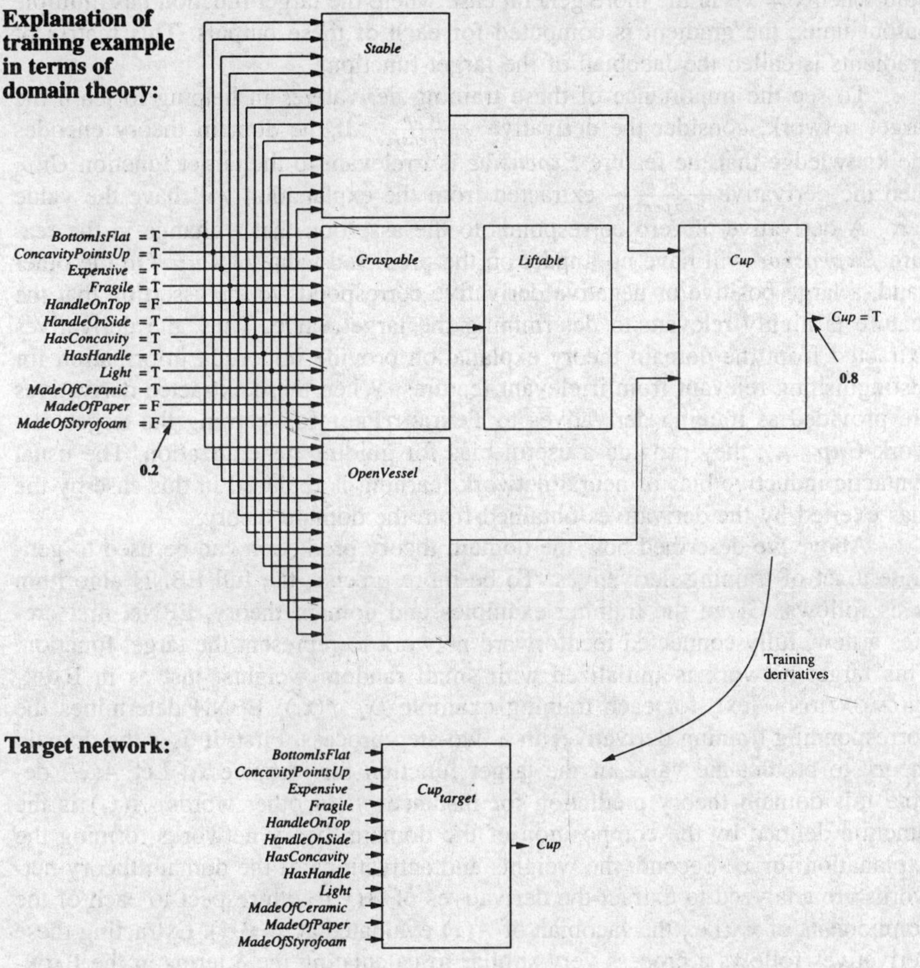

FIGURE 12.7
Explanation of a training example in EBNN. The explanation consists of a prediction of the target function value by the domain theory networks (top). Training derivatives are extracted from this explanation in order to train the separate target network (bottom). Each rectangular block represents a distinct multilayer neural network.

(i.e., *False*), and the domain theory prediction is that $Cup = 0.8$ (i.e., *True*). EBNN calculates the partial derivative of this prediction with respect to each instance feature, yielding the set of derivatives

$$\left[\frac{\partial Cup}{\partial BottomIsFlat}, \frac{\partial Cup}{\partial ConcavityPointsUp}, \ldots \frac{\partial Cup}{\partial MadeOfStyrofoam}\right]_{x=x_i}$$

This set of derivatives is the gradient of the domain theory prediction function with respect to the input instance. The subscript refers to the fact that these derivatives hold when $x = x_i$. In the more general case where the target function has multiple output units, the gradient is computed for each of these outputs. This matrix of gradients is called the Jacobian of the target function.

To see the importance of these training derivatives in helping to learn the target network, consider the derivative $\frac{\partial Cup}{\partial Expensive}$. If the domain theory encodes the knowledge that the feature *Expensive* is irrelevant to the target function *Cup*, then the derivative $\frac{\partial Cup}{\partial Expensive}$ extracted from the explanation will have the value zero. A derivative of zero corresponds to the assertion that a change in the feature *Expensive* will have no impact on the predicted value of *Cup*. On the other hand, a large positive or negative derivative corresponds to the assertion that the feature is highly relevant to determining the target value. Thus, the derivatives extracted from the domain theory explanation provide important information for distinguishing relevant from irrelevant features. When these extracted derivatives are provided as training derivatives to TANGENTPROP for learning the target network Cup_{target}, they provide a useful bias for guiding generalization. The usual syntactic inductive bias of neural network learning is replaced in this case by the bias exerted by the derivatives obtained from the domain theory.

Above we described how the domain theory prediction can be used to generate a set of training derivatives. To be more precise, the full EBNN algorithm is as follows. Given the training examples and domain theory, EBNN first creates a new, fully connected feedforward network to represent the target function. This target network is initialized with small random weights, just as in BACKPROPAGATION. Next, for each training example $\langle x_i, f(x_i)\rangle$ EBNN determines the corresponding training derivatives in a two-step process. First, it uses the domain theory to predict the value of the target function for instance x_i. Let $A(x_i)$ denote this domain theory prediction for instance x_i. In other words, $A(x_i)$ is the function defined by the composition of the domain theory networks forming the explanation for x_i. Second, the weights and activations of the domain theory networks are analyzed to extract the derivatives of $A(x_i)$ with respect to each of the components of x_i (i.e., the Jacobian of $A(x)$ evaluated at $x = x_i$). Extracting these derivatives follows a process very similar to calculating the δ terms in the BACKPROPAGATION algorithm (see Exercise 12.5). Finally, EBNN uses a minor variant of the TANGENTPROP algorithm to train the target network to fit the following error function

$$E = \sum_i \left[(f(x_i) - \hat{f}(x_i))^2 + \mu_i \sum_j \left(\frac{\partial A(x)}{\partial x^j} - \frac{\partial \hat{f}(x)}{\partial x^j} \right)^2_{(x=x_i)} \right] \tag{12.2}$$

where

$$\mu_i \equiv 1 - \frac{|A(x_i) - f(x_i)|}{c} \tag{12.3}$$

Here x_i denotes the ith training instance and $A(x)$ denotes the domain theory prediction for input x. The superscript notation x^j denotes the jth component of the vector x (i.e., the jth input node of the neural network). The coefficient c is a normalizing constant whose value is chosen to assure that for all i, $0 \leq \mu_i \leq 1$.

Although the notation here appears a bit tedious, the idea is simple. The error given by Equation (12.2) has the same general form as the error function in Equation (12.1) minimized by TANGENTPROP. The leftmost term measures the usual sum of squared errors between the training value $f(x_i)$ and the value predicted by the target network $\hat{f}(x_i)$. The rightmost term measures the squared error between the training derivatives $\frac{\partial A(x)}{\partial x^j}$ extracted from the domain theory and the actual derivatives of the target network $\frac{\partial \hat{f}(x)}{\partial x^j}$. Thus, the leftmost term contributes the inductive constraint that the hypothesis must fit the observed training data, whereas the rightmost term contributes the analytical constraint that it must fit the training derivatives extracted from the domain theory. Notice the derivative $\frac{\partial \hat{f}(x)}{\partial x^j}$ in Equation (12.2) is just a special case of the expression $\frac{\partial \hat{f}(s_j(\alpha, x_i))}{\partial \alpha}$ of Equation (12.1), for which $s_j(\alpha, x_i)$ is the transformation that replaces x_i^j by $x_i^j + \alpha$. The precise weight-training rule used by EBNN is described by Thrun (1996).

The relative importance of the inductive and analytical learning components is determined in EBNN by the constant μ_i, defined in Equation (12.3). The value of μ_i is determined by the discrepancy between the domain theory prediction $A(x_i)$ and the training value $f(x_i)$. The analytical component of learning is thus weighted more heavily for training examples that are correctly predicted by the domain theory and is suppressed for examples that are not correctly predicted. This weighting heuristic assumes that the training *derivatives* extracted from the domain theory are more likely to be correct in cases where the training *value* is correctly predicted by the domain theory. Although one can construct situations in which this heuristic fails, in practice it has been found effective in several domains (e.g., see Mitchell and Thrun [1993a]; Thrun [1996]).

12.4.5 Remarks

To summarize, the EBNN algorithm uses a domain theory expressed as a set of previously learned neural networks, together with a set of training examples, to train its output hypothesis (the target network). For each training example EBNN uses its domain theory to explain the example, then extracts training derivatives from this explanation. For each attribute of the instance, a training derivative is computed that describes how the target function value is influenced by a small change to this attribute value, according to the domain theory. These training derivatives are provided to a variant of TANGENTPROP, which fits the target network to these derivatives and to the training example values. Fitting the derivatives constrains the learned network to fit dependencies given by the domain theory, while fitting the training values constrains it to fit the observed data itself. The weight μ_i placed on fitting the derivatives is determined independently for each training example, based on how accurately the domain theory predicts the training value for this example.

EBNN has been shown to be an effective method for learning from approximate domain theories in several domains. Thrun (1996) describes its application to a variant of the *Cup* learning task discussed above and reports that

EBNN generalizes more accurately than standard BACKPROPAGATION, especially when training data is scarce. For example, after 30 training examples, EBNN achieved a root-mean-squared error of 5.5 on a separate set of test data, compared to an error of 12.0 for BACKPROPAGATION. Mitchell and Thrun (1993a) describe applying EBNN to learning to control a simulated mobile robot, in which the domain theory consists of neural networks that predict the effects of various robot actions on the world state. Again, EBNN using an approximate, previously learned domain theory, outperformed BACKPROPAGATION. Here BACKPROPAGATION required approximately 90 training episodes to reach the level of performance achieved by EBNN after 25 training episodes. O'Sullivan et al. (1997) and Thrun (1996) describe several other applications of EBNN to real-world robot perception and control tasks, in which the domain theory consists of networks that predict the effect of actions for an indoor mobile robot using sonar, vision, and laser range sensors.

EBNN bears an interesting relation to other explanation-based learning methods, such as PROLOG-EBG described in Chapter 11. Recall from that chapter that PROLOG-EBG also constructs explanations (predictions of example target values) based on a domain theory. In PROLOG-EBG the explanation is constructed from a domain theory consisting of Horn clauses, and the target hypothesis is refined by calculating the weakest conditions under which this explanation holds. Relevant dependencies in the explanation are thus captured in the learned Horn clause hypothesis. EBNN constructs an analogous explanation, but it is based on a domain theory consisting of neural networks rather than Horn clauses. As in PROLOG-EBG, relevant dependencies are then extracted from the explanation and used to refine the target hypothesis. In the case of EBNN, these dependencies take the form of derivatives because derivatives are the natural way to represent dependencies in continuous functions such as neural networks. In contrast, the natural way to represent dependencies in symbolic explanations or logical proofs is to describe the set of examples to which the proof applies.

There are several differences in capabilities between EBNN and the symbolic explanation-based methods of Chapter 11. The main difference is that EBNN accommodates imperfect domain theories, whereas PROLOG-EBG does not. This difference follows from the fact that EBNN is built on the inductive mechanism of fitting the observed training values and uses the domain theory only as an additional constraint on the learned hypothesis. A second important difference follows from the fact that PROLOG-EBG learns a growing set of Horn clauses, whereas EBNN learns a fixed-size neural network. As discussed in Chapter 11, one difficulty in learning sets of Horn clauses is that the cost of classifying a new instance grows as learning proceeds and new Horn clauses are added. This problem is avoided in EBNN because the fixed-size target network requires constant time to classify new instances. However, the fixed-size neural network suffers the corresponding disadvantage that it may be unable to represent sufficiently complex functions, whereas a growing set of Horn clauses can represent increasingly complex functions. Mitchell and Thrun (1993b) provide a more detailed discussion of the relationship between EBNN and symbolic explanation-based learning methods.

12.5 USING PRIOR KNOWLEDGE TO AUGMENT SEARCH OPERATORS

The two previous sections examined two different roles for prior knowledge in learning: initializing the learner's hypothesis and altering the objective function that guides search through the hypothesis space. In this section we consider a third way of using prior knowledge to alter the hypothesis space search: using it to alter the set of operators that define legal steps in the search through the hypothesis space. This approach is followed by systems such as FOCL (Pazzani et al. 1991; Pazzani and Kibler 1992) and ML-SMART (Bergadano and Giordana 1990). Here we use FOCL to illustrate the approach.

12.5.1 The FOCL Algorithm

FOCL is an extension of the purely inductive FOIL system described in Chapter 10. Both FOIL and FOCL learn a set of first-order Horn clauses to cover the observed training examples. Both systems employ a sequential covering algorithm that learns a single Horn clause, removes the positive examples covered by this new Horn clause, and then iterates this procedure over the remaining training examples. In both systems, each new Horn clause is created by performing a general-to-specific search, beginning with the most general possible Horn clause (i.e., a clause containing no preconditions). Several candidate specializations of the current clause are then generated, and the specialization with greatest information gain relative to the training examples is chosen. This process is iterated, generating further candidate specializations and selecting the best, until a Horn clause with satisfactory performance is obtained.

The difference between FOIL and FOCL lies in the way in which candidate specializations are generated during the general-to-specific search for a single Horn clause. As described in Chapter 10, FOIL generates each candidate specialization by adding a single new literal to the clause preconditions. FOCL uses this same method for producing candidate specializations, but also generates additional specializations based on the domain theory. The *solid* edges in the search tree of Figure 12.8 show the general-to-specific search steps considered in a typical search by FOIL. The *dashed* edge in the search tree of Figure 12.8 denotes an additional candidate specialization that is considered by FOCL and based on the domain theory.

Although FOCL and FOIL both learn first-order Horn clauses, we illustrate their operation here using the simpler domain of propositional (variable-free) Horn clauses. In particular, consider again the Cup target concept, training examples, and domain theory from Figure 12.3. To describe the operation of FOCL, we must first draw a distinction between two kinds of literals that appear in the domain theory and hypothesis representation. We will say a literal is *operational* if it is allowed to be used in describing an output hypothesis. For example, in the Cup example of Figure 12.3 we allow output hypotheses to refer only to the 12 attributes that describe the training examples (e.g., $HasHandle$, $HandleOnTop$). Literals based on these 12 attributes are thus considered operational. In contrast, literals that occur only as intermediate features in the domain theory, but not as

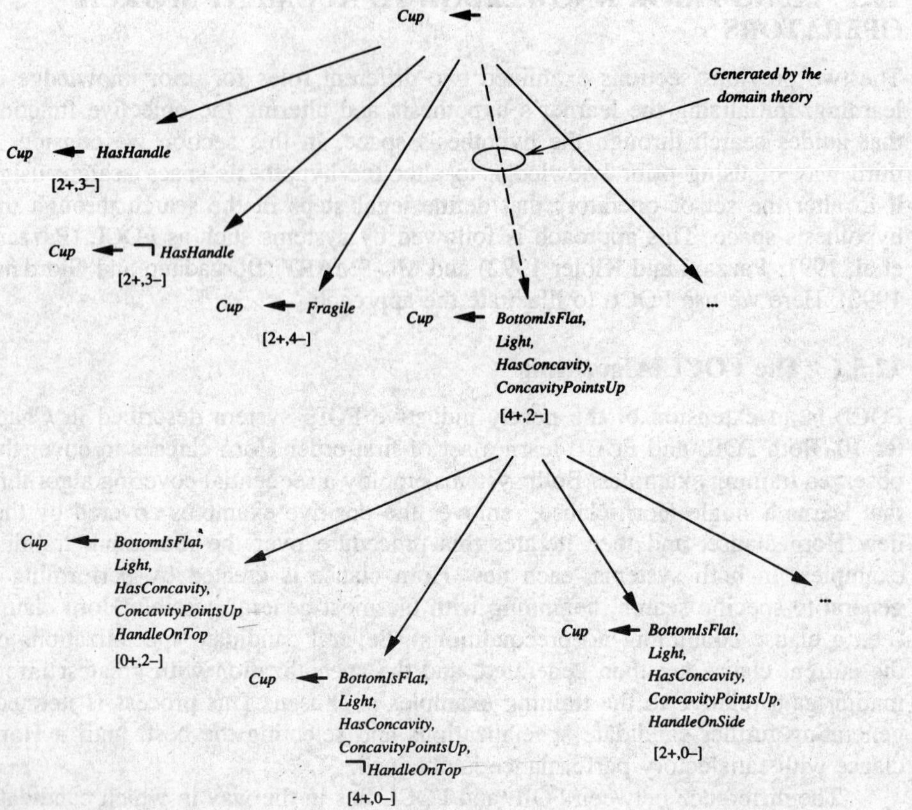

FIGURE 12.8
Hypothesis space search in FOCL. To learn a single rule, FOCL searches from general to increasingly specific hypotheses. Two kinds of operators generate specializations of the current hypothesis. One kind adds a single new literal (solid lines in the figure). A second kind of operator specializes the rule by adding a set of literals that constitute logically sufficient conditions for the target concept, according to the domain theory (dashed lines in the figure). FOCL selects among all these candidate specializations, based on their performance over the data. Therefore, imperfect domain theories will impact the hypothesis only if the evidence supports the theory. This example is based on the same training data and domain theory as the earlier KBANN example.

primitive attributes of the instances, are considered nonoperational. An example of a nonoperational attribute in this case is the attribute *Stable*.

At each point in its general-to-specific search, FOCL expands its current hypothesis h using the following two operators:

1. For each *operational* literal that is not part of h, create a specialization of h by adding this single literal to the preconditions. This is also the method used by FOIL to generate candidate successors. The solid arrows in Figure 12.8 denote this type of specialization.

2. Create an operational, logically sufficient condition for the target concept according to the domain theory. Add this set of literals to the current preconditions of h. Finally, prune the preconditions of h by removing any literals that are unnecessary according to the training data. The dashed arrow in Figure 12.8 denotes this type of specialization.

The detailed procedure for the second operator above is as follows. FOCL first selects one of the domain theory clauses whose head (postcondition) matches the target concept. If there are several such clauses, it selects the clause whose body (preconditions) have the highest information gain relative to the training examples of the target concept. For example, in the domain theory and training data of Figure 12.3, there is only one such clause:

$$Cup \leftarrow Stable, Liftable, OpenVessel$$

The preconditions of the selected clause form a logically sufficient condition for the target concept. Each nonoperational literal in these sufficient conditions is now replaced, again using the domain theory and substituting clause preconditions for clause postconditions. For example, the domain theory clause *Stable* ← *BottomIsFlat* is used to substitute the operational *BottomIsFlat* for the unoperational *Stable*. This process of "unfolding" the domain theory continues until the sufficient conditions have been restated in terms of operational literals. If there are several alternative domain theory clauses that produce different results, then the one with the greatest information gain is greedily selected at each step of the unfolding process. The reader can verify that the final operational sufficient condition given the data and domain theory in the current example is

$$BottomIsFlat, HasHandle, Light, HasConcavity, ConcavityPointsUp$$

As a final step in generating the candidate specialization, this sufficient condition is pruned. For each literal in the expression, the literal is removed unless its removal reduces classification accuracy over the training examples. This step is included to recover from overspecialization in case the imperfect domain theory includes irrelevant literals. In our current example, the above set of literals matches two positive and two negative examples. Pruning (removing) the literal *HasHandle* results in improved performance. The final pruned, operational, sufficient conditions are, therefore,

$$BottomIsFlat, Light, HasConcavity, ConcavityPointsUp$$

This set of literals is now added to the preconditions of the current hypothesis. Note this hypothesis is the result of the search step shown by the dashed arrow in Figure 12.8.

Once candidate specializations of the current hypothesis have been generated, using both of the two operations above, the candidate with highest information gain is selected. In the example shown in Figure 12.8 the candidate chosen at the first level in the search tree is the one generated by the domain theory. The search then proceeds by considering further specializations of the theory-suggested preconditions, thereby allowing the inductive component of learning to refine the preconditions derived from the domain theory. In this example, the domain theory affects the search only at the first search level. However, this will not always be the case. Should the empirical support be stronger for some other candidate at the first level, theory-suggested literals may still be added at subsequent steps in the search. To summarize, FOCL learns Horn clauses of the form

$$c \leftarrow o_i \wedge o_b \wedge o_f$$

where c is the target concept, o_i is an initial conjunction of operational literals added one at a time by the first syntactic operator, o_b is a conjunction of operational literals added in a single step based on the domain theory, and o_f is a final conjunction of operational literals added one at a time by the first syntactic operator. Any of these three sets of literals may be empty.

The above discussion illustrates the use of a propositional domain theory to create candidate specializations of the hypothesis during the general-to-specific search for a single Horn clause. The algorithm is easily extended to first-order representations (i.e., representations including variables). Chapter 10 discusses in detail the algorithm used by FOIL to generate first-order Horn clauses, including the extension of the first of the two search operators described above to first-order representations. To extend the second operator to accommodate first-order domain theories, variable substitutions must be considered when unfolding the domain theory. This can be accomplished using a procedure related to the regression procedure described in Table 11.3.

12.5.2 Remarks

FOCL uses the domain theory to increase the number of candidate specializations considered at each step of the search for a single Horn clause. Figure 12.9 compares the hypothesis space search performed by FOCL to that performed by the purely inductive FOIL algorithm on which it is based. FOCL's theory-suggested specializations correspond to "macro" steps in FOIL's search, in which several literals are added in a single step. This process can be viewed as promoting a hypothesis that might be considered later in the search to one that will be considered immediately. If the domain theory is correct, the training data will bear out the superiority of this candidate over the others and it will be selected. If the domain theory is incorrect, the empirical evaluation of all the candidates should direct the search down an alternative path.

To summarize, FOCL uses both a syntactic generation of candidate specializations and a domain theory driven generation of candidate specializations at each step in the search. The algorithm chooses among these candidates based solely on their empirical support over the training data. Thus, the domain theory is used in a fashion that biases the learner, but leaves final search choices to be made based on performance over the training data. The bias introduced by the domain theory is a preference in favor of Horn clauses most similar to operational, logically sufficient conditions entailed by the domain theory. This bias is combined with

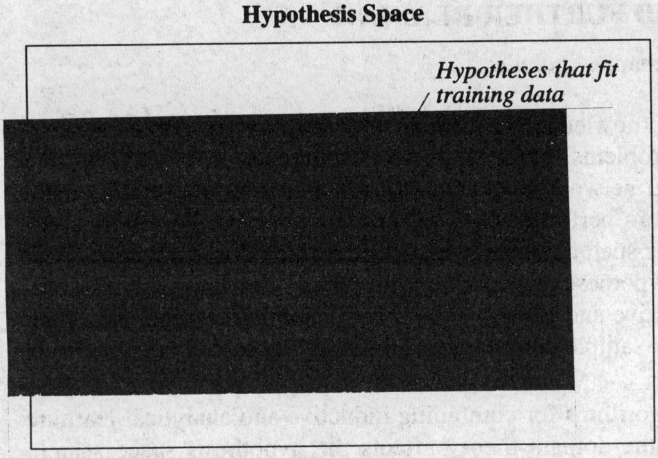

FIGURE 12.9
Hypothesis space search in FOCL. FOCL augments the set of search operators used by FOIL. Whereas FOIL considers adding a single new literal at each step, FOIL also considers adding multiple literals derived from the domain theory.

the bias of the purely inductive FOIL program, which is a preference for shorter hypotheses.

FOCL has been shown to generalize more accurately than the purely inductive FOIL algorithm in a number of application domains in which an imperfect domain theory is available. For example, Pazzani and Kibler (1992) explore learning the concept "legal chessboard positions." Given 60 training examples describing 30 legal and 30 illegal endgame board positions, FOIL achieved an accuracy of 86% over an independent set of test examples. FOCL was given the same 60 training examples, along with an approximate domain theory with an accuracy of 76%. FOCL produced a hypothesis with generalization accuracy of 94%—less than half the error rate of FOIL. Similar results have been obtained in other domains. For example, given 500 training examples of telephone network problems and their diagnoses from the telephone company NYNEX, FOIL achieved an accuracy of 90%, whereas FOCL reached an accuracy of 98% when given the same training data along with a 95% accurate domain theory.

12.6 STATE OF THE ART

The methods presented in this chapter are only a sample of the possible approaches to combining analytical and inductive learning. While each of these methods has been demonstrated to outperform purely inductive learning methods in selected domains, none of these has been thoroughly tested or proven across a large variety of problem domains. The topic of combining inductive and analytical learning remains a very active research area.

12.7 SUMMARY AND FURTHER READING

The main points of this chapter include:

- Approximate prior knowledge, or domain theories, are available in many practical learning problems. Purely inductive methods such as decision tree induction and neural network BACKPROPAGATION fail to utilize such domain theories, and therefore perform poorly when data is scarce. Purely analytical learning methods such as PROLOG-EBG utilize such domain theories, but produce incorrect hypotheses when given imperfect prior knowledge. Methods that blend inductive and analytical learning can gain the benefits of both approaches: reduced sample complexity and the ability to overrule incorrect prior knowledge.
- One way to view algorithms for combining inductive and analytical learning is to consider how the domain theory affects the hypothesis space search. In this chapter we examined methods that use imperfect domain theories to (1) create the initial hypothesis in the search, (2) expand the set of search operators that generate revisions to the current hypothesis, and (3) alter the objective of the search.
- A system that uses the domain theory to initialize the hypothesis is KBANN. This algorithm uses a domain theory encoded as propositional rules to analytically construct an artificial neural network that is equivalent to the domain theory. This network is then inductively refined using the BACKPROPAGATION algorithm, to improve its performance over the training data. The result is a network biased by the original domain theory, whose weights are refined inductively based on the training data.
- TANGENTPROP uses prior knowledge represented by desired derivatives of the target function. In some domains, such as image processing, this is a natural way to express prior knowledge. TANGENTPROP incorporates this knowledge by altering the objective function minimized by gradient descent search through the space of possible hypotheses.
- EBNN uses the domain theory to alter the objective in searching the hypothesis space of possible weights for an artificial neural network. It uses a domain theory consisting of previously learned neural networks to perform a neural network analog to symbolic explanation-based learning. As in symbolic explanation-based learning, the domain theory is used to explain individual examples, yielding information about the relevance of different example features. With this neural network representation, however, information about relevance is expressed in the form of derivatives of the target function value with respect to instance features. The network hypothesis is trained using a variant of the TANGENTPROP algorithm, in which the error to be minimized includes both the error in network output values and the error in network derivatives obtained from explanations.
- FOCL uses the domain theory to expand the set of candidates considered at each step in the search. It uses an approximate domain theory represented

by first order Horn clauses to learn a set of Horn clauses that approximate the target function. FOCL employs a sequential covering algorithm, learning each Horn clause by a general-to-specific search. The domain theory is used to augment the set of next more specific candidate hypotheses considered at each step of this search. Candidate hypotheses are then evaluated based on their performance over the training data. In this way, FOCL combines the greedy, general-to-specific inductive search strategy of FOIL with the rule-chaining, analytical reasoning of analytical methods.

- The question of how to best blend prior knowledge with new observations remains one of the key open questions in machine learning.

There are many more examples of algorithms that attempt to combine inductive and analytical learning. For example, methods for learning Bayesian belief networks discussed in Chapter 6 provide one alternative to the approaches discussed here. The references at the end of this chapter provide additional examples and sources for further reading.

EXERCISES

12.1. Consider learning the target concept *GoodCreditRisk* defined over instances described by the four attributes *HasStudentLoan, HasSavingsAccount, IsStudent, OwnsCar*. Give the initial network created by KBANN for the following domain theory, including all network connections and weights.

$$GoodCreditRisk \leftarrow Employed, LowDebt$$
$$Employed \leftarrow \neg IsStudent$$
$$LowDebt \leftarrow \neg HasStudentLoan, HasSavingsAccount$$

12.2. KBANN converts a set of propositional Horn clauses into an initial neural network. Consider the class of *n-of-m clauses*, which are Horn clauses containing m literals in the preconditions (antecedents), and an associated parameter n where $n \leq m$. The preconditions of an n-of-m Horn clause are considered to be satisfied if at least n of its m preconditions are satisfied. For example, the clause

$$Student \leftarrow LivesInDorm, Young, Studies; \quad n = 2$$

asserts that one is a *Student* if at least two of these three preconditions are satisfied.

Give an algorithm similar to that used by KBANN, that accepts a set of propositional n-of-m clauses and constructs a neural network consistent with the domain theory.

12.3. Consider extending KBANN to accept a domain theory consisting of first-order rather than propositional Horn clauses (i.e., Horn clauses containing variables, as in Chapter 10). Either give an algorithm for constructing a neural network equivalent to a set of Horn clauses, or discuss the difficulties that prevent this.

12.4. This exercise asks you to derive a gradient descent rule analogous to that used by TANGENTPROP. Consider the instance space X consisting of the real numbers, and consider the hypothesis space H consisting of quadratic functions of x. That is, each hypothesis $h(x)$ is of the form

$$h(x) = w_0 + w_1 x + w_2 x^2$$

(*a*) Derive a gradient descent rule that minimizes the same criterion as BACKPROPAGATION; that is, the sum of squared errors between the hypothesis and target values of the training data.

(*b*) Derive a second gradient descent rule that minimizes the same criterion as TANGENTPROP. Consider only the single transformation $s(\alpha, x) = x + \alpha$.

12.5. EBNN extracts training derivatives from explanations by examining the weights and activations of the neural networks that make up the explanation. Consider the simple example in which the explanation is formed by a single sigmoid unit with n inputs. Derive a procedure for extracting the derivative $\frac{\partial \hat{f}(x)}{\partial x^j}|_{x=x_i}$ where x_i is a particular training instance input to the unit, $\hat{f}(x)$ is the sigmoid unit output, and x^j denotes the jth input to the sigmoid unit. You may wish to use the notation x_i^j to refer to the jth component of x_i. Hint: The derivation is similar to the derivation of the BACKPROPAGATION training rule.

12.6. Consider again the search trace of FOCL shown in Figure 12.8. Suppose that the hypothesis selected at the first level in the search is changed to

$$Cup \leftarrow \neg HasHandle$$

Describe the second-level candidate hypotheses that will be generated by FOCL as successors to this hypothesis. You need only include those hypotheses generated by FOCL's second search operator, which uses its domain theory. Don't forget to post-prune the sufficient conditions. Use the training data from Table 12.3.

12.7. This chapter discussed three approaches to using prior knowledge to impact the search through the space of possible hypotheses. Discuss your ideas for how these three approaches could be integrated. Can you propose a specific algorithm that integrates at least two of these three for some specific hypothesis representation? What advantages and disadvantages would you anticipate from this integration?

12.8. Consider again the question from Section 12.2.1, regarding what criterion to use for choosing among hypotheses when both data and prior knowledge are available. Give your own viewpoint on this issue.

REFERENCES

Abu-Mostafa, Y. S. (1989). Learning from hints in neural networks. *Journal of Complexity*, 6(2), 192–198.

Bergadano, F., & Giordana, A. (1990). Guiding induction with domain theories. In R. Michalski et al. (Eds.), *Machine learning: An artificial intelligence approach 3* (pp. 474–492). San Mateo, CA: Morgan Kaufmann.

Bradshaw, G., Fozzard, R., & Cice, L. (1989). A connectionist expert system that really works. In *Advances in neural information processing*. San Mateo, CA: Morgan Kaufmann.

Caruana, R. (1996). Algorithms and applications for multitask learning. *Proceedings of the 13th International Conference on Machine Learning*. San Francisco: Morgan Kaufmann.

Cooper, G. C., & Herskovits, E. (1992). A Bayesian method for the induction of probabilistic networks from data. *Machine Learning*, 9, 309–347.

Craven, M. W. (1996). *Extracting comprehensible models from trained neural networks* (PhD thesis) (UW Technical Report CS-TR-96-1326). Department of Computer Sciences, University of Wisconsin-Madison.

Craven, M. W., & Shavlik, J. W. (1994). Using sampling and queries to extract rules from trained neural networks. *Proceedings of the 11th International Conference on Machine Learning* (pp. 37–45). San Mateo, CA: Morgan Kaufmann.

Fu, L. M. (1989). Integration of neural heuristics into knowledge-based inference. *Connection Science*, 1(3), 325–339.

Fu, L. M. (1993). Knowledge-based connectionism for revising domain theories. *IEEE Transactions on Systems, Man, and Cybernetics*, 23(1), 173–182.

Gallant, S. I. (1988). Connectionist expert systems. *CACM*, 31(2), 152–169.

Koppel, M., Feldman, R., & Segre, A. (1994). Bias-driven revision of logical domain theories. *Journal of Artificial Intelligence*, 1, 159–208. http://www.cs.washington.edu/research/jair/home.html.

Lacher, R., Hruska, S., & Kuncicky, D. (1991). *Backpropagation learning in expert networks* (Dept. of Computer Science Technical Report TR91-015). Florida State University, Tallahassee.

Maclin, R., & Shavlik, J. (1993). Using knowledge-based neural networks to improve algorithms: Refining the Chou-Fasman algorithm for protein folding. *Machine Learning*, 11(3), 195–215.

Mitchell, T. M., & Thrun, S. B. (1993a). Explanation-based neural network learning for robot control. In S. Hanson, J. Cowan, & C. Giles (Eds.), *Advances in neural information processing systems 5* (pp. 287–294). San Mateo, CA: Morgan-Kaufmann Press.

Mitchell, T. M., & Thrun, S. B. (1993b). Explanation-based learning: A comparison of symbolic and neural network approaches. *Tenth International Conference on Machine Learning*, Amherst, MA.

Mooney, R. (1993). Induction over the unexplained: Using overly-general domain theories to aid concept learning. *Machine Learning*, 10(1).

O'Sullivan, J., Mitchell, T., & Thrun, S. (1997). Explanation-based learning for mobile robot perception. In K. Ikeuchi & M. Veloso (Eds.), *Symbolic Visual Learning* (pp. 295–324).

Ourston, D., & Mooney, R. J. (1994). Theory refinement combining analytical and empirical methods. *Artificial Intelligence*, 66(2).

Pazzani, M. J., & Brunk, C. (1993). Finding accurate frontiers: A knowledge-intensive approach to relational learning. *Proceedings of the 1993 National Conference on Artificial Intelligence* (pp. 328–334). AAAI Press.

Pazzani, M. J., Brunk, C. A., & Silverstein, G. (1991). A knowledge-intensive approach to learning relational concepts. *Proceedings of the Eighth International Workshop on Machine Learning* (pp. 432–436). San Mateo, CA: Morgan Kaufmann.

Pazzani, M. J., & Kibler, D. (1992). The utility of knowledge in inductive learning. *Machine Learning*, 9(1), 57–94.

Pratt, L. Y. (1993a). *Transferring previously learned* BACKPROPAGATION *neural networks to new learning tasks* (Ph.D. thesis). Department of Computer Science, Rutgers University, New Jersey. (Also Rutgers Computer Science Technical Report ML-TR-37.)

Pratt, L. Y. (1993b). Discriminability-based transfer among neural networks. In J. E. Moody et al. (Eds.), *Advances in Nerual Information Processing Systems 5*. San Mateo, CA: Morgan Kaufmann.

Rosenbloom, P. S., & Aasman, J. (1990). Knowledge level and inductive uses of chunking (ebl). *Proceedings of the Eighth National Conference on Artificial Intelligence* (pp. 821–827). AAAI Press.

Russell, S., Binder, J., Koller, D., & Kanazawa, K. (1995). Local learning in probabilistic networks with hidden variables. *Proceedings of the 14th International Joint Conference on Artificial Intelligence*, Montreal. Morgan Kaufmann.

Shavlik, J., & Towell, G. (1989). An approach to combining explanation-based and neural learning algorithms. *Connection Science*, 1(3), 233–255.

Simard, P. S., Victorri, B., LeCun, Y., & Denker, J. (1992). Tangent prop—A formalism for specifying selected invariances in an adaptive network. In J. Moody et al. (Eds.), *Advances in Neural Information Processing Systems 4*. San Mateo, CA: Morgan Kaufmann.

Sudharth, S. C., & Holden, A. D. C. (1991). Symbolic-neural systems and the use of hints for developing complex systems. *International Journal of Man-Machine Studies*, 35(3), 291–311.

Thrun, S. (1996). *Explanation based neural network learning: A lifelong learning approach*. Boston: Kluwer Academic Publishers.

Thrun, S., & Mitchell, T. M. (1993). Integrating inductive neural network learning and explanation-based learning. *Proceedings of the 1993 International Joint Conference on Artificial Intelligence*.

Thrun, S., & Mitchell, T. M. (1995). Learning one more thing. *Proceedings of the 1995 International Joint Conference on Artificial Intelligence*, Montreal.

Towell, G., & Shavlik, J. (1989). An approach to combining explanation-based and neural learning algorithms. *Connection Science*, (1), 233–255.

Towell, G., & Shavlik, J. (1994). Knowledge-based artificial neural networks. *Artificial Intelligence*, 70(1–2), 119–165.

Towell, G., Shavlik, J., & Noordewier, M. (1990). Refinement of approximate domain theories by knowledge-based neural networks. *Proceedings of the Eighth National Conference on Artificial Intelligence* (pp. 861–866). Cambridge, MA: AAAI, MIT Press.

Yang, Q., & Bhargava, V. (1990). Building expert systems by a modified perceptron network with rule-transfer algorithms (pp. 77–82). *International Joint Conference on Neural Networks*, IEEE.

CHAPTER 13

REINFORCEMENT LEARNING

Reinforcement learning addresses the question of how an autonomous agent that senses and acts in its environment can learn to choose optimal actions to achieve its goals. This very generic problem covers tasks such as learning to control a mobile robot, learning to optimize operations in factories, and learning to play board games. Each time the agent performs an action in its environment, a trainer may provide a reward or penalty to indicate the desirability of the resulting state. For example, when training an agent to play a game the trainer might provide a positive reward when the game is won, negative reward when it is lost, and zero reward in all other states. The task of the agent is to learn from this indirect, delayed reward, to choose sequences of actions that produce the greatest cumulative reward. This chapter focuses on an algorithm called Q learning that can acquire optimal control strategies from delayed rewards, even when the agent has no prior knowledge of the effects of its actions on the environment. Reinforcement learning algorithms are related to dynamic programming algorithms frequently used to solve optimization problems.

13.1 INTRODUCTION

Consider building a learning robot. The robot, or *agent*, has a set of sensors to observe the *state* of its environment, and a set of *actions* it can perform to alter this state. For example, a mobile robot may have sensors such as a camera and sonars, and actions such as "move forward" and "turn." Its task is to learn a control strategy, or *policy*, for choosing actions that achieve its goals. For example, the robot may have a goal of docking onto its battery charger whenever its battery level is low.

This chapter is concerned with how such agents can learn successful control policies by experimenting in their environment. We assume that the goals of the agent can be defined by a *reward* function that assigns a numerical value—an immediate payoff—to each distinct action the agent may take from each distinct state. For example, the goal of docking to the battery charger can be captured by assigning a positive reward (e.g., +100) to state-action transitions that immediately result in a connection to the charger and a reward of zero to every other state-action transition. This reward function may be built into the robot, or known only to an external teacher who provides the reward value for each action performed by the robot. The task of the robot is to perform sequences of actions, observe their consequences, and learn a control policy. The control policy we desire is one that, from any initial state, chooses actions that maximize the reward accumulated over time by the agent. This general setting for robot learning is summarized in Figure 13.1.

As is apparent from Figure 13.1, the problem of learning a control policy to maximize cumulative reward is very general and covers many problems beyond robot learning tasks. In general the problem is one of learning to control sequential processes. This includes, for example, manufacturing optimization problems in which a sequence of manufacturing actions must be chosen, and the reward to be maximized is the value of the goods produced minus the costs involved. It includes sequential scheduling problems such as choosing which taxis to send for passengers in a large city, where the reward to be maximized is a function of the wait time of the passengers and the total fuel costs of the taxi fleet. In general, we are interested in any type of agent that must learn to choose actions that alter the state of its environment and where a cumulative reward function is used to define the quality of any given action sequence. Within this class of problems we will consider specific settings, including settings in which the actions have deterministic or nondeterministic outcomes, and settings in which the agent

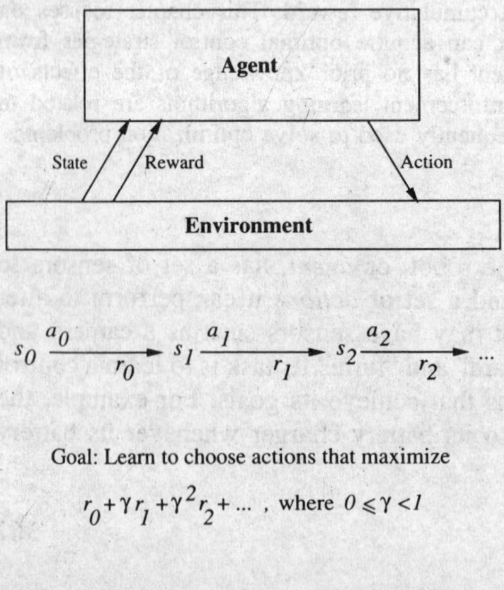

FIGURE 13.1
An agent interacting with its environment. The agent exists in an environment described by some set of possible states S. It can perform any of a set of possible actions A. Each time it performs an action a_t in some state s_t the agent receives a real-valued reward r_t that indicates the immediate value of this state-action transition. This produces a sequence of states s_i, actions a_i, and immediate rewards r_i as shown in the figure. The agent's task is to learn a control policy, $\pi : S \rightarrow A$, that maximizes the expected sum of these rewards, with future rewards discounted exponentially by their delay.

has or does not have prior knowledge about the effects of its actions on the environment.

Note we have touched on the problem of learning to control sequential processes earlier in this book. In Section 11.4 we discussed explanation-based learning of rules to control search during problem solving. There the problem is for the agent to choose among alternative actions at each step in its search for some goal state. The techniques discussed here differ from those of Section 11.4, in that here we consider problems where the actions may have nondeterministic outcomes and where the learner lacks a domain theory that describes the outcomes of its actions. In Chapter 1 we discussed the problem of learning to choose actions while playing the game of checkers. There we sketched the design of a learning method very similar to those discussed in this chapter. In fact, one highly successful application of the reinforcement learning algorithms of this chapter is to a similar game-playing problem. Tesauro (1995) describes the TD-GAMMON program, which has used reinforcement learning to become a world-class backgammon player. This program, after training on 1.5 million self-generated games, is now considered nearly equal to the best human players in the world and has played competitively against top-ranked players in international backgammon tournaments.

The problem of learning a control policy to choose actions is similar in some respects to the function approximation problems discussed in other chapters. The target function to be learned in this case is a control policy, $\pi : S \rightarrow A$, that outputs an appropriate action a from the set A, given the current state s from the set S. However, this reinforcement learning problem differs from other function approximation tasks in several important respects.

- *Delayed reward.* The task of the agent is to learn a target function π that maps from the current state s to the optimal action $a = \pi(s)$. In earlier chapters we have always assumed that when learning some target function such as π, each training example would be a pair of the form $\langle s, \pi(s) \rangle$. In reinforcement learning, however, training information is not available in this form. Instead, the trainer provides only a sequence of immediate reward values as the agent executes its sequence of actions. The agent, therefore, faces the problem of *temporal credit assignment*: determining which of the actions in its sequence are to be credited with producing the eventual rewards.
- *Exploration.* In reinforcement learning, the agent influences the distribution of training examples by the action sequence it chooses. This raises the question of which experimentation strategy produces most effective learning. The learner faces a tradeoff in choosing whether to favor *exploration* of unknown states and actions (to gather new information), or *exploitation* of states and actions that it has already learned will yield high reward (to maximize its cumulative reward).
- *Partially observable states.* Although it is convenient to assume that the agent's sensors can perceive the entire state of the environment at each time step, in many practical situations sensors provide only partial information. For example, a robot with a forward-pointing camera cannot see what is

behind it. In such cases, it may be necessary for the agent to consider its previous observations together with its current sensor data when choosing actions, and the best policy may be one that chooses actions specifically to improve the observability of the environment.

- *Life-long learning.* Unlike isolated function approximation tasks, robot learning often requires that the robot learn several related tasks within the same environment, using the same sensors. For example, a mobile robot may need to learn how to dock on its battery charger, how to navigate through narrow corridors, and how to pick up output from laser printers. This setting raises the possibility of using previously obtained experience or knowledge to reduce sample complexity when learning new tasks.

13.2 THE LEARNING TASK

In this section we formulate the problem of learning sequential control strategies more precisely. Note there are many ways to do so. For example, we might assume the agent's actions are deterministic or that they are nondeterministic. We might assume that the agent can predict the next state that will result from each action, or that it cannot. We might assume that the agent is trained by an expert who shows it examples of optimal action sequences, or that it must train itself by performing actions of its own choice. Here we define one quite general formulation of the problem, based on Markov decision processes. This formulation of the problem follows the problem illustrated in Figure 13.1.

In a Markov decision process (MDP) the agent can perceive a set S of distinct states of its environment and has a set A of actions that it can perform. At each discrete time step t, the agent senses the current state s_t, chooses a current action a_t, and performs it. The environment responds by giving the agent a reward $r_t = r(s_t, a_t)$ and by producing the succeeding state $s_{t+1} = \delta(s_t, a_t)$. Here the functions δ and r are part of the environment and are not necessarily known to the agent. In an MDP, the functions $\delta(s_t, a_t)$ and $r(s_t, a_t)$ depend only on the current state and action, and not on earlier states or actions. In this chapter we consider only the case in which S and A are finite. In general, δ and r may be nondeterministic functions, but we begin by considering only the deterministic case.

The task of the agent is to learn a *policy*, $\pi : S \rightarrow A$, for selecting its next action a_t based on the current observed state s_t; that is, $\pi(s_t) = a_t$. How shall we specify precisely which policy π we would like the agent to learn? One obvious approach is to require the policy that produces the greatest possible cumulative reward for the robot over time. To state this requirement more precisely, we define the cumulative value $V^\pi(s_t)$ achieved by following an arbitrary policy π from an arbitrary initial state s_t as follows:

$$
\begin{aligned}
V^\pi(s_t) &\equiv r_t + \gamma r_{t+1} + \gamma^2 r_{t+2} + \dots \\
&\equiv \sum_{i=0}^{\infty} \gamma^i r_{t+i} \qquad (13.1)
\end{aligned}
$$

where the sequence of rewards r_{t+i} is generated by beginning at state s_t and by repeatedly using the policy π to select actions as described above (i.e., $a_t = \pi(s_t)$, $a_{t+1} = \pi(s_{t+1})$, etc.). Here $0 \leq \gamma < 1$ is a constant that determines the relative value of delayed versus immediate rewards. In particular, rewards received i time steps into the future are discounted exponentially by a factor of γ^i. Note if we set $\gamma = 0$, only the immediate reward is considered. As we set γ closer to 1, future rewards are given greater emphasis relative to the immediate reward.

The quantity $V^\pi(s)$ defined by Equation (13.1) is often called the *discounted cumulative reward* achieved by policy π from initial state s. It is reasonable to discount future rewards relative to immediate rewards because, in many cases, we prefer to obtain the reward sooner rather than later. However, other definitions of total reward have also been explored. For example, *finite horizon* reward, $\sum_{i=0}^{h} r_{t+i}$, considers the undiscounted sum of rewards over a finite number h of steps. Another possibility is *average reward*, $\lim_{h\to\infty} \frac{1}{h} \sum_{i=0}^{h} r_{t+i}$, which considers the average reward per time step over the entire lifetime of the agent. In this chapter we restrict ourselves to considering discounted reward as defined by Equation (13.1). Mahadevan (1996) provides a discussion of reinforcement learning when the criterion to be optimized is average reward.

We are now in a position to state precisely the agent's learning task. We require that the agent learn a policy π that maximizes $V^\pi(s)$ for all states s. We will call such a policy an *optimal policy* and denote it by π^*.

$$\pi^* \equiv \underset{\pi}{\operatorname{argmax}}\, V^\pi(s), (\forall s) \tag{13.2}$$

To simplify notation, we will refer to the value function $V^{\pi^*}(s)$ of such an optimal policy as $V^*(s)$. $V^*(s)$ gives the maximum discounted cumulative reward that the agent can obtain starting from state s; that is, the discounted cumulative reward obtained by following the optimal policy beginning at state s.

To illustrate these concepts, a simple grid-world environment is depicted in the topmost diagram of Figure 13.2. The six grid squares in this diagram represent six possible states, or locations, for the agent. Each arrow in the diagram represents a possible action the agent can take to move from one state to another. The number associated with each arrow represents the immediate reward $r(s, a)$ the agent receives if it executes the corresponding state-action transition. Note the immediate reward in this particular environment is defined to be zero for all state-action transitions except for those leading into the state labeled **G**. It is convenient to think of the state **G** as the goal state, because the only way the agent can receive reward, in this case, is by entering this state. Note in this particular environment, the only action available to the agent once it enters the state **G** is to remain in this state. For this reason, we call **G** an *absorbing* state.

Once the states, actions, and immediate rewards are defined, and once we choose a value for the discount factor γ, we can determine the optimal policy π^* and its value function $V^*(s)$. In this case, let us choose $\gamma = 0.9$. The diagram at the bottom of the figure shows one optimal policy for this setting (there are others as well). Like any policy, this policy specifies exactly one action that the

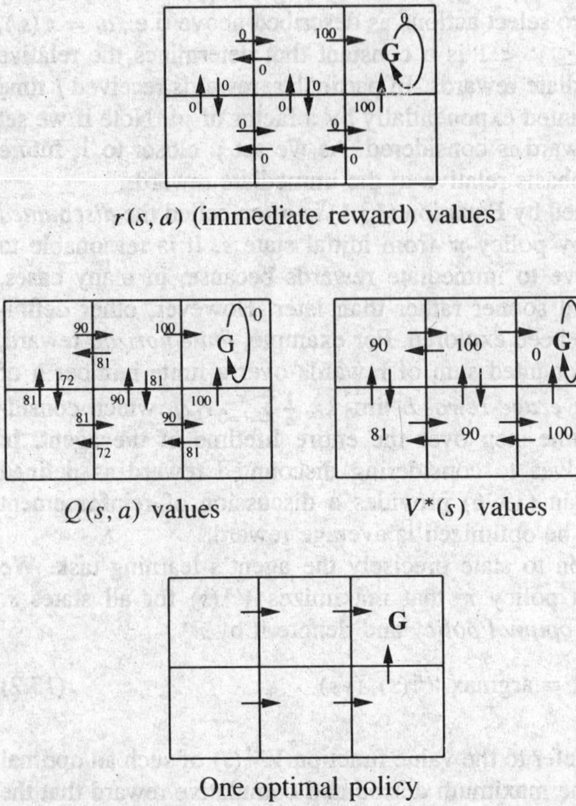

FIGURE 13.2
A simple deterministic world to illustrate the basic concepts of Q-learning. Each grid square represents a distinct state, each arrow a distinct action. The immediate reward function, $r(s, a)$ gives reward 100 for actions entering the goal state **G**, and zero otherwise. Values of $V^*(s)$ and $Q(s, a)$ follow from $r(s, a)$, and the discount factor $\gamma = 0.9$. An optimal policy, corresponding to actions with maximal Q values, is also shown.

agent will select in any given state. Not surprisingly, the optimal policy directs the agent along the shortest path toward the state **G**.

The diagram at the right of Figure 13.2 shows the values of V^* for each state. For example, consider the bottom right state in this diagram. The value of V^* for this state is 100 because the optimal policy in this state selects the "move up" action that receives immediate reward 100. Thereafter, the agent will remain in the absorbing state and receive no further rewards. Similarly, the value of V^* for the bottom center state is 90. This is because the optimal policy will move the agent from this state to the right (generating an immediate reward of zero), then upward (generating an immediate reward of 100). Thus, the discounted future reward from the bottom center state is

$$0 + \gamma 100 + \gamma^2 0 + \gamma^3 0 + \cdots = 90$$

Recall that V^* is defined to be the sum of discounted future rewards over the infinite future. In this particular environment, once the agent reaches the absorbing state **G** its infinite future will consist of remaining in this state and receiving rewards of zero.

13.3 *Q* LEARNING

How can an agent learn an optimal policy π^* for an arbitrary environment? It is difficult to learn the function $\pi^* : S \rightarrow A$ directly, because the available training data does not provide training examples of the form $\langle s, a \rangle$. Instead, the only training information available to the learner is the sequence of immediate rewards $r(s_i, a_i)$ for $i = 0, 1, 2, \ldots$. As we shall see, given this kind of training information it is easier to learn a numerical evaluation function defined over states and actions, then implement the optimal policy in terms of this evaluation function.

What evaluation function should the agent attempt to learn? One obvious choice is V^*. The agent should prefer state s_1 over state s_2 whenever $V^*(s_1) > V^*(s_2)$, because the cumulative future reward will be greater from s_1. Of course the agent's policy must choose among actions, not among states. However, it can use V^* in certain settings to choose among actions as well. The optimal action in state s is the action a that maximizes the sum of the immediate reward $r(s, a)$ plus the value V^* of the immediate successor state, discounted by γ.

$$\pi^*(s) = \underset{a}{\operatorname{argmax}}[r(s, a) + \gamma V^*(\delta(s, a))] \tag{13.3}$$

(recall that $\delta(s, a)$ denotes the state resulting from applying action a to state s.) Thus, the agent can acquire the optimal policy by learning V^*, *provided it has perfect knowledge of the immediate reward function r and the state transition function* δ. When the agent knows the functions r and δ used by the environment to respond to its actions, then it can then use Equation (13.3) to calculate the optimal action for any state s.

Unfortunately, learning V^* is a useful way to learn the optimal policy *only* when the agent has perfect knowledge of δ and r. This requires that it be able to perfectly predict the immediate result (i.e., the immediate reward and immediate successor) for every possible state-action transition. This assumption is comparable to the assumption of a perfect domain theory in explanation-based learning, discussed in Chapter 11. In many practical problems, such as robot control, it is impossible for the agent or its human programmer to predict in advance the exact outcome of applying an arbitrary action to an arbitrary state. Imagine, for example, the difficulty in describing δ for a robot arm shoveling dirt when the resulting state includes the positions of the dirt particles. In cases where either δ or r is unknown, learning V^* is unfortunately of no use for selecting optimal actions because the agent cannot evaluate Equation (13.3). What evaluation function should the agent use in this more general setting? The evaluation function Q, defined in the following section, provides one answer.

13.3.1 The Q Function

Let us define the evaluation function $Q(s, a)$ so that its value is the maximum discounted cumulative reward that can be achieved starting from state s and applying action a as the first action. In other words, the value of Q is the reward received immediately upon executing action a from state s, plus the value (discounted by γ) of following the optimal policy thereafter.

$$Q(s, a) \equiv r(s, a) + \gamma V^*(\delta(s, a)) \tag{13.4}$$

Note that $Q(s, a)$ is exactly the quantity that is maximized in Equation (13.3) in order to choose the optimal action a in state s. Therefore, we can rewrite Equation (13.3) in terms of $Q(s, a)$ as

$$\pi^*(s) = \underset{a}{\operatorname{argmax}}\, Q(s, a) \tag{13.5}$$

Why is this rewrite important? Because it shows that if the agent learns the Q function instead of the V^* function, it will be able to select optimal actions *even when it has no knowledge of the functions r and δ*. As Equation (13.5) makes clear, it need only consider each available action a in its current state s and choose the action that maximizes $Q(s, a)$.

It may at first seem surprising that one can choose globally optimal action sequences by reacting repeatedly to the local values of Q for the current state. This means the agent can choose the optimal action without ever conducting a lookahead search to explicitly consider what state results from the action. Part of the beauty of Q learning is that the evaluation function is defined to have precisely this property—the value of Q for the current state and action summarizes in a single number all the information needed to determine the discounted cumulative reward that will be gained in the future if action a is selected in state s.

To illustrate, Figure 13.2 shows the Q values for every state and action in the simple grid world. Notice that the Q value for each state-action transition equals the r value for this transition plus the V^* value for the resulting state discounted by γ. Note also that the optimal policy shown in the figure corresponds to selecting actions with maximal Q values.

13.3.2 An Algorithm for Learning Q

Learning the Q function corresponds to learning the optimal policy. How can Q be learned?

The key problem is finding a reliable way to estimate training values for Q, given only a sequence of immediate rewards r spread out over time. This can be accomplished through iterative approximation. To see how, notice the close relationship between Q and V^*,

$$V^*(s) = \max_{a'} Q(s, a')$$

which allows rewriting Equation (13.4) as

$$Q(s, a) = r(s, a) + \gamma \max_{a'} Q(\delta(s, a), a') \tag{13.6}$$

This recursive definition of Q provides the basis for algorithms that iteratively approximate Q (Watkins 1989). To describe the algorithm, we will use the symbol $\hat{Q}$ to refer to the learner's estimate, or hypothesis, of the actual Q function. In this algorithm the learner represents its hypothesis $\hat{Q}$ by a large table with a separate entry for each state-action pair. The table entry for the pair $\langle s, a \rangle$ stores the value for $\hat{Q}(s, a)$—the learner's current hypothesis about the actual but unknown value $Q(s, a)$. The table can be initially filled with random values (though it is easier to understand the algorithm if one assumes initial values of zero). The agent repeatedly observes its current state s, chooses some action a, executes this action, then observes the resulting reward $r = r(s, a)$ and the new state $s' = \delta(s, a)$. It then updates the table entry for $\hat{Q}(s, a)$ following each such transition, according to the rule:

$$\hat{Q}(s, a) \leftarrow r + \gamma \max_{a'} \hat{Q}(s', a') \tag{13.7}$$

Note this training rule uses the agent's current $\hat{Q}$ values for the new state s' to refine its estimate of $\hat{Q}(s, a)$ for the previous state s. This training rule is motivated by Equation (13.6), although the training rule concerns the agent's approximation $\hat{Q}$, whereas Equation (13.6) applies to the actual Q function. Note although Equation (13.6) describes Q in terms of the functions $\delta(s, a)$ and $r(s, a)$, the agent does not need to know these general functions to apply the training rule of Equation (13.7). Instead it executes the action in its environment and then observes the resulting new state s' and reward r. Thus, it can be viewed as sampling these functions at the current values of s and a.

The above Q learning algorithm for deterministic Markov decision processes is described more precisely in Table 13.1. Using this algorithm the agent's estimate $\hat{Q}$ converges in the limit to the actual Q function, provided the system can be modeled as a deterministic Markov decision process, the reward function r is

---

Q learning algorithm

For each s, a initialize the table entry $\hat{Q}(s, a)$ to zero.

Observe the current state s

Do forever:

- Select an action a and execute it
- Receive immediate reward r
- Observe the new state s'
- Update the table entry for $\hat{Q}(s, a)$ as follows:

$$\hat{Q}(s, a) \leftarrow r + \gamma \max_{a'} \hat{Q}(s', a')$$

- $s \leftarrow s'$

TABLE 13.1

Q learning algorithm, assuming deterministic rewards and actions. The discount factor γ may be any constant such that $0 \le \gamma < 1$.

bounded, and actions are chosen so that every state-action pair is visited infinitely often.

13.3.3 An Illustrative Example

To illustrate the operation of the Q learning algorithm, consider a single action taken by an agent, and the corresponding refinement to $\hat{Q}$ shown in Figure 13.3. In this example, the agent moves one cell to the right in its grid world and receives an immediate reward of zero for this transition. It then applies the training rule of Equation (13.7) to refine its estimate $\hat{Q}$ for the state-action transition it just executed. According to the training rule, the new $\hat{Q}$ estimate for this transition is the sum of the received reward (zero) and the highest $\hat{Q}$ value associated with the resulting state (100), discounted by γ (.9).

Each time the agent moves forward from an old state to a new one, Q learning propagates $\hat{Q}$ estimates *backward* from the new state to the old. At the same time, the immediate reward received by the agent for the transition is used to augment these propagated values of $\hat{Q}$.

Consider applying this algorithm to the grid world and reward function shown in Figure 13.2, for which the reward is zero everywhere, except when entering the goal state. Since this world contains an absorbing goal state, we will assume that training consists of a series of *episodes*. During each episode, the agent begins at some randomly chosen state and is allowed to execute actions until it reaches the absorbing goal state. When it does, the episode ends and

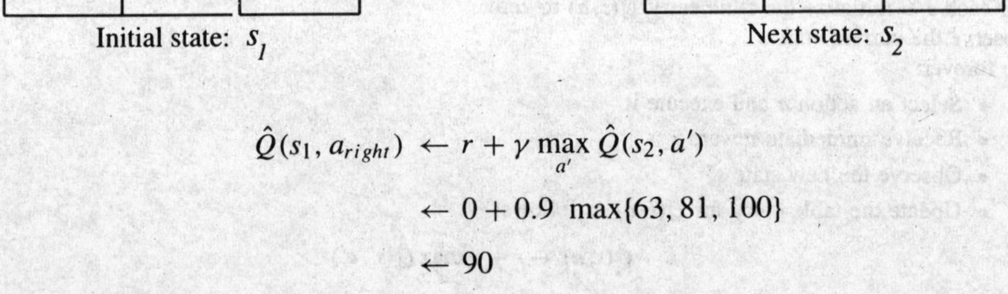

$$\begin{aligned}\hat{Q}(s_1, a_{right}) &\leftarrow r + \gamma \max_{a'} \hat{Q}(s_2, a') \\ &\leftarrow 0 + 0.9 \max\{63, 81, 100\} \\ &\leftarrow 90\end{aligned}$$

FIGURE 13.3
The update to $\hat{Q}$ after executing a single action. The diagram on the left shows the initial state s_1 of the robot (**R**) and several relevant $\hat{Q}$ values in its initial hypothesis. For example, the value $\hat{Q}(s_1, a_{right}) = 72$, where a_{right} refers to the action that moves **R** to its right. When the robot executes the action a_{right}, it receives immediate reward $r = 0$ and transitions to state s_2. It then updates its estimate $\hat{Q}(s_1, a_{right})$ based on its $\hat{Q}$ estimates for the new state s_2. Here $\gamma = 0.9$.

the agent is transported to a new, randomly chosen, initial state for the next episode.

How will the values of $\hat{Q}$ evolve as the Q learning algorithm is applied in this case? With all the $\hat{Q}$ values initialized to zero, the agent will make no changes to any $\hat{Q}$ table entry until it happens to reach the goal state and receive a nonzero reward. This will result in refining the $\hat{Q}$ value for the single transition leading into the goal state. On the next episode, if the agent passes through this state adjacent to the goal state, its nonzero $\hat{Q}$ value will allow refining the value for some transition two steps from the goal, and so on. Given a sufficient number of training episodes, the information will propagate from the transitions with nonzero reward back through the entire state-action space available to the agent, resulting eventually in a $\hat{Q}$ table containing the Q values shown in Figure 13.2.

In the next section we prove that under certain assumptions the Q learning algorithm of Table 13.1 will converge to the correct Q function. First consider two general properties of this Q learning algorithm that hold for any deterministic MDP in which the rewards are non-negative, assuming we initialize all $\hat{Q}$ values to zero. The first property is that under these conditions the $\hat{Q}$ values never decrease during training. More formally, let $\hat{Q}_n(s, a)$ denote the learned $\hat{Q}(s, a)$ value after the nth iteration of the training procedure (i.e., after the nth state-action transition taken by the agent). Then

$$(\forall s, a, n) \quad \hat{Q}_{n+1}(s, a) \geq \hat{Q}_n(s, a)$$

A second general property that holds under these same conditions is that throughout the training process every $\hat{Q}$ value will remain in the interval between zero and its true Q value.

$$(\forall s, a, n) \quad 0 \leq \hat{Q}_n(s, a) \leq Q(s, a)$$

13.3.4 Convergence

Will the algorithm of Table 13.1 converge toward a $\hat{Q}$ equal to the true Q function? The answer is yes, under certain conditions. First, we must assume the system is a deterministic MDP. Second, we must assume the immediate reward values are bounded; that is, there exists some positive constant c such that for all states s and actions a, $|r(s, a)| < c$. Third, we assume the agent selects actions in such a fashion that it visits every possible state-action pair infinitely often. By this third condition we mean that if action a is a legal action from state s, then over time the agent must execute action a from state s repeatedly and with nonzero frequency as the length of its action sequence approaches infinity. Note these conditions are in some ways quite general and in others fairly restrictive. They describe a more general setting than illustrated by the example in the previous section, because they allow for environments with arbitrary positive or negative rewards, and for environments where any number of state-action transitions may produce nonzero rewards. The conditions are also restrictive in that they require the agent to visit every distinct state-action transition infinitely often. This is a very strong assumption in large (or continuous!) domains. We will discuss stronger convergence results later. However, the result described in this section provides the basic intuition for understanding why Q learning works.

The key idea underlying the proof of convergence is that the table entry $\hat{Q}(s, a)$ with the largest error must have its error reduced by a factor of γ whenever it is updated. The reason is that its new value depends only in part on error-prone $\hat{Q}$ estimates, with the remainder depending on the error-free observed immediate reward r.

Theorem 13.1. **Convergence of Q learning for deterministic Markov decision processes.** Consider a Q learning agent in a deterministic MDP with bounded rewards $(\forall s, a) |r(s, a)| \leq c$. The Q learning agent uses the training rule of Equation (13.7), initializes its table $\hat{Q}(s, a)$ to arbitrary finite values, and uses a discount factor γ such that $0 \leq \gamma < 1$. Let $\hat{Q}_n(s, a)$ denote the agent's hypothesis $\hat{Q}(s, a)$ following the nth update. If each state-action pair is visited infinitely often, then $\hat{Q}_n(s, a)$ converges to $Q(s, a)$ as $n \to \infty$, for all s, a.

Proof. Since each state-action transition occurs infinitely often, consider consecutive intervals during which each state-action transition occurs at least once. The proof consists of showing that the maximum error over all entries in the $\hat{Q}$ table is reduced by at least a factor of γ during each such interval. $\hat{Q}_n$ is the agent's table of estimated Q values after n updates. Let Δ_n be the maximum error in $\hat{Q}_n$; that is

$$\Delta_n \equiv \max_{s,a} |\hat{Q}_n(s, a) - Q(s, a)|$$

Below we use s' to denote $\delta(s, a)$. Now for any table entry $\hat{Q}_n(s, a)$ that is updated on iteration $n + 1$, the magnitude of the error in the revised estimate $\hat{Q}_{n+1}(s, a)$ is

$$\begin{aligned} |\hat{Q}_{n+1}(s, a) - Q(s, a)| &= |(r + \gamma \max_{a'} \hat{Q}_n(s', a')) - (r + \gamma \max_{a'} Q(s', a'))| \\ &= \gamma |\max_{a'} \hat{Q}_n(s', a') - \max_{a'} Q(s', a')| \\ &\leq \gamma \max_{a'} |\hat{Q}_n(s', a') - Q(s', a')| \\ &\leq \gamma \max_{s'', a'} |\hat{Q}_n(s'', a') - Q(s'', a')| \end{aligned}$$

$$|\hat{Q}_{n+1}(s, a) - Q(s, a)| \leq \gamma \Delta_n$$

The third line above follows from the second line because for any two fu[illegible]ns f_1 and f_2 the following inequality holds

$$|\max_a f_1(a) - \max_a f_2(a)| \leq \max_a |f_1(a) - f_2(a)|$$

In going from the third line to the fourth line above, note we introduce a new variable s'' over which the maximization is performed. This is legitimate because the maximum value will be at least as great when we allow this additional variable to vary. Note that by introducing this variable we obtain an expression that matches the definition of Δ_n.

Thus, the updated $\hat{Q}_{n+1}(s, a)$ for any s, a is at most γ times the maximum error in the $\hat{Q}_n$ table, Δ_n. The largest error in the initial table, Δ_0, is bounded because values of $\hat{Q}_0(s, a)$ and $Q(s, a)$ are bounded for all s, a. Now after the first interval during which each s, a is visited, the largest error in the table will be at most $\gamma\Delta_0$. After k such intervals, the error will be at most $\gamma^k\Delta_0$. Since each state is visited infinitely often, the number of such intervals is infinite, and $\Delta_n \rightarrow 0$ as $n \rightarrow \infty$. This proves the theorem. □

13.3.5 Experimentation Strategies

Notice the algorithm of Table 13.1 does not specify how actions are chosen by the agent. One obvious strategy would be for the agent in state s to select the action a that maximizes $\hat{Q}(s, a)$, thereby exploiting its current approximation $\hat{Q}$. However, with this strategy the agent runs the risk that it will overcommit to actions that are found during early training to have high $\hat{Q}$ values, while failing to explore other actions that have even higher values. In fact, the convergence theorem above requires that each state-action transition occur infinitely often. This will clearly not occur if the agent always selects actions that maximize its current $\hat{Q}(s, a)$. For this reason, it is common in Q learning to use a probabilistic approach to selecting actions. Actions with higher $\hat{Q}$ values are assigned higher probabilities, but every action is assigned a nonzero probability. One way to assign such probabilities is

$$P(a_i|s) = \frac{k^{\hat{Q}(s,a_i)}}{\sum_j k^{\hat{Q}(s,a_j)}}$$

where $P(a_i|s)$ is the probability of selecting action a_i, given that the agent is in state s, and where $k > 0$ is a constant that determines how strongly the selection favors actions with high $\hat{Q}$ values. Larger values of k will assign higher probabilities to actions with above average $\hat{Q}$, causing the agent to *exploit* what it has learned and seek actions it believes will maximize its reward. In contrast, small values of k will allow higher probabilities for other actions, leading the agent to *explore* actions that do not currently have high $\hat{Q}$ values. In some cases, k is varied with the number of iterations so that the agent favors exploration during early stages of learning, then gradually shifts toward a strategy of exploitation.

13.3.6 Updating Sequence

One important implication of the above convergence theorem is that Q learning need not train on optimal action sequences in order to converge to the optimal policy. In fact, it can learn the Q function (and hence the optimal policy) while training from actions chosen completely at random at each step, as long as the resulting training sequence visits every state-action transition infinitely often. This fact suggests changing the sequence of training example transitions in order to improve training efficiency without endangering final convergence. To illustrate, consider again learning in an MDP with a single absorbing goal state, such as the one in Figure 13.1. Assume as before that we train the agent with a sequence of episodes. For each episode, the agent is placed in a random initial state and is allowed to perform actions and to update its $\hat{Q}$ table until it reaches the absorbing goal state. A new training episode is then begun by removing the agent from the goal state and placing it at a new random initial state. As noted earlier, if we begin with all $\hat{Q}$ values initialized to zero, then after the first full episode only one entry in the agent's $\hat{Q}$ table will have been changed: the entry corresponding to the final transition into the goal state. Note that if the agent happens to follow the same sequence of actions from the same random initial state in its second full episode, then a second table entry would be made nonzero, and so on. If we run repeated identical episodes in this fashion, the frontier of nonzero $\hat{Q}$ values will creep backward from the goal state at the rate of one new state-action transition per episode. Now consider training on these same state-action transitions, but in reverse chronological order for each episode. That is, we apply the same update rule from Equation (13.7) for each transition considered, but perform these updates in reverse order. In this case, after the first full episode the agent will have updated its $\hat{Q}$ estimate for every transition along the path it took to the goal. This training process will clearly converge in fewer iterations, although it requires that the agent use more memory to store the entire episode before beginning the training for that episode.

A second strategy for improving the rate of convergence is to store past state-action transitions, along with the immediate reward that was received, and retrain on them periodically. Although at first it might seem a waste of effort to retrain on the same transition, recall that the updated $\hat{Q}(s, a)$ value is determined by the values $\hat{Q}(s', a)$ of the successor state $s' = \delta(s, a)$. Therefore, if subsequent training changes one of the $\hat{Q}(s', a)$ values, then retraining on the transition $\langle s, a \rangle$ may result in an altered value for $\hat{Q}(s, a)$. In general, the degree to which we wish to replay old transitions versus obtain new ones from the environment depends on the relative costs of these two operations in the specific problem domain. For example, in a robot domain with navigation actions that might take several seconds to perform, the delay in collecting a new state-action transition from the external world might be several orders of magnitude more costly than internally replaying a previously observed transition. This difference can be very significant given that Q learning can often require thousands of training iterations to converge.

Note throughout the above discussion we have kept our assumption that the agent does not know the state-transition function $\delta(s, a)$ used by the environment to create the successor state $s' = \delta(s, a)$, or the function $r(s, a)$ used to generate rewards. If it does know these two functions, then many more efficient methods are possible. For example, if performing external actions is expensive the agent may simply ignore the environment and instead simulate it internally, efficiently generating simulated actions and assigning the appropriate simulated rewards. Sutton (1991) describes the DYNA architecture that performs a number of simulated actions after each step executed in the external world. Moore and Atkeson (1993) describe an approach called *prioritized sweeping* that selects promising states to update next, focusing on predecessor states when the current state is found to have a large update. Peng and Williams (1994) describe a similar approach. A large number of efficient algorithms from the field of dynamic programming can be applied when the functions δ and r are known. Kaelbling et al. (1996) survey a number of these.

13.4 NONDETERMINISTIC REWARDS AND ACTIONS

Above we considered Q learning in deterministic environments. Here we consider the nondeterministic case, in which the reward function $r(s, a)$ and action transition function $\delta(s, a)$ may have probabilistic outcomes. For example, in Tesauro's (1995) backgammon playing program, action outcomes are inherently probabilistic because each move involves a roll of the dice. Similarly, in robot problems with noisy sensors and effectors it is often appropriate to model actions and rewards as nondeterministic. In such cases, the functions $\delta(s, a)$ and $r(s, a)$ can be viewed as first producing a probability distribution over outcomes based on s and a, and then drawing an outcome at random according to this distribution. When these probability distributions depend solely on s and a (e.g., they do not depend on previous states or actions), then we call the system a nondeterministic Markov decision process.

In this section we extend the Q learning algorithm for the deterministic case to handle nondeterministic MDPs. To accomplish this, we retrace the line of argument that led to the algorithm for the deterministic case, revising it where needed.

In the nondeterministic case we must first restate the objective of the learner to take into account the fact that outcomes of actions are no longer deterministic. The obvious generalization is to redefine the value V^π of a policy π to be the *expected value* (over these nondeterministic outcomes) of the discounted cumulative reward received by applying this policy

$$V^\pi(s_t) \equiv E\left[\sum_{i=0}^{\infty} \gamma^i r_{t+i}\right]$$

where, as before, the sequence of rewards r_{t+i} is generated by following policy π beginning at state s. Note this is a generalization of Equation (13.1), which covered the deterministic case.

As before, we define the optimal policy π^* to be the policy π that maximizes $V^\pi(s)$ for all states s. Next we generalize our earlier definition of Q from Equation (13.4), again by taking its expected value.

$$\begin{aligned} Q(s,a) &\equiv E[r(s,a) + \gamma V^*(\delta(s,a))] \\ &= E[r(s,a)] + \gamma E[V^*(\delta(s,a))] \\ &= E[r(s,a)] + \gamma \sum_{s'} P(s'|s,a) V^*(s') \end{aligned} \tag{13.8}$$

where $P(s'|s, a)$ is the probability that taking action a in state s will produce the next state s'. Note we have used $P(s'|s, a)$ here to rewrite the expected value of $V^*(\delta(s, a))$ in terms of the probabilities associated with the possible outcomes of the probabilistic δ.

As before we can re-express Q recursively

$$Q(s,a) = E[r(s,a)] + \gamma \sum_{s'} P(s'|s,a) \max_{a'} Q(s',a') \tag{13.9}$$

which is the generalization of the earlier Equation (13.6). To summarize, we have simply redefined $Q(s, a)$ in the nondeterministic case to be the expected value of its previously defined quantity for the deterministic case.

Now that we have generalized the definition of Q to accommodate the nondeterministic environment functions r and δ, a new training rule is needed. Our earlier training rule derived for the deterministic case (Equation 13.7) fails to converge in this nondeterministic setting. Consider, for example, a nondeterministic reward function $r(s, a)$ that produces different rewards each time the transition $\langle s, a\rangle$ is repeated. In this case, the training rule will repeatedly alter the values of $\hat{Q}(s, a)$, even if we initialize the $\hat{Q}$ table values to the correct Q function. In brief, this training rule does not converge. This difficulty can be overcome by modifying the training rule so that it takes a decaying weighted average of the current $\hat{Q}$ value and the revised estimate. Writing $\hat{Q}_n$ to denote the agent's estimate on the nth iteration of the algorithm, the following revised training rule is sufficient to assure convergence of $\hat{Q}$ to Q:

$$\hat{Q}_n(s, a) \leftarrow (1 - \alpha_n)\hat{Q}_{n-1}(s, a) + \alpha_n[r + \max_{a'} \hat{Q}_{n-1}(s', a')] \tag{13.10}$$

where

$$\alpha_n = \frac{1}{1 + visits_n(s, a)} \tag{13.11}$$

where s and a here are the state and action updated during the nth iteration, and where $visits_n(s, a)$ is the total number of times this state-action pair has been visited up to and including the nth iteration.

The key idea in this revised rule is that revisions to $\hat{Q}$ are made more gradually than in the deterministic case. Notice if we were to set α_n to 1 in Equation (13.10) we would have exactly the training rule for the deterministic case. With smaller values of α, this term is now averaged in with the current $\hat{Q}(s, a)$ to produce the new updated value. Notice that the value of α_n in Equation (13.11) decreases as n increases, so that updates become smaller as training progresses. By reducing α at an appropriate rate during training, we can achieve convergence to the correct Q function. The choice of α_n given above is one of many that satisfy the conditions for convergence, according to the following theorem due to Watkins and Dayan (1992).

Theorem 13.2. Convergence of Q learning for nondeterministic Markov decision processes. Consider a Q learning agent in a nondeterministic MDP with bounded rewards $(\forall s, a)|r(s, a)| \leq c$. The Q learning agent uses the training rule of Equation (13.10), initializes its table $\hat{Q}(s, a)$ to arbitrary finite values, and uses a discount factor γ such that $0 \leq \gamma < 1$. Let $n(i, s, a)$ be the iteration corresponding to the ith time that action a is applied to state s. If each state-action pair is visited infinitely often, $0 \leq \alpha_n < 1$, and

$$\sum_{i=1}^{\infty} \alpha_{n(i,s,a)} = \infty, \quad \sum_{i=1}^{\infty} [\alpha_{n(i,s,a)}]^2 < \infty$$

then for all s and a, $\hat{Q}_n(s, a) \rightarrow Q(s, a)$ as $n \rightarrow \infty$, with probability 1.

While Q learning and related reinforcement learning algorithms can be proven to converge under certain conditions, in practice systems that use Q learning often require many thousands of training iterations to converge. For example, Tesauro's TD-GAMMON discussed earlier trained for 1.5 million backgammon games, each of which contained tens of state-action transitions.

13.5 TEMPORAL DIFFERENCE LEARNING

The Q learning algorithm learns by iteratively reducing the discrepancy between Q value estimates for adjacent states. In this sense, Q learning is a special case of a general class of *temporal difference* algorithms that learn by reducing discrepancies between estimates made by the agent at different times. Whereas the training rule of Equation (13.10) reduces the difference between the estimated $\hat{Q}$ values of a state and its immediate successor, we could just as well design an algorithm that reduces discrepancies between this state and more distant descendants or ancestors.

To explore this issue further, recall that our Q learning training rule calculates a training value for $\hat{Q}(s_t, a_t)$ in terms of the values for $\hat{Q}(s_{t+1}, a_{t+1})$ where s_{t+1} is the result of applying action a_t to the state s_t. Let $Q^{(1)}(s_t, a_t)$ denote the training value calculated by this one-step lookahead

$$Q^{(1)}(s_t, a_t) \equiv r_t + \gamma \max_a \hat{Q}(s_{t+1}, a)$$

One alternative way to compute a training value for $Q(s_t, a_t)$ is to base it on the observed rewards for two steps

$$Q^{(2)}(s_t, a_t) \equiv r_t + \gamma r_{t+1} + \gamma^2 \max_a \hat{Q}(s_{t+2}, a)$$

or, in general, for n steps

$$Q^{(n)}(s_t, a_t) \equiv r_t + \gamma r_{t+1} + \cdots + \gamma^{(n-1)} r_{t+n-1} + \gamma^n \max_a \hat{Q}(s_{t+n}, a)$$

Sutton (1988) introduces a general method for blending these alternative training estimates, called TD(λ). The idea is to use a constant $0 \leq \lambda \leq 1$ to combine the estimates obtained from various lookahead distances in the following fashion

$$Q^{\lambda}(s_t, a_t) \equiv (1 - \lambda) \left[Q^{(1)}(s_t, a_t) + \lambda Q^{(2)}(s_t, a_t) + \lambda^2 Q^{(3)}(s_t, a_t) + \cdots \right]$$

An equivalent recursive definition for Q^{λ} is

$$Q^{\lambda}(s_t, a_t) = r_t + \gamma [\ (1 - \lambda) \max_a \hat{Q}(s_t, a_t) + \lambda\ Q^{\lambda}(s_{t+1}, a_{t+1})]$$

Note if we choose $\lambda = 0$ we have our original training estimate $Q^{(1)}$, which considers only one-step discrepancies in the $\hat{Q}$ estimates. As λ is increased, the algorithm places increasing emphasis on discrepancies based on more distant lookaheads. At the extreme value $\lambda = 1$, only the observed r_{t+i} values are considered, with no contribution from the current $\hat{Q}$ estimate. Note when $\hat{Q} = Q$, the training values given by Q^λ will be identical for all values of λ such that $0 \leq \lambda \leq 1$.

The motivation for the TD(λ) method is that in some settings training will be more efficient if more distant lookaheads are considered. For example, when the agent follows an optimal policy for choosing actions, then Q^λ with $\lambda = 1$ will provide a perfect estimate for the true Q value, regardless of any inaccuracies in $\hat{Q}$. On the other hand, if action sequences are chosen suboptimally, then the r_{t+i} observed far into the future can be misleading.

Peng and Williams (1994) provide a further discussion and experimental results showing the superior performance of Q^λ in one problem domain. Dayan (1992) shows that under certain assumptions a similar TD(λ) approach applied to learning the V^* function converges correctly for any λ such that $0 \leq \lambda \leq 1$. Tesauro (1995) uses a TD(λ) approach in his TD-GAMMON program for playing backgammon.

13.6 GENERALIZING FROM EXAMPLES

Perhaps the most constraining assumption in our treatment of Q learning up to this point is that the target function is represented as an explicit lookup table, with a distinct table entry for every distinct input value (i.e., state-action pair). Thus, the algorithms we discussed perform a kind of rote learning and make no attempt to estimate the Q value for unseen state-action pairs by generalizing from those that have been seen. This rote learning assumption is reflected in the convergence proof, which proves convergence only if every possible state-action pair is visited (infinitely often!). This is clearly an unrealistic assumption in large or infinite spaces, or when the cost of executing actions is high. As a result, more practical systems often combine function approximation methods discussed in other chapters with the Q learning training rules described here.

It is easy to incorporate function approximation algorithms such as BACKPROPAGATION into the Q learning algorithm, by substituting a neural network for the lookup table and using each $\hat{Q}(s, a)$ update as a training example. For example, we could encode the state s and action a as network inputs and train the network to output the target values of $\hat{Q}$ given by the training rules of Equations (13.7) and (13.10). An alternative that has sometimes been found to be more successful in practice is to train a separate network for each action, using the state as input and $\hat{Q}$ as output. Another common alternative is to train one network with the state as input, but with one $\hat{Q}$ output for each action. Recall that in Chapter 1, we discussed approximating an evaluation function over checkerboard states using a linear function and the LMS algorithm.

In practice, a number of successful reinforcement learning systems have been developed by incorporating such function approximation algorithms in place of the lookup table. Tesauro's successful TD-GAMMON program for playing backgammon used a neural network and the BACKPROPAGATION algorithm together with a TD(λ) training rule. Zhang and Dietterich (1996) use a similar combination of BACKPROPAGATION and TD(λ) for job-shop scheduling tasks. Crites and Barto (1996) describe a neural network reinforcement learning approach for an elevator scheduling task. Thrun (1996) reports a neural network based approach to Q learning to learn basic control procedures for a mobile robot with sonar and camera sensors. Mahadevan and Connell (1991) describe a Q learning approach based on clustering states, applied to a simple mobile robot control problem.

Despite the success of these systems, for other tasks reinforcement learning fails to converge once a generalizing function approximator is introduced. Examples of such problematic tasks are given by Boyan and Moore (1995), Baird (1995), and Gordon (1995). Note the convergence theorems discussed earlier in this chapter apply only when $\hat{Q}$ is represented by an explicit table. To see the difficulty, consider using a neural network rather than an explicit table to represent $\hat{Q}$. Note if the learner updates the network to better fit the training Q value for a particular transition $\langle s_i, a_i \rangle$, the altered network weights may also change the $\hat{Q}$ estimates for arbitrary other transitions. Because these weight changes may increase the error in $\hat{Q}$ estimates for these other transitions, the argument proving the original theorem no longer holds. Theoretical analyses of reinforcement learning with generalizing function approximators are given by Gordon (1995) and Tsitsiklis (1994). Baird (1995) proposes gradient-based methods that circumvent this difficulty by directly minimizing the sum of squared discrepancies in estimates between adjacent states (also called Bellman residual errors).

13.7 RELATIONSHIP TO DYNAMIC PROGRAMMING

Reinforcement learning methods such as Q learning are closely related to a long line of research on dynamic programming approaches to solving Markov decision processes. This earlier work has typically assumed that the agent possesses perfect knowledge of the functions $\delta(s, a)$ and $r(s, a)$ that define the agent's environment. Therefore, it has primarily addressed the question of how to compute the optimal policy using the least computational effort, assuming the environment could be perfectly simulated and no direct interaction was required. The novel aspect of Q learning is that it assumes the agent does *not* have knowledge of $\delta(s, a)$ and $r(s, a)$, and that instead of moving about in an internal mental model of the state space, it must move about the real world and observe the consequences. In this latter case our primary concern is usually the number of real-world actions that the agent must perform to converge to an acceptable policy, rather than the number of computational cycles it must expend. The reason is that in many practical domains such as manufacturing problems, the costs in time and in dollars of performing actions in the external world dominate the computational costs. Systems that learn by moving about the real environment and observing the results are typically called *online* systems, whereas those that learn solely by simulating actions within an internal model are called *offline* systems.

The close correspondence between these earlier approaches and the reinforcement learning problems discussed here is apparent by considering Bellman's equation, which forms the foundation for many dynamic programming approaches to solving MDPs. Bellman's equation is

$$(\forall s \in S) V^*(s) = E[r(s, \pi(s)) + \gamma V^*(\delta(s, \pi(s)))]$$

Note the very close relationship between Bellman's equation and our earlier definition of an optimal policy in Equation (13.2). Bellman (1957) showed that the optimal policy π^* satisfies the above equation and that any policy π satisfying this equation is an optimal policy. Early work on dynamic programming includes the Bellman-Ford shortest path algorithm (Bellman 1958; Ford and Fulkerson 1962), which learns paths through a graph by repeatedly updating the estimated distance to the goal for each graph node, based on the distances for its neighbors. In this algorithm the assumption that graph edges and the goal node are known is equivalent to our assumption that $\delta(s, a)$ and $r(s, a)$ are known. Barto et al. (1995) discuss the close relationship between reinforcement learning and dynamic programming.

13.8 SUMMARY AND FURTHER READING

The key points discussed in this chapter include:

- Reinforcement learning addresses the problem of learning control strategies for autonomous agents. It assumes that training information is available in the form of a real-valued reward signal given for each state-action transition. The goal of the agent is to learn an action policy that maximizes the total reward it will receive from any starting state.
- The reinforcement learning algorithms addressed in this chapter fit a problem setting known as a Markov decision process. In Markov decision processes, the outcome of applying any action to any state depends only on this action and state (and not on preceding actions or states). Markov decision processes cover a wide range of problems including many robot control, factory automation, and scheduling problems.
- Q learning is one form of reinforcement learning in which the agent learns an evaluation function over states and actions. In particular, the evaluation function $Q(s, a)$ is defined as the maximum expected, discounted, cumulative reward the agent can achieve by applying action a to state s. The Q learning algorithm has the advantage that it can be employed even when the learner has no prior knowledge of how its actions affect its environment.
- Q learning can be proven to converge to the correct Q function under certain assumptions, when the learner's hypothesis $\hat{Q}(s, a)$ is represented by a lookup table with a distinct entry for each $\langle s, a\rangle$ pair. It can be shown to converge in both deterministic and nondeterministic MDPs. In practice, Q learning can require many thousands of training iterations to converge in even modest-sized problems.
- Q learning is a member of a more general class of algorithms, called temporal difference algorithms. In general, temporal difference algorithms learn

by iteratively reducing the discrepancies between the estimates produced by the agent at different times.

- Reinforcement learning is closely related to dynamic programming approaches to Markov decision processes. The key difference is that historically these dynamic programming approaches have assumed that the agent possesses knowledge of the state transition function $\delta(s, a)$ and reward function $r(s, a)$. In contrast, reinforcement learning algorithms such as Q learning typically assume the learner lacks such knowledge.

The common theme that underlies much of the work on reinforcement learning is to iteratively reduce the discrepancy between evaluations of successive states. Some of the earliest work on such methods is due to Samuel (1959). His checkers learning program attempted to learn an evaluation function for checkers by using evaluations of later states to generate training values for earlier states. Around the same time, the Bellman-Ford, single-destination, shortest-path algorithm was developed (Bellman 1958; Ford and Fulkerson 1962), which propagated distance-to-goal values from nodes to their neighbors. Research on optimal control led to the solution of Markov decision processes using similar methods (Bellman 1961; Blackwell 1965). Holland's (1986) bucket brigade method for learning classifier systems used a similar method for propagating credit in the face of delayed rewards. Barto et al. (1983) discussed an approach to temporal credit assignment that led to Sutton's paper (1988) defining the TD(λ) method and proving its convergence for $\lambda = 0$. Dayan (1992) extended this result to arbitrary values of λ. Watkins (1989) introduced Q learning to acquire optimal policies when the reward and action transition functions are unknown. Convergence proofs are known for several variations on these methods. In addition to the convergence proofs presented in this chapter see, for example, (Baird 1995; Bertsekas 1987; Tsitsiklis 1994, Singh and Sutton 1996).

Reinforcement learning remains an active research area. McCallum (1995) and Littman (1996), for example, discuss the extension of reinforcement learning to settings with hidden state variables that violate the Markov assumption. Much current research seeks to scale up these methods to larger, more practical problems. For example, Maclin and Shavlik (1996) describe an approach in which a reinforcement learning agent can accept imperfect advice from a trainer, based on an extension to the KBANN algorithm (Chapter 12). Lin (1992) examines the role of teaching by providing suggested action sequences. Methods for scaling up by employing a hierarchy of actions are suggested by Singh (1993) and Lin (1993). Dietterich and Flann (1995) explore the integration of explanation-based methods with reinforcement learning, and Mitchell and Thrun (1993) describe the application of the EBNN algorithm (Chapter 12) to Q learning. Ring (1994) explores continual learning by the agent over multiple tasks.

Recent surveys of reinforcement learning are given by Kaelbling et al. (1996); Barto (1992); Barto et al. (1995); Dean et al. (1993).

EXERCISES

13.1. Give a second optimal policy for the problem illustrated in Figure 13.2.

13.2. Consider the deterministic grid world shown below with the absorbing goal-state G. Here the immediate rewards are 10 for the labeled transitions and 0 for all unlabeled transitions.

(*a*) Give the V^* value for every state in this grid world. Give the $Q(s, a)$ value for every transition. Finally, show an optimal policy. Use $\gamma = 0.8$.

(*b*) Suggest a change to the reward function $r(s, a)$ that alters the $Q(s, a)$ values, but does not alter the optimal policy. Suggest a change to $r(s, a)$ that alters $Q(s, a)$ but does not alter $V^*(s, a)$.

(*c*) Now consider applying the Q learning algorithm to this grid world, assuming the table of $\hat{Q}$ values is initialized to zero. Assume the agent begins in the bottom left grid square and then travels clockwise around the perimeter of the grid until it reaches the absorbing goal state, completing the first training episode. Describe which $\hat{Q}$ values are modified as a result of this episode, and give their revised values. Answer the question again assuming the agent now performs a second identical episode. Answer it again for a third episode.

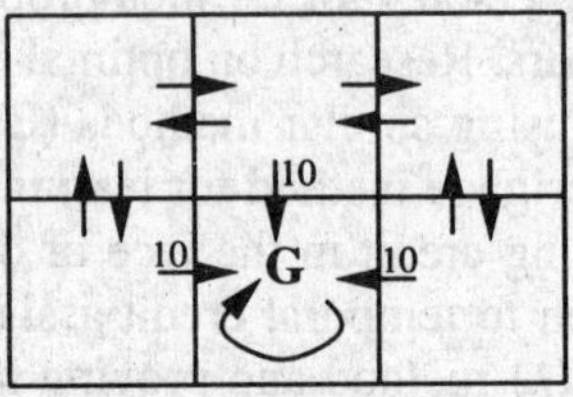

13.3. Consider playing Tic-Tac-Toe against an opponent who plays randomly. In particular, assume the opponent chooses with uniform probability any open space, unless there is a forced move (in which case it makes the obvious correct move).

(*a*) Formulate the problem of learning an optimal Tic-Tac-Toe strategy in this case as a Q-learning task. What are the states, transitions, and rewards in this non-deterministic Markov decision process?

(*b*) Will your program succeed if the opponent plays optimally rather than randomly?

13.4. Note in many MDPs it is possible to find two policies π_1 and π_2 such that π_1 outperforms π_2 if the agent begins in some state s_1, but π_2 outperforms π_1 if it begins in some other state s_2. Put another way, $V^{\pi_1}(s_1) > V^{\pi_2}(s_1)$, but $V^{\pi_2}(s_2) > V^{\pi_1}(s_2)$. Explain why there will always exist a single policy that maximizes $V^{\pi}(s)$ for *every* initial state s (i.e., an optimal policy π^*). In other words, explain why an MDP always allows a policy π^* such that $(\forall \pi, s)\ V^{\pi^*}(s) \geq V^{\pi}(s)$.

REFERENCES

Baird, L. (1995). Residual algorithms: Reinforcement learning with function approximation. *Proceedings of the Twelfth International Conference on Machine Learning* (pp. 30–37). San Francisco: Morgan Kaufmann.

Barto, A. (1992). Reinforcement learning and adaptive critic methods. In D. White & S. Sofge (Eds.), *Handbook of intelligent control: Neural, fuzzy, and adaptive approaches* (pp. 469–491). New York: Van Nostrand Reinhold.

Barto, A., Bradtke, S., & Singh, S. (1995). Learning to act using real-time dynamic programming. *Artificial Intelligence*, Special volume: Computational research on interaction and agency, 72(1), 81–138.

Barto, A., Sutton, R., & Anderson, C. (1983). Neuronlike adaptive elements that can solve difficult learning control problems. *IEEE Transactions on Systems, Man, and Cybernetics*, 13(5), 834–846.

Bellman, R. E. (1957). *Dynamic Programming*. Princeton, NJ: Princeton University Press.

Bellman, R. (1958). On a routing problem. *Quarterly of Applied Mathematics*, 16(1), 87–90.

Bellman, R. (1961). *Adaptive control processes*. Princeton, NJ: Princeton University Press.

Berenji, R. (1992). Learning and tuning fuzzy controllers through reinforcements. *IEEE Transactions on Neural Networks*, 3(5), 724–740.

Bertsekas, D. (1987). *Dynamic programming: Deterministic and stochastic models*. Englewood Cliffs, NJ: Prentice Hall.

Blackwell, D. (1965). Discounted dynamic programming. *Annals of Mathematical Statistics*, 36, 226–235.

Boyan, J., & Moore, A. (1995). Generalization in reinforcement learning: Safely approximating the value function. In G. Tesauro, D. Touretzky, & T. Leen (Eds.), *Advances in Neural Information Processing Systems 7*. Cambridge, MA: MIT Press.

Crites, R., & Barto, A. (1996). Improving elevator performance using reinforcement learning. In D. S. Touretzky, M. C. Mozer, & M. C. Hasselmo (Eds.), *Advances in Neural Information Processing Systems*, 8.

Dayan, P. (1992). The convergence of TD(λ) for general λ. *Machine Learning*, 8, 341–362.

Dean, T., Basye, K., & Shewchuk, J. (1993). Reinforcement learning for planning and control. In S. Minton (Ed.), *Machine Learning Methods for Planning* (pp. 67–92). San Francisco: Morgan Kaufmann.

Dietterich, T. G., & Flann, N. S. (1995). Explanation-based learning and reinforcement learning: A unified view. *Proceedings of the 12th International Conference on Machine Learning* (pp. 176–184). San Francisco: Morgan Kaufmann.

Ford, L., & Fulkerson, D. (1962). *Flows in networks*. Princeton, NJ: Princeton University Press.

Gordon, G. (1995). Stable function approximation in dynamic programming. *Proceedings of the Twelfth International Conference on Machine Learning* (pp. 261–268). San Francisco: Morgan Kaufmann.

Kaelbling, L. P., Littman, M. L., & Moore, A. W. (1996). Reinforcement learning: A survey. *Journal of AI Research*, 4, 237–285. Online journal at http://www.cs.washington.edu/research/jair/-home.html.

Holland, J. H. (1986). Escaping brittleness: The possibilities of general-purpose learning algorithms applied to parallel rule-based systems. In Michalski, Carbonell, & Mitchell (Eds.), *Machine learning: An artificial intelligence approach* (Vol. 2, pp. 593–623). San Francisco: Morgan Kaufmann.

Laird, J. E., & Rosenbloom, P. S. (1990). Integrating execution, planning, and learning in SOAR for external environments. *Proceedings of the Eighth National Conference on Artificial Intelligence* (pp. 1022–1029). Menlo Park, CA: AAAI Press.

Lin, L. J. (1992). Self-improving reactive agents based on reinforcement learning, planning, and teaching. *Machine Learning*, 8, 293–321.

Lin, L. J. (1993). Hierarchical learning of robot skills by reinforcement. *Proceedings of the International Conference on Neural Networks.*

Littman, M. (1996). *Algorithms for sequential decision making* (Ph.D. dissertation and Technical Report GS-96-09). Brown University, Department of Computer Science, Providence, RI.

Maclin, R., & Shavlik, J. W. (1996). Creating advice-taking reinforcement learners. *Machine Learning*, 22, 251–281.

Mahadevan, S. (1996). Average reward reinforcement learning: Foundations, algorithms, and empirical results. *Machine Learning*, 22(1), 159–195.

Mahadevan, S., & Connell, J. (1991). Automatic programming of behavior-based robots using reinforcement learning. In *Proceedings of the Ninth National Conference on Artificial Intelligence*. San Francisco: Morgan Kaufmann.

McCallum, A. (1995). *Reinforcement learning with selective perception and hidden state* (Ph.D. dissertation). Department of Computer Science, University of Rochester, Rochester, NY.

Mitchell, T. M., & Thrun, S. B. (1993). Explanation-based neural network learning for robot control. In C. Giles, S. Hanson, & J. Cowan (Eds.), *Advances in Neural Information Processing Systems 5* (pp. 287–294). San Francisco: Morgan-Kaufmann.

Moore, A., & Atkeson C. (1993). Prioritized sweeping: Reinforcement learning with less data and less real time. *Machine Learning*, 13, 103.

Peng, J., & Williams, R. (1994). Incremental multi-step *Q*-learning. *Proceedings of the Eleventh International Conference on Machine Learning* (pp. 226–232). San Francisco: Morgan Kaufmann.

Ring, M. (1994). *Continual learning in reinforcement environments* (Ph.D. dissertation). Computer Science Department, University of Texas at Austin, Austin, TX.

Samuel, A. L. (1959). Some studies in machine learning using the game of checkers. *IBM Journal of Research and Development*, 3, 211–229.

Singh, S. (1992). Reinforcement learning with a hierarchy of abstract models. *Proceedings of the Tenth National Conference on Artificial Intelligence* (pp. 202–207). San Jose, CA: AAAI Press.

Singh, S. (1993). *Learning to solve markovian decision processes* (Ph.D. dissertation). Also CMPSCI Technical Report 93-77, Department of Computer Science, University of Massachusetts at Amherst.

Singh, S., & Sutton, R. (1996). Reinforcement learning with replacing eligibility traces. *Machine Learning*, 22, 123.

Sutton, R. (1988). Learning to predict by the methods of temporal differences. *Machine learning*, 3, 9–44.

Sutton R. (1991). Planning by incremental dynamic programming. *Proceedings of the Eighth International Conference on Machine Learning* (pp. 353–357). San Francisco: Morgan Kaufmann.

Tesauro, G. (1995). Temporal difference learning and TD-GAMMON. *Communications of the ACM*, 38(3), 58–68.

Thrun, S. (1992). The role of exploration in learning control. In D. White & D. Sofge (Eds.), *Handbook of intelligent control: Neural, fuzzy, and adaptive approaches* (pp. 527–559). New York: Van Nostrand Reinhold.

Thrun, S. (1996). Explanation-based neural network learning: A lifelong learning approach. Boston: Kluwer Academic Publishers.

Tsitsiklis, J. (1994). Asynchronous stochastic approximation and *Q*-learning. *Machine Learning*, 16(3), 185–202.

Watkins, C. (1989). *Learning from delayed rewards* (Ph.D. dissertation). King's College, Cambridge, England.

Watkins, C., & Dayan, P. (1992). *Q*-learning. *Machine Learning*, 8, 279–292.

Zhang, W., & Dietterich, T. G. (1996). High-performance job-shop scheduling with a time-delay TD(λ) network. In D. S. Touretzky, M. C. Mozer, & M. E. Hasselmo (Eds.), *Advances in neural information processing systems*, 8, 1024–1030.

APPENDIX

NOTATION

Below is a summary of notation used in this book.

(a, b]: Brackets of the form [,], (, and) are used to represent intervals, where square brackets represent intervals including the boundary and round parentheses represent intervals excluding the boundary. For example, (1, 3] represents the interval $1 < x \leq 3$.

$\sum_{i=1}^{n} x_i$: The sum $x_1 + x_2 + \cdots + x_n$.

$\prod_{i=1}^{n} x_i$: The product $x_1 \cdot x_2 \cdots x_n$.

$\vdash$: The symbol for logical entailment. For example, $A \vdash B$ denotes that B follows deductively from A.

$>_g$: The symbol for the *more general than* relation. For example, $h_i >_g h_j$ denotes that hypothesis h_i is more general than h_j.

$\underset{x \in X}{\operatorname{argmax}} f(x)$: The value of x that maximizes $f(x)$. For example,

$$\underset{x \in \{1,2,-3\}}{\operatorname{argmax}} x^2 = -3$$

$\hat{f}(x)$: A function that approximates the function $f(x)$.

δ: In PAC-learning, a bound on the probability of failure. In artificial neural network learning, the error term associated with a single unit output.

ϵ: A bound on the error of a hypothesis (in PAC-learning).

η: The learning rate in neural network and related learning methods.

μ: The mean of a probability distribution.

σ: The standard deviation of a probability distribution.

$\nabla E(\vec{w})$: The gradient of E with respect to the vector $\vec{w}$.

C: Class of possible target functions.

D: The training data.

$\mathcal{D}$: A probability distribution over the instance space.

$E[x]$: The expected value of x.

$E(\vec{w})$: The sum of squared errors of an artifial neural network whose weights are given by the vector $\vec{w}$.

$Error$: The error in a discrete-valued hypothesis or prediction.

H: Hypothesis space.

$h(x)$: The prediction produced by hypothesis h for instance x.

$P(x)$: The probability (mass) of x.

$\Pr(x)$: The probability (mass) of the event x.

$p(x)$: The probability density of x.

$Q(s, a)$: The Q function from reinforcement learning.

$\Re$: The set of real numbers.

$VC(H)$: The Vapnik-Chervonenkis dimension of the hypothesis space H.

$VS_{H,D}$: The Version Space; that is, the set of hypotheses from H that are consistent with D.

w_{ji}: In artificial neural networks, the weight from node i to node j.

X: Instance space.

INDEXES

AUTHOR INDEX

Page numbers in italics are references to the bibliography.

SUBJECT INDEX

Page numbers in italics refer to tables; numbers in bold to figures. An "*n*" following a page number refers to a footnote on that page.

D

E

F

G